WILLIAM III

William III, in the manner of Willem Wissing. Rijksmuseum, Amsterdam

WILLIAM III

FROM PRINCE OF ORANGE TO KING OF ENGLAND

A HISTORY
1650–1689

WILLIAM PULL

UNICORN

This edition first published in the UK by Unicorn
an imprint of the Unicorn Publishing Group LLP, 2021
5 Newburgh Street
London W1F 7RG

www.unicornpublishing.org

10 9 8 7 6 5 4 3 2 1

ISBN 978-1-913491-60-4

Edited by Elisabeth Ingles
Design by Vivian@Bookscribe

Printed in Turkey by FineTone Ltd

PICTURE CREDITS
The author and publishers are grateful to the following for permission to
reproduce works in their collections:
National Galleries of Scotland: Image 12 (p.574)
Rijksmuseum, Amsterdam: Cover, Images 1 (p.2), 2 (p.22), 3 (p.32),
    4 (p.35)
Stiftung Preußische Schlösser und Gärten Berlin-Brandenburg: Image 7
    (p.216)
Walker Art Gallery, Liverpool: Image 5 (p.93)

CONTENTS

LIST OF ILLUSTRATIONS

Note on Dates, Names and Currencies

England in the 17th century followed the Old Style, Julian, calendar, whilst the New Style, Gregorian, calendar, which England did not adopt until the middle of the 18th century, was used on the European continent. This book follows the New Style throughout, except where the context makes the difference significant, when both styles are given.

Place names present a little difficulty – the Meuse in Belgium becomes the Maas when it flows into the Dutch Republic, and so forth. To arrive at some consistency, therefore, modern German practice has been adopted, which readers will hopefully not find difficult to follow; though we have retained the English version of 'Rhine'. Leyden is given rather than the modern spelling of Leiden, since that was how it was spelt in the 17th century. Names of people are very variously spelt in the sources, and we have tried to make them consistent throughout.

Like all exchange rates the Dutch guilder fluctuated, but to give some indication of values the exchange rate has been taken at 10 guilders to the English pound, and similarly the French *livre* has been taken at 12.5 *livres* to the pound. Converting historic currencies to present-day values is a very inexact exercise, but for what it is worth the Bank of England's inflation calculator produces a multiple of 203.5 at 2019 for 1675 prices (£10 in 1675 = £2,035.15 in 2019).

Acknowledgements

The late Dr Jeremy Catto, for many decades history fellow of Oriel College, Oxford, was an outstanding Oxford personality whose polished methods, almost imperceptible in their operation, reached throughout the globe – *suaviter in modo, fortiter in re*. I am deeply grateful for his unstinting encouragement in writing this book and to Professor David Parrott of New College, who so kindly read a large part of it and whose wise advice was so invaluable. All errors are, of course, exclusively mine.

I am also very grateful for the inexhaustibly patient and professional support of Lord Strathcarron and his team at Unicorn Publishing and my editor, Elisabeth Ingles. The staff at the British Library and the London Library, particularly during the tiresome tribulations of the lockdown, have been beyond praise. Both have extraordinary resources but the treasures of the latter which so often emerge unexpectedly from the most unsuspected corners of the collection never cease to amaze. I am grateful to the Royal Collections in The Hague, courtesy H.M. The Queen of the Netherlands, for their help. My thanks too to Heather Holden-Brown for her introduction to Ian Strathcarron.

The book is dedicated to all those jolly dogs from Oriel College with whom I have so often heard the chimes of midnight.

But only in the second degree.

My wife, Andrea, occupies the first place, whose 'When will it be finished?' ensured that it was.

PREFACE

William III was so called not only because he was the third Prince of Orange of that name, but also because he was the third king named William to accede to the throne of England. Although he invaded England from the Dutch Republic, he was neither Dutch nor English, but a cosmopolitan European aristocrat. His family's origins did not lie in the Principality of Orange, which William never visited, which was situated far away in the south of France, and which was tiny and insignificant in every way, save for one supremely important and overriding attribute – it conferred sovereignty. The Princes of Orange were independent sovereign princes.

Where their origins did lie was in Germany, and the clan never lost touch with their German roots.

They acquired – largely through marriage – considerable wealth in the Low Countries and the other lands that the dukes of Burgundy governed; by this means and through their prestige as sovereign princes, the clan acquired formidable powers of patronage and an extensive client system in the Netherlands and Germany. Through the marriage of William's father, William II of Orange, to Mary, the daughter of King Charles I, this was extended into England.

The clan's system could be put at the disposal of the Dutch political class when the Low Countries rebelled against the Habsburg successors of the dukes of Burgundy and established their independence in the Dutch Republic after a war lasting 80 years. It could also be put at the disposal of the English political class when they turned against King James II in 1688.

A number of books have been written about William III, but this one deals with his career before he became King of England; it examines in detail how his patron/client relationships worked across the European scene and explores the inevitable conflict that arose with the rival system of King Louis XIV of France.

THE HOUSE OF ORANGE-NASSAU

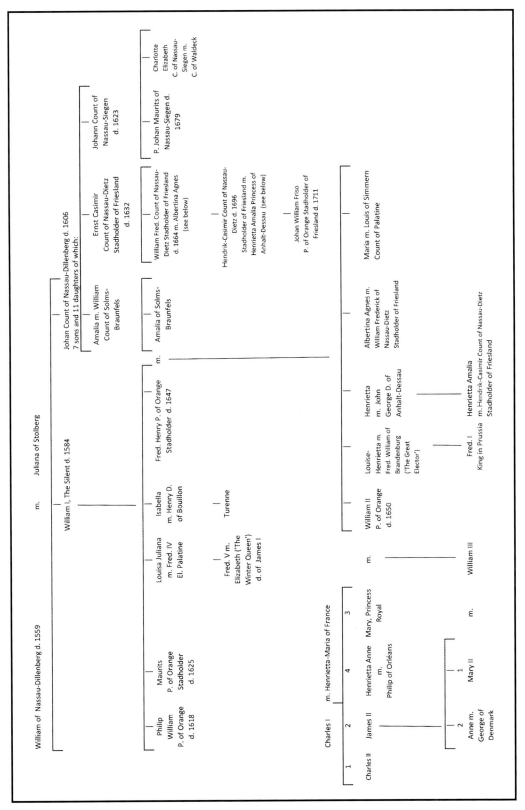

THE HOUSE OF ORANGE-NASSAU

Illegitimate Branches of Princes Maurits and Frederick Henry

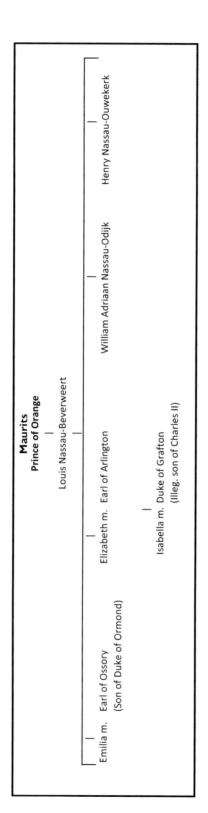

Maurits
Prince of Orange

Louis Nassau-Beverweert

Emilia m. Earl of Ossory
(Son of Duke of Ormond)

Elizabeth m. Earl of Arlington

Isabella m. Duke of Grafton
(Illeg. son of Charles II)

William Adriaan Nassau-Odijk

Henry Nassau-Ouwekerk

Frederick Henry
Prince of Orange

Frederick Nassau-Zuylenstein Snr.

Frederick Nassau-Zuylenstein Jnr.

1 1650: THE DYNASTIC LEGACY

He did not know that he was dying as the waters lapped against the yacht that was carrying him through the river and canal systems of the United Provinces to The Hague. The day before he had been hunting at his country house at Dieren, near Arnhem, returning with a fever. But a couple of days after his arrival at his quarters at the Binnenhof at The Hague the rash that had broken out over his body was recognised as smallpox. On Sunday 6 November 1650, at about 9 o'clock in the evening, Prince William II of Orange died.[1]

In the same quarters, in the evening of Monday 14 November, between 8 and 9 o'clock, his son, William III, was born.[2]

It was the birthday of his mother, Mary, who was 19 years old.

William III's family of Orange-Nassau derives its origins from the hilly country of Nassau in Germany, through whose territory there flows the pleasant Lahn river, which joins the Rhine just south of Coblenz; and in the surrounding areas the little towns of Dillenburg, of Siegen and of Dietz provided the different branches of the family with distinguishing suffixes to add to the Nassau name. By the second half of the 12th century the counts of Nassau had acquired a modest significance, accompanying the Holy Roman Emperor, Frederick Barbarossa, on his wars in Italy, in the Holy Land, and in Germany itself.[3] Their aims were those of their military caste, to gain reputation, to increase their status, and to extend their territorial possessions. But, until the latter end of the Middle Ages, they remained on a middling footing.

What raised them from the position of run-of-the-mill German counts were shrewd marriages and the skilful exploitation of relations with the powerful dynasties of their day. In 1403 one of them married an heiress, the great-niece of a banker who had financed the princes and rulers of the Netherlands, and whose political influence had become as extensive as his fortune.[4] The Nassaus were solidly established in the Netherlands, a position, as the Dutch royal family, they have retained to this day.

Making use of these firm foundations, they developed ties, which, despite some setbacks, became ever closer, with the dukes of Burgundy,[5] a cadet branch of the French royal family, who had in the 15th century become the major power in the Low Countries.

When in 1482 the line of the Burgundian dukes in the Netherlands became extinct and the rich inheritance passed to the Habsburgs[6] the ascent of the Nassaus was not impeded; rather it accelerated. Count Henry became a confidential friend of the Habsburg emperor, Charles V. In 1515 he was appointed Stadholder, or Governor, of Holland, Zeeland, and West Friesland,[7] offices which it was to become a tradition for members of his family to hold and which were to be of the first importance in the future political roles they were able to play.

Count Henry entered into yet another propitious marriage for his House by marrying Claudia of Châlons.[8] The Châlons had extensive properties in France and Germany, especially in Burgundy and Franche-Comté, and tucked away amongst their possessions was the little Principality of Orange, in the south of France. When the Châlons's male line became defunct the inheritance passed to Henry's and Claudia's son, René, in 1530; and with it the Châlons's motto 'Je maintiendrai Châlons', later to be adapted to 'Je maintiendrai Nassau',[9] and later still to the rather more pithy, and perhaps more usefully vague 'Je Maintiendrai', in which form – whether attracted to the first or to the second quality is not recorded – it was taken up by the English royal family after William III became king of England.

But more important than the motto was the Principality of Orange. Small and insignificant in every other way, it brought with it one overriding attribute. The sovereignty, which had once been bestowed upon it by the Holy Roman Emperor, Barbarossa, had been confirmed by Louis XII of France.[10] The Princes of Orange were accordingly sovereigns in their own right. The House of Nassau had become the House of Orange-Nassau and it had risen to the foremost rank in the Netherlands.

René too became Stadholder of Holland and Zeeland, as well as Utrecht, and, at the end of his life, of Gelderland[11] too. When he died of wounds in battle, in 1544, he named as his heir his eleven-year-old cousin, William, who, as the son of Henry's younger brother, William, Count of Nassau-Dillenburg, had been brought up in the considerably less glittering Dillenburg milieu.[12] Later he was to be called 'the Silent' and he was William III's great-grandfather.

William the Silent was the first, and the greatest, of three outstanding men who preceded William III as head of the House of Orange-Nassau and who secured the independence of the Northern Netherlands from Habsburg rule. In doing so they vouchsafed for the House a unique position of prestige and acquired an almost royal eminence.

The close relationship between Nassau and Habsburg at first continued; and Charles V took a personal interest in the education of the young Prince of Orange, who was by far the richest nobleman in the Netherlands. Indeed, his position was deemed so important that it was Charles V who had persuaded René to skip a generation and to draw up his will, not in favour of the natural heir, his uncle the Count of Nassau-Dillenburg, a Lutheran, but in favour of his still young cousin, whose religion could yet be changed.[13] When the world-weary emperor decided to transfer the sovereignty of the Netherlands to his son, Philip, in 1555 it was on the shoulder of the Prince that he leaned to deliver his abdication speech to the assembled States-General and dignitaries in Brussels.[14]

Things changed under the son, who became Philip II of Spain, when his father also abdicated from Spain and its empire a year later, with the Holy Roman Empire ending up in the hands of the Austrian branch of the Habsburgs. At first, indeed, there was a good relationship between the Prince of Orange and the new King: and the Prince, like the earlier members of his family, was appointed Stadholder of Holland and Zeeland, and also of Utrecht.[15] But the middle of the 16th century was beset by the storms of the Reformation, and everywhere in the Low Countries disturbances were taking place. Philip saw himself as the defender of the Catholic Church and was determined upon the eradication of Protestant heresy, using the Inquisition as one of his instruments.

William the Silent, moved by a combination of his self-interest, his ambition, and his humanity, his hand finally forced by Philip's inept confiscation of his property and abduction of his eldest son and heir, changed from being a supporter to being an opponent of the dynasty in whose service his family had risen so high. At the beginning of 1568 he came out in open rebellion.[16] The revolt of the Netherlands against Philip II of Spain had found its leader.

In July 1572 a majority of the large towns of the Province of Holland met as the States of Holland. They accepted Orange's claim that he was still Stadholder of Holland, Zeeland and Utrecht (he was not present, but was represented by his secretary, Marnix) and recognised him as Captain-General of these Provinces.[17] The fiction was maintained that the revolt was directed against the evil advisers of the King, not the King himself.[18] Hence the vexed question, which was to bedevil the future, of where sovereignty was to lie was not then addressed, at any rate for the time being. It remained with the King.

In 1575 the Provinces of Holland and Zeeland formed a Union which was followed in 1579 by the Union of Utrecht: this was entered into initially and in the main by the Provinces of Holland, Zeeland and Utrecht, to be followed by most of the other Northern Provinces.[19] There were existing fault lines[20] between the Northern and Southern Provinces – the Catholic Church and its institutions and the nobility were more powerfully entrenched in the south – but the fault lines now widened further; and they still exist in modern times in the present-day form of the Netherlands and Belgium. Whilst the Southern Provinces gradually returned to Spanish rule, the Northern Republic, which owed its origins to the Union of Utrecht, was to continue the long struggle against Spain until complete independence was recognised at the treaty of Westphalia in 1648, after a war which had lasted eighty years.

With Spanish successes in the south, Orange was to leave the Southern Netherlands in 1583 and establish himself in a former convent at Delft in Holland. He was to be followed by the States-General who left Antwerp and who too ended up in Delft before moving to The Hague, where the Southern Provinces eventually lost their representation.[21] The Province of Holland was increasingly confirmed as the core centre from which the revolt against Spain was to be conducted.

The Union of Utrecht made up the constitution of the United Provinces, as they were to become known. It was improvised in the midst of the turbulence of a desperate revolt; it inherited many of the institutions from the Burgundian dukes and their Habsburg successors, although not, however, without modifications, which we will come to examine in due course. Amongst these institutions were the Provincial Stadholderships, which were looked up to as providing a role of leadership politically, diplomatically, and, especially, militarily in time of war; and which were already closely associated with the House of Orange.

The issue of sovereignty could not be wholly ignored for much longer. In June 1580 Philip issued a ban on William the Silent which laid him open to assassination with impunity. In July 1581 the States-General entered into an act of abjuration with the formal renunciation of Philip's sovereignty. An attempt was by then already under way to arrive at a new answer to address the issue of sovereignty by bestowing it, with strict limitations, on the brother of the King of France, the Duke of Anjou.[22] It proved not to be workable, however, and, after a failed coup by Anjou, he returned, disappointed, to his homeland in 1583.[23]

Negotiations were under way to bestow sovereignty on Orange when he was struck down in his former convent by an assassin's bullets on 10 July 1584. 'Mon dieu, mon dieu', he muttered in his dying moments, 'aye pitié de mon âme et de ce pauvre people.'[24]

William the Silent was succeeded by his eldest son, Philip William, as Prince of Orange until his death in February 1618. However, as we have mentioned, this son had been abducted by the Spaniards when still a boy, and, having been brought up by them, retained his allegiance to the Spanish cause throughout his life. The headship of the House of Orange in the United Provinces consequently devolved upon William the Silent's second son, the sixteen-year-old Maurits, the second of the remarkable leaders produced by the House in the struggle against Spain. Although he was called such he did not in fact become Prince of Orange until he succeeded his brother in 1618; but in 1585 the traditional appointments of Stadholder of Holland and Zeeland were granted to him and he became as well Captain and Admiral-General of those provinces.[25] The Province of Friesland in the meanwhile appointed (in 1584) his cousin, William Louis, the eldest son of William the Silent's brother, Johan, as its Stadholder; whilst Maurits was also in due course to become Stadholder of Utrecht, Gelderland and Overijssel.[26]

There was a short interregnum from 1584 to 1586 when, as a result of an alliance entered into with Elizabeth I of England, her favourite, the Earl of Leicester, became Governor-General of the United Provinces. But this arrangement, like the one with Anjou, was also unsuccessful and after his return to England the leading figure in the country was not Maurits but Johan van Oldenbarnevelt, the 'Advocate' of the Province of Holland since 1586 and the Province's chief spokesman at the States-General of the Republic as a whole.[27] The wealth of Holland gave it the most powerful single voice in the assembly and Oldenbarnevelt was established in a position that has been described as analogous to prime minister and foreign minister of the Republic.[28]

Maurits initially matched, in the military sphere, Oldenbarnevelt's achievements in the political. He was perhaps the greatest general on the European stage during his lifetime; the Dutch army under his leadership was the model of its age; and he led it to a series of dazzling successes against the Spaniards in the 1590s.[29]

But the partnership was soured when Oldenbarnevelt manoeuvred a 12-year truce with the Spaniards in 1609, in the teeth of the opposition of Maurits, for whom the Spaniards were the arch-enemy. In his mind the seed was sown that Oldenbarnevelt might be prepared to betray the country to that arch-enemy; and that it might become his duty to prevent this from happening. In Oldenbarnevelt's mind, on the other hand, the suspicion was sown that Maurits was aiming at supreme power, sovereignty, which the continuance of war would facilitate.[30]

The rift was widened by a religious conflict, which began as a sophisticated theological dispute between two Dutch theologians, Jacobus Arminius and Franciscus Gomarus, relating to the refinements of the doctrine of predestination; but which, in accordance with the temper of the times, widened into a serious political confrontation that threatened to tear the young Republic apart.

Theologically, Gomarus adhered to the strict orthodox Calvinist doctrine of predestination, which derives from St Paul and St Augustine, and which holds that God has for all time predestined certain people to eternal salvation, with the concomitant that the rest are predestined to eternal damnation. Arminius modified the doctrine by stating that the damned are those who chose to reject the offer by God of His grace, something foreseen, but not decided, by God.[31]

Politically, the adherents of Arminius, who coalesced into a party to be called the Remonstrants, aimed at a Calvinist church which was as broad and tolerant as possible, and subject to the civil authority. The adherents of Gomarus, who became known as the Counter-Remonstrants, aimed at theological purity and a Church independent from the civil authority; in their minds lay the fear that the toleration advocated by the Remonstrants would lead to Catholics re-establishing themselves and hence open up a fifth column.

Oldenbarnevelt was drawn into the dispute on the side of the Remonstrants because he believed that the Church should be subordinate to the civil powers, by which he meant not the States-General, but the individual provinces, his own Province of Holland in particular. Ultimately Maurits, a military man whose grasp of the slippery subtleties of predestination never reached even the elementary stage, came down on the other side; he saw an attack on the orthodox Calvinist Church, the true Reformed Church, the symbol of the revolt against Catholic Spain, as treason; and he feared for the unity of the country and for its continued independence.[32]

Underlying the political struggle between the two lay the rivalry between the two main power centres that had evolved in the United Provinces. The striking expansion in commerce had created a wealthy, self-confident ruling class, known as the Regents, which had taken root as an urban elite particularly in the Western Provinces, and especially in Holland and Amsterdam.[33] In Holland, the wealthiest and most important of the provinces, they commanded the Town Councils, who elected the representatives to the Holland Provincial States; they, in turn, appointed their representatives at the States-General. A sufficient number of them in the province had seen their financial interest in supporting the 12-year truce with Spain – they were persuaded that the war against Spain could not continue without a further major fiscal effort.[34] And in the Remonstrants' support for the civil authority to supervise the Church there was a further appeal to many of them; for as rulers of the Town Councils that authority was wielded by them. Oldenbarnevelt's strength lay in the support he could garner from these Regents; his weakness lay in their not constituting a homogeneous and united group in all circumstances.

The alternative main centre of power lay with the House of Orange. Its influence was sustained by its own enormous wealth; by its customary hold on the offices of Stadholder and of the armed forces, with the patronage that both bestowed; by its prestige in leading the struggle against Spain; and by its supporters in the more backward provinces outside Holland. Everywhere it had widespread popular support. Peace diminished its power base in the armed forces and the scope for enhancing its leadership in war. In the religious dispute the Counter-Remonstrants were adamantly opposed both to the peace with Spain,[35] the Catholic arch-enemy, and the interference by the State in Church affairs,[36] and its preachers were fervent supporters of the House of Orange.

Whilst the strength of Oldenbarnevelt lay with his Regent supporters in Holland his support there was far from unanimous,[37] and in the States-General Maurits had a majority.[38]

The religious and the associated political dispute developed by twists and turns over the years until events moved to a crisis in 1617, when it became clear that Maurits was not prepared to use regular troops to curb disturbances caused by Counter-Remonstrants. Oldenbarnevelt and the Remonstrants took measures in Holland to raise auxiliary troops who were to owe their obedience not to the central authority of the Republic, the States-General, but to the town which paid them; and at the same time they issued instructions to those units of the regular army whom the province was paying that they also owed their first allegiance to that province.

Maurits took this as a personal affront.[39] It was a threat to his own authority over the armed forces, and to the union of the United Provinces; and to be asked to use troops against orthodox Calvinists confirmed his worst suspicions that Oldenbarnevelt was planning to betray the Dutch revolt and the country.[40] In his slow, ponderous, but deadly way he took time to prepare his ground and his support in the States-General, until finally, using his majority there, he arrested Oldenbarnevelt and some of his main adherents on 29

August 1618; on 13 May of the following year the old statesman's head was severed by the executioner's sword.[41]

Maurits had by then set about reviving the historical powers of the Stadholder, dating from Burgundian times – using, however, methods that lay outside the law[42] – to supervise municipal elections to purge the Town Councils in Holland and replacing Oldenbarnevelt's supporters with his own.[43] And in Oldenbarnevelt's place as 'Advocate' he appointed a nominee, in future to be called 'the Pensionary' of Holland.[44]

The 12-year truce with Spain expired in 1621 and the long struggle resumed. But Maurits's old vigour was lacking. Sunk in gloom and prematurely aged, he died four years later.

He was succeeded by his half-bother, the 41-year-old Frederick-Henry, grandfather of William III. Following the now very strong historical tradition the new Prince of Orange was appointed Captain-General of the Union by the States-General and he became Stadholder of Holland and Zeeland.[45] As a general he showed a mastery of war on the same level as that of Maurits.[46]

The Dutch Republic had now become a great power and one of the wealthiest countries in Europe, and it may be helpful to pause to appreciate how power operated at this stage in its development. Every province had its own Provincial States, whose membership was determined by the widely differing constitutions each province possessed; and the Provincial States sent delegates to the States-General of the Republic as a whole. In Holland, for example, there were 18 towns – of which Amsterdam was by far the most powerful – who could vote in that province's States. In addition the nobility was represented collectively, not individually, its representatives being elected through co-option; and it always spoke and voted first. In Zeeland there were seven voting towns in its Provincial States, with the nobility represented by the First Noble, who was the Prince of Orange.[47]

From 1620 each province chose its own Stadholder, which it was the custom to pair with the Captaincy-General. There was also a Captain-General and Admiral-General of the Union who was appointed by the States-General. The Stadholders had responsibility for the oversight of the administration of justice in each province where he held the post and he could exert influence in judicial appointments. He appointed magistrates in the towns from lists submitted by the Town Councils, and he could supervise the electoral processes under which these were chosen; and in some towns – Amsterdam was an important exception – he had the right to choose Burgomasters from lists provided by the Councils; and through these means of influence he could predispose those by whom he himself was ultimately elected. He also had a duty to maintain the Reformed Religion.[48]

In foreign affairs Frederick-Henry was able to exert considerable influence by means of a committee, the *Secrète Besogne*, on which he sat and which could take binding decisions.

As part of the arrangements for his succession Maurits, himself a confirmed bachelor with a vigorously irregular private life, to which his illegitimate offspring bore fruitful testimony, but no doubt anxious that there should be a legitimate Orange heir, saw no contradiction between the life he himself led and bringing pressure to bear on Frederick-Henry to marry his long-standing mistress, Amalia von Soms-Braunfels.[49] She was a relation of the Nassaus – she was a great-granddaughter of a sister of William the Silent[50] – and she had been a lady-in-waiting to Queen Elizabeth of Bohemia, the daughter of James I of England, the 'Winter Queen' (so-called because of her short tenure for a winter as Queen of Bohemia), who had taken refuge in the Dutch Republic after her husband, the Elector Palatine, had launched a disastrous attempt to assume the crown of Bohemia, thus igniting the Thirty Years' War, which was now devastating Europe.

The court of the Nassaus now moved on to a higher, more splendid, more ostentatious and more cosmopolitan plane. Frederick-Henry's mother, Louise de Coligny, was French and in his youth he had been sent to France, mingling with his mother's relations in the high nobility.[51] French was generally spoken at his court[52] and it was dominated by French culture. His income in 1627 has been estimated to amount to 250,000 guilders from his offices and to 573,000 guilders from his private resources,[53] and it was matched by the gleam and glitter of his court. He built new palaces and restored old ones; he installed gardens; and he collected art. His collection of paintings included works by Rembrandt, by Honthorst, by Rubens and by Van Dyck – but Rembrandt fell out of favour, being somewhat dilatory in the completion of his commissions.[54]

The dynastic ambitions of Frederick-Henry and Amalia, too, were on a large scale. In 1630 they arranged for their son, the future William II, to be appointed a general of cavalry at the age of three. Holland and Zeeland granted the boy the continuance of the Stadholderships in their provinces, in which they followed the example of Utrecht and Overijssel; but perhaps with a degree of reluctance evinced by the proviso that he should be of age at his father's death.[55] Nevertheless an element of heredity was thus unmistakably attached to the Orange grip on the Stadholderships. It was reinforced by a change in style in addressing Frederick-Henry. In 1636 Louis XIII decreed that he should be addressed as 'Altesse', instead of 'Excellence', a style adopted by the States-General the following year.[56]

In 1638 Marie de Médici, the Queen Mother of France, paid a visit to the Netherlands – she had fled France and was then kept in exile by her son, Louis XIII, who had finally been driven to exasperation by the old woman's incessant intrigues against his chief minister, Richelieu. She was received sumptuously and was much impressed by the palaces of the princes, of the nobility, and of the leading burgesses.[57] As she was about to depart for England, on her way to her daughter, Henrietta Maria, Charles I's Queen, Amalia waited on her to bid her farewell. The two arch-intriguers then hatched a plot to marry the future William II of Orange to the daughter of the King of England.[58]

The negotiations for this marriage were much prolonged, but at each stage the negotiating stance of Charles and Henrietta Maria was weakened both by their political position, which was to lead to the English Civil War, and by their need for finance, which they hoped the wealthy House of Orange would help to alleviate. It was not until 21 February 1641 that Charles I wrote to Frederick-Henry agreeing to the marriage of his eldest daughter, Mary, instead of her younger sister, which was all the English royal couple had originally been prepared to contemplate for the, in their eyes, comparatively *arriviste* Orange House.[59]

They were anxious to do all they could to maintain their daughter's royal status. The marriage contract stipulated that she should retain all the English servants chosen by her father, provided they did not exceed more than 26 male, and not more than 14 female, attendants.[60] The head of the household was to be Jan van der Kerkhoven, Lord of Heenvliet, whom Frederick-Henry had sent to England to conduct the marriage negotiations in their earlier stages, and who was married to an English widow, Lady Stanhope.

Young Prince William arrived in England in splendid manner. He was escorted across the North Sea by 20 vessels commanded by the renowned admiral Maarten Tromp; and when he arrived in the English capital[61] he was greeted by the sound of 100 cannon fired from the Tower of London. The marriage took place, with full royal ritual, pomp and pageantry, on 2 May 1641. Mary was nine years old and her husband was just short of his 15th birthday.[62] We find the Venetian ambassador reporting: 'to render it [the marriage] irrevocable so far as the tender age of the bride would allow, their Majesties agreed that the Prince should associate with her [*sunisco seco*]. This was done for two hours only in the presence of their Majesties and all the Court…'.[63]

The young husband returned to the Dutch Republic on his own at the end of May 1641; and it was not until March 1642 that Mary left England to join him, with an English civil war now increasingly likely. She was accompanied by her mother, Henrietta Maria, who was to seek money, arms and support from Frederick-Henry for her husband's increasingly difficult position. It was a sad parting, as the Venetian ambassador again noted. 'His Majesty accompanied his wife as far as the shore, and did not know how to tear himself away from her, conversing with her in sweet discourse and affectionate embraces, nor could they restrain their tears, moving all those who were present.'[64] As the ship departed, escorted by a fleet of 15 sail, once more commanded by Tromp, he climbed the battlements of Dover castle to gaze after it until it was lost to view.[65] Mary was never to see him again.

The Queen and the little Princess were met outside The Hague by the King's sister, Elizabeth of Bohemia, together with one of her sons, Prince Rupert – known in English history as Rupert of the Rhine – and two of her daughters.[66] Mary was treated with great, perhaps inordinate, respect by her father-in-law, Frederick-Henry. 'The princess … was received by … the old Prince of Orange as did become the daughter of so great a king, into whose presence he would never approach but with a reverence more like a subject towards his sovereign than the freedom of a father towards his son's wife; by no means suffering

Mary Stuart and William II of Orange, William III's parents,
as child bride and bridegroom, 1641, by Sir Anthony van Dyck.
Rijksmuseum, Amsterdam

either himself or his son, much less his servants, to come near the place of her residence, but bare-headed, and to his dying day – yea, even in his death-bed – maintained the same, as due to the greatness of her birth and excellent virtues.'[67]

It was an obsequiousness which may well have irked the Prince's wife Amalia von Solms. We hear of a quarrel between her and Mary in September 1642. 'The Princess Mary, in speaking recently with the Princess of Orange, her mother-in-law, of the interests of her House, and complaining to her of the suspicion shown by frequently sending spies to her apartments, gave way to a passion of anger against her, clearly expressing her contempt, hatred and dissatisfaction, affording an unhappy augury for the marriage of the Prince's son.'[68]

Charles I raised his standard at Nottingham, thus formally commencing the English Civil War, on 22 August: and at the beginning of 1643 Henrietta Maria departed from the United Provinces,[69] leaving her little daughter to face married life alone. In February 1644 Mary was officially installed in her full conjugal position.[70] Her husband was frequently absent, campaigning with the army, but, despite his infidelities, she clearly became greatly attached to him, as her grief at his early death was to testify. And she was much comforted by her aunt, the Queen of Bohemia, who took a maternal interest in her. Devoted to her clan and her family and living in exile from the Palatinate, her dead husband's electorate, this good woman had established a somewhat rickety and financially precarious court in The Hague.

Mary fought to preserve her royal dignities, and she refused to attend the wedding of the Elector of Brandenburg at the end of 1646 to Louisa, the eldest daughter of Frederick-Henry and Amalia von Solms, when it was claimed that henceforth Louisa, as the new Electress, should take precedence over her.[71]

Frederick-Henry and Amalia had advanced their ambitions by an impressive marriage into one of the major royal houses of Europe, however uncertain the fortunes of that house at present appeared to be. But there was a price to be paid. The pretensions of the House of Orange, or the Maison as it was universally called, smacked too much of royalist ambitions and were greeted with suspicion by many of the Dutch Regents. There were fears, as there had been with Maurits, that Frederick-Henry was aiming to make himself sovereign of the country. He was also supporting his Stuart in-laws in England, financially and with arms, a further cause for concern in the Regent circles in Holland and Amsterdam who wished to maintain neutrality in the English Civil War.[72]

Frederick-Henry's power base was dependent on divisions within the Province of Holland, which had arisen during the 12-year truce with Spain and which both Maurits and he had been able to exploit. In the 1640s these divisions lessened and with it the influence of Orange.[73] In the 1630s a peace party, under the leadership of Amsterdam, had come into existence, which was opposed by a faction led by the textile towns of Leyden and Haarlem.

After the capture of Breda from the Spaniards in 1637 and the safeguarding of Holland's territory the peace party gained in strength, with many of the smaller Holland towns as well as the eastern provinces adhering to Amsterdam's position. Frederick-Henry, however, supported by Leyden and the provinces of Zeeland and Utrecht, favoured the continuance of the war until the borders of the Republic were secured by a series of fortresses on the Ijssel, the Rhine and the Mosel. By 1646 this had been achieved and the ageing and sickly Frederick-Henry was at last prepared to yield to the Amsterdam faction and enter into peace negotiations with Spain.[74]

But not everybody in the Orange clan was so amenable and willing to cede ground to the pre-eminence of Amsterdam. The conflicts between the two major power centres in the United Provinces, the House of Orange and the Province of Holland led by Amsterdam, would soon again become manifest when Frederick-Henry, who, like Maurits, aged prematurely, died on 17 March 1647.

The life of William III's father was as filled with drama as it was short. At the time he succeeded, as Prince William II of Orange, negotiations were far advanced for the Peace Treaty of Westphalia which was to end both the Thirty Years' War in Europe and the long war of independence between the Dutch and the Spaniards. As with Maurits, when Oldenbarnevelt had entered into the 12-year truce with Spain a split now occurred between the two Dutch power centres. The Regents of Holland and Amsterdam, oppressed by the costs of the war and seeing that Spain was prepared to give full recognition to the independence of the United Provinces, saw no further gain in continuing the fight. William, however, with a relentless hatred of Spain, and no doubt aware of the diminution in his power base if peace were established, wished to continue the war to liberate the Southern Netherlands. Besides, the United Provinces had entered into an alliance with France in 1635 under which both sides had agreed not to enter into a separate peace with Spain without the consent of the other. And France wished to continue the war.

Furthermore, a split had occurred within the Orange clan itself: Amalia von Solms, who had been promised substantial territorial concessions in the Spanish Netherlands by the Spaniards, was supporting the peace party.[75]

Then, as well, William II was much more eager than Frederick-Henry had been to support the Stuarts. Frederick-Henry had followed a nuanced policy; whilst lending support to the Stuarts, he had also tried to pursue a policy of mediation between Parliament and Charles I. William II wanted to give active support to his brother-in-law, the future Charles II – who in 1648 had arrived in the Dutch Republic – very much against the wishes of the Holland towns, anxious as ever to avoid Dutch involvement in the English Civil War.[76]

Amsterdam and Holland were successful in pushing through the peace with Spain in the spring of 1648;[77] and with its coming into effect the size of the army was reduced. By 1648 it was down to 35,000 men; but Holland pressed for greater cuts. To this William II was strongly opposed and, whilst the final figure between him and Holland was reduced to a few hundred men, deadlock ensued.

Behind the numbers lay hidden a constitutional conundrum. Holland wished to have the right to disband those troops for which she paid under the prevailing system of quotas for sharing the financial burden of the army between the provinces. But if an individual province was able to do this in disregard of the States-General and the Stadholder it would imply a major diminution in the power of these authorities and an increase in that of the individual provinces, particularly Holland and its wealthy and powerful city, Amsterdam. In William's eyes, this was a major threat to the Union and, worse, to his own position.[78] The dispute thus shares many similarities to that between Maurits and Oldenbarneveldt.

To counter this William planned a coup, with his cousin, William-Frederick, the Stadholder of Friesland. On 30 July 1650 he arrested six principal Regents in The Hague; and this was followed by the appearance of William-Frederick before the gates of Amsterdam with 12,000 troops. Unfortunately, however, a postal courier, on his way from Hamburg, had passed through this army in the night, and Amsterdam had been alerted. William-Frederick found the gates of the city closed against him. Nevertheless when William II himself arrived he was able to demand the dismissal of two leading Regents from the Amsterdam Town Council; Holland agreed to cancel the orders for the disbandment of the troops whom she financed; and she submitted to accepting such troop levels for the army as was decided by the States-General.[79]

The authority of William had – very narrowly – been asserted.

But then, as we have seen, he caught smallpox, and died on 6 November. He left behind him an affronted and offended section of the Regent class; and these Regents were to take immediate advantage of the gaping political void left by his death. A counter-coup against Orange was soon set in motion.

When she was told of her husband's death the destitute and distraught Mary was led weeping to her bed.[80]

For this she had much cause.

1 A. Wicquefort, *Histoire des Provinces-Unies*, Amsterdam, 1861, I, pp.327–28; *Journaal. Heenvliet. Historish Genootschap*, Utrecht, 1869, pp.541–4.

2 L. van Aitzema, *Saken van staet en oorlog*, The Hague, 1669, III, p.459. *Journaal Heenvliet*, p.552.

3 N. Japikse, *De Geschiedenis Van Het Huis Van Oranje-Nassau*, The Hague, Zuid-Hollandsche Uitgevers Maatschappij, 1937–38, I, p.24. One of them indeed was elected to be king of Rome, but rather because of his weakness than his strength. Those who elected him did not want a strong king; and when he tried to exert himself he was soon deposed in favour of a Habsburg. See also article by H.P.H. Jansen in *Nassau en Oranje*, ed. C.A. Tamse, Alphen, 1979, p.16.

4 Japikse, *op. cit.*, I, p.34; Jansen, *op. cit.*, pp.17–21.

5 Japikse, *op. cit.*, I, p.37; Jansen, *op. cit.*, p.32.

6 Through the marriage of Mary of Burgundy to Maximilian of Habsburg. J. Israel, *The Dutch Republic: Its Rise, Greatness, and Fall 1477–1806*, Clarendon Press, Oxford, 1995, p.29.

7 Japikse, *op. cit.*, I, p.45; Jansen, *op. cit.*, pp.36–7.

8 Count Henry made no bones about his motives. As he bluntly wrote to his father, he did it to please both his own sovereign and the French king and 'in particular for my own renown and profit' ('sonderlinge om mijnder eere ende proufijtswille'). See Japikse, *op. cit.*, I, p 48.

9 *Ibid.*, I, pp. 58–61.

10 *Ibid.*, I, p.63.

11 *Ibid.*, I, p.58; K.W. Swart in *Nassau en Oranje*, p.48.

12 C.V. Wedgwood, *William the Silent: William of Nassau, Prince of Orange, 1553–1584*, Cassell, London, 1944, p.11.

13 *Ibid.*, p.11.

14 Japikse, *op. cit.*, I, p.71. Swart, *op. cit.*, p.48.

15 *Ibid.*, p.49; H. Rowen, *The Princes of Orange: the Stadholders in the Dutch Republic*, Cambridge University Press, Cambridge, 1988, p.16.

16 Swart, *op. cit.*, pp.51–59.

17 Israel, *op. cit.*, p.175.

18 Swart, *op. cit.*, p.65; Rowen, *op. cit.*, p.16.

19 Israel, *op. cit.*, pp.197, 201–2.

20 Swart, *op. cit.*, p.69.

21 Israel, *op. cit.*, pp.213–14, 225.

22 *Ibid.*, pp.209–10.

23 *Ibid.*, p.213.

24 Japikse, *op. cit.*, I, p.124.

25 Rowen, *op. cit.*, p.35; Israel, *op. cit.*, p.224; A. Th. van Deursen in *Nassau en Oranje*, pp.87–8.

26 Rowen, *op. cit.*, pp.34, 38.

27 Israel, *op. cit.*, p.223; van Deursen, *op. cit.*, p.93.

28 Rowen, *op. cit.*, p.37.

29 Israel, *op. cit.*, pp.242–3; van Deursen, *op. cit.*, p.96.

30 Israel, *op. cit.*, pp.403–5; van Deursen, *op. cit.*, pp.100, 103; Rowen, *op. cit.*, p.45.

31 Diarmaid MacCulloch, *Reformation Europe's House Divided 1490–1700*, Penguin, 2003, p.376.

32 Rowen, *op. cit.*, pp.41, 46; Israel, *op. cit.*, p.433; Van Deursen, *op. cit.*, pp.103, 105.

33 Israel, *op. cit.*, pp.341–2, 344–5.

34 *Ibid.*, p.404.

35 *Ibid.*, p.423.

36 *Ibid.*, p.426; P.J. Blok, *Geschiedenis van het Nederlandsche Volk*, Groningen, J.B. Wolters, 1892–1908, 1899, IV, p.108.

37 Blok, *op. cit.*, IV, p.145.

38 *Ibid.*, IV, p.136.

39 Israel, *op. cit.*, p.441; Jan den Tex, *Oldenbarnevelt*, Cambridge, 1973, p.583.

40 Van Deursen, *op. cit.*, p.106.

41 Israel, *op. cit.*, pp.449, 459.

42 Blok, *op. cit.*, IV, p.177.

43 Israel, *op. cit.*, p.453.

44 *Ibid.*, p.454.

45 Rowen, *op. cit.*, pp.56, 58, 59.

46 *Ibid.*, p.61.

47 Israel, *op. cit.*, pp.278–81.

48 *Ibid.*, pp.304–5.

49 Rowen, *op. cit.*, p.59.

50 J.J. Poelhekke, *Frederik Hendrik, Prins van Oranje: een biografisch drieluik Zutphen*, Walburg, 1978, pp.568–9.

51 Rowen, *op. cit.*, p.60.

52 Japikse, *op. cit.*, p.202.

53 *Ibid.*, p.196. As Japikse points out, these figures must have been subject to considerable fluctuations.

54 Japikse, *op. cit.*, p.200.

55 Rowen, *op. cit.*, p.71.

56 Israel, *op. cit.*, p.537.

57 Japikse, *op. cit.*, p.210; A. Levi, *Cardinal Richelieu and the Making of France*, Constable, London, 2000, pp.133–4.

58 Japikse, *op. cit.*, p.211. However, P. Geyl, *Orange and Stuart 1641–72*, Weidenfeld & Nicolson, London, 1969, p.6, n.8 doubts that Marie de Médici favoured the match, preferring, as did Henrietta Maria, a Spanish alliance.

59 G. Groen van Prinsterer, *Archives ou corréspondance inédite de la maison d'Orange-Nassau*, Leyden, 1847, series 2, III, p.357.

60 M.A. Everett Green, *Lives of the Princesses of England*, Henry Colburn, London, 1855, VI, p.109.

61 *Ibid.*, VI, p.111.

62 William II was born on 27 May 1626. Poelhekke, *op. cit.*, p.150; Everett Green, *op. cit.*, VI, p.113.

63 Venetian State Papers, 1640–42, XXV. The French ambassador's despatch, with less theatre, stipulates half an hour with the bed curtains undrawn.

64 Venetian State Papers, 1642–3, XXVI, p.5. She stayed in the Netherlands until 26 February. S. van Zuylen van Nyevelt, *Court Life in the Dutch Republic, 1638–1689*, J.M. Dent & Co., London, 1906, p.60.

65 Everett Green, *op. cit.*, VI, pp.125–26.

66 Ibid., VI, p.127.

67 Quoted by Everett Green, *op. cit.*, VI, p.128.

68 Venetian State Papers, 1642–3, XXVI, p.158.

69 Geyl, *op. cit.*, p.16.

70 Entry on Mary by Marika Keblusek in *Oxford Dictionary of National Biography*, Oxford, 2004.

71 Everett Green, *op. cit.*, VI, p.138.

72 Geyl, *op. cit.*, pp.13–14.

73 Israel, *op. cit.*, pp.540–1.

74 S. Groenveld, *The House of Orange and the House of Stuart, 1639–1650: A Revision, Historic Journal* XXXIV (1991), pp.956–7, 964; Poelhekke, op. cit., p.139.

75 See Groen van Prinsterer, *Archives*, series 2, IV, pp.159, 163.

76 See Groenveld's article, *The House of Orange and the House of Stuart*, pp.967, 970. I have tried to steer a somewhat middle course between Groenveld's revisionist article and Geyl's version in *Orange and Stuart* (*op. cit.*).

77 Israel, *op. cit.*, pp.596–7.

78 Ibid., pp.602–4; Rowen, *op. cit.*, pp.84, 85, 87.

79 Israel, *op. cit.*, p.607; Rowen, *op. cit.*, pp.90–91.

80 *Journaal Heenvliet*, p.545.

2 THE DYNASTY AT BAY

THE FAMILY IN DISARRAY

In the middle of the 17th century three dynasties, bound by ties of blood and by marriage, the Bourbons, the House of Orange and the Stuarts, were in disarray. Yet they had the potential of being, with the Habsburgs, the four most influential in Europe. We will come to the Stuarts. Let us glance at the Bourbons.

All his adult life William III was to battle with the hegemonic power of France and of her Bourbon king, Louis XIV, a confrontation which was to be the central facet of his life; hence in this story we will need to give a special focus to France and her king. Louis has been seen as the exemplar of Absolute Monarchy in his lifetime and since; and yet his youth and his early manhood were precarious in the extreme. On that gloomy day in November 1650 when William was born, Louis was 12 years old and France was enveloped in the civil wars known as the Frondes.

The administration of France had broken down; and during the minority of her son, Louis's mother, Anne of Austria, and her wily Italian minister, Mazarin, were clinging to the maintenance of an uncertain regency. In 1648 the Crown had defaulted on its debts. The country's highest court of law, the Parlement of Paris, which could also cluster around itself formidable political power, was in opposition to the regime. There were disorders amongst the peasants in the countryside and amongst the mobs in Paris. The plots and revolts of the nobility were endemic. Whilst one of France's leading generals, Turenne, was in open revolt, another, Condé, was under arrest, and the king's uncle, Gaston of Orléans, was plotting against his sister-in-law's minister.

In February 1651 Mazarin left Paris to go into exile. On the night of 9 February it was rumoured that Louis and his mother were about to flee the capital. To reassure the Parisian mob that that was not the case, a delegation was allowed into the Palais-Royal. There, whilst Louis pretended to be asleep, it filed past his bed.[1]

In the north, in the United Provinces, it might have been thought that there was little to be feared from the might of France.

There in The Hague William and his clan of Orange-Nassau too confronted an unstable present and a precarious future. Family discord stalked around the cot of the new-born Prince. At once disturbing questions began to trouble the minds of his immediate family, and of its various supporters. Who amongst the members of the clan were to be his guardians and who would become master, or mistress, of the wealth, the political position, and the patronage of the House? And who would safeguard it against its enemies amongst those groups of Regents whom it had so recently and so deeply offended?

Both the chief protagonists within the family turned towards the States of Holland for support for their antagonistic positions. To them Mary submitted a memorandum, as did her formidable mother-in-law, the Princess Dowager, Amalia von Solms-Braunfels. Amalia asked their Noble High Mightinesses, as the States of Holland were termed, to appoint guardians for the child. Mary, who, as the eldest daughter of Charles I of England, bore the title of Princess Royal, submitted a claim, based on the unsigned will of her dead husband, that she and nominees appointed by the States of Holland should assume the task. She left vague the exact role to be played by the Holland nominees, manifesting the clear intention that the foremost role should be played by herself. To this the Princess Dowager retorted that, as the Princess Royal was herself under age, she could scarcely take on the tutelage of her under-age child.[2]

Not to be left behind in the dispute, another member of the clan, related by marriage, and, more distantly, by blood,[3] and also of high status, the Elector of Brandenburg, hastened to intervene. He was married to Louise-Henrietta, the eldest daughter of Amalia and Frederick-Henry; and, in the event of the death of William, she would become the heiress of the House of Orange.

'It has come to the astonished notice of His Electoral Serene Highness', it was reported in a memorandum to their Noble High Mightinesses, the States of Holland, 'that attempts were here in progress to dismiss and completely exclude Her Most Excellent Serene Highness and Beloved and Most Esteemed Lady, his Mother-in-Law, as well as other close Blood Relations, from the Guardianship and Administration of the Infant's estate, in an unheard of manner and against all justice, reason, and fairness, which His Electoral Serene Highness views in the most fraught and serious terms.'[4]

Thus confronted, their Noble High Mightinesses judged it best to refer the matter, and the attendant files, to the Province's Court of Justice, to see whether it couldn't find some middle way, or 'viam concordiae', as their Noble High Mightinesses, rather optimistically, put it, between the wrangling relatives.[5]

In the midst of all this there was the baptism of the child and the burial of the father to attend to. The baptism came first. It occurred at the beginning of 1651, in the afternoon of 15 January, a Sunday.

The long-standing custom of deference towards the House of Orange was too long established, too widespread, and too deeply rooted in the history of the Republic to be disregarded. The baptism was attended by delegates from the States-General, from the States of Holland and of Zeeland, and from the towns of Delft, Leyden, and Amsterdam, all of whom were to act as sponsors. A large crowd had gathered in the church, the Groote Kerk, or Great Church, in The Hague. Driven by curiosity to see the spectacle, they had clambered wherever they could, up to the organ, up the walls, up to the church furnishings, the better to obtain a view. As the crowd, and the tumult, increased, the pastor, the Reverend Tegnejus, was reduced to clapping his hands for silence, so that he could deliver his address; but, this producing no effect, he judiciously decided that the best course was to cut it short.

The Stuart representative, James, Duke of York, brother of the Princess Royal, had taken refuge in The Hague from a troubled England, which was beset by its civil war, and which would cost their father, Charles I, his head. But the duke refused to attend the ceremony. Some said he thought it beneath his dignity; others that it was because of the disagreements between his sister and her mother-in-law.

There were bitter disputes as to who was to carry the child, and who was to carry his train. Finally, the admirable Elizabeth of Bohemia, the exiled queen, managed to present the baby for baptism. The Princess Royal, it was rumoured, had wanted to have him called Charles William, so linking a Stuart with an Orange name. But the Princess Dowager was adamantly opposed to this; and she made it clear that if it were insisted upon she would absent herself from the proceedings. In the end he was christened William Henry.[6]

The scene was indeed reminiscent of a Jan Steen picture with the Lord of Misrule firmly installed on the House of Orange's ancestral seat of authority.

But matters did then somehow take a turn for the better. The States-General waited upon the Princess Royal after the ceremony; and the presentation of their compliments was attended with the donation of an elegant golden box containing securities worth 8,000 guilders (£800) per annum. And similar *douceurs* arrived from Holland, Zeeland, Delft, Leyden and Amsterdam. These were welcome additions to the income of the princely House, which at this time, we are told, amounting to 500,000 guilders (£50,000), was exceeded by its outgoings.[7] The princes of Orange had received prize money from the Dutch fleet and from the fleets of the Dutch East India and West India Companies, as well as booty gained from the Republic's military campaigns. After the Treaty of Westphalia these were partly lost, and, after the death of William II, entirely so. The House now had to rely solely on the income from its private domains; and whilst these were generally sufficient to cover its ordinary expenses – the Princess Royal and the Princess Dowager between them cost 189,000 guilders (just under £19,000) a year – they were insufficient to cover extraordinary expenses, including interest on its substantial debts, or the repayment of the debts.[8]

It was taken amiss by staid republicans that the little Prince had been accompanied by halberdiers, and that his baptismal swaddling clothes were lined with ermine.[9] It smacked, the staid republicans thought, too much of royal symbolism.

The baptism was followed by the burial of William II on Wednesday 8 March, attended by more pomp and ceremony – the mourning and the burial cost 118,277 guilders (nearly £12,000).[10] Too much royalism again.

There is a portrait of Princess Mary by Van der Helst in the Rijksmuseum in Amsterdam which shows a face weary, haughty, defensive and worn. She sits a little stiffly and awkwardly, conveying a sense of precarious self-control, 'my poor Neece,' wrote her aunt, Elizabeth of Bohemia, when Mary's husband died, 'is the most afflicted creature that ever I saw and is changed as she is nothing as skin and bone…'.[11]

She lacked the common touch and the cynical, polished, political skills of her brother, Charles II, and gave the appearance of taking for granted the services rendered to the House of Orange by its supporters. A French observer noted that 'elle ne descend pas volontiers a des demonstrations de bonté et de caresses aux personnes de l'Etat, croyant les choses trop au dessous de sa condition et se persuadent que les amis de la Maison d'Orange, en luy demeurant fidelles, ne feront que ce qu'ils doivent'.[12] She never learnt Dutch,[13] preferring English and French, and she developed an aversion to the country in which she lived.[14] She travelled incessantly outside that country, visiting her Stuart relations, and she has been accused of neglecting the true interests of her son.[15] But such charges, often repeated by historians, do not give full weight to her predicament nor to the values of the times in which she lived.

Two years before the baptism of her son, almost to the day, her father, King Charles I, had stretched out before the executioner's block on the scaffold in Whitehall in London before a taut and silent crowd. He extended his arms as a signal to the executioner to do his work, and his head was severed by a single blow. A strange sound, a sort of groan,[16] emanated from the watching multitude. By the quality of the speeches he delivered before a large audience at his trial; by his address to the little group that surrounded him on the scaffold; by the dignity of his bearing; and by his courage he had metamorphosed from an inept into a martyr king. The snow fell heavily as his coffin was carried to the entrance of St George's Chapel at Windsor Castle for burial so that the funeral pall was covered in white, the colour associated with innocence.[17] Parliament had destroyed the king; the 'White King', the 'Martyr King', had taken the first step towards the restoration of the monarchy.

But that was not, at this time, apparent.

In The Hague with Mary then was her refugee brother, now become Charles II. He did not yet know that he had inherited the throne, nor for many years did it become discernible that the manner of his father's death had helped to open a path, however long and tortuous, to the Restoration. Still hoping for his father's reprieve, he was anxiously waiting for news. It was brought to him by his chaplain, Dr Goffe. He heard himself addressed as 'Your Majesty'. He realised the import at once: he broke down in tears, and gestured to bear the shock and grief alone.[18]

To Charles, and to Mary, brought up on the doctrine of divine right, this was a horror which was more than the execution of a father: it was the murder of a divinely appointed monarch, the Lord's Anointed. The shock reverberated across Europe. And the trauma was never fully erased from the minds of William III's English royal uncles, Charles II and

Mary Stuart, William's mother, 1652, by Bartholomeus van der Helst.
Rijksmuseum, Amsterdam

James II, with, in the case of the latter, important consequences for his conduct when he fled from England on William's invasion of England in 1688.

For Mary, a teenager still at the birth of her son, the shock of her father's death was followed by that of her husband's. She was now isolated in a foreign country, a large part of whose power elite were republican in sentiment, and she had to contend within the House of Orange with her formidable mother-in-law. It was both very natural and, as events in the end were to prove, very shrewd that she now directed all her energies towards her Stuart family.

But at the beginning of 1651 their plight seemed to carry with it very little hope. At the end of April 1648 James, as the Duke of York, had arrived in The Hague, having contrived to escape from England, dressed as a girl.[19] Mary's younger sister, Elizabeth, had died – in September 1650 – a captive of Parliament whose prisoner as yet was still another brother, the Duke of Gloucester. Her eldest brother, Charles II, was by now, in 1651, in Scotland where his coronation as king of that country had just taken place; but only as the result of the support of the severe Calvinist party, whose inflexible principles he had been forced to swear to uphold and which, in every way, were wholly abhorrent to him.[20] He was to embark later in the year on a desperate campaign from Scotland to recover his English crown. Mary's mother, Henrietta Maria, the aunt of Louis XIV, had sought refuge in Paris, dependent on the uncertain charity of her French royal relations, themselves facing the turbulence of the Frondes.

In attaching importance to her family and to her clan, and in the manner in which she did it, Mary was a creature of her times. 17th-century Europe was dominated by these identities, with their inseparable adjuncts, the complicated substructures of patrons and clients, on which we shall expand later in this chapter.

Mary indeed laid enormous emphasis on her royal status, all the more so, perhaps, because she was aware that her marriage into the House of Orange was not as elevated as it would have been had her parents not been forced into it by the harsh realities of the circumstances they faced. But rank, or degree, was supremely important in an age in which all authority, whether in the Catholic monarchy of France or in the Calvinistic republic of the United Provinces, carried divine sanction – 'the powers that be are ordained of God'.[21] Even republicans recognised that royal rank was a political fact going beyond mere status. The Orange-Nassaus attached the importance they did to the minute Principality of Orange, which had no strategic or economic value, precisely because it conferred sovereignty upon them, even if only as princes and not as kings, and they were prepared to spend very large sums of money on its defences as a result. Hence also what appear to us now absurd disputes over precedence. But precedence was politically supremely important and it brought with it material benefits. It could not be ignored, which is why the disputes were carried to such inordinate lengths.

Mary's rival within the House of Orange, Amalia von Solms, was 49 in 1651. The sexual allure of her earlier portraits stares brazenly at us across the centuries and she remained still a handsome woman. She was intelligent and worldly, with a practical appreciation of the importance of money. Her relationship with the Elector of Brandenburg was influenced not only by the prestige brought by his marriage to her daughter, Louise-Henrietta, but also by the consideration that should William III, a weakly child, die, Louise-Henrietta would be heiress to the Orange fortune.[22] And the stance she adopted with regard to the States of Holland was tempered by her hopes of obtaining a pension from them, as was usual for the widow of a Stadholder[23] – although she, uncharacteristically, did not help herself when she rejected one offer and insisted on receiving double the amount decreed by custom.[24] Mature, experienced, earthy, and with far greater roots in the Netherlands, she had more developed political skills than her teenage daughter-in-law. It has been pointed out that she was from now on to become a central figure on the Dutch scene, recognised as such internationally.[25]

She was closely connected to the Nassaus. We have seen that her grandmother on her father's side was a sister of William the Silent. Her mother, who died young, was Agnes von Sayn-Wittgenstein, and had Orange blood, as did her stepmother, who succeeded Agnes as the wife of her father, the ruling Count of Solms-Braunfels. He had been the Court Chamberlain at the court of the Palatinate, where his nephew was the Elector, and Amalia's early years were spent at the castle at Heidelberg. Unlike Mary, she did speak Dutch, although French was her working language – her version of it was atrocious, but, like most things about her, very effective. Her mother tongue, German, was just as bad. Her husband, Frederick-Henry, had very much relied on her political abilities and she exercised considerable influence on her son-in-law, the Elector of Brandenburg. Like Mary, she travelled extensively, for example to Spa, and most of the winter of 1655 was spent with her daughter in Berlin, who together with the Elector also spent much time at Cleves within easy reach of her mother. The family connections in Germany were further extended by Amalia's marrying two of her other daughters to Johann Georg, Prince of Anhalt-Dessau (in 1659), and Louis of Zimmern, the Count Palatine (in 1666).[26]

The antagonism between the Princess Royal and the Princess Dowager has been seen by historians as a source of weakness that divided the Orange camp; and this to a degree it did. But – much more importantly – the antagonists supplemented and complemented what each could bring to the cause; Amalia with her shrewd and practical comprehension of Dutch politics assisted the House to survive in the present; Mary, by insisting on maintaining close contact with her Stuart clan and on her royal status, prepared the ground for the future – culminating in the throne of England for her son. It was a future to which Amalia also contributed by maintaining the extensive relationships that the clan of Orange-Nassau had in Germany, which it derived from its origins there and which it had never lost – the marriages of her daughters were part of this. Both sets of relationship constituted

Amalia von Solms-Braunfels, 1650, workshop of Gerard van Honthorst.
Rijksmuseum, Amsterdam

a potentially invaluable asset for the House, for both, if the House wished to act as broker, could be put to work on behalf of the Dutch Regents – and indeed, subsequently, on behalf of the English political class as well. But that, for the moment, was not apparent – the relationship with the English royal house, indeed, was viewed as a particular disadvantage. The two princesses were flanked by their advisers, Jan van Kerckhoven, Lord of Heenvliet, and Constantijn Huygens. Heenvliet had been head of Mary's household since her marriage and his English wife, Lady Stanhope, had been Mary's governess. He has been depicted as an upstart, 'the son of a Leyden professor of theology' who 'had merely bought the manor of Heenvliet'.[27]

Constantijn Huygens was of a different hue. As Frederick-Henry's former secretary he was devoted to the House of Orange; he was a man of great culture, a leading connoisseur, and a poet;[28] he was instrumental in extending Frederick-Henry's patronage to Rembrandt,[29] and he was involved in the building of the Orange palaces, the Mauritshuis and the Huis ten Bosch, both in The Hague.[30]

There was one other figure circulating within the firmament of the House, Count William-Frederick of Nassau-Siegen, head of the cadet branch of the Nassaus, whose side of the family were traditionally Stadholders of Friesland. With William III but a child, he saw himself as the potential candidate to become the leader of the Orange party. But he was suspected by both Mary and Amalia of wanting to pursue his own ends at the expense of the child Prince, particularly after December 1650, when he had accomplished his aim of becoming Stadholder of Groningen to add to the position he held in Friesland.[31] But whatever his ambitions might have been to fill the leadership void in the country as a whole, they were frustrated by his association with William II's coup before the gates of Amsterdam in 1650; and after William's death he went in fear of reprisals from the Holland Regents.[32]

It was thus that the family and clan of William III was to face a very hostile world.

THE REGENTS ON THE OFFENSIVE

If the question as to who should gain control of the House of Orange was preoccupying the members of the family, the question as to how to fill the constitutional void in the country as a whole was preoccupying the whole Dutch political elite. Events evolved with great rapidity. Mary's concern for the position of her son, who, however young, was the nominal head of the Orange clan, was evinced by despatching, on the day itself of her son's birth, a request to the States-General that he should acquire the dignities of his father. Amalia von Solms followed suit a few days later.[33]

It was to no avail. Able and determined Regents in the Province of Holland were moving with equal despatch to take over the leadership of the Union left vacant by the death of William II, in a series of movements so swift as to amount to a counter-coup. It was decided at once, in November 1650, to leave unfilled the position of Stadholder in Holland and pressure was put on a wobbly Zeeland, where there was a strong Orangist faction, to do the same.[34] On 8 December the powers which the Stadholder had had in Holland over political appointments in the towns with votes in the Province's States were acquired by the towns themselves; whilst, at the same time, the town councils were to appoint their own membership through co-option. The councils of towns without votes were in future to be appointed by the Holland States.[35] The ruling elites, it was clear, intended to become self-perpetuating.

The other Provinces adopted similar regimes and also left their Stadholderships vacant, except for Friesland and Groningen. There, in the east of the country, William-Frederick hurried to have himself elected Stadholder of Groningen to add to that of Friesland, which he already held.[36] The Regents in Holland did not allow the pace to slacken. They summoned a Great Assembly to determine the measures that would be required to govern the Union in the new circumstances, and this was attended by delegates from all the Provinces. They began to arrive at the end of December and the official opening took place on 18 January 1651 in the splendid surroundings of the Knights' Hall in the Binnenhof at The Hague.[37] There the Holland Pensionary, Jacob Catz, addressed the crucial question of the command of the armed forces, a role which, as Captain-General and Admiral-General, had traditionally been performed by a member of the House of Orange. In presenting the case for leaving these positions unfilled he observed that the country had been free from war since the conclusion of peace with Spain; that the House of Orange had no one who could aspire to the command of the army; and that for several years there had been a field-marshal who could and should command the army.[38]

But Holland did not have it all its own way. The deputies of Friesland, thereto motivated by William-Frederick, championed, if not entirely the rights of the infant Prince, at least those of the House of Orange; or, if not entirely the House of Orange, then those of the cadet branch, the House of Nassau, in the shape of William-Frederick himself. In times of peace, they said, one should not neglect to prepare for war; and, while it remained that in the House of Orange there was at present no person who could exercise the actual command of the armies, there was such a one in the House of Nassau. Whilst the country would gain immortal glory in appointing the young Prince as Captain-General, so that he could enter into the actual exercise of his duties at such time as his age would allow him to add his personal capacities and merit to the services which his predecessors had performed, William-Frederick could in the meantime stand in for him.[39]

To this the Holland representatives responded that the post of Captain-General was not hereditary and it was unheard of, in a free republic, for such a charge to be given to an infant in swaddling clothes.[40]

Furthermore, to appoint William-Frederick as deputy, in the guise of Lieutenant-General, as far as the army was concerned, would cause offence to Van Brederode, who was already Field-Marshal, and, as far as the navy was concerned, to Tromp who was already Lieutenant-Admiral.[41]

There was, of course, deep suspicion of William-Frederick, because of the role he had played in William II's coup against the Amsterdam Regents in the previous year; and it was universally recognised that, once he had established himself by deputising for the infant William III in the traditional roles carried out by the princes of Orange, the true heir would find it very difficult to replace him when he, William, came of age.[42]

The two princesses, despite their differences, did their best to stem the currents which were flowing so strongly against the interests of the baby Prince. They had after all a joint interest in preserving as much as they could of the influence of the House, even if each then sought to capture it for herself. In February Amalia von Solms made another move on behalf of her grandson by submitting a memorandum in which she observed that she was aware that the military and political offices of her deceased husband were under discussion and that she hoped cognisance would be taken of the young Prince. She acknowledged that the eminent offices held by his predecessors were not hereditary, but expressed the wish that the Prince might receive them as a pure grace and favour, and as a mark of respect for the memory of his ancestors.[43]

This initiative again proved fruitless, as did an intervention by Mary in Zeeland. There the position of First Noble, who represented the nobility in the States of this Province, had become vacant as the result of her husband's death, and Mary maintained that this was a position tantamount to being hereditary in the family, both because of the important services which the princes of Orange had rendered to the country in general and to Zeeland in particular, and because of the extensive property interests the family possessed there. And, she indicated, if the position were left open it would, in effect, leave a constitutional void in the Province.[44]

Although Mary was to fail in her immediate aim, it nevertheless became apparent that she had managed to arouse sufficient feeling in Zeeland to cause alarm in Holland that the Province was wavering in its support on the issue of the young Prince's appointment as Captain-General. Holland was compelled to send a delegation to steady Zeeland's resolve.[45] It was successful, thanks in large part to a rising young politician from Dort, a town in Holland where he had just become Pensionary. He was destined in a short time to take over the leadership of the Republic for nearly two decades and his complicated relationship with the young Prince was to be central to both their lives. His name was Johan De Witt, and he was not yet 26 years old.

The upshot of the Great Assembly when it came to an end in August was that no Captain-General and no Admiral-General were appointed. In the Dutch Republic the Regents tended to leave military leadership to the traditional aristocracy, at any rate as far as the army was concerned. Nor was there a lack of supplicants amongst the higher aristocracy to take on this role. However much they were previously identified with William II, immediately after his death military members of his own family such as William-Frederick, Johan Maurits of Nassau-Siegen, and Jan Wolfert van Brederode, a brother-in-law of Amelia von Solms, had not hesitated to recommend themselves to the States-General;[46] and Holland's championship of Brederode, a citizen of that Province, confirmed his appointment as Field-Marshal.

But the position Brederode was to hold was infinitely weaker than the traditional military-political position of the princes of Orange. Holland made certain that it was entangled by a lumbering, complicated system under which the Provinces assumed control of the troops they paid for and of troop movements. It was further debilitated by jurisdiction over the troops being transferred to magistrates, with the army's own jurisdiction being confined solely to cases of desertion and insubordination.[47] The settlement of the Great Assembly before its dissolution in August left the Republic considerably enfeebled militarily, particularly on land. Whilst she was about to be proved vulnerable on the sea as well, it was fortunate that no land threat was to develop for many years. But when it did it was to prove devastating.

Despite their efforts on behalf of the young Prince there was little that Mary, or her dowager mother-in-law, could do to prevent the *coup d'état* that was occurring under Holland's leadership. And further dangers still were emerging from a background already sufficiently bleak.

EXCLUSION

Even whilst the Great Assembly was still sitting there disembarked at Rotterdam towards the end of March 1651 Oliver St John, Chief Justice of England, and his fellow ambassador, Walter Strickland.[48] They had come on a mission to settle the strained relations between their country and the Republic.

The economic differences between the two were of long standing. But they were affected by two very new developments. The Dutch were the pre-eminent trading power in the world and the English were finding it increasingly difficult to compete. As Jonathan Israel[49] has pointed out, the English had lost their markets to the Dutch in the northern reaches of Europe, but the trade embargoes imposed by the Spaniards in their wars against the Dutch and the privateering activities carried out by them and their Flemish subjects had enabled the English to compensate in southern Europe and the Mediterranean for what they had lost in the north. With the peace established between the Dutch and the Spaniards in 1648, this position was transformed and transformed very rapidly. In the face of Dutch competition the English became as helpless in the south as they had been in the north.

The second major development was that the new Commonwealth or Republic which had come into existence as a result of the Civil War in England had built a powerful and large navy, more modern than the Dutch. There was the temptation at hand, therefore, to seek assuagement on the military front for England's deficiencies on the economic. Would she succumb to that temptation?

The auspices for the English mission were not good. A previous mission had been sent a couple of years before, which was in Holland at the time of Charles I's execution; its main aim had been to expel English royalists from the Republic and royalist ships from Dutch ports. A member of that mission, Isaac Dorislaus, an Englishman of Dutch extraction, had been assassinated by the royalists and the mission had been withdrawn.[50]

The present mission, too, began badly. It was very large, consisting of 246 people.[51] The official lodgings reserved for Ambassadors Extraordinary were occupied by the French ambassador, who refused to vacate them. In the alternative and dispersed lodgings that were found for the English ambassadors and their suite they were exposed to the insults of the mob, then, as always, staunchly Orangist in its sympathies and hence strongly in favour of the Stuarts with whom the House was so closely associated.[52]

From the moment they arrived in The Hague the servants of the Princess Royal and of the Queen of Bohemia harassed the ambassadors and their train. Mary's brother, the Duke of York, and the Queen of Bohemia's sons, Prince Edward of the Palatinate and his brother, Prince Rupert of the Rhine, who had commanded the troops of Charles I in the English Civil War, took the lead. Shouts of 'king-murderers' and 'Cromwell's bastards' were hurled at the mission.

The States of Holland did their utmost to quell these disturbances. They provided a guard for their diplomatic guests whilst the Provincial court took proceedings against Prince Edward – who, however, escaped punishment – and others, who, it was felt by the ambassadors, got off very lightly.[53]

In this atmosphere it was not surprising that the negotiations between the English and Dutch proved difficult to resolve. The English ambassadors were rather vague in their proposals, but it gradually became apparent that what they had in mind was a full political union between the two countries, a single state. The rather startled Dutch quickly saw this as a somewhat naïve and crude attempt to subordinate them, which, of course, it was.[54] Then the English were also showing considerable concern for the threat that the Stuarts presented to their fledgling English Republic. They had seen both the popular support which could be mustered on the Stuarts' behalf and the numbers and distinction of the royalist exiles. They submitted a clause to be inserted in the draft treaty which barred the Princess Royal and, for good measure, the baby Prince, her son, from sheltering or assisting the enemies of the English Republic on pain of confiscation of their property.[55]

This was a politically impossible demand, for, despite the disarray in the Orange camp, popular opinion in the streets would never have tolerated it. The English ambassadors concluded that there was little point in their remaining in the Dutch Republic and on 30 June they took their formal leave and departed its shores the following day.[56]

The Orangist party and the Princess Royal in particular have been blamed for the breakdown in negotiations, and the outbreak of the subsequent war.[57] But the causes of dispute between England and the Dutch Republic, such as the resentment of powerful merchant interests at Dutch competition, were well beyond the powers of the Princess Royal either to instigate or to control. They continued to operate when the Stuarts were restored and were a factor in contributing to two further Anglo-Dutch wars.

From Mary's point of view the representatives of the new English Republic were a threat. They had chopped off her father's head and she was right to anticipate that they would soon be menacing the interests of her son.

Aside from Anglo-Dutch relations, and prior to the end of the year, in August, the legal dispute between Mary and Amalia von Solms and the Elector of Brandenburg over the guardianship of William III was resolved. All three were to act as co-guardians with Mary having one vote and the other two one vote between them: thus creating a deadlock position, which would require mutual agreement to make it work.[58]

Then, in September, further disaster overtook the Stuarts. Charles II's invasion of England at the head of the Scottish army had ended in total defeat at the battle of Worcester.[59] He was now wandering in the English countryside to find a means of escape from Cromwell's searching soldiers.

In the meantime the Dutch and English Republics were gradually moving towards war, which was to bring further set-backs to Mary and her cause. England passed the Navigation Act, directed against the use of Dutch shipping for goods traded with England. It was accompanied by increasing harassment of Dutch shipping at sea by the English navy and privateers. By the end of June 1652 the English and Dutch were at war.[60]

The outbreak of war was to bring Johan De Witt, in rapid succession, first to greater prominence and then to the supreme leadership of the Dutch Republic. The absence of a suitable member of the House of Orange to lead the country had left a gap and the pressures of war were to demonstrate that the collegiate system of government of the Regent oligarchies was not sufficient to fill it. A strong leader was required. De Witt, by family background – his father had been one of the Regents imprisoned by William II – and deep conviction, carried the banner of the anti-Orangist republican party. This had always been profoundly suspicious of the position of 'eminent head', which, since the origins of the Dutch Republic, had been filled by members of the House of Orange. It was therefore not without irony that a not dissimilar role should be played by De Witt himself.

At the conclusion of the Great Assembly the aged Jacob Catz had resigned as Pensionary of Holland, to be succeeded by another aged elder statesman, Adriaan Pauw, who had played a leading part in negotiating the peace with Spain in 1648. Now that war had broken out it was decided to send Pauw, as Ambassador Extraordinary, to England to see what he could rescue. Dort, where De Witt was Pensionary, was historically the first town in the Province of Holland and accordingly and fortuitously the task of deputising for Pauw fell to him; and he continued to act as Pauw's assistant on his return a short while later.[61]

The war, from the Dutch viewpoint, did not open well and the interruption of trade and of the fishing industry began to be manifested in social unrest, which was fomented by preachers and expressed itself in a strong surge in Orangist sentiment. Once again Zeeland was vacillating and in August 1652 the town of Middelburg in that Province had submitted to the Provinces' States proposals to appoint William III as Captain – and Admiral-General. Holland at once reacted by despatching a mission which included De Witt. The delegation was menaced by mobs and was in some danger, although it was successful in heading off the immediate threat. But feeling in favour of the young Prince was not stilled,[62] and it grew as the failures of the war increased and the economic situation deteriorated further.

The Regents in Holland, who had in any case always dreaded the war, were therefore under considerable pressure to reach a settlement with the English before its economic and social effects were to become too menacing. They were assisted by the growing power of Cromwell in England, who had been sceptical from the beginning about the purposes of a war with as Protestant a country as the Dutch Republic. By the end of 1652 it became clear that Holland, the strongest, but not the exclusive, voice in the Dutch Republic, and Cromwell, the most influential, but not yet the all-powerful, voice in that of England, were ready to parley.

But they both had to carry others with them. A curious duality of parallel negotiations therefore commenced, partly in the open and partly secretly. Shortly before he died, in February 1653,[63] Pauw had written a letter to the English government in a personal capacity, indicating Holland's desire for peace. The States of Holland, persuaded by De Witt, followed this up in March with an official letter;[64] that is to say, Holland was taking the initiative in commencing negotiations itself, rather than doing so through the States-General, who of course represented the country as a whole. The secret letter was published in England as a piece of propaganda as evidence that the States of Holland were suing for peace, and, although De Witt was subsequently able to gain the support of the States-General, it caused a stir in the Orangist party, which accused Holland of acting unconstitutionally.[65]

Following his crushing defeat at the battle of Worcester, Mary's brother, Charles II, after many adventures which for the rest of his life he never tired of telling – either always in complete accordance with the facts or consistently[66] – had at length managed to make his way to France. In the spring of 1653 he was in Paris and contacted the Dutch ambassador there with the suggestion that, if the Dutch were to provide him with a fleet, he would personally join it for an expedition against England. De Witt and the Holland Regents took the view that an alliance of this nature would scupper any hopes of peace.[67] And when it became apparent that Charles planned to come to The Hague, the States of Holland made it clear to Mary, in the politest but most unmistakable terms, that they considered it inadvisable, adding that any future visit should be cleared both with them and the States-General.[68]

Meanwhile in England Cromwell seized supreme power. On 20 April he stalked into the House of Commons and called in his soldiers to disperse the members. Although it was not to be until the middle of December that he was formally installed as Lord Protector, from now on he was able to pursue his own policy towards the Dutch unhampered. The English, too, were experiencing the penalties of war. If the Dutch were facing set-backs in the North Sea, everywhere else they were inflicting losses as great if not greater on the English in the Baltic, in the Mediterranean, in the Indian Ocean and in the Far East.[69]

In June the Dutch Admiral, Maarten Tromp, suffered a major naval defeat, which set off the most violent Orangist riots everywhere, including the Province of Holland. William-Frederick took occasion to visit Texel in the northern part of the Province and was treated and cheered as though he was a sovereign.[70] Mary saw him as a clear threat to her baby son. 'The Princess Royal', it was recorded, 'is passionately against the having of Count William to be Lieut.-General'.[71] In The Hague a mob shot a flag to pieces from which the arms of the Prince of Orange had been removed. Cromwell's spies reported from The Hague in August, 'The young Prince with the Princess-Royal, are to return hither this week. Already the boys at The Hague are eagerly carrying Orange placards about, but at the coming of the Prince this will be redoubled. All the people, except in Holland, are for the Princess-royal and her son, and Prince William [i.e. William-Frederick] his deputy.' And a month later, 'The young Prince, being sent for, is come to The Hague with his mother, whom to congratulate the young fry were in arms after their fashion, and broke the windows of those who offered to oppose them. If no agreement is made in England, 'tis thought the States will have the young babe, and make them their general.'[72]

The rise to supreme power of Oliver Cromwell, the opponent of the House of Stuart in England, was echoed on 30 July by the appointment, as Pensionary of Holland, of Johan De Witt, the opponent of the House of Orange in the Dutch Republic. Negotiations with England could now begin in earnest. Four ambassadors, two from Holland, one from Zeeland, and a fourth from Friesland to keep an eye on the negotiations on behalf of William-Frederick, had already been appointed. The first of them, Hieronymus van Beverninck, who was very close to De Witt, arrived in London on 17 June, and the others were not far behind.[73] The negotiations dragged on until the spring of 1653 when the key outstanding question was the position of William of Orange and his family.

Cromwell was most concerned that the security of the new regime in England should not be undermined by the Stuarts operating from a Dutch base and supported by their relations in the House of Orange. He demanded a clause in the peace treaty which would debar William 'and all members of his family' from the traditional high offices held by his family of Stadholder, Captain-General or Admiral-General. This, as it stood, was wholly unacceptable to the States-General, who felt unable to face down the ensuing popular uproar. But a clever compromise, which became known as 'the temperament', was devised. The treaty was to contain an article by which both countries undertook not to aid each other's rebels; and the clause explicitly debarring, or excluding, the Prince from the traditional high offices was dropped. However, if he did accept those offices he would have to swear to abide by the terms of the treaty, including the clause relating to rebels, which, of course, would include his Stuart relations. All seemed well. This was acceptable to the States-General, who approved the Treaty on 22 April 1654.

But all was not as it seemed. 'The temperament' by itself had not after all satisfied Cromwell. He had insisted that a secret Act of Exclusion should be entered into by the Province of Holland, which would give an undertaking that the Province would exclude the Prince from the traditional high offices. De Witt had withheld this not only from the States-General but also from the States of Holland themselves. Nevertheless, by extremely able manoeuvring, he managed to get the States of Holland to pass the Act of Exclusion on 4 May; and Cromwell's ratification arrived on the 7th.[74]

However, De Witt's clerk had revealed the passing of the secret Act by Holland to Count William-Frederick; and a huge Orangist furore broke out.[75] But, once again, not all the members of the House were solidly on the same side. Amalia von Solms played an ambivalent role with the powers of the hour. Her ostensible opposition to exclusion in public was tempered in private when she told De Witt that if she had been a Holland deputy she would have voted in its favour. It was whispered that her position was not uninfluenced by her hopes of receiving fruitful compensation in the form of the pension she had been claiming from Holland since the death of Frederick-Henry.[76] And Field Marshal Brederode, who had his own interests to secure in safeguarding his military position, played a key role in managing to get the Holland nobility to support De Witt.[77]

The House faced a *fait accompli*. The situation was succinctly summed up by Mary when she received a delegation from Holland, led by De Witt, who had arrived to explain Holland's stance. 'Things now are as they are,' she said. 'I must be patient and know how to accept things as long as I am in the country.'[78]

It is still disputed by historians whether De Witt contrived to persuade Cromwell in demanding the Act of Exclusion, or whether the two were complicit in achieving their joint objective of excluding the House of Orange from positions of power.[79] But whatever the truth of the matter, one of the most authoritative of Dutch historians has argued convincingly that the Act of Exclusion was a mistake committed by both Cromwell and De Witt. It enduringly embittered popular feeling against De Witt's regime and undermined it, thereby in the long run strengthening the cause of Orange.[80]

The man who was now the leading figure in the United Provinces has been described as the head and chief proponent of the 'Republican Party'. But De Witt's republicanism was not the result of abstract principle, but of pragmatic consideration. He told William Temple that 'if he had been born under a king, he could never have consented to what his ancestors did towards the king of Spain; but being born under a commonwealth [republic], and sworn to maintain it, he could consent to nothing that should destroy it.'[81]

His political principles are enunciated in a document called, in shorthand, 'the Deduction', which was written by him as an apologia for the Act of Exclusion; and as such it was inevitably directed at the House of Orange and its adherents. He insisted that the individual Provinces within the United Provinces fully retained their sovereignty, thus bestowing authority on the main alternative power centre to the House of Orange, the Province of Holland; he denied that the Prince of Orange, or anyone else, could hold high office by right of birth; he warned of the dangers of conferring high military offices on a hereditary basis, citing the example of the Visconti in Milan, who had turned themselves into sovereign princes; and the combination of high civil with high military office was full of danger and totally unacceptable.[82]

Johan De Witt was from an old Regent family and he was a Regent through and through. His philosophy was rooted in Dutch history from the second half of the 16th century up to his own time, with its conflicts between the Regent class and the House of Orange: it was essentially a justification of the system of rule by a predominant Regent class to which the House of Orange should only be allowed to make a contribution provided its position was subordinated to the authority and the interests of that class, which De Witt also considered to be the interests of the country as a whole.

We need to be careful, when considering the language he used, not to give it too much of a modern slant. In practice the Regents, whose power base rested on co-option and family and clan relationship, were themselves firmly rooted in heredity; they believed solidly in hierarchy; and, like most people in De Witt's time, they tended to seek divine sanction for their authority. This tendency was not to be seriously undermined until the new writing of such as Spinoza, in particular, began the very long process – it is easy to underestimate how long – of challenging this element in all the ancient regimes. When the process did finally result in turning upside down the notion that political legitimacy descended not from above, from God, to the political authorities set over the people, but that it ascended from below, resting in the people themselves, it did so with revolutionary force.

The political philosophy of De Witt was to prevail and to hold sway in the United Provinces for nearly two decades. Sincerely, honestly, and honourably held, it was to become known as the 'True Freedom'.

MARY'S TRAVELS WITH CHARLES II

With the tide running so strongly against her and her son there was nothing for it but for Mary to prepare for the future as best she could. Arrangements for William's upbringing had already been made. In May 1653 an independent household had been established for him, which consisted of some 20 people, including a doctor and two pages. It was by the standards of the time not lavish. Some time earlier a governess had been appointed. She was Mrs Howard, a daughter of Heenvliet and the widower of Thomas Howard, who had been Mary's Master of Horse. The total cost of William's establishment was about 30,000 guilders (£3,000), on top of the salary of 1,000 guilders (£100) for Mrs Howard, 10,500 (£1,050) for living expenses, 3,500 (£350) for clothes, and more than 2,400 (£240) for the stables.[83]

With William so taken care of Mary could take steps to keep the closest possible contact with the Stuart clan and its connections. She never wavered in her fundamental belief that there ultimately lay the salvation for her son's cause. To this end she travelled extensively. The storm over the Act of Exclusion was still raging in the United Provinces when at the beginning of July 1654 she set out on a journey to meet her brother Charles II at Spa.

She did not forget her son. On the way she wrote to Mrs Howard (in French), setting out her instructions. The young Prince should be taken for walks when the weather was fine, or he should be taken to see his grandmother – the relationship between Mary and Amalia von Solms, it appears, was not totally disharmonious (Constantijn Huygens observed in January 1656, for example, that the Princess Royal had assured him that she was on a very good footing with her mother-in-law[84]). William was to be available to callers twice a day at 11 o'clock in the morning and at 3 o'clock in the afternoon. At such time the lackeys should be standing at the door or in the gallery and the halberdiers should also be in their appointed places.[85]

When brother and sister met the royal party made the best of their reduced circumstances and took their pleasures where they could. When smallpox broke out at Spa they moved on to Aix-la-Chapelle, where Mary booked the two largest hostels for their use. The king's train consisted of 80 people and the expenses were borne by Mary.[86] At the beginning of October they moved on to Cologne, where they were greeted by the salute of 30 cannon, followed by the firing of a triple salute by 300 musketeers.[87] Their sumptuous entertainment culminated in a final banquet at the *hôtel de ville* arranged by the magistrates of Cologne and they embarked to sail along the Rhine to Düsseldorf on the 29th.[88] At the end of the journey Mary made her way along the Rhine first to Delfthaven and then to her country house at Teyling, where she arrived in November to be met by her son. There the winter was enlivened by frequent visits from Elizabeth of Bohemia.[89]

We hear of William in January 1655, in a report from Elizabeth, writing to Charles II's Secretary of State, Sir Edward Nicholas, on the 10th. 'Mr Secretarie, I beleeue you will hear at Collein [Cologne] how I haue beene debauched this last week in sitting up late to see dancing. Wee made Friday out and every night, which lasted till Saterday at fiue a clock in the morning, and yesterday was the christening of P.Will; childe[90] [William-Frederick's child]; I was at the supper: my Neece the Ps douager, the little Prince [William III] and P. Maurice were gossips: the States generall. I mean their Deputies and the Counsell of State … were there as guests after supper was dancing [till] three a clock. My little Nephue was at the super and satt verie still all the time: those States that were there were verie much taken with him.'[91]

It is the first time that we hear of taciturnity with regard to William. Like his ancestor, William the Silent, it was a feature which he was to cultivate as he grew older.

On the next day Elizabeth again wrote: 'We had a Royaltie, though not vpon twelf night, at Teiling, where my Neece [Mary] was a gipsie and became her dress extreame well…; Mrs Hide a sheperdess and I assure [you] was verie handsome in it, none but her Mistress looked better than she did.'[92] The 'Mrs Hide' here referred to was Anne Hyde and the looks the Queen of Bohemia commented on were not without effect on James, Duke of York. She was indeed first to become pregnant by him and then to marry him, eventually becoming the mother of two queens of England. One daughter became the wife of William III, and the second succeeded him as Queen Anne.

This was not the only gallantry taking place. On 21 June Mary wrote to Charles II: 'Your wife desires me to present her humble duty to you, which is all she can say. I tell her, it is because she thinks of another husband, and does not follow your example of being as constant a wife as you are a husband it is a frailty they say is given to the sex therefore you will pardon her, I hope.'[93]

'The wife', who was no wife, but the butt of Mary's teasing of her brother, was Lucy Walters, and this liaison, too, had far-reaching consequences. The illegitimate son it produced, the Duke of Monmouth, was to lead his ill-conceived rebellion against James, when James became king after Charles, and he received his retribution by perishing on the block.[94]

In July Mary again travelled to meet Charles in Germany and they spent the summer in much the same way as the previous year, with Mary returning home in November.[95]

There, according to Constantijn Huygens, Prince William was no longer a child; Huygens saw with astonishment how much he had grown in body and in mind.[96] Mary's health, on the other hand, was not good. 'I have not been well since I came home,' she wrote to Charles from The Hague on 2 December.[97] It was one of the reasons why she was now planning a trip to Paris, where she would be able to obtain medical advice.[98] From her brother Charles's point of view there were diplomatic reasons against the trip. In October Cromwell had entered into a treaty of friendship with France, which country was now denied to Charles as a refuge.[99] He was negotiating for the support of the Spaniards, who continued to be at war with France and who since the autumn of 1655 were also at war with Cromwell.[100] But there was no moving Mary: '[I] beseech you first to consider,' she wrote to him, 'how reasonable a thing all the world must think it in me to desire to see the queen, my mother, which I have not done since I was a child, and next you know that there has been ill offices done me to her majesty, which I hope, by my going quite to remove, as also to put it out of all malicious people's power to make me again so unhappy.'[101] One of the points at issue between mother and daughter was Mary's intention to appoint Anne Hyde as a maid of honour.[102]

Mary left The Hague on 17 January 1656 with a large train and with no expense stinted so that she might appear with appropriate splendour in the French capital.[103]

MARY'S VISIT TO FRANCE AND REFLECTIONS ON EARLY MODERN EUROPEAN SOCIETY

The war between France and Spain did not prevent Mary travelling through the Spanish Netherlands on her way south. She was treated with as much ceremony there as she was when she entered French territory.[104] At length, on 3 February, Mary met her mother just outside Paris. They had not met for a couple of decades, and Mary and her younger sister, Henrietta, who was with her mother, had never met at all. Shortly afterwards, at St-Denis, Mary was met by the whole court of France, the 17-year-old King, Louis XIV, the Queen Mother, Louis's brother, the Duke of Anjou, and Cardinal Mazarin; and so she was accompanied to the apartments at the Palais Royal which had been prepared for her.

The Paris Mary entered was settling down in the aftermath of the storms caused by the Frondes. Louis's majority, which he reached at the age of 13, had been officially declared in September 1651,[105] and his coronation had taken place in June 1654. His mother's regency was at an end. It was no longer possible for those challenging the king's government to cast a doubt on the authority of those acting on his behalf: authority now stemmed directly from the king himself. Mazarin had returned from exile in February 1653.[106] But, although Turenne had resumed his allegiance to the Crown as early as April 1651, Condé was still in open revolt, fighting for the Spaniards, and the upper nobility, of which he was so potent an example, still needed to be managed; the memory of what it had been capable of remained a constant undercurrent in Louis's considerations.

As Mary settled into her quarters in the Palais Royal, she was treated by the French court as one of its own, with a mother who was the daughter, the sister and the aunt of French kings. Amid the sparkle and glitter by which she was surrounded she was able to observe the French court with which she, her Stuart family, and the retinue of the House of Orange strongly empathised, which they tried to emulate and whose values they absorbed.

Throughout Europe loyalties were much more concrete and personal and much less centred on the abstractions which we call the 'State', the 'People' or the 'Nation'. The complicated webs of family, clan and patron/client relationships operated within states but they could also transcend frontiers and, at the level of Louis XIV and William III, they extended over the whole of Europe. Power had to be exercised through these relationships. If, for example, the king were to attempt to dismiss a minister or secretary of state he could not ignore the fact that their departure was likely to be accompanied by that of their immediate personnel and their own webs of clients, who regarded themselves as being beholden to them personally. Hence the families who provided the membership of the *Conseil d'en Haut*, effectively the king's cabinet, amounted to little more than a handful in over half a century of Louis's personal rule – he rarely dismissed them because the implementation of effective government occurred through the channels of their personal networks of influence. He rarely dismissed them, in short, because he rarely could. The king's territorial disputes were framed in terms of his personal rights, not those of the State, the People or the Nation.[107]

Throughout Europe anyone in authority was expected to display his status. This, of course, Louis XIV was to carry to its apogee. A great man had to behave as a great man, with all the appropriate pomp, circumstance and the pursuit of the appropriate codes which at the same time was both an expression of status and a buttress to it. At every turn standing and renown, particularly in the eyes of history, was a consideration, what was called *gloire*.[108] La *Gloire* was something of practical political importance, and the primary aim of display, which was a constituent of it, was the outward manifestation of political strength, more than an indulgence in personal vanity. The greater one's *gloire*, the greater one's following. They fed on each other.

Amongst the French aristocracy, and the European aristocracies which emulated this example, including the House of Orange, every generation aimed to rise to a higher rank, or, if one was a king, to a higher rank in the order of European monarchs. *Gloire* could be passed on to the next generation. Nobody expressed it better than Louis XIV himself in his *Mémoires*, written for the instruction of the Dauphin: '...quand il s'agira du rang que vous tenez dans le monde, des droits de votre coronne, du Roi enfin et non pas du particulier, pressez hardiment l'élévation de coeur et d'esprit dont vous serez capable, ne trahissez point la gloire de vos prédécesseurs ni l'intérêt de vos successeurs à venir, dont vous n'êtes que le dépositaire....' Hence the great importance attached to precedence. Battles lost there would diminish the family's standing, its influence amongst potential clients would melt away, and its own claims to rewards and to advancement would be that much reduced.[109]

Loyalty to country as a vague concept existed but it was not yet what nationalism or patriotism in the future was to make it, the supreme good that overrode all family and other personal considerations. In the middle of the 17th century it lay side by side with, and could be tempered, and was as often as not overridden, by personal loyalties based on family, clientship and local and communal ties – and by religion, another form of patron/client relationship, but this time with God.

Mary's insistence on her royal rank, her constant travelling to keep in touch with her clan, her financial support for her brothers so that they could maintain their state, especially that of Charles, king and head of the clan, her own expenditure for this visit to France, her use of French (the common language of cosmopolitan aristocratic society) in preference to

Dutch, were not only the common currency of her time but were reinforced by very practical political considerations.[110] Her style of behaviour was indeed the subject of reproaches by her contemporaries and these have been repeated by modern historians. Frequently they originate with political opponents of the House of Stuart and the House of Orange in Mary's own times. But those opponents themselves could not, in the 17th century, avoid the overarching presence of clanship, with its adjuncts of client/patron relationships, even in the Dutch Republic where the old aristocracy had ceded so much of its power and influence to the predominant Regent families – in the Province of Holland in particular, although less so elsewhere.

These Regent families were small in number, and not the least of the pillars supporting De Witt's power was his blood ties with many of them. He had married the daughter of a former Amsterdam burgomaster, Wendela Bicker, and the Amsterdam clans of the Bickers, De Graeffs, the Trips (whose wizened faces Rembrandt captured) and the Deutzen intermingled their influence with the clans closely allied with the De Witts, the Van Sypesteyns, Van Beverens, Van Slingelandts, Hoeufts, De Veers, Coolwijcks and Viviens. For his brother De Witt procured the position of steward of Putten, for his father the membership of the audit office in The Hague, for Van Slingelandt and for Van Vivien the posts of Pensionary, which he had himself held, of Dordrecht, and numerous relations were embedded in town and provincial posts. It was their knowledge of local problems, local personalities and local politics that made government possible just as the webs of clan and clientship did in France and England.[111]

The Regents, too, were jealous of their reputations, their 'Honour' – only honourable people, those recognised as honourable, could hold public office, although the Regent code of honour had different emphases reflecting the mercantile society of the Dutch Republic. An essential component of honour among the Regents, for instance, was creditworthiness. Nevertheless a Regent's honour was to him and to his family as important as was *gloire* to Louis XIV; and the Regents too were as obsessed as Louis with precedence and protocol, for example in the seating arrangements at the States-General, lest these reflect on their honour.[112] But the values of the Dutch aristocracy, of its gentry, and of its military class – those who moved most closely in the ambit of the House of Orange – were nearer the mores of France.

Mary's stay in France extended to almost a year. Even by the high standards of the French court she cut a splendid figure, which impressed no less a personage than Louis XIV's very rich niece, la Grande Mademoiselle. As Princess of Orange and as Princess Royal she was surrounded by her magnificent entourage, whilst her imposing ear pendants, her pearls, her clasps of large diamond bracelets and her diamond rings were set off by the black widow's weeds she wore in memory of her dead husband. It was to la Grande Mademoiselle that she confided that she was very happy in France, that she had an 'aversion horrible' for her adopted country and that as soon as the king, her brother, was re-established in England she would go to live with him.[113]

Her eventual departure was hastened by the news that her son had smallpox, which in the event turned out to be measles and from which he made a good recovery.[114] On 21 November she left Paris, and she met Charles at Bruges on the 29th.[115] She returned to The Hague on 2 February 1657.

MARY'S COURT

On her return to the Dutch Republic her first care was the restoration of her son's health. After his recovery mother and son were able to make full use of the various Orange palaces in the Republic. One of these was close to Breda, which had for generations been a major seat of the princes of Orange. Their ancient palace lay a short distance from the small town and enjoyed both spacious rooms and splendid gardens.[116] It was convenient for Bruges, where Charles had established himself with his brother Henry, the Duke of Gloucester, and where he summoned his other brother, James, who was thus compelled to leave the French army. In the Spanish army he was soon fighting against his old comrades.

A major event was the betrothal of the Queen of Bohemia's youngest daughter, Sophie, to Duke Ernest Augustus of Hanover. On 24 June 1658 the Queen wrote archly to her son Charles Louis, the Elector of Palatine, complaining of being kept uninformed of the progress of the match. She had no objection to Ernest Augustus: 'I doe not all dislike the match concerning the person, being no exceptions against him, for whome I haue a great esteeme'; but, she continued, 'since neither my opinion nor consent hath bene asked, I haue no more to say, but uish that it may proue for Sophies content and happiness.'[117]

In one of the ironies of history Ernest Augustus was not deemed a great catch. 'In the present condition of our family,' Charles Louis remarked, 'we must be satisfied to take hold of what we can.'[118] It was not to be anticipated that the young couple's son was to succeed to the English throne as George I.

A more dramatic event was to electrify the exiled royalists. Cromwell died on 3 September 1658. On the 30th the Queen of Bohemia wrote to her son: '…he liued uith the curse of all good people and is dead to their great ioye so as, though he haue gained three kingdoms by undoubted wrong and uickedness, wants that honnour to leaue a good name behinde him in this worlde, and I feare, he is not now much at his ease where he now is. All the French court went to congratylat this monsters death uith the Queene my sister [Henrietta Maria], and the Cardinal himself, and he called him ce vipere.'[119]

For the moment, however, there was no sign of a possible Restoration of Charles II. Indeed, so remote did this prospect seem that that most astute of social climbers, Amalia von Solms, let slip a gilded prize and vetoed the proposed marriage to the king-in-exile of her daughter Henrietta,[120] who subsequently married the Prince of Anhalt. That did, however, strengthen the clan's connections in Germany, and Anhalt was to become a useful component in Prince William's German system of patronage.

WILLIAM'S EARLY UPBRINGING

In the meantime thought was being given to William's education, although there are few hard facts as to what he was actually taught as opposed to instructions on what he should be taught. But from the man whom we subsequently get to know we must strongly suspect that some of the instructions given for his education were not without lasting effect.

The first of these instructions is an undated and anonymous memorandum, 'Discourse sur la nourriture de S.A. Monseigneur le Prince d'Orange' – Dr Japikse dates this from the earliest period in the Prince's life, as it envisages an education from the fourth to the sixteenth years. It lays stress on physical exercise; on current affairs; on geography and history to develop his judgement; the Calvinist religion; and the study of warfare. It contains a conventional warning against gambling, wine and women – although, perhaps, given the character of William's father, the author may also have been reflecting, as much as he dared, on the hard facts of recent experience.

It contains one element of practical advice, which the Prince did not imbibe. It draws a distinction between 'deception', which is not acceptable, and 'dissimulation', which is, because 'il appartient quelques fois à la civilité de faire paroitre de ne voir ou de n'ouir point ce que l'on sçait ou voit ou oyt'. Whatever William was prepared to acknowledge in the sphere of manners, in the sphere of politics certainly he was to prove himself to be a performer in the first rank as a dissimulator, and deception also was not always far absent from his repertoire. But in politics, as in war, these are not always heinous qualities. Breaching his given word, however, was another matter – that would have been in contradiction with his *gloire*, which was to become as important to him as to his cousin, Louis.

Other advice was absorbed, such as the dictum 'Qui est maistre de soy mesme, il est maistre de tout autres.' Whilst William did have a temper, to which he was known to give vent on occasion – sometimes with calculation – he was from his earliest years known for his deep reserve, and his ability to hide his thoughts and emotions. He was not, when he so wished, a man easy to read.

There was a word of political advice, which did not go unheeded and which was to prove of the first importance – the Prince should maintain a strict understanding with the Province of Holland. There were occasions when he found it difficult to adhere to this principle, and, indeed, there were occasions when the Province of Holland – Amsterdam in particular – had to learn the corollary of cooperating with him. But when the two power centres in the Dutch Republic found ways of uniting they became, together, one of the great powers of Europe.[121]

Whilst Mary was away in France, Amelia von Solms had, in 1656, turned to the States of Holland to appoint tutors for the Prince, a request which these States refused. A minister of religion, however, took office in April 1656, Cornelius Trigland, to address his spiritual education. The substantial time of one and a half hours a day was set aside for this. Although no religious fanatic, Trigland, who was noted for his learning, was an orthodox Calvinist, with the unavoidable attachment to the Calvinist doctrine of predestination.[122]

Trigland was an adherent of the Voetian school of Calvinism and his appointment should be seen in the context of the division in the Dutch Church at this time between the adherents of Voetius and Cocceius, which was reminiscent, but not so divisive, as the dispute between the Remonstrants and Counter-Remonstrants earlier in the century.

The Voetians were the stricter Calvinists; they believed in the literal truth of the Bible; and this led them to be proponents of a more Godly way of life, particularly on Sundays. The Cocceians did not adhere to a literal interpretation of the Bible, parts of which, they maintained, should be understood in the context of the development of the ancient Israelites at the time. In this they were more in tune with the new science and the new sceptical philosophy which was emerging and one of whose major proponents was Descartes.[123] But for many in Dutch 17th-century society to question the literal meaning of the Bible, the source of all religious authority in a Protestant society, was to question faith itself: it was the first step to atheism.

And, of course, these religious divisions had, as usual, a political dimension. At its centre was the old Erastian dispute as to whether ecclesiastical affairs should be subordinate to the State, or whether the Church should maintain its independence. The Cocceians supported the first principle, and had the sympathy of many of the Regents. The Voetians championed a Church independent of the State, that is to say independent from the predominant Regent party to whom the Orangists were also opposed. It was natural therefore that a Voetian should have been chosen as Prince William's religious instructor, albeit not one who was an extreme proponent of his school.[124]

When William was 16 Trigland published the 'idea or portrait of a Christian Prince', which contained maxims clearly directed at the young Prince of Orange. Much of Trigland's tract contains the commonplace pieties of the age, but one or two quotations have resonance in the way the Prince behaved throughout his life.

'It is required of kings and princes', Trigland says in his opening paragraph, 'that they foster piety and judgement.... O blessed servitude, sole method of happy government: above all for thee, Most Noble Prince, since God brought thee in such wondrous wise into this earthly scene'. The Prince, thus, would be called upon to fulfil a special political destiny in his life to accompany his special status.

At a less elevated level there is the admonishment that 'A faithful friend is a strong defence and he that hath found him hath found a treasure.... A faithful friend is a medicine for life, and they that fear the Lord shall find him.'[125] It was an admonishment that may perhaps have encouraged what was in any case already in William's nature; it was to be a characteristic, perhaps to a fault, that he relied on a very small but very close coterie of friends throughout his life – a characteristic that left an opening for his political opponents to exploit, to the point of accusations of homosexual scandal.

It was not till the end of 1659 that William's education was put on a more formal footing when it was decided that he should attend the university of Leyden, a strongly Orangist institution which had been attended by the Princes Maurits and Frederick-Henry before him – it had also been attended by his uncle, the Elector of Brandenburg. His household was expanded and a governor was appointed to head it, who was to oversee the young Prince's education. He was Frederick of Nassau, Lord of Zuylenstein, an illegitimate son of Frederick-Henry, and another uncle of William. He was married to an Englishwoman, Mary Killigrew. With his preoccupations markedly more centred on this world than were those of Trigland, he was somewhat idle and he had had a reputation of being something of a rake in his youth. William became very attached to him.[126]

Charles Henri van den Kerckhoven, Baron Wotton and Lord of Blydenstein, a son of Heenvliet, became Gentleman of the Bed Chamber, and two other appointments, Johan Boreel, Steward of the Household, and Frederick van Reede, Master of the Horse, were to remain closely associated with the Prince in the future.

We now come to the second set of instructions for the Prince's upbringing; they were detailed and they were drawn up by Constantijn Huygens.[127] The reader will note echoes in places of the earlier 'Discours'. The structure of Huygens's *Mémoire* follows a hierarchical pattern that was almost second nature to the 17th-century mind; it begins with God, it moves on to the Prince's personal education, and it ends with the regulation of the personnel of his household.

The first and principal care of his governor was to bring up the Prince in the love and fear of God, from whom his every action, every word and every thought was never hidden. Every day he should study extracts from the Bible, with explanations being given of the more obscure passages. He should be armed with quotations to counter the arguments of the Popish religion and great care should be taken to bar from his presence any advocates of atheism. Combining religious instruction with the practical, Huygens stipulates that the Prince should attend sermons twice on Sundays alternating between the Dutch and the French churches, to enable him to acquire facility in both languages.

Huygens then addresses the Prince's political education. He should acquire a style of conversation suitable to his rank, honest, civil, and obliging to all. And Huygens goes on to reinforce and expand on the principles set out in the earlier *Discours* relating to relations with the Regents. William should be taught that, following the eclipse of the fortunes of his House, the goodwill which the people of the country owed to his illustrious predecessors should be re-established by a manner of behaviour which would remove the rancour of the opposition whilst animating the affections of the well-disposed. Neither the Prince nor any in his entourage should speak with disrespect of the government of the country or of its leading figures. On the contrary he should be made aware that his princely ancestors had always deferred to the Republic and its component members and by these means had strengthened the basis of their authority and standing. This profound principle must have stuck in the memory of the Prince, for he eventually followed it, although not without difficulty, first in the Dutch Republic and later, *mutatis mutandis*, in England.

If the central political precepts were thus once more reiterated on the lines of the first *Discours*, Prince William was at the same time also to be imbued, from the start, with the *gloire* of the House to which he belonged; the glorious acts of his ancestors for the good and for the service of the country should be held before him and he should be taught history in general and the history of the United Provinces in particular, in which connection he should compare and contrast the actions of the great men of old.

Huygens touches on the general tone of the company surrounding the Prince, which should be devoid of blasphemy or coarse language, and rigorous measures should be taken against any vices such as drunkenness, gluttony and suchlike. Precautions should be taken against his being furnished with lewd books.

Huygens hints at a short temper in the Prince, due either to a natural inclination or to his tender years – it was in fact the former – and should it manifest itself, it should be corrected on the spot with as much discretion as possible, whilst he should be taught the need for self-control in dealing with servitors – which was not always to be the case.

The governor should let the Prince out of his sight as little as possible and to this end he should sleep in his bedchamber, it not being reasonable to leave him under the sole watch of his valets. Privacy was not a requisite in a prince's education in the 17th century.

As regards the Prince's studies, Huygens lays great emphasis on the need for him to be able to write letters in an easy and gracious style, dignified and appropriate to a prince. As regards languages, without detracting from the importance of Latin, at that stage in his life it wouldn't be necessary to press it too hard. As his mind matured it was important that he should be thoroughly drilled in the two languages that were most necessary to him, apart from Latin, that is to say Dutch and French, whilst the English which he had already acquired should be retained. Care should be taken that he should learn to spell correctly in all three languages and to acquire a flawless pronunciation.

It appears therefore that, in the very English environment with which Mary had surrounded him, William's first language was English. But it seems equally likely that he would have heard a great deal of French from his earliest infancy spoken both by Mary and her court – Huygens's *Mémoire*, for example, is most typically written in French. And he must, of course, have heard Dutch spoken on a daily basis. The evidence of his correspondence is that he used French, the language of the officer corps in the Dutch army, of the Dutch aristocracy and of diplomacy, and Dutch, the language used in the Provincial Estates and the States-General, with equal facility; but that he was less comfortable in English – the later English ambassador in The Hague, Sir William Temple, for example, makes mention of the occasions when the Prince used English expressions in their conversations, making clear that the bulk of their intercourse was in French.

As regards other subjects Huygens lays particular emphasis on arithmetic, and on mathematics generally, which he calls 'la vraye science des Princes, et de laquelle ils ne sçauroyent se passer ni en paix ni en guerre.' As far as music is concerned, if the Prince had a disposition towards singing no harm could result. More important was drawing, which could be used to employ an idle hour.

These, in summary, says Huygens, are more or less the preliminary disciplines which the tender years of the Prince would allow. As he increases in age, by God's good grace, their Highnesses (the two princesses) would be able, through appropriately qualified people, to regulate and adjust the process by which he could acquire the skills and knowledge to render him capable of the great employments for which it was hoped he was destined through the bounty of God.

On bodily nourishment and exercise, Huygens admonishes Zuylenstein to have a care of the Prince's constitution 'qui n'estant pas des plus robustes doibt estre mesnagée discrètement'. It would appear appropriate that he should go to bed between 9 and 10 at night and rise between 7 and 8 in the morning. The morning should be devoted to his lessons, and, if there is time before dinner, that would be the most appropriate time to have dancing lessons to improve his deportment. More violent exercises such as fencing, horse *manège* and tennis would have to be postponed until his physical strength allowed. He could, however, play billiards indoors, and out of doors he could take the air in a carriage, on foot or on horseback. In this way a good part of the time after dinner could be employed and if any time remained before supper some of the morning's lessons could be revised.

We have here one of the first hints that Prince William had a weak constitution, of which historians have made a great deal; but we will need to judge the evidence carefully as to how serious a defect this was at various stages during his life; certainly in his earlier years as a military commander he was capable of great physical energy, living in very rough conditions whilst on campaign, and he was capable as well of sustaining long periods in the saddle in pursuing his favourite form of relaxation, hunting.

The *Mémoire* finishes with short instructions as to how the staff of the Prince's establishment are to be managed. On no account were any of the servants to be allowed to behave in an insolent or disorderly fashion either indoors or out and become a source of scandal.

In view of Governor Nassau-Zuylenstein's rakish antecedents, one cannot but be aware of a certain irony in some of Huygens's stricter admonishments. Indeed, we do not know how much of these instructions was put into practice but equally, as we have indicated in the case of the first *Discours*, the subsequent development of the Prince's character leaves ample scope for believing that they were by no means ignored. It is true that the French ambassador remarked in August 1660, thus getting on for a year after the Prince moved to Leyden, that not enough care was being taken of his education, 'estant encore en quelque façon entre les mains des femmes, qui le destournent de ses estudes'; and he made mention of it to the Princess Dowager, who undertook to remedy this.[128] Thus the easy-going Nassau-Zuylenstein may himself, on occasion, have had need of correction.

It is to the point, however, that in these instructions of Huygens, there is no mention at all of the military education which had been mentioned in the first *Discours*. This was a marked gap in the Prince's upbringing, and was to handicap him throughout his career. In contrast to William the Silent's two sons, who were regarded as amongst the great generals of their age, William was to be a very brave but pedestrian military commander.

But despite Nassau-Zuylenstein's possible shortcomings, Huygens's design for the Prince's education, combined as it later was with De Witt's practical instructions in statecraft, even if it was an ill preparation for the career of a general, was a very solid preparation for that of a statesman.

On 4 November 1659, ten days before his ninth birthday, Prince William rode through cheering crowds in Delft to take up his residence and commence his studies, accompanied by the Princess Royal and his grandmother, and a few days later he was regaled by one of the professors on the deeds of the House of Orange.[129] The weight of his family's role in history – so important a constituent of his *gloire* – was never to be kept from his mind. And nor were the expectations that rested on this boy with a constitution which, it was said, was not amongst the most robust.

DISPUTES OVER THE PRINCIPALITY OF ORANGE. LOUIS XIV'S OCCUPATION

On 20 January 1660 Elizabeth of Bohemia wrote to her son, the Elector Palatine, '…there is an ill favoured business fallen out between my Neece [Mary] and the governor of [the Principality of] Orenge, which I feare vill go neere to a cause of the loss of that place. It is too long to relate, I beleeue there is fault on both sides. The French king takes my Neeces part highlie, the Elec[tor] of Brandenburg and the dowager, the Count of Donas', that is to say of the governor.

Elizabeth was referring to a long-standing dispute between Mary, Amalia von Solms, and the Great Elector over the guardianship of the Principality of Orange which had existed ever since the death of William II in 1650. Prior to his death, Mary's husband had given instructions to Count Donha that he was to obey Mary's orders concerning Orange and 'to hold the place on her behalf against all others laying claim to it'. But the governor, who had been appointed in 1649, was both the son of Amalia's elder sister and a subject of the Elector of Brandenburg, in whose territories his estates lay.[130] He was also related to the Elector by marriage through the Elector's marriage to Louise-Henrietta, the daughter of Amalia and Frederick-Henry. Louise-Henrietta, it will be remembered, was the potential heiress of the House of Orange's estates and of the Principality in the event of the demise of William III, and hence the Elector had a direct interest in the Principality's affairs. The essence of the dispute was Mary's claim of sole guardianship of the Principality on behalf of her infant son against the claim of Amalia and of the Elector, on behalf of his wife, for a joint guardianship between all three. This, of course, would result in Mary being outvoted by the other two acting in concert[131] – unlike the settlement of the guardianship in the United Provinces where Mary had one vote and the other two one vote between them.

The geographical situation of the Principality had always presented a problem of control for the princes of Orange and there had been a long history of the governors they appointed establishing semi-autonomy.[132] Donha acted in accordance with this tradition to assert as high a degree of independence as possible.

Key to the situation was the Parlement (the Supreme Court) of the Principality, which would have to decide on the legalities of the conflicting claims. Mary sent emissaries to the Principality who were, however, promptly arrested by Donha, and counter-representations were produced by the emissaries of Amalia and the Elector. In these circumstances, and in the light of the pressure that the governor was able to exert on the spot, it was perhaps not surprising that the Parlement gave judgement in 1652 in favour of joint guardianship.

Mary eventually decided to bow to the *fait accompli* by entering into an agreement in 1654 with Amalia and the Elector to allow the *status quo* thus established by the court to stand until 17 February 1657, but without prejudice to her rights in the future.[133] Donha's own commission expired on 13 June of that year.

Nevertheless, in 1658 Donha was still in practical control of the Principality; but he was then no longer assured of the support of the Parlement, and he accordingly took steps to protect his position by arranging for the appointment of two new members to this body.[134] Far from achieving his end, however, this *démarche* infuriated the Parlement, which, on 24 August, decreed in favour of Mary as the sole regent of the Principality. Donha retorted by imprisoning Mary's supporters and confiscating their property, amongst whom were the advocate-general, Sylvius, and his father.[135]

Mary sought the intercession of her mother, Henrietta Maria, in Paris, who in turn sought the intervention of the French Queen Mother, Anne of Austria, who turned to Cardinal Mazarin.[136] A precedent for such an appeal to a king of France existed when Philip William, the then Prince of Orange, had appealed to Henri IV, Louis XIV's grandfather, for his support against a similarly recalcitrant governor of Orange. Indeed, the situation of the Principality had always meant that its tenure by the princes of Orange necessarily involved the goodwill of the kings of France.

In response to Mary's appeal the French sent a frigate up the Rhône to compel the payment of the river tolls, which amounted to more than half the revenues of the Principality, to Mary's representative. Then, at the beginning of 1660, Louis XIV was himself in Provence both to quell disturbances in that part of France and because he was on his way to marry Maria-Theresa of Spain in accordance with the Treaty of the Pyrenees which had established peace between that country and France in 1659.

Negotiations were entered into with Donha, who, once his own interests were safeguarded – including the payment of a hefty sum of money – surrendered the Principality to the French under an agreement reached on 20 March 1660. Donha was to remain as nominal governor, but without discharging the functions of the office, whilst Louis took possession of the Principality during the minority of Prince William, promising to return it to him when he became of age. In the event of his death it would revert to the Elector of Brandenburg.[137]

A symbolic story is told that on 27 March, the Saturday before Easter, Louis XIV paid a visit to Orange and climbed the highest bastion of the citadel. There he remained in silence, affronted by the sight of this proud fortification appearing so challenging in the midst of his demesnes. He took a stone and let it fall over the parapet. To his entourage it was taken as a signal that the place should be demolished without delay. Still in silence, Louis descended into the town where the local notabilities vainly tried to persuade him to partake of the collation prepared for him. But he would partake of neither the food nor the drink. He mounted his horse and left for Avignon.[138]

To Louis the signal to demolish the fortifications at Orange was an assertion of his royal authority. To Prince William, when the news reached him, it was the declaration of a challenge to his very status as a sovereign prince.

Before the reports of these events reached the two princesses in the Netherlands they had realised that their quarrels were threatening the total loss of the Principality. They patched up their differences and appealed to the Dutch States-General to lend their diplomatic support to their intercession with the French King, which the States agreed to do.[139]

But to no avail. The fortifications of Orange were levelled – their remains can be seen to this day, still gazing across the plains of Louis's former kingdom – and the reply came from the French court that these served no other purpose but to be a charge on the resources of the Prince of Orange and to disturb the peace of the kingdom of France.[140]

The French ambassador, De Thou, was aware of the long-standing damage this could do to relations with the House of Orange. 'Je fus hier à Honslardick', he reported on 11 June, 'voir la Princesse mais je la trouvay fort esmue et toute affligée de la nouvelle qu'elle avoit recue d'Orange, me disant qu'on n'en vouloit pas seulement aux fortifications, mais aux droits et prérogatives de la souveraineté; qu'on ne manqueroit pas d'aigrir le Roy son frére sur ce sujet.'[141]

Two major European clans were thus involved in Mary's mind, the House of Orange as well as the more senior House of Stuart. In everyone's thoughts there was the threat to the sovereign status possessed by the House of Orange through the medium of the Principality.

De Thou suggested a solution. The King of France could augment the revenues of the Principality. This would turn the Prince into a 'pensionnaire de France', binding him to the King's interests,[142] that is, the Prince would become part of Louis's European network of clients. We shall see that this was a theme which for some time formed a continuum in Louis's policy towards the House of Orange and the Dutch Republic. It was to prove a grave miscalculation.

In a despatch to Cardinal Mazarin on 26 August De Thou again suggested that it might be opportune to do the young Prince a good turn 'pour adoucir un peu cette amertume de la démolition de la place [i.e of Orange's fortifications],' adding 'dont il sera difficile qu'il ne se souvienne quelque temps et que le mal-intentionnez contre nous se servent de ce prétexte pour envenimer l'esprit de ce jeune Prince, dans l'esprit duquel se descouvre desjá quelque semence de fierté.'[143]

It remained that in 17th-century terms Louis had inflicted a personal insult, a mortal insult. A threatening shadow had emerged, a challenge both to the pride and to the very status on which William's House depended for its position in the constellation of the powers of Europe, a threat to his *gloire*.

After long negotiations extending over five years Constantijn Huygens eventually managed to gain the return of the Principality and the French troops withdrew on 25 March 1665.[144]

But its vulnerability and the menace from Louis remained.

---

1 J.-C. Petitfils, *Louis XIV*, Perrin, Paris 2008, pp.94–9; G. Treasure, *Mazarin*, London and New York, p/b, 1997, pp.177–9; E. Le Roy Ladurie, *The Ancien Régime*, Blackwell, p/b, 1998, p.115: 'There were numerous provinces where resistance to taxation became something of a guerrilla war.' For the default of the crown on its debts see Roger Mettam, *Power and Faction in Louis XIV's France*, Oxford, Blackwell, 1988, p.107.

2 Aitzema, *op. cit.*, III, pp.462, 464; Wicquefort, *op. cit.*, I, pp.346–7; Geyl, *op. cit.*, p.75.

3 He was a great-grandson of William the Silent through his daughter, Louise Juliana. See family tree pp.272–3 in Derek McKay, *The Great Elector*, Harlow, Longman, 2001.

4 '…zijn Keur-Vorstelijke Doorluchigheid tot verwonderinghe is voorkomende dat alhier wereden getracht om hare Hoogkeyt zijne Cheur-Vortreffelijcke Doorluchtigheyts Lieve ende Hoogh-ge-eerde Vrouw Schooon-Moeder, nefers andere naeste Bloedverwanten uyt gemelde Tutele ende Administratie van den Pupilli goederen, op een ongehoorde manier ende tegens alle Rechten, reden, ende billichleyt te verstooten ende uyt[te] sluyten, waer by also zijn Keur-Vorstelijke Doorluchtigheid in gantsch pregnante ende serieuse termen is…', Aitzema, *op. cit.*, III, p.465 .

5 *Ibid.*, III, p.466.

6 *Ibid.*, III, p.551.

7 B.J. Veeze, *De raad van den Prinsen van Oranje tijdens de minderjarigheid van Willem III, 1650–1668*, Assen, 1932, p.12.

8 *Ibid.*, p.74.

9 Aitzema, *op. cit.*, III, p.552; Wicquefort, *op. cit.*, I, pp.354–5.

10 *Ibid.*, III, pp. 552–3; Veeze, *op. cit.*, p.74.

11 *Letters of Elizabeth, Queen of Bohemia*, Bodley Head, London, 1953, p.179.

12 Groen van Prinsterer, *Archives, op. cit.*, series 2, V, p.169.

13 Geyl, *op. cit.*, p.77.

14 Van Nyevelt, *op. cit.*, p.173: 'elle avoit an aversion horrible pour la Holland et que dès que le Roi son frère serait retabli, elle irait demeurer avecc lui', quoting the *Mémoires de Mademoiselle de Montpensier*. See also Geyl, *op. cit.*, p.77.

15 N. Japikse, *Prins Willem III, De Stadthouder-Koning*, Amsterdam, 2 vols., 1930, 1933, J.M. Meulenhoff, I, p.23.

16 C.V. Wedgwood, *The Trial of Charles I*, London, Collins, 1964, p.193.

17 W. Davenport Adams, *The White King*, London, George Redway, 1889, I, pp 91–126. Leanda de Lisle suggests the snow may be a myth but if so it had, like many myths, considerable impetus. See L. de Lisle, *The White King, The Tragedy of Charles I*, London, Penguin Random House, 2018, p.282.

18 Wedgwood, *Charles I, op. cit.*, pp.199–200; R. Hutton, *Charles II*, Clarendon Press, Oxford, 1989, p.33.

19 Hutton, *op. cit.*, Oxford, 1989, p.23; Venetian State Papers, XXVI, p.58.

20 *Ibid.*, pp.59–60.

21 'Let every soul be subject unto the higher powers … the powers that be are ordained of God'. Romans, 13:1.

22 Groen van Prinsterer, *op. cit.*, IV, p.163, V, p.170; Israel, *op. cit.*, p.596; De Witt Huberts, *Uit de jeugd jaren van stadhouder Willem III*, The Hague, 1925, p.70.

23 *Ibid.*, V, pp. 148, 171.

24 *Ibid.*, V, p.171.

25 Poelhekke, in *Nassau en Oranje, op. cit.*, p.119.

26 Poelhekke in *Amalia van Solms in Vrouwen in Het Landsbestuur*, ed. C.A. Tamse, The Hague, 1982, pp.114–26.

27 Geyl, *op. cit.*, p.10.

28 Israel, *op. cit.*, p.486.

29 *Ibid.*, p.561.

30 *Ibid.*, p.554.

31 Groen van Prinsterer, *op. cit.*, V, p.7.

32 *Ibid.*, V, p.32.

33 H. Rowen, *John De Witt, grand pensionary of Holland, 1625, 1672*, Princeton, N.J., Princeton University Press, 1978, p.47.

34 Israel, *op. cit.*, p.703.

35 *Ibid.*, pp.703–4.

36 *Ibid.*, p.705. He also arranged to have himself appointed Stadholder of Drente, which, however, had no votes in the States General.

37 Wicquefort, *op. cit.*, I, p.3.

38 *Ibid.*, II, p.6.

39 *Ibid.*, II, p.12.

40 *Ibid.*, II, p.15.

41 *Ibid.*, II, p.16.

42 *Ibid.*, II, p.17.

43 *Ibid.*, II, pp.18–19.

44 *Ibid.*, II, p.19.

45 *Ibid.*, II, p.20.

46 Japikse, *Willem III, op. cit.*, I, p.40.

47 Geyl, *op. cit.*, p.80; Israel, *op. cit.*, p.710.

48 Rowen, *De Witt, op. cit.*, p.54; Wicquefort, *op. cit.*, II, p.78.

49 Israel, *op. cit.*, pp.713–14.

50 C. Wilson, *Profit and Power*, Longmans Green, 1957, p.48.

51 S. Gardiner, *History of the Commonwealth and Protectorate, 1649–1660*, London, 1894–1901, Longmans Green, 1894, I, p.359.

52 Wicquefort, *op. cit.*, II, pp.78–81.

53 Gardiner, *op. cit.*, I, p.360.

54 Geyl, *op. cit.*, p.83.

55 *Ibid.*, p.88.

56 Rowen, *De Witt, op. cit.*, p.55.

57 Geyl, *op. cit.*, pp.88–9. 'The troubles of 1651 were clearly rooted in the marriage of 1641 by which the House of Orange, the Orangist party and popular feeling had become disastrously entangled with the Stuart family…. It was this very

involvement which also lay at the heart of the ensuing war, from which the Netherlands had nothing to gain, but a great deal to lose.'

58 Entry by Marika Keblusek in *Dictionary of National Biography*, Oxford, 2004.

59 Geyl, *op. cit.*, p.86.

60 Israel, *op. cit.*, pp.714–15; Geyl, *op. cit.*, p.91.

61 Rowen, *De Witt, op. cit.*, pp.69, 91.

62 Wicquefort, *op. cit.*, II, pp.188–9, 191–2.

63 The letter was written in early February: Geyl, *op. cit.*, pp.94, 95. Pauw died on the 21st. Rowen, *De Witt, op. cit.*, p.92.

64 Geyl, *op. cit.*, p.95.

65 Blok, *Geschiedenis, op. cit.*, V, p.73.

66 Gardiner, *op. cit.*, I, 1649–51, p.457.

67 Israel, *op. cit.*, p.720; Wicquefort, *op. cit.*, 2, pp.204–5.

68 Wicquefort, *op. cit.*, II, p.228.

69 Israel, *op. cit.*, p.721.

70 Blok, *Geschiedenis, op. cit.*, 1902, V, p.76.

71 Geyl, *op. cit.*, p.110.

72 John Thurloe, State Papers, 1742, I, p.237. Quoted in Agnes Strickland, *Lives of the Last Four Princesses of the House of Stuart*, London, 1872, p.47.

73 Gardiner, *op. cit.*, II, 1651–4, p.340.

74 Rowen, *De Witt, op. cit.*, p.218; Israel, *op. cit.*, p.723.

75 Geyl, *op. cit.*, p.119.

76 Rowen, *De Witt, op. cit.*, pp.220, 222.

77 *Ibid.*, p.213.

78 *Ibid.*, p.231.

79 See, for example, Israel, *op. cit.*, p.722, who takes the view that it is probably right that the demand originated with De Witt; Geyl, *op. cit.*, p.116, for the opposite view. There is no conclusive evidence. The Dutch Ambassador closest to De Witt, van Beverninck, destroyed all but a few of the letters between him and De Witt, besides which there were plenty of opportunities for De Witt to give verbal instructions.

80 Blok, *Geschiedenis, op. cit.*, 1902, V, p.91.

81 W. Temple, *The Works of Sir William Temple*, Bt, London, 1770, II, p.11.

82 Rowen, *De Witt, op. cit.*, pp.385–8.

83 Japikse, *Willem III, op. cit.*, p.56.

84 *Briefwisseling van Constantijn Huygens*, ed. J.A. Worp, The Hague, Martinus Nijhof, 1916, V, p.250.

85 Japikse, *Willem III, op. cit.*, p.59. His source: letter 13 July. Diest: H.A. 2583, fol.106. Also quoted by S. Baxter, *William III*, Longmans, 1966, p.21. Koninklijke Huis Archief, inventaris 15, XIII, 4, 106.

86 Everett Green, *op. cit.*, p.215. Her source: Clarendon, iii, p.270.

87 *Ibid.*, VI, p.217.

88 *Ibid.*, VI, p.218.

89 *Ibid.*, VI, p.222.

90 William-Frederick, the Friesian Stadholder.

91 *Letters of Elizabeth, op. cit.*, p.227.

92 *Ibid.*, pp.228–9.

93 Everett Green, *op. cit.*, p.229, without quoting her source. Baxter, *op. cit.*, p.22, gives the same quote and gives his source as Thurloe, *State Papers*, I, 664.

94 Most historians discount the thesis that Charles and Lucy were married. Mary's use of 'wife' was light-hearted raillery.

95 Everett Green, *op. cit.*, VI, pp.230, 233.

96 Huygens, *Briefwisseling, op. cit.*, VI, 1663–87, p.159.

97 Everett Green, *op. cit.*, VI, p.233, quoting Lambeth MS, No.645, art.19.

98 *Ibid.*, VI, p.234.

99 A secret article in the Treaty stipulated that Charles and the Duke of York (and others) should no longer be harboured in France. Henrietta Maria, related as she was to three kings of France, was permitted to remain. Gardiner, *op. cit.*, III, 1654–6. In practice, too, the Duke of York was able to remain to pursue his career in the French army.

100 Geyl, *op. cit.*, p.126.

101 Everett Green, *op. cit.*, VI, p.238, quoting letter dated The Hague, 29 Nov. Lambeth MS, art.3.

102 *Ibid.*, VI, p.234.

103 *Ibid.*, VI, p.244; Geyl, *op. cit.*, p.128.

104 Everett Green, *op. cit.*, VI, pp.245–6.

105 F. Bluche, *Louis XIV*, Blackwell, 1990, p.45.

106 *Ibid.*, p.54.

107 I am much indebted for these observations to Dr M.A.M. Franken, *Coenraad van Beuningen's Politieke and Diplomatieke activiteiten in de jaren 1667–8, Institut voor Geschiedenis der Rijksuniversiteit te Utrecht*, 1966, p.21.

108 Ragnhild Hatton, ed., *Louis XIV and Europe*, Macmillan, 1976, pp.20–1.

109 *Oeuvres de Louis XIV*, ed. Ph.A. Grouvelle, Paris, 1806: III. *Mémoires Historiques et Instructions de Louis XIV pour le Dauphin, Année 1661*, p.139.

110 See p.31 for the case levelled against Mary by Geyl and Japikse.

111 Blok, *Geschiedenis, op. cit.*, 1902, V, p.93.

112 W. Frijhof and M. Spies, *Dutch Culture in a European Perspective*, Royal van Gorcum, Assen, 2004, pp.187ff.

113 *Mémoires de Mlle de Montpensier*, Charpentier, Paris, 1891, pp.385, 435–6.

114 Everett Green, *op. cit.*, VI, p.253, her source: Thurloe, *op. cit.*, IV, p.593.

115 *Ibid.*, VI, p.254, her source: Thurloe, *op. cit.*, IV, pp.609, 650, 665.

116 *Ibid.*, VI, p.256.

117 *Letters of Elizabeth, op. cit.*, p.275.

118 Quoted in Alison Plowden, *The Stuart Princesses*, Sutton, 1997, p.107. No source given.

119 *Letters of Elizabeth, op. cit.*, p.278.

120 Geyl, *op. cit.*, p.134.

121 Japikse, *Willem III, op. cit.*, I, pp.57–8. Japikse suggests that Heenvliet or one of his circle could be the author, although it surely has a whiff of Huygens about it.

122 Geyl, *op. cit.*, p.131; Japikse, *Willem III, op. cit.*, I, pp.59–61.

123 The new philosophy was to lead to the publication of Spinoza's *Tractatus Theologico-Politicus* in 1670, whose biting criticism of theological authority based on the Bible was too strong meat for all but a few of the Regents. Israel, *op. cit.*, pp.787–8.

124 For a discussion of the dispute between the Voetians and Cocceians see Israel, *op. cit.*, pp.661ff; Troost, *William III, the Stadhoulder-King, A Political Biography*, Ashgate, 2005, pp.35–6.

125 Nesca Robb, *op. cit.*, London, 1962, I, pp.135, 136, 140.

126 Japikse, *Willem III, op. cit.*, I, p.70.

127 *Mémoires de Constantin Huygens*, The Hague, 1873, Martinus Nyhoff, pp.163ff.

128 Groen van Prinsterer, *op. cit.*, series 2, V, p.199.

129 Japikse, *Willem III, op. cit.*, I, pp.72–3.

130 Baxter, *op. cit.*, p.9; A. de Pontbriant, *Histoire de la Principauté d'Orange*, 1891, pp.197, 201.

131 Pontbriant, *op. cit.*, p.201; Wicquefort, *op. cit.*, II, pp.661–2.

132 See Pontbriant, *op. cit.*, pp.176ff.

133 *Ibid.*, pp.201–3. Wicquefort, *op. cit.*, II, p.662.

134 Pontbriant, *op. cit.*, p.203.

135 *Ibid.*, p.206.

136 Wicquefort, *op. cit.*, II, pp.663–4; Pontbriant, *op. cit.*, pp.209, 211, 212.

137 Pontbriant, *op. cit.*, pp.216–17, 220; Wicquefort, *op. cit.*, 2, pp.664–6.

138 Pontbriant, *op. cit.*, pp.220–21.

139 Rowen, *De Witt, op. cit.*, p.288. In backing the House of Orange over the Principality the States-General was sending a signal to the French in their negotiations with France over the introduction of trade impositions, which had been festering since 1659.

140 Wicquefort, *op. cit.*, II, pp.661–7.

141 Groen van Prinsterer, *op. cit.*, series 2, V, p.197.

142 *Ibid.*, p.199.

143 *Ibid.*, p.205.

144 *Briefwisselingen van Constantijn Huygens, op. cit.*, VI. Introduction, p.xii.

3 THE STUART RESTORATION

THE DUTCH WELCOME

William had barely been at his studies at Leyden for a few months when events in the spring of 1660 at long last portended the restoration of his uncle, Charles II, to his throne in England. The French ambassador, De Thou, in a despatch in April, noted the possible implications that the restoration of the uncle to the throne of his ancestors would have for the restoration of the nephew to the traditional offices held by his. He reported that De Witt had held a dinner, to which had been invited several adherents of the House of Orange. There a toast to the young Prince's health was solemnly drunk and proposed by De Witt's father, who had always been a leader of the anti-Orangist party.[1] Barely nine months earlier De Witt had refused Mary's request that her brothers, the dukes of York and Gloucester, should be allowed to visit her for a few days at her country house at Honselaarsdijk.[2]

On 14 May the Princess Royal received the news at Breda that Charles had been proclaimed king in London on the 11th; and, writing in her own hand, she immediately conveyed this to the States-General.[3] As it happened Charles and the dukes were staying with her, and both the States-General and the States of Holland resolved to send delegations to Breda to invite him to make his way to England via the United Provinces and for the party to stay as their guests. The two sets of delegates were soon vying with each other over precedence and over who should do the honours in entertaining the restored monarch. Underlying the bickering there was, as always in the 17th century, an important issue. It was the old question in the United Provinces of where sovereignty lay. The States-General claimed overall sovereignty, and hence overall precedence. The States of Holland claimed sovereignty within their Province and hence precedence in entertaining the King whilst he was there.[4]

The King and his entourage departed from Breda on 24 May by boat, wending their way to Moerdijk, in the Province of Holland, where De Witt had arranged a military reception.[5] From there they proceeded to Dordrecht, De Witt's home town, to be greeted by the local militia decked out in orange ribbons, and from there to Delft where the Grand Pensionary himself greeted the royal party. A very large number of coaches had been assembled. The Princess Royal and the King settled into one of these with their backs to the coachman, and were faced by the two royal dukes, York and Gloucester, whilst young Prince William had to be content with being deposited near the window. So arranged, the procession of 72 coaches progressed to The Hague, where the militia and a regiment of guards formed a double hedge at the entrance of the palace of Prince Maurits of Nassau-Siegen – nowadays the Mauritshuis museum with its magnificent collection of Dutch art. Here the King was to lodge during his stay in the United Provinces, and this was where he was officially proclaimed king by a delegation from the English Parliament.

The States-General had allocated 300,000 guilders (about £30,000) just to provide for the King's table, at which there were always present eight of its deputies to attend upon him. The table took the form of a double T, in the midst of which the King was seated between the Queen of Bohemia and the Princess Royal, whenever they were present. The royal dukes occupied one end of the table and young Prince William another, whilst in between were ranged the deputies to the States-General. The service, the food and the wines were of equal splendour. And outside in the city of The Hague the fountains ran with wine, without intermission, day and night.[6]

Everything possible was done by the Dutch to gain the goodwill of the restored King of England and of his family. The States of Holland, not to be outdone by the States-General, allocated 600,000 guilders (£60,000) for the royal party and for donations which it was judged the circumstances required. The dukes of York and Gloucester received 60,000 guilders (£6,000) each. For Charles himself a number of rare articles were to be assembled, but, as these would not yet be ready prior to his departure, he was initially presented with a splendid bedstead – are we permitted a wry smile? It had originally been ordered by William II for Mary's lying-in and was purchased from her for 100,000 guilders (£10,000).[7]

When the so-called 'Dutch gift' was finally delivered to the King at the Banqueting House in London in November it included a Titian, a Tintoretto, a Saenredam, two Gerhard Dous and antiquities from the ancient world. And all of this was rounded off with a yacht, provided by Amsterdam.[8]

What were the aims of the Dutch in organising these effusive arrangements? A cynic amongst them observed that the expense would have been better employed in the purchase of powder and lead.[9] And indeed it was to be not many years before the Dutch and the English were once again engaged in war. For the Dutch Republic, however, trade was everything. The Dutch merchant establishment remembered the costly first Dutch war with its devastating effect on the country's trade and wealth. Cromwell and De Witt had brought that war to an end. It was in the minds of all at The Hague at this time that part of Cromwell's price for ending it had been the Act of Exclusion, banning the young Prince of Orange from the offices held by his forefathers, and effectively banning the Stuarts, other than Mary herself and her son, from the Republic. Others could have added that De Witt instigated this. The Regents were now as eager to maintain good relations with the English government under the restored Charles II as they had previously been when the English were governed by the Lord Protector.

The actions taken against the Stuarts were accordingly explained away as dictated by the necessities of the times. At a ceremony attended by the King and the States of Holland the day after Charles arrived in The Hague, De Witt delivered a speech pleading in extenuation for the events of the past 'interest of state' and proposing a formal alliance between the two countries. To this the King replied that he too was determined on such an alliance and that he would be jealous if the States should enter into a closer alliance with anyone else.[10]

Perhaps these general terms of friendship were all that time allowed, for the King was under pressure to leave for England as soon as possible. But for him these were early days and he needed to assess the state of opinion in England before committing himself definitively to Continental alliances. For De Witt it might have been another matter to safeguard the mercantile interests of the Republic by negotiating and signing an alliance there and then.[11]

There was, however, another issue which raised itself with obvious clarity in the new circumstances. What was to be the position of the young Prince, Charles's nephew, William III of Orange? Would Charles demand that he should be raised to the offices traditionally held by the Prince's ancestors, as Stadholder of Holland and of other Provinces and as Captain-General and Admiral-General of the Dutch Union? It clearly presented De Witt with a considerable dilemma. He needed the goodwill of the uncle: his republican principles opposed the elevation of the nephew. De Witt finessed. He advised the King against haste on the issue and suggested that he should content himself with recommending the Prince to the goodwill of the States of Holland. One should allow a free people, he added, to advance in their own free way.[12]

Charles conducted himself in accordance with this advice. On the day before his departure for England, at De Witt's request he penned a note in the room of the Princess Royal to the States of Holland: 'Gentlemen, as I am leaving here in your hands the Princess, my sister, and the Prince of Orange, my nephew, two people who are extremely dear to me I pray you, Gentlemen, to take their interests to heart and to let them have the benefits of your favour, on those occasions when the Princess, my sister, asks you for it, whether for herself, or for the Prince, her son. Assuring you that the outcome of your goodwill towards them will be recognised by me as though I had received them in my own person.'[13]

De Witt had played for time. He had gained it. He knew however that matters could not remain as they had been and that the question of the Prince of Orange would soon have to be addressed.

In writing the note Charles failed, by accident or design, to make mention of Amalia von Solms, an omission which caused such pique in William's grandmother that she said that she no longer wished to meddle in the affairs of the Prince, and even that she wished to resign her position as guardian.[14] It must indeed have been hard for the old lady to see the attention and deference with which Mary, her adversary of old, was now treated. She must have smarted at the difference in rank between herself and her royal daughter-in-law, which was now so clearly emphasised. 'My neighbour in the Northend would faine haue bene the States guest at the feasts but they answered all was done onelie for the king and his familie and for none else,' wrote Elizabeth of Bohemia about Amalia.[15]

The next day, 2 June, the royal party made for Scheveningen, just outside The Hague, where the English fleet was awaiting them, accompanied by Prince William, his mother the Princess Royal, and the Queen of Bohemia. A huge crowd had gathered, which Elizabeth of Bohemia estimated to be 'at least aboue an hundred thousand men',[16] and the departing members of the royal family were escorted to the very edge of the beach by the solicitous delegates of the States of Holland.[17] Elizabeth and the King travelled out together to the fleet in a long boat amidst cries, as she reports – with rather inconsistent spelling – of 'we haue him, wee haue him, God bless King Charles!'[18]

At length the King, the two royal dukes, the Queen of Bohemia, the Princess Royal and young Prince William came aboard the man-of-war. There Samuel Pepys, obsequious, watchful, ready to record every detail, awaited them to kiss their hands. Finally, having eaten a repast together for the last time, the moment for departure arrived: '…the Queen', the observant Pepys duly recorded in his diary, 'Princesse Royalle, and Prince of Orange, took leave of the King, and the Duke of York went on board the London, and the Duke of Gloucester, the Swiftsure. Wich done, we weighed anchor, and with a fresh gale and most happy weather we set sail for England.'[19]

Sad, cynical, witty King Charles had developed a genuine fondness for his young nephew. As his fleet disappeared over the horizon, what had William made of him?

GUARDIANSHIP OF THE PRINCE: DE WITT AND MARY

A series of reactions followed the radical change in the circumstances of the House of Orange. The French ambassador expressed his view that, there being no longer any doubt that the Prince of Orange would acquire the offices of his forefathers, it was absolutely necessary to gain the favour of the Prince's governor, Nassau-Zuylenstein, and that of his English wife – whose influence over the Prince, he maintained, was as great as that of her husband – by means of 'quelque gratification considerable et réglée'.[20] The combination of a considerable bribe regularly administered adds an undoubted savour to the prescription recommended by this seasoned practitioner.

But he was reckoning without De Witt, who, on principle, was as determined to prevent the elevation of the Prince to his family's ancestral offices as he was to forestall the interference of English influence in the internal affairs of the United Provinces. Nevertheless, in achieving these aims he had to take account of the surge in support for the Prince of Orange.

William and his mother were invited to visit Amsterdam and Haarlem during June and the first two days of July 1660.[21] There they were greeted with glittering receptions by the notabilities of the two cities and with rapturous joy by the common people. On 27 June, in the Province of Gelderland, the Nijmegen Quarter passed a resolution to designate William as Captain-General of the Union, supported by the appointment of Prince William-Frederick of Friesland and Prince Maurits of Nassau-Siegen as field-marshals.[22]

Mary supported the resolution – whilst, however, warily omitting the proposals relating to the field-marshals. In so doing she, of course, revealed both her suspicions of other members of the House of Orange and the disunity in the Orangist camp. She made overtures to an influential Regent in Amsterdam, Cornelis de Graeff, Lord of Zuidpolsbroek, who, as an ex-burgomaster, retained substantial influence in the city. A connoisseur of art, he had been instrumental in arranging the 'Dutch gift' for King Charles;[23] but he was also an uncle of De Witt's wife, and De Witt was in close touch with him.

At the same time Mary also entered into discussions on a couple of occasions with De Witt himself. The second of these occurred in The Hague on 22 July, of which De Witt wrote a detailed report to de Graeff on the 23rd.[24] She urged the designation of William in accordance with the Nijmegen resolution (without the appointment of the field-marshals); and she asked De Witt for his views and advice. De Witt demurred and suggested instead that the Prince's upbringing should be supervised by the States of Holland, who, he added as inducement, would also provide him with a substantial yearly pension.

This seemed to strike a chord. But, whilst De Witt gained the impression that the Princess herself was persuaded of his view, she nevertheless replied that she would have to consult her brother, King Charles. When Charles duly replied that he had come down in favour of the designation Mary read out his letter to De Witt, and to his every objection answered 'that it was the King's command, which she dared not disregard in the least detail' ('que c'estoit le commandement du Roy, qu'elle n'oseroit s'en dispenser en le moindre circumstance'). It summed up in succinct form Mary's attitude towards her royal brother, the head of her clan. She added, however, that De Witt could convey his reasons for rejecting the designation through the medium of the Dutch ambassador in London, Nassau-Beverweert. She was about to arrive in Amsterdam and De Witt added in his letter to de Graeff that he hoped that the latter with his prudent and wise advice would succeed in persuading her Royal Highness to accept his proposal that the Prince's upbringing should come under the supervision of the States of Holland. This, in his judgement, would be far better for the House of Orange and for the Prince and would avoid trouble and disunity in the State.

Mary was under no illusions as to the difficulties she faced. '…de Witt does continue so wilfully in the opinion I ought not to desire my son's designation, that that will give me many difficulties to surmount', she wrote to Charles on 22 July. She made clear what her aims were. The States of Holland were about to recess 'so that', wrote Mary, 'if I possibly can, I will make some proposition before they separate, that at their next coming together, which will be about a month hence, they may make some resolution, that at the least I may know who are my friends and who are not'.[25]

She arrived in Amsterdam on the same day and began to sound out opinion there through De Graeff. She soon discovered that in the upshot she could make no further progress with him in Amsterdam than she had done with De Witt in The Hague. De Graeff, as flexible as a politician as he was cultured as a man, may at first have been disposed to make concessions to the Princess. But if that was indeed the case he was headed off by the Burgomasters of the city. Nor was this surprising, as the equally elastic De Witt had taken the double precaution of priming them as well through one of his allies among their number.[26] De Graeff accordingly informed Mary of their position[27] and she was compelled to moderate her stance.

She announced to the States of Holland on 30 July that she was planning a visit to England and dangled a carrot by offering her support in the diplomatic negotiations which were taking place with Charles to settle relations with the Republic. In her absence she recommended her son to them. She mentioned that she in no way doubted that they would – in consideration of the services which had been rendered by his eminent forefathers to the country as a whole and in particular to the Province of Holland – wish to employ him when he came of age in the offices and dignities held by them. She went on to indicate that she would find it most pleasing if they would give her cause for hope to that end now by taking on the task of educating him as a Child of State so that he could be brought up in the true Protestant religion, in all the princely virtues, and in the knowledge of the humours, laws and customs of the country. In that way he would become fit to discharge the offices in question.[28]

She had to content herself, in short, with no more than the 'hope' that in due course her son would be elevated to the offices of his ancestors.

A similar memorandum was presented by Mary to the States-General, who responded on the same day. They accepted her offer of support in the negotiations with England and they established a commission, of which De Witt was to be a member, to look into the matter of the Prince's upbringing.

It looked as though the Grand Pensionary had succeeded in blocking Mary's aim to obtain the designation of her son to the ancestral offices and that she had had to bow to political realities. But then on 7 August her position was forcibly strengthened when the States of Zeeland passed a resolution to ask the States-General to designate the Prince with the Captain-Generalship and Admiral-Generalship of the Union. And they accompanied this by designating him to become First Noble of the Province, at the same time inviting the States of Holland to designate him as Stadholder of both Provinces – 'designate' because all the appointments were to become effective not immediately but on the Prince's 18th birthday. The Stuart clan in unison – that is, the Princess Royal, King Charles II, and the Duke of York – as well as Amalia von Solms on behalf of the Orange clan, all wrote to Zeeland to express their thanks.[29]

The designation as First Noble would give the Prince, on his 18th birthday, one of the seven votes in the States of Zeeland, of which he already had two by virtue of his ownership of two of the six towns with the remaining votes.[30] The combination of the federal military offices with the Stadholderships, which, as we have noted, carried with them rights of appointment to the town councils choosing the representatives to the Provincial States, who in turn were represented in the States-General – the highest bodies, on the one hand, in the Provinces and, on the other, in the whole country – was tantamount, in De Witt's eyes, to creating a 'sovereign'. The danger was particularly threatening as the young Prince was the nephew of the King of England, whose influence in the Republic by means of these clan relationships De Witt wished to forestall.[31] A formidable movement, it seemed, was deploying in favour of Prince William.

But then the very wellspring wavered that Mary counted on most to sustain her. Charles was still uncertain of his position in England and was aware that the financial resources of the Dutch might not come amiss in assisting him to maintain his political independence.[32] The search for foreign financial help to bolster his domestic position was a constant throughout his reign and he engaged in it from the start. He made soundings in the Netherlands to ascertain the political practicality of designating Prince William at this stage. And Nassau-Beverweert, the Dutch ambassador in London, was a persuasive force in putting De Witt's point of view. An illegitimate member of the House of Orange, he maintained good relations with both the Princess Royal's faction in that House and with De Witt's faction amongst the Regents.[33] Charles seems to have decided that the time was not ripe to press for the designation and through the medium of Mary's secretary, Nicholas Oudart, she was asked to desist from her efforts.[34]

Mary's discouragement was reflected when she wrote to her brother from her country house, Honselaarsdijk, on 20 August: 'I hear you are changed in your opinion concerning my son, which if it be true and that you continue in it, I fear it will be our total ruin, in this conjuncture of time that our friends are so well disposed. The party in the province of Holland that are against us, though now governing, are so few that, if you will but continue in your first resolution, they will not be able to resist, for you will so encourage our friends that they will not fear to avow themselves to be so; as for example, Zeeland, who were strangely much encouraged to do what they did, with the assurance I gave them that their kindness to my son would be acceptable to you. M. Beverweert is I am confident, deceived into that opinion, for otherwise I am sure he considers his relations too near my son's to be against his interest; and though I am far from trusting to my own reason, yet I will believe, by the justice of my opinion, to change his, when I see him. Therefore I humbly pray you that no aplausible story work any effect upon you, till I have the happiness to see you; for hearing all sides, you will then be better able to judge who is in the right.'[35]

Mary was looking to the head of her clan to extend his protection. At the same time she was, as part of that clan, exerting herself in every way she could to promote the clan's interest through her son. She saw Nassau-Beverweert as fitting in as part of the structure of the clan/client relationships of the Stuart and Orange families, notwithstanding his ties with De Witt. It may be remarked, too, that her indefatigable efforts on behalf of her son sit ill with the accusations of her neglecting him which have been levelled by historians. At the same time she also reveals a touching consciousness in this letter of her limited political judgement: 'I am far from trusting to my own reason'.

She was indeed, as she seemed to recognise, no match for De Witt, and her judgement was indeed at fault. When the French ambassador met with her after dinner at Honselaarsdijk in August he suggested that, with the young Prince being the grandson of a daughter of France and the son of a daughter of England, combined support from both countries for his designation should be more than enough to overcome all opposition. Whether or not he was right in this, Mary did not even try to finesse this formidable combination, being, in the ambassador's opinion, of the view that the King of England was sufficiently influential to carry the matter alone and that the Dutch were too much in fear, and had too much need, of England not to defer entirely in the matter.[36]

De Witt, on his side, was totally confident that he would carry matters against the Princess. He genuinely thought that she was playing her hand badly by trying to force matters through. The way to handle Holland was not through 'force and constraint, but through gentleness and with time'. As for her reliance on Charles II, his shrewd assessment was 'that one should not expect the same vigour of the present government of England as of that of the former Protector' ('qu'on ne debvoit pas attendre le mesme vigour du gouvernement présent d'Angleterre que de celuy du defunct Protecteur').[37]

He still had to deal with Zeeland, however. On 9 September a delegation from that Province arrived at The Hague to submit their proposals to the States of Holland. They soon obtained the support of Friesland and of Gelderland, whilst in Holland itself De Witt was having more difficulty in agreeing a common line than he had anticipated.

But his assessment of Charles II's lack of 'vigour' was to prove correct. On 22 September an English fleet arrived at Hellevoetsluis to carry Mary over to England. It brought with it a messenger, Daniel O'Neile, from the King to De Witt. O'Neile raised the question of Charles's obtaining a loan from the Dutch for 2 million guilders. And as far as designation was concerned, the message he carried was that, whilst Charles's initial opinion was based on the advice he had received, he was not so wedded to it that if the Dutch gave sufficient reasons he would not submit to their views.[38]

The response of the Holland States on the 25th was to agree to undertake the education of William 'so that he could become fit to serve in the high charges and offices' held by his ancestors. They would also supervise his estate and there was to be a yearly pension of 5,000 guilders (about £500). On the 26th they repealed the Act of Exclusion. Whilst Mary thanked them for their goodwill she indicated that she looked forward to a 'further and complete' resolution – that is to say the designation to the offices now – which would encourage her all the more to support the interests of the Republic when she arrived in England.[39] And with that sally she joined the fleet which was waiting to take her there.

On the surface it appeared that, despite their differences, there was the making of an understanding between Mary and De Witt. Before her departure she nominated the committee to supervise William's education and the most significant name amongst the members was that of the Grand Pensionary himself. It seemed a shrewd and far-seeing move. No one was more fitted to prepare William for the role of statesman than the great statesman himself, who was then ruling the Dutch Republic. Furthermore, De Witt and his supporters were under enormous pressure to maintain good relations with Charles II. And the leverage this gave Mary could, in her eyes, be used to inch her son closer towards his elevation to the ancestral offices.

From De Witt's point of view it was a matter of 'needs must'. The House of Orange was a force too strong to resist. The policy of attempting its almost complete marginalisation, which had been pursued with some success since the death of William II, was no longer feasible after the restoration of the House of Stuart with which it was so powerfully linked. Instead De Witt was prepared to explore the possibility of deflecting the strength of Orange and to use it to further his perception of the interests of the Dutch Republic. With himself in charge of the young Prince's upbringing, he would educate him as far as possible with a thorough understanding of the 'True Interests' of the Republic, as De Witt saw them, and to remove him as far as possible from the baleful influence of his Stuart uncle. If, at some indeterminate point in the future, the Prince was to play a role in public affairs, De Witt was determined that he should at least do so imbued with the right principles.

But it could, of course, be a short step from exerting influence over the House through the education of its prince to the subordination of its power, patronage and prestige to meet De Witt's objectives. It was a danger which was soon to be presented to Mary's eyes.

In making her nominations to the education committee she had conceded a great deal, whether by accident or design. The members of the committee did not include Orangist supporters – no one from the loyal Province of Zeeland, no one from the loyal town of Leyden. Amelia von Solms, with her earthy sense of reality, was quick to seize the point. Her temper is not likely to have been improved by her having travelled to Mary's port of departure, Delfshaven, only to find that she had set sail on 1 October without bidding her farewell. On the 6th she wrote in her usual forceful way to the Holland States complaining that Mary's nominations had been made without the consent of the Prince's other guardians, that is, herself and the Elector of Brandenburg; and she put forward a number of names for inclusion from staunchly Orangist towns and from the nobility. Nor would it have improved her mood any further when she found she could make no progress with these demands.[40]

But the fundamental difficulties of the understanding between Mary and De Witt, which the old dowager had pinpointed, were real enough. The education committee met on 7 December, when its minutes made clear what De Witt's objectives were: 'The knowledge of the rights and customs of this country and the character and humour of this nation' were to be instilled into the Prince. He was to move from Leyden to the Binnenhof at The Hague, which was also used by the States of Holland and therefore physically immediately 'under their eye.' And his present governor, Nassau-Zuylenstein, to whom William was very attached, was to be removed, his removal being sweetened by his appointment to the Governorship of Orange.[41]

When this was reported to Mary in London by Nassau-Beverweert she was agreeable enough to Prince William's moving from Leyden to The Hague but her body language revealed that she jibbed at the replacement of Nassau-Zuylenstein.[42] De Witt wrote to the ambassador on 23 December emphasising that the committee 'had no other object but to procure and to advance the good of monsieur the Prince of Orange and to neglect nothing which could serve his advancement, which is also the wish of madame the Princess Royal' ('n'ont autre but que de procurer et avancer le bien de monsieur le Prince d'Orange et de négliger rien de ce qui pourrait servir à son avancement, qui est aussy le souhait de madame la Princesse Royale').[43] Which was all very well – but the removal of Nassau-Zuylenstein, a member of the Orange clan, was a step too far for Mary. It is true that he would have taken over the governorship of the Principality of Orange from Count Donha, with whom Mary was in bitter conflict. Nevertheless, it is not unlikely that she may have felt that she had already gone very far in ignoring the House's supporters when she nominated the education committee. If she was now to be seen to consent to the removal of members of the family – even those on the wrong side of the blanket – from positions of patronage in the House of Orange, would she not be in danger of undermining the morale of the House's supporters and the prestige of the House itself?

De Witt's motivation was certainly to remove the English influence which Nassau-Zuylenstein, with his English wife, could exercise over Prince William; but he must also have been conscious of the impact that it would have on the standing of the Orange clan, just as he must have been fully aware that the appointment of Nassau-Zuylenstein to the governorship of Orange was a sop to disguise the reality in a wider struggle for power.

The Regents whom De Witt represented were part of complexes of familial and patron/client relationships, the interests of which were, De Witt thought, at odds with those of the Stuarts and the House of Orange. He genuinely identified their interests with those of the Republic, whilst in practice making the Republic the servant of those interests. He himself, as we have indicated, was at the centre of a web of familial relationships amongst the powerful ruling Regent clans. With the passage of time the Regents were becoming a closed hereditary caste, holding office through co-option and birth.[44] The struggle for power in the Republic, at every turn, was set in the framework of struggles between contesting and ever-changing family and clan alliances. The importance of clan would have been imbued in both Mary and De Witt with their mothers' milk.

Of all the clans in the Dutch Republic that of the House of Orange, because of its international connections, its historical role, its status and its prestige, was the most prominent and the most complex. For De Witt this political reality was a constant consideration for the maintenance of his power and for the pursuit of his political beliefs. How was he to manage the most important clan of all?

We do not know how the relationship between the Grand Pensionary and the Princess Royal would have been resolved. Mary was engaged in another demonstration of clan and patron/client politics. True to her word, she did intercede on behalf of the United Provinces with her brother the King and pleaded the case for an alliance between the Dutch and the English. The Dutch, she said, in a memorandum she submitted to him after she had arrived at Whitehall, 'have requested me, both in confidential letters and in interviews, to intercede on their behalf, well knowing that my welfare and their own also depends on the good and peaceable conditions of the United Netherlands.'[45] She was, in short, to take on the role of patron using her power of patronage with her brother to broker an understanding between the rulers of her country by adoption ('yea, as a fellow citizen of the same', as she put it) and the King of her country by birth. It was exactly the role, making full use of birth and clan, which a powerful noble was expected to play in 17th-century Europe, in both internal and international politics, with suitable reciprocal obligations being, of course, expected from the client.

DEATH OF MARY

But Mary's powers of patronage were not to be brought to a conclusion. Even as she had arrived at the fleet waiting to take her across the North Sea to England the black wings of the smallpox were beating relentlessly above her. She then learnt that it had killed her brother, the Duke of Gloucester. And on 3 January 1661 it killed her, too.

On her deathbed her thoughts were on her absent son: 'My greatest pain is to depart from him. Oh my child, give him my blessing.'[46] She lies in Westminster Abbey amongst her Stuart relations, close to where her son was eventually to join her.

William had accompanied her to the fleet to say farewell. Not yet eleven years old, he had rested his eyes on her for the last time on the day before her fleet, delayed by the tides, finally set sail. We have it from one authority that William – when told of the news at Leyden, by Elizabeth of Bohemia – was laid low by grief and that 'shortly afterwards he fell seriously ill'.[47] With no siblings, with a mother from whom, however committed she was, he was separated for long periods, and inevitably aware of the feuding between her and his other nearest relation, his grandmother, Amalia von Solms, William developed deep reserves. But, nevertheless, beneath these reserves, he was able, all his life long, to develop strong emotional attachments to those very few he came to trust.

His mother's legacy in the United Provinces had immediate repercussions. 'I, Mary, princess of Great Britain, Dowager of Orange. ec., being visited with sickness, and probably at this time to exchange this life for a better, do hereby resign my soul into the hands of God my Creator…. My body I bequeath to the earth, to be buried in such decent, Christian manner, and in such place, as the king my royal brother, shall be pleased to appoint…. I earnestly beseech his majesty, as also the queen my royal mother, to take upon them the care of the Prince of Orange, my son, as the best parents and friends I can commend him unto, and from whom he is with most reason, to expect all good helps, both at home and abroad, praying to God to bless and make him a happy instrument to his glory, and to his country's good, as well as to the satisfaction and advantage of his nearest friends and allies. I entreat his majesty most especially to be protector and tutor to him and to his interests by his royal favour and influence.'[48]

Thus sounds the last will and testament of the Princess Royal, made on the day she died. As a creature of her age, it succinctly encapsulates the interaction in her mind between God, Clan, Patron, Client, and Country.

THE GUARDIANSHIP OF THE PRINCE: DE WITT AND AMALIA VON SOLMS

To De Witt it was all very unwelcome. He expressed his alarm shortly after the news of Mary's death was received in The Hague on 13 January 1661. At this time he had an extract but no exact copy of the will. He was concerned that the King would arrogate too much to himself in assuming the rights of guardianship that it looked as though the will had bequeathed him. The best course of action would be to persuade the King, as well as Amalia von Solms, to leave the Prince's education in the hands of the States of Holland, although only time would tell if this could be successfully done.[49]

In a further letter, written on 21 January, he expressed the view that if this could not be done then the Holland States should wash their hands of the affair and 'leave the high born claimants to worrit amongst themselves'.[50]

The King, as it turned out, wrote a conciliatory letter to the Prince's education committee on the same day, noting that their correspondence with Mary indicated that they were in agreement with her on 'the form and manner of proceeding', as he also wished to be.[51]

But De Witt remained unsatisfied. 'The Princess Royal makes a will', he tartly wrote on the 27th, 'and not only does she not name her only son her sole heir, but leaves him not so much as a penny; recommends him true enough to the care of the King her brother, and of the Queen, her mother, but makes not the least mention of the States, or even those of Holland, to whom she entrusted her child whilst she was alive as his chief guardians.'[52]

Apart from giving vent to his views of the defunct Princess Royal, however, the letter also indicates very clearly that, in De Witt's opinion, by accepting Holland as having responsibility for the education of the Prince, the Province had also become the Prince's 'chief guardian'. However, putting this across to a King, Charles II, and eliminating his claim to guardianship under Mary's will, was something that, De Witt was aware, would –

as he noted in an earlier letter – require proceeding with 'exceptional moderation and great discretion'.[53]

In the same letter of the 27th in which he berated Mary he also expressed his views of Charles II, this time in the context of events unfolding in London. Before her death Mary, as well as her mother, Henrietta Maria, who had hurried to come there from France, had done all they could to prevent the recognition of the marriage of James, Duke of York, to Anne Hyde, who, as we have seen, had been a Lady-in-Waiting to Mary, a marriage which was considered beneath the rank of the royal duke. Nassau-Beverweert reported that the English court was so transfixed by the affair as to preclude the pursuit of his diplomatic business,[54] and it was finally left to Charles II to insist that there was nothing for it but that his brother's marriage should be endorsed. 'The king, so it appears,' wrote De Witt, resorting to the cadences of bitter invective, 'allows himself to be led by the nose by his servants; the king's only brother clandestinely marries a miss in waiting to his sister and his majesty is not alone not jealous of his vilified authority, but takes the part of the aggrieved lady against his recalcitrant brother, against his own mother and against his sister, and deems it glory to force the marriage through.' Where a modern republican would have applauded the King, the leading European republican of the times condemned the lack of decorum. The Dutch republican oligarchy, it must be observed, was nothing if not hierarchical.

In the end, however, it seemed that the relationship with the King could be satisfactorily managed. On 4 February Nassau-Beverweert reported from London with assurances that the King was prepared to entrust not just the education of the Prince but the whole guardianship to the States of Holland – provided he could acquire the Regency of the Principality of Orange during William's minority....[55] Whatever else Charles failed to be true to, he was always true to himself.

But then a notorious episode, the episode of the iron chest, intrudes itself into our story. This chest, which had been in Mary's safekeeping, contained documentary material relating to William II's coup of 1650 which could be used against prominent supporters of the House of Orange. On Mary's death the education commission asked for it but it was refused by the Prince's council, who had overall responsibility for his possessions and estate. On 1 February the education commission, of whom, we must remember, De Witt was a member, very unwisely prevailed upon the court of Holland to send the clerk of the court, accompanied by court servants and a locksmith, to force open the room containing the chest and remove it to the court, ostensibly so that the contents could be kept in safekeeping until the Prince came of age.[56]

Amalia von Solms wrote from Cleves, where she was staying, to object to this high-handed measure, as did the Elector of Brandenburg, both of whom still regarded themselves as the Prince's guardians. It caused De Witt to write with great pungency to Nassau-Beverweert on 11 February that to claim that the Prince and his council were not subordinate to the court of Holland was 'something which no Prince of Orange had ever dared to raise his mind to' and that if these sentiments were instilled into the young Prince it would 'oblige the State never to entrust him with any authority or power.'[57]

In the meantime, in one of the earliest letters we have written by him, William had written to Charles II from Leyden on 2 February thanking him for extending his protection and for declaring himself his guardian and pleading that the King should exert pressure for him to obtain the offices held by his predecessors in the United Provinces. Clearly, given his age, the instigation must have come from someone in his circle, possibly Nassau-Zuylenstein, who had become aware of De Witt's manoeuvrings to remove him from his position as the Prince's governor.[58]

Amalia and the Elector of Brandenburg decided on sending an embassy to King Charles, consisting of Prince Maurits of Nassau-Siegen, on behalf of Amalia, and Daniel Weiman, on behalf of the Elector – the ties between Maurits and the Elector were in fact also very close, Maurits having served the Elector in numerous capacities, militarily, diplomatically and politically, as we shall later see.[59] Their instructions, dated 11 February, were to argue the case that it had not lain within the powers of Mary to appoint the King as sole guardian.[60] Their aim was to persuade Charles to hand over the guardianship entirely to Amalia; and on their way to England they stopped off to meet De Witt at The Hague. The removal of the King was, of course, in accordance with the policy of De Witt but the substitution of Amalia was, just as obviously, not.[61] He made it clear that if difficulties were to arise concerning Holland's assumption of responsibility for the Prince's education it would be best for Holland to withdraw completely from the matter.

At this stage the iron chest again obtruded itself, creating an even greater commotion than on its first appearance. The States of Holland passed a resolution on 9 March, with total unanimity, stating that they approved everything that the education commission had done, including both the seizure of the iron chest and the commission's plans for the education of the Prince. For good measure they issued instructions to transfer the chest from the court of Holland to their own safekeeping. The iron chest thus became the instigator of deep diplomatic discord.

At once an official protest flew in from the Princess Dowager, Amalia, and, quite as inevitably, from the Elector of Brandenburg, Frederick-William. And from London ominous rumblings of regal thunder rolled across the North Sea. There the ambassadors from Amalia and the Elector had arrived, and they were only too ready to exacerbate matters by emphasising the significance of Holland's actions, which was already obvious enough to the King and his advisers. Both to take possession of the Prince's property and to take command of his education, without reference to the other guardians, manifestly demonstrated De Witt's presumption that the Prince's chief guardian was the Province of Holland. Nassau-Beverweert and one of his ambassadorial colleagues were admonished in London by the Lord Chancellor, Clarendon, who conveyed the King's great displeasure that the States of Holland were acting as if the Prince's guardians did not exist, and this at the very time when he was pondering over how best to regulate the guardianship. Never, Clarendon was able to assure them, had he seen the King so angry.[62]

However, Charles's shift in stance was not entirely through considerations relating to the guardianship. The old English antagonisms against the Dutch that had manifested themselves in the first Dutch war under the Commonwealth were very deep-rooted and were not altered by the restoration of the monarchy. It was too strong a tide to be left out of the considerations of a newly restored King, still testing the strength of his position. The Navigation Act, on the repeal of which the Dutch set great store, had instead been renewed in September 1660. This in turn, alas, put paid to Charles's hopes of obtaining a Dutch loan. At the same time commercial rivalries across the globe were as acute as ever and, nearer to home, there were disputes over the fisheries in English waters involving the formidable Dutch fishing industry.[63]

The response from the States of Holland to Clarendon's admonishment to the Dutch ambassadors was not long in coming. They intimated on 1 April that they would withdraw from taking responsibility for the Prince's education if the King and the Great Elector persisted in their opposition and unless they were recognised as guardians-in-chief.[64]

It was clear to Charles, a keen sailor, that he would have to go about and complete another of his tacks. On the one hand he did not want to lose all influence over so important a member of his clan, his nephew William, who after the death of Mary and the Duke of Gloucester had moved closer to the English throne. William was next in succession immediately after James and his offspring, and behind the King's last remaining sibling, his sister, Henrietta, known as Minette, who had just married Philippe, Duke of Orléans, the brother of Louis XIV. Then there was also the influence which could be exercised through the guardianship in internal Dutch affairs by means of the House of Orange, a theme which, as we shall see, was to characterise his foreign policy both in peace, and when it came to it, in war.

On the other hand, he could not go bull-headed at the States of Holland in view of the firm stance they had taken. Charles, and particularly Clarendon, realised that the States of Holland would never tolerate the foreign ruler of a substantial European power being allowed to exercise so much blatant influence in their country.[65] An understanding with the Princess Dowager and the Great Elector suggested itself as a possible means to address the King's predicament. This was entered into on 17 May and under it Amalia von Solms was to exercise the guardianship on behalf of the King and the Elector, thereby lowering the profile of the two foreign rulers. Holland would be asked to nominate a new education committee to advise Amalia, with a good sprinkling of representatives from Orangist towns. And Nassau-Zuylenstein was to continue as the Prince's governor.

These proposals were put to Holland by George Downing, who had arrived in The Hague in June, and from the Dutch perspective it could not have been a more ominous choice. His father had been a puritan lawyer who had emigrated to America and Downing had been educated at Harvard to enter the ministry. He had risen in the Commonwealth to serve in the same ambassadorial role he was now undertaking, and, like so many important servitors of that regime, he had exchanged his allegiance to the Crown with lithe timing just before the Restoration. Evelyn said of him that 'from a pedagogue and a fanatic preacher, not worth a groat' he was 'becoming excessive rich'. He has lent his name to Downing Street. He combined his ambassadorial role with being Member of Parliament for Morpeth. He had an extensive knowledge of commerce and was a major protagonist of those commercial interests in England imbued with animosity towards the Dutch. He was indeed the chief instigator of the renewal of the Navigation Act.[66]

But if during Downing's embassy mercantile matters were to be a matter of acute concern, a prime objective of the King was to foster and maintain the edifice of his clan, of his clients and of his related allies on the continent of Europe. In his instructions relating to the Prince of Orange, Downing was told:

1. That he should keep good correspondence with the Princess Dowager or the ministers of the Elector of Brandenburg.
2. That with them he shall consider of what is to be demanded to the benefit of the Prince of Orange, and consequently
3. That with them he shall endeavour as much as possible he can, to the end that the true friends of the house of Orange may be conserved … to the service of those houses, that are interested.[67]

Downing, the instructions made clear, should so endeavour matters that Holland, under pressure from the other Provinces, would 'give the Prince of Orange some assurance, that at his coming to his aage [sic] of discretion he shall be provided with those charges, which his ancestors have been provided withal.' In addition he was to pursue Holland's involvement in William's education, but in accordance with the agreement reached on 17 May between the three guardians, Charles II, Amalia and the Elector.

Downing was completely clear in his mind that the Prince of Orange was the key to Charles II establishing a power base in the United Provinces, a tenet which was to run through Charles's foreign policy in the coming years: '…its a playne case', he wrote to Clarendon on 1 July 1661, 'that the King can have no firme friendship in this Country without the Prince of Orange, and his restitution and his designation for the present in order thereunto would be matter of great reputation to the King'.[68] He ignored De Witt's warning 'that any foreign interposition' on the Prince's behalf 'would but make it recayle [recoil]'.[69]

He set about it with a will to garner support for William on two fronts – the elevation to the ancestral offices, and acceptance by the States of Holland of the understanding between Charles, Amalia and the Elector for the education of the Prince. He met with Prince William himself in Leyden and held discussions with leading Orange supporters. But on the Prince's elevation he made little progress.

In England Clarendon, who did not want to risk a break with the Dutch, was trying to exert a moderating influence whilst the Grand Elector, an ultra-cautious man, was also reluctant to antagonise them.[70] Clarendon contended that the best way to promote William's interests was for England first to enter into a trade treaty with the Dutch. After such a treaty had been made, Dutch mercantile interests would have too much to lose to risk the loss of English friendship and at that stage the English King would be in a position to assert maximum pressure in favour of the Prince of Orange. He was very concerned that the newly restored English monarchy was insecurely based, both domestically and internationally. Domestically there was 'nothinge the seditious and discontented people do so much feare as a peace with Hollande, from the contrary to which they promise themselves infinite advantages.' Internationally the restored monarchy was without allies – 'we have yet no alliance made with France, Spain, or the United Provinces'.[71]

But Clarendon's policy was based on very uncertain foundations, given Downing's simultaneous policy of aggressively pursuing English mercantile interests. The Dutch Regents, in bestowing the 'Dutch Gift' on King Charles, had been seeking the English King's patronage to further their commercial interest. If it became obvious that Charles was one-sidedly extending his patronage to that alternative Amsterdam, the City of London, without seeking in any way to address Dutch concerns, they would need to revise their views. And there were sound reasons for believing that Charles was moving in that direction. There was the renewal of the Navigation Act; there were frictions off the coast of Africa, where an English fleet under Sir Robert Holmes had appeared to challenge Dutch interests;[72] and the very points at issue which were on the agenda for the negotiations for the proposed Trade Treaty revealed the extent of the commercial differences between the two countries.

Neither King Charles nor Downing appreciated the repercussions this would have on the position of the Prince of Orange and his House within the Republic. If the patronage of King Charles was becoming of somewhat uncertain value, so was the need to reach a compromise with the House of Orange through the education of the Prince. At the end of September the Grand Pensionary formally informed the States of Holland of what they already knew, that William's three guardians had rescinded the proposal that Holland should take charge of his education; and on 30 September the Holland States themselves resolved to withdraw from that commitment and disbanded the education committee.[73] Far from strengthening the position of the Prince, the King and Downing had strengthened that of De Witt at the Prince's expense. De Witt drove through his advantage to reach an agreement between Holland and Zeeland under which the two Provinces undertook not to consider the elevation of William until he was 18.[74]

The surge in Orangist fortunes resulting from the Stuart restoration had been contained.

THE ORANGE COURT AFTER THE DEATH OF MARY

William III matured early. The Queen of Bohemia had reported in April 1661 that 'You cannot imagine the witt that he has, it is not a witt of a childe who is suffisant, but of a man, that doth not pretend to it, he is a verie extraordinary childe….'[75] And when Amalia von Solms took him for a visit to Cleves in the same month to stay with the Elector of Brandenburg, Frederick-William had observed that 'he is the dearest child that can be, and for his age very mature'. It was the Elector who had introduced him to hunting, a passion that was to remain with him all his life. Some symptoms of bad health, it seems, may again have begun to manifest themselves. There is some evidence that he had begun to develop a hump-back and that he wore a corset as a counter-measure, as well as signs that he had begun to suffer from the asthma that later was to become such a burden – but there is no evidence that the symptoms became serious until 1688. Another uncle, the Prince of Anhalt, was also there as part of the family party and extended clan, a further connection of which Prince William was to make full use later in his career.[76]

Constantijn Huygens noted that there were bickerings amongst his Leyden tutors and entourage, who had accompanied him to Cleves, with disputes regarding precedence; and one of them complained openly about 'la vie de Leyden', which may have been indicative of a lack of control over his upbringing.[77] Certainly within nine months it was being reported that Amalia was aiming at removing Nassau-Zuylenstein from his governorship and substituting her nephew, Count Donha, the former governor of Orange, in his place.[78] William left Cleves on 8 June by yacht to travel to Leyden by way of Utrecht, where he was received with considerable pomp and ceremony.[79]

The issue of his education was continuing to exercise Amalia after the States of Holland washed their hands of all responsibility at the end of September. Moreover, she was now confronted by the agreement between Holland and Zeeland to leave any decision on the Prince's elevation until his 18th birthday. In the light of this she gradually began to waver in her resolution on the question of the guardianship. By July 1662 she approached the States of Holland, asking them to reconsider their position, although she did not yet unequivocally meet De Witt's stipulation that Holland should have sole control.[80] But at the same time she was getting very little support from Charles II – he omitted to take the opportunity to exert pressure on Louis to return the Principality of Orange when he was negotiating the sale of Dunkirk to the French in September and October 1662 – and by the beginning of 1663 she was ready to surrender totally to De Witt's demand when she persuaded Charles that meeting De Witt's criterion was a prerequisite to the Prince's prospects of elevation.

With that somewhat lackadaisical inconsistency which characterised so much of his policy-making, good uncle Charles concurred. 'Nephew,' he wrote to William on 28 February O.S., 'The Princess Dowager, your grandmother, hath sent hither an express to mee, desiring I would concur in the opinion of having your person and affaires put into the care of the States of Holland to which I have – as far as depends on mee – consented, assuring myself that your grandmother cannot but know what is best for you … and I presume likewise your owne inclinations concurre therein because I have nothing from you or any body, relating to you, contradicting this opinion….'[81]

Consequently, on 17 March, the Princess Dowager formally approached the States of Holland and asked them to take responsibility for William's upbringing. But to this the Holland States gave a negative reply.[82] Their mood had changed; the resurging power of the House of Orange in the wake of the Stuart Restoration had been contained – and even pushed back; and the considerations which had led to the understanding between Mary and De Witt – so far as they went – had become, from Holland's point of view, no longer applicable.

As for Amalia, she received the rebuff with some equanimity and it was not long before, in June, she was dining amicably with De Witt.[83] He on his part supported her in August in her attempt to get Charles to repay the debt that the Stuarts owed the House of Orange, a matter of some 2 million guilders or about £200,000, and a month later he did so in relation to the even larger debts owed to the House by the Spanish King,[84] although both attempts proved abortive.

William, meanwhile, had been moved from Leyden to The Hague at the end of 1662. The control of his education remained with Nassau-Zuylenstein as governor – despite Amalia's misgivings – and his religious education continued to be conducted by Pastor Trigland. The routine was that he received instruction in religion from Trigland from 8 to 9am and another tutor, Bornius, taught him Latin, further languages and other disciplines from 9 to 11am and then for another two hours in the afternoon.[85]

In his entourage there was a swashbuckling French soldier, somewhat in the same mould as Nassau-Zuylenstein in his youth, hard-drinking and of a dissolute disposition. With English connections Buat was in nominal receipt of a pension of £500 from Charles II and he bore a marked antipathy to the States party led by De Witt. We shall encounter him later in William's life, when he has a not unimportant part to play in our story.[86]

One other figure also enters the stage, to remain a dominant feature throughout William's life. Hans Willem Bentinck, later Duke of Portland, came from an old gentry family from Overijssel, in the eastern Netherlands, and joined William's household as a page in 1664.[87] In a life which was to have very few close personal relationships this bond was to become perhaps the closest, equalled perhaps only by William's future wife, Mary, and, possibly, and for a much shorter time, with somebody of the same familial background as Bentinck, Joost

Keppel, created by William Earl of Albemarle.[88] Despite vicissitudes the relationship with Bentinck was to survive until William's deathbed.

At this time also we can perceive the beginnings of another relationship which – despite their never meeting and being conducted at long distance – was to develop and remain with him to his dying day, his relationship with his cousin, Louis XIV. Amalia had sent Constantijn Huygens to France in 1661 to negotiate the return of the Principality of Orange. He complained bitterly about the behaviour of the French: 'they are self-satisfied and proud beyond measure, so that in the matter of our authority in Orange I have had to swallow a lot of talk and arrogant conclusions…'.[89] The Princess Dowager was deeply affronted. 'I would say to you,' she had written in November 1661 to Huygens, 'that the princes of Orange have always been of service to the Kings of France, but never their subjects, and much less their slaves.'[90] Nor was she very pleased when she and William had an interview with the new French ambassador, D'Estrades, in The Hague in January 1663 who indicated that it was Louis's intention to return Orange, provided that it should have a Catholic governor.[91] Given the intense sensitivity about the sovereignty of the Principality, the imposition of such a condition was bound to cause unease.

At the interview William made an impression on the ambassador: 'This little Prince promises much in himself.' He was soon to have a further sharp encounter with 'the little Prince', in which it is reasonable to suppose that the rancour, the personal insult, over Orange played no small part. On May Day afternoon in 1664 William took to his coach to enjoy the *kermis*, or annual fair, in The Hague. He encountered D'Estrades going in the other direction on his way home in a fashionable thoroughfare, the Voorhout. William's coach hugged the recognised place of honour near the railing bordering the road and neither side was prepared to give way on this issue of precedence.

An ugly scene began to develop. There was a large crowd attracted by the *kermis*. This began to congregate around the contestants and became menacing to the point where matters might have got completely out of control had the situation not been rescued, according to d'Estrades's despatch to Louis XIV, by the arrival of De Witt on the scene. The Pensionary persuaded William to send a messenger – Nassau-Zuylenstein, it transpired, who was with him in the coach – to give warning to Amalia. Acting on De Witt's advice, which was conveyed to her by this means, she gave orders for the Prince's coach to turn round, which was done, but only after he had vacated it to observe the fun of the fair on foot. The point of precedence was thus neatly averted.[92]

The incident attracted a great deal of attention at the time. William's claim to precedence over the ambassador was based on his being a grandson of a King of England. Now, Louis XIV much savoured matters of precedence; he had made of them a particular study – there was no one who could possibly dispute precedence with himself, and, from this elevated vantage point, he was able to appraise the scramble below with detached nicety. Carefully assessing all the relevant considerations in the present circumstances, he waved aside William's pretensions. In a despatch to D'Estrades his full authority on the subject was displayed; and he concluded, magisterially, that William's claims came through the female line, which 'signified nothing in the case in question'.[93]

In April 1665 Louis returned the Principality of Orange to William but only after four years of hard negotiation by Constantijn Huygens; and the stipulation that its governor should be Catholic was met.[94]

If William had displayed a flash of steel in his make-up when confronting the ambassador of his French cousin, we also have another glimpse of him. In June 1665 he wrote a letter in his own hand to Johan Theodore, Baron van Friesheim, a former page in his service, who was now serving as an ensign in the army: 'I hope that you have not been debauched by drink', he wrote, before continuing, 'I fear that you have become much more so by women.'

What escapades the deficient Baron, who was about 23 years old, had enacted to deserve these strictures from the Prince, who was 14, is not detailed in the sources, but the matter did not end there. A further letter followed in September in which the Prince assured the Baron of his regard and that he would not forget him, before returning to the former theme, 'abstain as far as you can from drink and principally from women'.[95]

As it happened neither the drink nor the women retarded the delinquent Baron. He ended his days as a general of infantry and died in his 91st year.

But at the age of 14 there does seem to have been somebody in the Prince's entourage – certainly not Nassau-Zuylenstein; possibly Trigland – prompting in him a touch of the prig.

1 Groen van Prinsterer, Archives, op. cit., series 2, V, p.195.
2 Geyl, *op. cit.*, p.135.
3 Rowen, *De Witt*, *op. cit.*, p.442.
4 Wiquefort, *op. cit.*, II, pp.647–8.
5 Rowen, *De Witt*, *op. cit.*, p.443; Wiquefort, *op. cit.*, II, p.649. Rowen says the 23rd, Wiquefort the 24th as does Geyl, *op. cit.*, p.135.
6 Wicquefort, *op. cit.*, II, pp.653–4.
7 *Ibid.*, p.660.
8 Israel, *op. cit.*, p.750.
9 Wicquefort, *op. cit.*, p.656.
10 Rowen, *De Witt*, *op. cit.*, p.444; Japikse, *De Verwikkelingen tuschen de Republiek en Engeland van 1660–1665*, Leiden, S.C. van Doesbergh, 1900, p.13.
11 Japikse, *Verwikkeling*, *op. cit.*, p.17.
12 Japikse, *Verwikkelingen*, *op. cit.*, p.18. The account is based on the report to the Elector of Brandenburg by his representative, Weiman.
13 Wicquefort, *op. cit.*, II, p.660.The original was written in French.
14 Groen van Prinsterer, *op. cit.*, series 2, V, p.197.
15 *Letters of Elizabeth, Queen of Bohemia*, *op. cit.*, p.308.
16 *Ibid.*, p.309.
17 Wicquefort, *op. cit.*, II, p.661.
18 *Letters of Elizabeth*, *op. cit.*, p.310.

19 *Diary of Samuel Pepys*, London, 1875, 1, pp.127–8, 23 May 1660, Old Style. The King was soon regaling Pepys with a version of his escape after the battle of Worcester.

20 Groen van Prinsterer, *op. cit.*, series 2, V, pp.197–8.

21 *Ibid.*, series 2, V, p.198; Japikse, *Verwikkelingen, op. cit.*, p.19.

22 Geyl, *op. cit.*, p.140.

23 Israel, *op. cit.*, p.750.

24 *Brieven van Johan De Witt*, Hist. Gen. Utrecht, series 3, No.25, II, 1909, pp.240–2.

25 Everett Green, *op. cit.*, VI, p.306, quoting Lambeth MS, p.645, art.15.

26 Japikse, *Verwikkelingen, op. cit.*, p.24.

27 Rowen, *De Witt, op. cit.*, p.515.

28 Aitzema, *Saken van Staet en oorlog*, IV, pp.635–7; Wicquefort, *op. cit.*, 2, p.669; Japikse, *Verwikkelingen, op. cit.*, pp.25–6; Rowen, *De Witt, op. cit.*, pp.515–16.

29 Geyl, *op. cit.*, p.142; Japikse, *Verwikkelingen, op. cit.*, p.25.

30 Baxter, *op. cit.*, p.49.

31 Japikse, *Verwikkelingen, op. cit.*, p.25. Rowen, *De Witt, op. cit.*, p.516; Groen van Prinsterer, *op. cit.*, series 2, V, p.200.

32 He approached them for a loan of two million guilders in September, see Japikse, *Verwikkelingen, op. cit.*, p.47; Geyl, *op. cit.*, p.142.

33 He was an illegitimate son of Prins Maurits. Japikse, *Verwikkelingen*, pp.42–3. See also Mary's letter to Charles in Everett Green, *op. cit.*, VI, p.306, in which she says Nassau-Beverweert 'has always been my friend'.

34 Rowen, *De Witt, op. cit.*, p.517.

35 Everett Green, *op. cit.*, VI, p.308, quoting Lambeth MS, art.28. Holograph.

36 De Thou, despatch, 19 August. Groen van Prinsterer, *op. cit.*, series 2, V, p.202.

37 De Thou, despatches, 26 August and 2 Sept. Groen van Prinsterer, *op. cit.*, series 2, V, pp.204–6.

38 Rowen, *De Witt, op. cit.*, pp.518–19; Japikse, *Verwikkelingen, op. cit.*, Appendices I and II.

39 Japikse, *Verwikkelingen, op. cit.*, p.29. There is a copy of the resolution in 'Resolutiën van consideratie der Ed. Groot. Mog. Heeren Staten van Holland ende West-Friestland genomen zedert den aenvang der bedieninge van den Heer Johan de Witt', Johannes Oosterwijk, *Steenhouwer en Uytwerf*, Amsterdam & The Hague, 1719.

40 Rowen, *De Witt, op. cit.*, pp.520–21; Geyl, *op. cit.*, p.146; Japikse, *Verwikkelingen, op. cit.*, p.32; Wicquefort, *op. cit.*, II, p.677.

41 Rowen, *De Witt, op. cit.*, p.525; Japikse, *Verwikkelingen, op. cit.*, p.132.

42 Nassau-Beverweert to De Witt, 17 Dec.1660, *Brieven geschreven tuschen de Heer Johan de Witt ende gevolmaghtigden van den Staadt*, Hendrick Scheurleer, The Hague, 1724.

43 *Brieven van de Witt, op. cit.*, II, 1657–64, p.255. With the aristocratic Nassau-Beverweert (with rare exceptions) and with the Princess Royal, De Witt's communications were in French.

44 Rowen, *De Witt, op. cit.*, p.135.

45 Quoted in Everett Green, *op. cit.*, pp.322–4.

46 Quoted in entry under Mary by Marika Keblusek, *Oxford Dictionary of National Biography*, based on royal archives, The Hague. Report by her secretary Nicholas Oudaerdt, 1661, inv. G1–6, II–H fol.41.

47 Nesca Robb, *op. cit.*, p.102, citing *Histoire de Guillaume III* (Amsterdam, 1692), I, p.12, *Kingsdon's Weekly Intelligence*, 7 January 1661, and a contemporary poem by an unknown author. The two other main authorities with detailed biographies throw no light on William's reaction. Japikse says he does not know, *Willem III, op. cit.*, I, p.90, and Baxter is silent.

48 Everett Green, *op. cit.*, p.326.

49 *Brieven van De Witt, op. cit.*, II, pp.277–8, letter dated 15 Jan. 1661.

50 *Ibid.*, p.279, letter dated 21 Jan. 1661.

51 Japikse, *Verwikkelingen, op. cit.*, Appendix VI, p.XIV.

52 *Brieven van De Witt, op. cit.*, II, p.283, letter dated 27 Jan. 1661 to Godard van Reede van Ginkel.

53 Geyl, *op. cit.*, p.163; *Brieven van De Witt, op. cit.*, II, pp.283, 290.

54 Scheurleer, *Brieven, op. cit.*, 22 Oct. 1660.

55 Japikse, *Verwikkelingen, op. cit.*, p.135, citing Nassau-Beverweert to De Witt, 4 Feb.

56 Japikse, *Verwikkelingen*, p.135; Geyl, *op. cit.*, p.165; Rowen, *De Witt, op. cit.*, pp.529ff; Fruin, *Verspreide Geschriften*, The Hague, 1901, IV, pp.149ff.

57 *Brieven van de Witt, op. cit.*, II, p.286.

58 The text is given in Japikse, *Verwikkelingen*, *op. cit.*, Appendix VI, p.XIV. On Zuylenstein's knowledge of his proposed removal see Rowen, *De Witt*, *op. cit.*, p.529, and Nassau-Beverweert's letter to De Witt of 31 Dec. 1660, Scheurleer, *Brieven*, *op. cit.*

59 Geyl, *op. cit.*, p.164.

60 Rowen, *De Witt*, *op. cit.*, p.530.

61 Japikse, *Verwikkelingen*, pp.139–41.

62 Japikse, *Verwikkelingen*, pp.142–3; Geyl, *op. cit.*, p.165.

63 Geyl, *op. cit.*, pp.166–7; Israel, *op. cit.*, p.752.

64 Geyl, *op. cit.*, p.168; Rowen, *De Witt*, *op. cit.*, p.534; Japikse, *Verwikkelingen*, op. cit., pp.143–4.

65 See Japikse, *Verwikkelingen*, pp.145–6 and his Appendix VIIIa for this and some of the other considerations which appeared in the King's mind. See also Geyl. *op. cit.*, p.168; Rowen, *De Witt*, *op. cit.*, p.536. Certainly by August 1661 Clarendon asked Downing: 'What harangues would De Witt make upon that subiect, that the King of England will not make a peace with [the Dutch] excepte he may give them a Generall, Admirall and Stateholder, who must always remember to whome he owes the benefit?' T.H. Lister, *Life and Administration of Clarendon*, London, 1837, p.167.

66 *History of Parliament: The Commons 1660–1690*, section on Downing.

67 Japikse, *Verwikkelingen*, *op. cit.*, Appendix VIIIb.

68 *Ibid.*, Appendix IX, p.XXII.

69 *Ibid.*, p.XXI.

70 Geyl, *op. cit.*, pp.171–2; Japikse, *Verwikkelingen*, *op. cit.*, pp.149–51.

71 Lister, *op. cit.*, 1837, pp.167–70.

72 Japikse, *Verwikkelingen*, *op. cit.*, pp.164–5.

73 Rowen, *De Witt*, *op. cit.*, p.539.

74 Israel, *op. cit.*, p.757.

75 Quoted in Robb, *William III*, *op. cit.*, his source letters of Elizabeth to the Elector Palatine, p.342, 11 April 1661.

76 Japikse, *William III*, *op. cit.*, I, pp.100–2.

77 Huygens, *Briefwisseling*, *op. cit.*, V, p.359.

78 *Ibid.*, V, p.385.

79 *Ibid.*, V, p.361.

80 Geyl, *op. cit.*, p.185.

81 Japikse, *Correspondentie van William III en van Hans Willem Bentinck*, II, Pt 1, Martinus Nijhof, The Hague, 1932, p.6. The date there given is 28 Feb.1662 O.S. Under the Julian calendar the new year began on 25 March so that 28 Feb. 1662 translates into 10 March 1663 N.S. The actual letter is undated. See Japikse, *Verwikkelingen*, App.XL, for his dating of the letter.

82 Geyl, *op. cit.*, p.186.

83 *Ibid.*, p.186.

84 Rowen, *De Witt*, *op. cit.*, p.543.

85 Japikse, *Willem III*, I, pp.110–12.

86 *Ibid.*, I, p.112; Japikse, *Verwikkelingen*, *op. cit.*, p.250.

87 Japikse, *Willem III*, *op. cit.*, I, p.114.

88 *Ibid.*

89 Huygens, *Briefwisseling*, *op. cit.*, V, p.369.

90 Groen van Prinsterer, *op. cit.*, series 2, V, p.213. Letter dated 9 Nov.1661. Copy also in Huygens, *Briefwisseling*, V.pp.369–70.

91 Groen van Prinsterer, *op. cit.*, series 2, V, pp.231–3.

92 D'Estrades's version, including De Witt's role, is contained in his despatch to Louis XIV dated 8 May. *Lettres, Mémoires et Négociations de Monsieur Le Comte d'Estrades's*, London, 1743. Huygens, *Briefwisselingen*, *op. cit.*, V, p.61 gives Amalia's version of the incident, which does not mention De Witt's intervention and suggests that Nassau-Zuylenstein came to her of his own volition. Downing also has a version: letter to Clarendon, 29 April O.S., Lister, *op. cit.*, pp.312–13. In this version De Witt happened to be present and was threatened by the crowd 'so that [he] began to be afraid of himselfe'.

93 D'Estrades, *op. cit.*, Letter from Louis XIV, 30 May 1664.

94 Pontbriant, *op. cit.*, p.222.

95 Groen van Prinsterer, *op. cit.*, series 2, V, p.xxxvii.

4 CHARLES II'S DUTCH WAR

THE ORIGINS OF WAR

After the initial attempts by the Regents in the Dutch Union to establish a good footing with the restored monarchy of Charles II, relations began to deteriorate.

The treaty of friendship with England, on which the Dutch initially had laid such store, was indeed signed in September 1662 and ratified in January 1663,[1] but it did not resolve the underlying commercial frictions with England. At every point in the globe there were rivalries. In the Indonesian archipelago trade and territorial disputes between the Dutch and the English East India Companies were decades old – so old that the execution of English merchants in Ambon in 1623 had entered English folk memory as 'the Ambonia Massacre', a phrase to be deployed with all its emotional resonance whenever tensions rose high. The treaty of 1662 stipulated the handing over of an island, Pulau Run, to the English East India Company, but local resistance by the Dutch East India Company prevented compliance. In the United Provinces Amsterdam merchants were particularly closely associated with the Dutch company, with all the influence they could bring to bear on the Republic's policies.

Off the coast of Africa the slave trade was growing in importance as the demand for labour for the sugar industry in the West Indies expanded. The English Royal African Company began to trade there in 1660, its initial interest being in gold, but the switch in emphasis to slaves – 'for £17 a head or 24,000 lbs of well cured muscovado sugar'[2] – was marked by the grant of a new charter in 1663.[3] This brought it into competition with the Dutch West India Company, which was closely associated with the Province of Zeeland. At the same time those who had an interest in the Royal African Company sounded like a roll-call of the royal family, the aristocracy and the political elite in England – the Queen, the Queen Mother, the Duchess of Orléans, Prince Rupert, the Duke of Buckingham, the Earls of Manchester, Pembroke, St Albans, Bath, Sandwich and Lauderdale – and so the list continues.[4] Its chairman was James, Duke of York.

But the Royal African Company was not very profitable, its capital was not very large, and most of the shareholdings were small or represented only a small proportion of the shareholders' wealth.[5] The latest historiography tends to reduce the emphasis on commercial factors as a direct cause of the Second Dutch War and instead points to the personal ambitions of key players, particularly those associated with the Duke of York, who made skilful use of the commercial grievances to obtain support and drive forward their aims.

The Duke of York was Lord Admiral and regarded the navy as his special preserve, from which he could exercise power and patronage. He was, furthermore, a frustrated condottiere looking for a role, as, his father-in-law, Clarendon, remarked. 'Having been even from his childhood in the command of armies and in his nature inclined to the most difficult and dangerous enterprises, he was already weary of having so little to do and too impatiently longed for any war, in which he knew he could not but have the chief command.'[6] The aristocratic militarism of the French court in which James had moved during the royalist exile, with its concomitant values, had clearly left its mark. Clustered around the Duke of York were naval officers for whom war represented prize money and career advancement, and politicians, both at court and in Parliament, plotting to ascend the greasy pole. The King was persuaded that a war resulting in a greater share of trade would lead to greater royal revenues.[7]

Clarendon, indeed, and the Lord Treasurer, Southampton, feared a war without allies[8] and in this Clarendon was, to James's unfeigned annoyance, deviating from the clan/client relationship of which he had become part when his daughter had married the Duke.[9] But although the King relied heavily on the experience and standing of Clarendon, he did not do so exclusively,[10] and less so as time moved on. Clarendon was not the King's first minister, nor did Charles perform that role himself.

There was therefore no central directing force in English politics and the conflicting forces within the government led to inevitable contradictions and incoherence.[11] Charles's own position was not at all clear but rather, probably intentionally, opaque as he played off the competing parties against each other.

Parliament was, of course, crucial in finding the finance if a war was to be fought. Clarendon had a following in Parliament based on his family, his servants and his close friends. But his management of Parliament was being rivalled by Sir Henry Bennet, since 1662 one of the two Secretaries of State. He had served the Duke of York as secretary and was also, or had been, a client of the Earl of Bristol, whose former secretary he had also been.[12] Bristol had been dismissed as Secretary of State and as a Privy Counsellor after his conversion to Catholicism and was a bitter opponent of Clarendon, whom he tried to impeach in 1663. Close associates of Bennet in Parliament were Sir Charles Berkeley, who was captain of the Duke of York's lifeguards and groom of his bedchamber, and Sir Thomas Clifford.[13] Berkeley was later to join the Duke at sea – to be killed in battle – and Clifford too was to participate in the sea war.

De Witt calculated that Parliament would not vote the King the necessary supplies lest he should use them to make himself independent of that body; and indeed it is not immediately obvious why its members, dominated by the gentry, who would largely have to pay for the war, were persuaded otherwise.[14] Mercantile interests in the House of Commons were numerically not great – and nor was the City of London united in its support for a war.[15] In his diary entry for 23 March 1664 Pepys noted that he was informed that there were 'not above 20 or 30 merchants' in the House of Commons,[16] a figure which modern research suggests is not significantly wide of the mark at the time Pepys wrote, and there was not a large number of naval officers. It is however true that in this Parliament never less than 20 per cent of the members held office at court.[17] These sources of support seem to have provided a sufficient base for the pro-war party to manoeuvre their aims through the House. Paul Seaward has emphasised the mutual dependency of the English Crown and the English gentry – the gentry's standing in the country depended on the Crown; the Crown depended on the gentry for the administration of the country.[18] This may have been a factor at a time, moreover, of undoubted, passionately strong popular feeling against the Dutch.

In the spring of 1664 the House set up a committee whose terms of reference embraced the general decay of trade. Its members included Bennet;[19] and Clifford, who had hitched his star to that of Bennet, and who was later to become a Catholic, chaired its first meeting.[20] The committee presented its conclusion to the House 'that all those damages & affronts [from the Dutch] be reported to the House as the greatest obstruction to our foreign trade & should be represented to the King & he be moved to take speedy and effectual course for redresse'. The Commons not only adopted the resolution without a single dissenting vote but – such was the fervour of the moment – they offered their lives and fortunes as well.

A few indeed were to lose their lives and, as a body, they certainly voted what seemed ample supplies – £2.5 million in the 1664–5 session of Parliament and £1.25 million in October 1665.[21] Despite his pacifist leanings Clarendon played a part in obtaining the supplies when – so as to avoid too obvious a link being made between the supplies and the court – he persuaded Robert Paston, a Norfolk MP from an old family, but in some pecuniary straits, to propose the motion for the £2.5 million.[22] Clarendon's motive was to use the supplies as a lever to bring the Dutch to negotiate,[23] a view which must have been fostered by Downing's despatches from The Hague. It was a woeful miscalculation.

George Downing was an extremely unpleasant man, for whom no contemporary had a good word at a personal level – 'a crafty fawning man', as Burnet describes him[24] – but nevertheless he was possessed of considerable drive. He had a detailed grasp of Dutch trade and, imbued with the mercantile thinking of the time, but in extreme form, he saw the Dutch as usurping in the area of trade the position which should rightly have been held by the English. At every turn he neglected no opportunity to raise matters in dispute between the two countries.

His line of thought, from which he was not subsequently to deviate, was expressed in a letter to Clarendon on 20 January 1662: '…lett the King of England continue firme, where he hath justice on his side, and they [the Dutch] will doe him justice, and, if otherwise, not, but instead thereof, doe him one injury after another, of which what can be ye issue but warr at last.'[25] He greatly underestimated De Witt's resolve. 'Let me tell you, I know I am sure of it, and from his most intimates, he dreads a warr,' he wrote to Clarendon in August 1662.[26] His judgement did not change as war approached. In reporting to Clarendon in May 1664 the intense preparations the Dutch were making for war, he added: 'It is their opinion that, by shewing their teeth, they shall be able to fright you into compliance and obtaine their ends, though I am sure they doe dread a warre as ye Devill.'[27]

These thoughts seem to have influenced Charles II, who wrote to his sister, Minette, in France on 2 June that the Dutch 'keep a great bragging and noise, but I believe, when it comes to it, they will look twice before they leap'. And he remarks on the feverish war atmosphere in England, 'I never saw so great an appetite to a war as is in both this town and country, especially in the Parliament men, who I am confident, would pawn their estates to maintain a war.' And again in September, 'The truth is they [the Dutch] have no great need to provoke this nation, for except myself I believe there is scarce an Englishman that does not desire a war with them.' But how sincere was the King in demonstrating his pacifism? He was using Minette as his private conduit for communicating with Louis XIV and he was anxious to demonstrate – admittedly somewhat feebly – that he himself was not the aggressor in this war and in this way to absolve Louis from coming to the aid of the Dutch under the French treaty with them of 1662.

In May the Dutch West India Company had reported to the States-General that English ships under Captain Holmes had captured three of their ships, as well as Cape Verde off the Guinea coast of Africa. When the news of these hostilities was confirmed in July by a returning Dutch skipper who reported that the capture of Cape Verde (more accurately an island, Goeree, just off its coast) had occurred in February, and that he had witnessed the English firing on another Dutch possession, Cape Corso (although he did not report its capture), the Dutch ambassador in London received little satisfaction from Charles, who denied that Holmes had acted on his orders and who presented counter-grievances against the West India Company. There was no question of returning what Holmes had seized.[28]

Holmes was in fact in command of an expedition sent out by the Royal African Company at the end of 1663 and the Council had authorised the support of three royal men of war. His instructions were to act defensively to protect the interests of the Company off the African coast, instructions which he blatantly exceeded.[29]

On 11 August the States-General sent secret orders to De Ruyter, the Dutch admiral based in the Mediterranean, to retrieve the situation off the African coast.[30] In October the capture by Holmes of Cape Corso was authenticated in the Netherlands – according to Charles II it was 'a stinking place', worth at most a hundred pounds. But all the same he now admitted to the Dutch ambassador that Holmes had acted with his knowledge and under his orders as regards this capture, something he had hitherto denied in connection with Holmes's earlier actions. And he supported the English claim to the place, 'stinking' or not.[31]

At the end of October the Dutch West India Company told the States-General that its colony in America, New Netherlands, with the town of New Amsterdam, had been seized by the English on 6 September. The town, which was to become the property of the

Duke of York and renamed New York, at that time was a place of little significance – the Indonesian island of Pulau Run was considered of much greater value.[32] But there was no vacillating this time. The King acknowledged his responsibility for the action.[33]

Since the despatch of the orders to De Ruyter rumours had been circulating of his likely destination, which, however, had been discounted both by Downing in The Hague and by the English government. Late in October, Lawson, the commander of the British fleet in the Mediterranean, returned to England with two of his ships with the news that he had parted from De Ruyter at Cádiz. The Dutch admiral beguiled him with the story that he was heading for Salé, a corsair base on the Atlantic coast of what is now Morocco, and he extended all the courtesies, striking his flag and firing a nine-gun salute, an honour which Lawson reciprocated.[34]

Whilst there was still no definite confirmation of where De Ruyter was heading for, premonitions began to grow in London. On 24 October the Dutch ambassador reported that very strong rumours were circulating that he was heading for the Guinea coast, and that this was causing great consternation. The King and the Duke of York in particular were markedly stirred, with their personal prestige and authority now at stake. The English fleet was brought up to a high state of preparedness for war.[35] At last, on 22 December, Pepys recorded in his diary: 'I hear fully the news of our being beaten to dirt at Guinny, by De Ruyter with his fleete.'

In January 1665 the English launched an unsuccessful attack on the homecoming Dutch Smyrna fleet. In March England officially declared a war which in reality had existed for some time. James and his associates had got the war which they had so longed for, but the English government had drifted rather than steered into a situation which was to have a calamitous outcome.

THE WAR AND THE PRINCE OF ORANGE

The outbreak of war between England and the Dutch Republic presented the House of Orange with a dilemma. In April Downing, who remained as English ambassador in The Hague, wrote to Clarendon that it was being mooted that the Prince should visit the Dutch fleet at Texel and indicated the embarrassment this might give rise to: 'no doubt, if he should go, he would be put upon drinking ye prosperity of the fleet, and such kind of things, as his Matie would have no great excuse to be over satisfied with'.[36] At the same time if the war had great popular support in England there was also, if the French ambassador in The Hague is to be believed, considerable popular enthusiasm for it at its inception in the Dutch Republic.

The dilemma was, in fact, handled, on this occasion, with some skill by the leading members of the House – we must consider Amalia von Solms to be at their head. When William did visit the fleet at Texel he did so in the presence of the Elector of Brandenburg, the Duke of Holstein and other German princes, thus with a greater emphasis being laid on the German,

Charles II, *c.*1685, by Godfrey Kneller.
Walker Art Gallery, Liverpool

rather than the English regal connection.[37] It can also be read as a hint to the Dutch Regents that the usefulness of the Orange clan and patronage system was not confined to England, and that it could function as a power broker elsewhere on the Continent as well.

We may mention that the Prince was not the only one who had split allegiances. There were four English regiments and three Scottish ones in the service of the Republic. They were given the choice of swearing a new oath of loyalty and fighting on behalf of the Dutch, even against the King of England, or of returning to England, and new regiments were formed from those who chose the former option.[38]

Even if the French ambassador was right that there was enthusiasm for the war in the Republic – and he was not always a very reliable witness – it was not universal. Among certain sections of the population the English royal connection was deemed not a disadvantage, but an advantage. The war began badly for the Dutch, who suffered a heavy defeat at the battle of Lowestoft in June 1665, and in the States of Holland there were demands that the Prince should be elevated to his family's traditional offices.[39] Orangists believed that the war was the outcome of the King of England's concern for his nephew and that his elevation would bring peace.[40] Downing reported that seamen in the Dutch fleet had refused to fight at Lowestoft unless the Prince of Orange's flag was raised. When drums beat in Leyden to recruit more men in the name of the States-General a mob of women tore the drums to pieces, crying out 'yᵉ Devill take yᵉ States; – beat for yᵉ Prince of Orange'.[41]

In October 1665 Charles II indicated to the Dutch ambassador in London, who like Downing had remained at his post, war or no war, that he would be receptive to Dutch peace offers. This initiative interacted with the invasion of the eastern part of the Republic by Freiherr von Galen, the Prince-Bishop of Münster, a belligerent prelate whose warlike reputation had gained him the sobriquet of 'Bomber Galen', and who had entered the war on the English side. His Münster territories were adjacent to a very large part of the eastern borders of the Republic, where he had territorial claims; he had ambitions to turn Münster into a personal absolutist state; and he was a fierce adherent of the Counter-Reformation. His invasion threatened the Province of Overijssel, which now seized the opportunity presented by King Charles's peace overtures to put forward a resolution in the States-General to pursue the King's initiative. The Province proposed that the Dutch embassy King Charles called for should be headed by the Prince of Orange; and, to enhance his standing, he should be appointed Captain- and Admiral-General, albeit, having regard to his youth, with the support of a lieutenant. There was sympathy for this proposal not only in Zeeland and Friesland but also in several Holland towns. A member of the Prince's Council, its secretary Buysero, engaged in intense lobbying for his elevation. And at this point a heavyweight Dutch politician from Holland, the veteran Hieronymus van Beverninck, whose career reached back to negotiations with Cromwell in the early 1650s, resigned his post as Treasury General in protest at the state of the country.[42]

In addressing these challenges De Witt was helped by divisions within the Orange House. William-Frederick, Count of Nassau, who headed the cadet branch of the family in the east of the country and who held the positions of Stadholder of Friesland, Groningen and Drenthe, was accidentally killed when examining a pistol in October 1664. His widow was William's aunt, Albertina-Agnes, who was acting as deputy Stadholder for her infant son, Hendrik-Casimir, and she was at loggerheads with her mother, Amalia von Solms. Her support was useful to De Witt in bringing to naught the suggested embassy of Prince William to England;[43] and the family rift was to be a lasting factor in the life of William III.

On their side of the Channel the English government saw an opportunity to make use of the Orange clan, in its eyes, of course, an extension of that of the Stuarts, to further its interests in Dutch politics. In November it tried to persuade the Elector of Brandenburg, with his close ties to the Orange House, to desist from trying to induce Bomber Galen to withdraw from the war. The King's instructions to the English emissary to the Elector stated: 'You shall let [the Elector] know that wee looke upon the rise of this warre betwixt us and the United Provinces to bee, not from the Estates, but only from de Witte and his faction and adherents out of an animosity to our Nephew the Prince of Orange and his family, and therefore that wee doe not thinke that wee or the Elector can have any friendshippe with that country'. The Elector was to be persuaded to use his influence in the Dutch Republic to 'sturre up the friends of the family of Orange' to 'laye hold of this opportunity for the shaking of the Act of Seclusion'.[44]

The Elector, however, was an independent spirit with his own views of where his interests lay, and he was proof against English seductions. Instead he entered into an agreement with the Republic, in return for subsidies, to continue to put pressure on the Bishop of Münster, backed up with the threat of military force, and this, combined with French intervention, to which we shall come, forced the Bishop to make peace in due course in April 1666.

But the endeavours of Charles II and his government to make use of the Orange clan were not at an end.

In the late summer of 1665 Downing had left The Hague because of concerns for his safety,[45] and Arlington, who had been appointed Secretary of State in October, sought two other channels for conducting the English government's diplomacy, both of which consisted of long-standing Orange-Stuart clients. One was Buat, an expatriate French soldier long resident in the Dutch Republic (his father had served in the Dutch army); he was wholly devoted to Prince William, whom he called his 'little master', and we have met him as a member of William's household (see p.82). He had accompanied William's mother, the Princess Royal, when she went to England and he was in receipt, as we have indicated, of a – characteristically irregularly paid – pension from Charles II. Although a rollicking soldier, a *bonhomme*, fond of his wine and of convivial company – much at home in the court of Charles – he was not, as a diplomat, perfectly chosen.[46] The other channel chosen by

Charles was Gabriel Sylvius, who had been knighted by the King, and who originally came from Orange, where his family were staunch supporters of the Princess Royal, and who, coming to England as one of her servitors, had taken up residence there after her death. He was closely connected with Arlington.[47] But, as a diplomat, he too was to prove defective.

Communication was established with the discontented Dutch elder statesman, Hieronymus van Beverninck, loquacious, inclined to indiscretion and, like Buat, not averse to his tipple, but, unlike the *bonhomme*, deft, shrewd and able. The cause of his discontent was his opposition to the alliance between the Dutch and Louis XIV, but at the same time he was nevertheless also suspicious of the relationship between Charles II and the French King. At the end of 1665, Buat and Sylvius joined each other near Rotterdam and Sylvius conferred with two of Buat's key allies, Kievit, burgomaster of Rotterdam, and another Rotterdam Regent, Van der Horst. Sylvius thought that Van Beverninck would be a much more formidable centre of opposition to De Witt than was Amalia; but in this he underestimated Van Beverninck's profound distrust of Charles II, which in the event caused him to move back more closely into the orbit of De Witt, with whom by the beginning of 1666 he was in close touch.[48]

Buat also established contact with De Witt himself, presenting the Grand Pensionary with English peace proposals, which were both 'ambiguous and opaque', in De Witt's words. The Pensionary did not expect very much to come of all this, but nevertheless saw no reason why he should not test the waters; and he continued the contacts through the rather unorthodox channels which Charles II was using, although they fell somewhat short of impressing him.[49] There was in any case a diplomatic void left in The Hague by the departure of Downing, which was followed by a similar void in London when Van Goch, the Dutch ambassador, had also been recalled in December 1665. Through the Sylvius–Buat duo Charles's strategy consisted of two prongs – official peace feelers towards De Witt, whilst at the same time building up contacts with the Orange clan which were designed to subvert his regime in order to create the conditions in which to obtain the best peace terms.[50]

In January 1666 Louis XIV, in accordance with his treaty obligations with the Dutch, reluctantly declared war on England, and to Charles II's diplomatic strategy there was now added the further objective of prising the Dutch away from his French cousin.

At about this time support for Prince William in the Republic was markedly increasing. Five out of the seven Provinces, supported moreover by several Holland towns, were demanding that he should be appointed Captain-General of the army. Retreating a little in the face of this pressure, De Witt floated the possibility that he could be made a Cavalry-General to serve under the French Marshal, Turenne, who would take overall command; and he told Amalia von Solms of what he had in mind. He also discussed the idea with the French ambassador, D'Estrades, on the basis that it would be a pre-condition of the appointment that the Prince should renounce his English ties. He went on to suggest that Louis should use his good offices in the Dutch Republic to promote the matter on William's behalf.[51]

In the event Turenne turned down the proposal, or rather he was not allowed to pursue it by Louis XIV, who took the view that to expect the Prince to give up his ties with England was 'pure illusion and a total chimera'; and as for the suggestion that Louis should intervene on his behalf so that he should feel obligated to the French King, the Prince 'would be the first to laugh at it' with the English. Louis in short regarded Prince William as belonging irretrievably to the Stuart clan.[52]

We are, however, left with an interesting counter-factual historical hypothesis. Prince William was never to be given a thorough military training. If he had served his apprenticeship with Turenne, perhaps he might have become a better general than was in the event the case. The association with Turenne would also have revived a family connection. Turenne's mother was a daughter of William's great-grandfather, William the Silent.[53]

The Turenne proposal was significant in one other respect. The Dutch Republic had at its disposal great admirals of non-aristocratic origin, of the calibre of De Ruyter and the elder Tromp, interspersed with commanders of higher birth – De Witt was himself not averse to joining the fleet in a significant leadership role, as was his brother Cornelis. But on land the burger oligarchy was in large part dependent on the remaining indigenous aristocracy supplemented by cosmopolitan aristocratic professionals, a sort of quasi-*condottieri*, it being a widely held tenet in the 17th century that only commanders of a certain social rank would be able to exert the necessary authority attendant on their military position. These *condottieri* figures in Europe were much in demand and many pursued highly respected careers of much distinction. They moved with ease across country borders. In England Prince Rupert of the Rhine fell into this tradition and his cousin the Duke of York had pursued such a career during the interregnum. Later in the century Georg Friedrich, Count of Waldeck, was to be employed by Prince William, and Prince Eugene of Savoy was to take on the role for the Austrian Habsburgs in a career which saw both the 17th and 18th centuries. In France Condé and Turenne had lent their hand to the trade when they served the Spanish monarchy before returning to the French fold. Part of the traditional role of the very cosmopolitan House of Orange was, effectually, to perform a somewhat similar function; and after the death of William III the Dutch Republic sought a substitute in the Duke of Marlborough. The refusal of Turenne compelled the Dutch burgers to continue to rely on the member of the cadet branch of the House who had been leading the army, the ageing Prince Maurits of Nassau-Siegen, who himself had previously served the Elector of Brandenburg.

In the meantime De Witt still needed to address the problem of what to do about Prince William in response to the pressure from his Orangist supporters, which had not ceased. The clergy were pursuing their traditional pro-Orange agitation from the pulpits. Despite the war, the daughter of Nassau-Beverweert, the ex-ambassador to London and the illegitimate son of William's great-uncle, Prince Maurits of Orange, had, after her father's death, become betrothed in January to Charles II's minister, Arlington, and her brother, Nassau-Odijk, was fostering the enthusiasm of Orangist followers in the Dutch Republic through lavish entertainments. The Prince himself was greeted by Van der Horst, Buat's close associate, amidst cheering crowds in Rotterdam whilst he was similarly received in Amsterdam. There, according to D'Estrades's despatch in March, a vociferous crowd of 4,000 gave vent to their support and, upon his departure, acclaimed him beyond the confines of the city.[54] To add to all these pressures the Province of Zeeland was demanding his elevation to the high military offices and to the Council of State.

The French ambassador had reported at the end of February that De Witt was deeply despondent, remarking that 'a lawyer from Dort does not have the same steadiness as a man of quality'.[55] But the ambassador, as we have already noted, is not considered too reliable a witness,[56] and the remark does rather smack too much of matching his tone to harmonise with that of his lofty interlocutors in France for it to reflect very accurately the state of De Witt's morale. But despite D'Estrades's attempts do his utmost to exert French influence in the towns of the Dutch Republic to counteract the Orangist upsurge,[57] De Witt's difficulty was not abated.

CHILD OF STATE

In the predicament he now faced cooperation came to him from an unexpected quarter – Amalia von Solms. The Dowager on 2 April submitted a memorandum to the States of Holland which in effect revived the idea of the Province's taking over the education of William as a 'Child of State'. This was a response to a resolution of the Holland States passed on 31 March that they would comply with the suggestion if it were made by the Prince's guardians, or by Amalia on their behalf, and this itself was a response to the pressures to which De Witt was reacting, outlined below. The proposals were essentially a reformulation of those discussed with William's mother, the Princess Royal, in October 1660.[58]

De Witt's motives for pursuing the matter are contained in a letter of 3 April to one of the Amsterdam Regents, Reynst. For some time, he acknowledged, there had been great pressure to force the Prince's elevation to the highest military ranks, and, in some cases, also to appoint him to the Council of State. There was support for this in the body of the Province of Holland itself, which gave Zeeland, together with, at its own instigation, several other Provinces occasion to apply serious pressure in favour of that movement. There was grave danger that the State would be torn apart unless this was prevented by necessary compromises and he went on to point at the need to maintain unity at a time of war.[59]

The constraint he was under is revealed by the speed with which he acted. The Holland resolution on 31 March and Amalia's request on 2 April had themselves been preceded by a tense meeting between De Witt and a Zeeland delegation on the afternoon of 26 March.

Following Amalia's request the Holland States set up a committee to deal with the details of the proposals on 9 April; this included De Witt, and he had a report ready the next day. On the 13th the details were agreed by the Holland States, and by the 15th they came into effect. The education committee of 1660 was re-established with four members, including De Witt and – a reluctant member – Gillis Valckenier, a rising Regent and a Burgomaster of Amsterdam whom Reynst had consulted on receipt of De Witt's letter of 3 April.[60]

If these were De Witt's motives why did Amalia, on her part, act in the way she did? She had always taken a practical view of the need to cooperate with the powerful Regents of the Republic, dating back to the time of her husband Frederick-Henry and the peace with Spain established by the Treaty of Westphalia which was entered into under pressure from the Regents, and the unavoidability of which she was to perceive before her husband did. De Witt's predicament opened up the opportunity for him to take on the education of her grandson which, she had consistently seen, could be the first step in the rehabilitation of the House of Orange. But the House would have to pay a price, which she may have underestimated, or which she may have thought worth paying. Her grandson William certainly thought it was a bitter price indeed.

A thorough purge of Prince William's household was instituted at once. Less than two weeks were allowed to Nassau-Zuylenstein, the governor of his household, who, it will be remembered, had an English wife, to depart from his position. The Prince's *maitre d'hôtel*, Johan Boreel, his two gentlemen of the bedchamber (one of whom, Lord Bromley, was an appointee of Charles II and who had been sent the previous year by the King with a gift of horses), and Buat, all were dismissed. Their replacements were carefully chosen. Baron van Ghent, a close supporter of De Witt, took the place of Nassau-Zuylenstein; and when De Witt was warned by a cousin of his, Cornelis Fannius, that one of those recommended for posts, Jonkheer Cabeljauw, was a cornet of horse in Buat's company, a great friend of Buat, and probably part of a scheme for Buat to retain influence in the Prince's court, the cornet failed in his candidature.[61] The Grand Pensionary, in short, had performed a sharply executed *coup d'état* to bring the House of Orange under his control.

Prince William was desolated, worse, humiliated. In 1660 his mother, the Princess Royal, had jibbed when De Witt proposed to remove Nassau-Zuylenstein as his governor. De Witt had now purged the household of him who was the Sovereign Prince of Orange. In 1660 he was but ten years old. He was now in his 16th year and very capable of feeling the personal affront and perceiving the pernicious political consequences. Two years before he had, as a grandson of the King of England, disputed precedence with the ambassador of the King of France in his coach in the Voorhout. Now his personal household was to be dictated to him by the descendant of a merchant family from Dort. He would have been very well aware of the threat these measures would present to the prestige, the patronage and the influence of the House of Orange.

He was very attached to Nassau-Zuylenstein,[62] and did all in his power to retain him. As early as 12 April he came to see D'Estrades with tears in his eyes, so the ambassador reported, begging him to intercede with De Witt to allow him to retain his governor. He promised to send Nassau-Zuylenstein's English wife to one of his estates and would not see her until peace was established with England. He himself would do nothing but in accordance with the wishes of the Province of Holland. He wished to put himself entirely in the hands of De Witt and to regard him as a father. He was addressing himself to D'Estrades, he said, to emphasise his desire to follow the example of his ancestors in attaching himself entirely to the interests of Louis XIV and it was a mistake to think that he had, because of their relationship, any attachment to the King of England – being a Child of State he would have no other attachment but to the States and their friends and allies.

How much dissimulation was there in the Prince when he thus appeared to submit entirely to the Grand Pensionary and appealed for the protection of his cousin, Louis XIV, whilst renouncing that of his uncle, Charles II? And were his tears the tears of grief at the loss of Nassau-Zuylenstein or were they the tears of insulted pride and of mortification? We suspect that we find here a 15-year-old politician, who was conducting this interview on his own without any supporting presence, and who was showing a hard grasp of the realities. De Witt was in command, and, for the moment, he had succeeded in neutralising the Orange clan – with the cooperation, moreover, it appeared, of the Prince's grandmother. A show of submission to the aims of the ruling faction in the Republic was what was now called for and he would wait to fight another day.

The apparent submission reached the ears of De Witt. The conversation, as the Prince would have anticipated, was relayed to him by the French ambassador.[63] Seeing him in action, D'Estrades had no doubt about his interpretation: 'Ce Prince a de l'esprit, & aura du mérite. Il est fort dissimulé, & oublie rien pour venir à ses fins.'[64]

The wish to retain Nassau-Zuylenstein was the consequence not only of personal affection but also of the need to protect William's clients; or, at the least, to be seen to be making an effort on their behalf. His efforts were not totally abortive – Nassau-Zuylenstein was assured of receiving his stipend for another five years. And to another of the Prince's retainers, Johan Boreel, the promise was given of the first available military command of a company that became vacant, although in this instance Boreel was also assisted by his father's being the Dutch Republic's ambassador in Paris.[65] The Prince personally wrote to the father that he had done what he could to retain his son and that he would make restitution as soon as circumstances allowed.[66]

He was not in fact devoid of all influence. His becoming a 'Child of State' – a term widely used, although it was not an official title – was, on the contrary, a recognition by De Witt of his clan's position and of the following it gave him: it was an attempt to direct the influence of the House of Orange into channels that De Witt deemed beneficial to the true interests of the State.

But the influence of the House was nevertheless impaired; its following in Zeeland had been diverted and the education commission contained no representatives from Orangist towns.

William manifested his resentment towards his grandmother. He made his disapproval of the management of his affairs crystal clear when he met the members of the education committee. He caustically told them that, since they had removed his household and governor, and since they wished to take charge of his education, he prayed them also to take care of his affairs and present an audit to his council and his treasurer of the administration of his estate. Every day his property was being sold at a vile price. None of his debts were paid. And, although his expenses were not large for a man in his position, he owed his butcher, his baker and other suppliers for years on end. These remarks were a reflection on Amalia's direction of his affairs and she defensively expressed her opposition when a scrutiny of the princely accounts was suggested.

His relations with De Witt did not please her either. Adapting to the circumstances, he moved closer into De Witt's orbit, personally assuring him that he regarded him as a father and that he would follow his advice in all things. He met with the Pensionary nearly every day by himself, and for Amalia the close relationship was going too far. When she remonstrated he told her that, since she herself had judged it appropriate to entrust him into the hands of the Province of Holland, as much for his education as for other advantages, he would regard its representatives as those whom he would look to for his future; that he would abide with them and with De Witt with every vestige of respect, of deference and of amity; and that, if she had the true feelings of a grandmother, she would easily accommodate herself to these sentiments.[67]

We may note the combination of resentment, of personal affront, of strength of personality and of political realism. The Prince was handling the first political crisis which he had to confront on his own authority – apparently entirely on his own and without advisers – and he was doing so with skill, with self-assurance, with cool dissimulation, and with deft ruthlessness.

William's household, although substantially reconstructed, retained nevertheless a thoroughly aristocratic flavour. His new governor, Van Gent, was a nobleman from Gelderland, which did not prevent the Prince from overcoming his strong aversion to him. He was a strong supporter of the French, who were expecting him to work on William in their interests. He was not very well off and Louis proposed that he should be paid a gratification of 4,000 *livres* a year, as a mark of 'my benevolence and of my esteem'. This Van Gent refused but as he obtained a French military appointment for his son this made not too great a difference and he made no secret of the fact that he regarded the French King as his friend and protector.[68]

De Witt took care to discuss the appointments with Amalia von Solms as well as Van

Gent,[69] which seems to have led to a degree of compromise. One of Nassau-Beverweert's sons, Hendrik, Lord of Ouwekerk, became Master of Horse. Nassau-Beverweert himself had as long ago as 1657 come to terms with the Grand Pensionary, who had been able to make full use of his services as ambassador to England prior to his death, with Nassau-Beverweert performing a skilful balancing act between his obligations to the Orange clan and De Witt's party; and it was presumably this which induced De Witt to make the appointment. But in the event a close relationship was to develop between William and Nassau-Ouwekerk, just as it did with his brother, Nassau-Odijk, who, as we have seen, even at this time was very active in the Orangist cause. And, as we have also seen, their sister – Isabella – had only recently married Charles II's minister, Arlington.

Another member of the household important for the future was Hans Bentinck, who retained his position as a page. Pastor Cornelis Trigland, in charge of the Prince's religious education since 1656, ceased to perform that role, presumably because, the Prince having reached his present age, Trigland's task was deemed complete.[70]

If De Witt and his supporters did what they could to accommodate the Prince, he reciprocated on his side. He again visited the Dutch fleet at the Texel in May 1666 where he was received with joy by the officers and sailors and where, D'Estrades claimed, his presence was worth the recruitment of a thousand sailors.[71]

A special room, the chamber of education, was set aside for William, where his preceptor, Bornius, arrived daily and instructed him in history and politics and someone else taught him mathematics. De Witt took a close interest in his education. Every Monday he paid a visit to check on his progress and they appeared to have met more frequently still. Nor was William totally ungrateful for what he owed De Witt in his lessons on statecraft. De Witt, he acknowledged later in his life to an Englishman, had given him 'very just notions of every thing relating to their State'.

Constant discussions of affairs of state gave him a very practical grounding, and he was, not least, able to benefit from the Pensionary's very considerable expertise in public finance.[72] A parallel process had occurred in France, where the Prince's cousin, Louis XIV, had also benefited from lessons in practical statecraft through observing Cardinal Mazarin at close quarters. In both cases, indeed, their political education was far superior to those two kings of England, William's uncles Charles II and James II; a not unimportant factor, perhaps, in William's ability to outmanoeuvre the latter in particular.

At the social level, as well, William and De Witt adjusted themselves as best they could to each other's company. D'Estrades was very pleased when he played against them at tennis and won. 'It is thirty years,' the overjoyed, if rather oleaginous, ambassador told Louis's foreign minister, 'since I played tennis. You can judge from that that I am no more feeble than in my youth, and that I still have arms and legs to serve the King, when he judges me worthy of it.'

As far as the differences between William and Amalia von Solms are concerned the rights and wrongs may appear evenly balanced; but perhaps we may heed the warning which a member of the States-General proffered his colleagues at the time. In making the Prince of Orange a Child of State, he said, they should beware lest he should turn the State into a child of his.[73]

BUAT

The Prince's Orangist supporters continued their intrigues on his behalf. One of the staunchest of these was Admiral Cornelis Tromp, who, whilst he was not as accomplished an admiral as his father, Maarten, nevertheless was held in considerable regard. In August he was serving in the fleet under De Ruyter when the Dutch and English fleets clashed for a second time in the North Sea after a previous engagement, the Four Days' Battle in June, which had ended in an English withdrawal. This second engagement, the Two Days' Battle, reversed the outcome of the first, leaving the English cruising off the Dutch coast. The impetuous Tromp had led his squadron in pursuit of an English squadron, which left De Ruyter and the main fleet dangerously exposed. The resultant very public quarrel with De Ruyter, who was politically a supporter of the republican party, was followed by the dismissal of Tromp by the States-General despite De Witt's attempts at mediation.

Tromp was the brother-in-law of Kievit, the Rotterdam Regent who was in close touch with Sylvius and Buat. Kievit at the time held an important position as a member of the Delegated Council – the body that held delegated responsibility from the States of Holland when they were not in session. A pamphlet appeared, whose author, it soon transpired, was Kievit, glorifying Tromp and traducing De Ruyter. The Dutch fleet, and the country as a whole, divided into two camps, supporters of Tromp and the Orangists and supporters of De Ruyter and the republicans. Intermingled with this there were strong feelings against the allies of the Dutch: the French, whose fleet, it was felt, had been tardy in travelling from the Mediterranean to lend its support.[74]

In the midst of all this Charles II was attempting to make progress with his rather unsteady and precarious diplomatic strategy. On the one hand he continued to put general peace proposals to De Witt, and on the other he continued with his aim to build up an Orangist party to subvert his regime, so that he could obtain peace on the most favourable terms, a two-pronged strategy which he continued to combine with attempts to separate the Dutch from their French allies.[75] And in this Sylvius and Buat continued as his chosen instruments.

On 18 August the two prongs of this policy conjoined in a manner not foreseen by Charles. Sylvius had written, at the King's behest, two sets of letters to Buat. One, containing nothing new, was intended for De Witt and the other was marked for Buat himself, 'pour vous même'. This second letter indicated that it was opportune for the Dutch party favourable to an accommodation with the English to pursue a solution backed by force, in which event they would be provided by the English with 'all the means they could wish for'.[76]

Hence it was rather unfortunate that Buat, at 9 o'clock on the morning of the 18th, handed *both* sets of letters to De Witt. Returning home, he realised his mistake and a couple of hours later he was back with De Witt asking for the return of the letter that was intended for himself, Buat, alone. The Pensionary told him that he had handed it to the Delegated Council. Curiously, however, Buat was not arrested on the orders of the Council until half past six in the evening, by which time, of course, anyone else but he would have disappeared over the Dutch border, which was not very far away.

At his house, a minute Buat had kept of a further incriminating letter to Arlington dated 9 March was found relating to the conspirators' formation of a large party favourable to peace and consequently to his 'little Master … which had high import for' the ruling party. Buat asked Arlington to reflect on the satisfactory situation the English King and 'his little Master' would find themselves in once the desired peace was obtained. Charles II would be the 'plus grand Roy du monde'.[77] In the state of war that existed between the Dutch Republic and England these intrigues were, of course, inevitably regarded as treasonable.

Following his arrest Buat began to reveal to the Delegated Council some of the people who had had an involvement in his movement. They included Fagel, the Pensionary of Haarlem, who was later to succeed De Witt as Pensionary of Holland and to become a close collaborator of Prince William. He revealed also that he had met Kievit and Van der Horst at the house of Nassau-Zuylenstein. The Delegated Council put the matter in the hands of the Court of Holland, who also summoned Kievit and Van der Horst to appear before them in September. The latter two, however, more astute than the unfortunate Buat, had made good their escape to the Spanish Netherlands.

The court was noticeably dilatory in the prosecution of the case – so much so that it received a summons from the Delegated Council where De Witt urged them on to greater diligence. But even so nothing was done to track down those associated with Buat. There appeared to be a marked reluctance amongst the Dutch establishment to pursue the matter with great vigour; and De Witt himself appears to have allowed Buat very considerable time to escape arrest after he had handed over the fatal letters. Kievit and Van der Horst had fled, which left only Buat to be made an example of. On 11 October, wearing a black cloak and attended by servants also in black, he doffed his hat to his judges, to his friends, and to the empty chamber of William III in the Binnenhof as he passed on his way to meet a soldier's death on the scaffold. He bequeathed what was later to become a martyr's memory to the Orangist cause.[78]

Despite the closeness of Buat, and those associated with him, to Prince William there were no direct repercussions for the Prince himself. It was fortunate that he and Amalia von Solms were out of the way at this critical time. At the end of July De Witt had given his consent for the Prince to attend a family wedding in Cleves; and in August he also gave his consent for the Prince to travel to Maastricht.[79] He took pains to keep William informed during August of the incriminating evidence relating to Buat, as he did Amalia.[80]

The Prince lost no time in reassuring the Grand Pensionary that he had had no part in, or knowledge of, Buat's activities and that he candidly and most decidedly disapproved of them. De Witt, on his part, told him that he had advised his fellow guardians and others of William's assurances, and that he would do the same elsewhere where it would do most good.[81] It was not in De Witt's interest to exacerbate divisions in the Dutch Republic; and the Prince had every reason to distance himself as far as possible from these developments. But the Buat affair was nevertheless to be of long-lasting symbolic importance in Orangist mythology.

THE END OF THE WAR

For the moment De Witt's position appeared as strong as ever. Tromp's dismissal from the fleet was soon forgotten,[82] and the English enemy was soon to be brought to the negotiating table in earnest. In 1665 the plague had devastated London; worse was to follow with the Great Fire which swept through the city in September 1666; and the adverse effects of the war had depressed trade. The combination of all three had their consequences for the finances of the English government and on the ability of the City of London to advance further credit.

A wrangle – symptomatic of deteriorating relations generally – between the King and the House of Commons over the House's intention to investigate the expenditure on the war caused the Commons to delay voting supplies for it until February 1667: and, when it did, most of the money had to be used to repay existing debts and could not be used for current needs. The King was forced to lay up his largest ships.

Peace negotiations with the Dutch commenced at Breda in May 1667. But, with the large ships out of commission, the Dutch had control of the seas. De Ruyter, accompanied by De Witt's brother, Cornelis, and a large naval force were on their way to plan a descent on the Thames. In June they attacked in the Medway, burning the laid-up ships and towing away the 'Royal Charles', the ship that had conveyed Charles II to England from Scheveningen at his restoration seven years before.[83]

Pepys's fears, and very human reactions, were typical of the climate now pervading London. 'And the truth is, I do fear so much that the whole kingdom is undone, that I do this night resolve to study with my father and wife what to do with the little that I have in money by me.… So God help us! And God knows what disorders we may fall into', he wrote in his diary entry for 12 June (O. S.). As he wrote in the entry for the following day, there was a general panic and a run on the bankers.

The war which the King had thus drifted into, and with such reluctance as regards himself and Clarendon, ended in calamity. There was nothing for it but to make peace on the best terms possible. This was done at Breda on 31 July. In the Dutch Republic the conclusion of the war and the brilliance of the naval campaign which brought it to an end were a triumph for De Witt personally and for his immediate associates.

But already the constellation of forces on the European diplomatic scene had begun to shift. Within five years De Witt and his brother would be dead, their bodies mutilated by an incensed mob, and in the place of the Grand Pensionary William III of Orange would be propelled to power.

1 Japikse, *Verwikkelingen, op. cit.*, p.263.

2 C.H. Wilson, *op. cit.*

3 *Ibid.*, p.112.

4 Japikse, *Verwikkelingen, op. cit.*, p.349.

5 J.R. Jones, *The Anglo-Dutch Wars of the Seventeenth Century*, Longman, London and New York, 1996, p.91. P. Seaward's article 'The House of Commons committee of trade and the Anglo-Dutch war, 1664', *Historical Journal*, XXX, 1987, p.442.

6 J. Miller, *James I*, Yale University Press, New Haven and London, 2000, p.50.

7 J.R. Jones, *op. cit.*, pp.8–9.

8 K. Feiling, *British Foreign Policy 1660–1672*, Macmillan, London, 1930, p.131.

9 J. Miller, *James II, op. cit.*, p.50.

10 R. Hutton, *Charles the Second: King of England, Scotland, and Ireland*, Clarendon Press, Oxford, 1989, p.216.

11 J.R. Jones, *op. cit.*, pp.145–6.

12 P. Seaward, *The Cavalier Parliament and the reconstruction of the old regime*, Cambridge University Press, 1989, pp.14, 84.

13 *Ibid.*, p.85.

14 J.R Jones, *op. cit.*, p.148.

15 *Ibid.*, p.90.

16 *Diary of Samuel Pepys, op. cit. History of Parliament*, The Commons 1660–90, I, p.7 states 'actually only 28 had been returned at the 1661 election (two had died before Pepys wrote) … though subsequently another 28 came in at bye-elections', without specifying when. There were only 19 naval officers during the period covered, p.7.

17 *History of Parliament, op. cit.*, I, p.26.

18 P. Seaward, *The Cavalier Parliament, op. cit.*, pp.51–2.

19 *History of Parliament*, Section on Henry Bennet.

20 *History of Parliament*, Section on Thomas Clifford. P. Seaward, *Historical Journal*, XXX, *op. cit.*, p.445.

21 J.R. Jones, *op. cit.*, p.93.

22 *History of Parliament*, Section on Robert Paston. Paston's financial embarrassments were relieved and he ultimately received a peerage, as Earl of Yarmouth, in 1673 as well.

23 P. Seaward, *Historical Journal*, XXX, *op. cit.*, p.451.

24 Quoted in Lister, *op. cit.*, p.134.

25 *Ibid.*, pp.181–2.

26 *Ibid.*, p.217.

27 *Ibid.*, p.325.

28 Japikse, *Verwikkelingen, op. cit.*, pp.346, 348, 349.

29 *Ibid.*, p.352.

30 Geyl, *op. cit.*, p.192.

31 Japikse, *Verwikkelingen, op. cit.*, pp, 393–4. As Japikse suggests, it is possible that Charles had decided, now that Cape Corso had been captured and the English had decided to hold on to it, that he would take responsibility for Holmes's action. Alternatively, he might have sent orders for its capture to supplement the original orders given to Holmes.

32 C.H.Wilson, *op. cit.*, p.117.

33 Japikse, *Verwikkelingen, op. cit.*, pp.396–7.

34 *Ibid.*, pp.411–12.

35 *Ibid.*, p.412–13.

36 Lister, *op. cit.*, III, p.375.

37 Israel, *op. cit.*, pp.771–2.

38 Wicquefort, *op. cit.*, III, pp.195–6.

39 Geyl, *op. cit.*, p.197, citing D'Estrades, *Lettres et négociations*, III.

40 Rowen, *De Witt, op. cit.*, p.667.

41 Lister, *op. cit.*, III, p.381.

42 Geyl, *op. cit.*, pp.207, 210. Wicquefort, *op. cit.*, III, pp.211–12 and footnotes. For Galen's ambitions see Israel, *op. cit.*, pp.733, 735.

43 D'Estrades, *op. cit.*, Letter to Louis XIV 5 November 1665, p.505. Geyl, *op. cit.*, p.212. Rowen, *De Witt, op. cit.*, pp.666–7.

44 Geyl, *op. cit.*, pp.218–19.

45 Rowen, *De Witt, op. cit.*, p.615.

46 R. Fruin, *Verspreide Geshriften*, The Hague, 1901, IV, p.268 footnote.

47 Geyl, *op. cit.*, pp.220–2.

48 Rowen, *De Witt, op. cit.*, pp.613–16. Geyl, *op. cit.*, pp.222–4, 227.

49 *Brieven van De Witt, op. cit.*, III, p.222.

50 Rowen, *De Witt, op. cit.*, p.616.

51 Geyl, *op. cit.*, pp.228–30. Rowen, *De Witt, op. cit.*, pp.669–70. D'Estrades, *op. cit.*, IV, pp.103, 125.

52 D'Estrades, *op. cit.*, IV, p.131.

53 Geyl, *op. cit.*, pp.229–30.

54 *Ibid.*, p 239. D'Estrades, *op. cit.*, IV, p.172.

55 D'Estrades, *op. cit.*, IV, p.147.

56 Geyl, *op. cit.*, p.213 and footnotes.

57 D'Estrades, *op. cit.*, IV, p.172.

58 Geyl, *op. cit.*, p.241. Rowen, *De Witt, op. cit.*, p.671.

59 The letter is quoted in Wicquefort, *op. cit.*, III, p.286 note.

60 Geyl, *op. cit.*, pp.241–2.

61 Wicquefort, *op. cit.*, III, p.288. *Brieven van De Witt, op. cit.*, II, p.281. Rowen, *De Witt, op. cit.*, p.673.

62 Wicquefort, *op. cit.*, III, p.288.

63 D'Estrades, *op. cit.*, IV, pp.223–4.

64 *Ibid.*, p.245.

65 Japikse, *op. cit.*, *Willem III*, I, p.127.

66 Japikse, *ibid.*, I, p.128.

67 D'Estrades, *op. cit.*, IV, p.242.

68 *Ibid.*, pp.259, 262, 311.

69 *Brieven van De Witt, op. cit.*, III, p.175.

70   Japikse, *Willem III, op. cit.*, I, p.131. Rowen, *De Witt, op. cit.*, p.157. Worp, *op. cit.*, VI, p.181.

71 D'Estrades, *op. cit.*, IV, p.282.

72 Japikse, *Willem III, op. cit.*, I, p.135. Aitzema, *op. cit.*, VI, p.607.

73 Aitzema, *op. cit.*, V, p.787.

74 Geyl, *op. cit.*, pp.245–8.

75 Fruin, *op. cit.*, IV, p.278. Rowen, *Brieven van De Witt, op. cit.*, p.619.

76 Wicquefort, *op. cit.*, III, p.260 note gives the text of the letter.

77 Rowen, *De Witt, op. cit.*, p.620. Fruin, *op. cit.*, IV, p.271. Text of the minute in Wicquefort, *op. cit.*, III, p.262.

78 Geyl, *op. cit.*, pp.249–55.

79 *Brieven van De Witt, op. cit.*, III pp.177–9; II, note 3 to pp.281–2.

80 *Brieven van De Witt, op. cit.*, III, pp.212–13, 219–20.

81 *Ibid.*, p.220, note 3.

82 Geyl, *op. cit.*, p.256.

83 J.R. Jones, *Charles II Royal Politician*, Allen & Unwin, London, 1987, pp.72–3. J.R. Jones, *The Anglo-Dutch wars, op. cit.*, pp.174–7. Israel, *op. cit.*, p.773. Geyl, *op. cit.*, p.265.

5 THE MOUNTING THREAT FROM LOUIS XIV

LOUIS'S ASSUMPTION OF PERSONAL RULE

At two o'clock in the morning of 9 March 1661 Giulio Mazarin, Cardinal, Prince of the Church and first minister of France, died at the Château of Vincennes. On the 10th, Louis XIV, aged 22, summoned the nobility and grandees of the court to the chamber of his mother, Anne of Austria, and announced that he was taking personal direction of the State.[1] Henceforth he was to be his own first minister. His personal rule had begun and he was to be the chief protagonist in Europe for the next 54 years.

In the 1660s the geo-political constellation in Europe, in which Louis's assumption of personal rule was central, was taking clear shape. When the exhausted Habsburg Holy Roman Emperor, Charles V, gave up the sovereignty of the Netherlands in 1555, the massive power of the Habsburgs was perceived to present the threat of a 'Universal Monarchy', extending throughout the continent of Europe, and from thence to the New World, and to the Pacific Ocean. Upon Charles's full retirement a year later, when he gave up sovereignty over Spain and Spanish America and then abdicated as the Holy Roman Emperor, the vast inheritance was to rest henceforth upon the two pillars of the House, one based in Spain, the other on the hereditary lands in Austria and upon the standing of the Habsburgs as customary, but not hereditary, emperors of the Holy Roman Empire.

By 1648 the brittleness of both these pillars was fully revealed: that of the Spanish pillar by the ending of the Eighty Years' War that led to Dutch independence; and of the Austrian pillar by the simultaneous ending of the Thirty Years' War, which led to greater independence for the German princes in the Empire. Their right to determine the religion of their subjects was reaffirmed and reinforced by extending the principle of *cuius regio eius religio* ('he who is the ruler, his shall be the religion') to include Calvinists as well as Lutherans – and they were entitled to pursue their own foreign policy provided it was not directed against the Emperor. Both these mighty wars came to an end with the twin treaties of Westphalia and Münster in 1648 (collectively usually referred to as the Treaty, or Treaties, of Westphalia).

The diminution of the Habsburgs made room for a new power to take their place both as the dominant power in Europe and as presenting another perceived threat of a 'Universal Monarchy' in a new form. This was to be the French monarchy of William's cousin, Louis XIV.

But, as so often in history, there was a protracted time-lag between cause and effect. France had become directly involved in the Thirty Years' War by declaring war on Spain in 1635.

The heavy taxation this demanded contributed to profound popular discontent. At the same time the power of the State, and of the Crown, had been expanding under two formidable first ministers, Cardinal Richelieu, until his death at the end of 1642, and then Cardinal Mazarin. We have touched upon, in earlier chapters, how that expansion was challenged by two main sources of opposition; both could attract and exploit the discontented and the position of both was strengthened by the fact of Louis XIV's minority – he had succeeded his father in 1643 at the age of five.

One source lay with the judges of the Parlements, of which the Parlement of Paris was the most important. These were law courts, not representative bodies in the Westminster sense. They were required to register the laws before they could take effect and they thus acquired formidable political power. They had a right to remonstrate before registering a law and they made full use of this to pursue their own considerable political ambitions. They could indeed be overruled by the King attending in person at a *lit de justice* to force a law through, but the legitimacy of this procedure when the King was a minor was contested. The other source of opposition was the high nobility, many of whom were closely related to the Crown and who resented being edged out by the cardinals from the political influence they had exercised in the past and which they regarded as theirs of right.

Until these competing sources of opposition had been contained the French monarchy was not in a position to exert its full authority on the European scene. The instability culminated in a series of civil wars between 1648 and 1653, the Frondes, which so threatened the authority of the Crown that it came close to collapse.

The Frondes did not come to a clean-cut end. They began to peter out in the early 1650s and the restitution of the Crown's authority, over both the nobility and the Parlements, was slow and gradual.[2]

It was complicated by the French war with Spain, which did not benefit from the general settlement elsewhere in Europe imposed by the Treaties of Westphalia. The Frondes gave Spain the opportunity to intervene in France itself. In particular she supported the revolt of the Prince of Condé, a prince of the blood, against Louis XIV's government. It was a sign of Spain's debility that despite the profound internal crisis and despite the defection of Condé, and his outstanding military skills, France was able to fight the war to a successful conclusion. But it was not until the Peace of the Pyrenees was signed on 7 November 1659 that the war with Spain was brought to an end. Condé was granted full restitution of his position and of his estates. The Crown in the process regained a general of genius who was to be used to the full in Louis's later wars.

The Peace Treaty had another provision. Under its terms Louis married the Spanish Infanta, Maria Theresa, King Philip IV's daughter by his first marriage. In consideration of the payment of her dowry she renounced all her rights to the Spanish throne – but only in consideration of that payment, or so the French were to claim. As, in the event, the dowry was never paid by an impoverished Spanish Crown, Louis, and his advisers, were presented with the opportunity to deny that Maria Theresa's renunciation remained valid.[3]

Philip's heir was his very sickly son, Carlos, by his second marriage, to Maria Anna, the sister of Leopold I of Austria. Not only were the Habsburgs a diminished force in Europe, but their power base, first in the Provinces which they had managed to retain in the Southern Netherlands, and then, increasingly, as the second half of the 17th century progressed, their citadel in Spain itself, were to become vulnerable to the pretensions of the King of France, and to his claims to the Spanish throne through his wife, and hence, in due course, through his children by her. For over half a century, from the day he assumed his personal rule of France until the day he died, the question of the Spanish Succession was central to all his foreign policy considerations.

As we have indicated, the France of that king was much less homogeneous than the epithet which has been applied to it, 'absolute monarchy', implies. In the Frondes the government of the king had faced open rebellion from the king's uncle, Gaston of Orléans – and from Gaston's daughter, la Grande Mademoiselle, who had personally directed cannon fire on the king's troops in the king's very presence – from the princes of the blood like Condé and Conti, and from the higher nobility, peers like the Duc de la Rochefoucauld. Although the rebellions of the nobility failed, the ordeal was to remain in all the men's minds, not least in the mind of the king.

Ruling the nobility was complicated by it not constituting a single noble class. There was the famous distinction between the nobility of the sword – the ancient nobility deriving its status, broadly, from military service to the crown in the distant past – and the more recent, and less prestigious, nobility of the robe – deriving its status from a ministerial or legal background. There were legitimate, and illegitimate princes of the blood. There were 'the foreign princes', such as the Duc de Bouillon, who, until recently, had been sovereign princes in their own right.[4]

If, after the Frondes, the capacity of the French nobility to resort to armed rebellion would not revive, it remained necessary that the control of the aristocratic clans, and of the complex of patron and client relationships, was to require all the political skills, all the powers of patronage and all the force of personality that Louis XIV, with his rare talent, possessed. But his success lay in managing, not in eliminating, the latent power of both the nobility and the Parlement of Paris, and when his management was gone after his death, both were to revive, to weaken the monarchy in the next century.

It was a highly militarised society, a trait of which Louis was both to make full use and of which he had to take full account. Excepting only the heir to the throne, he excluded the Nobility of the Sword from any role at the highest level in his government. For that he relied on new men like the Les Telliers and the Colberts, who were to become part of the Nobility of the Robe. But both the Nobility of the Sword and that of the Robe provided military service, paying for their privileges with their blood. It was not a token payment. After the great campaigns of the reign Versailles was littered with men in bandages and on crutches. 'Everyone mourns a son, a brother, a husband or a lover', Madame de Sévigny noted in her correspondence.[5] The highest nobility provided a reservoir for the outstanding generals of the age – Condé, Turenne, who was the brother of the Duc de Bouillon, Luxemburg, Vendôme. And, until he was prevented by age, Louis himself was frequently at the front, not averse to sharing the hardships of the campaign in a bivouac or in a barn.

France was a rich country with a population of about 22 million people. Its armed forces were reorganised by the Les Telliers family. Its finances were put on a sound footing by Louis's finance minister, Colbert, in the years of peace that followed the Frondes. It was a formidable force at the disposal of a formidable young monarch. The King, first very cautiously and then more boldly, was beginning to edge his way to the wars which, from the later 1660s, were to dominate his very long reign.

THE SPANISH NETHERLANDS

The outbreak of the Anglo-Dutch war had posed a dilemma for Louis XIV. In 1662 he had entered into a treaty with the Dutch, France's traditional ally against the Spaniards, whose terms included a mutual guarantee of each party's territorial integrity.[6] But, as Downing reported in January 1664, 'I find him [De Witt] infinitely apprehensive of France its getting Flanders', that is, the Spanish Netherlands.[7]

The failure of the Spanish Crown to pay Maria Theresa's dowry laid the ground for Louis to revive her claims and to expand territorially into the Provinces of the Spanish Netherlands once his wife's father, Philip IV of Spain, should die, and if Carlos, the sole male heir, should also die without issue, something which the state of his health made extremely likely.

The Alps, the Mediterranean, the Pyrenees and the Atlantic constituted natural defences for France, as would the Rhine if it were possible to bring the kingdom's frontiers into closer alignment with that river. But the northern and eastern frontiers of France in particular were indented by a complex of small states and feudal relics, and by the possessions of the King of Spain. The position of Paris itself, close to the borders of the Spanish Netherlands, constituted one of the kingdom's greatest vulnerabilities – it had been a particular preoccupation of Mazarin.[8] These territories had always been a traditional invasion route for the enemies of the kings of France and it was natural that Louis should be sensitive to the threats from that direction.[9] Whilst the decline of Spain meant that there was no immediate risk, Spain's weakness also presented an historical opportunity to secure for the future those borders of his kingdom.

But the acquisition of those territories would make Louis a powerful and alarming neighbour immediately next to the Dutch Republic, 'a very worrying and dangerous business for this State', as De Witt described it in a memorandum he prepared in (probably) May

1663.[10] If Louis's concerns were defensive – as has been alleged – they themselves triggered Dutch defensive concerns.

The problem, part of the problem of the Spanish Succession as a whole, was to preoccupy the statesmen of Europe, not least William III and Marlborough, until the Treaties of Utrecht were finally entered into shortly before the death of Louis in 1715; and it may be worth a little attention to summarise the possible solutions to the problem in the analysis contained in De Witt's memorandum, seen from the Dutch point of view. He was not alone in being unable to arrive at an answer. But his own failure to do so was to destroy his regime and to cost him his life.

The first course of action that came to mind, he suggested, was to establish the Southern Netherlands as an independent republic allied with the Dutch and supported by an alliance with England and, if possible, with France. This would, of course, have created a buffer between the United Provinces and the French. But, as De Witt pointed out, the ways towards achieving this lay in either obtaining the consent of Philip IV, the King of Spain (whose territories they were), or the King of France (who laid claim to them) – which, in both cases, was unlikely; or it required the use of force, with such allies as could be persuaded to join the Dutch, to protect the newly independent state in opposition to the King of Spain or his son or, if they were both deceased, in opposition to the King of France, which would be 'too heavy and dangerous an enterprise' for the Dutch to undertake.

A second possibility was for the Spanish King to transfer the Southern Netherlands into the more powerful hands of the German Emperor, Leopold I, by incorporating them into the dowry of Philip's daughter, Margarita Theresa, who had just become engaged to Leopold and who was the daughter of Philip's second wife (and niece), Leopold's sister, Maria Anna. But the Emperor was heavily engaged in a war with Turkey and, given the alliances of many of the German princes with France, it would be difficult for him to defend the territories with any appearance of success, even if he was prepared to do so.

Thirdly, the United Provinces could endeavour to defend the Southern Netherlands against the French in conjunction with the German Empire and England. But this would imply a very dangerous war, which, if the French claims to the Spanish succession proved justified, would also be difficult to defend as being a just one.

Fourthly, the United Provinces could safeguard themselves by securing appropriate towns and fortifications in the Southern Netherlands – what later was to become known as 'the Barrier'. However, there was no point in coming to any agreement with the Spanish to achieve this as their weakness would leave the Dutch having to deal with the French in any event.

All these possibilities were to be tried in the course of the best part of the next 50 years.

De Witt, with misgivings about proceeding on any of these fronts, nevertheless made an initial attempt with the first possibility; he concluded that conversations should be opened with the French which should lead to the establishment of the Spanish Netherlands as 'a free and independent Republic, allied with this State [that is, the Dutch] as a Catholic canton and supported by an alliance with France provided that could be worked out or achieved'.

Should these conversations lead to no satisfactory outcome, and should the decease of both the King of Spain and his son Carlos lead to the King of France forcibly annexing the Spanish Netherlands as compensation for the non-payment of his wife's dowry, then, as a fall-back position, the Dutch would receive territory in the Spanish Netherlands to provide for the security of the Dutch State – the 'Barrier', in short. If the French King was prepared to listen to these proposals the boundary between the Dutch and France would follow a line from Ostend to Maastricht, and, if possible, beyond to Liège.

De Witt thus began a series of tortuous negotiations with the above considerations in mind.

In the absence of a revolt against Spain in the Southern Netherlands – De Witt had reported a possible plot against the Spanish in March 1663 – his plans presupposed that Louis could establish a valid claim on his wife's behalf. In July the French ambassador discussed with De Witt a further basis for these claims, additional to the non-payment of Maria Theresa's dowry – the Brabant 'law of devolution', which applied in Brabant and some other parts of the Spanish Netherlands.

Under this law children of a first marriage had precedence in inheriting over children of subsequent marriages: so that Maria Theresa, the daughter of Philip IV of Spain's first marriage, would have precedence over his son, Carlos, the issue of his second marriage. Maria Theresa's claims in the Spanish Netherlands therefore would now come into effect, not on the death of both her father and brother as before, but on the death of her father alone.

Hence, Louis now had two sets of claims, one relating to the Spanish Netherlands which would come into force on the death of Philip IV, and another relating to the Spanish Empire as a whole, which would come into force on the death of both Philip IV and of Carlos.

Unfortunately, in De Witt's view – and in the view of most historians – the Brabant law applied only to private individuals and did not affect the transmission of sovereignty. And he also needed convincing that the non-payment of Maria Theresa's dowry invalidated her renunciation of the Spanish Empire as a whole.[11]

Another obstacle, furthermore, lay in the Dutch acquiring territory on the Ostend-to-Maastricht line under the proposed partition. This would have incorporated Antwerp into Dutch territory and thus run counter to Amsterdam's insistence that any treaty should be conditional on keeping intact the closure of the Scheldt to prevent Antwerp from being able to re-emerge as an important competitor; an instance in the 17th-century mindset of how loyalty to a local identity – Amsterdam – could overrule loyalty to a wider one – the Republic.[12]

Apart from their negotiations with France the Dutch also had before them earlier overtures from the Spanish with proposals for a league between the 17 original Provinces of the Low Countries, an alliance thus between the Dutch and the Spanish territories.[13]

But for De Witt there was no doubt at all that an arrangement with a powerful France was infinitely preferable to one with an enfeebled Spain.[14]

Louis, on his side, eventually came to the conclusion that as, in his eyes, he had valid rights to the Spanish Netherlands, there was no reason why he should have to share them with a third party; and he accordingly allowed the negotiations to drag on inconclusively.[15]

LOUIS'S DUTCH ALLIANCE

So matters stood when the English and the Dutch drifted into the second Dutch war at the end of 1664 and the beginning of 1665, at which point the Dutch turned to Louis to honour his treaty with them of 1662. Now, Louis's central concern was his ambitions in the Spanish Netherlands, for which the Dutch war was an annoying distraction. If he joined either the Dutch or the English he risked the other joining Spain. He did not, indeed, relish the prospect of a victorious Charles II establishing English maritime supremacy or installing his nephew, William of Orange, as a client in power in the Dutch Republic; but for a year he maintained a precarious neutrality and tried to act as mediator between the warring parties.

However, the intervention of the Bishop of Münster on the English side, the English naval victory at Lowestoft on 3 June 1665, raising the threat of English maritime supremacy, and the possibility of the English and Dutch coming to an arrangement, possibly with Spanish involvement, in the Spanish Netherlands weighed on his mind. Furthermore, on 7 September 1665 Philip IV of Spain died, leaving the semi-imbecilic four-year-old Carlos II as his successor. For Louis it became all the more compelling that the distraction of the Anglo-Dutch war should be ended as soon as possible so that he could concentrate on the Spanish Netherlands. In January 1666 he grudgingly declared war on England.[16]

He played as reluctant a military role as was compatible with his treaty obligations to the Dutch, and his Admiral, the Duke of Beaufort, failed to effect a junction with the Dutch fleet.[17] However, on land he did send troops, before the end of 1665 and even before his declaration of war on England, to confront the invasion of the United Provinces by the Bishop of Münster, who was thus driven to make peace in the spring of 1666. But the behaviour of his troops on that occasion rather lessened the gesture in Dutch eyes – a taste of matters to come.[18]

Louis continued to focus on pushing forward his central interest, the Spanish Netherlands. Philip IV's will had been uncompromising in stating the 'incompatibility' of uniting the Crowns of France and Spain; and, as for the non-payment of Maria Theresa's dowry invalidating the renunciation of her rights of succession to the Spanish throne and dependencies, the renunciation had not been registered by the Parlement of Paris in the accustomed manner, thus voiding the need for the payment; but, nevertheless, payment would now be made, leaving the other clauses of her marriage treaty in full force.[19] There was a further provision in the will of Philip IV; should the frail Carlos II die without issue then his sister, Margarita Theresa, would inherit the vast Spanish empire; and in 1666 Leopold of Austria married her. Leopold's sister, Maria Anna, was already the Queen Regent of Spain and Leopold's marriage threatened Louis with the revival of the empire of Charles V.[20]

LOUIS'S WAR OF DEVOLUTION

Louis was well on the way to preparing the ground for his invasion of the Spanish territories. During the course of 1666 and 1667 he entered into secret treaties with the Duke of Neuburg, the Elector of Cologne, the Elector of Mainz and the Bishop of Münster, in exchange for subsidies, whose aim was to block the possibility of the German Emperor coming to the aid of the Spanish Netherlands.[21] At the beginning of 1667 D'Estrades reported De Witt's concerns about the rumours circulating about a possible French attack on Flanders.[22]

In England Charles II, in the meantime, was pursuing his policy of dividing, however he could, the French from the Dutch, and was seeking a way to obtain French support in the peace negotiations which were leading up to the Treaty of Breda. There was a hint that such French support might be forthcoming when reciprocal letters were exchanged in April between Charles and Louis, via Henrietta Maria, in which each king undertook for a period of a year not to enter into any arrangement with another power which was against the other's interests and that during that period they intended to enter into a close association.[23]

On 16 May 1667 Louis left St-Germain to join his army for the invasion of the Spanish Low Countries, to commence what became known as the War of Devolution.[24]

De Witt's reaction to this invasion had of necessity to be tempered by his being engaged in the delicate negotiations leading up to the Peace of Breda, in which he was anxious not to be divided from his French ally, although he did express his surprise to D'Estrades that the Dutch had not been informed and treated with greater confidence by Louis.[25] His diplomatic hand was strengthened, however, by the successful attack on the Medway in June which led to the rapid signing of the Treaty of Breda on 31 July.

Louis had indicated, in a memoir for D'Estrades dated 4 July, the terms to be conveyed to De Witt on which he was prepared to settle his Queen's claims under the laws of devolution in the Spanish Low Countries with a list of places to be ceded to the French. On the 21st De Witt replied with a modified list: he suggested that a three-month truce be entered into by the French and Spanish during which the Dutch would commence negotiations with the Spanish and the Austrian Habsburgs to persuade the Spanish to accept the terms; and if these negotiations failed the Dutch would impose the terms upon the Spanish by force.

He addressed the wider problem of the circumstances which would arise if the new King of Spain should die without legitimate children, which would trigger Louis's claims to the Spanish inheritance as a whole. In that case he suggested the cantonment of the Spanish Netherlands, leaving Louis to pursue his wider pretensions to the whole Spanish Empire.

Louis, after a delay of two months, moderated his original proposals to bring his list of places in line with those of De Witt, and these were conveyed in a despatch to D'Estrades on 27 September. He would content himself with the Duchy of Luxemburg, Cambrai, Douai, Aire, St-Omer, Bergues and Furnes; he proposed to raze Charleroi and to cede his other conquests; and he was willing to accept Franche-Comté instead of Luxemburg to meet Dutch concerns that Luxemburg would be too much of a threat to them; or, in lieu of the foregoing, he would accept all the conquests he had made in the Low Countries. He was prepared to enter into a reciprocal truce with Spain until the end of March – that is a six months' truce instead of De Witt's proposed three months – to give the Dutch time to persuade the Spanish to enter into these proposals.

To Louis's indignant surprise, however, his proposals were not met with immediate acceptance by De Witt, who told D'Estrades that there were internal Dutch political obstacles to overcome. He said that the influential Regent, Coenraad van Beuningen, who was ambassador in Paris, was on his way back to the Republic and Van Beuningen was strongly persuaded that peace would not be of long duration if Louis did not renounce his Queen's rights; others shared his views; and De Witt said that he was not far from doing so himself.[26]

In a letter to the Dutch ambassador in London on 14 October De Witt expressed the hope that the business of the Spanish Netherlands could in time be brought to an accommodation; but his judgement was that nothing could ever be expected to come of this unless France could be deprived of the means of seizing the rest of these territories; it was incumbent, therefore, to pursue every conceivable association to defend them. And he asked Meerman, the ambassador, to seek some assurance from the English court for English cooperation to that end.[27]

In England King Charles now affably awaited whoever could offer him the best terms, against a domestic political background where the pro-French Clarendon was in the process of being treated, through impeachment, as the scapegoat for the disastrous outcome of the Dutch war; he was eventually forced to flee the country on 13 December; and he was succeeded in prominence by the pro-Spanish Arlington.[28]

Louis despatched his ambassador, the Marquis de Ruvigny, to London at the beginning of September with instructions to pursue the 'strict union' which had been mooted in April when the two kings had exchanged their letters through Henrietta Maria. Ruvigny was soon reporting on the strong anti-French feeling in England and the threat of a 'Universal Monarchy' which the warlike Louis was seen to present.

Ruvigny met Charles on 21 September, who declared his inclination for the union with Louis, and his aversion and mistrust of the Spanish. But, he said, there were few people who shared his view; above all his Parliament and the majority of his Council were fearful of Louis's power. He needed to manage Parliament and to demonstrate to it the advantages of a liaison with the French King, or – in so many words – what would Louis put on the table?[29]

By 17 October he thought it expedient to amplify a little further on this. He sought money; he sought territory in Flanders; and he sought commercial advantages.[30]

At the same time, when the Dutch ambassador said, on 28 October, that he trusted that His Majesty was of the same view as the Dutch, that it was against the common interest that the French should make themselves masters of the whole of the Spanish Netherlands, Charles – that most adaptable of men – replied that he was 'also absolutely of that understanding'.

THE TRIPLE ALLIANCE

With Charles thus negotiating on both fronts, the pace of events now advanced very rapidly. On 22 December Arlington proposed a secret offensive and defensive alliance between France and England against the Dutch.[31] Concurrently, on the 30th a client of Arlington, the English diplomat Sir William Temple, arrived in The Hague and began negotiations with De Witt;[32] and so eager was King Charles to arrive at a rapid conclusion that Temple was instructed to tell De Witt that the Prince of Orange's interests should not stand in the way.[33] On 10 January 1668 Louis's rejection, dated the 4th, of Arlington's proposal was received in London.[34] On 23 January Temple signed a Treaty of Alliance in The Hague with the Dutch, whilst the Swedish ambassador signed a separate article providing for Sweden's participation, subject to further negotiations which related principally to agreement for the payment by the Spaniards for Swedish troops.[35] These dragged on until 11 May, when Sweden also formally joined the Alliance.[36]

The Triple Alliance, as these arrangements became known, was a treaty for armed mediation in the Franco-Spanish dispute in the Low Countries. It contained the terms of a defensive alliance between Britain and the United Provinces; and then addressed the terms on which mediation was to be imposed on the warring parties in the Spanish Netherlands.

Louis was to be granted either all the conquests which he had made or the alternative of a list of places on the lines suggested by himself to De Witt on 27 September the previous year, and England and the Dutch would mediate with the French and Spanish to that end. The subsequent peace would be guaranteed by England and the Republic, as well as by the Emperor and other neighbouring states. A truce would be entered into until the end of May and, if the Spaniards had not been induced to agree to the proposals by then, the terms would be imposed upon them by the English and Dutch by 'more effectual means', that is, armed force.

But there was a sting in the tail of the treaty, which was contained in a secret clause. If Louis did not comply, England and the Republic would unite with the Spaniards against him and push him back, if possible, to the frontiers established by the Peace of the Pyrenees. It was this requirement which had brought the Swedes into the arrangements, as they had armed forces which they were willing to make available in exchange for subsidies.[37]

The secret clause did not remain secret for long; D'Estrades was complaining to De Witt about it on 10 February.[38] At this time Louis was engaged in the conquest of Franche-Comté, for which he had departed on the 2nd. In this brilliant, lightning winter campaign Condé completed the conquest in 14 days and Louis was back at St-Germain on the 24th.[39]

It was then that a hint of the rancour which the Triple Alliance was to elicit in Louis first became apparent. Lionne offered the Dutch ambassador in Paris at the end of February his personal comment that peace would have been obtained without the Triple Alliance, voluntarily, from the King and 'pour acquérir la gloire de modération'; now it would be made to appear to the world that Louis would be forced into it by the Alliance, a hard matter for the King, 'qui préfère sa réputation à toute autre considération' – an instance of how central *la Gloire* and its reputational connotation were to both the King and the 17th century.[40]

A further development had taken place, which may reinforce Lionne's assertion that Louis would in any case have yielded without the Triple Alliance. On 19 January agreement was reached at Vienna between Louis and the Austrian Emperor for the partition of the Spanish Empire in the event of the death of Carlos II without heirs.

Under this treaty the Emperor accepted Louis's claims immediately to Luxemburg – or Franche-Comté instead – and the list of places in the Spanish Netherlands agreed between him and De Witt; and Leopold undertook to use his influence to persuade the Spanish Queen Regent to do the same, whilst Louis undertook to cede his conquests made in the Spanish Low Countries. Should little Carlos die without heirs, Louis and his heirs would acquire the whole of the Spanish Low Countries, including Franche-Comté, plus the Philippines, the kingdom of Navarre, and the kingdoms of Naples and Sicily. The Emperor's share would include Spain itself, Spanish America, the Duchy of Milan, Sardinia, and the Canaries and Balearic Islands.[41] Unlike the Triple Alliance, the secret of the Partition Treaty was confined to a comparatively narrow circle.[42]

Why did Leopold sign the treaty? There were divided views in Vienna and Leopold vacillated, but the views of his minister, Prince Lobkowitz, prevailed; he believed that the resources of the Emperor, menaced as he was by the Turks, were insufficient to come to the aid of the Spanish in the Low Countries without support from other powers.[43] The treaty was a compromise to keep Louis's ambitions within bounds. Although dated 19 January, it was signed towards two o'clock in the morning of the 20th. And that very morning Leopold showed signs of regretting the deed.[44]

The Partition Treaty would require Spanish consent, and the lightning conquest of Franche-Comté was designed to put pressure on the Spanish Council of State, which conceded to both the Partition Treaty and the proposals to settle Louis's claims in the Spanish Netherlands.[45]

Louis's generals, Turenne and Condé, argued strongly for the continuation of the war. But with the Partition Treaty safely secured – unknown to the generals – Louis himself knew that he would be in a very strong position eventually to obtain the whole of the Spanish Netherlands in any case. In his *Mémoires* he set out his reasons for pursuing the pacific course but, as these were written many years after the event, there is a large element of *post-facto* justification which makes them unreliable as an historic record. Nevertheless, one of the observations which he made there, that by yielding to the pressure of the Triple Alliance he would dissolve it, was indeed true.[46] And we may note that the fact that in public he had to appear to yield to that pressure must have made the humiliation all the more bitter.

He conceded and peace was obtained when the Treaty of Aix-La-Chapelle was signed on 2 May. Rather than choosing the places agreed between De Witt and Louis in September 1667, the Spaniards chose to settle with Louis on the basis of his conquests of 1667. This gave Louis Charleroi, Binch, d'Ath, Douai, Scarpe, Tournai, Oudenarde, Lille, Armentières, Courtrai, Bergues, and Furnes. These places presented a greater strategic threat to the rest of the Spanish Netherlands and therefore to the Dutch, and the Spanish aim was by this means to draw the Dutch closer to Spain in the future. Franche-Comté was returned to Spain.[47]

Louis had yielded. But for how long?

LOUIS'S WAR PLANS: TREATY OF DOVER WITH CHARLES II

He lost little time in setting about trying to dismantle the Triple Alliance. He sent a new ambassador to England, Colbert de Croissy, the brother of his minister of finance, whose instructions in August 1668 were to detach England from the Alliance and from the Dutch.[48]

The date of 4 February was the day on which the Catholic Church celebrated the conversion of St Paul, and on that symbolic date in 1669 a portentous meeting took place. It was attended by Charles II, by his brother James, Duke of York, by Arlington, by Clifford and by Lord Arundell. There a much moved and tearful King proclaimed his own Catholicism, and he asked those present for their advice on how to re-establish it in his kingdom, and on the most favourable moment to make an open declaration of his faith. There was a long consultation after which the meeting decided to approach Louis XIV to enlist his cooperation.[49]

Or did Charles do any such thing?

The only evidence for the meeting is in James's unreliable memoirs and some historians have doubted that the meeting ever occurred. Whatever the truth of the matter, Arundell did arrive in France in March with proposals for Charles to be provided with 2.4 million *livres tournois* (£200,000) for his conversion and with troops to enable him to support his declaration of Catholicism. Charles wrote on 21 March to his sister Minette, the Duchess of Orléans and Louis's sister-in-law, to whom Louis was much attached, and who played a major role in the negotiations about to unfold, underlining the need for caution – Buckingham, for instance, knew nothing about his intentions regarding Catholicism. It may be that, as Charles's biographer suggests, the Catholic conversion was a bait for Louis to take his proposals seriously.[50]

This Louis ultimately did. Indeed, he had been so intent upon establishing close relations with Charles that he turned to every resource. Learning of Charles's weakness for astrology, he had, in February, hit upon the stratagem of sending one skilled in this art to ingratiate himself with his English cousin. An Italian monk, the Abbé Pregnani, had established a considerable reputation in Paris in this field – he was especially popular with the ladies. He had also much impressed the Duke of Monmouth, Charles's illegitimate son by Lucy Walters, when he was in Paris. Alas, when despatched to England and tested on the horses at Newmarket, his predictive proficiency proved incomplete.[51]

'The abbé Pregnani', Charles wrote on 22 March to Minette, 'was there [at Newmarket]…, and I believe will give you some account of it, but not that he lost his money upon confidence that the Starrs could tell which horse would win, for he had the ill luck to foretell three times wrong together, and James [the Duke of Monmouth] believed him so much as he lost his money upon the same score.'

Failing by means of the Abbé Pregnani, Louis returned to diplomatic orthodoxy; instructions were soon conveyed to Croissy to bribe Lady Castlemaine.[52]

The lengthy negotiations so begun culminated in the secret Treaty of Dover, which was signed on 1 June 1670. In this Charles affirmed his intention to declare his Catholicism as soon as circumstances in his kingdom allowed. His piety was to be rewarded with 2 million *livres tournois* (£166,000), payable as to half three months after ratification of the treaty and half three months later; and, if needed, Louis would also furnish him with 6,000 troops to deal with internal opposition.

Louis undertook not to breach the Treaty of Aix-la-Chapelle with Spain, although Charles agreed, somewhat vaguely, to support any new rights to the Spanish monarchy which might accrue to Louis in the future.

The two kings also agreed to wage war on the Dutch. And here Louis's injured prestige manifested itself – 'to mortify their pride' and to 'destroy the power of a nation which was so often blackened by extreme ingratitude towards the true founders and creators of this republic, and which now even had the audacity of wanting to set itself up as the arbiter and judge of all other powers'. The Dutch, in short, as ungrateful clients, would be made an example of. For this Louis would pay Charles 3 million *livres tournois* per year (£250,000), whilst Charles's share of the conquered territories would consist of Walcheren, Sluys and Cadsand – which would give him control over the mouth of the Rhine and of its trade. And insofar as the division of Dutch territory could be prejudicial to the interests of the Prince of Orange, the two kings undertook to do what was possible for him so that he could identify his interests with the war.

As to the timing for the declaration of the war, the treaty contained a nice circularity.

The war would follow the declaration of Charles's Catholicism, the timing of which was for Charles to decide, whilst thereafter the timing devolved on Louis.[53]

The treaty was signed at Dover, where its secrecy was maintained under the cover of a family reunion. Minette came over from France for the signing. Before doing so the objections to her doing so from Louis's brother, Monsieur, the Duke of Orléans, Minette's homosexual husband, with whom her relations were strained, had to be overcome. His mood was particularly sensitive at this time because he had been parted from his lover, the Chevalier de Lorraine, whom Louis had banished to Italy for his insolence. Jealous of the distinction which would devolve on his wife, the Duke at first refused permission for her to go and it required Louis's personal intervention to overcome his antipathy.[54]

Charles was very fond of his sister and we have a source which claims that, at a meeting between the two of them, where only a lady in waiting to the Duchess was present, the Duchess assured her brother that he would draw incomparable advantages from the French alliance; it would deliver him from his dependence on Parliament and it would give him the means to re-establish the Roman Catholic religion in his domains. So touched was the King by this, the source goes on, that tears – again – came to his eyes.[55] But perhaps we need not attach too much credence to this report, there being only one witness, and the historian who records it was a republican supporter of De Witt – although nevertheless an historian of some repute.

Minette's marital tribulations were soon over. On her return to France, before June was out, she died amidst rumours of poison. Louis himself had left her deathbed in tears and Charles was now inconsolable.

But, despite the rumours of poison, Arlington, who had not allowed his pro-Spanish sympathies to override his master's wishes to enter into the French alliance, came to reassure Croissy personally that nothing had changed.[56]

Louis sent Marshal de Bellefonds to present his condolences to Charles on Minette's death, and the Duke of Buckingham offered to go to France to deliver Charles's formal reply to the French court. Although Buckingham had participated in some of the interchanges which had taken place with the French, he was ignorant, as Charles had indicated to Minette, of the details surrounding the negotiations with Louis. The Duke had become a fervent proponent of a French alliance and, perceiving what he saw as a chance of achieving a diplomatic triumph for himself, he now urged that the occasion of his mission to France should be used to secure a treaty, unaware that exactly such a treaty had just been signed; an ignorance, indeed, which he shared with Charles's other leading ministers, apart from Arlington and Clifford.

For Charles it was a jest to be savoured. Buckingham was despatched to negotiate a treaty and returned in September with exactly the same terms as the Treaty of Dover, but minus the 'Catholic' clauses. Louis – eager to lend verisimilitude to the proceedings – had eased the 'negotiations' along with the grant of an annual pension of 10,000 *livres* to Buckingham's mistress, the Countess of Shrewsbury.[57]

Charles, pushing the jest a stage further, now took the opportunity to better the terms of the original Treaty of Dover. The new secret 'Treaty of London' was signed by all five of Charles's leading ministers on 31 December and essentially conformed to that of Dover save for three points. Charles's declaration of Catholicism was omitted, and the money for this was rolled up into the other subsidies payable by Louis; two further Dutch islands (Goeree and Voorne) were added as Charles's share of the spoils; and the war was to start in the spring of 1672.[58] But the original Treaty of Dover remained in existence and it therefore became ambiguous whether Charles's declaration of Catholicism should still precede the declaration of the war or not.

LOUIS'S WAR PLANS: TREATIES WITH THE GERMAN PRINCES

Whilst Louis had brought Charles II into his schemes against the Dutch, this was only part of an overall plan. He needed the support, or at least the neutrality, of those German princes whose territories bordered on, or were in the neighbourhood of, the Rhine, which was the strategic route he was planning to use in his attack on the Dutch Republic. But he had not been finding this easy: as he mentioned in his despatch to Croissy of 7 October, 'je trouve de plus grands obstacles que je n'avais cru à ajouster avec les princes d'Allemagne'.[59] He was not helped by his invasion, in the autumn of 1670, of the Duchy of Lorraine; this was also strategically placed, and its duke, Charles IV, who had for long been a thorn in Louis's side, had been intriguing for the Austrian Emperor, the Electors of Mainz and of Trier, and himself to enter into the Triple Alliance.[60] But the invasion naturally aroused German fears and suspicions and made Louis's task more difficult.

His efforts to win over the German princes proved unsuccessful as regards the Duke of Neuburg and two of the Brunswick princes, namely the dukes of Zell and Wolfenbüttel. Nevertheless the House of Brunswick, whilst maintaining a loose association amongst itself, pursued different allegiances – the Duke of Zell, for example, was a Protestant whilst the Duke of Hanover was a Catholic,[61] and, in the course of 1671, the Duke of Hanover and the fourth member of the House, the Bishop of Osnabrück, allied themselves to cooperate with Louis, which included allowing the French limited rights to cross their territory and raise provisions there. Similar treaties were entered into with the Elector of Cologne, who was also the Bishop of Liège, and the Bishop of Münster, the ever-bellicose 'Bomber Galen'.[62]

Louis also, under a treaty which he entered into with the Emperor on 1 November 1671, and in consideration of his observing the Treaty of Aix-la-Chapelle, obtained Austrian neutrality in any war between France and any of the members of the Triple Alliance, which, of course, included the Dutch. This Franco-Austrian Treaty, however, had an important exception; it applied only to a war outside the Holy Roman Empire and unfortunately, from

Louis's point of view, his military plans involved infringing imperial territories. Possible Austrian intervention in the war was not therefore precluded.[63]

In January 1672 Louis further strengthened his alliances with the Elector of Cologne and with Galen, the Bishop of Münster, by turning them into offensive alliances against the Dutch.[64] His planned invasion route from the south and from the east of the United Provinces, it appeared, was now secure.

And on 14 April 1672, six days after his declaration of war on the Dutch, Louis and Sweden entered into a three-year treaty, which, under the pretext of preserving the peace in the German Empire, engaged the Swedes to oppose by arms the Emperor or any German princes who should come to the aid of the Dutch in the war Louis had just launched, a provision aimed at containing the Elector of Brandenburg should he come down in favour of the Dutch. The impoverished Swedes were always in need of funds and were ready to lend their swords to anyone prepared to pay for them.[65]

There were, however, two weaknesses in Louis's diplomacy. There was the exception in his Austrian treaty where Austrian neutrality applied only to a war outside the Holy Roman Empire. And the Elector of Brandenburg had not committed himself to the French King. The war, which Louis launched at the beginning of April 1672, and which had all the promise of being the greatest of military and diplomatic triumphs, was the greatest mistake of his long life. It laid the foundation for the career of William III.

1   Geoffrey Treasure, *op. cit.*, Routledge, London, 1997, pp.308–9. François Bluche, *op. cit.*, p.95.
2   See Roger Mettam, *op. cit.*, pp.154, 160.
3   Bluche, *op. cit.*, pp.87–8. Mignet, *Négociations Relatives à la Succession d'Espagne sous Louis IV*, 4 vols., Paris, 1835–42, I, p.52 contains the relevant clause.
4   Bluche, *op. cit.*, pp.52–4.
5   Quoted in Bluche, *ibid.*, p.310.
6   Geyl, *op. cit.*, p.177. Rowen, *De Witt, op. cit.*, p.469.
7   Lister, *op. cit.*, p.27.
8   Mignet, *op. cit.*, I, p.180.
9   *Ibid.*, p.190, Louis to D'Estrades, 6 April 1663.
10 The text is in *Brieven van De Witt*, II, pp.579–88.
11 Rowen, *De Witt*, pp.474, 480. Geyl, *op. cit.*, pp.188, 189. Mignet, I, p.219ff. D'Estrades, *op. cit.*, II, Letter to Louis XIV, 23 August 1663, pp.303ff. Letter to Louis XIV, 11 Oct. 1663.
12 D'Estrades, *ibid.*, p.388. Letter to Louis XIV, 21 Feb. 1664.
13 Mignet, *op. cit.*, II, p.212. D'Estrades, *Mémoires, op. cit.*, despatch to Louis XIV, 26 July 1663.
14 Mignet, *op. cit.*, II, pp.266–8. De Witt, *mémoire* for the deputies of the States of Holland. Copy sent by d'Estrades in his despatch 7 March 1664. *Mémoires, op. cit.*
15 Mignet, *op. cit.*, II, Louis XIV to D'Estrades, 23 April 1664.
16 Keith Feiling, *op. cit.*, pp.139–50. D'Estrades, *Mémoires*, III, pp.5–6, despatch from Louis 2 Jan. 1665, pp.277–8. Louis, despatch to D'Estrades, 7 August 1665.
17 J.R. Jones, *Anglo-Dutch Wars, op. cit.*, pp.167–73.

18 Geyl, *op. cit.*, pp.207, 216.

19 Mignet, *op. cit.*, I, pp.383–4.

20 Olaf van Nimwegen, *The Dutch Army and the Military Revolutions*, trans. Andrew May, The Boydell Press, Woodbridge, 2010, p.429.

21 Mignet, *op. cit.*, II, p.22ff.

22 D'Estrades, *op. cit.*, V, p.37. Despatch to Lionne, 14 Feb. 1667.

23 Mignet, *op. cit.*, II, pp.42–5.

24 Mignet, *op. cit.*, II, p.119.

25 D'Estrades, *Mémoires, op. cit.*, V, pp.233–4, despatch to Louis, 19 May 1667.

26 Mignet, *op. cit.*, II, pp. 486–90, 492–5, 497–9. Louis's terms of 27 Sept. are incorrectly stated in Rowen, *De Witt, op. cit.*, pp.686–7. D'Estrades, *Mémoires*, VI, pp.62ff., pp.73ff.

27 Scheurleer, *op. cit.*, IV, p.490.

28 K.H.D. Haley, *An English Diplomat in the Low Countries*, Clarendon Press, Oxford, 1986, p.158.

29 Mignet, *op. cit.*, II, pp.514–15.

30 *Ibid.*, pp.521–2.

31 *Ibid.*, p.537.

32 K.H.D. Haley, *An English Diplomat, op. cit.*, p.158.

33 T.H. Courtenay, *Memoirs of the Life, Works and Correspondence of Sir William Temple*, 1836, II, p.383.

34 Mignet, *op. cit.*, II, pp.539ff. Haley, *An English Diplomat, op. cit.*, p.161.

35 Haley, *ibid.*, p.171. Temple, *Works, op. cit.*, 1770, I, p.324.

36 Haley, *op. cit.*, p.205.

37 The text of the Triple Alliance is contained in Temple, *Works, op. cit.*, 1770, I, pp.362–84.

38 D'Estrades, *Mémoires, op. cit.*, VI, p.272.

39 Mignet, *op. cit.*, II, pp.607–8.

40 D'Estrades, *Mémoires, op. cit.*, VI, p.304, Lionne to d'Estrades, 2 March.

41 Mignet, *op. cit.*, II, pp.441–9 contains the French translation of the Latin text.

42 Feiling says that Louis revealed it to William III in 1698 and that the Prussians knew about it by March 1669, *op. cit.*, p.240.

43 *Louis XIV and Europe*, Ragnhild, ed. Hatton 1976, art. by Jean Bérenger, pp.139, 142.

44 A. Legrelle, *La Diplomatie française et la succession d'Espagne*, ed. Pichon, Libraire Cotillon, Paris 1888, p.144. John Spielman contends that the treaty was never signed (see *Leopold I of Austria*, London, 1977, p.56). The original treaty is certainly missing from the French archives (see Legrelle, p.518) but both Leopold and Louis acted as if it had been ratified. See Leopold's response to the French ambassador, Grémonville, in March 1669 ('Per l'amore di Dio, teniamo il tratto celato', Legrelle, p.169), and see Louis's proposals to Leopold to publish the secret treaty as soon as the news of the death of Carlos should be received together with the measures which he and Leopold would then take to give effect to it (Legrelle, pp.167–8).

45 Jean Bérenger's art., *op. cit.*, p.240.

46 Mignet, *op. cit.*, II, pp.621–5.

47 Mignet, *op. cit.*, II, p.639. Temple, *Works, op. cit.*, I, pp.413–17.

48 Mignet, *op. cit.*, III, p.34.

49 *Mémoires de Jacques*, II, Paris, 1824, II, pp.102–3.

50 Mignet, *op. cit.*, III, p.84. Ronald Hutton, *op. cit.*, pp.263–4. P. Sonnino, *Louis XIV and the Origins of the Dutch War*, Cambridge University Press, 1988, pp.54, 60.

51 Mignet, *op. cit.*, III, pp.73–4.

52 *Ibid.*, p.85.

53 *Ibid.*, pp 187–97. See also Hutton, *op. cit.*, p.266 for control of the Rhine trade.

54 Mignet, *op. cit.*, III, p.178. Sonnino, *op. cit.*, p.111.

55 Wicquefort, *Mémoires sur la guerre faite aux provinces-unies en l'année 1672*, Bijdragen en mededeelingen van het historisch genootschap gevestigd te Utrecht, XI, 1888, p.95.

56 Mignet, *op. cit.*, III, p.208.

57 *Ibid.*, pp.215–22.

58 *Ibid.*, pp.256–67.

59 *Ibid.*, p.233.

60 Sonnino, *op. cit.*, pp.110–11, 119.

61 *Ibid.*, p.88.

62 Mignet, *op. cit.*, III, pp.290–94.

63 Text in Mignet, *op. cit.*, III, pp.548–52. See also Rowen about the exception of imperial territory. *John De Witt, op. cit.*, p.777.

64 Mignet, *op. cit.*, III, pp.705–7.

65 The text of the treaty is in Mignet, *op. cit.*, III, pp.365–74.

6 THE ASCENT TO POWER

DEVELOPMENTS FAVOURING THE PRINCE

It took Louis four years from the signing of the Treaty of Aix La Chapelle in the spring of 1668 to make the laborious diplomatic and military preparations to launch his Dutch War in the spring of 1672. Despite De Witt's personal triumph with the Dutch fleet's raid on the Medway and the Thames, the questions raised by the need to face Louis's more hostile stance began to weaken his supremacy in Dutch politics, commencing with the War of Devolution in 1667. And as his position weakened that of William of Orange correspondingly and gradually strengthened.

In April 1667 Colbert published a new tariff which had wide-ranging, adverse effects on the Dutch economy, including Amsterdam; and the same month marked the start of the French invasion of the Spanish Netherlands and the War of Devolution. The view of the former Dutch ambassador to France, Coenraad van Beuningen, that the right response was an alliance against France with Spain and the Holy Roman Emperor, Leopold I of Austria, combined with retaliatory tariff measures, found resonance in Amsterdam, where Spain and its Empire had emerged as important markets.[1]

At the same time the War of Devolution raised difficult questions as what to do to put the Republic's very weak army into better condition to defend the country – the early successes of 'Bomber Galen', a minor power in the European context, and the need for Louis to come to the Republic's rescue, had already demonstrated the woeful state of the Dutch land forces.

To the Orangists the obvious candidate to head the armed forces was Prince William, who would become 18, the age of majority, they claimed, in the following year, 1668. The French ambassador, D'Estrades, reported on 16 June that they were exerting every effort to have the Prince appointed as Captain-General and Admiral-General; and that, to facilitate those aims, they were prepared to renounce his claims to the Stadholdership.[2] On the 30th he wrote that De Witt's rejection of these proposals was meeting with stiff opposition, and that his contention that the Prince was too closely connected to Charles II would no longer have validity once peace with England was obtained. He remarked upon the skill shown by the Prince in his encounters with the representatives of the towns and with the people when he adopted the political line, amidst these controversies, that he had no other interest than that of the State and that he would let himself be conducted by his tutors appointed by the State.

The ambassador, indeed, went so far as to question whether it was the right policy for France to support De Witt. He was sure that the Prince of Orange, 'having as much intelligence and ambition as he did, and his strong passion being war', would be compelled by his own interests to attach himself to Louis XIV. If the Prince were established in power, the Ambassador's argument in effect ran, he would not be able to establish his authority as his ancestors had done without a war, which he could obtain by joining Louis in a war against Spain; in short, D'Estrades had in mind the old alliance of the House of Orange with the House of Bourbon against the House of Habsburg.[3]

It was not a suggestion that Louis was yet ready to adopt.

The ambassador did not consider the more original, and diplomatically more revolutionary, alternative that, whilst the Prince of Orange's role and authority could indeed be enhanced by a war, that war could be against, rather than in alliance with, the King of France.

THE HARMONY AND THE PERPETUAL EDICT

On 5 August the States of Holland passed three resolutions which were designed to arrive at a compromise between the Orangist and republican parties, and which, for that reason, became known as the Harmony. Under the first resolution Prince Maurits of Nassau-Siegen and a Holsteiner, Wirtz, were to be appointed as First and Second Field-Marshals; and under the second resolution the Prince of Orange was to be invited to join the Council of State, it being left open for him in the future to pursue a military career.

The functions of the Council of State included advising on, and making proposals for, the defence budget; it put into execution resolutions of the States-General; it had supervisory powers in the military sphere; and it was involved in the administration of the Generality Lands, the lands conquered by the Republic in the wars against Spain, which did not belong to any particular Province and which were administered by the States-General.[4] But the Council's practical powers were not extensive, being mostly of an advisory nature, with the final word resting with the States-General. Hence the issue of the Prince's membership was largely symbolic.

These two resolutions were conditional on a third, which became known as the Perpetual, or Eternal, Edict, and which was designed forever to separate command of the armed forces from the office of the Stadholdership. Under its provisions the States of Holland would not permit a future Captain-General or Admiral-General of the Union to combine these offices with the office of Stadholder of any Province; the other Provinces would be persuaded to adopt the same principle; oaths to support the principle would be requisite from all future Captain- and Admiral-Generals; the membership of the Town Councils of Holland and of the Province's nobility were to be co-opted by themselves and would also be required to swear an oath to the Perpetual Edict; and Holland abolished the Stadholdership in Holland for ever.

De Witt added the further provision that Prince William would not be considered for the post of Captain- and Admiral-General until he had completed his 22nd year rather than when he was 18.[5]

The authors of the Edict were Fagel from Haarlem, and the Amsterdam Regent Valckenier, not De Witt. Fagel had been an Orangist with close involvement in the Buat affair. It may be, as has been suggested, that he was trying to clear himself from that involvement, but he was to revert, to become a very close associate of William III in the future – and was then to remain so for the rest of his life. It is just conceivable that he was playing a very deep double game, which involved keeping in with both sides, both to cover himself from his association with Buat and to advance the Prince as far as was politically possible at the time; after all, both the membership of the Council of State and the possibility of the highest military commands were explicitly open to the Prince – and all resolutions can always be de-resolved, even 'perpetual' ones. An alternative explanation is that Fagel was either, for the time being, a genuine convert to De Witt's point of view, or that he genuinely thought the Edict would be a compromise to bring unity to the conflicting parties.[6]

De Witt himself did eventually accept the proposal as a unifying measure.[7]

But the other Provinces apart from Holland took a long time to be brought to agreement on the Edict – not indeed until 1670 did they all come into line – and meanwhile the Prince was not able to take up his place in the Council of State.

De Witt himself was sent as a deputy by the States of Holland to Prince William to facilitate the swallowing of 'the pill' of the Edict, as Wicquefort puts it, although, as we read Wicquefort's account, we may be surprised at the degree of bluntness and the modicum of tact in De Witt's explanation of the reasons for the measure.

He began, indeed, by saying that there was not a single member of the assembly of the Holland States who did not see His Highness as someone who should one day command the forces of the Province. But, he then continued, they trembled, all of them, when they relived what had happened in the time of his defunct father, who had the misfortune of falling into the hands of people who had thrown him into all sorts of excesses, and who had given him counsels calculated for his destruction, pulling the ruins of the State on top of him. He did touch upon the 'very excellent nature' of the Prince himself, but then harped on William's connection with the English Royal House; he indicated that his father had been ruined by his alliance with that House, and, for good measure, he added that the Holland States would have to approve his marriage if they were to give him command of their armed forces.

After these aspersions on both his father and his mother, the unruffled Prince – whose every day's existence was steeped in the consciousness of his illustrious ancestry – expressed his satisfaction, and prayed De Witt to thank the States of Holland for the care which they expressed for his person and his interests. The irony was noted by Wicquefort the historian; it would be surprising if it passed the Grand Pensionary by.[8]

It was not long before William had to put up with a further slight: he had a mortgage on certain property rights at Gertruydenberg in exchange for a loan, the repayment of which the States of Holland forced through in March 1667 in a high-handed manner, and when the Prince's Council refused to accept the repayment, the States resorted to armed coercion to take possession of the property. Furthermore, at the end of the year the widow of the Count of Brederode, the sister of Amalia von Solms, who had been enjoying exemption from paying a property tax at Viane, was compelled to commence paying the tax by having four companies of infantry and two of cavalry billeted on her *domaine*.[9]

And when William himself attended a review of troops at Bergen op Zoom their officers were forbidden to salute him.[10]

On 17 January 1668 the States-General voted through the Harmony. But it was passed only by a majority vote; Gelderland, Utrecht and Overijssel had joined Holland, but Zeeland, Friesland and Groningen remained opposed.

As a result Maurits of Nassau-Siegen was appointed the First, and Wirtz the Second, Field-Marshal of the army, although Wirtz had effective command in the absence of Maurits on a diplomatic mission.[11]

But, however intense, however fierce and – in the final outcome through no fault of William – however deadly the underlying conflict between the Prince and De Witt, the Grand Pensionary had developed a certain affection for his young opponent. He told William Temple at this time 'that for his own part, he never failed to see the Prince once or twice a week, and grew to have a particular Affection for him, and would tell me plainly, that the States designed the Captain-generalship of all the Forces for him, so soon as by his Age he grew capable of it.'[12]

FIRST NOBLE OF ZEELAND

In the Province of Zeeland an increasingly influential Orangist faction led by Pieter de Huybert, the Province's Pensionary – who, from 1667, was also a member of the Republic's Council of State – and by William's cousin, Nassau-Odijk, who had married into a rich family in the Province, were strongly committed to furthering William's cause.[13] In March 1668 Zeeland rejected the Perpetual Edict and confirmed that it would abide by its resolution taken in August 1660 to designate the Prince as First Noble of the Province on his 18th birthday.[14] As First Noble he would acquire a vote in the Zeeland States to add to the two votes he already possessed through his ownership of two towns, Flushing and Veere – where he was also the Marquis – giving him three votes out of the total of seven in the Provincial body.

Amalia von Solms's old retainer, Constantijn Huygens, was in Zeeland in March to settle disputes in Veere relating to the elections of the town's magistrates, and on 10 May D'Estrades was reporting that the Prince's friends were advising him to travel to Zeeland to be installed as First Noble, although not immediately. At the same time in Holland, according to the ambassador, efforts were being made to remove De Huybert, who was regarded as one of De Witt's great enemies, from his post as Zeeland Pensionary.[15] On 12 September Huygens wrote to the Prince (as always in French, as were his letters to Amalia) outlining the plans which he, Amalia and the De Huybert family had conceived for him to make an unexpected descent on Zeeland to be installed as First Noble. The Prince was at Breda, De Witt and William's governor, Van Ghent, having been informed that he had embarked on a hunting trip. From there, following the guidance of Huygens's letter, and under cover of the hunting excursion, he proceeded to Bergen op Zoom, and from there, by means of his grandmother's yacht, to Middelburg in Zeeland.[16]

There, on 19 September, seated in an armchair at the head of the table, he was installed as First Noble by the States of Zeeland, with no one – save the representatives from Zierikzee – daring to offer any opposition; and Zierikzee was soon brought into line by the violence of popular opinion. He had indeed been greeted with great popular acclaim on his arrival at Middelburg in the usual manner of the times – with his coach and six drawing him through crowded streets lined with the local militia, with the windows and roofs of the houses filled with people, and with the continuing noise of saluting ordnance.[17]

Huygens, in a letter to him dated the 20th, remarked that 'your highness cannot believe how universally our people [that is, the Orangists] are rejoicing at the good and happy success which your highness has encountered in Zeeland'. But it is clear that the practical and shrewd Amalia von Solms was anxious not to lose control of the situation. Huygens, mentioning that he wrote on her orders as well as that he was taking 'the liberty of an old servant', passed on the Dowager's advice that William should not allow resentments to arise from his visit and that he should accelerate his return from the Province. He was politely reminded to show his appreciation of De Huybert's efforts in conceiving and executing the design in Zeeland; and Huygens passed on Amalia's warning not to make a hasty judgement in the appointment of William's deputy as First Noble.[18]

It was customary, however, for the princes of Orange to appoint such a deputy and William had appointed Nassau-Odijk to the position on 21 September, before he received Huygens's letter. Nassau-Odijk was known, says Wicquefort, 'for his gaming, his debauches and his knavery, which surpassed those of the greatest rogues, ancient and modern'. Although Wicquefort was in De Witt's camp, historians have tended to follow this view, and Nassau-Odijk was indeed indicted for corruption after the death of William III.[19] But Nassau-Odijk was a very close member of the Orange clan, of undoubted loyalty, who had played a very successful role in the planning of the Zeeland trip; and, as we shall see, on other occasions these personal ties were often to be an overriding political consideration in William's calculations when he had need of clan/client support. In this he was not alone in the 17th century.

The appointment rankled, however, in another and important quarter when Nassau-Odijk broke a promise from William to appoint one of Pieter de Huybert's sons to the Zeeland audit office.[20]

As carefully orchestrated and controlled as was possible by Amalia and the House of

Orange's able and loyal servitor, Huygens, the *démarche* in Zeeland consolidated William's political position in the second most important Province in the Republic, after Holland; it was a further shift towards his re-establishment in the traditional offices of his House; and it was a further shift of power away from De Witt.

The popular acclaim for him in Zeeland was stupendous. When on 21 September he walked through the streets of Middelburg he was surrounded by so huge a crowd that he could barely make his way through the throng, which cheered him with repeated shouts of 'vivat Orangie'. Bells and trumpets played the Orange anthem 'Wilhelmus van Nassau' throughout the day and night, when fireworks were let off. When he arrived at Flushing on the 22nd the ships there fired their guns, and there were salvoes from the militia who lined the streets, whilst the town was black with people. On the 25th he proceeded to Veere and from there to Breda.[21]

As for De Witt, he again reiterated to William Temple on 6 September the position he had adopted when he had personally delivered 'the pill' of the Perpetual Edict to William the previous year and in very much the same terms. 'The States' intentions', the Grand Pensionary told Temple, 'were to make him [the Prince] captain-general and admiral too … and to this purpose they would already have brought him into the council of state in order to fit him for those charges, had it not been for some of those provinces that had hindered it upon pretence of more kindness to him, and designing greater matters for him' – that is, the Stadholdership; and he alluded again to the subversive role played by William's father, although he also spoke favourably of 'the great moderation' of the other princes of Orange which had contributed so much to the Republic's survival in the past; he clearly regarded them as role models for the present incumbent.

William did not push for the Stadholdership of Zeeland, which, under the terms of the Perpetual Edict, would have debarred him from holding the federal military posts which, as De Witt made clear, lay within his grasp. His abilities were certainly recognised by the Pensionary who at the same interview with Temple 'fell into commendations of this young prince's parts and dispositions'.[22]

William was indeed beginning to acquire international recognition – the previous March, Pomponne, who had succeeded D'Estrades as the French ambassador, had reported to Louis XIV that everybody told him that he was growing up with much intelligence and application.[23]

Another person had observed William's moves in Zeeland, not without a certain nervousness, his uncle Charles II in England. At this time Temple was negotiating what became the Triple Alliance in The Hague and, even prior to the Zeeland visit, Charles had been anxious that William's position in the Netherlands should not disturb the aims of his diplomacy, with Temple, according to his instructions, 'advising our nephew to depend rather upon [the States'] good will than any particular faction'.[24] When the Dutch ambassador in

London gave the King an account of what had happened in Zeeland, Charles took care to deny any previous knowledge of William's plans; and on 8 September Arlington wrote to Temple: 'I long to hear how the Prince of Orange's Acquisition [that is, his installation as First Noble] in Zeeland goes down in Holland; you know already you may with all Truth declare His Majesty's ignorance of it.'[25]

Temple was true to his instructions. 'Tho the King', he told De Witt, 'could not lose the affection he had for his Nephew; yet he was of Opinion he could not express it better than by infusing into him the Belief that he could make himself no way so happy as in the good will of the States, and trusting wholly to Them in the Course of his Fortunes, and not to private Factions, or Foreign Intrigues.' His Majesty's opinion was 'that Princes were not apt to do themselves more Hurt than by affecting too much Power, or such as was directly contrary to the Stomach and Genius of the Country which fell to their Share...'.[26]

But there were circumstances where the King could be stirred to take an interest on his nephew's behalf. Earlier that year, in April 1768, Arlington had heard that it was the intention to deprive William of his lodgings in The Hague 'and to take his stables from him'. The family's, and the clan's, prestige was at stake – 'if His Majesty's discretion [in not pushing for the Prince's advancement] should expose his Nephew to such a Mortification, what would his Highness, and all standers by say of it' – and Temple was instructed to make further enquiries. In the event the Prince's lodgings remained safe.[27]

The Zeeland visit did cause considerable indignation in Holland, whose States were in session at the time, particularly the deception imposed upon Van Ghent, but they soon accepted the *fait accompli*.[28] But then, at the end of October, further friction arose when Amalia von Solms, having consulted Charles II and the Elector of Brandenburg, informed the States-General that on reaching his 18th birthday, his coming of age in her view, William would take over the conduct of his own affairs. The proposal of several deputies at the States-General that they should send their compliments to the Prince was negated by the Holland representatives, who added that they would advise everybody in their Province that any contractual arrangement with the Prince would be invalid, because, without special dispensation from the Holland States, the legal coming of age was 25; and furthermore, they obtained an undertaking from Amalia that he would not sell any of his real estate until he reached that age.[29]

De Witt was irked both by William's becoming First Noble in Zeeland and by Amalia's unilateral announcement of his coming of age without the advice, consent, and legal dispensation of Holland; she was, in his view, acting as though he was not a subject of the Province; and he went so far as to write to Valckenier to ask whether it would not be advisable to bring an end to the education commission, and to reconsider the Prince's position so as to 'preserve the necessary harmony of the state together with the freedom so dearly bought'. But from Valckenier he received no support, and the education commission was left unchanged. One can only speculate if there was any change in atmosphere when he arrived in the Prince's quarters for his continuing educational visits.[30]

By the end of March 1669, Zeeland, William and Amalia von Solms recognised the political reality that those Provinces that had accepted the Harmony would veto his appointment as Captain-General if he accepted any of the Stadholderships. They accordingly accepted the principle of the separation of the two offices: as Wicquefort aptly put it, 'to get the prince back in the saddle it was necessary to get his foot into the stirrup'. If indeed the appointment to the main military charges could be obtained, the further objective of the Stadholderships might become feasible. Wicquefort said this was something that passed by those who were in prime authority in Holland.[31] It did not escape De Witt.

There was some delay in persuading the remaining two Provinces, Friesland and Groningen, to accept the Harmony. There the cadet branch of the House of Orange retained the Stadholderships – although the current holder, Hendrik-Casimir, was a minor and his mother was acting for him as his guardian – and hopes were entertained that, should Prince William die, they could aspire to the Captain-Generalship in their own right. Eventually in March 1670 Zeeland and the two recalcitrant Provinces jointly informed the States-General that they too would now support the Harmony.[32]

ENTRY INTO THE COUNCIL OF STATE

This, paradoxically, confronted De Witt with a dilemma. The Harmony promised William membership of the Council of State; so much was unavoidable. But his membership of the Council raised a number of awkward points, such as whether he should have purely advisory, or full, voting rights. De Witt exerted every effort to restrict the Prince's powers and influence, and to confine his vote to an advisory one.[33]

De Witt's ability, however, to direct affairs was continuing to ebb. In his bailiwick of Holland opposition was being led in Amsterdam itself by two powerful Regents, Coenraad van Beuningen and Gillis Valckenier. Both were forceful personalities – of Van Beuningen, Temple wrote to Arlington that he was 'not always so willing to hear as to be heard; and out of the abundance of his imagination is apt sometimes to reason a man to death', adding, however, 'for the rest, you will find him *fort honnête homme*'.[34] He had returned to the Republic in the autumn of 1668 from his post as ambassador in Paris, where his observations had turned him into a fierce opponent of France and an equally fierce supporter of the Triple Alliance. He had become a Burgomaster of Amsterdam on 1 February 1669 with the support of Valckenier's faction and against the opposition of Rijnst and De Graeff, the supporters of De Witt. His relationship with De Witt, however, was not straightforward, and despite the important differences now arising between them on foreign policy they managed to maintain a good working relationship at the personal level.

Valckenier and his faction were motivated by the interests of Amsterdam, in particular the impact of taxation, and of French tariffs, on the city and its trade.[35] Valckenier was a practical politician with a keen sense of which way the wind blew; at different times he dropped remarks that Hieronymus van Beverninck, another Regent with much influence, was a wise man to disassociate himself from the government; that De Witt was faltering; and that the Prince would become ruler.[36] Although neither Valckenier nor Van Beuningen were Orangists, they were both alarmed by the increasing threat from France, they both wanted to make economic reprisals against the French and they were both motivated by the desire to change the Republic's foreign policy against Louis. In that context, they wished to come to terms with the Prince of Orange and were in conflict with De Witt. Pomponne thought that, as both were opposed to De Witt, they allied themselves with William to pull the Pensionary down, if possible – a view which in the case of Van Beuningen seems somewhat overstated.[37] But Valckenier did resent the authority of De Witt at a personal level.[38]

They managed to throw Amsterdam's weight behind Haarlem and its Pensionary Fagel, who seems to have begun tacking back at this time towards his Orangist sympathies, if indeed he had ever abandoned them. Fagel argued that there were three considerations pointing strongly in favour of the Prince being granted the full vote in the Council of State: the affection of the people; his wealth in the country; and his illustrious connections outside it. We may, perhaps, make a small digression here to note a dissenting republican voice against these assertions: the affection of the people, an opposing Regent argued, was so dangerous in a republic, and so contrary to liberty, that in ancient times ostracism was resorted to for those who aspired to the people's adulation – which neatly encapsulates whose interests the Regents supporting De Witt thought the 'True Freedom' should serve.[39]

On 16 May the States of Holland resolved to give the Prince a full vote, but only with the very narrow majority of ten to nine. In an attempt at finding a compromise within the divided Province, De Witt came to an agreement with Coenraad van Beuningen, with Fagel and with Pancras, who was another of the four Burgomasters of Amsterdam. The Holland resolution was accepted but the Prince's entry into the Council would be conditional. He should not attend the Council when questions relating to his relatives were to be discussed – a reflection of the old fear of Stuart involvement in the country; he should not vote on taxation in the Generality Lands where he had large estates; and his eventual appointment to the Captain-Generalship should be for one year only unless agreed by the unanimous vote of the Holland States.

But it was a compromise rejected by Valckenier, who, in characteristically high-handed fashion and without putting the matter to the Amsterdam Town Council, repudiated the efforts of Pancras and of Van Beuningen. In the event the conditions were dropped other than the one relating to the Captain-Generalship. William, who according to Pomponne had engaged in intensive lobbying and whose conduct impressed the ambassador, declared himself very satisfied with the outcome, and much praise was also directed at De Witt for his skilful handling of the negotiations.[40] The Harmony passed the States-General on 31 May, and the Prince's induction to the Council of State took place on 2 June.[41]

The Prince's faction now worked to obtain his entry into the States-General, but this was a step too far, and De Witt's opposition ensured the failure of the manoeuvre.[42]

It seemed to De Witt that the time had come to dissolve the Prince's education committee and on 20 July he consulted Valckenier, who this time agreed. Van Ghent resigned, no doubt to William's relief, on the 26th and the commission was dissolved on the 29th.[43]

1 Israel, *op. cit.*, pp.780–83.

2 D'Estrades, *op. cit.*, V, p.348.

3 *Ibid.*, pp.379–82.

4 Temple, *Works, op. cit.*, 1770, I, pp.130–1.

5 Geyl, *op. cit.*, pp.270–1. Rowen, *De Witt, op. cit.*, pp. 676–8. Rowen says when he was 23, which is incorrect. See Japikse, *Willem III, op. cit.*, I, p.138. Wicquefort, *Histoire, op. cit.*, III, pp.373–4.

6 *Brieven aan Johan De Witt*, II, 1660–1672. *Historisch Genootschap te Utrecht*, Series 3, No.44, III, pp.362–4. Geyl, *op. cit.*, p.271. Rowen, *De Witt, op. cit.*, pp.678–80. Van Nimwegen, *op. cit.*, p.438 indicates that it was a device of Fagel and Valckenier to 'allay the concern among the regents about a repetition of the events of 1618 and 1650'. *Brieven aan De Witt*, II, 1660–72, pp.412–13 does show Fagel in the light of a true supporter of De Witt's philosophy at this time.

7 *Brieven van De Witt, op. cit.*, III, pp.367–9.

8 Wicquefort, *Histoire, op. cit.*, III, p.375. For a less ironic interpretation see Rowen, *De Witt, op. cit.*, n.132 p.681, where he cites Wicquefort's letters to the French Foreign Minister and the King of Denmark, in which he 'described the prince as very satisfied with De Witt, who defeated the efforts of deputies of several towns who wanted to deprive him of the hope of eventually becoming either stadholder or captain general'. But Wicquefort's subsequent history reads: 'Le Prince, *qui est naturellement artificieux et dissimulé* [my italics], témoigna estre fort satisfait des Estats de Hollande, et pria De Witt de les remercier de soins, qu'ils avaient de sa personne et de ses interests.' The less than flattering tone of De Witt's address is surely more compatible with an ironic interpretation of the Prince's reply and perhaps his history, written later, reflects Wicquefort's more considered view.

9 Wicquefort, *Histoire, op. cit.*, III, pp.375–6.

10 *Ibid.*, p.405.

11 Rowen, *De Witt, op. cit.*, pp.788–90. Israel, *op. cit.*, pp.791–2.

12 Temple to Arlington, 24 Jan. 1668. *Letters written by Sir W. Temple, Bart., and other ministers of state, both at home and abroad: containing an account of the most important transactions that pass'd in Christendom from 1665–1672*, publ. Jonathan Swift, MDCC, I, p.136.

13 Huygens, *Briefwisseling, op. cit.*, VI, n.5, p.226. Wicquefort, *Histoire, op. cit.*, p.410.

14 Geyl, *op. cit.*, p.282.

15 Huygens, *Briefwisseling, op. cit.*, VI, pp.225–8. D'Estrades, *op. cit.*, VI, p.438. Wicquefort, *Histoire, op. cit.*, III, p.379.

16 Huygens, *Briefwisseling, op. cit.*, VI, pp.235–6. Wicquefort, *Histoire, op. cit.*, pp.409–10. Huygens says the yacht was Amalia's, Wicquefort that it was a Middelburg yacht. It could, of course, have been a yacht put at the disposal of the Dowager.

17 Geyl, *op. cit.*, p.302.

18 Huygens, *Briefwisseling, op. cit.*, VI, pp.237–8.

19 *Ibid.*, p.42. Wicquefort, *Histoire, op. cit.*, p.410.

20 *Correspondentie Willem III en Bentinck, op. cit.*, II, Pt 1, pp.9–16.

21 Aitzema, *op. cit.*, VI, p.614.

22 Temple, *Works, op. cit.*, 1770, II, pp.11–12.

23 Mignet, *op. cit.*, III, p.579.

24 Haley, *An English Diplomat, op. cit.*, p 218.

25 Arlington letters to Temple, 1 and 18 Sept. 1668. See also his letter of 29 Sept.in similar vein. *Arlington's Letters to Sir William Temple*, ed. Thos. Babington, London, 1701, pp.350, 352, 356.

26 Temple to Arlington, 7 Sept. 1668, *Temple's Letters, op. cit.*, I, p.12ff.

27 *Arlington's Letters to Temple, op. cit.*, I, Arlington to Temple, 6 April 1668, p.308.

28 Wicquefort, *Histoire, op. cit.*, III, p.412. Aitzema, *op. cit.*, VI, p.631.

29 Wicquefort, *Histoire, op. cit.*, III, p.414.

30 *Brieven van De Witt, op. cit.*, II, pp.440–41.

31 Wicquefort, *Histoire, op. cit.*, IV, pp.67–8.

32 Geyl, *op. cit.*, p.280. Wicquefort, *Histoire, op. cit.*, IV, p.126.

33 De Witt's letter 1 April 1670 to Andries de Graeff, quoted in n.2 in Wicquefort, *Histoire, op. cit.*, IV, pp.128–31.

34 Temple, *Works, op. cit.*, II, pp.116–17.

35 M. Franken, *op. cit.*, pp.69–70, 76–7.

36 H. Bontemantel, *De Regeering van Amsterdam*, ed. Kernkamp, The Hague, 1897, II, p.157.

37 Israel, *op. cit.*, p.793. On one occasion Valckenier described a work of the republican Grotius as 'being the political testament of those who loved freedom'. Reynst to De Witt, 20 Sept. 1668, *Brieven aan De Witt, op. cit.*, II, p.417. Pomponne to Louis XIV 1 May 1670. Mignet, *op. cit.*, III, p.611. Franken, *op. cit.*, pp.79, 91–2.

38 Wicquefort, *Histoire, op. cit.*, IV, p.143.

39 *Ibid.*, pp.133–4.

40 *Ibid.*, pp.137–9. Haley, *An English Diplomat, op. cit.*, p.263. Geyl, *op. cit.*, pp.310–12. Mignet, *op. cit.*, III, p.612. Rowen, *De Witt, op. cit.*, pp.794–5. Bontemantel, *op. cit.*, I, pp.107–9. Temple, *Works, op. cit.*, III, pp.434–5. Stephen Baxter's account states that the condition relating to the Captain-Generalship was dropped and the other two conditions retained (Baxter, *op. cit.*, pp.53–4). Wicquefort implies that all three conditions were maintained, which is at variance with the other authorities.

41 Rowen, De Witt, *op. cit.*, p.795. Haley, *An English Diplomat, op. cit.*, p.264.

42 Wicquefort, *Histoire, op. cit.*, IV, pp.141–3 and notes.

43 *Brieven van De Witt, op. cit.*, IV, Note 1, p.50.

7 ON THE EVE OF LOUIS XIV'S DUTCH WAR

THE ENGLISH VISIT – REASONS FOR THE VISIT

The advancement of Prince William did not stop at the borders of the Dutch Republic. At the international level, too, plans were afoot to raise his profile. A project was set in train for him to establish a closer relationship with the head of the Stuart clan by a personal journey to England to visit Charles II, whom he had not seen since the Restoration in 1660. In 1669 he had indeed invited himself to England on a number of occasions; and in March 1670 Charles asked him to come across so that he could be invested with the Order of the Garter on 23 April, the day of the Order's patron saint, St George.[1] Had he gone to England then he would have been there during the family gathering attended by Henrietta of Orléans which accompanied the signing of the Treaty of Dover on 1 June.

But the journey was prevented by his preoccupation at that time with the politics leading to his appointment to the Council of State. The King's invitation, however, was repeated in June. It is important to remember that the visit took place after the Treaty of Dover had been signed and it overlapped with Charles II's and Louis XIV's surreptitious planning of their Dutch war.

One reason for the journey, from William's point of view, was financial. The Stuarts were heavily indebted to the House of Orange – Princess Mary's dowry of £40,000 had never been paid and the Orange princes had lent the Stuarts very large sums of money, so that by the time the Prince came of age in November 1668 the English debt was reckoned at about 1.9 million guilders or about £190,000.[2] Constantijn Huygens had been in London in 1663 and negotiations with Charles II and his ministers had been dragging on ever since.[3] Arlington wrote to Temple in November 1668 saying: 'We shall be very sorry to find his Highness, the Prince of Orange, call to His Majesty for the Payment of his Debt; when it is impossible for His Majesty to do it. He hath solemnly acknowledged it by the Form of a Privy Seal, and means, whenever the Parliament is in disposition to pay his other Debts, to add to them this to the Prince.'[4] In November 1668 there was a similar debt due to the House of Orange from Spain amounting to about 2.4 million guilders or about £240,000. To put this in context the total annual revenue, which Parliament judged necessary for Charles II to conduct his government at the beginning of his restoration, amounted to £1.2 million.[5]

The non-payment of these debts naturally weighed heavily on the financial affairs of the Prince, 'which', as Charles II said in his instructions to William Temple, 'we hear are running into great disorder'; and he instructed Temple to seek the assistance of De Witt in the matter. The Pensionary told Temple in August 1668 that the Prince's finances 'were in ill condition, but he thought not so bad as they were said to be: … he had that very morning been instructing [the Prince] in the business of the finances of this state' and 'he had taken occasion likewise to put him in mind of his own particular revenue, and hoped that he would fall into the care of it.'[6]

The Prince could not ignore the implications his finances had for his power base. Despite his appointment as First Noble in Zeeland and to the Council of State, his authority in the Dutch Republic still needed bolstering. Patronage and the demonstration of wealth were factors in calculating political strength, and for this money was required.

He sought to further his prestige on another front as well. Upon his entry into the Council of State he intimated to Pomponne how useful to him a compliment from Louis XIV on this event would be. As it happened the secret Treaty of Dover had been signed the day before he joined the Council, and, unbeknown to him, this envisaged a role for him – however ill-defined – to identify his interests with the war which Louis and Charles were planning to make on the Dutch Republic. It is not surprising, therefore, that Louis was only too happy to provide the desired compliment, which was contained in instructions to Pomponne on 13 June. In these the King said that he foresaw that membership of the Council of State 'would be but a stage to be followed swiftly by other greater' offices, 'that is to say by [William's] establishment in the same authority which his ancestors had held in the state with so much justice and merit, to which I would be very glad to have occasion to contribute'. Pomponne let these sentiments of the French King be known in a public ceremony which was deliberately designed to enhance esteem for Prince William.[7]

As regards William's visit to England, Pomponne reflected many years later that it was important for him to let himself be seen by the English people, who regarded him, after the daughters of the Duke of York, as the closest heir to the throne, and that the marks of consideration which he would receive from the King and the court would much augment the position which he had begun to build up in the Dutch Republic.[8]

THE ENGLISH VISIT – THE PREPARATIONS

The Prince's lack of confidence in his authority in the Republic is demonstrated in the very cautious and covert way that he prepared for the English visit – which left the way open for him to withdraw if it was unlikely to enhance his prestige. At the end of June he sent over an inconspicuous figure, his personal physician, Dr Peter Rumpf, who had cared for him at the time of his birth. Rumpf, who had a good command of English, was to sound out Arlington, who, it will be remembered, had married Isabella, Nassau-Beverweert's daughter, and who was therefore a member of the Orange clan. Dr Rumpf's instructions, signed by William, were translated into English and were handed over to Arlington.

No bones were made that William had 'greate neede' for the repayment of the Stuart debt without which 'his princely house kould [*sic*] not possibly subsist and bee brought in order'. Some of his supporters had concerns regarding the English visit 'if the same should bee without good effect', given that the Prince had only just joined the Council of State, which was regarded as but 'a weake business'. Their concerns were, first, that if he returned from England without payment of his debts 'his credit [his authority is meant] should be so much weakned [*sic*] by the States and the common people, that the dommage never kould be repared': and secondly, that Coenraad van Beuningen had just arrived in England as an Extraordinary Ambassador to buoy up the incompetent Boreel in negotiations relating to a trade agreement between the English and the Dutch, and there was concern that the Prince, on the one hand, should not be associated with the negotiations should they fail, but, on the other hand, if they looked likely to succeed, he should be present in England to claim the credit through 'his interposition and solicitation'. What would Arlington advise?

It was deemed so important that Dr Rumpf's visit and soundings should remain secret that melodramatic expedients were resorted to; at Lady Arlington's suggestion Rumpf donned a wig to escape recognition for a first preliminary meeting with her. This was followed by a subsequent meeting with Arlington himself, held – with the precautions continuing – in Arlington's garden. This minister's advice was that the Prince's personal visit would be helpful as regarded the Stuart debt but that the risks of failure feared by the Prince's supporters on this score should be offset by other considerations. As Charles II had no children (legitimate, that is) and as the Duke of York had few and very frail children, and with the Duchess of York unlikely to have more, it would not require a miracle for Prince William in due course to come to the throne, and it would therefore serve no ill purpose if he should show himself to the people. Besides which, His Majesty, with great impatience, was longing to see him.

Another meeting was arranged – in the garden again – at which Arlington reported that he had read Dr Rumpf's instructions to the King who, after consulting the Duke of York, advised the Prince to come over to England at the beginning of October, so that the question of the debt could be settled in consultation and with the help of Parliament. The negotiations with Coenraad van Beuningen were proving problematic, which was another reason why the King advised the Prince to postpone his journey until October, by which time, possibly earlier but not later, Van Beuningen should have departed.[9]

RUMOURS OF THE TREATY OF DOVER IN THE DUTCH REPUBLIC

The question that arises in relation to the Treaty of Dover and its plans was how far Prince William's knowledge of it extended, prior to and during his visit to Charles II.

There was inevitably much speculation at the time, both before the Duchess of Orléans's visit to England and afterwards, about the purpose of her visit. The contemporary historian Wicquefort says that Pomponne advised the Prince to make his voyage to England to fall in with the Duchess's plans to go to Dover; he also says that he assured the Prince that she would render him services which would not be disagreeable to him, letting it be known that the meeting between King Charles and the Duchess would witness the taking of decisions which would change his fortunes, and which would produce an inevitable revolution in the Dutch Republic. Historians have discounted the version given in Wicquefort's history – it was written long after the events it relates, Wicquefort was an ally of De Witt with a motive to denigrate William, and there is no corroboration in the French archives. A contemporary newsletter stating on 11 April that Pomponne had assured the Prince that the Duchess of Orléans would carry particular orders for him of a satisfying nature has also been dismissed on the grounds that the newsletter had merely, perhaps, picked up a rumour.[10] Wicquefort's version and the newsletter's story look therefore unlikely.

Nevertheless it remains that the newsletter does bear witness at least to the speculations that were current about the purpose of the Duchess's visit. These, in as small a political community as The Hague, are unlikely to have escaped the attention of the Prince's court; and, even if they had, the Prince and his entourage, which included intelligent, experienced and well-informed advisers such as Amalia von Solms and Constantijn Huygens, are likely to have asked themselves, without any further prompting, what the Duchess was up to on her excursion to England. Furthermore, they had also received the hint from Louis himself in June when Louis sent his compliment to William upon his joining the Council of State and when Louis remarked that he foresaw the Prince swiftly taking over the offices of his ancestors, to which Louis would be very happy to have occasion to contribute.

Let us now examine the intelligence conveyed to De Witt by the Dutch embassy in Paris beginning in March 1670 and ending in February 1671, keeping in mind that the Prince of Orange left for England on 6 November 1670 and returned to Holland on 23 February 1671.

In March the secretary of the Dutch legation in France, Christiaan Rumpf, who was Dr Peter Rumpf's brother,[11] reported that some in Paris were of the opinion that the forthcoming visit of Henrietta of Orléans to England was the pretext for something else, of considerable advantage to France, which required this last effort to bring about a conclusion.[12] On 11 April he indicated that wise heads in Paris were saying that the forthcoming journey of the Duchess to England and the projected trip of the Prince of Orange needed to be thought through and reflected upon.[13] On 4 July he warned De Witt of the English change of sides after Dover without knowing the exact terms of the treaty.[14] At the end of August he again warned De Witt that the purpose of the visit of the Duke of Buckingham to Paris was to negotiate an Anglo-French alliance, a warning of which De Witt took note without giving it credence.[15] On 4 September De Groot, the Dutch ambassador in Paris, sent further confirmation to De Witt, who, although he was at this time sceptical that Charles II and Louis would in fact act together, doubted, in the event of a French attack on the Spanish Netherlands and on the Dutch, that Charles II would act with sufficient vigour to meet his obligations to the Republic under the Triple Alliance, and by 3 October he had come round to the view that, because of the likely lack of support from Charles, it behoved the Dutch to strengthen their military both on land and at sea.

All these despatches preceded the arrival of the Prince in England. Moreover the Paris embassy continued to give its warnings of an Anglo-French alliance throughout the winter whilst he was in England; and certainly the full import of the Treaty of Dover was revealed to De Witt at the end of February 1671 – just as William was returning to Holland – when the ambassador reported that he had it on the very best authority that France and England had entered into a treaty which envisaged the total overthrow of the constitution of the Dutch Republic and the conferring of the sovereignty of the country upon the Prince of Orange.[16]

We shall see that the Prince's subsequent actions demonstrate that he had no knowledge of the contents of this latest despatch then or later; but how credible is it to believe that the court of William of Orange had no hint at all of what was being discussed in Paris over such a lengthy period of time and which formed the basis of these despatches, bearing in mind that William's close confidant, Dr Peter Rumpf, was also the brother of Christaan? Indeed, how secure were all the contents of the despatches themselves in the Dutch Republic, where secrets were notoriously difficult to keep? It is true, as historians have asserted,[17] and as we shall see, that William was not aware of the exact terms of the Treaty of Dover, but surely the probability must be that, well before his departure for England, he, and his advisers, did have cause for suspicions of a possible combination of some sort between Louis XIV and Charles II directed against the Republic.[18] There was time for rumination before he finally embarked on his journey to England at the beginning of November and during his lengthy stay until the end of February 1671,[19] during which indeed there would have been further evidence of the war-like preparations being made in England itself. If it were true that the French and English Kings were planning an alliance of some sort against the Dutch, how should he play his hand?

The eagerness of Charles II that his nephew should come over to England was manifest during Dr Rumpf's visit and was of long standing. The timing of the Prince's visit and the signing of the Treaty of Dover had been linked in Charles's mind – Arlington wrote to Temple on 29 April regarding Henrietta of Orléans's visit to Dover that 'I am sorry that the Prince of Orange is not like to make a Figure in that Interview',[20] and, as we shall see, Charles was toying with the idea of taking William into his confidence and revealing the terms of the Treaty of Dover when he came to England. Perhaps Louis was as well, as his hint when he complimented the Prince on his membership of the Council of State indicates – although, if so, he changed his mind.

THE PRINCE'S DEPARTURE FOR ENGLAND

The Prince sought the consent of the States-General and the States of Holland before he embarked on his journey – although he gave offence to Dordrecht by describing the King of England rather regally as 'our uncle' rather than 'my uncle'.[21] As it turned out, Van Beuningen was still in London in October and some of the Provinces wished to pass a resolution requesting William 'to support and to second' his Embassy, but De Witt managed to water this down so that the final resolution passed on 1 October was to be regarded, so De Witt instructed Van Beuningen, only as a compliment to the Prince and was not to be seen as involving him either 'directly or indirectly' in Van Beuningen's negotiations – something which, as we have seen, William himself was in any case eager to avoid for his own reasons.[22]

King Charles sent two yachts to Holland under the command of Lord Ossory, the son and heir of the Duke of Ormond; like Arlington, Ossory too was married to one of Nassau-Beverweert's daughters: he acted as the Prince's guide during his stay in England and became a close friend. Whilst in Holland he met with De Witt and tried to persuade him that neither De Witt's own interests nor those of the Dutch State were incompatible with reinstating the Prince in the offices held by his father. The King of England would be put under an obligation and his amity would act as an 'anker' (sic) in the storm which was to be feared from the direction of France – arguments which left the Dutch statesman unimpressed.[23]

William, who before his departure had entertained De Witt and all the notable personages of the Republic to a sumptuous feast,[24] had taken care to assemble a large and imposing entourage, amounting to some 100 people, to accompany him on the journey in which the Nassau clan and its closest associates were well represented. They included – although they did not all travel together – Willem Albert von Donha, Otto van Limburg-Stirum, Hans Willem Bentinck, Beverweert's sons Nassau-Odijk and Nassau-Ouwerkerk – the brothers of Ossory's and Arlington's wives – his old governor Nassau-Zuylenstein and, to negotiate on the financial front, Constantijn Huygens.[25]

POMPONNE'S CHARACTER SKETCH
What was this young man like, embarking on this important mission to his English uncle? One character sketch that we have of him at the age of 19 – just before this time – is from Pomponne. Born with intelligence, his judgement was equal to his intelligence, says Pomponne, and he knew how to hide his feelings beneath a dissimulation which was natural to him. Except for hunting he had none of the enthusiasms natural to one of his age. He was extremely regular in his habits. His natural demeanour was judicious, pleasant and courteous. His application and intelligence were in advance of his years. He was well aware of his own interests and knew how to manage them with address. His inclination, or perhaps the state of his private affairs, appeared to predispose him a little too much to economy, although Pomponne admired the way he laboured to restore the finances of his house. He was a private and retiring personality, a little too withdrawn from the world, a handicap at the popular level. The love which the people at large had for him, and which caused them

never to call him anything other than 'Our Prince', needed to be cultivated with more of a common touch. His supporters regretted that this lack of communication worked against his interests whilst his opponents attributed it to pride in his English royal connections, a pride which he did not seem to have for his own country. Pomponne also remarked that more dealings with women, who, more than anywhere else in the world, had considerable influence with their husbands in Holland, would have been a great advantage and that, with many qualities beyond his years, one would have wished for him the enjoyment of company, parties and diversions usual with young people.[26]

Temple gave a very similar, but slightly earlier, picture in February 1668. The Prince, according to Temple, was 'something much better than he expected, and a young Man of more Parts than ordinary, and of the better sort, that is, not lying in that kind of Wit, which is neither of use to oneself, nor any body else, but in good plain Sense, which shows Application, if he had business that deserved it, and with extreme good and agreeable Humour and Dispositions; and thus far of his way without any vice; besides being sleepy always by Ten a Clock at Night, and loving Hunting as much as he hated Swearing and preferring Cock-Ale before any Wine ... and never any body raved so much after England, as well the language as all else that belonged to it.'[27]

THE PRINCE IN ENGLAND

Leaving Holland on 6 November, the Prince landed at Margate 36 hours later and travelled via Canterbury, Rochester and Gravesend to London; the last part of the journey was by States Yacht amidst the thunder of cannon and ceremonial salutes. At Whitehall he was received by the King with tears in his eyes and repeated kisses, and later on by the Queen and the Duke of York; and in the evening bonfires were lit. 'L'accueil qu'on luy a fait icy', Constantijn Huygens wrote from London on 10 December, 'est splendide et noble et, qui est bien plus, tres cordial'. But this was not entirely the case; the Duke and Duchess of York seemed somewhat more reserved and refused to give up their children's lodgings at St James's Palace, which had been originally prepared for him and which would have ceded him precedence over their offspring, so that he was housed at the Cockpit instead.[28]

His social activities were intense, so that he was more often than not out of his lodgings. He was entertained by the Lord Mayor, attended sessions of the House of Lords, and was sumptuously feasted by the French ambassador, Colbert de Croissy.[29] Croissy noted the great familiarity which had developed between Arlington and the Prince, who, Croissy said, daily took his meals at Arlington's house.[30] At his entertainment by the Lord Mayor the Prince's sober attire and his wearing his own hair contrasted with the exuberant luxury and powdered wigs of those who surrounded him; and, it was said, during his stay in England the ladies were much taken with him.

Hunting trips were specially arranged for him; one such was during his visit to Newmarket where he also inspected the King's racehorses.[31] This was followed, at the King's request, by an investiture at Cambridge, 'we desiring', the King wrote to the vice-chancellor of Cambridge, 'that in all places where he shall pass within this our Kingdom [the prince was] to be received with those regards that are due to his birth and quality, and to the near relation that he hath to our person, and that may express the particular affection and kindness we have for him.'

There came into Cambridge on 26 November, a contemporary recorded, 'the Prince of Orange … a well countenanced man, a smooth and smeeger face, and a handsome head of hayre of his owne, there were in all 3 coaches 6 horses a piece, the Prince was in the middlemost, and sat at the head end thereof … the Lord Ossory sat in the same end with him.' Degrees were conferred on William and on Bentinck, amongst others, but he could stay in Cambridge for only one day.[32]

At Oxford, on a dark winter's day, he arrived somewhere around five in the evening on 19 December; he was received by the vice-chancellor and others in their scarlet gowns and was then conducted between lines of scholars forming a guard with lighted torches to be welcomed by Dr Fell, the Dean of Christ Church, where he was to be accommodated in the Dean's lodgings. At eight the next morning an extensive tour of Oxford and its colleges, beginning with Oriel, was arranged for him, followed by morning prayers at Christ Church Cathedral. There he was seated next to Dr Henry Compton, who helped him with the Church of England service, with which he was of course unfamiliar, and who was to play crucial roles in William's life: he was to be charged with the spiritual upbringing of William's future wife, Mary, the daughter of James, Duke of York – he conducted their marriage service; and he was to be one of 'the immortal seven' leading figures who invited William to England in 1668, leading to the deposition from the throne of his father-in-law.

The party then proceeded to the Sheldonian Theatre, newly built by Wren, where convocation was to be held. When the door of the theatre opened the Prince appeared in the scarlet gown and hood and velvet cap of a Doctor of Law; Ossory was on his right and the Professor of law on his left; they were conducted 'by the beadles with their silver staves erected, and chains about their necks'; and music was played from the music gallery. Degrees were presented to the Prince and to members of his suite including Baron Opdam, Nassau-Ouwerkerk, and Bentinck again; and there followed two learned disputations, the first on the question 'are brutes mere machines', which received a negative verdict.

When the Prince departed the next morning at seven or eight his bearing, and especially his devotion, created a great impression.[33]

How did William get on with his uncle? According to Pomponne's account, although the Prince was at first received with every mark of friendship, the differences in temperament soon began to show, with the King outgoing and informal, devoted to pleasure, particularly where women were concerned, even to the point of debauchery, whilst the Prince was the contrary, by nature careful of his reputation, serious and reserved, removed from any appearance of vice, and only entering into the King's diversions in so far as good manners required. The Prince's restraint seemed to rebuke the King and appealed to the English. But that which moved the people even more was his assiduous fulfilment of his religious duties and the revelation of his great zeal for Protestantism. Hence the Prince departed from London, little regretted by the King, who had found his presence a constraint, but loved by the people.[34]

Pomponne indeed is not the only source that remarked upon the contrast between Charles's initial warm welcome for William and the subsequent change in his feelings at the end of his stay.[35]

It is conceivable that political as well as personal considerations played a role in this change of attitudes. On the eve of the Prince's visit Charles continued to toy very strongly with the idea of confiding to him the secrets of the Treaty of Dover, as he had all along wished to involve him in the project. Croissy reported to Louis XIV at the end of October that Charles had suggested to him that he should detain the Prince in England and dangle the bait of Dutch sovereignty before him: an alarmed Louis replied on 2 November warning of the imprudence of revealing a secret (the Dover Treaty) of this importance to someone so young, and whose true sentiments were furthermore still uncertain.[36] Charles concurred – or seemed to – and Croissy informed his master that whilst the King of England was 'much satisfied with the parts of the Prince of Orange', he 'finds him so passionate a Dutchman and protestant, that even although your Majesty had not disapproved of his trusting him with any part of the secret, these two reasons would have hindered him'.[37]

But did the King wholly resist the temptation of finding out what Prince William's possible reaction might be to what was envisaged for him by the Treaty of Dover, or, at least, of making some tentative soundings whilst he had him in England, where he was for almost four months? The Treaty left vague how the interests of the Prince were to be aligned with the war which Louis and Charles were planning. At the conclusion of a successful war, however, it was undoubtedly Charles's intention to continue with the policy which he had consistently pursued since his restoration, which was to regard the Prince as a very useful instrument to further the interests of the Stuart clan in the Dutch Republic.[38] One might anticipate a certain curiosity in Charles's mind as to whether this scion of the Stuart clan would, in the event, play the rather important part envisaged for him, and one may suspect that a few flies were cast over Prince William.

According to Burnet the King indeed 'tried the prince, as [the Prince] himself told me, in the point of religion … spoke of all the protestants as a factious body'; urged him 'not be led by his Dutch blockheads' in these religious matters; and he revealed his papist convictions. William, so says Burnet, 'amazed' at this politically extremely sensitive revelation, evermore judged the King's intentions in the light of this disclosure, and did not in the future expect 'any real assistance' from this quarter.[39]

However, in telling Burnet this, well after the event, we must not discount the fact that the Prince had a propaganda motive to present himself as the resolute Protestant champion, unalloyed by other considerations, who rejected his uncle's advances from the outset. There may be a kernel of truth in Burnet's account, which the Prince's slant has glossed over. As we shall see, he did not in fact act as if he did not expect 'any real assistance' from Charles. Suspicions arise that, on the occasions when uncle and nephew met and when the King was trying to size up his nephew, hints were dropped, which may well have fallen short of revealing the existence of the Dover Treaty and its full terms, but from which the Prince may have learnt rather more about the direction in which his uncle was travelling and of his uncle's plans for himself than historians have allowed – and furthermore that the Prince reacted in a rather more neutral fashion than he was prepared to reveal to Burnet.[40]

There was no need to repulse his uncle completely on the lines suggested in Burnet's account. He was still very uncertain of his position in the Dutch Republic and there was no utility in forgoing the potential support of the Stuart clan before he had to. King Charles himself acted throughout as if he had received no irretrievable rebuff from his nephew – on the contrary his plans continued to assume that his nephew would act as his client in the Netherlands. And William in fact had not foreclosed the option of working through the Stuart clan and his Stuart uncle to further his interests in the Dutch Republic.

To balance the observations on the Prince's character by both Pomponne and William Temple there is a well-known story, from the *Memoirs* of Sir John Reresby. On one occasion '…the King', Sir John records, 'made him drinke very hard one night at a supper given by the Duke of Buckingham. The Prince did not naturally love it, but being once entered was more frolick and merry than the rest of the company. Amongst other expressions of it he broake the windows of the maids of honour their chambers, and had gott into some of their apartments, had they not been timely rescued.'[41]

The court of Charles II certainly had an air to it of rather well-hung game, with his spaniels giving birth and suckling their pups in his bedchamber, making 'the whole court nasty and stinking', and with the King publicly 'sitting and toying with his concubines'.[42] William's conduct was undoubtedly more decorous, but the contrast which is often made between Charles's court and the Prince's standards is perhaps somewhat overstated and encapsulates rather more of the respectable mores of decorous Dutch professors in the earlier parts of the 20th century than aristocratic society in the Dutch Republic of the 17th.

And it may also very well be that in his public demeanour this very political young man may have deliberately exaggerated certain of his character traits, posing as the clean-living champion of Protestantism, from which, no doubt, it would be a short step to draw comparisons with the more dissolute lives of Louis XIV, the confirmed Catholic, and Charles II, enigmatic though he was, but with his suspected papist leanings. This, after a four months' sojourn, may well have been a cause for irritation, leaving Charles with the relief at the departure of his nephew on which contemporaries remarked.

There were two close relations of the Prince who did not view his visit with great warmth. The King compelled his cousin, Prince Rupert, to cede precedence to William, who was closer in the royal blood line, which caused the huffy departure of Rupert from the court; and the Duke of York, whose initial reaction when the Prince first arrived we have already noted, was observed to be most of the time in a dark mood.[43]

The visit was rounded off by William's receiving the Order of the Garter and by his taking a parade in Hyde Park.[44] When he departed from England on 23 February 1671 Constantijn Huygens was left behind to continue the negotiations regarding the Stuart debt. He was successful only in achieving the repayment of the dowry of William's mother, the Princess Royal, amounting to £40,000 in March 1672 – but not without, to the great indignation of the Prince, the deduction of £325 for fees payable to officers of the English exchequer.[45]

One important consequence of the Prince's lengthy visit was the knowledge that he, and many of his entourage, acquired of the country. It was not long before this knowledge was to be put to use to create support in England which could, at need, be used to assert pressure on the senior branch of the Stuart clan to move in the direction which the head of the junior clan desired.

When he returned to the Dutch Republic the plans of Louis XIV and his ally, the King of England, for its destruction had been delayed because Louis's negotiations with the German princes were taking longer than anticipated, but they had by no means been abandoned. The revised, sham, treaty to replace that of Dover which Buckingham had negotiated and which was signed on 31 December 1670 at Whitehall – just after the Prince of Orange left Oxford – now fixed the joint declarations of war by the two kings for the end of April, or at the latest, the beginning of May 1672.[46] For some time the French King's military preparations had been as increasingly manifest as they were threatening.

THE DUTCH PREPARE FOR WAR

'The firm conviction that there will be a war with your majesty next year is not disguised here', wrote Pomponne from The Hague to his master on 23 October 1670, and Dutch preparations both diplomatic and military began to be made to counter the threat from France. As we have seen De Witt was informed by the Dutch embassy in Paris of the full import of the Treaty of Dover by the end of February 1671.

The old veteran Hieronymus van Beverninck was, despite his reluctance, despatched to Madrid in December, arriving there at the end of February 1671, to seek a Spanish alliance. 'He is indisputably one of the most able members of the government', said Pomponne, although – referring to Van Beverninck's well-known love of wine – it was true that his performance varied during the day, and that once he had had his dinner the culmination of his sobriety tended to be followed as well by the culmination of the talent and capacity he displayed until then.[47] By the time he returned to the Republic in September 1671 the ground had been prepared for a treaty of mutual assistance between the Republic and Spain, which fell short of a full defensive treaty, but under which both sides undertook to provide auxiliaries to the other if attacked by France. Signed in December 1671, it was ratified in February 1672[48] and it exploited the loophole provided by Article 3 of the Treaty of the Pyrenees between France and Spain which allowed the despatch of auxiliary troops to friendly states.[49]

De Witt also sought ways to strengthen the Dutch military both on land and at sea. But for that large sums of money were required and he ran into difficulties from Amsterdam, which was not prepared to provide funds until she had received satisfaction on some outstanding fiscal grievances.[50] Amsterdam came to terms by the end of 1670 and in the Town Council elections in February 1671 Valckenier and his supporters – as well as Coenraad van Beuningen – were decisively beaten, which removed a thorn in De Witt's side; although the Council was by no means subordinate to De Witt and retained a large degree of independence of mind.[51]

But Zeeland, too, under the leadership of Nassau-Odijk, was refusing to cooperate. According to Wicquefort he wanted the command of a regiment for his brother, but, as the rearmament plans put a greater emphasis on the navy, there was no regiment for his brother to command. He therefore rejected the proposed military budget and claimed that he had the support of the Prince of Orange.[52]

That, however, proved not to be the case. When he arrived in The Hague on 28 February on his return from England – he had fleetingly passed through Zeeland on his way – William told De Witt that he had sent an urgent messenger telling Nassau-Odijk to desist.[53] Amalia von Solms, indeed, crisply described William's cousin as a 'muddlehead' capable of ruining his affairs.[54] She would have been very well aware that the expansion of the country's armed forces was in the interests of the House of Orange, especially if it resulted in the Prince's elevation as Captain and Admiral-General, but even without that, because the land forces were a natural constituency for Orangist support.

There is an undated letter from William to Ossory – in French – in which he reports that the talk in the Dutch Republic was about nothing but the war and the great preparations which 'the king of France is making to attack us. I hope that [Charles II] will not abandon us and that he will keep to the treaties which he has with the States. It is in his interest as well not to let us lose. I hope that my lord Arlington will also contribute all that he can to this effect.' He adds at the end of the letter, 'Have the goodness to give this letter to the Duke', that is, the Duke of York. The letter was intended therefore as a message to his Stuart uncles, with William hoping that Arlington would reinforce his case.

Japikse surmises from the content that the letter dates from not long after his return from England and places it in the summer of 1671, although it could be earlier. It shows that William hoped he could still persuade his uncle to adhere to his Dutch commitments; thus he was not definitely aware, whatever his suspicions might be, that Charles was already firmly committed to Louis under the Treaty of Dover of which, obviously also, he had no exact knowledge. Of course, too, if he could demonstrate the use of his connections with the Stuart clan to persuade it to act in the interests of the Republic his own influence there would be enhanced – he would be seen as the patron brokering a deal on behalf of his clients, in a manner, moreover, of which De Witt was not capable.[55]

William, who seems to have been quite ill with a swelling in the neck in April, made a journey, accompanied by Opdam and Nassau-Ouwerkerk, to Brunswick in June to see what military lessons he could draw from the siege of that city, which was in open revolt against its Duke – although, in the event, he arrived after the capitulation took place. He went on to Berlin where he visited and would have been able to assess, and be assessed by, his uncle, the wily, pragmatic, yet also staunchly Calvinist Elector of Brandenburg, known as the Great Elector, who, until his death in 1688, was to play an important role in William's diplomatic calculations for so many years. At this time he was having to decide whether he should support the Dutch or the French or remain neutral in the war which was threatening between these powers. Now 52 years old and a veteran of the Thirty Years' War, the Elector had lived in the Dutch Republic between the ages of 14 and 18, had attended Leyden university and was profoundly influenced by all things Dutch – although Dutch troops garrisoning fortresses in his Duchy of Cleves were a bone of contention. His marriage to William's aunt, Louise Henrietta, had ended with her death in 1667. Alas, we know nothing of the details of William's visit or what was discussed; but, like the Stuart connection, it was a hint of the ability of the House of Orange to act as a power broker on behalf of the Dutch Regents, particularly at the present time when they were coming under manifest threat. William was back in The Hague by the end of July.[56]

In the Republic his clientele in the Provinces was proving its worth. In Utrecht there was the Van Reede clan, an influential section of the Province's nobility. Jonkheer Frederick van Reede had been a page in his household from 1654 and became his Master of Horse from 1659 to 1666. Whilst he was still in England he wrote thanking Godard Adriaan van Reede, Lord of Amerongen, for his efforts in persuading the Province to support his being paid 50,000 guilders (£5,000) per annum as a member of the Council of State.[57] Amerongen increasingly used his weight in the Province of Utrecht on the Prince's behalf. When he was dispatched on diplomatic missions he made a point of keeping William informed, as he did when he was dealing with the Bishop of Münster and other German princes including the Great Elector,[58] thus extending the Prince's knowledge of affairs in the German Empire.

THE PRINCE APPOINTED CAPTAIN-GENERAL

Then, in May, the Province of Gelderland, where William paid a visit to Arnhem to organise support, proposed that he should be appointed Captain-General. Holland appealed to the Harmony, which envisaged such an appointment only in the Prince's 23rd year. But on 4 December a town in Holland itself, Enkhuizen, put the same proposal to the Holland States and, despite De Witt's strong opposition, on the grounds that under the Harmony it would be illegal, Amsterdam came out in support on 16 December.[59] William sought the intervention of Amerongen to gain the support of Utrecht in the matter.[60]

Negotiations began on the exact terms on which the appointment should be made, which lasted until the end of February 1672. The States of Holland proposed that the appointment should be for one campaign only, and after some hesitation, the Prince refused to accept the post on these terms. Negotiating by means of Hieronymus van Beverninck, who had returned to the Netherlands from his English embassy, and Fagel, De Witt eventually agreed that the appointment should be for a single campaign only, but that once William was in his 23rd year, which would be in November 1672, the appointment would be for life – the Grand Pensionary thus in effect conceded the point.

But all the same the Prince's authority remained extremely limited; he still could not hold the Stadholdership of any Province conjointly with his military posts – and he would have to swear to this; his responsibility was confined to giving effect to the decisions of the Field Deputies from the States-General who accompanied the army; and he was subject to the very cumbersome restriction that he could not move troops without the consent of these Deputies, who themselves could only act on the advice of the Council of State and with the approval of the Province or town which had financed and had primary authority for the recruitment of the relevant troops – a measure designed to prevent the recurrence of his father Willem II's coup against Amsterdam in 1650. On 25 February 1672 the States-General appointed him as Captain – and Admiral-General – with a remuneration of 48,000 guilders (£4,800) a year.[61]

There was huge popular rejoicing. The Hague was crowded with people from neighbouring towns; all night long there were volleys of musket fire; bonfires were lit by crowds of youths, who, amidst the beating of drums, cried 'viva Orange'; and the soldiers charged with maintaining order gave up the attempt lest they set off a riot. Women processed through the town, beating drums slung from their necks, and all was illuminated by hundreds of flares, torches and candles.[62]

The Prince of Orange himself resorted to conspicuous display to mark this further step in his elevation and he held a magnificent feast at great expense for the Holland States in their meeting hall, which lasted from three o'clock in the afternoon until one in the morning, with out-of-season delicacies, such as asparagus in the midst of winter, and with a splendid exhibit of preserved fruits.[63] And when Constantijn Huygens seized the moment to present his congratulations a smiling Prince thanked him by appointing his son, also called Constantijn, as his secretary, thus adding another member of this family to the long list who acted as servitors to the House of Orange.[64]

COMMUNICATIONS WITH CHARLES II

In the midst of the negotiations leading up the military appointments the Prince continued to leave open his options with his Stuart clan – this despite obvious signs on all sides that relations between the Dutch Republic and the King of England had seriously deteriorated.

William Temple, who had done so much to promote the Triple Alliance and had thus incurred the hostility of the French, was, as a gesture to France following the Treaty of Dover, recalled to England at the end of September 1670. At the same time, however, Charles II was trying to obtain subsidies from Parliament, ostensibly to bolster the Triple Alliance. He did not therefore wish to give credence to suspicions that Temple's recall signalled the change of policy which had in fact taken place. For that reason Temple nominally remained as ambassador to the United Provinces and he was told to leave his wife behind.[65]

Upon Parliament's prorogation on 22 April 1671 the need to preserve the façade of Temple's embassy receded and, furthermore, Charles was now ready to build up grievances with the Dutch to prepare the way for open hostilities. Temple's embassy was formally ended in June 1671.[66] The King's yacht, the *Merlin*, was sent to bring Lady Temple back to England, which gave occasion to foster the first of the King of England's grievances: when the *Merlin* sailed through the Dutch fleet on its return journey and when the Dutch refused to lower their top-sails in salute, its captain, in accordance with his instructions, opened fire. At the same time issues relating to the East Indies and Surinam were raised and the quarrelsome Downing was once more nominated to go to The Hague to replace the emollient Temple as Ambassador – he arrived in The Hague in January 1672.[67]

Reacting to the news of Temple's recall, William wrote to Arlington, Charles II's most influential minister, on 24 July 1671 expressing his fears that the recall was a bad sign, which may be read as a further attempt, on the same lines as his letter to Ossory, to dissuade the King from breaking with the Triple Alliance with which Temple was so intimately, even symbolically, associated.[68] But an even more significant message to the King was conveyed by the Prince shortly after 19 January 1672.

When he left England Charles had invited him, if there was anything of consequence which he wished to raise, to do so through the medium of Arlington. As it happened that long-term servitor of the Stuarts, Sir Gabriel Sylvius, was at present on his way through The Hague, returning from a diplomatic mission to the Great Elector; and Prince William decided to make use of him to communicate with the King. The message Sylvius was to convey reads as follows:

Unless His Majesty be too closely bound to France, he may never find a better opportunity for obtaining from the States whatever he wish, and should His Majesty be willing to let me know his desires, I am confident that, so long as they are not directly hostile to the foundations of this Republic, I shall be able to obtain them for him in spite of Mr Grand Pensionary De Witt and his cabal, who will thereby be worsted, while I and my friends, in whom His Majesty can place his trust, will be placed at the helm; once his Majesty has had his wish, he will moreover, be able to count on this state for all time. I have no doubt that His Majesty will believe that so long as I have any authority in this state, I shall be utterly devoted to His Majesty's interests, in so far as my honour and the faith which I owe to this country can allow me, being well assured that His Majesty would not wish it otherwise – Sylvius will also explain to His Majesty that no member of the government has any knowledge of this matter, and that I pray H.M. to keep it secret; I assure H.M. that I shall deal cautiously with his reply, whatever it may be, and that, in all this, I have no other aim than the interests of His Majesty.[69]

The Prince wrote covering letters to both the King himself and to Arlington saying that Sylvius would be speaking to them on his behalf.[70] We may note the suspicion that Charles had done a deal with Louis XIV ('Unless His Majesty be too closely bound to France...') but not the certainty.

The message is heavily qualified – 'so long as they [Charles's desires] are not directly hostile to the foundations of this Republic', and he is devoted to Charles's interests 'in so far as my honour and the faith which I owe this country can allow me'. These qualifications absolve the Prince from betraying his duty to his country even if the message is read through the spectrum of modern notions of patriotism or nationalism; but these have modern connotations, which did not exist in William's time, and we should instead read the message through the spectrum of 17th-century notions of identity. As the patron of the inhabitants of 'this country' his loyalties to them, his clients, could be taken as read – 'His Majesty would not wish it otherwise'. But that did not preclude him from also identifying himself with, and acknowledging, other loyalties, such as those to the Stuart clan and those which arose from the patron/client relationship he had with the head of that clan. It might be difficult to reconcile these different loyalties but – as yet – William obviously thought he could. Furthermore, he thought the clan relationship could also be turned to his own advantage: 'I and my friends, in whom His Majesty can place his trust, will be placed at the helm.'

Putting the Prince at the helm, with obligations to himself, was in fact exactly what Charles himself had in mind, although he thought that could only be achieved in cooperation with Louis XIV, and not through William alone. He replied to him on 26 February, 'I have made no haste to answer what you commanded Sylvius to say to me, because I am farr from beleeving you could effect what you should undertake....'[71]

ENGLISH AND FRENCH DECLARATIONS OF WAR

Charles was in any case too far on the road to join Louis in their war to be able to turn back. On 12 January he had resorted to the 'stop of the exchequer' – which suspended payments of the government's debts – as a means of financing the impending Dutch war. To the British public it was justified on the grounds that, as other European powers were preparing for war, the safety of the realm demanded from the King 'appropriate preparations of his own'.[72] On 3 February, in the midst of negotiations on the points of contention between Britain and the Dutch, in which the issue of maritime sovereignty and saluting the flag was being given particular emphasis, Downing informed De Witt of his recall – a gesture which, in De Witt's view, was 'tantamount to a declaration of War'.[73]

In a curious repeat of the opening of the Second Dutch War, the homeward-bound Dutch Smyrna fleet was attacked on 3 March, without a declaration of war, by Sir Robert Holmes off the Isle of Wight – with the same ignominious lack of success.[74] Charles did not declare his Catholicism but on 25 March he issued a declaration of indulgence suspending the penal laws against Protestant dissenters and Catholics alike.[75] And his declaration of war, dated 28 March, was published on the 29th. The French Ambassador to England, Colbert de Croissy, observed that it was greeted, both at court and at large in London, with more criticism than praise.[76]

In France Louis's elaborate preparations were finally in place. He too declared war, on 6 April. He announced that he could not, without detriment to his *gloire*, any longer dissimulate his indignation at the conduct of the Dutch which was so little in conformity with the great obligations which they owed him and the kings his predecessors.[77] The client Republic, in short, had bitten the hand of its patron, an affront which could not be tolerated without a weakening of the King's prestige and his *gloire*, and hence an important component of his power base. Four years of diplomatic manoeuvring and military preparation had elapsed since De Witt had entered into the Triple Alliance in January 1668 to check his ambitions in the Spanish Netherlands. That affront would now be avenged; and at the same time the defeat and, if possible, the annihilation of the Dutch Republic would provide him with the ultimate means of achieving his ambitions in the Spanish Provinces as well.[78]

1 Haley, *op. cit.*, p.261. Geyl, *op. cit.*, p.320. *Correspondentie Willem III en Bentinck, op. cit.*, II, Pt 1, pp.21–2. *Arlington's Letters, op. cit.*, I, p.430.

2 B.J. Vreeze, *De Raad van den Prinsen van Oranje tijdens de minderjaarigheid van Willem III 1650–1668*, Assen, 1932, p.78, which also mentions the Spanish debt.

3 Huygens, *Briefwisseling, op. cit.*, VI, Introduction p.x.

4 *Arlington's Letters, op. cit.*, I, p.364.

5 See C.D. Chandaman, *The English Public Revenue 1660–1688*, Oxford, 1975, pp.200, 207.

6 Courtenay, *op. cit.*, *Memoirs*, II, pp.394–5, I, p.281.

7 Mignet, *op. cit.*, III, pp.614–15. Pomponne, *Relation de mon Ambassade en Holland*, ed. H.H. Rowen, Utrecht, 1955. Issued by Hist. Genootschap gevestigd te Utrecht, Werken, 4th series, no.2, III, p.134.

8 *Ibid.*, pp.149–50. Although Pomponne was writing many years after the event he was one of the most astute diplomatic minds of his time and from his vantage point as ambassador in the Netherlands and subsequently as Louis's Foreign Minister he had access to information which few could rival. The Duke of York had two other children apart from Mary and Anne at this time, although they did not live for long.

9 *Correspondentie, Willem III en Bentinck*, II, Pt 1, pp.25–32. For Rumpf's medical care of the new-born Prince see De Witt, *Huberts, op. cit.*, p.11.

10 Geyl, *op. cit.*, p.403, n.57. Wicquefort, *Histoire, op. cit.*, IV, p.121. Rowen, *The Ambassador Prepares for War*, Martinus Nijhof, The Hague, 1957, p.57, n.2. Rowen notes the lack of any mention of such a meeting between Pomponne and the Prince, or of the hint of the encouragement given to the Prince, in either a despatch Pomponne sent on 10 April or any other in the Quay D'Orsay archives, which 'makes the whole story almost certainly untrue', and he suggests that the newsletter had perhaps picked up a rumour. It is furthermore true that in a despatch to Louis on 1 May 1670 Pomponne says that neither the Prince nor De Witt discussed their interests with him because they perhaps thought that they would render themselves suspect if they addressed themselves to France – although, of course, that would not preclude Pomponne himself from conveying to them what he wanted to convey if he were so instructed by Paris. The lack of corroboration in the Quay D'Orsay archives suggests that he was not so instructed and did not so act, although it is not conclusive.

11 See Fruin, *op. cit.*, IV, p.354n.

12 Rumpf to De Witt, 21 March 1670. H.A. van Dijk, *Bydrage tot the Geschiedenis der Nederlandsche Diplomatie*, Utrecht, 1851, p.73n.

13 Rumpf to Griffier Ruysch, 11 April 1670, Van Dijk, *op. cit.*, p.73.

14 Rowen, *De Witt, op. cit.*, p.732.

15 *Ibid.*, p.734. *Brieven van De Witt, op. cit.*, IV, pp.59, 81.

16 *Brieven van De Witt, op. cit.*, IV, pp.86, 90. *Brieven aan De Witt, op. cit.*, II, pp.481, 542–3. The evidence that warnings from the Dutch Embassy in Paris continued to come in during the winter is witnessed by a letter from De Groot to Wicquefort dated 21 November 1671 in which he stated that Charles II was the origin of all the mischief that existed in France regarding the Dutch Republic, 'having left the party of the States-General as early as the previous winter', and that without that the French would never have dared to contemplate their designs. It was 'not the work of now or yesterday but an engagement entered into during the previous winter'. He said he had warned De Witt, to whom he could write in cypher, at that time of Charles II's betrayal. The letter is missing from De Witt's papers, although the despatch at the end of February supports De Groot's assertion. Van Dijk, *op. cit.*, pp.104, 230.

17 See Japikse, *Willem III, op. cit.*, I, p.161.

18 Robert Fruin thinks the Prince must have had these suspicions, *op. cit.*, V, p.20.

19 Huygens, *Briefwisseling, op. cit.*, VI, Introduction p.xvii, J.H. Kernkamp, *De Reis van Prins Willem III Naar Engeland in het jaar 1670 in Koninklijke Bibliotheek Gedenkbook 1798–1948*, The Hague, 1948, p.190.

20 *Arlington's Letters, op. cit.*, I, p.433.

21 *Briefwisseling tusschen de Gebroeders (Willem, Martinus, Adriaen) van der Goes, 1659–1673*, C.J. Gonnet, 1899, 1909, II, p.159.

22 *Brieven van De Witt, op. cit.*, XIV, pp.92–3.

23 Wicquefort, *Histoire, op. cit.*, IV, p.123.

24 Rowen, *De Witt, op. cit.*, p.804.

25 Fruin, *op. cit.*, V, p.20. Geyl, *op. cit.*, p.322 and notes. Kernkamp, *op. cit.*, p.190.

26 Pomponne, *Relation, op. cit.*, pp.55–6.

27 *Courtenay Memoirs, op. cit.*, I, pp.285–6.

28 Kernkamp, *op. cit.*, pp.190–1. Huygens, *Briefwisseling, op. cit.*, VI, p.273.

29 Kernkamp, *op. cit.*, p.191. Japikse, *Willem III, op. cit.*, I, p.167. *Calendar of State Papers, Domestic 1670*, ed. Everett Green, 1895, p.531.

30 Violet Barbour, *Henry Bennet Earl of Arlington, Secretary of State to Charles II*, Oxford University Press, 1914, p.171n.

31 Kernkamp, *op. cit.*, pp.192–3.

32 Marion Grew, *William Bentinck and William III, Prince of Orange: The Life of Bentinck, Earl of Portland from the Welbeck Correspondence*, London, 1924, pp.18–20.

33 *Calendar of State Papers, op. cit.*, pp.589–90. Anthony Wood, *Athenaexonienses. Fasti*, London, 1820, IV, p.323. Grew, *Bentinck, op. cit.*, pp.21–3. The above account is an amalgam from all three sources.

34 Pomponne, *op. cit.*, pp.149–50.

35 See Wout Troost, *William III, op. cit.*, pp.63–4.

36 Croissy, letter to Louis XIV, 23 October 1670, quoted in Sir John Dalrymple, *Memoirs of Great Britain and Ireland*, London, 1790, I, p.121. Mignet, *op. cit.*, III, p.616. Louis replied on 2 November 1670.

37 Croissy, letter to Louis XIV, 4 December. Dalrymple, *op. cit.*, I, p.122.

38 It is difficult to credit the account of Wicquefort, who was in no doubt that Charles II tried to persuade Prince William that his only hope in the Dutch Republic was a revolution in the country, which could only be expected from the war that France was planning, and which would destroy the enemies opposed to his advancement. According to Wicquefort, the Prince resisted these blandishments either because he was expecting support from Amsterdam (which, of course, would obviate the need for external assistance) or because he was dissimulating. Wicquefort, *Histoire, op. cit.*, IV, p.125. But Wicquefort does not quote his sources, there is no corroborating evidence that the King did hold such an explicit conversation, and Wicquefort gives no motive for the Prince's dissimulation. In the absence of such evidence the most that can be said is that the Prince could obtain hints of what Charles and Louis were planning but nothing definite.

39 Burnet, *Burnet's History of my Own Time*, Clarendon Press, 1897, Part I, p.495.

40 See, for example, Japikse, *Willem III, op. cit.*, I, pp.168–9; Baxter, *op. cit.*, p.56.

41 Sir John Reresby, *Memoirs*, Royal Historical Society, 1991, p.82. The story is not wholly accurate as it depicts William coming to England 'to pretend to the Lady Mary', which is not true at this time, and is dated 1671, whilst the Prince's departure from England in February occurred before 1671 began in the old English calendar. Ronald Hutton thinks 'the story very doubtful. The incident is not recorded anywhere else, including the copious contemporary newsletters. Reresby was a Tory and supporter of James II, and he is wrong in other details of his account of Wilhelm's visit', *op. cit.*, p.510, n.88. There is however a curious echo in Pomponne's character sketch (paraphrased in English on page 144) when he says the Prince 'n'entroit dans les divertissements du roy, son oncle, qu'autant que la seule complaisance l'y obligeoit', which we can compare with the quote from Reresby.

42 *The Diary of John Evelyn*, ed. Guy de la Bédoyère, The Boydell Press, 1995 repr. 2002, pp.275–6.

43 Wicquefort, *Histoire, op. cit.*, IV, p.122.

44 Kernkamp, *op. cit.*, p.195.

45 Huygens, *Briefwisseling, op. cit.*, VI, pp.xvii, 302.

46 Louis to Croissy, 7 October 1670, article 6 of the treaty. Mignet, *op. cit.*, III, pp.233, 260.

47 *Ibid.*, pp.625–7, 638. Geyl, *op. cit.*, p.320.

48 Mignet, *op. cit.*, III, pp.663, 664, 690.

49 F.J.L. Krämer, *De Nederlandsche–Spaansche diplomatie voor de vrede van Nijmegen*, Utrecht, 1892, p.64.

50 De Witt to van Beuningen, 3 October 1670, *Brieven van De Witt, op. cit.*, IV, pp.90–91.

51 Geyl, *op. cit.*, pp.325–6. Rowen, *De Witt, op. cit.*, p.801.

52 Wicquefort, *Histoire, op. cit.*, IV, pp.288–9.

53 *Brieven van De Witt, op. cit.*, IV, p.160.

54 Wicquefort, *Histoire, op. cit.*, IV, p.259.

55 Geyl states, *inter alia* on the evidence of the letter, that 'in the conflict between England and the republic, he took his stand firmly on the Dutch side'. But that is to see matters somewhat too much in 20th-century nationalistic terms. William would not lightly have abandoned the Stuart clan, as Geyl suggests; nor did he: Geyl, *op. cit.*, pp.326–7. Letter to Ossory is in *Correspondentie Willem III en Bentinck, op. cit.*, II, Pt 1, pp.37–8.

56 *Briefwisseling, van der Goes*, II, pp.201, 206–7. Japikse, *Willem III, op. cit.*, I, p.171. D. McKay, *op. cit.*, pp.12–13, 36, 209–10.

57 *Correspondentie Willem III en Bentinck, op. cit.*, II, Pt 1, p.34. E. Mijers and D. Onnekink, *Redefining William III*, Ashgate, 2007, p.238.

58 See pp.35–8, *Correspondentie Willem III en Bentinck*, II, Pt 1.

59 Geyl, *op. cit.*, pp.327–9.

60 *Correspondentie Willem III en Bentinck*, II, Pt 1, p.38.

61 Geyl, *op. cit.*, pp.332–3, 336. Rowen, *De Witt, op. cit.*, pp.806–8. Troost, *op. cit.*, p.67. *Brieven van De Witt, op. cit.*, V, pp.256–8. Ten Raa & de Bas, Breda, 1911. *Het Staatsche Leger 1568–1795*, V, pp.29, 289–90.

62 Goes, *Briefwisseling, op. cit.*, II, pp.352–6.

63 *Ibid.*, p.356. Rowen, *De Witt, op. cit.*, p.809.

64 Huygens, *Briefwisseling, op. cit.*, p.301.

65 Haley, *An English Diplomat, op. cit.*, pp.272, 274, 275.

66 Haley, *An English Diplomat, op. cit.*, p.280; Hutton, *op. cit.*, pp.277, 282. The prorogation arose from a deadlock between the Lords and the Commons regarding a money bill on import duties with the Lords reducing imposts on sugar. Haley suggests that the reason for the prorogation was that the bill also contained duties on French brandy and other goods which would have embarrassed Charles *vis-à-vis* Louis (Hutton, *op. cit.*, p.279). Hutton rejects this and leans towards the view that the king was attempting to 'chasten the Houses and to dispose them to a reconciliation' (*ibid.*, p.277).

67 Haley, *An English Diplomat, op. cit.*, pp.282–3. Hutton, *op. cit.*, p.282. *Correspondentie, Willem III en Bentinck, op. cit.*, II, 1, n.2, p.40.

68 Haley, *An English Diplomat, op. cit.*, p.281.

69 The French original is in *Correspondentie, Willem III en Bentinck*, II, 1 Pt, p.41. I have made use of Geyl's English translation. *Op. cit.*, pp.333–4. The instructions are undated but Geyl plausibly puts the date as shortly after 19 January, n.108, p.406.

70 *Correspondentie, Willem III en Bentinck, op. cit.*, II, Pt 1, pp.40–1.

71 *Ibid.*, p.43.

72 Quoted in Haley, *An English Diplomat, op. cit.*, pp.286–7. See also Hutton, *op. cit.*, p.284.

73 Mignet, *op. cit.*, III, p.695. *Brieven van De Witt, op. cit.*, IV, p.273.

74 Mignet, *op. cit.*, III, p.702.

75 Hutton, *op. cit.*, p.284.

76 Mignet, *op. cit.*, III, pp.702–3. The decision to declare war was taken by the King in Council on 27 March and conveyed to the Dutch ambassadors that evening.

77 *Ibid.*, p.710.

78 *Ibid.*, p.665.

Louis XIV, c. 1670, after Claude Lefèbvre. Palace of Versailles

8 1672: LOUIS XIV'S DUTCH WAR

PRELIMINARIES

Louis XIV's war strategy was as ambitious as his preparatory diplomacy. The military plan was to envelop the Dutch Republic in a vast pincer movement, with a combined operation of the French army attacking down the Rhine from the east, with auxiliary support from the Bishops of Münster and Cologne, and a joint Anglo-French fleet attacking from the sea in the west, if possible landing an army on the Dutch coast.

The Dutch fleet was indeed a formidable force; but it would be outnumbered if the English and French fleets could combine. It was commanded by the redoubtable Admiral De Ruyter, and De Witt's brother, Cornelis, was attached to it as a Deputy from the States-General, a role which he had performed in the successful Second Dutch War. On 9 May 1672 the fleet managed to put to sea: but Zeeland, fearful of facing the enemy by itself, delayed joining De Ruyter until it had news of the departure of the main fleet; and this delay enabled the English and French fleets to join off the Isle of Wight on the 16th, which consequently outnumbered and outgunned the Dutch.[1]

Nevertheless Cornelis De Witt, judging it appropriate to take advantage of a favourable north-easterly wind 'to serve our dear fatherland', with the support of De Ruyter decided to fight a battle.[2] The Dutch fleet consisted of 61 large warships and 14 frigates, with further auxiliaries – a total of 4,484 guns and 20,738 men. They caught the allies on a lee shore at Sole Bay, off Southwold, where the allied fleet consisted of 87 warships and frigates, which, with auxiliaries, amounted in all to 5,100 guns and 33,000 men.[3] Commanding the *Victory* in the English fleet was the Prince of Orange's close friend and relation by marriage, the Earl of Ossory, who had looked after him so diligently during his visit to England.[4] A fierce and bloody battle ensued on 7 June during which William's uncle, the Duke of York, who was in overall command, had to abandon his flagship. Of Cornelis's bodyguard of 12 halberdiers who surrounded him on deck or who were stationed above the hut of the ship's helmsman, three were killed, one had his legs shot from under him and one or two were expected to die from their wounds. Although no decisive result followed, the battered fleets made for their respective coasts to repair their considerable damage. Some time after the battle the drowned body of the English Vice-Admiral, the Earl of Sandwich, was found floating in the water with the star of the Order of the Garter glinting on his chest.[5]

Cornelis De Witt had to return to land at the end of June because of illness, whilst on the 24th the States-General resolved to reduce the size of the fleet and to divert most of its soldiers and marines to strengthen the land defences, facing a French onslaught that had swept all before it.[6] In De Ruyter's view the Dutch fleet, thus reduced in strength, was in no position to venture out to challenge the combined Anglo-French fleets, and he took up a defensive station on the Dutch coast.[7] On 13 July, the Anglo-French fleet appeared off Den Helder and again five days later. But, although they had a formidable army on board, they attempted no landing on the practically undefended shore, before being driven off by fierce storms.[8] Meanwhile the richly laden Dutch East India fleet, which normally returned to the Republic once a year, had anchored off Delfzijl, on the mouth of the River Ems on the north-east frontier of the Republic, on 3 August. It was worth 14 million guilders (£1.4 million) and would have done much to ease Charles II's financial difficulties. There was nothing for it but for De Ruyter, leaving the Dutch coast exposed to invasion and risking defeat if his depleted force should encounter the Anglo-French fleet, to venture out; this he did and escorted the precious cargoes safely back to the homeland.[9] In September both the Dutch and the allied fleets were laid up for the winter.[10] The threat from the sea had been contained – for this year at least.

Far different were the fortunes of war on land. On 28 April Louis XIV left St-Germain and reached the camp of the first of his two armies at Charleroi on 5 May.

The need to manage his generals was a constant preoccupation for Louis and, behind the façade of the Absolute Monarch, he was required to exercise considerable political skill. He used as his intermediary his 31-year-old Minister of War, Louvois, of modest 'robe' background, but created a marquis. He was the son of another of Louis's ministers, Le Tellier, who had preceded his son in building what was in effect a new French model army. The young minister, with his *arriviste* background, did not hesitate to underline, when he wrote his somewhat imperious orders to the lofty aristocratic personalities in the field, that he was doing so under the instructions of the King: but, at the same time, should there be need for the King to give ground to his generals, the use of Louvois as a front reduced, or eliminated, any loss of regal authority. Both Condé and Turenne were too established in their fame, in their military abilities and in their birth always to comply with Louvois's demands when they thought them too contrary to their professional judgement. But Condé was more supple in his responses, accommodated himself to the need to preserve appearances, and took the trouble to explain his decisions in some detail in an attempt to persuade and to reach agreement. Turenne was of a different cut; being responsible he thought he should decide, without the distraction of explaining, and he was as much engaged in his struggles with Louvois as he was with the enemy commanders arrayed against him. He had one further opponent to dispute his views: that opponent was Condé.

Louis's army was initially divided into two. The part that assembled at Charleroi was under the nominal command of the King himself but under the effective command of Turenne, who, as we have seen, was connected to the House of Orange, being the great-grandson of William the Silent, and who had learnt his military craft under Frederick-Henry. Not until 1668 had he abandoned his family's traditional Protestantism for the Catholic faith. The other part of the army was mustered at Sédan under Condé. His military prowess had earned him the title of *le grand Condé* and, as head of the cadet branch of the Bourbon family, he was referred to as 'Monsieur le Prince'. He had had grave misgivings about the whole plan of campaign, which he had expressed in a prescient memorandum of November 1671; in this he had pointed out the great military difficulties the Dutch terrain presented, with its combination of the sea, the marshes and the great rivers, and the vulnerability to which the French armies would be exposed as a result of the logistical difficulties of supply so far from Louis's own territories. A modern historian has indeed surmised that he may have revealed the substance of the Anglo-French invasion strategy to the Dutch ambassador in Paris, Pieter De Groot, as early as February 1671. These two pre-eminent generals of the age, who during the Frondes at different times had fought both the royal government and each other, now combined to seek greater *gloire* for the King they now served, and for themselves. [11]

Louvois, able, unscrupulous and ruthless, had made every preparation to meet the colossal logistical challenges of supplying the King's forces; strategically placed magazines gave the new French army unprecedented logistical reach and every detail had been foreseen, down to providing equipment to build three bridges to cross the rivers, each bridge consisting of 100 boats stretched across on a pontoon system.[12] Like the Dutch army, the French army was recruited across Europe, and the English and Scottish regiments stood ready to confront the Scottish element in the Dutch army, which also contained regiments from France.[13] Amongst the officers in the 'Royal English' regiment in the French army were Charles's illegitimate son, the Duke of Monmouth; Thomas Armstrong, who was to become a close associate of Monmouth; and Sidney Godolphin.[14]

THE FRENCH INVASION

The two French armies joined at Viset, between Liège and Maastricht, and the huge army of perhaps 148,000 men advanced on the massive fortress of Maastricht. There the Bishop of Cologne, in his capacity as Bishop of Liège, exerted joint sovereignty *de jure* with the Dutch who, having a substantial garrison there, were in *de facto* possession. Condé was in favour of besieging Maastricht, but was opposed by Turenne, whose opinion prevailed. To enter into a siege would have been very time-consuming in an epoch where the campaigning season was short, and the French decided to leave Maastricht behind them, masked by a force which, if all went wrong, could also cover any possible French retreat. Maastricht's garrison amounted to some 6,000 men; it was well provisioned and commanded with determination by Count Frederick von Salm, known as the Old Rhinegrave to distinguish him from his son, Count Charles von Salm, the Young Rhinegrave, who was becoming a close confidant of the Prince of Orange.

The French marched up to the outer ring of fortresses the Dutch held on the Rhine, with the army once again divided into two: Condé on the right, and Turenne on the left bank of the river. Rheinberg, which like Maastricht belonged to the Bishop of Cologne and which also had a Dutch garrison, and Wesel, Büderick, and Orsoi in the Cleve territories of the Grand Elector of Brandenburg, likewise garrisoned by the Dutch, were swiftly captured; and the fortresses of Rees and Emerick surrendered as easily as the others. For the first time we now catch a glimpse of the Prince of Orange as a stern disciplinarian – one of the colonels commanding at Rheinberg was beheaded on his orders. The poor showing of the Dutch garrisons demonstrated the need for rigorous action.

Further north the Bishop of Münster had declared war on the Dutch on 18 May – followed shortly afterwards by the Bishop-Elector of Cologne. The numbers of the Bishop of Münster's army tended to oscillate, but they may have amounted to between 17,000 and 18,000 men. His bishopric stretched along nearly the whole of the eastern border of the Republic. He invaded the Dutch Province of Overijssel and a French force under Luxemburg – who had also rebelled under the Fronde and who was both a relation and a client of Condé – had been despatched in support of the two bishops.

By 12 June Louis's army was ready to cross the Rhine at Tolhuis to sweep across the vulnerable Republic.[15]

DUTCH DEFENCE

William had made his departure from the States-General on 19 April to take command of the Dutch army at Doesberg on the Ijssel river, which runs south on a north–south axis from the Zuiderzee to join the Rhine near Arnhem; it thus constituted the next natural line of defence in the east of the Republic behind the Rhine fortresses. By attacking through Germany on the eastern frontier Louis's strategy had outflanked the more formidable and huge river systems formed on an east–west axis by the Rhine estuary, created by the Rhine after it bends west from the German border to flow into the Republic. The Dutch fortresses on the Rhine outside the Republic, which succumbed so swiftly to the French attack, were intended to form the first line of defence. They had indeed proved formidable during the long wars of independence against Spain; but they had been allowed to deteriorate to a deplorable degree, and there were deficiencies of every sort, in the fortifications, in the provision of armaments and food, and in the garrisons themselves.[16]

The foremost of the Field Deputies nominated by the States-General to oversee the Prince was their President, Hieronymus van Beverninck, with the aged Maurits of Nassau-Siegen and Wirtz acting as field-marshals.[17] Circumscribed by the terms of his appointment and by the Field Deputies, William nevertheless managed to cooperate closely with the very forceful Van Beverninck, as well as with De Witt; and Van Beverninck's letters provide us with a clear picture of the developing crisis.

Shortly after William's departure for the Ijssel front Charles II wrote to his nephew on 2 May, 'I could not omit writing one word to you ... since I feare our correspondence must sease for some time, upon this misundestanding between the States and me, though I assure you my kindnesse shall never change to you in the least, and though our interests seeme to be a little differing at this present, yett I have done you that service, that if this warr had not falen out, I am confident you had not so soone at least been in the post you are at present; this is all I have to say at this time but I hope to live to be more usefull to you, and you may be assured I will slip no opportunity to lett you see how truly kinde I am to you.'[18] Contact with the clan was thus maintained, and, as we shall see, continued to be maintained, even though the lives and limbs of its members were hazarded on opposite sides in the war.

De Witt's and the Prince's cooperation was demonstrated by the Grand Pensionary's regularly keeping William informed on broad naval, military and diplomatic, as well as on practical, matters, whilst on 16 May William on his side wrote to set out his views on the situation he found on the front under his command. The Ijssel army was setting up camp the following morning between Zutphen and Deventer, a general review of the troops would follow and he would report further on their state after that. He could say now that the troops who were there were reasonably good but that God grant that there should be more of them, because certainly nobody could assume that it would be possible, with such a handful of men, to prevent so mighty an army as that of the King of France from crossing the Ijssel, given the extent of the front which had to be defended – it took 15 or 16 hours to traverse it. Without more men he foresaw great disasters. He was well aware of the overall shortage of troops that existed and that peasants were being brought under arms in the Province of Holland. If 15,000 or 20,000 of these could be sent to him they would in the absence of soldiers be of great utility. Everyone knew that the greatest disaster that could overwhelm the State would result from the enemy crossing the Ijssel. And he ends by assuring the Pensionary that he will continue to serve the country wherever possible. He wished he had to hand the necessary means of doing so and asked De Witt to lend a helping hand to that end.[19]

In a number of cogent letters at the end of April Hieronymus van Beverninck drew attention to the extremely cumbersome procedures required to give effect to troop movements, with messengers being dispatched to all corners of the Republic to obtain the necessary authorisations, whilst at the same time the Field Deputies from the different Provinces disputed amongst themselves as to who had authority over which troops. He was very concerned that the Deputies were exhibiting a greater regard for their specific interests rather than for those of the common cause, something which he anticipated would become worse in the event of setbacks arising from the fortunes of war, such as the army being cut off or the enemy breaking through at any point – a prescient observation. So bad was the position as regarded artillery that not a single cannon had arrived at the trenches dug to defend the Ijssel, driving the Prince into such a rage that he could hardly be restrained from going to The Hague himself to remonstrate.[20]

At the beginning of May, when the Grand Pensionary was visiting the fleet, one of his correspondents reported to him from The Hague how unbelievably alarmist people there were at the least news of the French troop movements, and, what was worse, the weakness was most to be observed amongst many Regents.[21]

On the 17th, the day before William was holding his planned review of the army, news was received at its newly established camp that the French army had bypassed Maastricht. Van Beverninck told De Witt that he was extremely concerned whether the army could now remain where it was, thus leaving Holland exposed to an attack from the direction of Brabant in the south and so losing all, poorly prepared as the Province was against a force that would overrun everything like a torrent. That afternoon indeed his Highness the Prince had whispered in his ear, 'We can't stay here and lose Holland.' Otherwise the troops were in better shape than he expected, 'and the Captain-General was full of action and courage'.[22] The day after the review the Field Deputies also expressed themselves satisfied with the quality of the troops, but, like the Prince, they too thought that the numbers were so small that it was absolutely impossible for them to defend an area of such a wide extent.[23]

Before the war began the total Dutch army amounted to about 84,000 men; on 28 March, the States-General had authorised an increase of 22,500 men, although about a third of these were still outstanding when hostilities began. Moreover, as Van Beverninck's despatch of 17 May indicates, the Dutch were uncertain of the direction of the French attack – there was a fear that French preparations along the Rhine might constitute a feint designed to draw Dutch troops away from Maastricht. The Dutch had accordingly responded to a request from Monterrey, the Spanish Governor-General, in February, to send 10,000 or 12,000 troops for the defence of the Spanish Netherlands, under the two countries' Defensive Alliance, by despatching regiments to Mechelen, Bergen op Zoom and Maastricht.[24] On 22 May Van Beverninck reported that the strength of the Ijssel army did not exceed 9,200 of foot and there were 4,800 horse. In addition there were 13 companies (round about 1,150 men) employed as garrisons in the Ijssel towns. These professional troops were being supplemented wherever possible by armed householders and he and the Prince asked that a further 4,000 of these should be sent from Holland.[25] By the end of May morale had clearly deteriorated and Van Beverninck wrote on the 28th that there were 'so many soldiers who had deserted during the marches and counter marches that it was difficult not to impute responsibility to the officers'.[26]

In the event the thrust of the French attack did not come from the south, through Brabant, but from the east, following the flow of the Rhine. With news of the French sieges of the Rhineland towns and fortresses the Field Deputies were acutely conscious of the massive peril advancing so relentlessly and remorselessly towards their front. 'From incoming intelligence we confirm beyond doubt', they wrote on the 28th to Fagel, who since

November 1670 had been the Griffier (Secretary) of the States-General,[27] 'that the entire French might is moving towards the Rhine and subsequently to the Yssel, and your grace knows in what posture of defence we are in. We find ourselves duty bound in all conscience to state, as we consider the great extent [of the area to be covered], and the terrifying might of the enemy mustering against the small handful that we have at our disposal for defence, that we are so perturbed that we hardly dare write. We hope that God will grant us his grace that duty and courage will not be lacking, but he is accustomed to work through his own designs, and we find these very sobering.'[28]

The strength of this French invading force may have constituted an initial 71,000 men, with another 25,000 to follow.[29]

William too could not fail to be intensely aware of the urgency of the situation. He wrote on the 28th to Van Beverninck at 6pm from the Orange hunting lodge at Dieren:

> Your grace will without doubt have received the same letters from the field deputies … which I have just received, from which it is apparent that the army of the king and that of the prince of Condé are marching in our direction; which news has caused me great anxiety, not knowing how we can put ourselves into a posture to defend the Yssel against such great forces. The more I look into it the greater the anxiety. The water has begun to fall at such a terrifying rate, that between Yselfoort and here there are well ten places which one can ride through. I believe that the only means now available to save the country is to order the despatch as soon as possible of all feasible forces for support here at the Yssel. For that reason I would ask your grace, without an hour's delay, to write to The Hague to ask for the withdrawal of as many men as possible from Maastricht, Breda, s'Hertogenbosch, Bergen op Zoom, and the Flanders quarters. I believe also that the cavalry which is in Holland should also be despatched here, as well as the little infantry that might be there; without the above I see no ostensible way to deny the crossing of the Yssel to the enemy. I don't have to tell your grace what a disaster it would be for the country if that came about, which God forbid. I believe that it would be the total ruin of the state; therefore we must put all the strength we have into preventing the aforesaid crossing, and knowing of no means other than more men, I would once again ask your grace most earnestly to put the same to The Hague so that we can receive here the little that is still there with all speed.[30]

After a night during which the whole of the army had stood to arms, although – unlike the previous night – in the event no alarm was sounded, Van Beverninck was full of admiration for the energy displayed by the Prince of Orange to bring everything as far as possible into the requisite state of readiness.[31]

William called a council of war of officers and Field Deputies on 3 June at which both the field-marshals, Wirtz and Prince Maurits of Nassau-Siegen, thought the Ijssel could not be defended. Prince William does not appear to have expressed an opinion other than to say that for the time being the army should remain where it was until further advice was received from the government and that a further meeting should be arranged with the military committee of the States-General at Arnhem;[32] and Van Beverninck accordingly sent an urgent missive to Fagel containing that request.[33]

The letter to Fagel was communicated to De Witt, who sent a response that there were immediate plans in hand to strengthen the Ijssel army, including five regiments which were being pulled back from the Spanish Netherlands, two other regiments, 2,000 Spanish cavalry, armed householders and above 18,000 *waartgelders* from Holland (special forces raised in the towns) as well as from elsewhere, so that one way and another the army's strength would be raised to 30,000 men; and both the States of Holland and the States-General were of the unanimous view that the enemy should be prevented from crossing the rivers, on which the delegation from the military committee, which was on its way, would expound further.[34]

The Grand Pensionary reported to the Holland States that Wirtz was dejected, but the Prince was resolute, having said that if anybody heard that the enemy had crossed the Ijssel then one could believe that he himself was dead.[35]

The minutes of the meeting between the Field Deputies, the Prince of Orange and the military committee of the States-General, which took place at Arnhem on 5 June, reveal the view that on the one hand the military position on the Ijssel was desperate, but that on the other hand to abandon that position would cause the utmost consternation amongst the country's inhabitants and the Provinces of the Union, and would leave the way open for the enemy to advance to the heart of the country. The result would be that each of the Provinces would look to its own defence and the outcome would be that 'neither order nor government would remain'. The resolution was therefore taken to defend the Ijssel 'to the utmost', a decision in which both the Field Deputies and the Prince of Orange unanimously acquiesced. According to Wicquefort the Prince offered no advice, confining himself to indicating that he would execute whatever was decided upon.[36]

The report of the meeting was presented on 7 June to the States-General, who resolved to back the decision taken at Arnhem, but very fortunately added that 'as matters of war can't be directed from afar' the actual decision on what to do should be left to the Field Deputies, after advice from the Prince of Orange, in the light of developments – and this left the way open for a sensible withdrawal of the army in due course.[37]

On that very day, with news emerging of the capture by the French of the Rhine towns and fortresses, Van Beverninck wrote to say that 'he would not be true to the state, and in *particular* [my italics] to the government of Holland' – thus revealing the duality of his own loyalty – if he did not warn the Grand Pensionary that it was impossible to prevent the enemy from breaking through the Ijssel line.

Again, on the 8th, he wrote that unavoidably and in a short time the French would break through. There was so great a 'terror panic and fright' amongst the officers of the army that Van Beverninck himself was frightened of what that entailed. Once the enemy had broken through, the Dutch army would have to retreat to avoid being surrounded, the cavalry towards Utrecht and the infantry, which was not required to garrison the Ijssel towns, evacuated if necessary via the Zuiderzee. In those circumstances he could not see of what further service he himself could be where he now was but that 'he might possibly be not wholly useless to my fatherland in our own province'; and he sought De Witt's guidance in the matter.[38]

Morale in the army was in a very bad state, he noted in the first of two letters on the 10th, and there was general defeatism in the towns amongst the Regents and the people. In Nijmegen and Arnhem there were full-scale revolts. At Zutphen, where he was quartered, the town was full of fright and irresolution. The Prince of Orange was full of animation but very downcast over the position the army faced and Van Beverninck 'feared indeed that, if his courage was not propped up, he might be brought to some extremity'.[39] It is difficult to know what Van Beverninck had in mind by 'extremity' but it is the only indication we have that, under the extreme pressures which he was under, the still only 21-year-old Prince may have wavered, uncertain though it is whether this was in his courage or in his loyalty to the Republic.

The Field Deputies that same day wrote to Fagel that the Ijssel was not defensible but that they would do all they could to hold it in accordance with what the States of Holland should resolve, which, however, they asked for in writing.[40] In the second of his letters on that day Van Beverninck wrote that the armed householders, on whom so much hope had rested, were proving to be of little value and it would be better to save the costs incurred in hiring them.[41]

De Witt, fully aware of the bleak situation, nevertheless wrote defiantly that should the French break through on the Ijssel front the seat of government should be moved to Amsterdam from where 'it would dispute the country with the enemy to the last man with Batavian doggedness'. Orders could be given for the inundation of the countryside. 'The Lord God has a hundred ways to save us. Should the fleet ... be successful ... England might take a different direction in accordance with her true interest and the whole of Europe might become more lively to her own enslavement as a result of the menacing defeat of this Republic.'[42] Van Beverninck thought Holland should look to its own defence; Amsterdam was impregnable and Dordrecht was also well positioned having regard to the buffer of Zeeland and Brabant, but Amsterdam had the advantage of being better situated to take advantage of the sea.[43]

On 10 June consent was given for the Ijssel army to retreat in the event that the French should break through its defences and on the 11th Van Beverninck, on his return to

Zutphen, having spent the night at Dieren with the Prince of Orange, reported that the enemy was approaching fast from all sides and that it was feared he would break through at Tolhuis.[44]

'Tuer! Tuer! Pas de quartier pour cette canaille', so cried Condé's young nephew, the Duc de Longueville, as he charged his horse at a group of Dutch soldiers who were on the point of surrendering as the French army was crossing the Rhine at Tolhuis on 12 June. But it was to his own death that his horse was carrying him. He was killed as, desperate and left with no alternative, the soldiers fired back.

Condé, too, nearly met his end. Coming to the young man's assistance, he was shot at by a Dutch officer with his pistol; Condé raised his left arm to shield himself, and the bullet struck his wrist, shattering the bone.[45]

The defence of Tolhuis had been entrusted to a Frenchman in the service of the Dutch, the Vicomte de Montbas, who was married to the daughter of Pieter de Groot, the Dutch ambassador to France. Montbas's orders, one set from the Field Deputies and another from the Prince of Orange, were conflicting and confused, with the result that Montbas arrived at the Prince's headquarters at Dieren, leaving Tolhuis undefended. His arrest was immediately ordered and Wirtz was rushed to Tolhuis where, however, he was unable to prevent the French from crossing.[46]

Tolhuis was situated where the Rhine, the Ijssel and the Waal rivers conjoin and the Ijssel was also soon crossed in the presence of Louis XIV himself. The memorable 'Crossing of the Rhine' having thus taken place, commemorated in the painted ceiling in the hall of mirrors at Versailles, the Field Deputies resolved on the retreat of the Dutch army, with the main army heading for Utrecht.[47] It left behind about 13,000 men out of its total strength of about 22,000, to garrison the Ijssel towns. These troops were regiments from Gelderland, Overijssel, Friesland and Groningen and their Provincial right to use them for their own defence was not disputed. Most of the remaining 9,000 or so men met at Arnhem on 13 June, with the artillery arriving at Utrecht on the same day. They barely escaped being cut off by Turenne, to whose army Arnhem surrendered on the 16th: its Town Council was compelled to swear an oath of allegiance to Louis XIV.

When the Prince of Orange arrived at the gates of Utrecht on the 15th negotiations began with the Town Council on whether his army should be allowed to enter the town. William asked that some of the suburbs should be razed to allow for appropriate fields of fire, whilst the Provincial States of Utrecht established that it would be possible to inundate land around the town. Before decisions on these matters were arrived at, orders reached the Prince from the States-General to retreat on Holland, which he now did. There his army took up position on the Provinces' borders on the 18th and 19th;[48] and on the 23rd Utrecht surrendered to the French.[49]

THE WATER LINE

The Holland States had commenced flooding to defend their Province, and it was on the Water Line which was now coming into existence that the Prince of Orange and his army made their dispositions. The main line stretched from the north at Muiden, which lies on the Zuiderzee and which guarded the approaches to Amsterdam, to Gorinchem on the north bank of the Waal river in the south of the Province; additional inundations stretched further south of the Waal and Maas rivers to Geertruidenberg and 'sHertogenbosch. It was by no means a straight line and took the shape required by the lie of the land to give maximum effect to the inundations. Once completed the Province was defended on all sides by water: from the east by the formidable, and, as it proved, nearly impregnable, Water Line; by the Zuiderzee in the north-east; by the North Sea towards the north and west; and by the massive Rhine tributaries and the island systems of Zeeland in the south. There were five so-called 'gateways'. These vulnerable places were defended by Prince Maurits of Nassau-Siegen, based at Muiden; the Prince of Orange himself in the centre at Bodegrave to the west of Woerden, near the narrowest point of the inundations; the Count of Hoorn at Goejan-Verwelle; the Count of Louvignies, who had been seconded by the Spaniards from the Spanish Netherlands, at Schoonhoven; and Field-Marshal Wirtz at Gorinchem.[50] The main line, as the crow flies, was about 55 kilometres, or just under 35 miles, in length, without taking account of the further inundations to the south of the Waal.

A little place, Hinderdam, a few kilometres south of the town of Muiden, was now crucial for the defence of the Province, for here were situated important sluices for flooding the country to the east of Amsterdam. On the 18th old Maurits of Nassau-Siegen had managed to occupy the place, arriving in all haste from Amsterdam, and on the 20th he also re-occupied Muiden, which a small detachment of French troops from the command of the Marquis de Rochefort had occupied for a short time.[51]

In their Eighty Years' War against Spain the Dutch had long perfected the technique of flooding their land, so much of which lay below sea level, as a most effective means of defence, although it had obvious adverse consequences for agriculture – particularly if salt water from the sea was used – and for property. It was natural to have recourse to this device in the present predicament and as early as 11 May the States of Holland had received a detailed report on the preparations for inundations which were already in hand. They were actively pursued, although opposition was not lacking – on 3 June, for instance, it was reported to the States of Holland that the town of Gouda wanted compensation for the damage to fields and property.[52] On 11 June the Holland States heard that commissioners had departed to commence the flooding. However, the engineering was complex and the Water Line could only be brought into being in a piecemeal fashion. We do not hear, for example, until the 19th that inundations had commenced at so important a part of the line as Goejan-Verwelle, and work on the inundations went on everywhere for some time afterwards.[53]

Nor were the problems of localism immediately overcome. On the 19th Gouda needed to be told in no uncertain terms to open the sluices or else the work would be put in hand by military means; and Hieronymus van Beverninck, who came from Gouda, also visited the town to persuade it to let the waters in. Another instance of a similar sort was manifested by the town folk of Schoonhoven where the troops under the command of the Count of Louvigny were barred from entry to the town and the citizenry refused to countenance the opening of the dykes or to defend themselves – on the contrary they wished to commence negotiations with the King of France. At Gorinchem armed peasants held watch on the approaches to the town whilst Prince Maurits was also opposed by a hundred armed peasants when he forced through the cutting of dykes.[54] De Witt told his brother that householders in the countryside had everywhere resisted the opening of the sluice gates and the cutting of the dykes, but that with the arrival of the army work had commenced at a number of places.[55]

Historians have much criticised the leaving behind of the garrisons in the Ijssel towns, citing this as an instance where local interests preceded the general interest; but, much as they denuded the army, the French did see the garrisons as a sufficient threat to their lines of communication to devote time to besieging them when every moment was vital to the Dutch. If the French had vigorously pursued the retreating Dutch army they would have found a very incomplete Water Line, and might have been able to capture The Hague, although Amsterdam might still have been another matter. In the time they were given the Dutch were able to work, in addition to the inundations, on the fortification of the Line, with the marines and sailors from the fleet brought in where they could be useful, whilst an inland fleet of flat-bottomed boats, mounted with guns, was a further aid to the growing strength of the defence.

NEGOTIATIONS WITH LOUIS

But by the time the States of Holland met on 13 June to discuss how to react to the French crossing at Tolhuis, the Water Line and its defences had not even taken on rudimentary form, and there were those who despaired of the country's plight when proposals were put to the meeting to transfer the seat of government to Amsterdam. When the Amsterdam delegates defiantly said that resistance should continue as long as possible and there should be no surrender of liberty the representatives from Gorinchem, whose geographic position was much more exposed than Amsterdam's, retorted that all was desperate, Amsterdam would be the last to be swallowed up, and they supported Leyden, which had suggested that a mission should be sent to England.[56] The following day the Holland States resolved, with the subsequent approval of the States-General, to send delegations to both Louis and Charles II – against the opposition of Fagel, who refused, as Griffier to the States-General, to sign the resolution. De Witt too thought no good would result from these missions.[57]

The delegation to Louis – consisting of Pieter de Groot, the previous ambassador to Paris, Nassau-Odijk, and Van Ghent, the Prince of Orange's former governor – left The Hague, and travelled via the Prince of Orange's headquarters at Utrecht, arriving with a French escort on the 22nd at the castle of Keppel, near Doesberg, where, still well in the east of the Republic ten days after the crossing of the Rhine and still not far from Tolhuis, the French King was quartered. They arrived at midnight and found a table laid with food, but there were no beds. At seven the following morning Louvois and Pomponne arrived, and asked them what they had to offer. To this they replied that the States-General believed that they would demonstrate greater respect for the King if their delegation could be the conduit for receiving his demands.

Having consulted Louis, Louvois and Pomponne returned at midday when they told the Dutch representatives that he wanted to await what the States-General had to offer, and that he would not negotiate other than with plenipotentiaries; that nevertheless he would go so far as to say that they needed to consider the state of affairs as they now stood, and what they could shortly become; that his conquests were already his, and it looked as if they could quickly be extended; that he would retain these or at least require an equivalent; that his costs in the war would have to be paid; and that his allies, such as the King of England and other princes, would need to be satisfied. With that De Groot, leaving Nassau-Odijk and Van Ghent behind, departed for The Hague to receive further instructions, stopping on his way to give a report to the Prince of Orange in the early hours of the 25th.[58]

When he arrived that day at The Hague, Johan De Witt had been removed from active participation in the Republic's affairs. He had become the object of a virulent pamphlet campaign and the target of accusations of all sorts; he had neglected, it was said, the country's defences; he had betrayed it to the French; he had plotted with Montbas to retain power under Louis XIV; he had sent his money to the safety of Venice. Late on the evening of 21 June two sons of a member of the court of Holland, an Orangist sympathiser, and two of their friends observed lights still burning in the assembly hall where the States of Holland met, and deduced that De Witt was working late. When he made his way home he was assailed by the brothers Peter and Jacob van de Graeff, and one of their friends, Cornelius de Bruyn. Jacob van de Graeff was arrested, condemned by the court of Holland and beheaded on 29 June. His brother Peter and the other two escaped.[59]

The States-General wrote to the Prince of Orange at his camp at Bodegrave saying that 'We have received news that they [the three felons] have saved themselves by resorting to the troops camped at Bodegrave, as known to Your Highness', although there is no corroboration of the accuracy of this report.[60] The outrage felt by the Regents at this assault on De Witt, and their support for him, are indicated by the States of Holland voting a reward of 5,000 guilders for the apprehension of each of the delinquents.[61] In the meantime, although his stab wounds were not fatal, the Grand Pensionary had to keep to his bed.

But, in contrast to the Regents, at the popular level there was much sympathy for De Graeff and his execution had aroused the anger of the people of The Hague.

Against this background, and amidst spreading popular disorders and riots, Pieter de Groot, on his return to The Hague, gave his advice to the Holland States on how to respond to Louis XIV. In his view what still remained of the Republic could react in one of two ways: either it could resort to armed resistance, or it could reach an agreement with the French King. Louis could be persuaded to allow the Union of the Seven Provinces to continue, in exchange for an indemnity for the areas he had conquered in the Republic and in exchange for the towns and fortresses lying outside it. He believed that the more offered, the better the terms that could be obtained, and that to engage in hard negotiations would be ruinous.[62]

Given the momentous issues involved it was not surprising that a long and, at times, acerbic debate ensued. Most of the Holland towns were inclined to follow the line advocated by De Groot. But the exception was the most important town of all, Amsterdam. The spokesman for Amsterdam began by saying that her delegates could not give any advice on so important a matter without referring back to their principals; he prayed the delegates to be resolute; and he added that the delegates present at the meeting did not have the authority to surrender the country. With De Witt's home town, Dordrecht, but also Delft and Leyden in particular taking the lead, Amsterdam came under considerable pressure to accommodate itself to the majority. Leyden's spokesman said that not all the Holland towns had the same strength of defence as Amsterdam; that Amsterdam had manpower and munitions, and the others not a man, nor powder, nor lead; that Leyden did not want to be deficient in generosity, but it did not want to perish on account of Amsterdam alone. Only from Alkmaar did Amsterdam get strong support, its delegation declaring that they would rather be struck dead by the enemy than by their own citizenry.[63]

Upon being asked for further advice, De Groot gave the warning – or rather he uttered the threat – that the French King would stay in the country until the winter to bring Amsterdam to heel, and, if Amsterdam detained him, he would let no stone of the city stand.

On that note the meeting adjourned until the following day, the 26th, whilst the Amsterdam delegates returned to their city to obtain further instructions.[64]

There, too, an anxious debate ensued in the Town Council. On the one side were those who favoured accommodating the French King; on the other were those who wanted to terminate the negotiations immediately. Neither could muster a majority. It was finally decided that, whilst the French demands could not be accepted – the Council would 'rather sacrifice their goods and their blood' – a substantial sum should be offered and the settlement should include 'freedom of religion and government'.[65] The decision was taken under great pressure from the populace and the militia, without which, it is said, it would have gone the other way, that is, to accommodate Louis XIV.[66]

The Amsterdam delegation was unable to return to The Hague on the 26th as anticipated, and was delayed until next day. In its absence, and in the absence as well of several other Holland towns, the States of Holland met at ten o'clock at night on the 26th. They passed a resolution to give De Groot plenipotentiary powers to negotiate with the French to obtain the best possible terms, provided the Union and freedom of religion and government could be preserved. A delegation from Zeeland, which had arrived in The Hague, expressly refused to associate itself with these negotiations. Nevertheless, the Holland States then made their way across the Binnenhof to the States-General. There the Provinces of Overijssel and Groningen were absent, and Zeeland declared that it had no instructions from its principals. Friesland, whose turn it was to take the chair, refused to put the resolution to the meeting, as did Utrecht and Zeeland: and in these very irregular circumstances the granting of plenipotentiary powers to De Groot was pushed through by Holland.

Fagel once again refused to sign this as Griffier of the States-General; and, turning to De Groot, told him that he might well depart to sell his country, but he would have difficulty in granting the purchaser possession of what he had bought. De Groot replied that it was better to save part of the country than to lose all of it. Fagel's response was that there was no need for De Groot to take similar trouble for his own estates; he would take care to have them strewn with salt, so that they would be useless unto the third generation.[67]

De Groot snatched five hours' sleep – he had not slept for two nights – with the intention of attending further deliberations of the States-General in the morning; his letters of credence by themselves gave him unlimited powers and he wished to clarify his exact instructions. But as soon as he awoke at seven on the morning of the 27th he came under considerable pressure from the Pensionaries of Leyden and Gouda to depart immediately, which he did, with the promise that the final text of the States-General's decision would follow. Apart from this lack of certitude in his negotiating position, his authority was further lessened by its being very questionable whether the whole procedure followed by both the States of Holland and the States-General was legal.

When he stopped on his way at the camp of the Prince of Orange at Bodegrave to inform him and Van Beverninck, who was also there, both told him they would not want to have his task. And William wrote to Fagel that De Groot had shown him 'the abundant authority' the States-General had granted him to negotiate with the King of France, at which he was 'not a little surprised'.[68]

His alarm is reflected in his letter. 'I think', he wrote, 'that it is also time that I begin to think of my own interests.' He asked Fagel to request permission from the States-General for him to send one of his entourage to Louis XIV to treat on his own behalf for his private concerns. He accompanied this with a letter to the States-General asking their permission to seek a safeguard from the French specifically for the town of Grave, which he owned, and to which he understood it was intended to withdraw the Dutch troops, something 'which there was all the less reason to refuse him as De Groot had shown him his plenipotentiary powers to come to an agreement with the French'.[69] If the States-General was looking to its own, so should he.

There were in fact historical precedents for this, and the subsequent discussion in the Holland States indicates that there was much sympathy for William's request, provided it related to his interests outside the Province; they resolved on 28 June to give their assent 'by turning a blind eye' as far as Grave was concerned.[70] And it is probable that the States-General did the same.[71] Before this, early in June, the States-General and the French had reached agreement to treat the town and county of Meurs, which William also possessed, as neutral territory;[72] and on 2 September the Dutch *chargé d'affaires*, Christiaan Rumpf, who had remained in Paris, was able to secure the assent of Louis XIV for the continuation of this agreement. He was not successful in trying to obtain the same for the Prince's castle of Buren, although he did obtain the promise that the Prince's dependants there would be treated with as much civility as possible.[73] There was nothing unusual, in the warfare of the time, in seeking and obtaining the neutrality of certain places if that suited both sides.

Passing through the Province of Utrecht, all of which the French now occupied, Pieter de Groot proceeded to Rhenen where he found Nassau-Odijk and Van Ghent, the former of whom was not prepared to support the conditions De Groot was proposing to put to the French, although he found Van Ghent more supportive. When negotiations began with Pomponne and Louvois, and when De Groot, in his own words, 'put all his wares on the table' ('nous deployons toute nostre boutique'), Nassau-Odijk did not hide from the two Frenchmen that his masters – the States of Zeeland – would not consent to them.[74]

Nevertheless, ploughing manfully on, De Groot, on condition that the Dutch Union was allowed to subsist with full sovereignty, offered to cede Maastricht and its dependencies, to pay a war indemnity of six million livres (£500,000), and to forgo certain places in the Generality Lands, to be agreed. Louvois laughing at this, De Groot's offer was increased to all the Generality Lands and an indemnity of ten million livres (£833,000). Louvois said that was more like it, and he and Pomponne went off to consult the King. The result of this offer would have been to interpose Louis between the United Provinces and the Spanish Netherlands; he would have established himself in an overwhelmingly powerful position on the southern borders of the Republic – provided, which was likely, that he could maintain his lines of communication through the territories of the Bishop of Liège; and the Spanish territories, which were so central to his ambitions, would be at his disposal at any time he pleased. It must be doubtful if De Groot, with his uncertain authority, could have pushed through the ratification of these terms on his return to his masters in The Hague.[75]

But Louis rejected the offer.

His demands included everything the Republic owned, in whatever capacity, outside the Seven Provinces; Delfzijl and 20 of its adjoining parishes; the county and town of Meurs for the Elector of Cologne, with the Prince of Orange, as its owner, receiving an appropriate indemnity from the States-General; a number of other towns, and everything that lay between the Rhine/Lek rivers and the Spanish Netherlands, with the option of exchanging certain additional towns for the Betuwe, which lay within this stretch of territory. In addition he demanded the lifting of trade barriers against the French (without reciprocation on the French side); freedom for Catholics to practise their religion in the Republic and to participate in the government; and a 20-million franc (£1.7 million) war indemnity.

And, finally, an annual embassy was demanded from the Dutch, with an appropriately inscribed medallion, thanking the French King for restoring their country to them.[76]

These exactions would have given Louis all the forts constituting the outlying Dutch defences on the Rhine and elsewhere, including Maastricht, and, in addition to the Generality Lands, it would have positioned him to the north of these lands as well, thus encroaching still further into the heartland of the Republic and weakening the Dutch defensive positions even further than under De Groot's proposals.

Further provision, De Groot was told, would also have to be made, in terms which were not clearly spelt out to him, for Louis's allies, the Bishop of Münster, the Elector of Cologne, and, above all, the King of England.[77]

If the invasion of the Dutch Republic was to haunt Louis's fortunes for the rest of his life, the terms he now demanded compounded the mistake. There was no point in the Dutch conceding them; they would have laid themselves open to any further moves which it pleased Louis to take against them in the future; and they would have been reduced to a plight not much worse than what they would have undergone if they had ceded total surrender immediately. All they would have gained was time. But, as we shall see, time was to tilt in their favour in any case, and on rather better terms.

Delfzijl and its 20 parishes, situated in the remote north-east corner of the Republic, were required so that Louis could give them to Charles II in exchange for Sluys and Cadsand, which the two kings had originally agreed should form part of Charles's booty, together with Walcheren in the south-west. Charles, Louis said in a despatch of 23 June to his ambassador to Britain, Colbert de Croissy, was just as suspect in his eyes as were the Dutch and the Spanish, and he did not want to establish him in too strong a position on the Continent.[78]

De Groot was given five days[79] to respond to the French demands.

But by the time he presented his report in The Hague on 1 July the whole political constellation in the United Provinces had changed: the regime of the 'True Freedom' which De Witt had created and led over a period of 19 years was about to be overthrown.[80]

---

1 Rowen, *De Witt, op. cit.*, pp.816–20.

2 Cornelis De Witt's letter to De Witt of 6 June, *Brieven aan De Witt, op. cit.*, II, pp.678–9.

3 De Jonge, *Geschiedenis van het Nederlandsche Zeewesen, op. cit.*, The Hague, 1833–48, pp.106, 108–9.

4 Richard Ollard, *Man of war: Sir Robert Holmes and the Restoration Navy*, Hodder & Stoughton, 1969, p.181.

5 J.R. Jones, *op. cit.*, pp.190–1. R. Hutton, *op. cit.*, p.288, *Brieven aan De Witt, op. cit.*, II, pp.680ff contain Cornelis de Witt's letters to his brother with details of the battle.

6 *Brieven aan De Witt, op. cit.*, II, p.688 and note to p.690. De Jonge, *op. cit.*, III, Pt I, pp.157–8. *Notulen gehouden ter Staten-vergadering van Holland (1671–1675) door Cornelis Hop en Nicolaas Vivien*, Historisch genootschap Utrecht, 3 ser., no.19, p.122.

7 De Jonge, *Zeewesen, op. cit.*, III, Pt II, pp.182–3. Jones, *op. cit.*, p.191.

8 De Jonge, *Zeewesen, op. cit.*, III, Pt II, pp.185–6.

9 De Jonge, *Zeewesen, op. cit.*, III, Pt I, pp.192–4.

10 *Ibid.*, p.195.

11 C. Rousset, *Histoire de Louvois et de son administration politique et militaire*, Paris, 1861–63, I, pp.348–54, 396–7. Condé's memoir is in Mignet, *op. cit.*, III, pp.666ff. De Groot's account of the revelation of the Anglo-French invasion strategy is contained in *Brieven aan de Witt*, II, *op. cit.*, pp.542–6. For the surmise that Condé may have been the author see Rowen, *De Witt, op. cit.*, p.747.

12 Robert Fruin, *De Oorlog van 1672*, Groningen, 1972, p.51.

13 Ten Raa and Bas, *op. cit.*, V, pp.229, 258, 318. Ten Raa and Bas maintain that the English and Scottish regiments in the Dutch army had to swear a special oath of allegiance to the Dutch authorities (see p.229). However, M.C. Trevelyan says there were no English regiments in Dutch service in the war of 1672 – the one English regiment having returned to England in 1665. English regiments were not reinstated by William III until after the treaty of Westminster in 1674 and the Scottish regiments were much diluted by non-Scottish recruits. *William III and the Defence of Holland 1672–4*, Longman, 1930, pp.121–2.

14 Anna Keay, *The last royal rebel: the life and death of James, Duke of Monmouth*, Bloomsbury, 2016, p.115.

15 Rousset, *op. cit.*, I, pp.354–9. Israel, *op. cit.*, p.797. Van Nimwegen, *op. cit.*, pp.436–7. It is difficult to be precise about the effective size of 17th-century armies at any particular time and estimates of the size of Louis's army differ widely. Van Nimwegen indicates 148,000 men; Rousset's estimate (p.347) is nearly 120,000 and Israel's 130,500. Wicquefort (*Mémoires sur la guerre faite aux Provinces-Unies en l'année 1672*, Historisch Genootschap Utrecht, 1888, p.158) says more than 160,600 men. For the course of the French march see Ten Raa and Bas, *op. cit.*, V, p.326. For the disagreement between Condé and Turenne see Mignet, IV, pp.4–5. For the size of the garrison at Maastricht see Van Nimwegen, *op. cit.*, pp.436–7. For the beheading of the colonel see Wicquefort's *Mémoires, op. cit.*, p.173. For the size of the Bishop of Münster's army see *Correspondentie Willem III en Portland*, II, Pt 1, *op. cit.*, p.36. For Luxemburg's relationship with Condé see P. de Ségur, *La jeunesse de Maréchal de Luxemburg*, Paris, 1900, pp. 318, 405–22. Luxemburg was a Montmorency who acquired the title of Duke of Luxemburg through his marriage to the heiress of the Duchy, arranged by Condé as a result of a rather disgraceful set of manoeuvres (according at any rate to the rather unreliable De Ségur's account).

16 Hop & Vivien, *op. cit.*, p.64.

17 Ten Raa and Bas, *op. cit.*, V, pp. 291, 320. M.C. Trevelyan, *op. cit.*, p.120.

18 *Correspondentie Willem III en Portland, op. cit.*, II, Pt 1, p.48.

19 *Brieven van De Witt, op. cit.*, IV, pp.328–35. *Brieven aan De Witt, op. cit.*, II, pp.628–9.

20 *Brieven aan De Witt, op. cit.*, II, pp.632–6, 638–9.

21 *Ibid.*, p.636.

22 *Ibid*, p.640.

23 De Jonge, *Briefwisseling tuschen Hieronymus van Beverninck en de Raadpensionaris Johan de Witt in het jaar 1672 in Verhandelingen en Onuitgegeven Stucken betreffende de Geschiedenis der Nederlanden*, Delft 1825, p.381.

24 Van Nimwegen, *op. cit.*, p.436.

25 *Brieven aan De Witt, op. cit.*, II, pp.643–4. I have taken 89 men per company of foot.

26 *Ibid.*, p.646.

27 A. De Fouw, *Onbekende Raasdpensionarissen*, The Hague, 1946, Section on Gaspar Fagel, p.98.

28 De Jonge, *Briefwisseling, op. ci*t., pp.383–4.

29 Van Nimwegen, *op. ci*t., p.439. Godard van Reede van Ginkel told his father, Van Reede van Amerongen, 80,000 men.

30 De Jonge, *Briefwisseling, op. ci*t., pp.385–6.

31 De Jonge, *Briefwisseling, op. ci*t., p.399. Beverninck to Fagel, undated but must be about the end of May.

32 J.W. van Sypesteyn and J.P. de Bordes, *De Verdedeging van Nederland in 1672 & 1673*, The Hague, 1850, Pt I, pp.107ff. Appendix III gives the minutes of the meeting.

33 De Jonge, *op. cit.*, pp.57–8, where the letter is dated 8 rather than 3 June.

34 *Brieven van De Witt*, IV, pp.345–7. The figure of 30,000 men is difficult to reconcile with Van Beverninck's figures contained in his letter of 22 May, unless the Waartgelders, and possibly the armed householders, are excluded.

35 Hop & Vivien, *op. cit.*, p.100.

36 Wicquefort, *Histoire, op. cit.*, IV, p.392.

37 Sypesteyn and Bordes, *op. cit.*, Pt I, pp.111ff.

38 *Brieven aan De Witt, op. ci*t., II, pp.648–50.

39 *Ibid.*, II, pp.650–1.

40 De Jonge, *Briefwissling, op. cit.*, pp.441ff. Strangely the resolution they referred to was that of 'their noble mightinesses', i.e. the States of Holland, rather than those from 'their high mightinesses', the States-General.

41 *Brieven aan De Witt, op. ci*t., II, pp.652–3.

42 *Brieven van De Witt, op. ci*t., IV, pp.350–1.

43 *Brieven aan De Witt, op. ci*t., II, p.652.

44 *Brieven van De Witt, op. ci*t., IV, p.352. *Brieven aan De Witt, op. ci*t., II, p.653.

45 Rousset, *op. cit.*, I, p.360. Eveline Godley, *The Great Condé*, London, 1915, p.552.

46 Wicquefort, *Histoire, op. ci*t., IV, pp.398–9. De Jonge, *Briefwisseling, op. ci*t., pp.453–4. Field deputies' letter to Fagel dated 11 June.

47 Rousset, *op. cit.*, I, pp.360, 365–6. De Jonge, *Briefwisseling, op. ci*t., pp.460–1. Field deputies to States-General, 12 June.

48 Sypesteyn and Bordes, *op. ci*t., Pt I, pp.74–5. Robert Fruin, *op. cit.*, pp.112–14, 141–2. Hop & Vivien, *op. cit.*, p.112. As regards the troops left behind on the Ijssel see Louvois's letter to his father Le Tellier on the 20th, where he remarks: '…l'armée ennemie que se dissipe tous les jours, tant par le terreur ou sont leurs troupes, que parce que chaque province redamande ce qu'elle paye pour l'employer à sa défense', Rousset, *op. cit.*, p.368.

49 Van Nimwegen, *op. ci*t., p.441.

50 Hop & Vivien, *op. ci*t., pp.112–13. Wicquefort, *Histoire, op. ci*t., IV, pp.417–18.

51 *Correspondentie Willem III en Bentinck, op. ci*t., II, Pt 1, pp.54–5. Robert Fruin, *De Oorlog van 1672, op. cit.*, pp.121, 141. Fruin says Maurits occupied Hinderdam on the 19th. The *Correspondentie* clearly states the 18th, Rousset, *op. cit.*, p.366. Hinderdam contained the crucial sluices. Japikse points out (*Willem III, op. ci*t., I, p.197) there were at that time no sluices at Muiden.

52 Hop & Vivien, *op. ci*t., pp.68–9, 82–3, 98.

53 *Ibid.*, pp.106, 114.

54 *Ibid.*, pp.115, 116. Groen van Prinsterer, *Archives, op. ci*t., 2nd series, V, 1650–88, p.252.

55 *Brieven van De Witt, op. ci*t., IV, pp.387–8. Letter from De Witt to Cornelis de Witt, 20 June.

56 Hop & Vivien, *op. cit.*, p.110.

57 *Brieven van de Witt, op. cit.*, IV, pp.385–6. Wicquefort, *Histoire, op. ci*t., IV, pp.422–4, 477.

58 Hop & Vivien, *op. cit.*, pp.127–8 contains the report of the delegation to the States-General. Rowen, *De Witt, op. cit.*, p.838 mentions de Groot's report to the Prince of Orange. See also Wicquefort, *Histoire, op. cit.*, IV, p.424, and Mignet, *Négociations, op. cit.*, IV, p.22.

59 Rowen, *De Witt, op. cit.*, pp.840–44. Geyl, *op. cit.*, pp.347–9 gives a slightly different version but is in substance the same. See also Wagenaar, *Vaderlandsche Historie*, Amsterdam, 1794, pp.68–70.

60 Quoted in J.E.Haijer, 'De moord op de Gebroeders De Witt', *Spiegel Historiael*, July/August 1967, 2 jaargang, nr.7/8.

61 Hop & Vivien, *op. cit.*, p.121.

62 *Ibid.*, pp.128–9.

63 *Ibid.*, pp.129–35.

64 *Ibid.*, p.135.

65 Geyl, *op. cit.*, pp.351–2.

66 Israel, *op. cit.*, p.800.

67 Hop & Vivien, *op. cit.*, pp.135–9. Wicquefort, *Histoire, op. cit.*, IV, p.431. Wagenaar, *op. cit.*, 14, pp.54–5.

68 See De Groot's letters to Wicquefort of 3 April 1674 and 20 March 1674 in Wicquefort, *Histoire, op. cit.*, IV, pp.476–80. The text of the States-General resolution of the 26th giving De Groot full powers is in Mignet, *Négociations, op. cit.*, IV, pp.30–1. See also Wagenaar, *op. cit.*, 14, pp.54–5 and, for the Prince's letter to Fagel and the States-General, pp.60–1. A different version of the letter to the States-General is contained in *Correspondentie Willem III en Portland, op. cit.*, II, Pt 1, p.56.

69 *Correspondentie Willem III en Portland, op. cit.*, II, Pt 1, p.56. Hop & Vivien, *op. cit.*, pp.151, 153ff.

70 See Wicquefort, *Histoire, op. cit.*, IV, p.432n.

71 See Wagenaar's reasons for coming to this conclusion, *op. cit.*, 14, p.61.

72 *Correspondentie Willem III en Portland, op. cit.*, II, Pt 1, pp.53–4.

73 *Ibid.*, II, Pt 1, p.97.

74 De Groot's letter to Wicquefort, 3 April 1674, in Wicquefort, *Histoire, op. cit.*, IV, pp.478–9.

75 Wicquefort, *Histoire, op. cit.*, IV, p.433. Hop & Vivien, *op. cit.*, pp.157–9.

76 Wagenaar, *op. cit.*, 14, pp.99–101.

77 Mignet, *op. cit.*, IV, pp.33–5.

78 *Ibid.*, IV, p.335.

79 Hop & Vivien, *op. cit.*, p.159.

80 His appointment as Councillor Pensionary of Holland dated from 30 July 1653. See Rowen, *De Witt, op. cit.*, p.95.

9 1672: THE ORANGE RESTORATION

THE BREAKDOWN OF ORDER

Fear, panic, confusion and disorder had escalated and spread in the Dutch Republic as the apparently irresistible might of the French armies relentlessly advanced. Amsterdam, even before the French crossing of the Rhine, was full of refugees, with many merchants doing what they could to transfer their wealth by means of bills of exchange to Hamburg and even to Paris, Nantes, La Rochelle, Bordeaux and Venice. After the crossing of the Rhine an English correspondent in Amsterdam in his newsletter of 14 June reported that 'Wee are in a sad condition (God help us): heare are many traytors in our land', and 'this city is full of thousands of fled people, rich and poor'. On the 16th the transfer of money out of the country caused the exchange rate of the guilder to fall by ten per cent and more.

An English merchant in Rotterdam wrote on the 17th that 'wee are all in an uproare, the common people tumult, and will permitt noe goods to go out, pretending the great ones send away their many and best things to Amsterdam, Antwerp, Zeeland and Hamburg and intend to follow after, and leave the people to the mercy of the French.' When he was in The Hague 'There were … seaverall boats laden with truncks and costly goods for Amsterdam which the people mutyned upon, and stopd…. The people of Leyden, Harlem, Dort [Dordrecht] and Rotterdam have been in like confusion.' On the 28th he wrote from Rotterdam that 'the generallytie of the people crye out upon the magistrates that they have sold the country and the people to the French'; and he remarked that 'abundance of people have left the country here … especyally women and the young and handsomer sort'.[1]

On 29 June the meeting of the States of Holland noted that in Dordrecht, the home town of the De Witts, a great tumult had broken out.[2] There demands – supported by Orangist preachers and by the civic guard – had been made by a crowd for the repeal of the Eternal Edict. The Town Council had been forced to send a delegation to the Prince on the 25th to ask him to come immediately: he showed some reluctance, fearing to revive memories of his father's intervention in municipal affairs in 1650; but, the delegation telling him that it was more than their lives were worth if he did not return with them, he was finally persuaded to accompany them to the town on the 28th. A declaration was drawn up repealing the Eternal Edict which William refused to accept until he was released from his oath by the States of Holland. The Town Council, however, was forced to sign it, with Cornelis De Witt, still ill after his return from the fleet, signing with 'v.c.' (*vi coactus* – under duress) after his signature. The Prince, otherwise silent, as was his wont, turned to the members of the Town Council with the words 'gentlemen, I feel for you'.[3]

A similar pattern emerged in other towns. On the 28th there were riots in Rotterdam, Gouda and Schiedam. Rotterdam rescinded the Eternal Edict on the 29th and Schiedam on the 30th. And Haarlem and several other towns followed.

In these cases the mobs too were supported by the civic guards.[4] These used to be under the control of the Regents – the colonels tended to be members of the Town Councils and the captains tended to be recruited from the patrician classes – with the poorer citizens being excluded because the members had to provide their own weapons. During the war, however, the numbers of civic guards had been considerably expanded and frequently included the poorer citizenry, with arms provided from the town arsenals.[5]

STADHOLDER, CAPTAIN- AND ADMIRAL-GENERAL

At the States of Holland meeting on 1 July reports of disturbances came pouring in from Delft, Rotterdam, Dordrecht and Gouda. It was impossible not to discuss the rescinding of the Eternal Edict, and the Holland States bowed to the irresistible threat of popular discontent to do so; but not without a long discussion in which Leyden in particular showed herself to be somewhat lukewarm in her support of this step.[6]

At four in the morning of 4 July the Holland States declared William of Orange Stadholder and Captain- and Admiral-General of their Province; they absolved him from the oath under the Eternal Edict which he had given when he was appointed Captain-General for the current campaign against France neither to solicit the Stadholdership nor to accept it if it were offered to him whilst he held that office; and a solemn delegation of 11 deputies carried the news to him at his army camp at Bodegrave.[7]

On 8 July the States-General too followed suit, appointing him to the offices of Captain- and Admiral-General of the Union, with all the prerogatives held by his predecessors; he was granted the right of patents – the right to give marching orders to troops on his own authority, the lack of which had proved such a handicap in the fighting to date – although on the clear understanding that this was only until further notice. He was also given a personal military escort of a regiment of horse and a regiment of foot, the command of which he gave to the young Rhinegrave, Charles Florentine van Salm, whose father, the old Rhinegrave, was still the governor of Maastricht.[8]

On the 9th the Prince took the oath of office; and on the same day the States of Zeeland resolved to offer him that Province's Stadholdership.[9] There too the tumults of the mob had played a decisive, intimidating part in persuading the Regents to bend before the popular will.[10]

He received a reproachful letter from his grandmother, the nearly 70-year-old Princess Amalia von Solms, in which she complained – in her distinctive French – that he never kept her informed of the occurrences in his life, in response to which he paid her a visit after taking his oath.[11] Her sentiments were reflected in a moving letter of about this time to Maurits of Nassau-Siegen. 'The grace which it pleases God to accord me, in putting my grandson in the offices which I have seen occupied by his illustrious predecessors, would have consoled me for all the vexations of the past if it had only occurred in less dangerous times; … if God grants us the peace which I wish for I hope He will confer on me the blessing of rejoicing in it with you.'[12]

After nearly a quarter of a century in abeyance the traditional offices of the House of Orange had been restored. But, if William had now ascended into the saddle, he was still not in full command of his steed. He would have to move with care to consolidate his position and to extend his power.

Three immediate and interacting tasks faced the 21-year-old Prince: the need to react to the negotiations which had taken place with Louis XIV, and which were about to commence with his uncle, Charles II; the need to establish his new regime; and the need to conduct the war with the enemies of the country where he now exercised the chief, albeit still limited, authority. The first two issues will be followed through in the rest of this chapter and continued in the next, after which we will resume with our account of the conduct of the war; but, in assessing the pressures under which the Prince was operating, the reader needs to keep in mind that he himself had to analyse and address the far-reaching complexities of all three issues in urgent combination on a daily basis.

REJECTION OF FRENCH TERMS

As to the negotiations with Louis XIV, when Pieter De Groot returned with the conditions the French King demanded it soon became clear that there was little chance of them being accepted by either the States of Holland or by the States-General. At the beginning of July the French occupied three of the Republic's Provinces, Utrecht, Overijssel and Gelderland, and in these circumstances the position of Holland, always the strongest Province in the Union in any case, was now of overwhelming importance. On 1 July Gaspar Fagel wrote to the Prince from The Hague that the unoccupied Provinces of Zeeland, Friesland and Groningen were flatly opposed to considering the French proposals; that most of the Holland towns and the most important ones, with the exception of Leyden, would rather be put to the sword than submit to the proposals; and that Amsterdam had that day told him that she was prepared to risk all in resisting the French. Speaking for himself, he said that he would rather die ten deaths than become a wretched slave of the French and blatantly permit the destruction of the body and soul of future generations; and this he was saying to all he met.[13]

When the Holland States convened on 4 July to discuss De Groot's report of his mission to Louis XIV, Alkmaar stated that when he had presented his first report nine days earlier matters were regarded as desperate. But now the situation had improved; the fortifications were better prepared; the inundations had taken place; the army had been strengthened and there was hope of assistance from abroad. Although Leyden did not share this view the mood of the majority was not with her.[14] Coenraad van Beuningen on behalf of Amsterdam made a powerful intervention, arguing that the negotiations with the French should be broken off, the sooner the better. Matters were capable of redress. All the princes of Europe had an interest in the outcome. It was possible to talk to England, where the Dutch were better placed – a reference, of course, to the Prince of Orange's family relationship with Charles II. France was demanding the towns in the Generality Lands, the better to conquer the Spanish Netherlands, and thereafter the Dutch – in which event they would still be subject to financial extortions.[15]

The outcome of these discussions produced the general sentiment that the French demands were unacceptable, although opinion was divided on whether to continue the negotiations or to break them off in a dignified manner, and that the opinion of the Prince of Orange should be sought on the matter.[16] Prince William's view was clear – the French terms were unacceptable. He was prepared to write to the King of England, but he would first hold discussions with Buckingham and Arlington, who had arrived in the Republic as Charles II's envoys to treat with both the Dutch and Louis XIV.[17]

THE ENGLISH NEGOTIATIONS AND SOVEREIGNTY

When the Dutch had sent their mission to England to negotiate with Charles in parallel with Louis XIV the English King refused to treat with them, fearing that Louis would see this as a wedge to prise them apart. He sent George Savile, Viscount Halifax, to Louis to reassure him that separate negotiations with the Dutch envoys were not taking place. At the same time he was receiving despatches from Sidney Godolphin, following in the train of the French army, who advised sending English emissaries to Louis before he captured the whole of the Dutch Republic. Halifax was sent via Zeeland to ascertain if that Province could not be persuaded to seek English protection, and thus to give Charles a bargaining counter. At the same time Arlington and Buckingham were sent as an Eminent Embassy to treat with Louis himself.[18]

The instructions that these two English ministers had received from Charles II on 1 July included demands for the right of the flag in British seas and the payment of an annual sum for the Dutch to fish in British waters; a war indemnity; the ceding of three or four 'precautionary towns' such as Flushing, Sluice, Brill 'or some others', with their garrisons to be paid for by the Dutch; and trade concessions in the East Indies.

The instructions also included provisions for the Prince of Orange: 'You shall make the best conditions you can for our nephew the Prince of Orange, by making him Prince (if possible) of Holland, as much of the other countryes [i.e. Provinces] as you can, or at least that he, and the heires males of his body be for ever stadtholders, generals and admirals.... But though you do not conclude a peace with the States-General yet you shall make conditions with [Louis XIV] for our nephew the Prince of Orange, as our treaty with the said King doth allow, and if it be possible you shall procure for him the places that shall be conquered in Holland or Zeeland (that is not our partage) or that shall submit upon owning him their Sovereign, but this must be left to you on the place, to get the best conditions you can for him.'[19] These were somewhat opaque demands and were more in the nature of a wish list; but clearly Uncle Charles was not willing to give up the dynastic cards that he held, without, however, being all that clear as to what to do with them.

The States of Holland had been forewarned of most of these terms by the Dutch delegation in England, including the hereditary right of Prince William to the Stadholdership and the military posts, but without mention of making him Prince of Holland and the other territorial concessions that Charles wished for him.[20] They had prepared a robust response. Even prior to obtaining the Prince's view on the French terms they had authorised him to commence negotiations with Arlington and Buckingham, in which, however, he was to be assisted by the two elder statesmen Coenraad van Beuningen and Hieronymus van Beverninck. It would be left to the discretion of this team whether they should display a certain 'liberality' to those whose good offices came to be employed for the benefit of the affairs of the Republic – that is to say, whether they should bribe the ambassadors. Otherwise their terms of reference contained restrictive provisos that no Province, towns or forts should be surrendered; nor any warships; and no annual payment for nautical rights or the right to fish should be admitted, although negotiations should not be broken off on this point.[21]

These terms reflected the new mood of defiance taking root in the beleaguered Republic, partly as a result of the changing European diplomatic situation to the advantage of the Dutch and partly because their defences on the Water Line were taking shape. But they may also have reflected other considerations. As we have seen, the States of Holland knew in advance the demands King Charles was going to make regarding the hereditary Stadholdership on behalf of his nephew; did they have an inkling, or did they anticipate, that there could also be demands of a territorial nature to include sovereignty on his behalf? Both the veto on granting any territorial concessions and the insistence on the involvement of Van Beuningen and Van Beverninck were clear restraints on his authority. Were they also designed to limit his freedom to manoeuvre on his own behalf? In any case, by design or not, when he did begin so to manoeuvre he had to take cognizance of these restraints.

The negotiations about to take place with Charles II's representatives need to be seen in the light of diplomatic shifts on the broader European scene, where the war had had the result of bringing the German powers into play. On 6 May Van Amerongen had finally succeeded in negotiating a treaty with the Elector of Brandenburg; in exchange for a subsidy of 220,000 thaler, and a commitment from the Dutch to pay half the cost of the Elector's army of 20,000 men, Frederick-William promised to have his army ready within two months of receipt of the recruitment money; these forces would advance through Westphalia to form a junction with the Dutch; and neither side would make a separate peace treaty with the French.[22]

The two-month period was stipulated to give the Elector time to negotiate a further treaty with the Austrian Emperor – something the Elector sorely needed. For it was a brave thing that he had done. His was the only European power that had entered into an alliance with the Dutch against the formidable might of Louis XIV – apart from the very limited Treaty of Mutual Assistance the Dutch had with Spain. According to Pagès, his motivation was his judgement that the preservation of the Dutch Republic was necessary for the preservation of the Reformed Church and the independence of Germany. As Pagès also notes, the Elector never in fact declared war on France – officially peace continued.[23]

The Elector was partly successful in his negotiations with Leopold I of Austria and a treaty between them was entered into on 23 June. This provided – with a delay of two months to enable the Austrians to build up their forces – for the formation of a combined army of 24,000 men, half Imperial and half Brandenburg. However, it did not oblige the Austrians to come to the assistance of the Dutch; rather it was a purely defensive treaty, with the Austrian troops solely committed to the defence of the Holy Roman Empire. Leopold was pre-occupied by discontent in Hungary and the threat from the Turks, whilst there was also profound suspicion of Frederick-William in Vienna.[24] Although neither their treaty with Brandenburg nor this limited Austro-Brandenburg treaty would bring immediate military relief to the Dutch, the treaties nevertheless put pressure on Louis XIV, presenting a potential future threat to his rear and to his very extensive lines of communication; and at the same time, of course, they were a welcome development for Dutch morale.

On the day the Holland States appointed William Stadholder, on Monday 4 July, the English ministers landed at Maassluis on their way first to The Hague and then to the camp of Louis XIV. As a safeguard for their personal security as they travelled through the terrain of the country with whom they were at war, they were escorted by a Utrecht Regent, Everart van Weede van Dijkveld, who had formed part of the Dutch mission to Charles II, and whom William was to use in the future both to consolidate his power base in the Province of Utrecht and to carry out many an important diplomatic mission on his behalf.

At Maassluis the English mission's hopes of bringing Zeeland into the English camp were raised by the manner of their greeting. There were cries of 'God blesse the King of England and the Prince of Orange and the Deville take the States', as Buckingham reported. The same state of affairs prevailed at Brill 'in soe much that I believe I might have taken that towne myselfe' – bravado and the Duke were never too far apart. But Arlington, too, thought that it would cost little to take most of the strong places of Zeeland 'who for their greate partiality to the Prince and feare of falling into French handes are saide to wish publiquely they were in his Majesty's [Charles II's]'.[25]

The two ambassadors sent Charles a copy of the demands Louis had made to Pieter De Groot 'in which', Buckingham noted, 'there is not the least notice taken of the King of England', adding 'the circumstances [surrounding these demands] I doe not like'. The suspicions of the King of France regarding his English ally were therefore clearly reciprocated on the English side.

Coenraad van Beuningen accompanied Arlington and Buckingham to the camp of the Prince of Orange at Bodegrave, but there the two Englishmen succeeded in having an initial meeting with William on their own late on 5 July. When the Prince reproached them about England's conduct regarding the war they replied that 'his Majesty would not be brought to begin it [the war] till hee had condiçoned the Prince should find his account in it in case of Successe'. They then drew him out on why he did not believe in that success, about which there was no doubt in their own minds. The Prince answered that the combination of the forces of the Elector of Brandenburg, of the Emperor of Austria, and of Spain would divert the French from their assault on the Dutch Republic. But more important than that was the belief that it was not in the interests of Charles II that the United Provinces should be totally overrun by France; the English should 'separate' from France and unite with the Dutch to constrain France to arrive at a settlement on more moderate terms; French demands were exorbitant and the Dutch 'would dy a thousand deaths rather then submitt to them'. As for the cautionary towns demanded by the English he was 'confident the States would never give them, and that for his owne part, hee could not in conscience advice them to it'. When they floated the possibility of his establishing his sovereignty 'over his country', secured by the Kings of England and France from foreign and domestic threats, 'hee replied hee liked better the condiçon of statholder … and that hee believed himselfe obliged in conscience and honour not to prefer his interest before his obligation'. His *gloire*, in short, needed to be preserved. Burnet says that, upon Buckingham asking the Prince if he could not see that the Dutch Republic was lost, he replied that 'he saw it was indeed in great danger, but there [was] a sure way never to see it lost, and that was to die in the last ditch'. So – to all appearances – there was not much progress there as regards the Prince of Orange.

At supper afterwards they were joined by Coenraad van Beuningen and Hieronymus van Beverninck, the former of whom, as was his wont, they found extremely voluble, 'with a multitude of arguments drawne from morality and conscience, which took up a great deal of time'. So definitely not much progress there either with the two elder Dutch statesmen. Van Beuningen's own report of this supper, which he made to the Holland States on 7 July, is further addressed below.

They did notice, however, that all the young men around William were of a contrary mind to himself, 'wishing there were a dozen of the States hanged soe the country had peace, and the prince were soveraigne of it'.

Yet, appearances to the contrary, behind the glacial, impenetrable façade of obduracy, the

Prince's talent for keeping his options open was at work. He agreed to keep confidential from Van Beuningen and Van Beverninck what had been discussed with the English ambassadors concerning 'sovereignty'. And when they left the next morning he made plans to send a personal emissary from himself to Charles to solicit his good offices to arrive at peace terms, 'upon the aforesaid grounds of honour and conscience', as the ambassadors put it.[26]

The man chosen for this task was a member of the Utrecht van Reede clan, Jonkheer Frederick van Reede van Renswoude, who had been first a page in his household and subsequently his Master of Horse, and who left for England on 6 or 7 July.[27] He was now about 42 years old.

On the 6th Arlington and Buckingham made their way to Zeist, near Utrecht, where Louis XIV was lodged, and where Charles II's illegitimate son, the Duke of Monmouth, was commanding an English contingent in the French army. Their despatch to Charles stated that they were received the following day with infinite grace by the French King himself, who assured them he would not do anything 'till the King our Master were intirely satisfyed'; indeed the King was so graceful that their suspicions of French intentions were for the moment stilled. The French 'expected speedily the returne of the States Deputies' and a discussion ensued with Pomponne and Louvois on the English requirements. These were conveyed in accordance with the ambassadors' instructions of 1 July and, as far as the Prince of Orange was concerned, he would be offered the Sovereignty of the United Provinces – the cautionary towns pertaining to the King of England excepted – under guarantee of the kings of France and England. A tripartite mission consisting of Henry Jermyn, the now knighted Gabriel Sylvius – who like Halifax had also travelled through Zeeland to assess the situation there – and Henry Seymour, the Speaker of the House of Commons, would be sent to William on the 9th with these proposals.[28]

Halifax, who had held conversations in Zeeland with Nassau-Odijk, the Dutch brother-in-law of Arlington, to explore the possibility of the Province asking for English protection,[29] had also arrived from there at Zeist the previous night. He assured Arlington and Buckingham – as they reported to Charles II – that there was 'all aversion possible towards France and a formal resolution [from the common people of Middelburg] to put themselves into English hands in case of extremity' had been passed. Arlington and Buckingham judged that, if the Prince of Orange could be persuaded to cooperate with this movement, the work would 'not bee hard' to win Zeeland over. But, it would be necessary first to disable, if not to destroy, the Dutch fleet – 'of the reasonablenesse of which', the ambassadors rather trailed off, as they appraised this obstacle, 'his Majesty is the best as the properest Judge'.[30]

In the meantime they settled down to await the arrival of the Dutch deputies with their response to Louis XIV's demands and the reaction of the Prince of Orange to the overtures being made to him.[31]

But, as for the Dutch deputies, they never arrived.

At the same time as Arlington and Buckingham were holding their discussions with the French at Zeist on 7 July the States of Holland were in session in The Hague to hear Coenraad van Beuningen's report of the supper which he, Hieronymus van Beverninck and Prince William had had with the two Englishmen on the 5th, following on from the meeting William had held with the two English ambassadors on his own. The English admitted, Van Beuningen reported, that matters had gone further than they had anticipated – a reference to the extent of the French conquests – but they said that they could not break with France. They pressed the Dutch representatives on what their proposals to England were and were told that there were none; matters were much changed, with the Prince's elevation to the Stadholdership being worth 12 towns to England (the English ambassadors interjected that if the Prince had been Stadholder in the first place there would never have been an issue between the two countries). On being asked about their proposals to the French the reply was that these came down to 'Maastricht and [French] garrisons in the Rhine towns up to Schenkenschans'. These proposals Arlington and Buckingham undertook to convey to Louis XIV, but they gave their view that not much would come from all this.[32] In the event the Dutch soon tacitly dropped even this offer.

In the ensuing debate within the States of Holland on whether they should continue with their negotiations with France on the terms demanded by Louis XIV the 50-year-old statesman[33] from Amsterdam, Coenraad van Beuningen, with all the prestige of his long experience, made a fiery, emotional, uncompromising speech which carried all before it. The offer of the Generality Lands to France had come as a great shock to Spain; it had come about without the consent of the Provinces and the advice of Amsterdam; the Prince of Orange was not only in good standing with Charles II but also with the common people in the Republic; he believed the English had good intentions; the Prince was in negotiation with them and De Groot's negotiations should not be allowed to prejudice them; the common people would beat them to death if they conceded to the French; the Emperor, Spain, the German princes, even Sweden could not contemplate the French King making himself master of Holland; De Groot should not return to the French because he had offered more than could be delivered – exceeded his powers, in other words – and negotiations with the French should be broken off.[34]

As far as Pieter De Groot's mooted return mission to Louis was concerned that was the end of the matter.

The tripartite mission of Sir Gabriel Sylvius, Henry Jermyn and Sir Edward Seymour arrived at the Prince's quarters carrying a covering letter from the English envoys dated 9 July and a draft agreement for him to sign, both written in somewhat haughty tones. The draft agreement committed the Prince to do everything possible to bring about a peace between the United Provinces and the English and French kings on terms that the two kings judged just and equitable, and to do everything possible to facilitate the granting of the cautionary towns to Charles II in perpetuity. In return the two kings would do everything possible to grant the Sovereignty of the United Provinces to Prince William, the Prince, so read the draft, 'being entirely persuaded and convinced in all conscience that the peace could not otherwise be arrived at for the benefit of [his] aflicted country'; and furthermore, the draft continued, he 'very humbly supplicated the said kings' to act as guarantors of his sovereignty.[35]

The covering letter stated that, if the Prince did not comply, the envoys would 'bee forced to returne home' and new measures would be proposed 'farr different from those' they were making now.[36]

Seymour departed for England immediately after this meeting, which, again, had taken place with the Prince alone; and he reported on his arrival home on the 21st 'that the Prince of Orange is not yet inclined to hearken to what has been proposed to him'. But the operative words here are 'not yet'. He was still leaving his options open. In Wicquefort's account the English delegation represented to William the miserable state of his country and said that there was only one way out, which was for the Prince to accept the sovereignty of the country, in which the two kings would assist him, if he would put the conquered towns and the Generality Lands in the hands of the French King. To this the Prince replied that they had come 24 hours too late, for as Stadholder and Captain-General he had sworn an oath of loyalty to the State. When Sylvius pointed out that he had also previously sworn not to accept the Stadholdership Prince William replied that the States-General had dispensed him from that oath and it was indeed true that they could also now grant him the same dispensation from his present one; one would have to see what would happen; he was not rejecting the offers from the two kings; and he thanked them for the goodwill they were showing him.[37] In Wicquefort's account, therefore, the Prince did not give a categorical rejection to the suggestion of sovereignty, as he had done at his earlier meetings with Buckingham and Arlington. Wicquefort was not an Orangist – on the contrary – but even if we dismiss his version on that account we shall see that the question of sovereignty was very much in the Prince's mind.

He, in the meantime, sent a report of the meeting to the States of Holland via Coenraad van Beuningen in which there was no mention of sovereignty. The English, he said, had asked for the immediate surrender of Sluys, Flushing and Brill and the Prince was writing to ask for clarification from Buckingham and Arlington on the precise terms the Dutch were being asked to comply with in a peace treaty.[38] He also wrote to the States-General indicating that his tactics were not to break off negotiations, but to try to arrive at an acceptable peace with both kings, hopefully with the goodwill of Charles II, and if that did not succeed, it might be possible, by dint of offering one side a bit more and the other side a bit less, to divide the two parties.[39]

On the 10th Louis XIV left Zeist with a large escort to return to France, leaving the Duke of Luxemburg in command of the occupying army in the captured Dutch territories. Buckingham and Arlington travelled in his retinue and on the 16th they entered into a treaty with the French at Heeswijk. They agreed not to enter into a separate peace with the Dutch and agreed the joint terms they would present to conclude a peace. On the French side these were essentially the same as the ones presented to De Groot and on the English side essentially those contained in Charles's instructions to Arlington and Buckingham on 1 July. The war indemnity for the English was fixed at £1 million; the island of Walcheren and the towns of Sluis, Cadzand, Goeree and Voorne would be ceded as pledges – cautionary towns – for the performance of the treaty; and sovereignty would be granted to the Prince of Orange over the remaining rump of the Dutch Republic.[40]

These Heeswijk demands were delivered to the Prince by Sylvius, with a covering letter dated 17 July from Buckingham and Arlington requesting a reply within ten days.[41]

The sovereignty question was now in the open for, on the 20th, the proposals were submitted to the Holland States. The submission was accompanied by these preliminary comments from the Prince: the proposals were, he said, unacceptable; there was not a single article which he would pursue; it would be preferable to be cut to pieces than enter into such an agreement; and as to what related to himself – that is to say, the proposed sovereignty – this came from his enemies and not his friends. This last – although literally true in the sense that the suggestion of sovereignty had not originated with him – was more than disingenuous, for the Prince had no intention of discarding this important card; it was too useful an option and it could be played in a number of ways.[42]

The following day Hieronymus van Beuningen told the Holland States that the unanimous advice of the Prince and of the Holland deputies acting with him was to let the French know, without further ado, that the Heeswijk proposals were unacceptable, whilst continuing to negotiate with the English whose demands 'did not come from the king, but from (his) ministers', which advice was accepted[43] by both the Holland States and the States-General.

Buckingham and Arlington, accompanied by Halifax, had left Louis XIV and, on their way back to England, had stopped at Antwerp. There Sylvius found them on the evening of the 20th and he reported on the outcome of his own conversations with the Prince of Orange regarding the Heeswijk proposals. Sylvius had 'found him in no small trouble att the propositions he [Sylvius] carried with him, saying he looks for easier ones from both the Kings *with a recommendation to the States of making him soverain of their countrys* [my italics]'. Van Beverninck, Van Beuningen and Van Amerongen 'were attending' the Prince, and Sylvius 'found him unwilling to answer, nay almost to open his letters, without [their] being by' – his initial remark about sovereignty must have been made before they came into the vicinity. Then, in their presence and whilst mounting his horse to depart for Schoonhoven, he remonstrated with Sylvius 'concerning the exorbitancy of the French propositions and the dificulty he should find in getting the English ones granted; he beleeved Sluse, Cadsande and the Brill might bee consented to, but that the people of Vlissing [Flushing] were so extravagant in their humours that they would never consent to putt themselves into the English hands.'

The English ambassadors decided that the best thing to do in these circumstances was to send Sylvius to Louis XIV to see whether he would be prepared to moderate his demands. If so they would also moderate theirs.[44]

But Louis, who had just captured two more towns, Crevecoeur and Bommel, was in no mood to be accommodating. He advised the English ambassadors to go straight to London in the same way as he himself was heading for Paris.[45]

Before they could continue their journey Coenraad van Beuningen arrived at their quarters at Antwerp on the 23rd, intent on prising the English apart from their French allies. He told them that, if Holland was to be ruined, she would give herself up to the French as a single undivided unit rather than submit to being partitioned between the English and the French. At dinner he continued on this vexatious course, as Williamson, the secretary to the English delegation, recorded in his diary. Chuckling to himself, he announced 'to thinke what a game we [the English] played for ourselves in suffering [the Dutch] to be lost ... we could last but three years after them.' Ridiculous behaviour, the English thought.

But a further development had taken place. The Prince's confidant, who commanded his military escort, the young Rhinegrave Charles Florentine van Salm, too had arrived at Antwerp. The Rhinegrave asked to speak to Henry Germain on his own and told him that he had come on the orders of the Prince of Orange to let the English envoys know that he did not seek, nor was he ready, at an early date, to accept an offer of sovereignty, but that he would willingly accept it 'if the people gave it him'. The ambassadors had only to tell Van Beuningen that Charles II 'would take it well, and desire [sovereignty] should be given' the Prince and 'certainly the thing would be done'.

The purpose of the Rhinegrave's mission was therefore to elaborate on what William told Sylvius, when Sylvius delivered the Heeswijk terms, that he was looking for 'a recommendation to the States of making him soverain of the country'. What he wanted was for sovereignty to come to him, not as a result of a clumsy bargain made between himself and Charles II and Louis – as embodied in the draft agreement of 9 July and its covering letter – but as a result of it being offered to him by 'the people', that is, the political class within the country. This class indeed would arrive at the decision to make the offer in the conviction that it would be pleasing to Charles II and that this was the route to a satisfactory peace. But there was a nice, though supremely important, difference between, on the one hand, the Prince accepting sovereignty from Charles and Louis on the basis of his own conviction that this was the best way to obtain peace and, on the other hand, receiving it from 'the people', even if 'the people' were convinced for the same reason. The first would put him in a tight client/patron relationship with the two kings, particularly with his uncle, backed up by a formal treaty between them – which was tantamount to a manumission; the second would very much strengthen the legitimacy of his sovereignty where it mattered, the political class of the United Provinces. It was the difference between the Prince acknowledging the two kings as his patrons and 'the people' of the United Provinces formally acknowledging themselves as his clients.

Of course, all this still left open William's vehement rejection of the Heeswijk peace terms, as Sylvius had emphasised to Arlington and Buckingham.

The Rhinegrave explicitly said that his orders were to talk to Arlington and not to Buckingham, perhaps because Arlington was married into the Nassau clan and had been used by the Prince in the past to convey his signals to his uncle. But when the Rhinegrave spoke to Arlington the nice distinction the Prince was trying to convey passed him by. The perplexed English minister asked the Rhinegrave, 'what shall wee gett, if wee doe this for' the Prince. 'What would you ask?' said the Rhinegrave. After talking to the more obdurate Buckingham the envoys offered some minor adjustments to the treaty terms. They had missed the point, or perhaps saw it all as a ploy to prise Charles away from Louis XIV to make a separate peace on his own – which indeed is likely to have been part, but by no means all, of what the Prince had in mind. The Rhinegrave shrugged, said that he would consult the Prince and promised to return immediately.

Waiting for a reply until the 25th, which did not arrive, the ambassadors decided to depart for Ghent where they found a letter from the Rhinegrave on the 26th and 'two lines of civility from the Prince of Orange's owne hand. But not one word of the business…. At which [they] wondered much.'

In this perplexed state they proceeded on their homeward journey with instructions for Sylvius to return to the Prince of Orange with the reply from Louis XIV that he would not moderate his demands, after which Sylvius too was to go on to England.[46]

As we have seen the Prince had sent a personal emissary, Jonkheer Frederick van Reede, to Charles II at the beginning of July. Van Reede arrived at Whitehall on the 14th, and, although his own account describes a very friendly reception, he made no progress in hiving off Charles II from France.[47] The Jonkheer brought two letters back with him which contained the King's replies. The first, dated 18 July (8th Old Style), was not in the King's hand, but only signed by him, and it was in French, and hence was intended as a formal official response: it laid the blame for the war on the regime of De Witt – with its 'insolences and perpetual machinations' – and it held out the promise, now that William had become Stadholder and if the King could be assured that the changed circumstances that now existed would continue, that Charles would do all he could as far as Louis XIV was concerned to facilitate an end to the war. This, of course, fell far short of breaking with Louis XIV, which the Prince of Orange and his countrymen were seeking. We shall return to this letter, and its publication at Fagel's instigation at the beginning of August, with its damaging effects on the position of Johan De Witt.

The second letter, dated 22 July, was in the King's own hand in English and was intended, therefore, as a personal letter for Prince William himself.

My deare Nephew, I have heard this bearer, Monsr. Reed, at large upon all you directed him to impart to me, and have had many conversations with him about your affairs, as matters now stand in Holland, in all which he will assure you that my kindnesse to you is not in the least deminished. The advice I give you by him, I am certaine is impartiall and most for your good, which you will not offten heare from those that I finde are about you, who will have ends very much contrary to your interest; but if you will follow my advice, I make little doute by the blessing of God of establishing you in that power there, which your forefathers alwaies aimed at, and I hope your ambission is not lesse, for being my nephew; I will say no more on this subject, haveing so fully instrueted the bearer, only to tell you that, though you may put it out of my power to expresse the kindness I have for you, I can never change in my harte from being, My deare Nephew,

your most affectionate uncle

Charles R.[48]

The letter indicates, therefore, that, whilst the King did not address the main point – he had no intention of breaking with France – neither was he breaking off negotiations with his nephew; and the bait of sovereignty continued to be dangled before the Prince of Orange, but it would be bestowed by Charles II, not by 'the people'.

Both Charles's letters were in the Prince's hands by 29 July.

When Sylvius – accompanied by Dr Rumpf – arrived in England on about 28 July he brought with him the Prince's answer to the Heeswijk proposals, which almost certainly were sent before he was in receipt of the two letters from his uncle.[49] These counter-proposals were that, on condition that Charles made peace with the Dutch Republic and ceased to assist France in any form, then the Prince offered to cede the right of the flag; pay 100,000 *livres* (just over £8,000) for fishing rights; cede Surinam; pay a war indemnity of 400,000 *livres* (£33,300); cede Sluys as a cautionary town; and the sovereignty of the seven provinces would accrue to himself.[50] Therefore, if, as the evidence strongly suggests, these proposals were sent to Charles before the Prince received his uncle's letters, he did not need any prompting from his uncle in pursuing the possibility of sovereignty – he was already pursuing it himself. He did not spell out how it was to be bestowed, but we have seen that in his mind it would have to come 'from the people'. He suggested that if these proposals were acceptable to the King then he could send further trustworthy emissaries who could act in his interests, when, no doubt, the means of bestowing sovereignty could be appropriately addressed. Of course, the proposals were dependent on his uncle's breaking with Louis XIV.

These proposals were naturally immeasurably more favourable to the Dutch than the Heeswijk terms. But it needs to be noted that the Prince was exceeding his authority – a proposal from Dordrecht that he should be given full powers to negotiate with England was rejected by the States of Holland on 14 July – and he had not agreed these terms in advance with either the States of Holland or the States-General.[51]

He must nevertheless have thought – he implied as much in September, when he sent Van Reede on a second mission to England – that there was a chance of being able to persuade them to accept the terms, and thus, possibly, also the point on sovereignty. We shall never know whether they would in fact have done so. It is true the Dutch Republic found itself in a precarious predicament; and, as the Rhinegrave told Henry Germain, as important a figure as Van Beuningen – who attached great store to William's connection with Charles – was, apparently, prepared to act to lend his support in procuring sovereignty on his behalf. It may be, therefore, that William's assessment of the chances of receiving it from both the States of Holland and the States-General, thus from 'the people', was worth a try. He could keep his options open – a consistent theme which, it will become apparent, characterised his whole career. Nevertheless, as we shall see in the next chapter, his own position in the Dutch Republic remained far from secure; Van Beuningen seemed to be a questionable basis for achieving his aims, despite the Rhinegrave's mention of him;[52] and it was just as implausible that Charles II would be prepared to countenance the independent form of sovereignty which he was seeking.

Indeed, in a letter dated 10 August that Rumpf brought over, Charles II rejected the proposals; these, he said, fell 'infinetly short of what I expected from you, not only in that you suppose, I can or will make conditions without France, but even in the conditions themselves, which I do not demande only for my owne security, but for yours also.… Bethinke yourselfe well what will become of you, when the warr shall be ended, if I have not a good footing in that country to stand by you against the designes and machinations of those that shall finde themselves throwne out of the governement, to which they have been so long accustomed.'[53] In this King Charles had a point, to which we shall return; but, for now, we need to heed the increasing note of asperity he is showing at his nephew's reluctance to fall in with his plans, and in particular at the Prince's attempt to separate him from Louis XIV.

In the meantime the two brothers De Witt had been murdered on 20 August, torn to pieces in horrific circumstances by an irate mob in The Hague. Charles wrote again at the end of August saying that the killing of these instigators of the war showed that the Dutch people were infinitely desirous of peace and that he was apprehensive for Prince William's person if they found out that he was opposing it. He suggested, therefore, that plenipotentiaries from England, France and the Republic should meet at Dunkirk, 'where a peace may be speedily concluded'.[54]

Sylvius, too, added his urgings to those of the King in a couple of long letters during

August, to which the Prince replied that, whilst he was prepared to oblige the King in all matters where he had the power to do so 'in this it is not'.[55] But, when Sylvius wrote again on 9 September[56] to say that his failure to reply to Charles II's letters of friendship could, he feared, have very ill consequences, Prince William once again turned to Jonkheer van Reede to carry out a second mission to England in the middle of September.

Van Reede's instructions were to tell the King in the politest terms that, whilst the Prince of Orange was still prepared to do all he could to persuade the States-General to accept the conditions which had been conveyed to the King by Sylvius – that is, Prince William's counter-offer to the Heeswijk proposals – public opinion in the Republic would not accept a peace with France and he himself was against it for a number of reasons; but they would accept a peace with England on reasonable terms. And the King was once again to be urged to break with France.[57]

Held up by bad weather, Van Reede did not arrive at Whitehall until 22 September. Once again he was well received by Charles, who embraced him with both arms; but when the message of the Jonkheer had been delivered the emollient mood of the monarch at once changed, and he began to fulminate against his nephew.[58] He expressed his exasperation in a letter of the 30th to Prince William, which Van Reede bore with him when he returned to Holland:

> I was very much surprised to finde my selfe so long without an answer to my two letters recommending to you sentiments of peace, and sheweing you a ready way to it, by an assurance of a moderation in the demandes, of France as well as England, and naming a place for the treaty so neare you. But I must confess to you, I was much surprised when after so long an expectation I had your answer by Monr. De Reede without the least siginification that my offers were acceptable to you, upon which I have taken the liberty to speake my minde very freely to Monr. De Reede and I hope you will take it for a great marke of my kindnesse to you that I have done so. I assure you, if I loued you lesse I would have taken an other course….

Threatening words indeed. But King Charles's ire had been triggered not only by his nephew's refusal to fall in with his plans for the Dutch Republic, but also by the suspicion that he was allying himself with persons in England who were intriguing against the King – Van Reede was warned by Charles in the presence of the Duke of York and Arlington that the Prince should not allow himself to be exploited by any malcontents. From the Prince's letters it seems that Arlington had threatened the Prince with the fate that befell the De Witts – the King could allow him to be torn to pieces by the mob.[59] But the King himself had also issued the same threat to Van Reede – 'He could with a little cost put the Prince where De Witt was' – which Van Reede passed on to William.[60]

Prince William tried to be conciliatory towards his uncle; he said he was 'in despair' at the King's reaction to Van Reede's mission, but that it did not solely depend on him to do what the King desired and, referring to the suspicions about his involvement with the English opposition, he begged the King to pay no credence to the false rumours that he was enmeshed in anything which ran counter to the King's interests.[61]

With Arlington a more brusque approach was deemed appropriate: 'Don't think your threats to have me torn in pieces by the populace will cause me any qualms; I am not very fearful by nature.'[62] The now just turned 22-year-old head of the House of Orange was not going to allow himself to be put upon by a servitor, minister of his Stuart uncle although he might be and linked by marriage to his own House through his wife Isabella Nassau-Beverweert.

Diplomacy having failed to detach Charles II from Louis XIV, the Prince very soon resorted to the alternative of which his uncle suspected him – use of the English opposition, in which context his membership of the Stuart clan was to be a key asset.[63]

1 H.T. Colenbrander, *Bescheiden uit vreemde archieven omtrent de groote Nederlandsche zeeoorlogen 1652–1676*, The Hague, 1919, II, 1667–76, pp.128, 130, 140–1.

2 Hop & Vivien, *op. cit.*, p.155.

3 There are various accounts of these events. I have followed in the main Rowen, *De Witt, op. cit.*, p.844, together with Wicquefort, *Histoire, op. cit.*, IV, pp.495–6, and Hop & Vivien, *op. cit.*, pp.160–62. The account in Geyl, *op. cit.*, pp.357–8 differs significantly as regards dates, which are incompatible with each other in his version.

4 D.J. Roorda, *Partij en Factie*, Groningen, 1978, pp.120–24.

5 *Ibid.*, pp.70–1, 85.

6 The debate in the States of Holland is contained in Hop & Vivien, *op. cit.*, pp.159–71.

7 Wicquefort, *Histoire, op. cit.*, IV, p.500. Roorda, *op. cit.*, p.126. Wagenaar, *op. cit.*, 14, p.87.

8 Wicquefort, *Histoire, op. cit.*, IV, p.502. Wagenaar, *op. cit.*, 14, pp.87–8.

9 Roorda, *op. cit.*, p.126.

10 *Correspondentie W.III en Portland, op. cit.*, II, Pt 1, pp.56–7, 59–61.

11 *Correspondentie W.III en Portland, op. cit.*, II, Pt 1, pp.62–3. The letter is undated, but Japikse dates it after 4 and before 9 July when the visit took place, p.62 n.4.

12 Groen van Prinsterer, *Archives, op. cit.*, V, p.263. Dated July 1672.

13 *Correspondentie W.III en Bentinck, op. cit.*, II, Pt 1, pp.57–8. Hop & Vivien, *op. cit.*, pp.172ff. gives the debate in the States of Holland on 4 July following De Groot's report on his mission to Louis XIV, which confirms Fagel's assessment of Holland's opinion.

14 Hop & Vivien, *op. cit.*, pp.173–5.

15 *Ibid.*, p.175 and n.2.

16 *Ibid.*, 178.

17 *Ibid.*, p.184.

18 Hutton, *op. cit.*, p.289.

19 Colenbrander, *op. cit.*, II, pp.142–3.

20 Hop & Vivien, *op. cit.*, pp.165–6.

21 *Ibid.*, p.180.

22 Wout Troost, 'William III, Brandenburg, and the construction of the anti-French coalition', *The Anglo-Dutch Moment*, ed. Jonathan Israel, 1991, p.303. J.W. Sypesteyn, *Nederland and Brandenburg in 1672 en 1673*, The Hague, 1863, p.45.

Albert Waddington, *Le Grand Électeur Frédéric Guillaume de Brandenbourg. Sa Politique Extérieure 1640–1688*, Paris, 1908, pp.263–4.

23 G. Pagès, *Le Grand Électeur et Louis XIV, 1660–1688*, Paris, 1905, pp.289. See also pp.287–90 on the treaty. Fred. William got very little for himself; the Dutch did not concede their fortresses in his territories and they barely paid for half of the costs of his troops. See also p.291 n.1.

24 *Ibid.*, pp.293, 298. Derek McKay, 'Small-power diplomacy in the age of Louis XIV: the foreign policy of the Great Elector during the 1660's and 1670's', *Royal and Republican Sovereignty in Early Modern Europe*, Oresko, Gibbs & Scott, eds, Cambridge University Press, 1997.

25 Colenbrander, *op. cit.*, II, pp.146, 147, 148. Wicquefort, *Mémoires, op. cit.*, p.226.

26 Colenbrander, *op. cit.*, II, pp.154–6. G. Burnet, *op. cit.*, 1897, I, p.585.

27 Fruin, *Verspreide Geschriften, op. cit.*, IV, p.354n.

28 Colenbrander, II, pp.156–7.

29 Geyl, *op. cit.*, pp.367–8.

30 Colenbrander, *op. cit.*, II, p.157.

31 *Ibid.*, p.159.

32 Hop & Vivien, *op. cit.*, pp.187–90. The Rhineland towns lay outside the United Provinces and so outside the prohibition on conceding towns and fortresses contained in the Dutch delegation's terms of reference.

33 Franken, *op. cit.*, p.44, states that he was assumed to have been born in 1622, but that this is not absolutely certain.

34 Hop & Vivien, *op. cit.*, pp.193–5.

35 Colenbrander, *op. cit.*, II, p.161.

36 *Correspondentie W.III en Portland, op. cit.*, II, Pt 1, p 65.

37 Colenbrander, *op. cit.*, II, *Inleiding*, p.XXV. Wicquefort, *Histoire, op. cit.*, IV, p.447.

38 Hop & Vivien, *op. cit.*, pp.209–10. The prince's undated letter is in *Correspondentie, W.III en Bentinck*, II, Pt 1, p.66.

39 Japikse, *Willem III, op. cit.*, I, pp.228–9. His source: undated letter in Public Record Office, state papers, foreign archives 101, fol.30.

40 Wagenaar, *op. cit.*, 14, pp.119ff.

41 Colenbrander, *op. cit.*, II, *Inleiding*, p.XXV n.4.

42 Hop & Vivien, *op. cit.*, pp.225–6.

43 *Ibid.*, pp 228–9. Wagenaar, *op. cit.*, 14, p.126.

44 Despatch Buckingham, Arlington and Halifax to Charles II, 21 July. Colenbrander, *op. cit.*, II, pp.168–9.

45 Despatch Godolphin to Arlington, 22 July, 'From the camp near Boisleduc (Hertogenbosch)'. Colenbrander, *op. cit.*, II, p.172.

46 Colenbrander, *op. cit.*, II, pp.164–6. Extracts from the diary of Williamson.

47 Elisabeth Korvezee, *De Zending van Frederik van Reede Naar Engeland in de jaren 1672–1674 Bijdragen voor Vaderlandsche Gechiedenis en Oudheidkunde*, 6th series, Pt 7, The Hague, 1928.

48 *Correspondentie W.III en Portland, op. cit.*, II, Pt 1, pp.73–4. Also in Schotel, *Bijdragen voor Nederlandsche Geschiedenis en Oudheidkunde*, 4th series, Pt 4, 1866, p.12.

49 See Fruin, *op. cit.*, IV, pp.353–4 n.3.

50 *Correspondentie W.III en Portland, op. cit.*, II, Pt 1, p.80.

51 Hop & Vivien, *op. cit.*, p.216.

52 The mention of Van Beuningen by the Rhinegrave as being prepared to further the Prince's assumption of sovereignty is indeed curious, given his subsequent career and opposition to the Prince. Possibly he was momentarily persuaded – he was notoriously volatile – that, in the dire straits in which the Dutch Republic found itself, William's good standing with Charles II and the common people (see p.185) at this time left no alternative.

53 Letter dated 31 July O.S., 10 August N.S. *Correspondentie W.III en Portland, op. cit.*, II, Pt 1, p.86. Also Schotel, *op. cit.*, pp.13–14.

54 Letter dated 20 August O.S., 30 N.S. *Correspondentie W.III en Portland, op. cit.*, II, Pt 1, p.96. Also Schotel, *op. cit.*, pp.14–15.

55 Colenbrander, *op. cit.*, II, pp.189–94. Japikse, *Willem III, op. cit.*, I, p.236.

56 Colenbrander, *op. cit.*, II, pp.194–5.

57 Schotel, *op. cit.*, p.13.

58 Korvezee, *op. cit.*, p.246.

59 *Ibid.*, p.249.

60 Haley, *William of Orange and the English Opposition, 1672–4,* Oxford, 1953, p.50.
61 Letter to Charles II, 7 October 1672, *Correspondentie W.III en Portland, op. cit.*, II, Pt 1, pp.114–15. Also Schotel, *op. cit.*, pp.16–17.
62 *Correspondentie W.III en Portland, op. cit.*, II, Pt 1, pp.115–16. Also Schotel, *op. cit.*, p.18.
63 Haley, *English Opposition, op. cit.*, pp.50–51. Haley thinks it not impossible, indeed, that the contacts with the opposition had already begun which would explain Charles II's outburst to Van Reede.

10 1672: THE DESTRUCTION OF THE DE WITT REGIME

THE PRINCE'S PRECARIOUS POSITION

When William took his oath of office his rule was far from being based on sure foundations. The Town Councils and the Provincial States of the unoccupied Provinces of Holland and Zeeland, followed by the States-General, were compelled to yield to popular violence and intimidation to restore to him his House's traditional offices of Stadholder and Captain- and Admiral-General. These were the same governments who for years had largely supported De Witt in his opposition to such a restoration: who had only as a compromise agreed to the possible elevation of the Prince to the military offices alone; who had only under the dire threat of war from France agreed to his actual appointment to the military offices; and who had only taken the final step of adding the Stadholdership under the cataclysmic consequences of the French invasion. There was still a great deal of anti-Orange sentiment, which reflected itself in pamphlets, which did not fall short of accusing the Prince of engaging in treasonable activities.[1] Fagel warned him on 1 July that 'the present affection for Your Highness very much displeases a lot of people',[2] and indeed it would have been surprising if there had not been feelings, ranging from suspicion to resentment, amongst many of the Regents, leaving scope for a reaction to develop against his power. It was an important factor and helps to explain the inflexible course that Prince William thought it necessary to follow against De Witt and his adherents.

THE REGENTS AND POPULAR DISCONTENT

The Dutch Regent class, particularly in the maritime provinces of Holland and Zeeland, had over the years grown increasingly rich, enjoyed an increasingly luxurious lifestyle, and had increasingly adopted French culture and mores, becoming bilingual in French and Dutch – a member of the Council of State did not scruple during this war against France to send his son to be educated in that country, after which he entered into service at the court of Prince William.[3] Since the establishment of De Witt's regime and the abolition of the Stadholdership it had become a self-appointed hereditary elite, with positions on the Town Councils taking place through co-option. It had in short become something of a quasi-aristocracy.[4] To qualify as a Regent one was expected to be a man of standing, as regards both wealth and lineage.[5]

This oligarchy was very much based on family relationships bound together by secret written agreements.[6] The patricians were closely linked to the judiciary and they could exercise considerable patronage, securing tens, or even hundreds, of jobs in countless ways – apart from their own expenditure they could control or influence expenditure in the municipalities – as a result of which they could build up an appreciable personal following amongst the middling sort in society.[7] They exercised considerable influence in the appointment of preachers, which required the approval, or the cooperation, of the Town Councils, who also met a large part of the Church's costs.[8] But they were split into factions, with a power base which very often tended to be local, and, supported by a local following, they strove for local power against each other. It would be an over-simplification, however, to describe the Regent power structure entirely in local terms. De Witt's family and connections, for example, transcended the localities and it was his achievement, by using families, clans and patronage at both the local and national level, to forge a regime that could govern the whole country.

As a governing class in the 17th century the Regents also had one particular weakness, which caused them to fall short of achieving full-blown aristocracy by the standards of the time. They had a close understanding of matters relating to finance and commerce – from which background their families tended to have arisen – and, to a large degree, of matters naval, but they had little family tradition in land warfare; for this they relied on the old aristocratic families and gentry, particularly in the land provinces, on foreign officers whom they hired for the purpose, and above all, when driven to it, to the House of Orange and its network of followers. This and their fear of the House had led them to neglect the army. In the defeats of the French war in which they were now involved their authority and prestige were badly afflicted; the daily exactions of their governments had built up long-standing resentments; and first the appearance, and then the fact, of anarchy created a popular hysteria.

The initial popular discontent was directed against the Regents as a class which had failed the country, and it was in favour of the Orangists.[9] But, once the disturbances arose, the temptation to exploit the discontent by Regent factions against each other was not resisted. To use the violence to unbalance their opponents the factions used intermediaries – the well-off in the class below them, officers and even non-commissioned officers in the militia, clergymen – to communicate with the agitators to ease themselves into, and their opponents out of, office.[10]

A fierce pamphlet war broke out in which vituperations of all sorts were heaped on the Regents both as a class and individually.[11]

THE PRINCE AND POPULAR DISCONTENT

The States of Holland turned to the Prince to defend the establishment against the menaces and violence of the mob.[12]

Radical change of the political and social structures of the Dutch Republic, or what remained of it, was not in his interests. The rump of the country could neither have been organised for the war nor could the war have been financed. He would need to conduct the war through the existing structures, as De Witt had done before him – clans and families, patrons and clients, local identities, religious affiliations and all – and like De Witt create a regime which could govern the whole country.

On 8 July he wrote a round-robin letter to the towns of Holland in which he defended the Regents against the accusations of betrayal, currently in vigorous circulation. He attributed the losses of the war in large part to the treason and cowardice of those to whom the most important posts had been entrusted. This had the effect, he said, of causing dismay amongst the inhabitants of the country and distrust of the Regents, and from this distrust there resulted worrying disturbances in a number of towns, which did not fall short of violating the respect and obedience that people owed the legal authorities. He was, he continued, disposed, on the one hand, to punish the disloyalty and cowardice of the military, but, on the other hand, he had no knowledge or even suspicion of any Regent from Holland being guilty of treason, being in cahoots with the enemy, or anything else in conflict with his oath of office. He would hold those responsible for the disturbances to be punishable in the highest degree as disturbers of the peace.[13]

But when this round robin did not have the desired effect – the riots continued – the Prince refused to follow it up with any action. He was asked to issue an ordinance against the disturbances, but replied on 15 July that he did not think that that would restore the peace and indeed that it would be counter-productive. The disturbances originated with leading citizens whom it would be better to lead than to force by means of harsh ordinances. He thought a commission made up of people of distinction to placate the populace would have the best effect; but he could not lead this in person himself as he could not leave his post with the army.[14]

It is indeed true that, given the force of the popular movements, and the fact that there was a hazardous war to be fought, there was little Prince William could do to stem the popular tide. He had tried to use his personal authority with his round robin, and this had failed. In the circumstances issuing ordinances without military backing would have risked the loss of further authority and the military could not be spared from the front line. The popular movement would have to run its course.

But that is not to say that, in adapting to the realities of the situation, the Prince could not use the disturbances for his own political purposes. An overthrow of the existing social and political structures was something wholly undesirable, but a change of personnel within those structures was something different altogether. He quickly realised that, as there was little he could do to stem the disturbances, the alternative was to make use of them – and in doing that he was doing what many of the Regent factions themselves were doing.

But the risks were not negligible and to change the personnel, without causing serious damage to the structures themselves or building up renewed opposition to himself within the Regent class, would require great skill and finesse.

Furthermore, there was another factor: as we shall see, the Prince was nowhere nearly as assured in his own mind of his position with the populace as has been maintained. Whilst he had to contend with residual opposition within the Regent class and the danger of counter-measures from De Witt's supporters, there was also a fear of the potential volatility of the popular mood, which he was by no means certain would always work in his favour. Hence there was an element of self-defence in the way he now proceeded.

The first substantial figure from the old De Witt regime to be the object of his carefully calculated and calibrated strategy, coldly and ruthlessly pursued, was Pieter De Groot. At the end of June the mob at Rotterdam had agitated against him and his authority was gravely undermined by the leading part he had played in trying to placate Louis XIV. When on 20 July the States-General began the debate on the Heeswijk peace terms the Prince was invited to expand further on his preliminary comments on the terms which in the event he made not to the States-General but to the States of Holland (see p.187 above). But he said he was only prepared to do so on condition that certain persons, whom he would name, would absent themselves. The representatives from Holland said that they feared that if this happened it would trigger further commotion amongst the populace. When the States of Holland met separately to discuss how further to proceed the nobles suggested that the persons the Prince had in mind should absent themselves from the debate but that secrecy should be preserved lest they become subject to the libels and maltreatment of the populace. They ended up by resorting to the device that the Prince should deliver his advice to the committee dealing with the Triple Alliance or such other committee as he should decide.[15]

But they dropped this when Haarlem, Fagel's home town, was not prepared to let matters rest there. On the 21st the town proposed that His Highness should be asked to name the persons involved and that they should be vigorously proceeded against; and it was then decided by the States of Holland to send a delegation to the Prince to ask him to name the people he had in mind.[16] He said that he had wanted to pursue the matter no further but nevertheless named De Groot who, in his view, had far exceeded what he was authorised to offer to Louis XIV.[17] According to Wicquefort, although Haarlem wished to take further action against De Groot, the States of Holland, which were still composed of people who had given him his orders, had too much honour to see a man lost who had been carrying out their intentions.[18] In any case Pieter De Groot, with his family, had fled the country to the Spanish Netherlands on 22 July.[19]

The Prince's designs were now directed against De Witt himself; and in this, as he had been in his move against De Groot, he was strongly supported by Fagel.

The fierce pamphlet campaign against the Grand Pensionary, who was still convalescing after the assassination attack against him, had continued in full flow: a particularly virulent version appeared which accused him of misappropriating secret funds held by the Delegated Council and of failing to lend full support to the army in the field. This was something which he felt could not be ignored. On 12 July he wrote to both the Delegated Councillors and to the Prince of Orange to obtain rebuttals of the charges.[20] He sent a copy of his letter to Prince William to Hieronymus van Beverninck, asking him to use his good offices with the Prince to assist him in defending 'his honour and good name'.[21] Clearly he regarded Van Beverninck as both being well disposed to himself and as having influence with William.

From the Delegated Council he received confirmation that it had 'no knowledge of his having received any secret funds'.[22]

As regards his letter to Prince William, Constantijn Huygens observed on 18 July – the Prince had received it only the previous evening – that the Prince's 'circular letter to the towns [the round robin of the 8th] had already caused sufficient whisperings amongst his supporters without his becoming involved anew in incurring the displeasure of the populace by declarations [in favour of De Witt] which ran counter to the populace's humour. Something was owed the populace.' His advice was to leave the letter unanswered.[23]

As Huygens indicates, the Prince needed to have regard not only to opinion in his own ranks but also to popular opinion, which had played such an important role in his elevation and which should not be alienated. It also indicates that Huygens was uncertain about the reliability of this popular support and that it could not be regarded as a given.

Although William did reply to De Witt, on the 22nd, it was in a letter which was intended for immediate publication and, politically deadly in its purpose, brought physical death in its train. He told him it did not lie within his power to remedy the insolences offered the Grand Pensionary by the pamphlets; and, he continued, with toxic irony, all one could do was to arm oneself with patience, as he had been constrained to do when the same excesses had not saved his own person nor the Princes of his House.[24] He did not doubt that De Witt had shown as much zeal for the army as the exigencies of the time allowed; but the multitudinous press of daily business prevented him from making an exact enquiry into what might have fallen short in the army's requirements and who was responsible for the failure in properly remedying these defects. As far as the secret funds were concerned, he would leave that to the Delegated Council but the justification asked from him could, he suggested, better be found from the evidence of De Witt's own records kept for the purpose.[25]

It could not have been made more manifest that the Grand Pensionary could not seek any remedies for his ills in turning to the Prince of Orange. On the contrary the Prince was engaged in a ruthless strategy to destroy his political power and that of his following, a strategy which ran out of control and ended in tragedy, the murder of Johan De Witt and his brother Cornelis at the hands of the mob.

ARREST OF CORNELIS DE WITT AND RESIGNATION OF JOHAN DE WITT

On 8 July a barber surgeon with strong Orangist sympathies, whose disreputable character has not been doubted then or since, Willem Tichelaar, came to visit Cornelis, who had not recovered from the illness that had caused him to leave the fleet and still lay sick in bed. According to Tichelaar's account he had come to seek the help of Cornelis, who was the Ruwaard (governor) of Putten, in a court case in which he was involved. Cornelis, thus went Tichelaar's story, promised to help him, but only on condition that he disposed of the Prince of Orange by means of 'poison, steel, or gun' to save the country from the Prince, who was seeking sovereignty over it and aiming to bring it under foreign domination. Tichelaar, according to his account, made his way to the Prince's camp at Bodegrave, where he met Van Albrantswaard, the Prince's Court Chamberlain, and subsequently Nassau-Zuylenstein, his old governor and now a general in the army. Van Albrantswaard accompanied Tichelaar to The Hague, where the matter was handed over to the court of Holland.[26]

The prosecutor of the court arrested Cornelis at his house in Dordrecht on 24 July and conveyed him by boat to The Hague. Subsequently, at the behest of the legal authorities of Dordrecht, Tichelaar was also arrested, although their pleas that Cornelis should properly, as a citizen of Dordrecht, be tried by them were ignored. Both Cornelis and Tichelaar were then held in the Gevangenpoort, the prison in The Hague situated between the Buitenhof and the square adjacent to the Binnenhof where the States of Holland and the States-General usually met.[27]

The strong popular antipathy against the De Witts, already powerful before the inflammation raised by Tichelaar's accusations, did not deter Coenraad van Beuningen from making an attempt to get the Prince and the Pensionary to work together. Wicquefort suggests that the Prince was not at first averse to making use of the services and the experience of Johan De Witt but that either he changed his mind or was persuaded to do so by pressure from his entourage.[28] Although he had worked closely with De Witt, as we have seen, in the opening phases of the French invasion, it seems unlikely that Prince William could have seriously entertained continuing the partnership in the circumstances that now pertained. On the contrary, he continued to do what he could to undermine the position of the Grand Pensionary.

De Witt did indeed pay a visit on 1 August to wish him luck with the eminent offices that he held. But he himself realised that in the current state of affairs and with the current state of popular opinion the time had come for him to withdraw from the pre-eminent position in public affairs that he had held for so long. On 4 August he appeared before the States of Holland to tender his resignation and asked that a promise that he should obtain a seat on the High Council should be met. Minutes of the meeting demonstrate the degree of respect and support he still had amongst the Holland Regents, with nearly all the towns expressing the wish that he should continue in office. However, they ceded to his reasons and resolved to grant him an honourable discharge. This, however, was not acceptable to the Prince of Orange. At his request it was amended to a simple discharge.[29]

Further steps were under way both to further the Prince's position and to undermine the reputation of De Witt's faction.

A few days before his resignation, on the night of 29 July, Montbas, who had been convicted of treason in allegedly allowing the French to cross the Rhine at Tolhuis, had managed to escape from custody to the French at Utrecht from the camp at Bodegrave. As the brother-in-law of De Groot, now an execrated figure, and with aspersions being made everywhere that Montbas's treason was conducted in association with De Witt, his successful escape from justice was calculated to raise popular tensions to a high level. He had been in the custody of two of the Prince's guards, who had connived in the escape and who had disappeared with him. That night William wrote in agitation to Fagel. He knew full well what a scandal this would provoke 'in particular amongst the commonalty, although it was not my fault', and he went on to give a detailed exoneration of himself, which demonstrated his deep anxiety, ending with a worried plea for advice from Fagel on how to proceed.

In the event his concern was misplaced and popular opinion did not swing against him – on the contrary, it further fed suspicions of treason in the government[30] – but the letter to Fagel does demonstrate William's apprehensions about the people.

Almost as an afterthought, amidst the distress of the moment, he added a postscript: 'I attach herewith the letter from the king of England which my friend the Heer van Reede has brought me. May it please your grace to communicate this or not as you judge fit.'[31]

The letter he was referring to was Charles II's, in French, of 18 July, which was intended to be treated as an official communication and which Van Reede brought back with him from his mission in England, together with the personal letter in English intended for William only, which we have already discussed. In the official letter in French the King made clear his affection and respect for his nephew and his gratitude for the services rendered to him personally by the Prince's father. It was 'the insolences and constant machinations' against himself of those who had recently played so large a part in the governance of the United Provinces that had caused him to ally himself with Louis XIV, who had the same cause for complaint, their sole aim being to crush the pride of the Louvestein faction.[32] If the inhabitants of the United Provinces had considered the error they were making in good time and had raised the Prince to the offices of his ancestors the French King and he himself would have lived in perfect amity with them.

In short, he said, he was now very satisfied with what the people of the United Provinces had just done in making William their Stadholder. And if he could ascertain that matters had reached such a state that they could no longer be subjected to the same faction or any other that could undo what had been done, and if he could guarantee his subjects against the violence and injustices that they had so long suffered and extend his protection to the Prince and his friends, he would do everything possible with regard to Louis XIV to put an end to the present dispute, so that the whole world would recognise the particular care he had for the Prince's person, and the regard he would have for the United Provinces out of consideration for him.[33]

Fagel did not hesitate. On 1 August he conveyed the letter to the States-General, which thanked William and resolved to return the letter via Fagel to him. But on the 5th Fagel's home town, Haarlem, proposed at the meeting of the Holland States that a copy should be obtained from the States-General and read out at the Holland meeting. This was resisted by Van Beverninck with the support of Dordrecht and Leyden. On the 6th Haarlem continued to press that a proposal be made to the States-General to 'communicate' the letter. It was in fact published on 15 August. But before that it had already reached the public domain, as it was bound to do.[34] It was far too easy to leak it and Fagel reached his objective by the back door.[35]

The letter, of course, did nothing to abate the popular anger against De Witt – on the contrary. In The Hague this anger was escalating, taking on a violent character which intensified by the day. Amidst rumours that Cornelis De Witt had escaped, an increasingly hysterical crowd gathered outside the prison where he was held.[36] In this extremely intimidating atmosphere his judges deliberated on how to proceed. The six of them decided, by a majority of one,[37] to apply torture to the prisoner in order to obtain a confession. Cornelis suffered this ordeal on the 19th without, however, breaking and admitting his guilt; and without this it was not legally possible to condemn him to death. At about 8.30 in the morning of 20 August the judges arrived at the prison to announce their sentence, which was put on display. Cornelis was to be deprived of all his offices, banished from the Province of Holland, and to pay all costs. But the court pronounced no verdict on the crimes of which he was accused and gave no reasons for its sentence.[38]

There is no doubt that Cornelis was wholly innocent of the accusations that Tichelaar had brought against him. But in the circumstances and in view of the menacing crowds it was the most humane and lenient sentence the thoroughly intimidated court could have arrived at, given the dangers to themselves they were running.[39] Outside the country Cornelis could find safety.

MURDER OF THE DE WITTS

But the difficulty was to get him there. Johan De Witt had arrived at the prison, where there were guards on duty, at about 9.30 to take his brother, crippled by his torture, away. But Tichelaar was released and, making his way through the streets of The Hague, he shouted that, as he was set free, Cornelis must have been guilty, and that the sentence pronounced was much too lenient. Death, was his underlying theme, should have been the verdict. He harangued the crowd from a window and then, for that day, disappeared from view.[40]

The Hague was in uproar: 'to arms, to arms, murder, murder, treason, treason' was everywhere the cry; and when, at about 10.30, Johan De Witt attempted to leave the prison he was turned back by the mob.[41] The brothers De Witt were trapped.

The States of Holland decided to put the garrison of The Hague, consisting of three companies of cavalry, that is to say professional soldiers, on an armed footing and at the same time the Delegated Council of Holland requested the Town Council of The Hague to summon the town's civic guards; they also sent a message to the Prince of Orange, who had left The Hague the previous evening to inspect the defences of Woerden,[42] asking him to return to restore order as a matter of urgency and to send a few companies of horse and foot by day or by night. According to one of the Van der Goes brothers the message would have taken about five hours to reach him and it was sent about midday. In that event even if the Prince had returned immediately to The Hague he would have arrived too late to save the De Witt brothers. The meeting of the States of Holland ended at about 11.30, leaving the Delegated Council with powers to manage the situation in consultation with the Town Council of The Hague.[43]

The civic guard were the first to arrive at the prison and its surroundings, at about 1pm, followed by the professional cavalry, and a tense relationship between the two was apparent from the start.[44] Part of the civic guard had already assembled earlier of its own accord.[45] According to Japikse's biography of Johan De Witt there was a minority amongst them who, deeming the sentence against Cornelis to be too lenient, wished to carry out a sentence of rough justice against him at once. As the day progressed it was they who gained the upper hand, led by a small number of trouble-makers, headed by a silversmith, Hendrick Verhoef, who were intent upon the murder of the two brothers.[46] There was a rumour that a swarm of unruly peasants was advancing on The Hague,[47] and the President of the Delegated Council and one other of its members decided to give the order to the commander of the cavalry, the Comte de Tilly, to remove two of his companies of cavalry to protect the approaches to the city. Tilly demanded that his orders should be in writing; and whether he ever said, as he departed, 'now are the De Witts dead men', that was nevertheless the truth of the matter.[48]

The two companies left at about 3pm, leaving the remaining company of a hundred or so troopers powerless to confront the much larger numbers of the civic guard where Japikse says the minority hostile to the De Witts prevailed over the majority.[49] At about 5pm[50] the door of the prison was beaten open; the De Witts were dragged outside and were then brutally murdered; their naked bodies were hung upside down on a nearby scaffold; their stomachs were sliced open; and a lively trade commenced in the purchase of their butchered body parts.[51] Prosperous burghers were amongst the principal participants.[52]

For nearly three and a half centuries, beginning immediately after the perpetration of the murders, the debate has swung to and fro on the role the Prince of Orange played in the affair. Most have absolved him of a direct involvement in managing the murders, but have not so absolved his adherents. To this we shall now turn.

EXCULPATION OF THE PRINCE

On the morning of 20 August William had arrived at 7.30 with a large retinue at Woerden. He stayed only an hour, after which he departed by yacht for Nieuwerburg, where he lunched.

In the evening he was at dinner at Alphen when the news of the murders was brought to him by means of the second of two missives from the States of Holland, which, as it was sent from The Hague at about 7pm, cannot have reached him until about midnight. The normally self-possessed Prince, who but rarely revealed his thoughts or feelings, turned pale and his discomposure was so manifest that his entourage took care not to reveal any satisfaction at the course events had taken. Years later Bentinck bore witness that he had never seen the Prince more affected than when he learnt of the tragic end of the brothers. And the English historian Bishop Burnet states that 'the prince spoke of it always to me with the greatest horror possible'.[53]

We need to remember that the relationship between the Prince of Orange and the Grand Pensionary was not one of straightforward antagonism. Prince William owed Johan De Witt a great deal; the Pensionary had taken on the responsibility for his political education; they had seen each other regularly on a weekly basis over a long period of time; they had not infrequently met socially; and in this war they had cooperated in close harmony. William later told Bishop Burnet that De Witt 'was certainly one of the greatest men of the age, and he believed he served his country faithfully'.[54] At the same time the Prince and his House also had many scores to settle with De Witt and his faction; for two decades they had been excluded from the positions and the influence which they regarded as their hereditary due, in an age where certain forms of political power were regarded as closely akin to a form of property;[55] they had been frequently humiliated; their political creed was the opposite of De Witt's republicanism; and two of their followers, Buat and De Graeff, had died, in the eyes of many of the House of Orange's retainers and supporters, as martyrs to the House's cause. Politics overrode any personal feelings the Prince had for his political tutor: but the politics of removing Johan De Witt was one thing; the ending in a profound and gruesome tragedy, which Prince William had neither aimed for nor expected, was another. And the surmise is unavoidable that the Prince of Orange was immediately aware of the damage that would result to his reputation – reason enough in itself for not having encompassed the murders in the first place. We need not wonder that he lost his composure.

One of the charges levied against him has been that he ignored the first of the messages sent to him from The Hague by the States of Holland which warned him of the disturbances and of the ugly humour of the crowd in their attitude towards the De Witt brothers, and yet that he did nothing. And the charge would stand even though, as it turned out, he could not possibly have arrived in time to save them. But it is not true, as has been said, that the withdrawal of the French from their advanced positions had begun so that Dutch troops could be spared to restore order in The Hague.[56] On the contrary, Prince Maurits of Nassau-Siegen wrote to the Prince on 5 August that he had received reports on all sides that the French had left Utrecht with a force of 6,000 or 7,000 infantry, a quantity of cavalry, artillery and boats to attack Hinderdam, where the important sluices required for the inundations protecting Amsterdam were situated; and on the 8th the Prince replied that he, too, had had reports from all sides warning that the enemy had designs on Prince Maurits's front, or wanted to pass through the gap between his front and the Prince's. On the 22nd Maurits reported that the Duke of Luxemburg had arrived in person with a large quantity of infantry to reconnoitre the sluice gates at Uytermeer; and on the 23rd the tension continued – 'we are everywhere on our guard', said the Field Marshal.[57] The military situation was not therefore auspicious for diverting forces from the front to deal with the unrest in The Hague. Moreover, we need to take into account the fact that the military pressures were such that the Prince of Orange could not devote his undivided attention to what was going on in the capital.

This was not the first time that he had refused to become personally involved in confronting the civil disturbances. Nor was it to be the last. He had been reluctant to go to Dordrecht to defend the Regents against the crowds there and he refused to become personally involved in restoring order after his round robin of 8 July had failed in its purpose to quell disturbances. If he had used troops against the civil guards, who were an important component of the disorders, he would not only have been distracted from his military and diplomatic preoccupations, he would have risked civil war at a time when the imperative was to bring as much unity as possible to what remained of the Dutch State. That would have been neither in the interests of the United Provinces nor of those of the House of Orange.

THE INVOLVEMENT AND REWARDS OF THE PRINCE'S ADHERENTS

Most historians have exculpated Prince William from direct involvement in the murders of the De Witt brothers; but many prominent ones have not so exculpated members, of one sort or another, of his following, with some going further than mere involvement and maintaining that Orangist adherents were engaged in, or played an important part in, a conspiracy.[58] Without reviewing the vast literature accumulated in the course of nearly two and a half centuries on this subject, we can address a central point – namely whether close associates of the Prince were involved in the murders or whether the involvement was confined merely to others at a lower level amongst the adherents of the House.

Perhaps the most damning of the accounts pointing to the involvement of Prince William's closest associates is contained in a diary of Copmoijer, who lived next door to the Gevangenpoort, the prison from which the two brothers were dragged to their deaths: this was not published until 1967. On the night of 17 August, so this account runs, the Prince arrived at the house of Nassau-Odijk in The Hague together with 'B', who it has been assumed was Bentinck; certain members of the court sitting in judgement on Cornelis De Witt were also there; the Prince left for Alphen at 2am on the 18th; at 5am on the day the De Witt brothers were murdered, the 20th, Nassau-Odijk, Nassau-Zuylenstein and Cornelis Tromp, a staunch Orangist and a prominent Admiral (although not as competent as his more famous father), arrived at an inn on a square next to the Gevangenpoort; they sent for the prison turnkey's maid and despatched her with a message to Johan De Witt to say that his brother wanted to see him and thus lured him to the prison; and at 3pm they summoned 15 members of Verhoef's blue regiment of civic guards to their inn, told them 'men it is running into the evening, if you have in mind to do the prince of Orange some good, now is the time', and these men, plied with drink, then returned to the prison to take the lead in beating the doors down and assaulting the De Witts.

The diary suffers, as evidence, from at least three defects: it is not in the hand of Copmoijer; it contains a passage indicating that it was written, not at the time of the murders on 20 August but probably between 1672 and 1690; and when Copmoijer wrote to a lawyer in Amsterdam on the 20th giving details of the murders he rather curiously made mention neither of Prince William's presence at Nassau-Odijk's house, nor of the involvement of Nassau-Odijk, Nassau-Zuylenstein or Tromp in either the events of the 20th or any of the preceding days or nights.[59] There are also certain inconsistencies in its relation of facts from what we know from other sources.[60] There are therefore serious doubts concerning the diary, but it is cited by the highly regarded modern historian Herbert Rowen.[61]

It should in any case be noted, however, that even if we accept the diary at face value it does not present a strong indictment of the involvement of Prince William himself in the murders. The diary says he left Nassau-Odijk's house in the early hours of the 18th and he could not possibly have foreseen the combination of events on the 20th which led to the murders and of which, if we accept the diary's account, his associates opportunistically made use as the events unfolded. From a political point of view the murders were crass – they left him, predictably, with a reputational stain which has not been wholly erased from that day to this.

It is a different matter when it comes to at least two of the House of Orange's more prominent supporters, Cornelis Tromp and his brother-in-law, Johan Kievit, of whom more in a moment. According to the much respected 18th-century historian Jan Wagenaar, Cornelis Tromp was certainly involved in encouraging members of the mob and he took up a position right in front of the scaffold where the De Witts were suspended; when the civic guard marched off after the murders, with drums beating as though after an execution, they passed Tromp and Kievit, who were peering from the windows of a house; and the two of them were greeted with shouts of 'Long live the Prince! Long live Tromp!'[62] Tromp and Kievit were therefore at least spectators, and in the case of Tromp, at any rate, an approving spectator of the violence inflicted on the De Witts.[63]

There is furthermore no doubt of the complicity of Orangists with no close connection with the Prince. Tichelaar; the silversmith Verhoef, who was intent on murder from the start; and an alderman of The Hague, Johan van Banchem, all were Orangists in their sympathies and all were major participants in what happened on 20 August.

When the Prince arrived at The Hague on the 21st he was faced with a profound dilemma. Undoubtedly members of his following had been involved, more senior members had been seen in the crowds, and maybe two of his entourage who were very close to him, his old governor Nassau-Zuylenstein and his cousin Nassau-Odijk, might have played an organisational role, although this seems very far from definite and William himself might not have been certain about the matter. The Prince of Orange was much more than a purely party leader in the modern sense. He was a great nobleman in a complex of almost feudal relationships, with bonds that tied patron and client in terms often tacit but nevertheless clearly understood in the 17th century; as a patron he had a duty to protect his clients, at whatever level, and to reward them for their services. Part of his appeal, even for as experienced and sophisticated a statesman as Coenraad van Beuningen, was the idea that, as a grandee with international grand connections, he could extend his protection to the people of the United Provinces. If he was seen not to be protecting his clientele, his standing and reputation as a grandee – his *gloire* – would be diminished and consequently his prestige, his authority and his power.

At the same time he would also have been all too conscious that his reputation had a moral component – he had to behave appropriately for a man in his position. And that reputation had been set at risk by the murders. Political opponents and pamphleteers could exploit this for their own advantage – and did. William himself, as we shall see, did precisely that in the case of Louis XIV when his generals and servitors, Louis's clients to whom Louis owed a duty of protection, and whom he did not punish, committed acts that redounded on his *gloire*. William therefore faced a very difficult choice.

Nearly all modern historians, even those sympathetic to the Prince who have exculpated him from direct involvement in the murders, have censured him for not taking firm action to punish at least the major perpetrator.[64] But the judgement he formed was that he could not. And more shocking still, in modern, though not entirely in 17th-century terms, he felt he had to reward them.

At first his acute dilemma caused him to hesitate and prevaricate. He didn't know, he said to a representative of the States of Holland, if it was appropriate to proceed with vigour against the culprits; the foremost citizens were involved; it would be dangerous; he would be grateful for the view of the States.[65] It is not surprising that, after this, any further official enquiry was dropped.

But subsequently Van Banchem became the bailiff in charge of policing The Hague, where his misdemeanours afterwards caused the court of Holland to complain of him to Prince William. The Prince replied that he was sorry to hear such things about him; he had always had a regard for him because he had at all times supported his House; he would summon him and let the court know his thoughts. Nevertheless, Van Banchem remained in his post until, as a result of his further activities, he was finally condemned to be beheaded, from which he was saved only by a timely death.[66]

Tichelaar too received his rewards, despite the Prince's lowly opinion of him. Tichelaar claimed he had been promised a post by Nassau-Zuylenstein and – whether through this influence or not – he ended up as Vice Governor of Putten. When a successor to Cornelis De Witt, as the governor of the town, complained in 1681 of his conduct and wished to dismiss him he asked the consent of William, enquiring at the same time if he felt bound to Tichelaar in any way. The Prince replied 'No', adding, to make his contempt, and perhaps his frustration, clear in the coarsest of terms, 'give the scoundrel a kick up the arse, and let him go'. Nevertheless Tichelaar received a pension from Prince William to the Prince's dying day.[67]

Adolphe Borrebach, one of the assailants, together with Jacob van der Graeff, in the assassination attempt on the De Witts on 21 June, also received a post-mastership, to be continued for his son.[68]

CONTINUING PRESSURE ON THE REGENTS

There was another aspect of the murders, from which the Prince of Orange benefited, albeit wholly unintentionally and without any form of premeditation – a rule of terror threatened the incumbent Regent classes.

Even before the murders had occurred, but on the very day that the anger of the crowds outside the Gevangenpoort was mounting against the two brothers, the States of Holland met in the complex of buildings adjacent to the scene. There they elected the candidate closest to the Prince, Gaspar Fagel, to Johan De Witt's old post as Grand Pensionary of Holland.[69] It is important to note, however, that, even threatened as they were, there was a continuing respect amongst the Holland Regents for De Witt. It is reflected in the humble tone of Fagel's own acceptance speech three days after his election; whether because he shared this respect and may have felt a sense of guilt at the unforeseen violence unleashed against the man he was succeeding, or because he deemed it politic so soon after the gruesome events, or perhaps a little of both, he said that he did not possess the qualities of his predecessor, who despite the good services he had rendered, could not prevent the mishaps that overcame him; and he accepted the office only in obedience to the wishes of their Noble High Mightinesses the States of Holland.[70] The Prince of Orange gave his approval to the appointment on the understanding that he was consulted on all material matters.[71]

The Secretaryship of the States-General, which Fagel already held, was now split into two, with a Secretary for Domestic and a Secretary for Foreign Affairs, the latter and more important post being entrusted to Fagel.[72] Even before his elevation to his new post Fagel, who was now 41 years old, had been an influential figure. Shortly after his initial appointment as Secretary (Griffier) of the States-General in November 1670 the powers of the office had, at his request, been extended (by a resolution dated 22 December 1670) – apart from attending meetings of the States-General he was entitled to attend all the committees of that body and to proffer advice to the deputies as required. One of the most important of the committees of which he was a member was the military one: in that capacity he was present at the conference in June to decide whether to abandon the Ijssel line; and, without

De Witt's knowledge, he had written to the Dutch ambassadors abroad asking them to maintain a secret correspondence with himself. He had therefore already for some time been able through these means to provide a certain counterweight to Johan De Witt.[73] The close partnership, which now began between Fagel and the Prince of Orange, was to last until Fagel's death in 1688.

The pressure on the Regents continued. The unrest amongst the people persisted in the Holland towns. On 22 August the civic guard at Rotterdam forced the resignation of those Regents of whom it disapproved, amongst whom was Pieter De Groot; the following day the mob presented the Town Council with some 50 names out of which the Council chose 27, and by 25 August the Prince of Orange finally nominated nine new Regents to serve on the Council. The first name on the list was Johan Kievit. Always a staunch Orangist, Kievit, it will be remembered, had fled the Netherlands as a fellow conspirator with Buat in 1666, after which he had taken refuge in England under the protection of Charles II, from whom he received a knighthood. He had returned to the Republic on 9 July, and at the beginning of August Prince William gave a nudge for the rescinding of the sentence of treason against him. Another of the clients of the extended Orange and Stuart clan thus received his reward under the protecting arm of his patron.[74]

In Amsterdam a seditious and threatening placard had been placed at the exchange and elsewhere demanding that the Town Council should be reconstituted anew, with the existing Regents being replaced from the citizenry and from 'respectable merchants'; and it was accompanied by the threat that, if the demands were not met, then 'house-keeping in The Hague manner' could be expected – a reference, of course, to the murders of the De Witts. Support for the Prince of Orange was apparent from the placard, and on 23 August an agitated, and perhaps rather too panicky, Town Council turned to William to advise him of the great mischief which, they asserted, was to be expected should the people resort to further disorders, and asked him to use his authority to restore calm to the town. When the delegation from the town arrived they found him at supper and, after a delay, he listened in an abstracted fashion to their message: he answered that he considered that his authority would not be sufficient; nor did he see any means of using the army. His advice was for them to come to an accommodation with the malcontents.[75]

THE PURGING OF THE TOWN COUNCILS

Against this menacing and sombre background the States of Holland were about to prorogue, at which time their Delegated Council would assume responsibility for maintaining order. This body submitted to the States an analysis of the situation with which it was confronted. In substance it echoed the advice William had given to the delegation from Amsterdam: the forces of law and order wielded no authority, the Councillors said, over a rebellious and armed commonality; the army was not in a position to bring it to heel; there was a powerful enemy on the borders, which could provide shelter for dissidents; the authority of neither the magistrates nor of Prince William could be put at hazard; and, they concluded, accommodating the commonality was thus the only expedient left. By this they meant that, if the Prince of Orange could not persuade the people to return to order, then he should be given the authority to ask those Regents who had incurred the displeasure of the people to lay down their governmental offices with an honourable discharge, and to appoint suitable replacements in the Town Councils to appease the discontent.[76] It needs to be noted that so great was the intimidation of the Regents that this initiative came from within the Regent establishment itself.

It was not received with approbation on all sides. Delft wanted the replacement of the unpopular Regents to occur in the 'ordinary way', that is, through the normal means of co-opting new candidates by the other Regents. Leyden feared that the proposal might lead to the commonality raising its demands. But Fagel put an end to the discussion with the argument that to accept the proposal would be to forestall further popular discontent, whilst hinting darkly that the fate of the De Witts might overcome those who continued to offer resistance to the popular mood. The States of Holland adopted the appropriate resolution on 27 August.[77] It made clear that the powers entrusted to the Prince to change the composition of the Town Councils were limited to meet the present predicament and were not to be repeated in the future; and they were only to be exercised at the request of the relevant towns – in the event all but one did so.[78]

On the face of it the Prince of Orange was now in a powerful position to purge the Holland Town Councils and reform them in his own image, and thus determine the composition of the States of Holland, the most powerful Province in the Dutch Union. But in practice how much of this was he able to achieve and, indeed, how much did he want to achieve? The time he could devote to the issue was limited because of his other preoccupations, whilst there was also the need for haste to react to the popular commotions, and he relied on the advice and assistance of Albrecht Nierop, a member of the court of Holland, and Johan Wierts, a member of the Council which ran the affairs of the House of Orange, where he had responsibility for the House's finances.[79]

Between 5 and 8 September the popular movements were at their high point, with petitions being presented ranging over a wide territory, including demands for the removal of the supporters of De Witt, demands for reverting to the political role the militias had played in the previous history of the Republic to counterbalance the power of the Regents, and demands for greater influence for Calvinist precepts in the Town Councils.[80] But, as the Dutch historian Roorda has argued, there was hardly any coordination between the popular movements in the various towns.[81] Changes to the composition of the governments of the local towns were made in the light of local politics and local pressures. There were occasions when William had to choose between factions loyal to De Witt's principles (Hoorn and,

Roorda argues, in actual fact, Amsterdam); others where he had to choose between two sets of Orangist supporters (Haarlem and Leyden); and others where the professed Orangist sympathies were of a rather dubious nature.[82]

Roorda's thesis, however, needs modification in the light of a further consideration. Prince William himself did not wish to undertake too radical a transformation in the personnel of the Town Councils. Fagel assured the States of Holland at their meeting on 27 August, when they resolved to grant the Prince the authority to change the Councils, that he would proceed with discretion and would preserve the governments as much as possible.[83] As we have earlier argued, it was not in his interest to risk a revolution, and the number of Regents with the necessary experience of government and with the necessary knowledge was limited. There was therefore both pragmatism and wisdom in adapting to the imperatives arising from local circumstances. One outcome was that the local factions with their knowledge of local conditions first out-manoeuvred, and then prevailed, over the popular movements. The system of local rule by the Regents in the Province of Holland was reaffirmed.

But we need to balance the depiction of the power of the localities described above by recognising the power which could be wielded by the Prince of Orange. If, in the end, the Regents were able to re-establish the existing social order and the existing system of government it was by making shrewd use of the prestige and the popular appeal of the Prince, with the changes in the Town Councils being made under the cover of his name. If the Prince had to work through the local factions, the local factions had to work through him. There were three other important factors: after the demise of De Witt the Prince of Orange remained the only player on the Dutch political scene who could assert his patronage across the whole country and thus unify it; in wartime conditions there was no other figure who could provide the military and diplomatic leadership the Regents required if they were to survive; and there was no one else whose family and patronage systems extended as widely into the other countries of Europe as did his, and which could be put at the disposal of the Regents – although they were only too well aware that all these factors put a double-edged sword into his hands.

One important outcome of the changes was that Amsterdam remained an independent power centre outside the control of the Prince. On 28 August the Town Council, bending before popular pressure, decided to put its membership at his disposal and on 10 September ten out of 36 members were removed and replaced by a list provided by the Prince on the 15th. But the replacements were in fact the choice of Valckenier, whose faction now became predominant, although not completely so – one of his opponents, Hooft, survived the changes. Coenraad van Beuningen became one of the Burgermasters. Valckenier, of course, was no convinced Orangist and was quite capable of taking an independent line.[84]

Whilst therefore 130 out of 460 Regents were replaced in Holland[85] these figures need to be qualified. They were not all William's adherents, and, even when they were, their views were capable of changing in the light of local and other circumstances. The changes did not preclude opposition arising in the future.

The events of 1672 may fairly be described as constituting a revolution, or, perhaps more accurately, a counter-revolution; the overthrow of De Witt's regime of 'the True Freedom' and the return to a Stadholder regime did represent such a profound change, with important consequences, particularly in foreign affairs and the conduct of war, thus deserving the name. But the Regent class and William between them forestalled a social and systemic revolution; and, if the forces unleashed by the French invasion had initially acquired a momentum of their own, it was not long before they were curbed and brought back into the framework of stable government that prevailed of old. Civil war such as occurred in the British Isles in the 1640s and with the Frondes in France, in that and the following decade, was avoided – as indeed was the far more radical change that Charles II and Louis XIV had in mind for the Dutch Republic. That most difficult of political feats, that of halting a revolution after it has begun, when it has achieved its ends, had been accomplished. It was one of the lessons that William carried with him when he invaded England in 1688.[86]

1 See Geyl, *op. cit.*, p.389.
2 *Correspondentie W.III en Portland, op. cit.*, II, Pt 1, p.58.
3 Roorda, *op. cit.*, pp.42–3.
4 *Ibid.*, p.48.
5 *Ibid.*, p.40.
6 *Ibid.*, p.256.
7 *Ibid.*, pp.49, 57.
8 *Ibid.*, p.61.
9 Israel, *Dutch Republic, op. cit.*, p.800.
10 *Ibid.*, p.800. Roorda, *op. cit.*, p.258.
11 Geyl, *op. cit.*, pp.372–4, 380–1. Israel says that the flood of pamphlets 'shows that the political impulse behind the popular movement went far deeper than a mere desire for the elevation of Orange. Militias and guilds wanted changes in the character of civic government'. Israel, *Dutch Republic, op. cit.*, pp.802–3.
12 Wagenaar, *op. cit.*, 14, p.89.
13 *Ibid.*, 14, pp.89–90.
14 Hop & Vivien, *op. cit.*, pp.217–18.
15 *Ibid.*, pp.222–4.
16 *Ibid.*, pp.226–7.
17 *Ibid.*, p.234. Wagenaar, *op. cit.*, 14, pp.125–6.
18 Wicquefort, *Histoire, op. cit.*, IV, p.509.
19 Rowen, *De Witt, op. cit.*, p.857.
20 *Ibid.*, p.855.
21 *Brieven van De Witt, op. cit.*, IV, pp.393–4.
22 Wagenaar, *op. cit.*, 14, p.139.
23 Huygens, *Briefwisseling, op. cit.*, VI, pp.306–7.
24 Wicquefort, *Histoire, op. cit.*, IV, p.519.
25 Wagenaar, *op. cit.*, 14, pp.139–40. Hop & Vivien, *op. cit.*, p.233.

26 Wagenaar, *op. cit.*, 14, pp.143–5. Rowen, De Witt, *op. cit.*, pp.864–5. Wicquefort, *Histoire, op. cit.*, IV, pp.514–15.

27 Wagenaar, *op. cit.*, 14, pp.142–3. Wicquefort, *Histoire, op. cit.*, IV, p.516. Rowen, *De Witt, op. cit.*, p.868.

28 Wicquefort, *Histoire, op. cit.*, IV, p.536.

29 *Brieven van De Witt, op. cit.*, IV, p.391. Rowen, *De Witt, op. cit.*, pp.857–8. Wagenaar, *op. cit.*, 14, pp.148–50. Franken, *op. cit.*, p.108 (citing Bontemantel, 'Regeering van Amsterdam', *Inl.* CIX 2, on the suggested reconciliation of De Witt and the Prince). Hop & Vivien, *op. cit.*, pp.244–7.

30 Wagenaar, *op. cit.*, 14, p.65.

31 Groen van Prinsterer, *Archives, op. cit.*, V, p.265. See also Wagenaar, *op. cit.*, 14, pp.63–4.

32 When William II had attempted his coup against the Regents in 1650 he had imprisoned several of them, including De Witt's father, in the castle of Louvestein, and 'Louvestein' became the name associated with the strong republican and anti-Orange party of which De Witt was the leader.

33 *Correspondentie W.III en Bentinck, op. cit.*, II, Pt 1, pp.71–2.

34 Hop & Vivien, *op. cit.*, pp.250–51, 253. Fruin, *op. cit.*, IV, p.341 n3. Geyl, *op. cit.*, p.393.

35 The letter has been much discussed. Wicquefort saw it as part of the Prince's campaign to ruin De Witt, *Histoire, op. cit.*, IV, p.519. Fruin argued that Fagel had meant nothing more than to strengthen the populace in its belief that peace with England was inseparable from the elevation of the Prince, *op. cit.*, IV, p.341. Japikse in p.266 n.2 of Hop & Vivien, *op. cit.*, suggests that the initiative for publication came not from Fagel but from somebody in the States of Holland. But it was Haarlem, with which Fagel was so closely connected, that had repeatedly urged that it should be read out in the States of Holland, and it was Fagel who had put it in the domain of the political class in the first instance by communicating it to the States-General, where it was unlikely to remain secret for long.

36 Colenbrander, *op. cit.*, II, pp.182–3.

37 Rowen, *De Witt*, Amsterdam, 1915, p.870. The number of judges and who they were is mentioned in Wagenaar, *op. cit.*, 14, p.156.

38 Wagenaar, *op. cit.*, 14, pp.153–7. Rowen, *De Witt, op. cit.*, p.874. Japikse, *De Witt, op. cit.*, p.340. *Briefwisseling, van der Goes, op. cit.*, II, p.404. Wicquefort, *Mémoires, op. cit.*, p.280.

39 Very little is known about the deliberations of the judges, as their minutes have disappeared: J.A. Wijnne, *Geschiedenis*, Groningen, 1872, p.254; A.W. Kroon, *Jan De Witt contra Oranje 1650–1672*, Amsterdam, 1868. Appendix C gives the minutes of the interrogations of Tichelaar and Cornelis De Witt in accordance with a copy made by a member of the court of Holland in 1748. It also contains a copy of the court's sentence, as does Wagenaar, *op. cit.*, 14, pp.155–6.

40 Rowen, *De Witt, op. cit.*, pp.874–5. Wagenaar, *op. cit.*, 14, p.160. Japikse, *De Witt, op. cit.*, p.341. Colenbrander, *op. cit.*, II, p.184.

41 Rowen, *De Witt, op. cit.*, p.876. Wagenaar, *op. cit.*, 14, p.160.

42 He had gone to see if the place could be made defensible. Hop & Vivien, *op. cit.*, p.283.

43 Japikse, *De Witt, op. cit.*, p.344. Wagenaar, *op. cit.*, 14, pp.161–2. Hop & Vivien, *op. cit.*, p.284. *Briefwisseling, van der Goes, op. cit.*, II, p.405. Rowen says that at this time the Prince was at Alphen about 15 miles away, *De Witt, op. cit.*, p.878.

44 Wijnne, *op. cit.*, p.267. Rowen, *De Witt, op. cit.*, p.877. Japikse, *De Witt, op. cit.*, p.344.

45 Wijnne, *op. cit.*, p.268.

46 *Ibid.*, p.268. Japikse, *De Witt, op. cit.*, pp.346–7. Wagenaar, *op. cit.*, 14, pp.164–5.

47 *Briefwisseling, van der Goes, op. cit.*, II, p.405.

48 Japikse, *De Witt, op. cit.*, p.349. *Briefwisseling, van der Goes, op. cit.*, II, p.405. Wicquefort, *Histoire, op. cit.*, IV, p.530. Wagenaar, *op. cit.*, 14, pp.168–9. According to Fruin, *op. cit.*, I, p.371, Tilly's words are supported only by tradition.

49 Japikse, *De Witt, op. cit.*, p.350. Japikse's view finds support in Wicquefort, *Histoire, op. cit.*, IV, p.526n and according to Wagenaar, *op. cit.*, 14, p.164. Verhoef's company in the civic guard, with a blue banner, was the most extreme in its attitude against the De Witts.

50 *Briefwisseling, van der Goes, op. cit.*, II, p.405.

51 Hop & Vivien, *op. cit.*, p.286. Rowen, *De Witt, op. cit.*, pp.878–82. Rowen says when Tilly's cavalry moved off 'it was not quite four o'clock'.

52 *Briefwisseling, van der Goes, op. cit.*, II, p.406. Japikse, De Witt, op. cit., pp.350ff. Wicquefort, *Histoire, op. cit.*, IV, pp.526n ff.

53 Bernard Costerus, *Historisch Verhaal*, Leyden, 1756, pp.110–18. Wicquefort, *Histoire, op. cit.*, IV, pp.535–6. Japikse, *Willem III, op. cit.*, p.252. *Correspondentie W.III en Bentinck, op. cit.*, II.2, p.745. Burnet, *op. cit.*, I, p.583.

54 Burnet, *op. cit.*, I, p.574.

55 See for example William's comment on his recent elevation to the Stadholdership of Holland in his letter to Louis XIV at the beginning of July 1672: 'La justice qu'il vient de rendre en ma personne à ce qu'ie doibt à mes ancestres', *Correspondentie W.III en Bentinck, op. cit.*, II, Pt 1, p.62.

56 Rowen, *De Witt, op. cit.*, pp. 878–89.

57 Groen van Prinsterer, *Archives, op. cit.*, 2nd series, V, pp.266–74.

58 See Rowen, *De Witt, op. cit.*, pp.891–2.

59 J.E. Haijer, *op. cit.* The letter, at least, appears to be authentic as it is signed by Copmoijer.

60 It states, for example, that the Delegated Council sent a message to the Prince at Alphen, reporting that there were tumults in The Hague and asking for troops, at 3pm on the 19th, rather than in the late morning on the following day.

61 See Rowen, *De Witt, op. cit.*, pp.871, 875, 879.

62 Wagenaar, *op. cit.*, 14, pp.173–6.

63 Japikse, *De Witt, op. cit.*, p.347 raises the question whether they were not amongst the principal cheerleaders instigating the mob. Geyl, *op. cit.*, p.304 says they were 'watching it [the disorderly mob] with great pleasure'.

64 See Wout Troost, *William III, op. cit.*, p.86. Rowen, *De Witt, op. cit.*, p.892. Geyl, *op. cit.*, p.396. Baxter, *op. cit.*, p.84. Nesca Robb, *op. cit.*, I, pp.248–9. Japikse, *Prins Willem III, op. cit.*, I, p.253. Fruin, *op. cit.*, IV, p.374.

65 Hop & Vivien, *op. cit.*, p.288.

66 Fruin, *op. cit.*, IV, p.375.

67 Wagenaar, *op. cit.*, 14, pp.180–82.

68 P.A. Samson, *Histoire de Guillaume III*, II, La Haye (The Hague), 1703, p.261.

69 The other candidates included Coenraad van Beuningen and Hieronymus van Beverninck. Wicquefort, *Histoire, op. cit.*, IV, pp.520–21.

70 Hop & Vivien, *op. cit.*, pp.284–9.

71 Wagenaar, *op. cit.*, 14, p.187.

72 Hop & Vivien, *op. cit.*, pp.294–5.

73 Franken, *op. cit.*, p.31. A. De Fouw, *Onbekende Raads Pensionarissen*, The Hague, 1946, pp.98–9.

74 Roorda, *op. cit.*, pp.153–4 says the Prince did not intervene directly with the justices, confining himself to scribbling a marginal note on Kievit's request for the rescinding. Wicquefort, *Histoire, op. cit.*, IV, pp.488–9 supports this. Geyl, *op. cit.*, pp.376, 388, 389. Wagenaar, *op. cit.*, 14, pp.193–4.

75 Bontemantel, *op. cit.*, pp.180–2. Wagenaar, *op. cit.*, 14, p.210.

76 Hop & Vivien, *op. cit.*, pp.295–6.

77 *Ibid.*, pp.299–301.

78 Wagenaar, *op. cit.*, 14, pp.192–3.

79 *Ibid.*, 14, pp.197, 201.

80 Israel, *op. cit.*, pp.804–5.

81 Roorda, *op. cit.*, p.241.

82 *Ibid.*, p.238.

83 Bontemantel, *op. cit.*, II, p.187.

84 Wagenaar, *op. cit.*, 14, pp.212, 216. Roorda, *op. cit.*, pp.185, 189. Israel, *op. cit.*, p.805. Franken, *op. cit.*, p.111.

85 Israel, *op. cit.*, p.808.

86 Tony Claydon has drawn attention to the application of William's experience in the Dutch Republic to Britain in 1688 and afterwards in his excellent short biography *William III*, Longman, Pearson Education, 2002.

Frederick-William, the Great Elector, and his Family, c. 1664,
by Jan Mytens. Stiftung Preußische Schlösser und Gärten Berlin-Brandenburg

11 1672: ALLIANCES AND THE CAMPAIGN

THE ALLIANCE WITH BRANDENBURG AND THE USE OF THE ORANGE-NASSAU CLAN IN GERMANY

We have seen on the diplomatic front that the Dutch had entered into a treaty in May 1672 with the Elector of Brandenburg, under which he undertook to raise a force of 20,000 men and to advance through Westphalia to join forces with the Dutch; and that he in turn had entered into a treaty in June with the Austrian emperor, with a commitment to contribute 12,000 men each, although the object of this was solely to defend the Holy Roman Empire.

Great emphasis has been laid by historians on the link that the Orange-Nassau clan had established in England. But it needs to be remembered that the origins of the House lay in Germany and that it was also well rooted in Central Europe. Indeed, it was more broadly based there than in England, compensating somewhat in breadth for the elevated, but less widespread, family connection with the English Royal House. Part of the strength of its position was that both these sets of relationships – the Continental and the English – could, certainly not on all occasions, but in the right circumstances, be put at the disposal, not only of the clan itself, but of the political classes in the United Provinces in an extensive and complicated web of mutually interacting and reinforcing patron/client relationships. This we can now see illustrated.

The connections of the House of Orange-Nassau in Germany had never been severed; Nassau served as a base, as a refuge and as a logistical centre for William the Silent in the most desperate years in the Dutch War of Independence against Spain; and more than 40 members of the House fought in that Eighty Years' War. The family name of William III's grandmother, Amalia von Solms-Braunfels, derives from two small places in the Nassau ancestral lands; Prince Maurits of Nassau-Siegen, whose father was a brother of William the Silent, was born at Dillenburg, where he maintained his ties;[1] and the family estates of the Count of Waldeck, whom we shall shortly be meeting, lay not far distant from the Nassau lands.

Through the Prince of Anhalt, who had negotiated the Brandenburg-Austrian treaty on behalf of the Elector, the clan had links with the courts of both Berlin and Vienna. He was married to Henrietta Catherine, a daughter of Frederick-Henry and Amalia von Solms, hence a sister of the Great Elector's first wife and the aunt of Prince William of Orange. Like the princes of Orange he was a sovereign prince and, as such, regarded himself, according to Albert Waddington, as the equal of the Grand Elector; he saw himself more beholden to the Emperor, whom he regarded as his true superior; and his tie to Frederick-William was dictated by his interests rather than personal loyalty. Anti-French, at Berlin his influence was intermittent. In the divided councils which there prevailed, Amerongen found, when he arrived, that the pro-Dutch party was primarily a military one; and here the Orange clan was well represented, apart from its strong links, of course, with the Elector himself. At the head of the pro-Dutch party stood the governor of Berlin and Grand Constable, the Baron von Pölnitz; he was married to Ellenor of Nassau, the illegitimate daughter of Prince Maurits of Orange, and thus he too, like the Prince of Anhalt, was related by marriage to both the Elector's first wife and to Prince William III. His wife had property in the Dutch Republic and he himself had been granted a company of cavalry by William II of Orange worth 10,000 francs a year, a post to which he was anxious his son should succeed. Count Christian Albert von Donha, whose mother was a sister of Amalia von Solms, was a lieutenant-general and governor of Halberstad, and, as a member of the Elector's Secret Council, he was the only minister to be a member of the pro-Dutch party. There were other officers who were pro-Dutch, the most notable being Field-Marshal Derfflinger, and, of course, Prince Maurits of Nassau-Siegen, who was the governor of Cleves, to whose many services the Elector of Brandenburg was much beholden, and who was able to act as a much-used bridge between the House of Orange, the Dutch Republic and the House of Brandenburg.

Opposed to the military were nearly all the Grand Elector's ministers. At their head was Baron Otto von Schwerin, the most influential of all his advisers, despite intermittent disagreements; he had been President of the Secret Council since 1658, and the Elector formed firm attachments to those who had been long at his side. Of two other advisers, Somnitz was pro-Austrian and pro-French and Frederic Jena, whom apparently nobody liked, was neither pro-French nor pro-Austrian, but had at this time rallied round to the French camp.[2]

For the time being the pro-Dutch faction prevailed in the councils of the Elector; but as the difficulties of the campaign intensified, opinion was in due course to swing the other way.

From the start there were hesitations both on the part of the Grand Elector and on the part of the Austrian Emperor. Formally the treaty between them was a purely defensive alliance to protect the Holy Roman Empire, which neither mentioned the Dutch Republic nor France, although its pro-Dutch and anti-French intent was clear enough. Neither the Elector nor the Emperor wished to act against the secret treaties that both had with Louis XIV – Frederick-William, indeed, was still receiving subsidies from the French King. Leopold and his councillors, the Grand Chamberlain, Prince Lobkowitz, and the Chancellor, Dr Hocher, believed that no 'rupture' with France would necessarily follow, whilst the Elector never declared war on France.[3]

THE DRAFT TREATY WITH AUSTRIA AND AUSTRIAN HESITATIONS
In the Austrian as in the Brandenburg camp there were divided opinions. Highly cultured, a gifted composer of music whose preferred language was Italian, the Austrian Emperor,

Leopold I, had a reputation for vacillating, not surprisingly in view of the dilemmas with which he was confronted. He was never a friend of France – he was too conscious of the hereditary feud between Habsburg and Bourbon. And at the personal level he disliked Louis XIV and his ways. The advice of the veteran and very able Italian general Montecuccoli, the President of the War Council, was to confront the French and their allies 'con animo, con risoluzione e con forza' ('with spirit, with resolution and with force'). Initially this advice prevailed in Vienna and in a conference held on 8 July an aggressive war strategy was decided upon. The Austrians would march on Frankfurt against the French and invest the Middle Rhine to prevent its use by the French; they would then unite with the Spanish troops from the Spanish Netherlands in order to threaten the French from the rear at Maastricht. And, whilst these views, for the time being, were in the ascendant, Leopold, who was receiving subsidies from Spain, raised his commitment to Brandenburg from 12,000 troops to 16,000 at the beginning of July, and on 18 and 29 June he authorised Lisola, his envoy in The Hague, to enter into an alliance with the Dutch.[4]

Baron Lisola, a native of Franche-Comté, was a vehement opponent of Louis XIV and was determined to build up an anti-French coalition. He made skilful use of pamphlets to conduct a propaganda war against Louis, which had resonance throughout Europe.[5] He accused the French King of aiming at hegemony in Germany and he inveighed against the intrigues of the brothers Fürstenberg on his behalf.[6] Under the draft treaty he entered into with the Dutch on 25 July the Austrian Emperor was not bound to break with France, but he was bound to maintain the Treaties of Cologne and Westphalia; and, as the Austrians regarded the French occupation of Cleves, which belonged to the Grand Elector, as a violation of the Holy Roman Empire, they used this to justify their intervention. The Emperor would raise 20,000 troops, for which the Dutch would pay him 200,000 *Reichstaler*, and thereafter 45,000 per month. He and the Republic agreed to assist each other against anyone who attacked them.[7]

But the treaty was to remain unratified for some time. It was opposed by the proponent of a pro-French policy, Prince Lobkowitz, at the time the most powerful man at the court of Vienna. In his view, if an understanding could be arrived at with Louis XIV in western Europe, Austria could obtain a free hand to deal with the problems she faced in the east, in Poland, in Hungary – where a revolt had only recently been suppressed – and against the Turkish Porte.[8] In the meantime no support was forthcoming from the other German princes[9] – Bavaria in August urged Leopold not to enter into warlike measures on the Rhine[10] – and there was distrust in Vienna of the Grand Elector.[11] The mood there became therefore less resolute, with consequences which will become apparent.

In the middle of July Pölnitz arrived in The Hague to discuss war strategy with the Prince of Orange. He told the Prince that the Elector dared not act on his own, and therefore the original plan to form a conjunction with the Dutch troops would have to await the assistance of the Austrian Emperor. The Dutch had hoped that the Elector could have marched up to, and captured, Cologne, which would have established a stronghold in the rear of the French lines of communication, and it would have opened up the possibility of his then marching on to join the Dutch army, thus further cutting off the French from their supply routes to France. Pölnitz was compelled to say that this would now have to be postponed, and the Prince of Orange was constrained to agree with him. Nevertheless the Elector himself returned to this plan after joining the Emperor's army, and it remained his personal objective throughout the campaign.[12]

Encouragingly, help from the Emperor appeared to be on its way. In August his army assembled at Eger with 15,000 men. Montecuccoli met the Great Elector at Halberstadt on 9 September; and there the war plan formulated at the conference of 9 July in Vienna was agreed in its essentials. Frederick-William had 10,000 men with him and the same number were positioned on the Weser and Lippe rivers. The combined Austro-Brandenburg army marched in a westerly direction and reached Wetzlar on 8 October. But there, instead of following the Lahn river to the Middle Rhine, they paused. The Elector of Trier forbade them to use the crossing of the Rhine at Coblenz; but that was not the real reason for the halt.

On 10 and 11 September Leopold had issued instructions to Montecuccoli, which reached him on the 28th, that he was to avoid a 'rupture' with the French as far as possible and to avoid anything that might lead to that result. On 10 September Lobkowitz promised the French ambassador in Vienna, Grémonville, that the Imperial troops would not be the first to attack. Much to the deep consternation of Montecuccoli, who, typically for the 17th century, feared for his reputation and his renown (his *gloire*) as a soldier, the conduct of the war from the Austrian side was to become a sham.[13] The more anxious and cautious mood in Vienna was reflected in the negotiations relating to the draft treaty Lisola had entered into with the Dutch; the Austrians wanted changes, the negotiations dragged on, and the treaty remained unratified.[14]

Although the Elector, on his side, remained eager to form a junction with the troops of the Prince of Orange and of Spain, the net result was that the Austro-German armies engaged in fruitless marches and counter-marches on the borders of the Empire, with fierce downpours of rain clogging the roads.[15] To add to his concerns the Elector feared that Saxony, which had designs on his possession of Cleves, might fall upon him if misfortune were to overtake him, and he was worried, too, about Sweden.[16]

THE RE-POSITIONING OF THE FRENCH ARMY AND THE RELIEF OF GRONINGEN AND FRIESLAND

Something, however, was achieved. Towards the end of August Turenne left the Dutch Republic to take up a position, with an army of 20,000 men, close to the Weser between the Rhine and the Roer river, with the aim of blocking any attempt by the Austro-Brandenburg army to cross the Rhine and of protecting the bishoprics of Cologne and Münster.[17] Louis XIV had left Zeist on 10 July to return to France, accompanied by the Duke of Orléans, and, travelling through the territories of the Bishop of Liège and the Spanish Netherlands, he arrived at St-Germain-en-Laye at 10pm on 1 August; whilst Condé, not yet fully recovered from his injury, had also left the Netherlands in August with the majority of the nobility and 'volunteers', including Monmouth. He was to take up a position in Alsace with 18,000 men to protect the eastern frontier of France.[18] Louis had realised that, as all the vulnerable points in Holland's defences were now protected by the inundations, the French would have to wait for the waters to freeze over during the winter and then see what opportunities that would offer.[19]

In the north-east of the Republic there were also favourable developments. Overijssel had surrendered to the Bishop of Münster at the beginning of July, but the threat from the Austro-Brandenburg army put pressure on this belligerent prelate and his fellow bishop, the Bishop of Cologne, to raise the siege of the town of Groningen on 27 August, after a heroic defence that inflicted considerable casualties – 11,000 men, including 5,600 deserters, against only around 100 defenders – on the joint armies of the two bishops, despite their widespread use of the bombs for which the Bishop of Münster was so notorious. This eliminated the threat to the Provinces of Groningen and Friesland.[20]

With the departure of Turenne and with the need to garrison the captured towns, the French army in the Dutch Republic was considerably reduced in strength.[21] Disease and desertion weakened it further.[22] The army in the conquered Netherlands consisted of 18–19,000 men in the Province of Utrecht and the Veluwe, and over 25,000 men around Zutphen and around Nijmegen; there were a further 7,000 cavalry in the vicinity of Maastricht.[23] In contrast to the French the Dutch army, secure behind its Water Line, was strengthened through new recruits, by the return to the colours of officers and men who had been scattered by the invasion, and by the return of prisoners of war: before leaving for France, Louis XIV, according to Rousset, released 20,000 prisoners for a small ransom, the majority indeed without the payment of any ransom at all.[24]

REORGANISATION OF THE DUTCH ARMY

The size of the Dutch forces has been the subject of considerable variation amongst historians. Indeed no one seems to have been more confused than the Prince of Orange himself; on 2 August he issued instructions to all the Dutch commanders to provide him with full lists of the men under their command and he carried out a further review at the end of October.[25] The total strength of the army at the beginning of August appears to have been in the region of 61,000 men, which the Dutch aimed to increase to about 72–82,000, a target they appeared more or less to have reached by the beginning of January 1673 with an actual strength of about 75,000 men.[26]

With much of the Republic under enemy occupation the Province of Holland was called upon to carry an even larger burden of the army's expenditure than customary; instead of about 58 per cent, its budgeted share for 1673 came to nearly 69 per cent, with the remainder being borne by the other still independent Provinces of Zeeland, Friesland and Groningen. From the Spaniards further help was forthcoming. With the addition of 6–7,000 troops the Spanish auxiliaries increased to 9–10,000 men in July; and, with the Spaniards taking over responsibility for garrisoning three towns in the Generality Lands, Dutch troops could be redeployed for the defence of Holland.[27]

The names of the Dutch commanders were a roll call of the aristocracy of the Dutch Republic and of Europe – including the Duke of Holstein, the Count of Königsmarck, the Count of Witgensteyn, and the Count of Limburg-Stirum. There were members of the Orange clan – the Count of Solms and William's old tutor Frederick-Henry of Nassau-Zuylenstein. There were also two names of whom we shall from now on hear a great deal as military commanders under William III – the Count of Waldeck, and a member of the Utrecht van Reede clan, Godard van Reede, Lord of Ginkel.[28] We have already met two other members of the latter's family, Van Reede van Amerongen, the ambassador to the Great Elector who was now plodding in the mud of Germany in the Elector's retinue, and Jonkheer Frederick van Reede, William's envoy to Charles II. Hieronymus van Beverninck remained a field deputy until 9 January 1673.

This increasingly formidable army was budgeted to increase to over 90,000 men in 1673, a figure that was inevitably theoretical and dependent on contingencies, but nevertheless the Dutch army was now becoming very different from the small force that had straggled into the uncertain defences of the Water Line in June. There were in addition the civil militia and the locally hired troops (*waardgelders*), together an unknown number but substantial, although perhaps of limited military value; and there were Spanish troops on loan from the Spanish Netherlands, which we have mentioned above.[29]

On 16 September, on the suggestion of the Prince of Orange, the Count of Waldeck was appointed the third Field-Marshal of the Dutch army, in addition to Prince Maurits of Nassau-Siegen and Wirtz. The reasons William gave for the appointment were that he anticipated that the war could last a long time, he himself could not be present everywhere, and Prince Maurits was getting older. He recommended Waldeck as the foremost commander in Germany: he had, as Count of Kuilenberg, a stake in the country, and he was a Lutheran.[30]

Waldeck, born in 1620, had a wealth of military experience behind him. From 1642 to 1651 he had begun his tutelage under Frederick-Henry; from 1651 to 1656 he served in the army of the Elector of Brandenburg, where he had been a lieutenant-general, and he also served the Elector as a minister; he had served in the Swedish army; he had fought the Turks; and from 1665 to 1671 he had been in the armies of the Brunswick-Lüneburg dukes.[31] As we have mentioned, the Waldeck family territories were not far from those of the Nassaus in Germany, and Waldeck had, furthermore, married into the Nassau clan – his wife was Charlotte Elisabeth, Countess of Nassau-Siegen, the sister of Prince Maurits of Nassau-Siegen.[32] When the Elector of Brandenburg's emissary, Crosigk, arrived in The Hague to consult with the Prince of Orange, Waldeck was described by him on 28 September as the Prince's 'factotum'.[33] William had found a man with the military experience that he himself so lacked to stand by his side; and he was also to be used for many a diplomatic mission.

Waldeck and William of Orange were to constitute a more formidable military combination than has perhaps been allowed – if not as outstanding commanders in the field, when they were facing opponents of the calibre of Condé, of Turenne and of Luxemburg, then well within the field of logistics, of supply and of military organisation. They were supported by the massively experienced and staunchly loyal Prince Maurits of Nassau-Siegen, handicapped though he was by his age and afflicted by gout. The two brothers-in-law had long experience of working together in the service of the Great Elector. Waldeck began at once with the reorganising and reforming of the Dutch army.[34]

Amid all his preoccupations the Prince found time to extend his patronage in favour of his client, Van Reede van Amerongen; when the vacancy of a regiment became available at the end of September he granted it to the Count of Warfusé, subject to the condition that the income from the post was paid to the Amerongen family.[35]

THE DUKE OF LUXEMBURG ON THE WATER LINE
Opposing the Dutch army on the French side was the Duke of Luxemburg, a ruthless, even sadistic, but very able general. His headquarters were established at Utrecht, where, in the early part of July and prior to Louis's return to France, the cathedral had been rededicated to Catholicism; where Monsieur, Louis's brother, had been sumptuously feasted by his lover the Chevalier de Lorraine; and where Louis himself had made a triumphant entry amid the sound of bells and cannon. Luxemburg's strategy was to attack the Dutch should the right opportunity present itself or, failing that, to await the ice of winter, thus opening the way for an assault over the frozen Water Line.[36]

Under Luxemburg's command the French occupation of the conquered territories in the United Provinces was harsh in the extreme. He wrote – with relish – to Louvois about punitive expeditions undertaken as reprisals against peasants who had fired on French troops – houses were set on fire, and all within, livestock, peasants, women and children, perished. The French troops exerted the utmost pressure on the inhabitants to extort the maximum contributions possible to pay for the war. Louvois, who was counting on this source of funds, 'exhorted Luxemburg to show himself inexorable', although this most adept man of affairs soon moderated his tone when Louis got a hint of what was afoot. 'The king', he wrote, 'is very surprised to see that the country is still subject to pillage and exposed to every sort of violence from the soldiers. You know as well as we do here that this is the best way of ruining the troops and the country…. His majesty has commanded me to let you know that he desires that you remedy [the excesses] by whatever means are available, so that the peasantry in the country return to as great a degree of repose as they were in when paying their taxes in the time of the Dutch regime.' But a reign of terror was, for Luxemburg, a deliberate policy from which he did not desist; and from which he was not prevented by Louis, either because the King was not fully aware of what was happening, as his biographer Petitfils has claimed, or perhaps because he was reluctant to discipline his client, linked as he was to the clan of that powerful Prince of the Blood, Condé, although, as we shall see, even Condé was shocked by Luxemburg's actions.[37]

PRINCE WILLIAM'S OFFENSIVE

The Prince of Orange now determined to go on the offensive. Maurits of Nassau-Siegen formulated a plan to capture Naarden, which, followed by a further move on Amersfoort and Hardewijk, would threaten the lines of communication of Utrecht and force Luxemburg back to the Ijssel, from where a further assault could be made in conjunction with the Dutch forces in Friesland and Groningen.[38] At the end of September the attempt on Naarden was made – the password given to the troops was 'vive Orange et Amsterdam' – by means of a surprise attack, which was to be supported by a seaborne force from Amsterdam. But this became becalmed, and thus the project was frustrated. Wicquefort says the young Rhinegrave, who commanded the seaborne force, did not depart on time because he was delayed by dissolute distractions. The tide was accordingly too low, which impeded the progress of the artillery and of the troops; and, after consulting Maurits, Prince William called off the attempt.

A further surprise attack on Woerden, which the French now occupied, was planned for 11 October; but the garrison there became aware of what was happening and, by means of the firing of guns from a tower, alerted the French at Utrecht. A relief force under Luxemburg himself attacked a post occupied by Nassau-Zuylenstein between Utrecht and Woerden. A sally by the garrison of Woerden against the Prince of Orange was driven back with substantial loss. But Nassau-Zuylenstein's post fell to Luxemburg's troops at a second assault, killing the Prince's old governor in the process. William then called off the attack. The body of Nassau-Zuylenstein was brought to his former pupil, who had been so attached to him: he had paid the blood money expected from the aristocracy in warfare; and the Prince arranged for the burial of his uncle at Breda, with its strong Orangist associations, where he had been governor.[39] There the young Rhinegrave was appointed governor in his place.[40]

One person did distinguish himself, a member of the important aristocratic Utrecht clan, closely associated with Prince William: Godard van Reede van Ginkel, the son of Amerongen, was on the periphery of the battle, in command of five gunboats, and his conduct was mentioned by Louvignies to the Prince of Orange. Embraced by the Prince, he was promised that his conduct would always be remembered; and thus the newly promoted Brigadier commenced his ascent, to become one of William of Orange's chief military commanders, ending his career as a field-marshal and the Earl of Athlone.[41]

THE PRINCE'S STRATEGY FOR THE AUSTRO-BRANDENBURG ARMY TO JOIN THE DUTCH

Undeterred by these setbacks, Prince William was determined to continue the counter-attack on the French that Naarden and Woerden had heralded. A bold and ambitious concept had been forming in his mind. He had written to Amerongen on 3 October, shortly before the attack on Woerden, that, if Austrian and Brandenburg troops could secure Coblenz and the passage of the Rhine they could join the Spanish and Dutch troops. What lay behind that letter was a crucial meeting at his headquarters at Bodegrave, which had taken place on the day he wrote, to discuss strategy, and which was attended by Colonel Crosigk, on behalf of the Great Elector, by the Prince himself, by Waldeck and by Prince Maurits of Nassau-Siegen.

In preparation for the meeting Waldeck had prepared a memorandum on a strategy which was to be based on the command of the Rhine, of the Mosel and of the Maas (Meuse) rivers, the supply routes used by the French. Cutting these supply lines would also sever the communications between the French and their allies, the bishops of Münster and Cologne; it would impede the levying of troops by France in Germany; it would facilitate the conjunction of Dutch troops with the Austrian and Brandenburg allies; and it would encourage the Estates and Chapters in the bishoprics to renounce their masters. The best way of achieving all this would be for the Austro-Brandenburg army to march on Cologne and Liège.[42]

Prince William spoke to this brief and amplified it, as is made plain by Crosigk's detailed account, which he submitted to the Great Elector.

The Prince said, according to this account, that much was hanging on the march of the Austro-Brandenburg army towards Coblenz; it would secure command of the Rhine and Mosel rivers, as well as Cologne. But whilst these were good objectives in themselves he had concerns that, given the lateness of the season, the bad roads and the remoteness of the territory, the march could extend into winter and therefore afford little relief to the Dutch Republic. Account needed to be taken of how matters there stood; if no prompt outside assistance was forthcoming to relieve its citizens and to revive trade, which had for some time been at a standstill, it would be impossible to persuade its inhabitants to contribute the levies with which to pay the subsidies of the allies.

He therefore urged the allies to march directly towards the Dutch and not to become bogged down in detours. Turenne's forces were not that considerable – Crosigk had already reported on 28 September that the Prince had received information from Grave that

Turenne's forces amounted to 19,000 men. And, in any case, if they went at him head on, and if he saw himself threatened in the van, that is, by the Austro-Brandenburg army, and in the rear, that is, by the Dutch army, he would find it very difficult to secure himself on all fronts. If, on the other hand, the Austro-Brandenburg army were to become mired in detours Turenne would be bound to learn of this; and – because of the reduced pressure on himself – he would be able to reinforce Luxemburg's army from his own.

Nor should the bishops of Cologne and Münster be spared. If Turenne learnt that there was no threat to them he would not need to dedicate an army to protect them, but would only need to provide for well-provisioned garrisons in the conquered territories, whilst using his main might against the Dutch.

The Prince urged, if Cologne could not be captured, that at least a few thousand men, perhaps 10,000, should be detached at Coblenz to cross the Rhine, to join up with several thousand Spanish and Dutch troops, or, if occasion allowed, even with the whole Dutch encampment – which, it was inferred, would be established at Maastricht, not far from Coblenz, as was, in the event, to be the case.

The Prince reverted to the treaty that the Elector had with the Dutch, which envisaged that the war would be pursued in Westphalia, to the north of Coblenz and Cologne.[43] He visualised the war being continued there, after the French lines of communication had been cut by means of the conjunction, in the approximate vicinity of Coblenz, of Austro-Brandenburg forces with Dutch and Spanish troops. We need to note that the territories of the Bishop of Cologne would stand on the line of march of an army moving up the Rhine from Coblenz to Cologne, and those of the Bishop of Münster were vulnerable to an attack through Westphalia.

The report was presented by Crosigk on 18 October at the Austro-Brandenburg headquarters, which were then at Bergen, north-east of Frankfurt-am-Main.[44]

The Elector wrote to the Prince from there on the 22nd saying that it had cost much trouble and inconvenience to reach the bridges of the Rhine and Main rivers, but he indicated that the intention was to cross the Rhine and then to act in accordance with the logic of the war situation and the movements of the enemy; and he offered the support of the troops he had retained in Westphalia, should William engage in any operations in the regions of Cologne or Münster.[45]

PROPOSED CAPTURE OF CHARLEROI

In the meantime, the Prince had written to Prince Maurits of Nassau-Siegen on 14 October that, in the light of the Austrian and Brandenburg troop movements, 'I believe that it will be very necessary that we take a firm resolution on what we can do on our side'; and he summoned Maurits and the other officers of the high command to a council of war to be held at Gouda on 16 October.[46]

The council was supposed to be held in great secret and even the States-General was not informed of its decisions.[47] However, a much alarmed Maurits wrote to William on 20 October reporting that one of his lieutenant-colonels, finding himself at table in an Amsterdam tavern, heard a mysterious gentleman, dressed in black mourning, giving an account, word for word, of what had happened at Gouda.[48] The notorious inability of public affairs to be kept secret in the Dutch Republic was therefore running true to form, although it was fortunate that what the gentleman in black knew does not appear to have reached the ears of the enemies of the Republic.

For what was decided at Gouda, at the meeting on 17 October, which included Waldeck as well as Prince Maurits, was a variation of Waldeck's original memorandum, discussed with Crosigk at Bodegrave – an audacious plan indeed, an attack on Charleroi. This French enclave in the Spanish Netherlands had been granted to Louis XIV under the treaty of Aix-la-Chapelle; it stood on the borders of France; it was the key to the communications between the French troops in the Netherlands and their magazines in France; and its capture would have constituted both the threat of carrying the war into France and a threat to the prestige and reputation of the French King himself. It was a bold and inspired move and the Prince's sudden appearance before the town, when it happened, was to cause consternation in the French capital.

But the military arithmetic made the expedition dependent on the support of the Austro-Brandenburg army. Waldeck calculated that the siege would require 12,000 men, supported by an army of observation of 25,000 men. There were about 41–43,000 troops in Holland and Zeeland of which 18,000 were required for the defence of the Water Line, leaving about 15,000 available for the Charleroi expedition. To this could be added about 10,000 Spanish troops, a total of 25,000 men, so that another 12,000 or so would be required from Austria and Brandenburg.[49]

THE MARCH TO MAASTRICHT

On 27 October the Prince issued an urgent order to Maurits to send all his cavalry from Muiden and Weesp for embarkation at Rotterdam – the Dutch army was about to commence its march.[50] A series of orders and missives flew back and forth between the Prince and his senior commanders, putting in train all the measures necessary in the exigencies of the circumstances – when there were insufficient funds for the immediate needs of the company commanded by the Prince of Brunswick-Wolfenbüttel, the Prince offered to pay with his own money.[51] About 25,000 men left from Rotterdam for Bergen op Zoom at the beginning of November, and from thence to Rozendaal, where they were met by 6–7,000 Spanish horse.[52]

On 2 November, before embarking himself, William wrote from Rotterdam to Maurits setting out his dispositions for the command of the troops remaining behind in Holland. The Count of Königsmarck was to take the place of the Prince in the centre of the Water Line at Bodegrave; Maurits was to continue to command in the north with Field-Marshal

Wirtz and the Count of Hoorn in the south. It was William's nature to act aggressively and Maurits was urged, if he saw the opportunity of taking appropriate action against the enemy in William's absence, 'pray to do so'.[53] As the Spanish commander, the Count of Louvignies, was accompanying the Prince, the Marquis of Westerloo took his place on the line at Schoonhoven. The Prince left behind for these defences more than 18,000 foot and a certain number of cavalry.[54] The possibility was anticipated – rightly as events were to prove – that, during his absence with his forces, the enemy might chance to break through the Water Line at its most vulnerable point, where Königsmarck commanded, to threaten the heart of the country, and to attack Königsmarck from the rear. In this event he was authorised to fall back on Leyden and await the orders of Prince Maurits or Field-Marshal Wirtz.[55]

Accompanied by Hieronymus van Beverninck, the Count of Waldeck, the young Rhinegrave and the Count of Louvignies, William arrived at Rozendaal on 7 November where he reviewed his army of 30,000 men – 18,000 cavalry (including the 6–7,000 Spanish), 2,000 dragoons and 10,000 infantry. On the 8th he marched towards Maastricht with 10,000 horse, including the Spanish, and 5,000 foot, leaving the rest of his army in the vicinity of Bergen op Zoom, where it could either join him or be used in Holland as circumstances warranted.[56] At Kastel he received news that French troops from Utrecht and its surroundings were marching in the direction of the Waal and Maas rivers so that he sent back the infantry to Bergen op Zoom to await the orders of Maurits and Wirtz, in the hope that, together with the troops whom he had left behind there, they could 'undertake something against the enemy' – he had in mind, for example, an opportunistic attack on some point left vulnerable by the French troop withdrawals such as Kampen or Swartsluis. Maurits recalled two of the regiments in the middle of November, leaving the other three at the disposal of Wirtz and Königsmarck, but no opportunity presented itself. On the 13th Prince William arrived at Lanaken, barely an hour's march from Maastricht. On the 15th he arrived at Eysden, two hours to the north of Maastricht.[57]

Before leaving The Hague William had sent Colonel Webenum at the end of October as his emissary to keep Amerongen, and hence the Elector of Brandenburg, informed of what was happening on the Dutch side, and his views on what the Austro-Brandenburg troops could do on theirs. Webenum and Amerongen submitted a joint memorandum, dated 6 November, to the Great Elector which reflected his thinking. It informed Frederick-William of his intended march to Maastricht where, in anticipation of the arrival of the Elector's troops, he would be laying in all necessary provisions. The Prince would do everything possible to incommode the French troops of the Duc de Duras – who had been masking the fortress of Maastricht – and he urged the Elector to cross the Rhine as soon as possible so that he could be near Cologne in the enemy's country, where he could be joined by the Dutch and Spanish army. Not only would it then be possible to cut the lines of communication between the King of France and his troops, but vigorous action on behalf of the Brandenburg troops would encourage the Spaniards so that they might come 'to break with', that is to declare open war on, France and its allies – instead of providing the 'auxiliary' aid which technically fell short of putting them on a war footing with France. It would also encourage the vacillating governing council of the Liège territories – at loggerheads with its bishop, who was also the Bishop of Cologne – to come down on the right side of the fence.[58]

FAILURE OF THE AUSTRO-BRANDENBURG ARMY TO JOIN THE DUTCH

But, alas, of the plans for Austro-Brandenburg troops to join with the Dutch and the Spaniards nothing was to materialise. Bruijninx, the Dutch envoy in Vienna, had written to Fagel as early as 2 October that he could say for certain that Montecuccoli had been ordered to avoid any major engagement.[59] Thus, well before the Prince's departure for Rozendaal, the suspicions of the lack of support forthcoming from the Austro-Brandenburg army with its endless and purposeless marches and counter-marches was causing a nagging anxiety amongst the Dutch. After all it was central to the campaign on which the Prince of Orange was embarking that the junction with this army should be effected, and there was not much sign that it was prepared to act in accordance with his plan. The tension was reflected in an acerbic letter from Fagel to Amerongen on 24 October: 'I will freely admit that I cannot understand the démarches of the elector…; all things considered they seem to bear comparison with nothing so much as the journey of the children of Israel to Canaan, who, arriving at the frontiers of that land, turned their back again and returned to the borders of Egypt.' If the Elector had marched into his own territories in Westphalia – under the terms of his treaty with the Dutch he should have been there by 25 July – he could have reckoned, Fagel remarked, on 16,000 Dutch troops who were observing the enemy from their side and who could have joined up with him.[60]

The Prince of Orange shared these worries to the full and he too tried to urge his uncle by marriage, and former guardian, to vigorous supportive action. He wrote – on the same date as Fagel – to Amerongen even whilst he was still at his camp at Bodegrave. He asked Amerongen to urge the Elector earnestly to commence marching towards the Dutch as rapidly as possible without embarking on so many detours. He was sending an express messenger to the Elector in a few days to inform him of his thinking and in what manner he intended to take action on his side – Colonel Webenum, we can take it. In the meantime he asked Amerongen to assure the Elector that he would neglect nothing in his power to divert the enemy and to instigate action with operations against him – although there is no evidence that the Elector was let into the full secret that the main objective was Charleroi.[61]

The Prince reinforced his message by writing – on the same date again – to another member of his clan, the Prince of Anhalt, in the same vein. He prayed him 'to hasten … the march of the Austro-Brandenburg armies … as much as possible' in the direction of the Dutch whilst he would make as great a diversion on the Dutch side as he could.[62]

At the beginning of November Amerongen conveyed William's message to the Elector, who thereupon undertook to break up his camp immediately together with the Austrians and to march first to below Frankfurt (on the Main) and then to below Mainz (on the Rhine). But nothing substantial resulted from these promises; and Amerongen formed the view that the Austrian troops had little inclination to fight, that they were the reason why the armies remained so far south in Germany, and why there had been such long delays – which, indeed, reflected the truth.[63]

On 23 November Prince William informed the States-General that he had crossed the Maas at Maastricht to take up quarters on the upper Maas to allow his troops to recuperate. His intention to 'pay the count of Duras a visit' was frustrated by Duras's withdrawal behind the Roer river and his retreat towards Cleves, whilst, at the same time, Turenne had crossed the Rhine and was moving towards the Prince's army; so that, as the Prince wrote, 'we will have to take other measures'.[64]

At the end of November he reinforced his army with infantry from Bergen op Zoom; he had also received reinforcements from the Spanish – 1,500 horse and about 3,000 infantry – and these forces were augmented by troops from the garrison from Maastricht, so that the joint Dutch and Spanish forces amounted to 24,000 men.[65]

He had already expressed his concern at the vacillation in the Austro-Brandenburg army about crossing the Rhine. 'I have to acknowledge', he told Amerongen, 'that I don't understand these maxims and wonder at them.'[66]

His concerns were not confined to what was happening on his own immediate front. He had to take into consideration the military situation which he had left behind him in Holland. From there Königsmarck warned him, on 18 November, that he had no more than 1,800 effectives to man his vulnerable section of the Water Line; should there be a frost, he wrote, one could count the section as lost. He feared that the orders which he had – which allowed him to withdraw once the enemy had broken through and attacked him in the rear – would leave the withdrawal too late if the waters had frozen over; and he asked the Prince to let him have written orders as to what he should do in those circumstances.[67] It was not long before these anxieties were to prove of more than theoretical interest.

In the meantime the Prince had an army to provision; 150,000 guilders had been requested by the Council of State from the States-General and the Prince urged that these sums should be made available as a matter of urgency at Liège or Maastricht and put at the disposal of Hieronymus van Beverninck. The old veteran was working closely with Waldeck to provision the army, in which they were assisted by some cooperation from the Liège territories, and by the Jewish contractor Moses Machado, with whom the Prince was to continue to work in the future. The Prince was then writing from Sichem, on 26 November, where he had moved because he needed the forage and because it was in accordance with his plan of campaign, of which, however, he said he dared not send details to the States-

General for fear they might be intercepted – they were, of course, the long-planned attack on Charleroi.[68]

At first he embarked on some minor engagements. On receiving news that Duras had crossed the river Roer at the beginning of December the Prince's troops recrossed the Maas but were prevented from pursuing the French forces by winter floods. When Duras retreated in disorder Prince William made the most of this rather minor success, as he did of the subsequent capture and raising of the fortress of Valckenburg, in despatches to the States-General on 6 and 10 December.[69]

The news that Amerongen was conveying from the Austro-Brandenburg camp was not encouraging – on 25 November he reported to the Prince that there were rumours that the Elector was going to withdraw his troops into winter quarters in his lands in Westphalia, and on 8 December he wrote to Fagel, with a copy to Prince William, saying there 'was little or nothing to be expected' from the two armies; and he recommended that the States-General and the Prince should take their measures accordingly and think of other expedients.[70]

The time had come to march on Charleroi.

THE PRINCE'S SIEGE OF CHARLEROI FAILS

William's army left Maastricht on 10 December and arrived at Gelly on the 16th, a quarter of an hour's distance from Charleroi, where the Counts of Nassau and of Louvignies had also arrived shortly before and had commenced the siege of the town. Its situation and fortifications were considerable, but its governor, the Count of Montal, was absent, having been lured away to defend the town of Tongeren which he feared was about to be attacked, leaving behind a weak garrison – some 700–800 men. However, a severe frost had set in two days before, which prevented the digging of earthworks in the hard ground;[71] the necessary equipment for the siege, which the Spanish had promised, did not materialise; and the count of Montal succeeded in returning from Tongeren and, by breaking through the Spanish lines, was able to re-enter Charleroi, where his presence lent spirit and vigour to the defenders. The continuation of the frost caused the ground to freeze to a depth of a foot and a half, and given the lateness of the season and in the light of the views of the Spanish officers, the decision was taken to raise the siege. 'Against the will of the Almighty there is nothing to be done', the Prince wrote with resignation to Amerongen on 23 December. He had resolved to return to Holland, leaving the larger part of his forces behind for the time being to inconvenience the French; they were beset by sickness and Van Reede van Ginkel had to be transported to Brussels to recuperate, lucky to survive with his life.

It was perhaps, at first sight, a disappointment, not compensated for by the subsequent capture of the town of Binch and the destruction of its fortifications by a joint force of Dutch and Spanish troops, however much William tried to emphasise Binch's importance in his despatch to the States-General. Waldeck had foreseen failure, even before the end of

November, but did not want to provide the Austrian Emperor with the excuse that Prince William had called off the expedition. It was the failure of the Austro-Brandenburg armies to conjoin with the Prince that frustrated the thrust of William's whole campaign to exploit the dangerously exposed and over-extended position of the French armies, of which Condé had warned all along before even the French invasion of 1672 was launched.

Nevertheless, the young Prince's entire plan for his expedition, culminating in the siege of Charleroi, had been imaginative in conception, resourceful in execution and valiant in spirit. And in Paris the threat to Charleroi had caused Louis himself, in the depths of winter and in a state of 'agitated anxiety', to leave St-Germain for Compiègne, to give orders for the despatch of his household troops, for the concentration of his garrisons situated in Flanders, and for the recall of Condé to the river Saar – a panic which only the inspired defence of the town by the Count of Montal was able to abate.[72]

Returning to the Republic as fast as he could with seven regiments of horse, the Prince found his march impeded by the severe weather. He complained of it to the States-General when staying at the abbey of Everboden near Zichem, and to Waldeck: 'God knows how I can return to Holland through this ice', he wrote on 26 December. It was not until the 31st that he arrived at Alphen in Holland, having learnt on the 30th of critical news. The ice that had impeded his plans at Charleroi and his return to Holland had provided Luxemburg with his long-sought opportunity. He had attacked the Water Line at its narrowest and most vulnerable point, at Bodegrave, where Königsmarck commanded.[73]

THE VULNERABILITY OF THE WATER LINE

When William departed from Rotterdam at the beginning of November 1672 he left no one in overall military command on the Water Line, a mistake that was now to have serious consequences. The States of Holland attempted to fill the void, and a number of meetings took place between delegates from these States, and from the States-General and the military commanders, to discuss and coordinate the defence of the homeland in the absence of the Prince. This included a meeting at Zwamerdam on 19 November at which the two field-marshals, Wirtz and Prince Maurits of Nassau-Siegen, were present, together with the Count of Königsmarck. But by the middle of December many of the necessary measures agreed upon were still lacking.[74] The shortage of cavalry, which could operate across ice, and most of which the Prince had taken with him, was a notable defect. Reduced by disease and other factors, the effective strength of the original 18,000 troops on the Water Line, even after the reinforcements of 5,000 men that the Prince of Orange had sent back in the middle of November, was about 19,000.[75]

Particularly exposed was Bodegrave, which was also the most obvious point for the French to attack; it was fortified only on the east, Woerden, side, leaving it vulnerable to an outflanking attack from the rear if the waters froze.[76] From the very beginning this problem had caused Königsmarck much concern, and we have already seen that he had asked for written instructions from the Prince on 18 November as to what he should do if ice should enable the enemy to break through and attack from the rear. William replied rather vaguely on the 27th that, as he had no cypher with him operative in the case of Königsmarck, he should act in accordance with the instructions he had given on 1 November when he left Holland – at which stage he had indicated that, if it was certain that a breakthrough had occurred, Königsmark should fall back on Leyden – or in accordance with whatever was decided upon at the conference at Zwamerdam.[77] When Fagel wrote to him asking for further clarification he replied on 18 December that 'his intention concerning the abandonment of the post at Bodegrave had been no other than in the utmost extremity'; and he asked Fagel to convey this to the Count, which Fagel did.[78]

The Dutch had managed, by opening and closing the sluices in combination with the tides in the Zuiderzee, to maintain the north/south flow of the waters in the Water Line, thus keeping the ice, especially at the narrowest points, comparatively thin.[79] But in the middle of December it began to freeze in earnest, and Luxemburg, seizing his chance, assembled his forces; by the 17th it had frozen so hard that in the course of a few days it was possible to cross the ice everywhere in the vicinity of Bodegrave; and by the 20th it was possible to cross on horseback. Königsmarck gave notice that in such weather he could not, without cavalry, hold his position.[80] News of Luxemburg's assembling of his forces was coming in from all sides and Königsmarck divined that their target was his position at Bodegrave.

He wrote to the Town Council at Leyden on 22 December that 'he had orders, in case of need, to retreat to their town' and he asked that the Council should make provision to house his command, consisting of 3,000 foot and 50 horse, and to lay in fuel. He informed the States of Holland of this and added that he had information that Luxemburg was mustering everything he could; Königsmarck's intelligence was that he had 2,000 horse and 1,000 dragoons at Utrecht and there were a further 2,500 men in garrison at Woerden; this, as it proved, was an underestimate. Königsmarck was sending his sick, his ammunition and his cannon – Luxemburg had no artillery at Utrecht – to Leyden. He would hold his position for as long as he could, after which he would march on Leyden and defend that town to the uttermost. Sending his artillery to Leyden seems to indicate that in his own mind he had abandoned hope for Bodegrave and that he saw Leyden as the more promising place to make his stand.[81] He had previously complained to the Holland deputies in the field that he had insufficient manpower and had asked them to remedy this; but in trying to respond the deputies found they were hampered by their lack of authority over the military.[82] The States of Holland, perhaps somewhat unrealistically, resolved on the 22nd to order Königsmarck to safeguard Bodegrave.[83]

In the extreme emergency they faced the States of Holland assembled on Christmas Day, a Sunday. They received news from Prince Maurits, dated the 23rd, giving confirmation that Luxemburg was concentrating all his forces based on the Ijssel river and elsewhere.[84] They also received news from the Field Deputies that Königsmarck now reported that the French were 9–10,000 men strong and that he had asked for definite orders on how he should proceed. It is clear from the minutes we have that the States of Holland were losing confidence in the Count, and that they were also aware of the problem of the lack of an overall chief. They resolved that overall command should be given to Field-Marshal Wirtz, although not without fear that it would raise Königsmarck's resentment.[85] On the 27th they approved measures proposed by the energetic and determined Fagel to put The Hague itself into a posture of defence.[86]

THE ASSAULT AND THE ATROCITIES

On that same day Prince Maurits reported to the Prince of Orange that Luxemburg had assembled from the French garrisons a force of 12–13,000 men, 'some said more'. Their aim was to bypass the main Dutch posts and head straight for Gouda and The Hague. There was a glimmer of hope for the Dutch – falling snow portended a thaw and by opening the sluices they had weakened the ice. But Luxemburg was not a man to allow this to deter him. He resolved to push forward. His forces came to a watercourse, which, because of the strength of the flow, had not frozen over; they built a bridge, which collapsed after some 3,500 men had crossed. Still undeterred, Luxemburg, with these troops, continued his advance. Some accounts relate that the remaining troops returned to Woerden, others that, after rebuilding the bridge, they followed a few hours later. The French general was on his way to Bodegrave, his ultimate objective being to put The Hague to the torch, and to force surrender on the Dutch.[87]

The weather conditions were increasingly turning against Luxemburg – a thaw had set in and the snow was becoming rain. Inflexible, he marched on, leading his army on foot through the night in the most appalling conditions, with the water at times reaching the men's necks. Amongst the officers there were some lucky escapes. The Marquis de Coevres fell through the ice and was saved only by being hauled up by the hair; Boufflers, a future marshal of France who was to be a successful opponent of Marlborough, also fell through the ice and was lucky to survive, as was a Lieutenant-Colonel Douglas, who fell through a hole and when his feet touched the bottom, managed to save himself by propelling himself upwards, where the ice was thin enough for his head to break through.[88]

Königsmarck fell back on the Goudsche Sluys and, later, on Leyden, where he found the town gates barred against him. The French captured the village of Zwamerdam, close to Bodegrave. 'The number of prisoners is small', Luxemburg reported to Louvois, 'because more were killed than it pleased us to take.' All those in the village were grilled alive, not one being allowed to leave their houses. The thaw impeded his further progress and, compelled to abandon his plan to move further into the Province of Holland, he embarked on his retreat. Before doing so he gave the village over to pillage and massacre and then applied the torch: 'I assure you', he again wrote to Louvois, 'that I took pleasure in ordering the burning before my eyes of the house of the prince of Orange and that of his favourite the Rhinegrave, which were two little châteaux, the prettiest in the world.' He personally revelled at the sight of the humiliating burning of the fallen bodies of enemy officers – he refused to return them to the Dutch – and the burning of people who had sought refuge in the houses. Then he returned via Bodegrave where the same atrocities were perpetrated. His aim was a deliberate act of terror; he wished to give the people of Holland 'a salutary fright', and to demonstrate that William of Orange could not protect his people, in 17th-century terms a patron who could not protect his clients or even his own property or that of his favourite.[89]

News of what had happened soon spread. 'Little girls of ten or twelve, mothers of newborn children and old women were not spared and hundreds were burnt alive in the houses', Adriaan van der Goes wrote. When the Prince of Orange arrived at the scene he found a baby boy of about nine months old lying in the road sucking his fingers, the offspring, it was thought, of parents killed in flight, and he took measures for his care.[90] Although it is disputed amongst historians whether the Prince was instrumental in it, a pamphlet war was launched in which no detail was spared. The pamphlets were translated into every language and spread throughout Europe, Germany in particular.[91] One such pamphlet was produced by the contemporary historian Abraham Wicquefort, with illustrations by Romeyn de Hooghe, appearing in 1673; both the pamphlet and the illustrations were based on the accounts of eyewitnesses and victims of the atrocities.[92]

Much to his surprise Luxemburg found the fort of Niewerbrugge, which barred his sole means of retreat, abandoned by its garrison and he and his surviving troops managed to find their way back to Woerden and Utrecht.[93] Prince Maurits reported that they had suffered considerable losses through the weather and with men falling through the ice; several thousand, so says Maurits, had drowned and Luxemburg was ill, having himself fallen into the water.[94] The Duke, however, found means to relieve the hardships of winter campaigning. The Marquis de La Vallière, the brother of Louis XIV's mistress, wrote to Louvois that at Luxemburg's instigation two beautiful creatures had arrived from Paris, one blonde and one brunette; and 'I surprised him yesterday in the most wicked *flagrante delicto* I ever found man in'.[95]

Letters captured by the Dutch revealed that Turenne reproached Luxemburg and told him that Louis XIV would not approve of his cruelties, which disfigured the fairest deeds of the French nation and sullied the most glorious deeds of the monarch.[96] It had no effect on Luxemburg, who had the backing of Louvois. The French Intendant, Robert, who was based at Utrecht, boasted to Louvois of the extortions he was inflicting on the occupied inhabitants to extract the utmost in contributions, resorting, as he himself admitted, to the most base and false of pretexts, backed up by the billeting of soldiers and threats of knocking down the houses of his victims. Louvois exhorted him further: 'drive on … with all vigour imaginable'.

When Condé arrived to take over command he was shocked, hardy warrior accustomed to the sights of 17th-century warfare though he was, at what his client Luxemburg had perpetrated. He felt compelled to write to Louvois on 25 April 1673 that the people were desperate because of the insupportable taxation that was daily inflicted upon them; the profit yielded beyond what could have been gained by gentler means was very small – and 'I do not know if it is in the interests of the king to continue.'

The reply that came from Louvois at the beginning of May was unyielding. The King's wishes were that 'Your Highness should appear as disagreeable and pitiless … as you can…. His majesty judges it *à propos* that you continue to burn all that you are capable of without relief to the Hollanders.' To this, it seems, Condé was unable to find an appropriate response. In February 1673 Amerongen's castle had been put to the torch, the diligent Robert justifying it on the ground that its owner was inciting the Great Elector and the German princes against Louis XIV.[97]

PRINCE WILLIAM'S DISCIPLINARY ACTION

Amongst the Dutch the expedition of the Duke of Luxemburg in the winter had caused similar disorders and the same lack of morale and discipline as had the previous breakthrough by the French at the Ijssel line in the summer. The Field Deputies noted on 23 December that Königsmarck's disposition to retreat to Leyden had resulted 'in much consternation and in the flight of many citizens; that it was unbelievable with what care the military was seeking its own salvation; and that the regiments of Polents and Degenfelt – they were commanded by two German colonels – were causing loss and much injury.'[98] Our troops, wrote Adriaan van der Goes, 'have caused much loss and plundered the peasantry, so that some have been hanged … order needs to be re-established amongst the soldiers. The lesson learnt is that it is not salutary to have many foreign and new recruits who treat our people badly in every way and exact a great deal of money, and when it comes to fighting don't fall in with much diligence, because', he added sardonically, 'it might invite death.'[99]

It was against this background that Prince William dealt with the case of Colonel Pain-et-Vin. The colonel was in command of the post at Niewerbrugge, which barred the way to Luxemburg's retreat, and which he abandoned to retire to Gouda. He was arrested by Wirtz. The States of Holland urged the Prince to administer vigorous justice. At his first court martial the colonel was sentenced to the dismissal of his posts, confiscation of his goods and imprisonment for life. With this, however, William expressed his dissatisfaction, upon which Wirtz and the other members of the court martial added the additional humiliation that the colonel should have his sword broken over his head in front of the ranks. The Prince remained obdurate, and he had the case brought before a court over which he himself presided, which condemned the colonel to beheading. The sentence was carried out in due form at Alphen on 23 January of the new year.[100]

The implacable sentence against Pain-et-Vin has been contrasted with the fact that no action was taken against Königsmarck, who had also abandoned his post. But Königsmarck had orders that allowed him to do so. Pain-et-Vin did not.

SUMMARY OF 1672

The year had begun with the intention of Louis XIV to invade and destroy the Dutch Republic. His immense, long-planned invasion, in alliance with the King of England and the Bishops of Münster and Cologne, and the speed of his victories seemed to portend the conclusion of the war in a matter of a few weeks, with an outcome exactly in accordance with his aims. The elevation of the Prince of Orange to the position held by his ancestors as a client of the King of England and, through him, as a client of the King of France would be the culmination of the plan that they had made all that time ago at the Treaty of Dover. But when the year ended the armies of France found themselves extended at the end of a long line of communications; the Dutch had a firm base behind their Water Line which, for the time being, had proved itself as resilient in the ice of winter as it had been in the summer, when the waters had – tantalisingly slowly – finally risen; and the Prince of Orange was not installed as the puppet ruler over the rump of the Dutch Republic, but was at the head of a resistance to his uncle of England and his cousin of France in a war that had already ceased to be confined to the Republic alone and that William was determined to extend further still.

But, whilst the capture of Coevorden from the two Bishops in the north-east of the country on 30 December provided a beacon of light, many vicissitudes still lay ahead.

---

1 See Oranien-Nassau, *Die Niederlande und das Reich*, ed. Horst Lademacher, Münster, Hamburg, 1995, Article by O. Mörke, pp.48–9, & by Murk van der Bijl, p.125.

2 Albert Waddington, *op. cit.*, pp.43, 46, 245–6. Van der Bijl, article, *op. cit.*, p.130. Ten Raa, *op. cit.*, VI, 1672–88, The Hague, 1940, p.3.

3 Oswald Redlich, *Welmacht des Barock, Österreich in der Zeit Kaiser Leopolds I*, Vienna, 1961, p.108. George Pagés, *op. cit.*, p.291.

4 Redlich, *op. cit.*, pp.108–11.

5 P.L. Müller, *Nederlandsche Eerste Betrekkingen met Oostenrijk 1658–1678, Verhandelingen der Koninklijke Akademia van Wetenschap*, IV, Amsterdam, 1869, p.17. Haley, *op. cit.*, p.52.

6 Pagès, *op. cit.*, p.271.

7 Müller, *op. cit.*, p. 37. Wout Troost, 'William III, Brandenburg and the Construction of the anti-French Coalition 1672–88' in *The Anglo-Dutch Moment, op. cit.*, p.303.

8 Redlich, *op. cit.*, p.111.

9 Pagès, *op. cit.*, p.299.

10 Redlich, *op. cit.*, p.111.

11 Derek McKay, in *Royal and Republican Sovereignty in Early Modern Europe: essays in memory of Ragnhild Hatton*, ed. Robert Oresko, G.C. Gibbs, Cambridge, 1997, p.206.

12 *Urkunden und Actenstücke Friedrich Wilhelm von Brandenburg*, III, Berlin, 1866, ed. Heinrich Peter, p.276.

13 Redlich, *op. cit.*, pp.112–13. Pagès, *op. cit.*, p.300. *Urkunden und Actenstücke, op. cit.*, III, p.294. Bruijninx to Fagel from Vienna, 2 October. Spielman, *op. cit.*, p.65. A.F. Pribram, *Franz Paul Freiherr von Lisola*, 1613–74, Leipzig, 1894, p.575.

14 Redlich, *op. cit.*, p.115.

15 *Urkunden und Actenstücke, op. cit.*, III, pp.286ff.

16 *Ibid.*, Amerongen to Fagel, 5 September, p.288, & Bruijninx to Fagel from Vienna, 2 October, p.294, when he also confirms that Montecuccoli had been ordered to avoid any major engagement.

17 *Ibid.*, III, p.288. Wicquefort, *Histoire*, IV, *op. cit.*, p.459. Rousset, *op. cit.*, I, p.383–4.

18 Ten Raa and Bas, *op. cit.*, V, pp.346–7. *Oeuvres de Louis XIV, op. cit.*, II, p.250. Van Nimwegen, *op. cit.*, p.446.

19 Sypestein and Bordes, *op. cit.*, II, p 137.

20 Van Nimwegen, *op. cit.*, p.446. Wout Troost, *William III, op. cit.*, p.92. *Oeuvres de Louis XIV, op. cit.*, II, p.245. Wicquefort, who gives the date of the raising of the siege as 6 September, *Mémoires, op. cit.*, pp.325–6.

21 Ten Raa and Bas, *op. cit.*, V, p.350.

22 Sypestein and Bordes, *op. cit.*, II, pp.111–12.

23 Van Nimwegen, *op. cit.*, p.446.

24 Sypestein and Bordes, *op. cit.*, II, p.113. Rousset, *op. cit.*, p.381. Hop & Vivien, *op. cit.*, p.235.

25 *Correspondentie Willem III en Bentinck, op. cit.*, II, Pt 1, pp.83, 123.

26 Hop & Vivien, *op. cit.*, p.250, covers the meeting of the States of Holland on 5 August when the target for the size of the army was given as 160 companies of horse and 666 companies of foot. Using Prince William's assumptions about company sizes (see below) with 80 men per company of horse and 89 men per company of foot this would give 12,800 horse and 59,274 foot, a total of 72,074 men. Furthermore the actual numbers at that time are given as 10,350 horse and 576 companies of foot (say 51,264 men), a total strength of say 61,614 men. On 12 January 1673 (see Hop & Vivien, *op. cit.*, pp.386–7) the Prince gave very similar figures to the States of Holland of the actual strength of the army then – 169 companies of horse (he stated 80 men per company), a company of miners (100 men), a company of grenadiers (100 men) and 689 companies of foot (each, the Prince said, of 89 men),which gives a total of about 75,000 men. Of these there were situated in Holland 10,320 horse (including 2,000 dragoons), about 39,000 foot and 58 companies of marines, as well as a small number of miscellaneous forces, including the Prince's personal regiment. Van Nimwegen indicates that in September approval was given for 781 infantry companies and 166 cavalry companies (*op. cit.*, p.330), which, on the Prince's above assumptions of the size of companies, gives a total of 82,789 men. Of course caution is required for an age when records were incomplete, with changes continually taking place, particularly in wartime conditions, and with assumptions about company sizes.

27 Van Nimwegen, *op. cit.*, pp.330, 444, 446.

28 Sypestein and Bordes, *op. cit.*, II, pp.217–18, 122.

29 Sypestein and Bordes, *op. cit.*, II, p.115.

30 Hop & Vivien, *op. cit.*, pp.304–5.

31 Von Rauchbar, *Leben und Thaten des Fürsten Georg Friedrich von Waldeck, 1620–1692*, 1867–70.

32 *Correspondentie Willem III en Bentinck, op. cit.*, II, Pt 1, p.256, n.4. Derek McKay, *The Great Elector, op. cit.*, p.66, see Erstes Buch Book 1.

33 *Urkunden un Actenstücke, op. cit.*, III, p.295, n.2.

34 Van Nimwegen, *op. cit.*, p.447.

35 *Correspondentie Willem III en Portland, op. cit.*, II, Pt 1, p.105.

36 Pierre de Ségur, *Le maréchal de Luxembourg et le prince d'Orange 1668–1678*, Paris, 1900, pp.52–3, 61, 68. Sypestein and Bordes, *op. cit.*, II, p.137.

37 Rousset, *op. cit.*, I, p.393. Petitfils, *op. cit.*, p.373.

38 Van Nimwegen, *op. cit.*, pp.448–9.

39 Wagenaar, *op. cit.*, 14, pp.226–7. Wicquefort, *Mémoires, op. cit.*, pp.332–4. Groen van Prinsterer, *op. cit.*, V, p.275, Prince William to the Rhinegrave dated 27 September; p.285, Prince William to Prince Maurits dated 10 October.

40 Luc Panhuysen, *Rampjarr 1672*, Amsterdam/Antwerp, 2009, p.226.

41 *Ibid.*, pp.224–5, 446.

42 Rauchbar, *op. cit.*, p.268.

43 *Urkunden und Actenstücke, op. cit.*, III, pp.295–7, p.296 n.1.

44 *Ibid.*, p.295 n.1.

45 *Correspondentie Willem III en Portland, op. cit.*, II, Pt 1, pp.123–4.

46 Groen van Prinsterer, *op. cit.*, V, p.286.

47 Wagenaar, *op. cit.*, 14, p.228.

48 Groen van Prinsterer, *op. cit.*, V, pp.287–8.

49 Van Nimwegen, *op. cit.*, pp.453–4.

50 Groen van Prinsterer, *op. cit.*, V, p.291.

51 *Correspondentie Willem III en Portland, op. cit.*, II, Pt 1, pp.129ff.

52 Van Nimwegen, *op. cit.*, p.454.

53 Groen van Prinsterer, *op. cit.*, V, pp.291, 294.

54 *Correspondentie Willem III en Portland, op. cit.*, II, Pt 1, pp.138–9.

55 *Ibid.*, II, Pt 1, pp.134–5.

56 Sypestein and Bordes, *op. cit.*, II, p.155. Van Nimwegen, *op. cit.*, p.454. *Correspondentie Willem III en Portland, op. cit.*, II, Pt 1, pp.138–9.

57 *Correspondentie Willem III en Portland, op. cit.*, II, Pt 1, pp.139–41. Groen van Prinsterer, *op. cit.*, V, pp.294–5.

58 *Correspondentie Willem III en Portland, op. cit.*, II, Pt 1, p.131. *Urkunden und Actenstücke, op. cit.*, III, p.321. The Prince expressed his approval of the memoir in his letter to Amerongen from Eysden dated 18 November. See *Correspondentie Willem III en Portland, op. cit.*, II, Pt 1, p.141.

59 *Urkunden und Actenstücke, op. cit.*, III, p.294.

60 Fagel to Amerongen on 24 October from The Hague. *Urkunden und Actenstücke, Correspondentie Willem III en Portland, op. cit.*, III, pp.308ff. For the treaty commitment to be in Westphalia by 25 July see Jan Willem van Sypestein, *Nederland en Brandenburg in 1672 en 1673*, The Hague, 1863, p.49.

61 *Ibid.*, pp.58–9. We are handicapped in the sources because many of Prince William's and Fagel's letters are missing in the archives as are many of the Prince's military instructions. *Urkunden und Actenstücke, op. cit.*, III, p.278.

62 *Urkunden und Actenstücke, op. cit.*, III, p.305.

63 *Correspondentie Willem III en Portland, op. cit.*, II, Pt 1, pp.135–6.

64 *Ibid.*, II, Pt 1, pp.145–6. Sypestein, *Nederland en Brandenburg, op. cit.*, pp. 66–7 gives the numbers of Duras's force.

65 Van Nimwegen, *op. cit.*, p.455.

66 Letter to Amerongen dated 18 November, *Correspondentie Willem III en Portland, op. cit.*, II, Pt 1, pp.141–2.

67 *Ibid.*, II, Pt 1, pp.144–5.

68 *Ibid.*, II, Pt 1, pp. 145, 147, 148, 149, 154, 158.

69 *Ibid.*, II, Pt 1, pp.157–8, 159–61. Hope & Vivien, *op. cit.*, p.339.

70 *Urkunden und Actenstücke, op. cit.*, III, pp.333, 340ff.

71 *Correspondentie Willem III en Portland, op. cit.*, II, Pt 1, pp.159–60. Van Nimwegen, *op. cit.*, p.456.

72 *Correspondentie Willem III en Portland, op. cit.*, II, Pt 1, pp.164–5. Mignet, *op. cit.*, IV, pp.124–5. For Louis's state of 'agitated anxiety' ('une inquiétude furieuse') see Rousset, *op. cit.*, I, p.407. For William's despatch to Amerongen on 23 December (from Binch) see *Urkunden und Actenstücke, op. cit.*, III, p.349. For Ginkel see Japikse, *Willem III, op. cit.*, I, p.280. For Waldeck's view see Van Nimwegen, *op. cit.*, p.455.

73 *Correspondentie Willem III en Portland, op. cit.*, II, Pt 1, pp.166–7.

74 Japikse, *Willem III, op. cit.*, I, pp.281–2. Wagenaar, *op. cit.*, 14, pp.229–30.

75 Van Nimwegen, *op. cit.*, pp.456–7.

76 Wagenaar, *op. cit.*, 14, p.230.

77 *Correspondentie Willem III en Portland, op. cit.*, II, Pt 1, pp.150, 135.

78 *Ibid.*, II, Pt 1, p.162. According to Japikse, *Willem III, op. cit.*, I, p.282 he conveyed much the same to Wirtz on 19 December, Wagenaar, *op. cit.*, 14, p.230.

79 Panhuysen, *op. cit.*, p.267.

80 Wagenaar, *op. cit.*, 14, p.231.

81 *Ibid.*, 14, pp.232–3. Hop & Vivien, *op. cit.*, pp.365–6.

82 Hop & Vivien, *op. cit.*, pp.364–5.

83 *Ibid.*, p.366.

84 *Ibid.*, p.369.

85 *Ibid.*, p.371–4.

86 *Ibid.*, p.377.

87 Sypestein & Bordes, *op. cit.*, p.173–7. Groen van Prinsterer, *op. cit.*, V, p.296.

88 Rousset, *op. cit.*, I, p.409.

89 Petitfils, *op. cit.*, p.337. Ségur, *op. cit.*, pp.176, 177, 180–3, 194. Japikse, *Willem III, op. cit.*, I, p.283. Rousset, *op. cit.*, I, p.411.

90 *Briefwisseling van der Goes, II, op. cit.*, p.448.

91 Ségur, *op. cit.*, pp.183, 197–8, in which he maintains the Prince's involvement in the pamphlet campaign. Japikse, *Willem III, op. cit.*, I, pp.288–9 bets against this.

92 Panhuysen, *op. cit.*, p.275.

93 Rousset, *op. cit.*, I, p.409.

94 *Correspondentie Willem III en Portland, op. cit.*, II, Pt 1, p.169. Groen van Prinsterer, *op. cit.*, V, p.297.

95 Ségur, *op. cit.*, p.204.

96 Wicquefort, *Histoire*, IV, p.469.

97 Rousset, *op. cit.*, I, pp.448–9. Panhuysen, *op. cit.*, pp.305–6.

98 Hop & Vivien, *op. cit.*, p.369. Wicquefort, *Mémoires, op. cit.*, p.340.

99 *Briefwisseling van der Goes*, II, pp.448–9.

100 Hop & Vivien, *op. cit.*, pp.383–4, 386. Wagenaar, *op. cit.*, 14, p.237.

12 SETBACKS AND SUCCESSES

BRANDENBURG FORCED OUT OF THE WAR

Before 1673 began, Louis managed to add to his alliances when the Duke of Hanover, on 10 December 1672, expanded his existing treaty of neutrality into a defensive and offensive alliance; in return for French subsidies, he agreed to provide an army of 10,000 men to be employed in the Imperial Circles of Saxony and Westphalia against all those who disturbed the peace of the Empire.[1] But a bigger prize awaited the French King.

On 20 February 1673 Amerongen wrote to the Prince of Orange from Bielefeld that the Elector of Brandenburg was considering an armistice in view of the state his affairs had been reduced to – the strength of his army had been much diminished as a result of its exacting marches in the winter weather and the Dutch were failing to pay his subsidies. Amerongen could not but see that the French party at the Electoral court was in the ascendant and that an attempt would be made to arrive at a truce, 'be it against the will of the states-general and your highness'. A truce, said Amerongen, did not accord with the instructions that the Austrian Emperor had given the new commander of his army, the Duc de Bournonville. He had taken over command on 1 February from Montecuccoli, who left for Vienna for health reasons on the 6th; but all the same Bournonville found himself unable to dispute the Elector's reasons for his conclusion.[2]

Prince William applied pressure to dissuade the Elector from his course; he had told Amerongen on the 24th that he was sending Waldeck to the Elector to coordinate the forthcoming campaign, and on 14 March he wrote a memorandum for both of them. They should protest against the proposal that the Elector had made to Turenne for an armistice, which ran counter to his treaty with the Dutch and which was counter to his 'given word'. Prince William explained that the Dutch had never refused to pay the subsidies – the delay in payment was due to a reluctance in the Dutch Republic to pay such heavy subsidies in the light of the 'strange conduct which prevailed' on the part of the Elector. Although the Elector's ministers had raised difficulties about the exchange rate, the subsidies had been ready for two months, albeit it was resolved not to pay them before it became apparent that the Elector was keeping to his side of the terms of the alliance he had with the Dutch.

Apparently fearing the worst, however, he gave instructions that, should the Elector nevertheless decide to breach the alliance, then Waldeck and Amerongen should insist that not only the Electoral troops raised on the back of the Dutch subsidies, but also as many as possible of the Elector's own soldiers as they could negotiate, should enter into Dutch service.[3] It may be that the subsidies Frederick-William ultimately received from the French were sufficient for him to maintain his much-depleted army in being, even if inactive, and that he was able to avoid these requests, although Japikse suggests that the troops were recruited by the Dutch in the open market.[4]

In the meantime Fagel amplified the position further in a despatch to Amerongen on 1 April. Money was very scarce in the Republic and, in the light of the non-fulfilment of Brandenburg's obligations, the Provinces could not be persuaded to furnish the money for so little advantage or profit; although, if the Elector had acted more vigorously and if something could have been achieved, they would certainly have hazarded the finance.[5]

But the army of Turenne was threatening Frederick-William with the loss or devastation of his territories; Amerongen wrote to Prince William from Minden on 9 March that, in the absence of an armistice, the Elector feared that what remained of Cleve, Mark and Ravensburg would be destroyed by the enemy; and on 10 April Frederick-William was forced to enter into a provisional treaty of peace with Louis, which was signed at St-Germain. The definitive treaty followed on 6 June at Vossem, and was ratified on 11 July. The Elector undertook not to lend any assistance to the United Provinces and to keep his army beyond the Weser; in return he received subsidies from France of 800,000 *livres* (£67,000), 300,000 up-front and the rest in six-monthly stages over five years. He was however left with some room for manoeuvre; he could defend the German Empire if it was attacked, although that would not be deemed the case if French troops entered Germany following any prince declaring against Louis or assisting his enemies contrary to the treaty of Münster.[6]

From the early months of 1673, therefore, the Dutch were left effectively without their staunchest ally.

LOSS OF MAASTRICHT

At the beginning of 1673 Louis had some 124,000 men at his disposal; of these 8,000 were required in the south to protect Roussillon, 7,000 in the east to protect Lorraine, and 1,000 in Italy to protect Pignerol. Of the rest he decided to devote 48,000 men to the Dutch Republic and 30,000 respectively to the Rhine and Flanders. The army in the Dutch Republic would consist of an active field army of 25,000, with the rest garrisoning the fortifications on the Maas, Ijssel and Waal rivers – the fortifications on the Zuyderzee would for the most part be abandoned and dismantled.[7]

On 1 May he departed from St-Germain for the frontier of the Spanish Netherlands with one army, one queen, and two mistresses. The ladies were left behind at Tournai, after which Louis was able to engross himself fully in the regal pursuit of war. At the beginning of June the French army made a feint towards Brussels, before marching on to its true destination – Maastricht. The violation of Spanish territory was justified on the grounds that the Spaniards had similarly violated that of France during the siege of Charleroi.

Under the supervision of Vauban, and with the presence of two young Englishmen, the Duke of Monmouth and John Churchill, the future Duke of Marlborough, the siege of Maastricht began on 6 June with a French army about 40,000 strong. The Maastricht garrison consisted of about 5–6,000 men commanded, after the death of the old Rhinegrave in January, by De Fariaux. The siege did not last long – with the Elector of Brandenburg out of the war and with the Prince of Orange having at his disposal a field army of not more than 18,000 men there was no hope of relief – and on 2 July the garrison was allowed to leave for s'Hertogenbosch. The siege had lasted 13 days from the opening of the trenches.[8]

Thus by the middle of 1673 the Dutch had lost not only their staunchest ally; they had also lost their strongest and largest fortress.

HIATUS ON THE WATER LINE

When the Prince of Orange returned from his attempt on Charleroi amidst the ice and cold at the end of 1672 and when the Duke of Luxemburg returned to Utrecht after his foray terminating in the destruction and the atrocities of Bodegrave and Zwamerdam, the beginning of 1673 saw a stalemate, with the two armies facing each other across the Water Line. William was still hoping to urge the Great Elector to take action against the French, and thus reduce pressure on the Dutch, and he wrote on 6 February to Amerongen to that effect.[9] But the disarray in the Austro-Brandenburg camp prevented any effective coordinated action with these allies.

As we have seen, it was in the Prince's nature to act aggressively, and he continued to search for opportunities to discomfit the enemy where he could. He aired the possibility of another attack on Woerden with Waldeck in the middle of February, which, however, came to nothing. He told Amerongen on the 17th that he continued to harbour a design, to be implemented as soon as a thaw opened a passage to Friesland, to send a good number of cavalry there, and in the meanwhile he was urging the commanders in that Province, Aylva and Rabenhaupt, to do their utmost to act against the enemy to divert French forces; he asked Amerongen to inform the Great Elector accordingly.[10]

But for the time being his ability to pursue his aggressive instincts when the campaigning season commenced in the spring was circumscribed by the threat presented by the combined Anglo-French fleet and the danger of invasion from the sea – in 1672 he had not embarked on his campaign culminating in Charleroi until November, after both the allied and Dutch fleets were laid up for the winter in September.

On the French side the Prince de Condé had arrived at Utrecht on 1 May to take over command from Luxemburg, who continued to serve under him: there, finding the Dutch defences too formidable for him to undertake anything of military significance, he was forced to kick his heels.[11]

LOUIS APPROPRIATES THE PRINCIPALITY OF ORANGE

This hiatus provided the opportunity to continue with the reorganisation of the Dutch army, which had begun the previous year. At the same time, the Prince and his colleagues used the time both to construct new alliances and to detach the King of England from the King of France, to both of which we will return later in this chapter. Success in these endeavours would offset the withdrawal of Brandenburg and the loss of Maastricht.

But there was some further bad news to come first. This the Dutch chargé d'affaires, Christiaan Rumpf, who all the time had remained in Paris, conveyed on 20 January as delicately as he could: 'I am obliged by my very respectful duty, although with much regret, to confirm to your Serene Highness, the rumour which I sent by the last ordinary courier [on the 13th] that the King has granted the principality of Orange to the comte d'Avergne [Auvergne] for the duration of the present war.' The Comte d'Auvergne was also the Marquis of Bergen op Zoom and he received the Principality in exchange for his properties near that town, which he lost when he chose Louis's side in 1672.[12] The French King was thus engaged in war not only with the Dutch Republic but also with the Prince of Orange himself.

FURTHER REORGANISATION OF THE DUTCH ARMY

Let us turn to the Dutch army, which had suffered more than two decades of neglect since the death of William III's father in 1650. To return it to approximately the state of European pre-eminence that it had enjoyed under his Orange predecessors, Prince Maurits and Prince Frederick-Henry, would be a considerable undertaking. The demoralised army that had shambled back behind the Water Line the previous summer did not promise much; and, although the army that embarked on the Charleroi expedition was considerably improved, there was still much that remained unsatisfactory. Waldeck submitted a memoir in January 1673 in which he provided a long list of what needed doing – although what has come down to us nevertheless remains incomplete. A considerable number of new regiments needed to be recruited, with good soldiers taking the place of those who were deficient, who should be dismissed; work on fortifications should be completed and, as there were several forts that were not manned, they should be either garrisoned or demolished, particularly those defending Brabant and Flanders; military justice was badly administered for the lack of a properly functioning war tribunal and this needed to be remedied; the payment of troops was so far in arrears that it was impairing the army; and the army needed to be assured of a good supply of bread with a proper transport system. Nor did Waldeck omit the need to care for the troops, with the sick properly looked after.[13]

That Waldeck's memorandum was very influential we can infer from the measures that were set in train; they evolved over time in the light of experience and of what was practical. One advantage was that, with the loss of the Provinces occupied by the French, Holland was bearing nearly 70 per cent of the army's costs[14] and this further increased the already substantial influence of Fagel, that Province's Grand Pensionary. To address regular pay, which was, of course, closely linked with discipline, he refined a system of army 'solicitors', each of whom was responsible for the pay of all the units assigned to them. They were financed out of Holland's taxes, but they were expected to provide bridging loans at a fixed rate of interest if occasion demanded and they received a fixed sum as remuneration for each company for which they were responsible. They had therefore to be men of substance and, after 1676, they were required to have sufficient resources for six months' pay and to pledge 5,000 guilders (£500) as deposit.[15]

To ensure that units were kept up to full strength and that they were properly equipped, a system was also established, improved over time, by which commanders were paid more per man than the minimum they were required to maintain under their command; if their units fell below the minimum level they were only paid for the actual numbers and, hence, they had a strong incentive to maintain their units at full strength. In return for the profit arising to them from this system, and for a deduction they were allowed to make from the pay of their men, they were responsible for restoring equipment lost during operations. They were also repaid recruitment money, again at a fixed rate, for men recruited to replace those killed – which removed the barrier to the rapid replacement of losses and the swift return to full strength and effectiveness of army units. With these carrots the commanders also faced the stick of disciplinary action if the strength of their units fell below a stipulated number. These measures had a dramatic impact on the effectives the Dutch army had at its disposal.[16]

We have already come across the name of Moses Machado during the autumn campaign in 1672, when he was involved in provisioning the army. With his Jewish connections he and his partner, Jacob Pereira, were able to arrange finance as well as providing the complicated logistics of supplying bread to the army. Machado was to retain his position as bread supplier until his death in December 1706.[17] The partnership's methods of supply also evolved over time and we shall see that they had a crucial effect in determining the range and scale of the operations the army would be able to undertake.

The Prince of Orange's correspondence is full of letters relating to the raising of new troop levies, many of which came from the ample recruiting grounds of Germany, and to the related finance and transport costs – Hamburg and Bremen were convenient embarkation ports to transport the recruits to the United Provinces.[18] The budget for 1673 was for 76,000 foot, 13,942 horse and 2,000 dragoons, a total of just under 92,000 men including the new recruits.[19] In a memorandum the Prince prepared for Waldeck in October he stated that the Province of Holland by itself had recruited 94 companies (say, 8,300 men) and that the 1674 budget was for 900 companies of foot (say, 80,000 men). If we allow around 13,000 for the horse and 2,000 dragoons this would give a total of around 95,000 men for 1674. The quality of the new troops, the Prince said, was better than that of many before.[20] In both numbers and in quality, therefore, the Dutch army was undergoing a thorough improvement.

The supply of soldiers was an activity in which the German princes and aristocracy participated avidly, and in all this Amerongen was closely involved. Both his and the Prince's tasks were facilitated by the technical efficiency with which bills of exchange could be drawn on Amsterdam – although money was becoming very tight, and in May the Prince had to ask Amerongen to draw funds in as small amounts as possible and staged over time to avoid pressure on the money markets, provided, he added, that that did not impede the recruitment of men.[21]

Waldeck's request that the sick should be properly cared for was not met in a systematic way until December 1673, when a field hospital, suitably staffed, was established whilst a surgeon-major was provided for each regiment and a barber-surgeon for every two companies, with each regiment being supplied with medicines.[22] But the Prince had taken action regarding the sick well before these measures were instituted. Before departing for the army at Geertruidenberg he wrote to Waldeck in July, 'I have taken care to give the necessary orders for the doctors and the surgeons and the medicines, and I have also spoken to Mr Hop about the tents for the sick; he is writing today to Amsterdam for them to be sent with dispatch to Geertruidenberg.'[23] Although care for the sick may be regarded as a matter of enlightened self-interest for a military commander, practical measures to do so were a novel concept in the second half of the 17th century.

A harsher, but just as necessary, side to the Prince's character was revealed by his approach to discipline, which remained an important issue if the Dutch army was to be restored as a coherent fighting force. Symptomatic was Waldeck's complaint in January that, in passing Bergen op Zoom, much shouting and blowing of a trumpet for a quarter of an hour failed to waken anybody in the entrenchments, and when eventually a single soldier appeared the barrier was raised without any proper precautions and without proper scrutiny from the commanding officer. Waldeck arrested three deserters – whilst he was about it, one rather feels – who had arrived from Zwamerdam, and awaited the Prince's orders as to what to do with them.[24]

Prince Maurits of Nassau-Siegen wrote in the same vein on 16 February: 'The negligence of all the captains, lieutenants, and ensigns and the disregard of their duty is so great that it is incredible and insupportable; so impertinent are they that they leave their posts at night, and go to lodgings to sleep between two sheets, something which I learnt when I did my rounds myself.' Repeated reprimands were ignored. When he did his rounds at about 4 am the previous night, despite the full alert having been sounded that the enemy was planning an attack on Woerden and was on the march, he found a captain, his lieutenant, his ensign, and his sergeant had left their post, and the sentinel was asleep – 'an unheard-of thing,' the shocked veteran Field-Marshal wrote, 'the alarm having sounded and the enemy all the time so close to us. Without discipline all is lost … if everyone does what he pleases, without reflecting on his duty or honour.'[25]

There are numerous instances of the Prince of Orange's obdurate stance on disciplinary matters – the exemplary execution of Colonel Pain-et-Vin was not unique; it had been preceded by that of other officers whose conduct fell short after the French invasion. Montbas would have shared their fate if he had not managed to escape. A further example was made when on 23 February the Prince gave orders for the execution of a major who had been found guilty at a court martial.[26] Strict discipline of both officers and men was to be a continuing feature of the Dutch army, enforced, in the case of officers, by disgrace, financial penalties and, on occasion, execution. Execution of ordinary soldiers was also to be expected but they were not easy to replace and so this was avoided or reduced as far as possible. In June 1673, out of 24 soldiers who were condemned for cowardice, lots were drawn for the execution of four, with the rest condemned to run the gauntlet.[27] In 1677 Prince William again resorted to the system of drawing lots and had one soldier from each company executed from a regiment which had fled during the battle of Mont-Cassel.[28]

FAGEL AND FINANCE

If, on the military front, a close partnership was developing between the Prince and Waldeck this was complemented, as we have already seen, by the close relationship he had with the Grand Pensionary, Fagel, in political and diplomatic affairs. But Fagel also made a substantial contribution to the finances of the Republic, an area in which Prince William had a less close personal interest – although he lent his political weight to support the Pensionary's financial policy when occasion demanded. Holland, which, as we have seen, was carrying about 70 per cent of the cost of the army, had a budget of 33.5 million guilders (£3,350,000) for 1673 (up 2.4 million guilders on 1672). To finance this Fagel resorted to extraordinary taxes, forced loans, interest-free gifts, wealth taxes, and a loan from the Dutch East India company. But the financial burden was stretching even the resources of the Province of Holland, which was heavily indebted, to the utmost; and when Fagel, towards the end of 1673, attempted to raise a tax on household income and property he came up against the resistance of Amsterdam. The Prince of Orange himself intervened in the debate and made a direct attack on Coenraad van Beuningen, whom he accused of being 'the sole mainspring' holding up 'the great work', and he would let the whole world know what was due to Van Beuningen's 'caprice'. Amsterdam gave way on 22 December, although practical difficulties in setting up the necessary registers and fear of popular opinion (the tax would have affected merchants and shopkeepers above all) prevented this particular measure from being implemented; the Amsterdam Regents ended up agreeing to a further forced loan instead. The incident does, however, indicate that Fagel and the Prince did not have matters all their own way and that they would have to carry the Regents, particularly of Amsterdam, with them if they were to obtain the finance they needed to pursue the war they wanted. As the Prince's outburst against Van Beuningen indicates, this was not yet something that he fully appreciated.[29]

REARRANGEMENT OF THE ARMY COMMANDERS AND STRENGTHENING OF FORTIFICATIONS

At the end of April the command structure of the Dutch army was reshuffled, with Prince Maurits of Nassau-Siegen being despatched to take command in Friesland; Field-Marshal Wirtz taking command in the States Flanders; Hoorn taking his place at Gorichem; and the Count of Limburg-Stirum taking over at Muiden in place of Maurits.

Prince Maurits's appointment above the two existing commanders, Aylva and Rabenhaupt, brought unity to the existing command structure in Friesland.[30] His instructions were to cooperate with William's aunt Albertina Agnes; she had married into the Friesian branch of the Orange family and, as Dowager Princess, was acting as trustee for her under-age son, Hendrik-Casimir, who despite his age had been recognised as Stadholder in Friesland in 1672. Prince William wrote to her on 28 April asking her to lend Maurits all her help.[31]

As we know, the reach of Prince Maurits stretched into central Europe. When the Great Elector, who regarded him as a relative and friend, appointed him as the governor of Cleves in 1647 he was the most important of a number of advisers from outside the Elector's domains, and therefore independent of their interest groups. Before he moved elsewhere and ultimately ended in Dutch service, Waldeck, married to Maurits's sister, was another and the Prince of Anhalt, who also, as we have seen, had married into the House of Orange, a third.[32] Prince William wrote to Maurits on 1 May asking him to inform the Elector that the object of his taking command in Friesland was to divert the troops of the Elector of Cologne and the Bishop of Münster, thus relieving the pressure on Frederick-William, and he was to coordinate his plans with those of the Elector.[33] Alas, with the Elector being forced to cease taking an active military role it was too late for this coordination to be put into practice, but it is illustrative of how central the Orange clan system, operating on a European scale, was to the Prince of Orange's methods of operation.

In the meantime appropriate measures were taken in Friesland to confront a possible attack from the Bishop of Münster. Coevorden's defences were put on the alert, as were those of the town of Groningen, and inundations were set in train in the wider Province of Groningen. The army in Friesland was reinforced and strongholds constructed to command the invasion routes into the Province. But when, later in the year, in June, the States of Friesland refused to comply with Prince Maurits's orders for inundations, Maurits found himself compelled to resort to the authority of the Prince of Orange.

The Prince's reply was not long in coming: 'I have received yours of the 20th of even date', he wrote on 25 June, 'and observe, with much astonishment, the insolent and impertinent resolution of the gentlemen of Friesland, which is much out of season. Should you find the inundations necessary, I pray you to execute them, without regard to the said resolution, and, if the Fries officers make any difficulty in obeying in this, as in any other, matter have them shot on the spot, without any further formality, on my authority.' It was as well for the unfortunate Fries officers that Prince Maurits bethought himself of the immediate need for the inundations, which were postponed for review in the light of the future military situation. But there was no question of the determination of the Prince of Orange to establish his authority in the north-east of the Dutch Republic as elsewhere – something, however, that was not always to happen easily.

In Holland the Water Line, and the towns and fortresses behind it, also had their fortifications strengthened, so that when Wirtz inspected the whole line in April he found it in the most formidable state.

To guard against a seaborne landing the coastal fortifications of both Holland and Zeeland were brought into a state of defence, as were those of States Flanders, which, being situated to the east of Zeeland, was exposed to the French on the landward side.[34] The Prince himself paid a ten-day visit, from 13 to 23 April, to Zeeland and States Flanders, attending a meeting of the Zeeland States, and, in States Flanders, inspecting the fortifications there – he was received with festivities at Aardenburg, where the streets were decorated with garlands and oranges and the ground was covered in palm leaves, whilst young maidens, bedecked in flowers, offered him the keys of the town on a silver salver.[35]

ABORTIVE ARMISTICE NEGOTIATIONS

Meanwhile the kaleidoscope of European diplomacy was not standing still. We have seen that Sweden had entered into a treaty on 14 April 1672 with Louis XIV to oppose the Emperor and any German prince, which included the Great Elector, should they come to the aid of the Dutch. She did not, however, anticipate the crushing success of the French, which threatened the complete destruction of the Republic and which would also bring in its train the dominance of England at sea. Anxious to avoid compliance with her commitment to France Sweden had, commencing in September 1672, sent emissaries to France, to England and to the Dutch Republic, offering her mediation between the conflicting parties.[36]

In accepting the Swedish mediation, Louis, at the beginning of December 1672, was also agreeable to accepting an armistice from which it appeared he had nothing to lose; it would not prejudice his existing gains and it would halt the advance – such, admittedly, as it was – of the Brandenburg and Imperial forces to the aid of the Dutch. In the meantime lengthy negotiations commenced on the choice of venue for the peace conference, which stretched well into the spring.[37]

When proposals for the armistice were put to the States of Holland the Prince of Orange appeared ambivalent at the meeting on 29 March. He enumerated the benefits of a short armistice; the Dutch army could be brought into shape, the fortifications could be addressed, the troops could be paid what they were owed, it would give time to coordinate further measures with the allies, Denmark and Celle could be brought into play and, in the absence of an armistice, France could mount a great force possibly before the Dutch were ready. But he warned against the disadvantages: France would retain and strengthen the places she occupied, and, after the ending of the truce, she could attack the United Provinces with greater force than before; in the meantime the German princes would not dare to declare themselves; and the Dutch resolve to finance the war, the need for which would remain as great as before, would weaken – he himself detected wavering in those who, he said, had particular responsibility for the conduct of the war. He stated that he did not know what was for the best; but he concluded that he could not advise entering into an armistice with an undefined duration, although one could be accepted for a short time. He suggested it should last until 1 June, a little longer at sea, during which time the Dutch could reorganise themselves and see how the peace negotiations were developing – which, the contending parties had now agreed, should take place at Cologne.[38]

This ambivalence may have been because of the internal politics with which he had to contend within the Republic. Five days before the meeting on the 29th he had recommended that Hieronymus van Beverninck (who came from Gouda) and Van Reede van Renswoude (a member of the Utrecht clan with whom he was so closely associated) should be the Republic's representatives at the Cologne conference. It was noticeable that the delegation did not include anyone from Amsterdam – there were murmurings from the great city, but she fell into line. The most obvious choice would have been Coenraad van Beuningen, and his biographer surmises that the reason for his omission was that his views diverged from those of the Prince – William was adamant in his opposition to peace, whilst Van Beuningen was prepared to look at peace proposals. From the Prince's point of view an armistice could be the thin end of the wedge leading to a definitive peace – hence his insistence that it should be of short duration, and his concern about any weakening of resolve or any wavering. He was only prepared to contemplate an armistice if 'the common good was in the interval [of the armistice] taken to heart', that is to say, he would expect total resolve from the Regent class.[39]

As it happened no agreement was reached on an armistice with the King of France or the King of England, and none occurred.

When, on 13 April, at Fagel's instigation, the States of Holland debated what instructions should be given to the Dutch delegation that was to attend the Cologne conference, Rotterdam proposed that all negotiations should be left in the hands of the Prince of Orange, who could appoint three or four deputies to aid him in the task.[40] The Prince – and Fagel: we must not omit him – thus had very tight control over foreign affairs at this time, albeit the States of Holland could not be entirely excluded from the picture, as the Prince and Fagel were well aware. We shall soon see what use they were to make of these powers.

AUSTRIA'S HARDENING STANCE AGAINST FRANCE

As the year 1672 had advanced the mood of the Austrian court had hardened in its opposition to France, and on 17 October the Austrian Emperor had ratified his treaty with the Dutch, the draft of which had been signed by Lisola as long ago as 25 July. In exchange for 45,000 *rijksthaler* (112,500 guilders, £11,250) per month Leopold would assist the Dutch with 24,000 men. The Prince of Orange pledged his own properties so that the up-front payment of 200,000 *rijksthalers* (500,000 guilders, £50,000) as subsidy to the Austrians could be advanced by a group of Amsterdam merchants – although the method of payment of the remaining subsidies was still unresolved. Unlike the Great Elector, at the commencement of 1673 Leopold was firm in his refusal to accept an armistice and in January 1673 he so informed the Swedish resident, Puffendorf, and the various Austrian representatives at the courts of Europe. He was prepared to take up the Swedish suggestion that a general congress should be convened, but the restitution of Cleves to Frederick-William, likewise the restitution of Lorraine to the Duke of Lorraine, and the clearance of French troops from German territories should form the basis for the negotiations.[41]

There was a change of mood, as well, amongst the German princes. The Elector of Trier, who had felt compelled to bend towards the power of France, had joined the Austro-Brandenburg league by the end of 1672; on 12 February the Archbishop-Elector of Mainz died and his successor, Lothar von Metternich, favoured the Austrian Emperor; and the Elector of Saxony, although never a strong force, had entered into a treaty with Leopold on 1 March 1673, under which he agreed to supply 3,000 men in exchange for subsidies.

Negotiations, too, were set in train in Vienna to arrive at a treaty with Spain;[42] something which, of course, received strong encouragement from the Dutch and the Prince of Orange. One of the Prince's reasons for the attack on the French possession of Charleroi with Spanish assistance was to push the Spaniards towards an open rupture with France. On 6 February Lisola reported to Vienna that he had had a meeting with Prince William, at which the Prince had said that the reason Spain had not declared war was because of the irresolution of the allies (Brandenburg and the Emperor); he asked Lisola expressly to enquire from the Emperor what he intended to do. William also championed the idea that Austria should enter into a treaty with the Duke of Lorraine, which could lead to an invasion of France, perhaps an insurrection – an idea with which he was to toy for some time – and in any case a great turn-round in the state of affairs there.[43]

All this was the kernel for the ideas which were to lead, before the end of the summer, to the formation of a grand alliance against the King of France.

Fagel reported to the Holland States on 14 February on the Prince's efforts to incline Spain to a rupture with France. De Lira, the Spanish ambassador in The Hague, had told the Prince that the Queen Regent of Spain was moving in that direction, but needed reassurance that the Dutch would not enter into a separate peace without Spain – a reassurance that the States of Holland were not slow in giving.[44] The attack on Charleroi and the general assistance that the Spanish auxiliary troops were lending the Dutch had irked Louis XIV to the extent that he confiscated the goods in France of all Spaniards serving with these auxiliaries. This had the result that, by the end of April, even those most obstinately opposed to a war with France within the Spanish government were brought round.[45]

As the year advanced Austria's resolve continued to strengthen. On 24 April Montecuccoli received orders to formulate a plan for the forthcoming campaigning season. On 25 May the Austrian Chancellor, Hocher, told Lisola that the Emperor wanted to send an army of 30,000 men to the Rhine if the States would pay him 80,000 *Reichsthaler* (£20,000) a month in cash (his subsidies from Spain were already in excess of this). On the 31st the Emperor instructed Lisola to reassure the Prince of Orange and Fagel that they need have no doubts about the availability of the 30,000 men, as at this time there was no fear of conflict with the Poles or the Turks. Shortly afterwards Hocher suggested that the Dutch subsidies previously paid to the Grand Elector should be paid to the Austrians who would then increase their army proportionately; but this proposal Fagel declined on 5 June because of the heavy burden of costs the Dutch were carrying to maintain their fleet.[46]

Notwithstanding this, the Dutch used all their persuasive powers to encourage the Austrians to continue to pursue their robust stance. Lisola wrote on 8 June concerning conferences he had had with the Prince and with Fagel at the end of May, which related to the terms to be demanded at the peace conference at Cologne. They had told him that, if the Emperor stuck to his 1672 treaty with the Dutch, very advantageous terms could be demanded, as France longed for peace; the Dutch had received secret proposals from the French a short time previously; even for a separate peace with the States the French offered to return all their conquests except for Maastricht (the French were anticipating the success of the siege, which did not in fact commence until the 6th); and from this William concluded that the French position was very weak. He quoted figures indicating that Louis had 21,000 men on the Maas, 14,000 men on the lower Rhine under Turenne, and 10,000 on the middle Rhine under Condé. The Prince's own strength was 60,000 men, of which he could bring half into the field; this, united with the Austrians and allies, was more than enough to force the French to come to an agreement.[47]

LOUIS'S PEACE OVERTURES

It was indeed true that Louis had approached the Dutch privately outside the usual diplomatic channels with peace overtures much more moderate than the extreme demands he was publicly to put forward at Cologne, after the peace conference commenced at the end of June, which were similar to those he had demanded from De Groot in 1672.[48] By means of a Benedictine abbot he conveyed his overtures to the Pensionary of Gouda, Jacob van der Tocht. His offer was to forgo all his conquests in the Dutch Republic, with the exception of one or two in the Generality Lands, if the Dutch would enter into a separate peace and forgo a treaty with Spain. Louis was, in short, trying to forestall the creation of the grand alliance against him on which the Prince, Fagel and Lisola were working. Fagel showed Lisola Van der Tocht's letter of 11 June in which the proposal was contained, and evinced a concern that, if it were to become public knowledge, it would encourage the peace party in the Republic. This was a further indication, perhaps, of Fagel's and the Prince of Orange's sensitivity to their possible exposure to risk from this quarter, although the hint that they might have to submit to this pressure to enter into a separate peace may also have suited their purpose to put pressure on the Austrians. To obviate bolstering the peace party Louis's proposals were kept secret, and it was decided, with Lisola's approval, to send to Vienna Coenraad van Heemskerk, an Amsterdam Regent – who too was kept in ignorance of Louis's proposals – to sound out the Austrian Emperor on his intentions.[49]

Fagel also informed Lisola about peace negotiations with England, to which we will return.

NEGOTIATIONS WITH SPAIN

At the meetings in May Lisola had emphasised the need to be assured of Spain, and the Prince accordingly decided to send Coenraad Van Beuningen to Brussels.[50] This might seem an odd choice, in view of the Prince's earlier refusal to include Van Beuningen in the Dutch delegation at the Cologne peace conference because of his pacific views. Nevertheless, in the negotiations with Spain and, indeed, with England, Van Beuningen was to play a leading role. It has been suggested that the reason for his change of view between March and the summer arose from the change in the Dutch Republic's diplomatic position. It now looked promising that she could obtain allies and form an anti-French coalition. But, whereas the Prince of Orange's interest in the alliance was its offensive aspect, Van Beuningen regarded it as a first step towards peace, at any rate with England, something to which he had always attached great importance to check French power. One reason to pursue the Spanish alliance was that it would increase the unpopularity of the war in England – Anglo-Spanish trade was of great importance and there was also the English concern about the strategic importance of the Spanish Netherlands if it fell into the hands of France.[51] From the Prince's point of view there were, of course, good reasons to use Van Beuningen, where he could, given his Amsterdam background, and the potential Amsterdam influence in the States of Holland.

According to Lisola's despatch of 8 June Van Beuningen was instructed by the Prince to tell Monterey that the predicament faced by the Dutch Republic could only be remedied either by her making peace or, on the other hand, by her entering into an offensive war. If Spain wished only to extend assistance by means of a defensive war and did not wish to break completely with France then the States would have to make peace, either by ceding part of their own territory to France or by negotiating swaps – that is to say, Spain would be asked to cede territory to France for which she would be compensated by receiving territory from the Dutch. Monterey replied that the Spanish government wanted nothing else but that the allies, in the first place Leopold, should take to the field, after which he would announce what he could do; and with this news Van Beuningen returned to his principals on 3 June. Monterey, Van Beuningen so informed them, was not interested in swaps; he wanted only a strong 'union', which bound all concerned not to make a separate peace and which guaranteed the integrity of the Spanish monarchy. Van Beuningen added that he understood from De Lira, who at this time was at Cologne, that Monterey had instructions to declare war shortly, hence Monterey's eagerness that the Austrians should also declare war openly.[52] We know that the Spanish Queen, in fact, was not prepared to declare war on France without the Austrian Emperor.[53]

On 10 July the Emperor instructed his representatives in the Dutch Republic to extend the 1672 alliance; and, in the middle of the month, Coenraad van Heemskerk returned to report the Emperor's preparedness to provide an army in exchange for Dutch subsidies. The Dutch did not tarry; at the end of July he was sent back to Vienna with a firm offer of Dutch money.[54]

In the meantime, the Holland States resolved on 19 July to make a counter-offer to Louis XIV's requests; they would concede to Spain, not to Louis, Maastricht and certain towns and territories in the Republic in return for which Spain would give him compensation in the Spanish Netherlands. This, of course, would have involved further negotiations with Spain and, as we know, Monterey had already informed Van Beuningen that he was not interested in swaps, so that we must regard the Dutch move rather in the nature of a public relations exercise for consumption by the rest of Europe, demonstrating their reasonableness, than as a serious proposal. The suggestion that it was also aimed at appeasing the internal Dutch peace party seems implausible; Van Beuningen was aware of Monterey's position that he was not interested in swaps and he at least would not have been convinced; nor presumably would any of his contacts amongst the other Regents.[55]

FORMATION OF THE QUADRUPLE ALLIANCE

Grémonville, the French ambassador in Vienna,[56] told Louis on 17 July that his capture of Maastricht had not deterred the Emperor; the pro-French party on the Imperial Council under Lobkowitz was rapidly waning; the anti-French party under Montecuccoli, Hocher and Schwarzenberg was gaining in strength; and the Imperial army was planning to muster in western Bohemia.

In August three treaties were concluded. The first was between the Emperor and the States-General; it stated that the Emperor's aim was to resist the hostilities of Louis in the Empire and to safeguard the treaties of Westphalia, Cleves and Aix-la-Chapelle; that his army of 30,000 men, which since 16 August had been in a state of readiness at Eger in Bohemia, would take the field and march to the Rhine; that he would receive 45,000 *rijksthaler* (112,500 guilders, £11,250) per month from the Dutch, with 100,000 paid up-front, and the Dutch would contribute an army of 20,000 men in support (Redlich says at least 14,000). In a secret article the Dutch also agreed to pay the Archbishop of Trier 3,000 *rijksthaler* (7,500 guilders, £750) a month.

The second treaty was between the King of Spain and the States-General: the parties agreed to come to each other's mutual assistance with, initially, 8,000 men, and then with all their forces if the war endured; they mutually guaranteed each other's possessions and their treaties with third parties; they would enter into no separate peace without the other's consent; Spain promised to declare open war on France, together with the Emperor, if peace were not concluded at Cologne, and to see that all the places lost by the Dutch during the war would be returned to them, whilst the Dutch guaranteed Spain's possessions under the treaty of Aix-la-Chapelle. This last indeed was further extended by the Dutch agreeing that Spain should be restored to the position she held under the Treaty of the Pyrenees, unless otherwise agreed at any future peace conference – that is to say that Louis would lose his conquests obtained under the War of Devolution – and the Dutch would also cede Maastricht to Spain. A separate article stipulated that Spain would delay declaring war on Great Britain until she had first interceded with the British government on behalf of the Dutch to endeavour to obtain a settlement between them on the basis of the Dutch conceding on the point of the flag and paying a war indemnity of 800,000 *écus*.

The last treaty, backdated to 1 July, was concluded between the Duke of Lorraine, the Emperor, the Dutch and the Spanish; it was an offensive alliance under which these allies agreed to form an army of 18,000 men, to be placed under the command of the Duke of Lorraine to restore him to the Duchy, which Louis had seized.

These three treaties had been preceded by an Austro-Spanish treaty on 28 August which reunited the two branches of the Habsburgs into a formal alliance under which Spain paid Leopold a monthly subsidy of 50,000 *Reichsthaler* (125,000 guilders; £12,500).[57]

The Quadruple Alliance had been formed; and the Dutch War was expanding on a scale which Louis's own system of alliances – so ingeniously conceived, so long planned, and so laboriously constructed – had been designed to prevent before he launched his fateful invasion of the Republic.

AUSTRO-FRENCH HOSTILITIES AND SPAIN'S DECLARATION OF WAR

On 26 August the Emperor reviewed his army of 30,000 men at Eger under the command of Montecuccoli; and on 16 September the French ambassador at his court, Grémonville, was handed his passports. We will remember that no war had been formally declared on France by Austria in 1672. Historians have claimed that she did so now, but that was not formally the case. Instead Leopold declared that France had made herself the Reich's enemy and he asked for assistance whilst forbidding any support for her. Leopold's reason for this was that under the Treaty of Westphalia the German Estates were entitled to participate in the negotiations of peace treaties where a war had been declared. By avoiding such a declaration Leopold retained the sole authority to negotiate peace on the Reich's behalf, which was to have important consequences.[58] Louis XIV himself finally declared war on Spain on 19 October,[59] although the Spanish Marquis de Villapondo had in fact anticipated him in Brussels on behalf of Spain three days earlier.[60]

THE BATTLE OF TEXEL

Before these events could take effect, the Prince of Orange remained distracted at the beginning of August, as it proved for the last time, by the imminent threat of invasion by the Anglo-French fleet. After the fall of Maastricht the French King had not continued his advance towards the north. On 14 July Prince William wrote to Waldeck that 'the King is going to Metz; this is undoubtedly to oppose himself to the troops of the Emperor which is not bad news'.[61] He himself had left The Hague on the 19th to join Waldeck at Geertruidenberg;[62] there, and at the neighbouring Raamsdonk, Dutch troops had assembled to protect the southern end of the Water Line. But despatches from De Ruyter, who had kept him closely informed of events at sea throughout the summer and continued to do so now, as well as other intelligence, warned him that the combined Anglo-French fleet was threatening the Dutch coast; and on 4 August he was back in The Hague, to which Waldeck and the Rhinegrave also came.[63] In this crisis part of the army at Raamsdonk was diverted to protect the coast.[64] According to one account they were supported by several thousand militia, bringing the total number of troops on the Holland coast to 10,000 whilst there were 5,000 under the command of Wirtz in Zeeland. Amidst the heightened tension prayers were said in the pulpits by the preachers.[65]

At The Hague the Prince of Orange 'found the enemy fleet had yesterday – that is on the 3rd – after dinner passed by Scheveningen [on the coast just outside The Hague]' and that it was planning to sail to Texel to make its descent on the coast there.[66] The allied fleet constituted a double threat for, as had been the case the year before, the richly laden Dutch East Indies fleet was completing its seasonal return journey by way of the northern approaches of the Republic. Important as it was for the finances of the Dutch, it was no less so for Charles II's plans to wage a profitable war to assure his fiscal independence from a troublesome Parliament.

On the 5th the Prince, with his lifeguard, and followed later by Waldeck, travelled to Texel to keep an eye on the allied fleet and to inspect the sea defences; he then returned to The Hague on the 11th, where he attended a meeting of the Holland States lasting until 11pm. At ten on the morning of the 12th William, with an entourage of noblemen and military commanders, was conveyed to the fleet in a flat-bottomed pink from whose masthead there flew his ensign of Admiral-General. As he boarded De Ruyter's flagship amidst the sounds of trumpets, the rolling of drums and the roar of ordnance he was greeted with huzzahs and 'long live the prince' from the crews of the fleet. There he had lunch and the commanders of the fleet were summoned on board for a two-hour council of war. De Ruyter received written instructions from both the Prince and the States-General to weigh anchor and to pursue the allied fleet in order to do the utmost to safeguard the returning East Indiamen.[67] Lest there were any doubt the Prince manifested his usual aggressive posture by confirming his instructions in a further letter to De Ruyter on 16 August, which also authorised him to sail to the Ems river, if that was where the allied fleet was heading to threaten the East India ships.[68]

As regards the panic that had drawn the Prince from the army camp to The Hague, he told Waldeck that 'the alarm was not as serious as I had thought, it was principally amongst the citizenry, but more so amongst some members of the government'. His confidence about the country's safety was manifested by his leaving The Hague on the 20th to rejoin Waldeck, who was once again at Raamsdonk. It was a confidence which was immediately justified by De Ruyter's successful battle off Texel on the following day.[69] The States of Holland ordered a day of thanksgiving and prayer[70] and, indeed, all was now changed; we shall see the effect it had in England, where it led to the ignominious withdrawal of Charles II from the war; and its effect on the war on the Continent was that, with the removal of the seaborne threat, and now that the Republic had the support of the Quadruple Alliance, the scope for military action open to the Prince of Orange widened considerably. It was not in his nature to let the opportunity pass him by without engaging in action.

THE PRINCE TAKES THE OFFENSIVE

The troops who had been diverted to defend against the threatened seaborne attack returned to Raamsdonk, and seven regiments, who were on their way to Friesland, were halted in Holland. The Prince made feints on Bommel and Grave which caused Luxemburg to divert 5–6,000 troops southwards to Tiel. But the Prince's true destination lay further north; he was aiming at Naarden, near Amsterdam, which constituted a threat to that city, whilst its capture, on the other hand, would open up the possibility of an attack on Utrecht. The Prince besieged Naarden on 6 September with 25,000 men. Luxemburg tried to march, with 10,000, to relieve the garrison of 3,000, but in vain – his force was too small; on the 12th, just as the Prince was giving orders for a prayer to be offered throughout the army to ask God to grant success for the general assault, the French commander of the town surrendered. The Prince of Orange's personal bravery in the most exposed trenches, where he appeared two or three times a day, was noted, as was the performance of the Dutch troops as a whole. Even Luxemburg was impressed by *ces coquins* whose conduct, in his eyes, was unexpected from Dutch soldiers.[71] But he wrote a plaintive letter to his friend Louvois: Condé had been recalled on 15 July to take up position in Brabant and if M. le Prince had not been moved from there to Flanders the Prince of Orange would not have dared to divert his troops to Naarden. 'Lord, why hast thou forsaken me?' he complained.[72]

He was acutely aware of how perilously over-extended the occupying French forces in the Dutch Republic were and he recommended to Louvois that the number of towns that were garrisoned should be reduced to increase the troops in those that remained. Louvois agreed and gave orders that not only should the defences be lifted but the towns as a whole should be put to the flames.[73]

At Naarden the reformed Dutch army had faced its first major test with success; and the Prince of Orange now fixed his attention on the east, on Germany and the Rhine. There it was clear that the Austrians, unlike in the previous year, were acting with vigour, with determination, and with great skill against the French, with the result that the abilities of their general, Montecuccoli, this time unleashed from restraining orders from Vienna, had opened up a promising strategic opportunity ripe for exploitation.

LOUIS'S MILITARY DISPOSITIONS AND MONTECUCCOLI'S SUCCESSFUL MARCH

Grémonville had warned Louis from Vienna on 17 July that plans were under way for the Imperial army to assemble in western Bohemia.[74] The French King was ready with his counter-measures; on 15 July Condé was recalled from Utrecht with part of his troops to take up position first in Brabant and then to command an army in Flanders to guard against the Spanish and the Dutch, with the command at Utrecht reverting to Luxemburg;[75] on the 23rd, orders were given for the Chevalier de Fourilles to occupy the Bishopric of Trier. Louvois had got wind that the Emperor and the Spaniards were in negotiations with the Bishop to garrison the city of Trier, with its command of the Mosel and hence French communications to the Dutch Republic; and on 19 August the Chevalier was ordered to invest the city of Trier itself.[76] No war had been declared on the Bishop and his territories suffered such devastation that it raised a whirlwind of protest at the Reichstag of the Holy Roman Empire at Regensburg.[77] On 24 August Louis himself left Nancy, the capital of Lorraine, for Alsace. This was a French dependency but Strasburg and ten surrounding towns – known as the decapolis – had remained independent; and these were now occupied and garrisoned by the French.[78] On 7 September Trier surrendered.[79] France's great fortress engineer, Vauban, had received orders in August to repair to Alsace to address the fortifications there.[80] Defensive action, together with the most stringent measures to deter those considering opposition to the French King, therefore appeared to be in place to protect the eastern borders of France, whilst Condé was in position to protect the north. What was also required was an attacking force to march on the Austrians; and for this Louis looked to Turenne.

This general, with his great reputation, after moving south from the Grand Elector's territories in Mark at the end of June, had first taken up position at Wetzlar on the Lahn river from the middle of July to the middle of August and thereafter moved just to the north of Frankfurt, on the Main river.[81] On 26 August the review of the Imperial army at Eger took place and, on 1 September, Montecuccoli reached Nuremberg to press forward swiftly to Windsheim.[82] When Turenne received the news at the end of August that Montecuccoli was about to advance into Germany, he crossed to the southern bank of the Main at Aschaffenburg and marched eastward along the river to seek a decisive battle with him.[83] It was not often that Turenne was outclassed, but, on this occasion, the veteran French general met his match: in a scintillating manoeuvre the wily Italian-Austrian commander bypassed him near Wurzburg, whose bishop had thrown in his lot with the Austrian Emperor and who made his bridge available, and then marched on Frankfurt. On 21 October news reached Turenne that he was advancing on Mainz, where the Main and Rhine rivers meet. The possibility of an offensive down the Rhine against the territories of the bishops of Cologne and Münster lay open before Montecuccoli; or, alternatively, even an offensive westward into France itself. To defend against the latter possibility Turenne retreated to the French dependency of Philippsburg, which he reached on 26 October, leaving Cologne exposed to the Austrian army.[84]

WILLIAM'S MARCH TOWARDS MONTECUCCOLI AND THE CAPTURE OF BONN

With the fall of Naarden, William determined on a repeat of his strategy of the previous year, but this time in much more propitious circumstances: he would once again march through the Spanish Netherlands to effect a junction with the troops of Montecuccoli. When he left for Rozendaal on 29 September Waldeck was left behind in overall command in the Republic and thus there was no repeat of the mistake made in 1672, when the vacuum in the supreme command had proved so perilous. Moreover, Waldeck was provided with a very substantial force indeed – according to one account, six regiments of horse (say 6,500 men, about half the total) and the greater part of the infantry, both to defend Holland and to threaten Luxemburg in the rear should he divert troops either to the Rhine or to the Spanish Netherlands.[85]

Pressing though his concerns were, Prince William found time to pursue his zest for hunting, an enthusiasm common to most of his class, although he possessed it, perhaps, to an even greater degree; he had arrived at Rozendaal on the 30th, and both the mornings of 2 and 3 October were devoted to this relaxation. On 4 October he conferred for three hours with Monterey between Rozendaal and Antwerp, accompanied by a small following of officers, returning at seven in the evening to ask, with a smile on his face, why his secretary, Constantijn Huygens junior, had not made an appearance – the unfortunate secretary's horses had been delayed, and his ill luck did not end there, for, as he complained, the fare at the second table, at which he sat, was *fort mediocre*. On the 7th the Prince went to Antwerp, where he was met with great ceremony and where he stayed the night, for further meetings with Monterey, so that we can assume that the discussions between the two of them must have been detailed and wide-reaching. Certainly the Prince reported to the *Secrète Besogne* (the Secret Foreign Affairs Committee) of the States-General that it was agreed that Spain should at once declare war on France in the week of the 9th – as we have seen, the Marquis de Villapondo did indeed do so on the 16th from Antwerp and the French declared war on Spain on the 19th, following the raising of contributions on Spanish territory by Condé and reprisals taken by the Spaniards on the 14th. Monterey gave orders for aggressive action to be taken by the Spaniards within the Spanish Netherlands against the French on the 26th.

On the 13th the Dutch army departed from Rozendaal to join Monterey's army. The Prince reported on the 15th to the *Secrète Besogne* that his effectives consisted of between 5,000 and 6,000 horse, 1,500 dragoons and three regiments of foot, the latter amounting, with the officers, to about 2,000 men, whilst the Spanish force was expected to come to about 3,700, although, in the event, only about 3,000 materialised. The combined forces came, therefore, to about 12,000 and, their junction having been effected between Mol and Balen, they commenced their advance on the 19th towards Venlo on the Maas river. Having crossed this they headed for Coblenz through the lands of the Bishop of Cologne: and, being now in enemy territory, their behaviour changed accordingly. 'The country here is being just as ruined as our own poor province [of Utrecht]',wrote Godard van Reede van Ginkel on 29 October. 'Nothing and no one is spared, many atrocities are committed. I fear that our army will become so wild that in the end there will be no command over the men.' More was to follow. On 1 November the army arrived at the little town of Rheinbach.[86]

It was ordered to surrender, but when this was refused and the gates barred against them, the Prince ordered an assault. This was successfully carried out by his guards and the Courland dragoons, and, in accordance with the customs of the times, the town was given over to pillage. It was not a pretty scene, as the diary of Constantijn Huygens demonstrates. The young Rhinegrave had warned members of the garrison that if they surrendered they would be provided with safeguards for themselves and their goods, but that otherwise their burgomasters would be seized, their town would be pillaged and burnt, and their women violated. They asked for two hours to consider this, which the Rhinegrave, riding off, refused – perhaps because military necessity made time too important. In the event the besiegers suffered considerable casualties but, when the town was given over to pillage, the order was given to spare the women, which Huygens says was well observed. Nevertheless, as he walked through the town after nightfall the pillage was still engulfing the town; when the Rhinegrave arrived he took personal charge to restore order, and measures were taken to save the women and girls; but there were plenty of bodies in the streets, and there were five or six dead even in the church, which, too, had been pillaged. In the kitchen next door to the room where Huygens and his companions settled down to dinner they found the body of a woman with a large sabre-cut through her belly and with her a small child, about a year old, who was still living but faring badly. When a peasant resisted having his smock wrenched from him by a Courland dragoon his head was cut off by another with a clean sweep.[87] The burgomaster, an old man who had exhorted the garrison to resist, was hanged from a tree, with the keys of the town round his neck and a dagger in his hand as a symbol of the causes of the bloodshed.[88]

But the accounts do not indicate the personal involvement of the Prince of Orange in these happenings. Furthermore, if we give credence to the picture that Wicquefort gives us of the Rhinegrave as a soldier who was not averse to the debaucheries common in his profession, Huygens, on his side, bears witness to the streak of humanity running through this favourite of the Prince. Apart from what he relates above of his attempts to mitigate the customary horrors of the sack he also tells us that the day before Rheinbach fell, when the two of them were on the road, they met a little boy lackey, dressed in green livery and in tears, who was struggling to carry a child of about a year old on his back on the way to Cologne, barely managing with his burden. The Rhinegrave transferred the child to a soldier and arranged for the little lackey to be transported by coach to his destination.[89]

The army left Rheinbach on the 3rd and resumed its march, the objective remaining, so the Prince of Orange wrote to the *Secrète Besogne*, Coblenz; but news being received that day from Montecuccoli that he was in the vicinity of Bonn, which he intended to besiege, and asking the Prince to join him there, it was decided to change direction.[90] The Prince arrived at Montecuccoli's quarters at a small village about half an hour from Bonn on the night of 4/5 November and found that the trenches had been opened the previous night. It was decided that he should mount an attack from the Cologne side as soon as his infantry arrived, whilst the Imperial army would do the same from two other directions. The Prince found time to thank Hieronymus van Beverninck for his 'usual diligence' in sending supplies to the besieging army. He took part in an attack on a ravelin in front of one of the gates of Bonn and on the 12th the garrison sounded the surrender. The following day, when it marched out, it consisted of about a thousand men, French and German, very many of whom sought service with the Imperial and Dutch armies. One of the officers of the garrison, marching at the head of some of the troops, had himself previously commanded a Dutch regiment; such, in the 17th century, were the rotations of war. Amongst the casualties on the Dutch side was the Count of Königsmarck, who died of his wounds.[91]

The Prince ordered his court preacher to deliver a sermon of thanksgiving outside the gates of Bonn – as an Imperial city only the Emperor's troops had entered it – and, in the Republic, the States-General also ordered a day of thanksgiving and prayer.[92]

On 15 November they wrote the Prince a fulsome letter of praise which portrayed him as God's instrument for the restoration of the State; but they had to reproach him for not taking more care for his own safety, and they urged him to have consideration for 'the total ruin which would befall the State' and for the Church and for the inhabitants of the country if anything untoward should happen to his person. State, Church and People, it was for these that the rulers of the Dutch Republic said they were fighting; and we cannot doubt their sincerity.

The letter mentions that 'Your Highness with God's blessing' had compelled the French to evacuate Woerden, Bommel and Crevecour and that they had received certain news that they would also evacuate the Province of Utrecht.[93]

THE FRENCH EVACUATE THE DUTCH REPUBLIC

It was indeed true that when France declared war against Spain on 19 October the threat that the military situation now presented to the exposed French position in the Dutch Republic had been thoroughly appreciated by Louis's closest military advisers. On 4 October Turenne had already written to advise Louis that, in the event of war with Spain, 'the sooner Holland is evacuated the better'. After the fall of Naarden, as we have seen, Luxemburg advised concentrating French forces in fewer fortresses, but at the end of October he went further. On the 24th he wrote privately to Louvois advising him that most of the French fortresses in the Dutch Republic should be dismantled and abandoned in preparation for war with Spain. Prior to this Louis had had to confront what must have been a bitter decision, but it was taken; he deliberated on the 20th and on the following day Louvois outlined a plan to Luxemburg to abandon the Dutch fortresses except for a few on the Maas and Rhine near the German frontier. Only Condé, amongst those at the summit of Louis's decision-making process, expressed his concern; he pointed to 'the loss of reputation and the discredit which this abandonment would give to the affaires of the king in the whole of Europe'.[94] It would be a serious loss of *gloire*.

The French planned to leave about 20,000 effectives in the fortresses that they wanted to retain, which included Arnhem as an advance post; the garrisons of the posts that were to be abandoned and the army corps that Luxemburg was ordered to assemble to conduct the retreat back to France have been estimated to amount to 20,000 foot and 10,000 horse. Even if this is deemed to be too high – by the time Luxemburg left Rijnberk at the beginning of December a contemporary Dutch historian put his force at 18,000/19,000 men – an evacuation on this scale, a sort of 17th-century Dunkirk without the ships, was not a small undertaking.[95] As French troops were withdrawn throughout the occupied territories, they demanded final ransoms, took with them prominent citizens as pledges for the ransoms, and encumbered themselves with long trains to carry their plunder.[96] At Utrecht troops left in various stages; the Queen's regiment left on 9 November; and at 9am on 16 November Luxemburg gave the order for the departure of a further substantial detachment of troops led by himself. This force of 6,000 men, with a large number of carts to contain the booty, marched through the streets to the sound of bells, drums and trumpets.[97] The perilous withdrawal had begun.

The Prince of Orange was aware of the opportunity that was presenting itself. After the capture of Bonn he wanted to cut off the French escape route – which, the Rhine route being blocked by the Imperialists, was likely to follow the Maas – by advancing westward on Maastricht and Charleroi. But this led to disagreement with Montecuccoli, who, under the pretext of sickness, departed for Vienna at the end of November, without taking leave of the Prince, and handed over command to the less than competent Duc de Bournonville.[98] The best chance therefore of heading off Luxemburg's retreat by the combined forces of the Emperor, of the Dutch and of the Spaniards was lost; although the Prince still had every intention of resuming it with the Dutch and Spaniards on their own.

But first the Prince deemed it necessary to pay a flying visit to The Hague.

POLITICAL IMPLICATIONS OF THE FRENCH EVACUATION

The recapture of Utrecht by the Dutch would have far-reaching political implications for the government of the Republic, which Prince William immediately appreciated. But he was not alone; the Van Reede clan, who were so entrenched in Utrecht, were also anxious about the position. Godard van Reede van Ginkel was in touch with His Highness concerning the future government of the Province of Utrecht; a letter of his of 21 November indicates that he understood from the Prince that 'most of the direction of the province' would be put in the hands of his father, Amerongen, and of his father's distant uncle, Johan van Reede van Renswoude.[99] Amerongen, too, had been in touch with him concerning the same matter but the Prince at this stage was leaving his options open and wrote to him – also on the 21st – that any decision on this score would have to await his arrival in The Hague, 'which I hope, God willing, will happen soon'. To Fagel he wrote: 'I share [your] sentiment that great changes need to be made in the governments of the province of Gelderland and Utrecht but that will have to wait until my arrival in The Hague, which I hope will happen shortly', but added in a postscript, 'I do not at all think it well that Amerongen should go to Utrecht; everything should remain as it is until my arrival.' The States-General, too, were told – on the 24th – that decisions regarding the Province of Utrecht should await his arrival in The Hague, although order needed to be restored there 'to prevent any innovations'.[100]

Definite news of the French evacuation of Utrecht reached William's camp on 28 November and Fagel sent news that he had gone to the city with other delegates from the States to establish order; he also indicated that the Bishop of Münster was inclining towards peace and his letter enclosed a resolution from the States authorising His Highness and the ambassadors at Cologne to come to an agreement with him.[101] Negotiations were also under way at the Cologne peace conference with the Bishop of Cologne.[102]

FAILURE TO CUT OFF LUXEMBURG'S RETREAT

The Prince marched back with his army to Brabant and met Waldeck at Diest on 5 December and Monterey the following day at Herenthals, to the south-west of Antwerp, where he must have discussed plans for impeding Luxemburg's retreat – the combined Dutch and Spanish army has been put at between 25,000 and 30,000 men compared with Luxemburg's force, which here is given as 16,000.[103] Leaving the army, Prince William arrived at The Hague on 8 December. There he received a hero's welcome; emerging from his quarters in the Binnenhof on the morning of the 9th, he inspected the civic guard drawn up outside, and, after his return to his quarters, three salvoes sounded, followed by adulatory speeches. As the signal for the salvoes was given by Nassau-Ouwekerk waving a handkerchief from one of the windows and as one of the speeches was delivered by Gaspar Fagel, we may assume that coordination was not lacking for these seemingly spontaneous manifestations of joy.[104]

At The Hague, William told Waldeck, he busied himself in preparing the military budget for the following year, which he anticipated would cause no difficulties with the States-General. He also worked on possible treaties with Denmark and the Lüneburg princes. He was well satisfied with affairs generally – everything was 'on a good footing' – and he also seems to have been satisfied that the political and constitutional position in Utrecht was being contained, for he confided to Waldeck that he had, after all, decided to postpone the settlement of Utrecht until the end of the campaign.[105] Meetings were held with the Council of State, with the States-General and the States of Holland.[106]

He was in The Hague for only a week, departing early in the morning on the 15th to join the Dutch army at Aerschot, close to Diest, and, after conferring with Monterey at midday on the 18th, he arrived later in the evening at Landen, which lay a little distance to the south-west of Maastricht, where Luxemburg had arrived some time before to rest the force he had managed to evacuate from the Republic. No sooner had the Prince arrived than he received news from Monterey that Luxemburg was now on the move and was heading for France; and he immediately decided to advance with the utmost speed to Namur, with the intention of overtaking Luxemburg's army. After reaching Namur and crossing the Maas there he, and an advance party consisting of all the cavalry, marched on Hamptiness, where this force was drawn up in battle array throughout the night, not more than two hours' distance from Luxemburg's army; but further action was precluded until his infantry arrived in support. By the time this arrived Luxemburg had retraced his steps and wended his way back to Maastricht.[107]

Luxemburg's peril had caused consternation in Paris, and plans were afoot to send an army of 30,000 to Charleroi under the command of Condé and Turenne. It was unnecessary; the season was far advanced; much had been demanded of the allied troops; and the possibility of substantial reinforcements for Luxemburg must have deterred the allies from pursuing matters any further. They decided to go into winter quarters; and by the middle of January Luxemburg entered Charleroi after a punishing march completed his masterly retreat from the Dutch republic.[108]

On 9 January 1674 the Prince of Orange returned to The Hague, leaving the Dutch-Spanish army in winter quarters in the Bishopric of Liège.[109]

CHARLES II FORCED OUT OF THE WAR

We have seen that William had consistently been unable to persuade Charles II that a French alliance was not in the latter's interest. He now resorted to putting pressure on his uncle by resorting to a campaign to influence English public opinion to drive him out of the war.

To achieve his aim he made use of a Huguenot, Pierre Du Moulin, a naturalised Englishman and former client of Arlington, who had fallen out with him. In August 1672 du Moulin had taken refuge in Holland and became a secretary of the Prince of Orange, who made use of his extensive knowledge of English affairs and also of Du Moulin's command of French to deal with correspondence in that language. In the autumn Du Moulin began to communicate with his contacts in England to keep himself, and Prince William and Fagel, informed of what was going on there.[110]

One of the influential figures with whom he tried to establish contact was Shaftesbury, to whom he wrote a letter dated 9 January 1673 asking to see him in private. He did not spell out what he had in mind but from his previous acquaintance with Shaftesbury he knew he was not wholeheartedly committed to the French alliance and it is a fair surmise that his underlying aim was to cause a split amongst Charles's ministers. This letter was carried over to England in January by two Dutchmen, Zas and Arton, who were immediately arrested when they landed at Harwich on suspicion of being Dutch agents – Charles and his ministers had a general suspicion that the Dutch were creating discontent in Parliament and a general warrant had been issued three days before for the arrest of all travellers arriving from Holland and Flanders.

This may have raised suspicions in Charles II's mind about Shaftesbury, and Professor Haley has surmised that, in order to allay these suspicions, this in turn may have caused Shaftesbury to show himself a particularly strong supporter of Charles's policy.[111] When the English Parliament met on 15 February it was addressed by the little Earl in a commanding Parliamentary and rhetorical performance when he quoted, in that classically educated age, Cato's admonition to the Senate of Rome that Carthage must be destroyed – *delenda est Carthago* – substituting the Dutch for the Carthaginians: 'Let this be remembered, the States of Holland are England's eternal enemy.' And against this background Parliament voted the necessary supplies for the war to continue – there was, at this stage, no strong anti-war feeling. But all the same there was a price to pay – in March Charles had to rescind the Declaration of Indulgence which he had issued at the beginning of the war when he used the royal prerogative to suspend the penal laws against Catholics and Dissenters alike. Worse, Parliament also insisted on forcing through the Test Act in the same month. This compelled office-holders to swear an oath renouncing the Catholic doctrine of Transubstantiation. This was to flush out Charles's brother, James, Duke of York, who resigned his offices on 15 June; and thus the heir to the throne was unambiguously confirmed to be a papist.

From now on this was to be a central conundrum in British politics, and it was to play out over time to provide the Prince of Orange with the opportunity to present himself as the Protestant alternative.[112]

During March Du Moulin – and hence William of Orange – arranged for an anonymous pamphlet to be distributed in great numbers. Entitled 'England's Appeal from the Private Cabal at Whitehall to the Great Council of the Nation and Commons in Parliament Assembled', it was a critique of Charles's ministers and their pursuit of the Dutch War, which it claimed they were supporting in the interests of France, influenced by French bribes, and against the interests of England, which would 'be made tributary to the French'.[113]

Ronald Hutton has argued that, based on the evidence of newsletters, the resignation by the Duke of York of his offices in June caused a substantial shift in English public opinion against the Dutch War and the French alliance.[114] By the beginning of August Colbert de Croissy, the French ambassador in London, reported that Charles II 'to tell the truth, is carrying a heavy load in favouring France against the inclinations of all his people and with only the support of the duke of York and Lord Arlington'.[115] Although 'England's Appeal' preceded James's resignation by a couple of months it, and the subsequent campaign supervised by Du Moulin, both exploited and fed the change in opinion.

It lent further impetus to the anti-French sentiments resulting from the naval campaign and the alleged behaviour of the French allies. Before the shift in public opinion occurred, Charles II still had Parliament's support for the war and he had his money; in April 1673 he had £1.25 million and he could fit out his fleet. It was commanded by Prince Rupert, and it joined with the French fleet, off Rye, on 27 May. Their objective was to clear the seas against the Dutch admiral, Michael De Ruyter, and to land an army in Zeeland: Rupert had secret orders to capture as much of Zeeland as possible and its inhabitants were to be lured with the promise of representation in the Parliament at Westminster.[116] The invasion force was to consist of 10,000 men, who were assembled at Blackheath and who were to be joined by 5,000 men from the fleet. Buckingham's combined incompetence and self-willed behaviour persuaded Charles to appoint a French general, Count Schomberg, to take over command of the Blackheath force; it was not to be long before he and Rupert were at loggerheads.[117]

The Anglo-French fleet significantly outnumbered the Dutch and De Ruyter adopted a defensive strategy of outstanding brilliance based on the Schooneveld sandbanks, behind which he could retire or sally forth as occasion demanded.[118] The naval war culminated in the battle of Texel on 21 August, which we have examined from the Dutch side. On the English side the battle had two far-reaching results; whilst it did not produce a decisive naval result, it did lead to the English government definitively abandoning its plans for an invasion of the Dutch Republic and to the English fleet being laid up for the winter on 16 September;[119] and it also led to recriminations against the French ally. Rupert blamed the failure to gain an outright victory on the French admiral, D'Estrées: 'if the French … had obeyed my signall and borne downe upon the enemy according to their duty, I must have routed and torne them [the Dutch] all to pieces. It was the plainest and greatest opportunity was ever lost att sea', he wrote in his account of the battle.[120] These criticisms became public and heightened the intense anti-French popular feeling triggered when James's public Catholicism had become known in the middle of June and to which the 'England's Appeal' pamphlet was able to add further fuel.

Then, whilst the King was once again running out of money, public opinion was further provoked. James entered into a second marriage on 20 September by proxy in Italy, and he did so to a staunchly Catholic wife. His first wife, Anne Hyde, had died on 31 March 1671,[121] and that marriage to one so inferior in rank, who, furthermore, was already pregnant, had caused sufficient consternation within the royal family to animate the court and diplomatic observers; his second marriage now was to cause consternation within the political nation. Two things were widely known about his new 15-year-old bride, Mary of Modena: first, her family, the D'Estes, had for long been clients of the kings of France and now of Louis XIV – he provided a dowry of £90,000;[122] and, secondly, she was an exceptionally devout Catholic, who would have much preferred to spend her life in a nunnery. James married her indeed because of the advice he received that he might be in need of the protection that Louis could extend to him.[123] If Charles was already very much in the position of a client to his French cousin, this marriage tightened that relationship yet more closely: hence further credence for 'England's Appeal'.

When Parliament met on 27 October – it had been adjourned on 29 March – Charles found it unwilling to vote him the supplies he asked for to continue the Dutch War; instead it called upon him to annul the Duke of York's marriage to Mary of Modena before it was consummated – she did not arrive at Dover until 1 December. This he refused, or was unable, to do, with James being too far committed; and he was compelled to prorogue Parliament until January.[124]

In the meanwhile, on 5 July, the States-General had resolved to send Coenraad van Beuningen to Brussels to pursue peace negotiations with the King through the good offices of Monterey and other Spanish representatives. The object was to induce England to enter into a separate peace with the Dutch and even to enter into an alliance with them against France. To coordinate negotiations with the Spanish ambassador in London, the Marquis Del Fresno, Monterey sent Don Bernardo de Salinas to England with a negotiating brief setting out the parameters of the Dutch negotiating position, which had been authorised by the *Secrète Besogne*.[125]

That William of Orange was the principal driving force behind the initiative is made clear by three letters that he wrote in the middle of July, which may well have been drafted by Du Moulin:[126] the first to Del Fresno; the second to Charles II; and the last to De Salinas himself. We need to note that the credentials given to De Salinas in the first two letters are the personal credentials of the Prince, not of the States-General or the *Secrète Besogne*, and William's primary role is further reinforced by the third letter, to De Salinas, in which the Prince – very politely – instructs this envoy in the arguments he is to deploy in the negotiations.

William's letter to Charles says that De Salinas will show his uncle 'what up till now the troublemakers of this war have concealed from you with such artifice. And if only Your Majesty would open your eyes you will clearly see in what manner your allies and those in whom you have the greatest confidence have abused your good will.' As regards the Prince himself he hoped that De Salinas would demonstrate that it was impossible for him to do more on the king's behalf and that, after serious reflection, Charles would not expect him to do anything that ran counter to his honour, or beyond what he could deliver. The King, in other words, should not anticipate that the Prince's influence in the Dutch Republic could be stretched to moderate the Dutch terms – which we may regard as a standard stratagem for someone who wishes to deflect responsibility for a hard negotiating stance. The letter ends: 'If, to the detriment of both England and the United Provinces, the good offices … of Don Bernard de Salinas bear no fruit, no other recourse will remain to me other than divine protection and to await in silence until it pleases God to inspire Your Majesty with other sentiments.' The King, in short, is being presented with what is tantamount to an ultimatum. The tone of this letter written from the 22-year-old nephew to his 43-year-old uncle, the King of England, is remarkable – he speaks as an equal and he manifests all the status with which he now wishes to be regarded on the European stage.

In his letter to De Salinas he spelled out what he meant by his allusions to Charles's allies. At the peace negotiations in Cologne the French King 'sought only his own particular advantage and paid little consideration to what England had already done and continued to do for him'; the French proposals were scarcely less disadvantageous to England than they were to the Dutch; the towns they were demanding would guarantee them the conquest of the Spanish Netherlands unless the English subsequently joined the Austrians and the Dutch to take them back again from the French in order to curb the power that the English King himself, through his bewildering policy, had contributed to making more formidable than ever.[127]

There was indeed much point in these arguments. If Charles had sought the patronage and the subsidies of his powerful cousin in France to wage a war against the Dutch, the booty which he had reckoned on was promising to be meagre indeed; and, as Prince William pointed out, the war threatened to leave the Low Countries in the hands of the dominant power in Europe, a menace of which politicians in England, reaching beyond those such as Sir William Temple, who had been conscious of the danger from the start, were increasingly aware. He ended this letter on much the same note as he had done in his own letter to Charles – if the King would not listen the Prince's own credit with the Dutch towns and Provinces would be insufficient to prevent them from concluding a separate peace with France 'at the expense of the whole of Europe'. The ultimatum, in short, was to be underlined.

The Dutch were in fact prepared to be more flexible than the Prince of Orange was prepared to reveal;[128] but the sea battle off Texel on 21 August reduced the need for such flexibility and caused them to harden their position. When they signed their treaty with Spain on 30 August the Spanish, under a separate, secret treaty, bound themselves to make an offer to the English on behalf of the Dutch. The Dutch would concede on the question of the flag (acknowledging English sovereignty in English waters); there would be a mutual return of conquered territories; and the Dutch would pay an indemnity of between one and two million guilders (£100,000–£200,000). If these terms were not met Spain would declare war on England within three weeks of the ratification of the main treaty by Spain.[129]

However, whilst on the one hand Spanish trade was of great importance to England, which was why the Dutch were using Spain to bring pressure on England with the threat of war, on the other hand Spain was very short of money to carry out the threat, which would also leave exposed her possessions in the Indies. The stipulated ratification was therefore much delayed – although dated 10 November it was not in fact delivered until January 1674, and then not in proper form. If the Prince had resorted to bluff in presenting his ultimatum to his uncle Charles, the threat of war from Spain was a double bluff.

Nevertheless, Del Fresno submitted a memorandum dated 20 December 1673 to the English government with the Dutch peace proposals, which were essentially those stipulated in the secret Spanish-Dutch treaty of 30 August. To placate King Charles the Dutch accepted some minor amendments in a letter dated 24 January 1674, behind which, as it was drafted by Du Moulin, we can again detect the hand of William of Orange. Charles submitted them for Parliament's approval which, in the strong anti-war mood that now prevailed, was forthcoming – an outcome that would have been influenced by the flow of Dutch pamphlets released at this time. And on 19 February 1674 the Treaty of Westminster was signed, ending the third and last of the 17th century's Anglo-Dutch wars, with, in order to hasten the proceedings, Del Fresno being authorised to sign on behalf of the Dutch.[130]

The Dutch conceded the flag; the departure of British subjects from Surinam was facilitated and New York, which the Dutch had recaptured during the war, was returned to England; a commercial treaty was left for further negotiation; and the Dutch agreed to pay two million guilders (£200,000) to King Charles. However, of this one and a half million guilders (£150,000) went to Prince William in payment of the debts the Stuarts owed to the House of Orange – the Dutch States binding themselves to pay it to him instead of to the King, although it was an obligation that they did not meet for many years.[131] For King Charles it was a meagre reward for the blood and treasure that his country had spent. For Prince William of Orange the outcome was one for which he had striven so long and so stubbornly. His uncle was forced into a separate peace and Louis XIV had lost his most prominent partner.

In March 1674 the Holland States were informed that Dutch policy all along, leading to the Treaty of Westminster, was to cause a schism between Charles II and his people, as well as to separate him from Louis XIV.[132] When William Temple was the English ambassador in The Hague later that year he probed the possibility at a meeting with William of Orange that 'discontented persons in England' had intrigued with the Dutch 'about raising seditions, and perhaps insurrections in England'. One such person Temple had particularly in mind was the Earl of Shaftesbury who, in Temple's view, following the change in parliamentary and public opinion, had switched from the position he had adopted in his *delenda est Carthago* speech. Temple told the Prince, without, however, mentioning any names, that the King had suspicions of some of his subjects and 'how much service it would be in his highness to discover them. The prince was stanch [staunch], and said, he was sure the king would not press him upon a thing so much against all honour, as to betray men that professed to be his friends' – in short, it would run counter to his *gloire* as a patron to cut loose his following of clients.[133]

How far these intrigues went – in this opaque world of espionage, agents, counter-agents and double agents – remains uncertain. Nor is this surprising for, as we shall see on p.327, William and Fagel took good care to cover their tracks. To this subject we will return.

SUMMARY OF 1673

During the year the Dutch had lost Maastricht and the Elector of Brandenburg as an ally and Prince William had been deprived of his, in any case indefensible, Principality of Orange. But he was the protagonist in the creation of the Triple Alliance, he had forced the French evacuation from the Dutch Republic – even if the chance of cutting off Luxemburg's masterly retreat was fluffed – and soon after the year's end Louis's primary ally, Charles II, had been knocked out of the war. It was no small embellishment to the *gloire* of the barely 23-year-old Prince of Orange and to that of his House.

1   Mignet, *op. cit.*, IV, pp.136–7.
2   *Urkunden un Actenstücke, op. cit.*, Dritter Band, pp.363, 366–9, 371.
3   *Ibid.*, p.372, 377.
4   Japikse, *Willem III, op. cit.*, pp.294–5.
5   *Urkunden und Actenstücke, op. cit.*, Dritte Band, p.381–2.
6   Mignet, *op. cit.*, IV, pp.132–136. Albert Waddington, *op. cit.*, pp.311–12.
7   Rousset, *op. cit.*, I, pp.428–30.
8   Carl Ekberg, *The failure of Louis XIV's Dutch war*, Chapel Hill: University of North Carolina Press, 1979, p.19. Nimwegen, *op. cit.*, pp.460–1.
9   *Correspondentie Willem III en Portland, op. cit.*, 2.1, p.184.

10 *Ibid.*, pp.187–8.

11 Rousset, *op. cit.*, I, pp.450–1. W. J. Knoop, *Krijgs- en geschiedkundige beschouwingen over Willem den Derde*, 1895, p.247.

12 *Correspondentie Willem III en Portland, op. cit.*, 2.1, p.179 & notes 3 & 4.

13 *Correspondentie Willem III en Portland, op. cit.*, 2.1, p.174.

14 Nimwegen, *op. cit.*, p.330.

15 *Ibid.*, pp.332–333.

16 *Ibid.*, pp.333, 334, 336, 337, 339.

17 *Ibid.*, pp.366, 368.

18 See, for example, the Prince's letter to Amerongen dated 30 January 1673, *Correspondentie Willem III en Portland,* 2.1, 1, p.181, and his letters to the same, pp.183–4, 186–7, 223.

19 *Vervolg van't Verwerd Europa*, Amsterdam, 1688, p.142.

20 *Correspondentie Willem III en Portland, op. cit.*, 2.1, pp.300–1. *Vervolg van't Verwerd Europa, op. cit.*, p.142.

21 *Correspondentie Willem III en Portland, op. cit.*, 2.1, pp.202, 219.

22 Nimwegen, *op. cit.*, p.349. See also *'t Onroerde Nederland*, Amsterdam 1676, pp.780 *et seq.*

23 *Correspondentie Willem III en Portland, op. cit.*, 2.1, p.267.

24 *Correspondentie Willem III en Portland, op. cit.*, 2.1, p.177.

25 Groen van Prinsterer, *Archives, op. cit.*, 2.V, pp.310–11.

26 Nimwegen, *op. cit.*, p.343. *Correspondentie Willem III en Portland, op. cit.*, 2.1, p.190.

27 Nimwegen, *op. cit.*, p.347.

28 *Ibid.*, p.348.

29 *Ibid.*, pp.356–7. Franken, *op. cit.*, pp.118–19. Hop & Vivien, *op. cit.*, pp.416, 418.

30 Knoop, *op. cit.*, pp.240–1.

31 Japikse, *Willem III, op. cit.*, I, p.293. *Correspondentie Willem III en Portland, op. cit.*, 2.1, pp.217–18.

32 Derek McKay, *op. cit.*, pp.53, 56, 66, 114.

33 Groen van Prinsterer, *Archives, op. cit.*, 2.V, pp.313–14. Maurits's instructions are contained in *Correspondentie Willem III en Portland, op. cit.*, 2.1, p.217. See also Ten Raa and Bas, VI, p.11.

34 Knoop, *op. cit.*, pp.240–2. Groen van Prinsterer, *Archives, op. cit.*, 2nd series 5, pp 325–7.

35 Japikse, *Willem III, op. cit.*, I, pp.292–3. *Vervolg van't Verwerd Europa, op. cit.*, p.136.

36 Mignet, *op. cit.*, IV, pp.139–140.

37 *Ibid.*, p.140.

38 Wagenaar, *op. cit.*, 14, pp.247–8. Hop & Vivien, *op. cit.*, pp.391–3.

39 Hop & Vivien, *op. cit.*, pp.389–390. Franken, *op. cit.*, pp.114–15.

40 Wagenaar, *op. cit.*, 14, pp.352–3.

41 P.L. Müller, *op. cit.*, pp.43, 47, 51, 57–8. Spielman, *op. cit.*, p.59. Pribram, *op. cit.*, pp.575–6, 584. For the guilder equivalent of a *rijksthaler* see Nimwegen, *op. cit.*, p.xxi.

42 Oswald Redlich, *op. cit.*, pp.116–7.

43 Müller, *op. cit.*, p.52.

44 Hop & Vivien, *op. cit.*, p.388.

45 Krämer, *op. cit.*, pp.97, 107.

46 Müller, *op. cit.*, pp.59/60. Redlich, *op. cit.*, p.117.

47 Müller, *op. cit.*, p.61. The Prince's figures appear to be reasonably consistent with Rousset's figures mentioned on p.242 for Louis's forces at the beginning of 1673, i.e. 30,000 on the Rhine and 48,000 in the Dutch Republic split between a field army of 25,000 and 23,000 in garrisons on the Maas and other river fortifications. The Prince's figures are lower but the usual attrition of war may help to account for this. If we add the Austrian force of 30,000 men to the same number on Prince William's side the total of 60,000 would be facing 45,000 French (21,000 from the Maas, 14,000 from Turenne, and 10,000 from Condé) and it would still leave 30,000 Dutch troops to contain the French field army of 25,000 men.

48 For these demands see Mignet, *op. cit.*, IV, pp.141–7. For the commencement of the Cologne conference see Wagenaar, *op. cit.*, 14, p.253.

49 Müller, *op. cit.*, pp.64 *et seq.*

50 *Ibid.*, p.61.

51 Franken, *op. cit.*, pp.116–18, 263.

52 Müller, *op. cit.*, p.61.

53 Krämer, *op. cit.*, pp.114–16.

54 Müller, pp.59–60. Ekberg, *op. cit.*, p.94.

55 Wagenaar, *op. cit.*, 14, pp.256–7. Japikse, *Willem III, op. cit.*, p.319.

56 Ekberg, *op. cit.*, p.31.

57 Mignet, *op. cit.*, IV, pp.206–8. Redlich, *op. cit.*, p.118.

58 J. Whaley, *Germany and the Holy Roman Empire*, II, OUP, 2012, p.35–6. Redlich, *op. cit.*, pp.120–1. He puts the Emperor's army at 36,000 men.

59 Mignet, *op. cit.*, 4, pp.215–16.

60 *Vervolg van't Verwerd Europa, op. cit.*, p.594.

61 *Correspondentie Willem III en Portland*, 2.1, p.256.

62 *Ibid.*, 2.1, p.267.

63 *Ibid.*, pp.275–282. *Vervolg van't Verwerd Europa, op. cit.*, p.408.

64 Wagenaar, *op. cit.*, 14, p.272.

65 *Vervolg van't Verwerd Europa, op. cit.*, p.408.

66 *Correspondentie Willem III en Portland, op. cit.*, 2.1, p.282.

67 De Jonge, *op. cit.*, III, I, pp.282–4. *Vervolg van't Verwerd Europa, op. cit.* p.408. *'T Onroerde Nederland, op. cit.*, II, p.552.

68 *Correspondentie Willem III en Portland. op. cit.*, 2.1, p.286.

69 *Ibid.*, pp.282, 287.

70 *'T Ontroerde Nederlandt, II, op. cit.* pp.570–1.

71 Wagenaar, *op. cit.*, 14, pp.272–3. Nimwegen, *op. cit.*, pp.462–3. Japikse, *Willem III, op. cit.*, I, p.308. *Vervolg van't Verwerd Europa*, p.488. See also Wicquefort, *Histoire, op. cit.*, IV, p.592.

72 Rousset, *op. cit.*, I.p.480.

73 *Ibid.*, p.484.

74 Ekberg, *op. cit.*, p.31.

75 Rousset, *op. cit.*, I, p.469.

76 Ekberg, *op. cit.*, p.24, 39. Rousset, *op. cit.*, I, p.471.

77 Redlich, *op. cit.*, p.123.

78 Ekberg, *op. cit.*, pp.35–6. Rousset, *op. cit.*, I, p.470.

79 Ekberg, *op. cit.*, p.41.

80 Rousset, *op. cit.*, I, p.409.

81 Ekberg, *op. cit.*, pp.64, 69.

82 Redlich, *op. cit.*, p.123.

83 Ekberg, *op. cit.*, p.69. Knoop, *op. cit.*, pp.278–9.

84 Ekberg, *op. cit.*, pp.70–75. Redlich, *op. cit.*, pp.120–1, 123. For the Bishop of Wurzburg see Rousset, *op. cit.*, I, p.497.

85 Knoop, *op. cit.*, pp.289–10. Constantijn Huygens the Younger, *Journaal*, Hist.Gen., Utrecht, 1881, p.3.

86 *Correspondentie Willem III en Portland, op. cit.*, 2.1, pp.299, 303, 305. Huygens, *Journaal, op. cit.*, pp.3–6. For Condé's contributions and Spanish reprisals see Rousset, *op. cit.*, I, p.489. L. Sylvius, *Willem de Derde*, Amsterdam, 1694, Parts I and II, pp.197–8. *Vervolg van't Verwerd Europa, op. cit.*, p.588.

87 *Correspondentie Willem III en Portland*, 2.1, p.307. Huygens, *Journaal, op. cit.*, pp.14–5. Panhuysen, *op. cit.*, p.394.

88 *Vervolg van't Verwerd Europa, op. cit.*, 1688, p.607.

89 Huygens, *Journaal, op. cit.*, p.13.

90 *Correspondentie Willem III en Bentinck, op. cit.*, 2.1, p.307, see William's letter to the *Secrète Besogne*. But according to Huygens's diary Huygens was told as early as 28 October that the army would march on Bonn on the 30th to besiege the city. Was the diary written up after the event and did Huygens confuse the dates?

91 Huygens, *Journal, op. cit.*, pp.16, 18, 19, 20. *Correspondentie Willem III en Portland, op. cit.*, 2.1, pp.307, 308–9, 311.

92 *Vervolg van't Verwerd Europa, op. cit.*, 1688, p.618.

93 *Correspondentie Willem III en Portland, op. cit.*, 2.1, pp.309–10.

94 Ekberg, *op. cit.*, pp.131–4. Rousset, *op. cit.*, I, pp.500–1.

95 Rousset, *op. cit.*, I, pp.500-2. Sylvius, *op. cit.*, I and II, p.221. See also *Vervolg van't Verwerd Europa, op. cit.*, p.660.

96 *Vervolg van't Verwerd Europa, op. cit.*, pp.652 *et seq.*

97 Le Ségur, *op. cit.*, p.275.

98 Redlich, *op. cit.*, p.124. Huygens, *Journaal, op. cit.*, p.23.

99 Panhuysen, *op. cit.*, p.403. See p.36 for Renswoude's family relationship with Amerongen.

100 *Correspondentie Willem III en Portland, op. cit.*, 2.1, pp.314–16.

101 Huygens, *Journaal, op. cit.*, p.25.

102 See Prince's letter to van Beverninck on 29 November. *Correspondentie Willem III en Portland, op. cit.*, 2.1, p.317.

103 Huygens, *Journaal, op. cit.*, p.27. The estimate of the armies' strengths is in Knoop, *op. cit.*, pp.302–3.

104 Japikse, *Willem III, op. cit.*, I, pp.316–17.

105 *Correspondentie Willem III en Portland, op. cit.*, 2.1, p.320.

106 *Vervolg van't Verwerd Europa, op. cit.*, p.619.

107 *Correspondentie Willem III en Portland, op. cit.*, 2.1, pp.326–7.

108 Rousset, *op. cit.*, I. pp.509–10.

109 Ten Raa and Bas, *op. cit.*, VI, p.22. *Vervolg van't Verwerd Europa, op. cit.*, pp.664–5.

110 Haley, *The English Opposition, op. cit.*, pp.219, 26, 52.

111 *Ibid.*, pp.74–7. Haley, *The First Earl of Shaftesbury*, Oxford, 1968, pp.313–15.

112 Jones, *op. cit.*, pp.198–201, 203. Hutton, *op. cit.*, p.301.

113 Haley, *The English Opposition, op. cit.*, pp.98, 100, 110, 111. There is no conclusive evidence that Du Moulin was the author, although, as Professor Haley has demonstrated, the probabilities point firmly in that direction.

114 Hutton, *op. cit.*, p.308.

115 Quoted in Ekberg, *op. cit.*, p.9.

116 Jones, *op. cit.*, p.201. Hutton, *op. cit.*, p.303.

117 Jones, *op. cit.*, p.201–2. Hutton, *op. cit.*, p.304.

118 Jones, *op. cit.*, p.205.

119 Hutton, *op. cit.*, p.305. C.R. Boxer, *The Anglo-Dutch wars of the 17th century, 1652-1674*, 1974, pp.57–8.

120 Colenbrander, *op. cit.*, II, p.308.

121 Miller, *op. cit.*, pp.69, 71, 73.

122 *Ibid.*, p.72.

123 *Ibid.*, p.72.

124 Hutton, *op. cit.*, p.309. Miller, *op. cit.*, p.74.

125 F.J.L. Krämer, *op. cit.*, pp.117, 118–19. See also Hop & Vivien, *op. cit.*, p.431.

126 On Du Moulin see *Correspondentie Willem III en Bentinck, op. cit.*, 2.1, n.3 and 4, p.257 and n.2, p.258.

127 *Correspondentie Willem III en Bentinck, op. cit.*, 2.1, pp.257–9.

128 See Krämer, *op. cit.*, pp.118–19.

129 Krämer, *op. cit.*, pp.121, 123, 127, 129, 133.

130 Krämer, *op. cit.*, pp.138–9, 146, 50. Ekberg, *op. cit.*, p.171. Haley, *The English Opposition, op. cit.*, pp.149, 163, 165, 166,175, 183. Hutton, *op. cit.*, p.316.

131 Haley, *The English Opposition, op. cit.*, pp.183–4. Wagenaar, *op. cit.*, pp.298–300.

132 Hop & Vivien, *op. cit.*, p.431.

133 Temple, *Works*, 1770, *op. cit.*, II, pp.286–7.

13 1674: THE ENTICEMENTS OF SOVEREIGNTY

CONSOLIDATION OF THE PRINCE'S POWER IN UTRECHT

The Prince of Orange had a reputation for reticence; but there were occasions when he let slip what was on his mind. On the march to Bonn in the middle of October, ruminating at table with his secretary, the younger Constantijn Huygens, on the execution of his grandfather, Charles I, and on English matters, he observed that, should his uncle the Duke of York die before Charles II, a dispute would arise if James's daughters took precedence over him in the succession to the English Crown.[1] But, if he was thus ruminating on the possibilities of acquiring sovereignty in the British Isles, in the Dutch Republic too his growing status and prestige gave rise to opportunities to extend the basis of his power there, with the enticement of sovereignty.

When the three Provinces of Utrecht, Overijssel and Gelderland had been overrun by the French they were, in September 1672, precluded from taking part in the meetings of the States-General. Now the States-General resolved by secret resolution on 18 November 1673 – that is, before the French had even departed from Utrecht – to suspend for the time being the government that now existed in the Province. The Count of Hoorn was named commander of the troops who were to occupy Utrecht, but it was also decided to send a commission from the States-General itself, to be headed by Fagel; and advice was sought as well from the Prince of Orange, who, as we have seen, urged delaying any decisions about the future government, beyond restoring immediate order. It is important to note that at this meeting of the States-General the representatives of the Province of Holland were predominant in numbers,[2] for Holland and Amsterdam were being drawn to the idea of treating the three Provinces as conquered territories and reincorporating them into the Union on the same lines as the Generality Lands, that is, without voting powers in the States-General. This would greatly have enhanced the power of Holland and of Amsterdam, and it would correspondingly have decreased that of the Prince of Orange; thus his anxiety to delay any decisions on the government. The role of Gaspar Fagel, the Grand Pensionary of Holland, was now central in deciding the outcome of these conflicting interests; how would he handle the situation?

The final French evacuation took place on 23 November 1673, following Luxemburg's own departure on the 16th. Even before this occurred the States of Utrecht wrote, on the 22nd, to the States-General saying that they had sent representatives to the Prince of Orange offering him the Stadholdership of their Province; and at the same time they asked to be allowed to resume their participation in the affairs of the States-General.[3] On the 24th the States of Holland decided to put aside this request pending the report from the delegation they were sending to Utrecht under Fagel's leadership.[4]

The Utrecht delegation that offered William the Stadholdership had left on 12 November, again well before the French evacuation, when the Prince was still with the army before Bonn. One of its members was a pliable politician, Everard van Weede van Dijkveld, who, unlike the aristocratic Van Reede clan, came from a Regent family – he was the son of a Utrecht Burgomaster. Once he had been a supporter of the Perpetual Edict against the Prince of Orange, but, like Fagel, he had switched in 1670 to become a proponent of the Prince's elevation to the Stadholdership. During the French occupation he returned, in July 1672, to Utrecht, where he held the position of President of the Utrecht States, and where he engaged in a range of transactions with the occupying forces, although he stopped short of taking the oath of allegiance to the French regime. He was now, once again, trimming his sails, and he was to be used by the Prince both as an alternative to the Van Reedes for exercising power within the Province and for important diplomatic missions.[5] The Prince's secretary records that during the march to Bonn the Prince had observed at dinner that Dijkveld had governed Utrecht by means of three women, his mistresses[6] – which was not, in the event, to stand in the way of his career, although, unsurprisingly in view of his cooperation with the enemy, he was unable, in the immediate circumstances, to avoid a diminution in his influence.

The French occupation of Utrecht, somewhat like the German occupation of France during the Second World War, had led to internal strife when the enemy retreated: a petition was raised amongst a faction within the Calvinist community in which accusations were levied at Regents who had submitted too readily to the French, were too accommodating to the Catholics, and had been too hostile to the preachers of the Reformed Church: in short, a cry was raised against those who had too closely collaborated with the occupying forces, but, in 17th-century fashion, with a religious theme. The petitioners had the support of the aged theologian Gisbertus Voetius, a veteran of the Remonstrant dispute on the Counter-Remonstrant side and hence a leading champion of Calvinist orthodoxy. The opponents of the Voetians were accused of being supporters of De Witt, and of being antagonistic to the Prince of Orange and the Reformed Church.[7] They came from fairly modest backgrounds and there were few patricians amongst them.[8]

With drums beating and with the bells ringing from the cathedral, where Mass had been said for the last time, the last of the French garrison, under the command of Stoupa, left Utrecht at 8am on 23 November 1673, with Stoupa ceremoniously handing back the keys of the town. By ten o'clock the whole garrison had departed. The citizenry now appeared and walked the streets bedecked with orange sashes, the youths of the town sported orange ribbons in their hats and the Orange flag was raised over the cathedral; there, images, altarpieces and anything that smacked of Roman Catholicism was dragged away and burnt in front of the town hall.[9] Throughout the country there was rejoicing; at the behest of the States-General a day of general thanksgiving took place, with the ringing of church bells, the firing of cannon, the lighting of bonfires and the release of fireworks.[10]

In the afternoon of that day, the first Dutch troops entered the city. The next day the Count of Hoorn arrived and suspended the government on the grounds that a petition had been presented to him by a number of citizens and that he was unacquainted with the agreements the sitting Regents had made with the French; and there was, furthermore, the uncertain military situation to take into consideration. Fagel and his delegation arrived in the evening and on the 26th, he dismissed the government, including Dijkveld.[11]

When Fagel made his report to the Holland States on 30 November on the Utrecht situation he recommended that the first priority was to re-establish order and to address a wide range of concerns, including the payment by the Province of the hefty ransoms that the French demanded for the release of the hostages they had taken with them as they retreated.[12]

But he did not remain inactive on constitutional issues. At a meeting of the Holland States on 23 January 1674 Haarlem maintained that the old form of government in the Republic under the Princes of Orange had been put aside, and that the woeful state the country had subsequently fallen into had demonstrated that it could not be governed without an eminent head. She accordingly proposed that, should His Highness marry, the positions he held as Stadholder and Captain- and Admiral-General should become hereditary in the male line.[13] Fagel came from Haarlem and we can safely assume that the hand of the Pensionary lay behind the proposal of his home town.

On 2 February the States of Holland gave effect to the Haarlem proposal – every member of the States was personally thanked by the Prince – and so, on the same date, did the States of Zeeland; Groningen offered him the position of hereditary Captain- and Admiral-General of that Province on 26 February, in spite of the fact that its Stadholder was William's cousin, Hendrik-Casimir – although he was still under age. At the Holland meeting some of those present had wondered what should happen if the Prince should acquire offices even greater still outside the Republic; it was thus not only Prince William himself whose mind had been turning over possible outcomes in England.[14]

In March the Holland States urged the Prince to marry, declaring that this 'needed to be the means of bringing to fruition the salutary decisions which had been taken on inheritance'. Goodwill was further demonstrated when Amsterdam suggested that the obligation for a loan of two million guilders (£200,000) which she had extended to Prince William II should be taken over by the Province of Holland – Amsterdam was, in fact, rather the gainer by the acceptance of her proposal as she obtained greater security from the credit of the Province of Holland than she could obtain by her mortgages on the properties of the House of Orange, which could hardly be foreclosed without some embarrassment.

Tokens of esteem – and ingratiation – did not end there; Zeeland bestowed 300,000 guilders (£30,000) in securities upon the Prince; and, in July, the East India Company granted him – and his heirs – three and a third per cent of all its dividends.[15] It was the 17th century's way of recognising the rising authority of the Prince of Orange, in the same way as did the lavish gifts bestowed by the Dutch on Charles II at his Restoration. Everybody now wished to be the client of this powerful patron.

On 24 January – the day after Haarlem had made her proposal that William's offices should become hereditary – the Holland States had also met to consider another issue with far-reaching implications: what was to be done with the three previously occupied Provinces?[16] We need to remember that, apart from Utrecht, two were still not completely cleared of the enemy. Attention was thus primarily fixed on Utrecht, although it was recognised that the other two were in much the same situation.

The meeting was attended by both Fagel and the Prince, and, once again, Fagel played a prominent role. It was not explicitly spelled out, but everybody was aware that underlying the discussions there were implications for power within the Republic if the three Provinces were not readmitted to the Union on the former terms. Fagel was the Pensionary of Holland and he could not ignore that power base – hence, if he wished to assist the Prince, he would need to finesse the politics.

He began by addressing the question of Holland's acquiring parts of Utrecht – Holland wanted greater control over her own security, including fortifications on Utrecht territory and access to the waters required for inundations. He pointed to Friesland's objection that not a foot of Utrecht's territory should be ceded or she would revive her long-standing claims to Den Briel and Voorne, which lay within the Province of Holland; and on this issue she was supported by Groningen. Then there were also the perennial controversies over precedence and whether Utrecht should resume her old ranking – something to which Zeeland was particularly opposed. Gaspar Fagel thus rather skilfully presented matters as consisting of disputes between the Provinces, and, in so doing, he created the opening for William to appear in the traditional role of the House of Orange, the mediator who was above the fray and who could restore harmony. Seizing the opportunity, Prince William remarked that these were matters that could be settled and overcome through discussion.

Fagel then gave matters a further steer by conceding that the access to water needed to be addressed, but he warned that there were people in Holland – and he knew who they were – who wanted to use Utrecht for their own purposes.

When William entered the discussion he maintained that no right or reason could exclude Utrecht from readmission to the Union. If it was true that she had shut her gates against the Dutch army retreating from the Ijssel line in 1672, there were also Holland towns which would not have done their utmost to defend themselves. Nor was it right to deprive the Province of any of her territories – God would punish them if they did. He successfully led the Holland States into allowing the three Provinces back into the Union with their territorial integrity intact. A practical way was found in due course of addressing Holland's concerns about her defences – she retained her fortresses on Utrecht territory, including access, and she obtained certain riparian rights to safeguard the inundations. In characteristic 17th-century fashion the point on precedence proved the most ticklish and William ducked the issue for the time being; it required, he said, 'sensitive consideration'. On readmission to the Union Dordrecht suggested that Utrecht should stay outside until she was able to meet her obligations to pay her quota of the Union's finances; her income was proportionately larger than Holland's and amounted in a good year to a million guilders or slightly less.

But matters now went beyond admitting the three Provinces back into the Union on the former terms, which would have restored matters to the *status quo* before the war. On 3 February Holland proposed to authorise the Prince to change the government in Utrecht and, eventually, in Gelderland and Overijssel as well. This, of course, had extensive implications for the future balance of power in the Dutch Republic; and it required a bit of time and a meeting of the States-General to pull all the strands together to arrive at the required settlement.

This meeting occurred on 20 April. There it was resolved that the three Provinces should not be re-admitted until they had sworn a new oath to the Union; the territorial question and Holland's concerns for her defence were settled on the lines indicated above – a settlement was also arrived at for Friesland and Gelderland, which had similar concerns – and the Provinces obtained their old order of precedence (a long-standing dispute between Zeeland and Utrecht was decided in favour of Utrecht through the arbitration of the Prince and Prince Casimir of Friesland); should all the Provinces fail to agree on quotas for their financial contributions this would be decided by His Highness; and, because of her stout performance in the war, Groningen should obtain a second seat in the Council of State at the expense of Gelderland, which would be reduced to one. And, finally, the States-General agreed that His Highness should be empowered 'to change the governments' of the three Provinces, albeit only on this occasion and without prejudice to the 'privileges' – that is, the accumulated historic rights of the Provinces.[17]

A remarkable turn of events was unfolding. The settlement was a balance – on the one hand, between the resentments that the war had raised in those Provinces which had been able to repulse the French and their allies, at considerable cost in blood and treasure, and those whom they saw as having submitted too easily to the enemy's yoke; and, on the other hand, the need for conciliation if the Union was to be restored with sufficient harmony to remain fit for the tasks, particularly in the war, that lay ahead. But we need to remember that, if reconciliation and unity were a benefit for the Republic as a whole, a strong Republic was also necessary for the pursuit of the Prince's personal ambitions and career.
The surge in his authority arose from his successes in the war, but he exploited this with deft political skill and his powers of persuasion were demonstrated by his handling of the Regents,

many of whom had held positions of importance under the regime of Johan De Witt. The Perpetual Edict of Exclusion had been turned on its head and turned into a perpetual edict of inclusion, with the House of Orange obtaining the hereditary right to its traditional offices. The partnership with the subtle and experienced Gaspar Fagel was crucial; and the weight the Grand Pensionary of Holland possessed can now also be seen in Holland's suggestion that the Prince should be empowered to change the governments of the three Provinces. Not only, therefore, was there no question of Holland extending her influence into the previously conquered territories but, on the contrary, they were, paradoxically with Holland herself taking the initiative, to fall within the tight grip of the Prince of Orange – and it is impossible not to detect Gaspar Fagel's hidden hand behind all this.

Prince William was not slow in taking advantage of the power the States-General's resolution accorded him. He arrived at Utrecht on 23 April and on the 26th he began a wholesale purge of the personnel of the Province's institutions. Although he had been authorised to do this by the States-General, he was empowered to do so only in conformity with the customary 'privileges', a restriction to which he did not hold himself.

The constitution of Utrecht derived from the old pre-Reformation bishopric that it had once been, and it was rooted in the Middle Ages. The Provincial States consisted of three bodies: the *geëligeerde*, the nobility, and the representatives of the Provincial towns. The *geëligeerde* consisted of seven members, all of whom were replaced, and an eighth was now added, who was also to become the President of the Utrecht States for life – an innovation. To this position, with the Prince resorting to his old clients, the Van Reede clan, the 80-year-old Johan van Reede van Renswoude was appointed – we have met his son, Frederick van Reede, when he was used by the Prince on his missions to Charles II.

Three new members were appointed to the nobility, all members of the military, which profession would previously have excluded them from this office, including two from the Prince's own family, the young Nassau-Zuylenstein and Nassau-Ouwekerk; and a sort of member-in-waiting was also appointed, Van Reede van Ginkel, who was to succeed his father, Amerongen, after his death.

Overall, 120 office-holders lost their places, a purge on a larger scale than had occurred in the Province of Holland in 1672. The presenters of the petition, who had raised their complaints against the Regents in office during the French occupation, were well represented. Many replacements were born outside Utrecht, which breached customary practice, and one was the Prince's doctor.[18]

But the Prince of Orange went further than changing the personnel; whilst the outward shape of the institutions remained the same, the reality of the changes introduced altered the whole constitution of the former Bishopric. Under the new regime the institutions of the Province fell under the almost total control of its Stadholder. Instead of holding the office for life the *geëligeerde* were appointed for three years and the Town Councils for one year, in each case by the Stadholder; the nobility were appointed for life, but the Stadholder could extend their number and appoint new members, as well as replace those who died; and he could declare 'unacceptable' anyone appointed by the States of Utrecht to the States-General, that is to say he had a veto, and therefore effectively the power of appointment, without providing any reason for his decision.[19]

The new rule was read out in the chamber of the States of Utrecht on the 26th, but no copies were distributed and the delegates were not aware of the proviso in the States-General resolution of the 20th that the Prince could act only in accordance with the 'privileges'. It was unanimously approved by the Utrecht States; those who expressed qualms were brushed aside by Fagel's telling them that the Province's re-entry into the Union depended on its adoption – the alternative was to be treated as conquered territory; and the Prince let it be known that it was demanded by necessity.[20] On the 27th the Prince took the oath as hereditary Stadholder and Captain- and Admiral-General of the Province.[21]

As in Friesland, where the Prince had appointed Nassau-Odijk as his representative to maintain his grip on the Province, so now in Utrecht he had his clients, the Van Reedes, to fulfil a similar function. But, very influential though they were over appointments within the Province of Utrecht, this clan was not to be the sole recipient of Prince William's trust – we have seen, at the end of the previous chapter, that he told Fagel, in his letter of 21 November 1673, that he was opposed to Amerongen going to Utrecht at that time. Amerongen and his wife deferred too greatly to the traditional authority of the States-General and it was not long before Dijkveld was reinstated to a position of influence; he became a member of the *geëligeerde* in 1677; and when Renswoude died in 1682 Dijkveld took over his position as President of the Utrecht States and permanent deputy to the States-General.[22]

Nevertheless, Renswoude arranged, at the end of October, that the Prince should receive from the States of Utrecht the manor of Zoest, 'not doubting', as Renswoude wrote, 'that Your Highness will always be a good stadholder and protector of the miserable province of Utrecht'.[23] It became one of Prince William's favourite country retreats.

With the military campaigning season approaching the Prince did not have time to address the definitive instalment of governmental institutions in Gelderland and Overijssel, the two other Provinces emerging from the French occupation; this would have to be deferred until he could return from the camp; and, in the meantime, the Count of Limburg-Stirum was appointed Military Governor, and two members of the Prince of Orange's Domestic Council, Wevelinckhoven and Wiertz, were appointed his deputies in the two Provinces.[24] When he did return the ground was prepared to offer him the sovereignty of Gelderland.

THE GRAND ALLIANCE AGAINST LOUIS XIV

Before addressing the 1674 military campaign we need to take a quick glance at the diplomatic scene.

The peace conference at Cologne was coming to nothing. Following the creation of the Grand Alliance with the treaties concluded in August 1673 between the Dutch, the Austrians, Spain and the Duke of Lorraine, Louis XIV indeed reduced his demands, including offering to cede Maastricht on condition that its fortifications were razed. But, as the Dutch pointed out, the whole situation had now changed; they could now only treat alongside their new allies who would need to be admitted into the negotiations. This had far-reaching implications which Louis was anxious to avoid – in particular, he bluntly refused to allow Lorraine to participate in the conference.

The chances of peace were further hampered by the heightening of personal antagonisms. Louvois gave instructions in January 1674 to the Count d'Estrades, the former ambassador to the Dutch Republic who now commanded at Maastricht, to abduct and even to kill Lisola – 'it would be no great inconvenience to kill him…; because he is a man very impertinent in his discourses'. Lisola's vigilance enabled him to avoid this fate. But Prince Wilhelm von Fürstenberg was not to be so fortunate, although what was in store for him fell short of assassination. The Electoral Bishop of Cologne, disheartened by the fall of Bonn and the threats to his territories, was wavering in his support for France, with only Prince Wilhelm morally propping up the distressed prelate. This prop the Austrians now determined to remove. Fürstenberg was attending the Cologne conference as the Bishop's official envoy, and, as such, should have enjoyed diplomatic immunity; but when, on 14 February, he was returning from visiting his mistress, the Gräfin von der Mark, he was abducted by the Austrians, who brought him first to the recently captured Bonn and then to Vienna, where he was treated as a traitor – a German prince furthering French interests.

On 1 March a further provocation occurred when French gold, on its way to the French garrison at Nuys, was seized at the gates of Cologne, which, as the venue for the congress, was deemed to be neutral. An indignant Louis recalled his envoys in the middle of April[25] – an open affront resulting from the seizure of a prominent client in Germany, as Fürstenberg was, was not tolerable, nor was the high tone in which Lisola refused to return the money.

The French King was to suffer further setbacks. On 4 April the Emperor concluded a military alliance with the Elector Palatine, despite the fact that the latter's daughter had married Louis's brother, the Duke of Orléans, upon the death of his first wife, Charles II of England's sister Minette; on the 22nd the Bishop of Münster made his peace with the Emperor and with the Dutch, to whom Bomber Galen restored all his conquests; and in May the unhappy Bishop of Cologne, the majority of whose council and Cathedral Chapter favoured the Emperor, too made his peace, also ceding all his conquests to the Dutch, for which he obtained the rather meagre concession of their withdrawing their rights to garrison Rhineberg. The new alliances did not end there.[26]

Fagel – we can assume the close involvement of the Prince of Orange – was concocting wide-ranging plans with the Republic's two major coalition partners, Austria and Spain.

At a four-hour meeting in Vienna at the end of January the Dutch envoys, Bruynix and Van Heemskerk, met with Montecuccoli and the Austrian chancellor, Hocher, and with the Spanish envoy, to hold a *tour d'horizon* of the European situation. Their aim was to forge alliances with Denmark and the Hanoverian Lüneburg and Brunswick princes, and to enter into a new alliance with the Elector of Brandenburg. The Austrians outlined the considerations in Leopold's mind: he had a total army of 60,000 men; he had to keep an alert eye on the situation in Hungary, always prone to rebellion; affairs in Poland were a concern – an election for a new king was under way following the death of Michael Wisnowiecki in November 1673; he had to subsidise Saxony, Trier and the Duke of Lorraine; and the Holy Roman Empire did not provide him with any money – it all had to come from the Habsburg hereditary lands. On their side the Dutch said that they had an army of about 94,000 men, the Dutch navy was to be brought up to 84 men-of-war plus frigates, and 11 frigates were to be kept in the Mediterranean during the winter; trade was at a standstill in Holland and the 'trading Provinces'; and much of the land which had lain under water, or still did, would need to recover.

The need to rein in Sweden was discussed and Hocher observed that not much could be expected from the Elector of Brandenburg, as he, too, had concerns about the Polish election and he had fears of being exposed to a potential threat from Sweden. They should, therefore, first concentrate on Denmark and the Hanoverian princes, whilst not neglecting the Elector.[27]

These negotiations bore fruit. An initial treaty had already been signed by the Emperor with Denmark on 26 January 1674. On 24 April Leopold signed a treaty with the Dukes of Brunswick and Lüneburg, who, in return for subsidies to be paid by the Dutch and Spaniards, would provide 13,000 men to the allied cause. On 1 July a new treaty was entered into with the Elector of Brandenburg; and on the 10th the Emperor, Spain and the Dutch entered into an alliance with Denmark which, again in return for Dutch and Spanish subsidies, undertook to raise an army of 15,000 men. In March Leopold had concluded defensive and offensive alliances with the Electors of Mainz, Trier and the Palatinate. And on 31 March he was successful in persuading the Diet of the Holy Roman Empire to approve assistance to the Palatinate and other areas threatened by the French King. With the exception of Bavaria and Hanover itself – the House of Brunswick's established practice of supporting opposite sides was maintained – practically the whole of Germany was arraigned against Louis.[28]

Hocher's concerns regarding the difficulties of bringing Brandenburg into the alliance were therefore overcome. As we know, the plight in which the Elector found himself at the end of 1672 and the beginning of 1673 had forced him to negotiate with France, culminating in the Treaty of Vossem on 26 June 1673. But this he soon regretted; the French envoy said that he 'could hardly bear to see or meet anyone and all felt he was ashamed and confused'.[29]

He did not receive all the subsidies due from France;[30] his appreciation of all things Dutch – with the exception of the old republican party of De Witt – and his ties with the House of Orange were always a strong influence in his thinking; the allies' treaty with Denmark provided protection against Sweden's openly joining France; and finally, the uncertainty in Poland was at last resolved by the election of John Sobieski in May. Whilst Sobieski's wife came from an aristocratic family in France and whilst Sobieski's own sympathies lay with that country, the Elector may nevertheless have seen him as a possible champion against the Turks.[31] But, as we shall see, the threat from Sweden was latent, not resolved.

As for William of Orange, he had proclaimed at the end of 1673 that 'the bond between the House of Orange and Brandenburg is as indissoluble as the bond between heaven and earth'.[32]

The main stumbling block in the negotiations between the Elector, the Dutch and the Emperor was that Frederick-William wanted to receive subsidies for 20,000 men, which would give him greater influence, whilst his counterparts were prepared to pay for only 12,000; a compromise figure of 16,000 was finally agreed, with the Dutch and Spain paying for half. We may note that the Elector always desired to maintain his standing army, which enabled him to override the estates in his various territories on the way to establishing his version of absolutism. On this occasion he would have turned to France if he could not have obtained the money from the Dutch.[33] In the Prussia which the Elector was crafting the army effectively became the State – to which, later in history, was added the bureaucracy.

The treaty with the Dutch was signed on 1 July, bringing Brandenburg into alliance as well with Austria and Spain. It contained, however, one provision which was to sour Brandenburg–Dutch relations in the future; at the Elector's own insistence, each of the allies could conclude a separate peace, or armistice, provided it notified the others and assured them of the same terms.[34] The treaty also left the Dutch with the impression that they were absolved from paying any amounts due under the old 1672 treaty.[35]

The Grand Alliance was thus reformed and expanded on a formidable scale. But, if the French were to suffer setbacks on the diplomatic front, events were to develop differently when it came to matters military.

THE WAR ON LAND: OPENING MOVES

France began the campaigning season very early in 1674. In the middle of February Louis learnt that the Elector Palatine had agreed on 14 January to transfer to the Emperor the small town of Germersheim; situated a little distance from the French stronghold of Philippsburg, it also constituted a threat to Alsace and Lorraine. Hearing the news, Louis XIV swiftly decided to occupy the town with his own troops. Although the Elector was about to abandon his neutrality, he had not in fact yet crossed that line, and the infringement of his still neutral state caused considerable commotion in Germany.

In the meantime Louis had already decided that he would also seize Franche-Comté from Spain. Whilst two of the French forces dedicated to this operation had been diverted to the Palatine, a third, under the Duke de Navailles, captured three of its towns in a little over three weeks between 20 February and 15 March. Louis himself left Versailles on 19 April, with Louvois hurrying before him to Franche-Comté to ensure that nothing should detract from his stately progress. On 2 May he arrived at Besançon. And, on the 21st, Vauban neatly presented him with the surrender first of Besançon and then, on 6 June, of Dôle. The rest of Franche-Comté soon followed. Its strategic importance lay in its check on the communications between the Spanish Netherlands and Spain's northern Italian possessions around Milan, the traditional 'Spanish Road' which Spain had used since the 16th century.[36]

Each of the allies opposed to the French King made their plans in 1674 to attack his kingdom in their own way, which, inevitably given the circumstances, could only be loosely cooordinated – there was no overall commanding figure as there was in France. In the event, attacks were mounted from nearly all points of the compass. On the sea the Dutch aimed to use their fleet to threaten the French Atlantic coast and on land they planned to operate in conjunction with Spain in the Spanish Netherlands. The Austrians, with their German allies, were to be divided into two armies, one of which under the Duke of Lorraine would operate on the Rhine and Mosel, and the other, under the Count de Souches – initially under the Count de Bournonville – would seek to join with the Dutch and Spanish armies in the Spanish Netherlands. The Spanish also planned to cross the Pyrenees and mount an attack on Roussillon. In the spring the French evacuated their remaining forces in the United Provinces until, by the beginning of May, all that remained in their hands was Grave and Maastricht, the former of which the Dutch planned to besiege under a force commanded by Rabenhaupt.[37]

THE NAVAL CAMPAIGN AND THE INTERNAL OPPOSITION TO LOUIS XIV

The Dutch aim at sea was to coordinate their actions to coincide with plans for internal revolts germinating in France. A scion of the grand Huguenot House of Rohan, the chevalier Louis de Rohan, was plotting to raise an insurrection in Normandy, as well as in the House's main power base in Brittany; his fellow plotters included a Norman gentleman, Tréaumont, and an aged Dutch philosopher of free-thinking republican inclinations, Van den Ende. There was another plot, inspired by another Huguenot, this time from Languedoc, whose real name – he appeared under a number of guises – was Sardan, an adventurer of dubious repute. There seems to have been some contact between the two sets of plotters and the Prince of Orange's Huguenot secretary, Pierre du Moulin, was also involved, although clarity is lacking. Coenraad van Beuningen, however, was prepared to listen to Sardan who was also able to obtain more than one meeting with Prince William.

The outcome was that the Prince signed an agreement with Sardan on 21 April 1674 in The Hague, which Sardan signed, he said, on behalf of a confederation in the French

Provinces of Guyenne, Languedoc, Dauphin and Provence. The Prince undertook to recommend to the States-General that the Dutch would provide a fleet and troops to support an insurrection by the confederation. The agreement was dependent on the Spanish King entering into a similar agreement under which he would provide a cavalry corps of 2,000 men, with assistance also provided by the Spanish fleet in the Mediterranean; and the intention was to bring the German Emperor into the arrangements as well as to support the troops of the confederation with a cavalry force that would enter France via Franche-Comté – although this part of the plan, of course, was pre-empted by the French seizure of that territory.

Why did Prince William enter into such an arrangement with a person of such uncertain credit as Sardan, of whom he was very mistrustful? He did believe, and consistently reiterated to Fagel, that there were serious discontents in France, but we can observe that the agreement was carefully drafted and committed the Prince to nothing concrete; under a long-standing plan the Dutch fleet was committed to going to sea in any case to harass the French coast and French possessions in the West Indies, and if Sardan could be the medium, however uncertain, for exploiting the discontents in France there was nothing to be lost. Ratification of the agreement by the States-General was dependent on the open declaration of the revolt by the heads of the confederate army and, as this did not materialise, nor did the ratification.[38]

The Prince of Orange wrote to Admiral Michiel De Ruyter on 6 May with detailed instructions for the campaign at sea.[39] De Ruyter had suggested to the Prince a plan to attack the French possessions in the West Indies: Martinique, Guadeloupe and Grenada; it was to be combined with an attack on the west coast of France, which the Prince had contemplated but rejected as impractical the previous year. On 24 May the Dutch fleet put to sea, with De Ruyter in overall command. Arriving off Torbay on 8 June, the fleet, and the soldiers on board, were divided, with De Ruyter and 18 warships and frigates and in excess of 3,300 men departing for the West Indies. Tromp took command of the other half, which consisted of 36 warships and frigates and between 3,000 and 4,000 soldiers and marines, who were commanded by the Count of Hoorn. He weighed anchor on 18 June and reached Belle-Isle, off the coast of Brittany, on the 23rd.[40]

But Louvois had been alerted and had made his preparations. In early 1674 he was warned that taxes and the levies of men for the war were causing discontent within Louis's kingdom. He was informed, too, in March, of Dutch plans to land on the coast of France, in particular, with the help of Huguenots, on the coast of Normandy. Further information reached him in the course of the spring, and by the beginning of June he was aware of the exact plans of the Dutch. These had been made available to him by a servitor in the Prince of Orange's entourage named Launoy, of whom more later. Tromp, therefore, found the coasts of France in such a state of defence that he was unable to achieve anything of significance.[41]

He accordingly sailed on to St Sebastian on the Spanish coast, where he arrived on 31 July and where he was persuaded by the Spaniards to sail into the Mediterranean, despite his lack of orders to do so, to assist them there in their endeavours against France. But a Spanish fleet with 7,000 veterans departed to Messina in Sicily, where a revolt against Spanish rule had broken out, and its departure prevented the plan that the Dutch had discussed with the Spanish court to attack French ships in their harbours – in particular to mount an assault on Toulon. Hence not much was achieved in the Mediterranean either. The Dutch refused a request from the Spanish Queen Mother to go to Messina; and on 2 October the States-General and the Prince of Orange sent a strongly worded missive disapproving of the conduct of the fleet's commanders and ordering them home.

In the West Indies, as well, the French had been forewarned of the Dutch plans and these too proved abortive.[42]

As for the conspirators against Louis XIV, Louvois was able to uncover the circle in Brittany and Normandy, with the consequence that Tréaumont was killed whilst being arrested and the Chevalier de Rohan and Van den Ende mounted the scaffold in Paris.[43] Sardan's identity was revealed to Louvois through Launoy at the end of July and his somewhat fantastical plans, which William of Orange considered chimerical, ran into the sand.[44] The Prince did send Riomal, a Protestant native of the Principality of Orange, to Genoa to cooperate with the insurrection should it happen and to deal with the financial aspects, although he made certain that the sums provided were very modest and subject to strict control lest the putative insurrectionists sought to divert them for their personal gain.[45] Riomal made a plan in July which envisaged sending a modest expedition up the Rhône to capture some of its towns, with Orange possibly foremost, and which, if successful, could then link up with a general revolt to be led by Sardan; but this did not materialise.[46] Prince William's scepticism about the whole of Sardan's plans was fully justified; but it was worth taking a chance that they might fly, and they did constitute a distraction for Louis XIV, with Louvois being compelled to send forces to man the French Atlantic coast.

The Prince was also unlucky. The fiscal demands of the war led a year later to very serious popular discontents in France; in March 1675 Louis faced rebellions in Bordeaux, which spread and soon extended to the rest of Guyenne and to Brittany, and which could be suppressed only by means of mass executions. The Dutch fleet in 1674 had arrived a year too early.[47]

And William, furthermore, had demonstrated that he was quite aware of the potential of sea-power in his strategic thinking.

THE LAND CAMPAIGN

On land Prince William set the Dutch campaign in motion by ordering the infantry and part of the cavalry to march to Bergen op Zoom in April and May – much later than the

French, who, as we have seen, were in action earlier in the year, their abilities enhanced by Louvois's much more sophisticated supply system based on well-stocked magazines. On 10 May Waldeck was in Brussels to coordinate plans with the Spanish commanders, the Count of Monterey and the Marquis d'Assentar, whilst the Marquis De Grana represented the Emperor. The next day the Prince of Orange took leave of the States-General in The Hague to join the army at its assembly point at Bergen op Zoom and the nearby Rozendaal, where he arrived on the 13th. There he reviewed his troops of 8,000 horse and 16,000 foot; he broke camp on the 15th and arrived with the army at Duffel, just to the south of Antwerp and within easy reach of Brussels, on the 17th.[48]

It may help to explain the peculiar nature of warfare in the Spanish Netherlands in this era. All the towns were fortified and garrisoned; and under the Treaty of Aix-la-Chapelle, the French had acquired towns which were very much intermingled with those of the Spanish.[49] The war was therefore a matter of sieges and presented a picture of some complexity, as the main field armies moved between the variously held towns either to besiege them or to relieve them from siege. The garrisons of towns belonging to the same side supported each other whilst doing what they could to impede the communications of the other side – many of the most important towns were situated on the rivers, which constituted the main supply routes.

On 12 May the Marquis de Bellefonds arrived at Maastricht at the head of the rest of the garrisons that Luxemburg had left in the Dutch Republic, and, without much difficulty, he captured the fortresses of Navagne and Argenteau, situated on the Maas, a little distance from Maastricht, where they could hinder the communications with Huy and Dinant. On the 23rd he handed over his command to Condé, who had come to meet him. Louis XIV had a soft spot for De Bellefonds and allowed him unusual licence. Of this the wilful Marquis had taken full advantage and Condé had been 'in mortal fear' that the insubordination and incompetence with which he had conducted his line of retreat would leave him exposed to surprise and defeat by the Imperial troops.[50]

On 18 May, at Duffel, the Prince of Orange was receiving intelligence of the French movements, of which he kept the *Secrète Besogne* of the States-General informed. On the 21st he reported the fall of Argenteau after a weak resistance and that Navagne was being besieged; but he was told that the Imperial army was on its way to lend assistance to the besieged fortress and that this army had made preparations to cross the Roer on the 19th, so that he expected its arrival in the region of Navagne at the time he was writing. He also had news that Condé was marching to join De Bellefonds and that, if this junction was successfully completed before De Bellefonds could be attacked by the Imperial army, it was to be feared that the rescue of Navagne would prove abortive. He had hoped that his own army could have rescued the place, but this proved impossible as all his troops had not yet joined him and the artillery and supply wagons had been held up.[51] As we have seen, the two fortified towns fell and the Imperial army did not materialise.

We have mentioned that Duffel was within easy reach of Brussels, where Monterey was based, and he and the Prince were in close communication. They had met on the 18th at Mechelen, outside Brussels, and they held a war council on the 22nd in Brussels itself, which was also attended by Waldeck and Prince Maurits of Nassau-Siegen, and where every honour was shown the Prince – a magnificent banquet was held in his honour.[52] On the main strategy they were of one mind, as is evident from their correspondence. Prince William wanted to march on Namur, which lay on the Maas, and this would have cut off the French communications between Charleroi and Maastricht whilst also threatening France itself. But this was subject to the Austrian commander, the Duc de Bournonville at this stage, agreeing to a junction of their armies, and also to Condé not making a threatening thrust towards the north – he was in fact moving in the opposite direction, south, back to France, to Perwetz near Charleroi, as Monterey confirmed on the 28th. Monterey's intelligence, which he fully shared with the Prince of Orange, was excellent. He agreed with the Prince's strategic thinking, but he anticipated difficulties from the Duc de Bournonville.[53]

At the end of May De Bournonville was succeeded by the Comte de Souches, a Frenchman by birth;[54] and, if the lack of vigour of De Bournonville had been frustrating the plans of the Prince of Orange, the indecisiveness, the incompetence, the eccentricity and the stubbornness of his successor were to bring disastrous consequences. June was devoted, both by the Dutch and the Spaniards, to trying to persuade him to formulate plans for a joint operation. His state of mind, however, was succinctly expressed by a Spanish representative, who had attended a long meeting, at the end of which he was told 'after much argument that [de Souches] would march, but he could not say where'.[55] During the first part of June the main camp of the Austrian army was situated between Düren, on the Roer river, and Lechenich, to the east of Aachen. On the 16th it left the Roer and arrived at Andenne, on the Maas near Namur, on the 27th.[56] But De Souches refused to cross the Maas to join with the Dutch and Spanish.

On 2 July a summit of the commanders of the allied armies took place at Landen, which included the Prince, Waldeck, Monterey and De Souches. Before the Prince arrived Waldeck sounded out De Souches on his views and was told that he could not cross the Maas because De Bournonville, who had taken over command of the allied troops on the Upper Rhine, did not have sufficient strength to confront Turenne. His orders were expressly not to abandon the Rhine, whilst he claimed that the diversion he was causing by his threat to Champagne would create space for the Dutch and the Spanish to act. But he then said in contradiction to that claim that the allied army, which he put at 45,000 men, lacked sufficient strength to carry out the contemplated plans. He added that his troops, who lacked money and victuals, might mutiny if they were ordered to cross the Maas.[57]

When Prince William arrived at seven o'clock in the evening these preliminaries were not very promising. The Prince argued that if the Imperial troops crossed the Maas Condé would have to choose between giving battle with inferior forces or retreating, leaving the allies masters of the country and being able to capture Charleroi without risk. It made no impression on De Souches, who cited the danger to the Palatinate and his orders from the Emperor. This set off a long harangue from the Prince of Orange.[58]

He represented to De Souches that the interests of Austria would be best served if some considerable town could be seized which would both secure the Spanish Low Countries and facilitate entry into France, thus safeguarding the German Empire and drawing the war away from the Rhine. It would also encourage the United Provinces to continue to provide the necessary means to continue the war. Otherwise it was to be feared that, if they stuck to the defensive, discontent in the United Provinces would become so widespread that a sudden precipitous outcome could result, with dangerous consequences. To maintain their troops the Dutch were having to spend their money outside their borders and they could not continue the war for long on this footing. There were too many ill-disposed people in the Republic; there were already thousands of false rumours concerning the Prince himself, which needed to be dissipated by a spectacular achievement that would provide justification for the great expenditure being incurred by the Dutch State. Finally, he said, the inhabitants of the Spanish Netherlands were seeing themselves being ruined by the allied armies, which could make them less inclined to submit to the contributions being levied on them for their own defence, with the consequence that a French conquest could become all too easy.

De Souches remained unconvinced and the meeting broke up without a decision. He was unable to decide on any of the numerous courses of action that presented themselves to his impractical imagination, and his changes of mind exasperated both the Prince of Orange and the Count of Monterey.[59]

On 6 July Prince William wrote to the Dutch envoy in Vienna, Coenraad van Heemskerk, urging him to get in touch with Montecuccoli to beseech him to use his influence with the Emperor to order De Souches to join forces with the Dutch and Spaniards and seek battle with Condé. The latter was situated at this time at Ath to the south-west of Brussels and since 11 June the Prince's army had been positioned around Vilvoorde just to the north-east of the city. Prince William's information was that Condé had an army of about 40,000 effectives, who, he said, were expected to be reinforced with a further 8,000 or 10,000 men. He maintained that the allied forces combined would far outnumber the French if only the Austrians could now cross the Maas and join him and the Spaniards.[60]

At last, after weeks when both the French and the allies in the Spanish Netherlands had engaged in sterile manoeuvring, matters were coming to a head. On 13 July Monterey advised the Prince that Condé was marching towards Charleroi. William at once beseeched Monterey 'in the name of God not to lose a moment of time to send the necessary orders' to those Spanish troops which were available to join him, so that they could march on Condé together without bothering about the Imperialists – it was the only way to force the hand of De Souches and overcome his indecision. On the 16th, the Dutch army marched to Louvain, where William reviewed his army of 30,000 men, and where he was joined by 10,000 Spanish troops. The desired effect was achieved; on the 25th the Dutch, the Spanish and – lo! – the Imperial armies under De Souches joined forces at Meerdorp, to the north of Namur. The Prince advised the *Secrète Besogne* of the States-General on the 29th, from Perwetz, that the Imperial infantry had now also arrived, and that the plan was to march the following day to seek out Condé, who was at Trazegnies, on a small river, the Piéton, between Charleroi and Seneffe.[61] At long last Prince William's overriding objective of combining the allied forces had been achieved and he was now looking forward to the battle that he had longed for.

THE BATTLE OF SENEFFE

The army advanced to Nivelle, from where the Prince again wrote to the *Secrète Besogne*, on 7 August, to say that the hope had been to bring the Prince of Condé to battle; he lay close by, but had not emerged from his strong position, protected by the Piéton; the allies would be at too great a disadvantage if they were to attack him there; and it had therefore been resolved to lure him from it by creating a diversion.[62] The following day the allies marched to pitch their camp between Arche and Seneffe. The diversion Monterey had in mind was to besiege Ath, which posed a threat to Brussels, but both the Prince and De Souches wanted something more spectacular – to advance southwards on Quesnoy, Douai or St-Quentin, and the latter opinion prevailed.[63] It would cut off Condé from France and force him to leave his position.[64]

As always there are no reliable figures on the strengths of the opposing armies; the allied army has been put at no more than 60,000 men (30,000 Dutch, 12,000 Spanish and the remainder, that is about 18,000, Imperial); and Condé's army at between 45,000 and 50,000.[65]

On the morning of the 11th the allied army began their march with the intention of next camping between Marimont and Binche. This necessitated their marching past the French army, which lay a short hour away on their left flank, but this flank was well protected by streams and woods. The Imperial troops formed the vanguard, the Dutch were in the middle, and the Spanish under the Prince de Vaudemont took up the rear. To protect the rear De Vaudemont had been supplied with a special detachment of 4,000 cavalry and 700 or 800 dragoons drawn from all three armies. The army was to advance in three columns, the one on the left, closest to the enemy, composed of the cavalry, the one in the middle the infantry, and the one on the right the artillery and baggage train.

A mistake occurred almost at once. It had been agreed the previous night, and it was reiterated in the morning, that the baggage train should be the first to leave camp and that De Souches should not do so before this had taken place; the reverse happened and the baggage train was left without sufficient protection. Nor did De Souches hold himself to the marching order of three columns. There was therefore some disorder from the beginning.

Observing the allied army from his horse as dawn broke was the Prince de Condé. For such an outstanding commander this was an opportunity not to be missed. He decided to attack the rearguard.

'And after we had been marching in this manner for a few hours', the Prince of Orange later reported in his official account to the States-General, 'the Prince de Vaudemont sent news that the enemy had appeared with some troops and that skirmishing had already begun, asking that two battalions of foot should be sent to him.' De Vaudemont found himself hemmed in, in broken country where it was difficult for his cavalry to operate, hence his request for infantry. The Prince decided to send him three companies from the regiments of Prince Maurits of Nassau-Siegen and of Maurits's young nephew and William's cousin, the Friesian Stadholder, Hendrik-Casimir, Count of Nassau, under the latter's command. Arraigned to defend the bridge at Seneffe, with the cavalry of De Vaudemont's special detachment in support behind them, they were vigorously attacked by the enemy's infantry, dragoons and cavalry. They were resisting strongly, but were then forced to retreat by an outflanking movement from the French. Condé himself led a cavalry charge at the head of the Maison du Roi, and the retreat turned to a rout despite the bravest attempts of the Prince de Vaudemont to stem the fleeing swarm.

The battle now commenced its second phase. The Prince of Orange, who himself had also participated in the latter part of the engagement at Seneffe, withdrew to a new location on a small hill at St-Nicholas-aux-Bois, half an hour south from Seneffe. It was occupied by Dutch troops, Spanish cavalry, commanded by the Duke of Villa Hermosa, and the remains of the rearguard detachment. Surrounded by orchards and hedges, it was a strong defensive post. A fierce conflict now developed in which the Spanish Marquis d'Assentar, displaying, Prince William said, extraordinary courage in trying to rally his troops, finally succumbed to the seven wounds he received. Waldeck, too, did what he could to counter the disorder into which the troops were falling. He took command of a squadron of cavalry to lead a charge against the enemy flank; but he found himself alone and cut off. Despite his wounds he managed to find his way back, cutting down two of the enemy in the process, and was forced to retire from the field. Once again the allied troops were driven from their position.

They retreated to the village of Fay, where Prince William took up another defensive position on an elevation protected on one side by hedges and small woods and on the other by a broad ravine, where the third and final phase of the battle took place. The Dutch commanders included Prince Maurits of Nassau-Siegen, the Rhinegrave and the Count of Nassau. Just as the retreating troops arrived at Fay they were joined by a large number of the Imperial troops. When he first received news of what was happening at Seneffe, De Souches was at Haine, about two hours south, and his return to the main army had been impeded by a French assault, which he had managed to beat off. It was now about midday and the battle raged late into the night, the terrain illuminated by the light of the moon.

In 17th-century battles the reputations of the aristocracy were at stake and were closely scrutinised, carefully assessed and minutely weighed. It led them to take huge physical risks. On the French side Condé, with his son, the Duc d'Enghien, at his side, personally led his troops forward and had three horses shot from beneath him. On the allied side Prince William in his official account of the battle took great care to address the personal performances of the commanders. He did not stint in his praise of Prince Maurits of Nassau-Siegen, who, he said, performed with a vigour beyond his years, even though he had only just emerged from a sickness from which he had not yet fully recovered; and the Rhinegrave also received fulsome praise from the Prince: 'one can say with truth that a great deal of the success of this battle was due to his courage and good leadership'. De Souches's bravery and vigour were also mentioned – his faults did not lie in that direction; but the Dutch lost their wagon train as a result of his failure to comply with requests to ensure its safety, and the Prince changed his despatch to add – and underline – a section to make very clear where the blame should lie. As for the Prince himself, the praise came from his opponent – 'a proven commander in the field', said Condé, 'except for the over-exposure of his own person'. William too, it is said, had several horses killed beneath him; and Nassau-Ouwekerk, the commander of his lifeguard, received a severe head wound when he tried to defend him from a pistol shot.

Not everyone was deemed to have done his duty; a major in the guard of the Prince of Orange was subsequently beheaded for dereliction in his conduct; and several other officers were court-martialled.

Finally the battle ceased from mutual exhaustion – it is not clear who left the field first: the Dutch accounts say the French, the French the reverse. Condé wished to renew the battle the following day, but found his men were too spent to do so; his army returned to the camp on the Piéton whence it had emerged.[66]

It had been a bloody battle and the casualties shocked contemporaries. The Intendant Robert, who had so oppressed the Dutch when he was in occupied Utrecht, now had the task of tending the French dead and wounded, 3,000 and 4,000 respectively. Prestige and status were paid for in blood; the Maison du Roi, which had fought so gallantly, lost 500 dead and 600 wounded; in the army as a whole one officer was a casualty for every seven men. When the news reached Paris, Madame de Sévigné expressed her reaction: 'We have lost so many in this victory that without the *Te Deum* and some flags carried to Notre-Dame we could believe ourselves to have lost the battle.'[67]

There is no reliable account of the losses on the allied side but they may have been much the same as those of the French, although the French may have lost proportionately more in dead and wounded and the allies in prisoners.[68]

It needs to be remembered that the allies had no overall commander; the Prince, De

Souches and Monterey had equal rights over decisions and dispositions. Even the well-disposed Monterey had initially refused to address the Prince as *Altesse* and the Prince had to have recourse to his own personal envoy in Madrid, Chiege, who operated there in parallel with the official Dutch representative, to remonstrate; and in 1673 Monterey had raised difficulties about the right to issue the password to the troops.[69] Orders had indeed been sent from Vienna to De Souches on 6 August that he was to act in accordance with the majority decision taken by the allies, but, as we have seen, this was something that he resolutely refused to do.[70] The lack, in practice, of an overall command to a degree reduced the advantage in numbers that Prince William had over Condé.

The Prince had, however, nothing to complain about over the quality of his troops: 'We have seen our infantry perform marvels,' he wrote to the Duke of Celle on the news that the Duke's troops were on their way to join the allies following the treaty he entered into in July. The efforts of the Dutch commanders to bring their troops up to the required level had borne fruit.

In his conduct of the battle William can be absolved from the accusation that he exposed the allies to a flank attack by marching past Condé's encampment – the protection afforded by the streams and woods decided the French general to launch his attack on the rearguard and not on the flank. When the day ended Condé had, with the expense of much blood, achieved a draw, as had the Prince of Orange, with the same cost.

Both sides decided to treat the outcome as a victory and Prince William received a generous letter of praise from the States-General, who urged him to take greater care of his person. Clearly word had spread of his heedlessness for his own safety. The Spanish ambassador in The Hague, De Lira, added his congratulations and he too admonished the Prince for not taking greater care of himself: 'I cannot omit the very humble prayer which I submit to Your Highness in the interests of the common cause that Your Highness in future should not expose his person for the sake of glory [*la gloire*], in the way he has done in this engagement.'[71] It was a shrewd observation.

From an early stage the Prince had been very determined to seek battle with Condé because, as his servitor, Launoy, revealed to the Count d'Estrades at the end of July, it would enable him 'to establish his reputation'; whatever the outcome, 'he could only but acquire reputation in fighting against such a great captain as M. le prince de Condé'.[72] When William Temple also added his voice to those urging greater caution on the Prince he replied that his 'life was less dear to him than the satisfaction of fulfilling that which was expected of him'.[73] These expectations were consonant with the heritage of great deeds which his ancestors in the House of Orange-Nassau had bequeathed him, the *gloire* which it was incumbent on him in turn to bequeath to history and posterity, gilded and embellished by his own deeds.

There was a religious aspect which should not be overlooked and which intertwined with political considerations. *Gloire* brought power in its train – the lustre, the status and the prestige of the Prince enhanced his allure as he stood at the centre of his patronage system – and power of itself was perceived as a manifestation of divine sanction; to repeat the quote, 'the powers that be are ordained of God'. In Calvinistic terms both the successful deeds that brought the *gloire* and the power could be seen as a sign of God's grace. Louis saw it in slightly different terms; he saw God as an extremely grand patron and himself as an extremely grand client, politely and respectfully below – although perhaps only a little below – the Divinity; two gentlemen, as it were, who understood each other and fundamentally had the same values. But he too looked for manifestations of God's favour; and, when matters did not go as he wished, grumbled, as a hardworking client would, that he deserved better after all he had done for his Patron.

On the 18th the army marched to Quiévrain, closer to France. There, on the 31st, a large convoy arrived from Brussels, consisting of several hundred wagons, bringing much-needed supplies, including money for a month's salary for the troops paid for under the reparation provided by the Province of Holland – the Prince urged the other Provinces to follow suit for the troops for which they were responsible. With the convoy arrived five Dutch regiments seconded to the Spanish garrisons, so that the loss in numbers suffered in the battle of Seneffe could be somewhat replenished.[74] William found time to negotiate a prisoner exchange with the Duke of Monmouth, Charles II's illegitimate son, who was serving with the French, for his grandmother's brother, the Count of Solms-Braunfels, who was a colonel in his guards and who had been captured during the battle.[75]

CONTINUING ECCENTRICITIES OF DE SOUCHES

On 23 August a council of war, attended by the heads of all the allied forces, was held, when Monterey's proposal to besiege Ath on 6 September was unanimously agreed, after which Monterey returned to Brussels to put in hand all the necessary preparations under his personal supervision. On 3 September a further council confirmed the resolution to besiege Ath and it was decided that a detachment of troops, 5,000 horse and all the dragoons, was to be sent on the 7th, under the command of the Duke of Lorraine, to commence the siege, to be followed the next day by the whole army. De Souches had withdrawn to Valenciennes, 'under the pretext of some slight indisposition', as the Prince was later to put it, but he returned late on the 6th. There the decisions taken on the 3rd were confirmed anew without any opposition from the Austrian commander. On the 7th he expressed his anxiety that the despatch of the detachment would weaken the army; but, when it was represented to him that without the detachment the French could throw reinforcements into Ath as soon as they detected the allies' intentions by their line of march, he conceded the point. Then, however, he again changed his mind, this time informing the Prince, at 4am on the 8th, when the main army was on the point of commencing its march, that he was after all opposed to the siege of Ath. This, to the consternation of the Prince of Orange, necessitated recalling the detachment and countermanding the orders given to the main body of the army. It looked as though the campaign would have to come to an unsatisfactory end. The young Prince wrote in frustration to Fagel, almost as though he were turning to a father figure, 'It will be a long time before I will come round to consoling myself.'

It was in sterner terms that he also wrote on the same day to Coenraad van Heemskerk in Vienna; he gave a detailed account of exactly what had happened, which was to be conveyed by the Dutch envoy to the Austrian Emperor; and he ended by saying that his narration demonstrated the ample grounds for complaint regarding the 'irresolution' of De Souches, 'not to say anything worse'. This intimation of cowardice was indeed as strong an indictment of a general as could be made – was there perhaps not even a suspicion of treason, given De Souches's French background? According to Burnet the Prince related to him that he told De Souches's son 'that his father had acted so basely that if it had not been for the respect he bore the emperor he would have shot him in the head'.[76]

The unpredictable Austrian commander now suggested the siege of Oudenarde instead of Ath. To this Prince William at once agreed – it would at least be something, although Oudenarde was well provisioned, could just as easily be reinforced as Ath, and, furthermore, could be protected on its north and south sides by flooding.[77] It lay on the Scheldt some distance due west of Brussels. The allied army arrived before the town on the 15th, work on the opening of the trenches having commenced the previous night. Prince William was informed that Condé had reached the neighbourhood of Leuze on the 17th.[78] He had been reinforced by drawing troops from the French garrisons and his army stood at about 50,000 men. In the meantime Vauban had been able to scramble into Oudenarde to conduct its defence.[79]

It did not take long before De Souches once more manifested the peculiarities of his personality. He refused to commence work on the circumvallation or to set up an appropriate camp. He asked Prince William for Dutch troops – the Prince, to avoid giving him any cause for complaint, sent him a brigade of cavalry and six regiments of foot, assuring him furthermore of other reinforcements if he had need of them. On the pretext of being indisposed De Souches did not attend a council of war. His cannon fired from a nearby height too distant to do the enemy any harm; and when he finally agreed to commence work on the lines he demanded 3,000 of the available 5,000 troops to do the work – 2,000 were put at his disposal, who even then were not immediately set to work.

On the 19th the allies received news that Condé had crossed the Scheldt at Doornik and was marching towards them. On the 20th it was decided to occupy a dominating height, but De Souches's absence prevented the execution of the plan until the following day. That night, without any consultation and after he had agreed that the allies should march towards the enemy, he sent all his artillery, powder and ammunition to Ghent. Furthermore, he left ten guns, which the Dutch had lent him, on the periphery of the post occupied by the Dutch troops that the Prince had seconded to the Imperial army. His intention was to blame the Dutch for their loss, but fortunately they were found in time and, just as fortunately, horses were also available to drag them away. On the 21st the enemy had arrived with his full might and the chance of occupying the strategic heights was lost. There was nothing to be done but for the allies to retreat as best they could, in which they were assisted by the descent of a thick mist.

But their travails at the hands of the Imperial commander were not yet at an end; instead of forming the rearguard, as had been agreed, he took a different direction, during which he managed to traverse the lines of the army and cause the utmost disorder. The rain came down and the infantry were compelled to march through watercourses up to their waists.

In view of the advanced season the Prince thought it would be very difficult now to do anything substantial in what remained of the campaigning season. The army retreated towards Ghent. It was left alone by Condé, and the French were satisfied that they had gained a considerable success;[80] the menacing threat that the combined allied army had presented to the borders of France itself and which lay at the heart of the Prince of Orange's strategy, as it did in 1672 with the thrust towards Charleroi, had again been headed off.

The Prince's anger was savage. The above account of what transpired at Oudenarde is contained in his very detailed despatch to the *Secrète Besogne* dated 25 September,[81] and he sent copies to both Monterey and the Austrian Emperor. 'As it is of the utmost importance', he wrote to Monterey, 'that the irreparable harm which this man [De Souches] has inflicted on Europe should not remain unpunished, I should say to Your Excellency that I shall always stand ready to join you in whatever you think appropriate should be done concerning him, and to employ my credit with the States to obtain their concurrence; I even believe that the majority of the officers of his army would take our part against him.' The Prince of Orange was a dangerous man to cross and he was relentless. De Souches was recalled and departed for Vienna on 1 November.[82]

So angry was the Prince, and so frustrated, that he proposed to leave the army and return in dudgeon to The Hague. It was Waldeck who saved him from this, perceiving at once the propaganda opportunity it could give his opponents, who could present him as having abandoned the army and vacated the field. He invoked both the Prince's *gloire* and God. What caused him to remonstrate as a loyal servitor, he wrote, was the service of the State, the wellbeing of the whole of Europe and the *gloire* of His Highness: 'The *gloire* of Princes who are in the position in which your Highness finds himself does not lie in abandoning in a mood of chagrin the cause of God and of the whole of Europe.' A beneficent God had miraculously guided the Prince through the disorders of the Dutch Republic, and thanks to God's benediction and the Prince's own steadfastness. Waldeck lists a whole range of achievements, which, indeed, were real enough – the Republic had been delivered from its miseries and the war had been pushed back from its frontiers; the most substantial powers in Europe had been brought on to the Dutch side; peace had been extracted from England; fortresses had been captured; alarm had befallen France; and in the battle of Seneffe the Prince had succeeded, in the midst of great disorders, in disengaging the army, with its artillery and equipment intact, and had conducted its withdrawal in full view of the enemy, whilst being deserted by De Souches. The Prince would not wish his vexation to injure his service to God, who was his 'Protector and Guide', nor to allow his enemies to use the occasion of his departure to attribute to fortuity what had been gained by his judgement and courage. The Prince alone was now, after God, arbiter of war and peace – as Louis XIV himself was aware. 'In the name of God,' Waldeck appealed, 'in the name of God again, remain steadfast, Monseigneur…'; and should the Prince decide to leave, let him at least do so in a manner which did not leave his *gloire* at risk.[83] It did the trick and the Prince abandoned his intention of returning to The Hague. There can be no doubt that Waldeck resorted to appealing to the Prince's *gloire* and presented him as God's instrument because he knew that these were William's own sentiments – we may note, too, the link between his *gloire* and his divine mission.

THE DUTCH SIEGE AND CAPTURE OF GRAVE

At hand there was one other enterprise which could still be undertaken, which would not look as though Prince William was abandoning the field, and which could to an extent offset the opportunities lost. Apart from Maastricht, Grave, near Nijmegen, was the last town in the Dutch Republic still occupied by the French. It had a garrison of 4,000 men and it was commanded by the Marquis de Chamilly; 38 years of age, he had earned his fame by serving in several European countries, and he had a considerable military reputation. Grave was well provisioned with munitions – the largest part of the French artillery had ended up there, perhaps 450 or 500 pieces.[84] It was, however, not so well provided with victuals for the men.

The siege had been entrusted to the Dutch commander Rabenhaupt, who had distinguished himself defending Groningen, in Friesland, in 1672. It had begun on 29 July, and by the middle of August it was conducted, it was said, by 16,000 men. But Rabenhaupt's abilities in attack did not equal his achievements in defence, and little progress was being made. Grave contained a large part of the Dutch hostages the French had taken with them when they evacuated the Republic, but the French managed to slip these past the besiegers to Maastricht at the end of August – they represented a considerable financial loss.[85]

When he learnt that Condé had put his army into winter quarters Prince William left the army in the Spanish Netherlands on 6 October under the command of Waldeck, and departed for Grave with the Count of Nassau, Nassau-Ouwekerk, Bentinck and a small following. He arrived at Grave in the evening of the 9th, having been in the saddle for 17 hours in order to avoid a French force which had been ordered from Maastricht and which was lying in wait for him. He told the *Secrète Besogne* that he found the siege not as advanced as he had hoped.[86] His determination, and his ruthlessness, now to capture Grave, and the price which he was prepared to pay, soon became manifest.

On the night of 11/12 October the town was stormed, with the Prince at the head of his troops. Chamilly, however, rallied his own troops, sword in hand, and the French remained masters of the points at which the assault was directed. The following night another assault took place, this time on all fronts, and this too failed, with the spilling of much blood; and yet again the action was resumed on the next night. Still the fortress held out. On the fourth night, the night of 16/17th, two storm columns attacked the covered way between 10 and 11pm led by Prince William in person, who put his life at risk with a courage bordering on recklessness; mounted on his horse he urged his men on. But again the resistance was too strong. Yet again, in the morning, the Prince ordered his tired troops to attack the covered way and yet again the Dutch failed and were driven back. The losses on both sides, but particularly amongst the attackers, were extremely heavy.

But the garrison was running out of food[87] and it was too distant to be rescued. Then, in the evening of the 24th, Chamilly finally received the consent of Louis XIV to capitulate. On the 28th he marched out of Grave with the full military honours the Prince of Orange granted him and which he so richly deserved.[88] The Prince wrote to D'Estrades at Maastricht that he had provided horses to pull the boats required to evacuate the French wounded and that he would provide them with bread – 'he was firmly persuaded that they would not complain of the treatment they received'; and he was confident that he had sufficient credit with the Imperialists and with the Spaniards to assure D'Estrades that he did not envisage any difficulties regarding the passports the wounded would require. Some 24 pieces of cannon were also returned to Maastricht. Why did he do it? Old Le Tellier, the father of Louvois, thought that it was done to cause himself to be honoured and to demonstrate that 'il estime les honnêtes hommes et aime la vertu'[89] – he respected gallant behaviour. But, in sending the cannon to Maastricht, there was also a touch of hauteur – a gesture approaching contemptuous condescension for his French cousin.

The Prince ordered a service of thanksgiving and at the beginning of November the States-General, too, ordered services throughout the land.[90]

The Prince did not neglect to maintain good relations with the Austrian Emperor, despite the unfortunate experiences he had had with De Souches; Leopold had written to him a letter which is now lost but whose contents we can guess from the Prince's reply on 25 October. He would, William wrote, always commit his utmost *gloire*, that is, in this context, his personal standing and prestige – perhaps also his clientship – to reciprocate the generous sentiments of the Emperor. He also wrote on the same date and in similar terms to the Spanish Queen Mother and Regent when he said that 'his greatest passion would always be to give her proof … of the part he would play for the *gloire* and advancement of the very august House of Austria'.

On the 29th the Prince left Grave to return to the army in the Spanish Netherlands for a few days and thence to The Hague, where he arrived on 10 November.[91]

The Imperial army, now commanded by Count Sporck, went into winter quarters in the Liège and Cologne territories, having first captured Huy and Dinant, whilst the Spanish took up their quarters within their fortified towns.[92] It was a disappointing end to the campaign that at one stage had promised so much. The Prince of Orange's fundamental plan of striking deep towards the frontiers of France to threaten that country and to cut the enemy's line of communications, as in the two previous campaigning seasons, was fundamentally sound. In its execution he had been severely handicapped by the vagaries of De Souches, but nevertheless he had rescued the allied army from the confusion at Seneffe, for which those vagaries were much to blame – from Condé himself. He did have superior forces and, given that, his essential aim of seeking battle with Condé was the right one, but it did presuppose intelligent cooperation from his ally. Nevertheless, it cannot be claimed that the military attainments of Prince William III of Orange could reach the same tactical level as those of a Condé or a Turenne. It was in his expansive vision and the imaginative combination of military strategy, of politics and of diplomacy across the whole European scene that his talents lay.

THE CAMPAIGN ON THE RHINE

The efforts of the allies on the Rhine had also not met with success. On 16 June Turenne had defeated, at Sinzheim, near Baden-Baden, the Duke of Lorraine and the Imperial general Caprara, who were on their way to the Palatinate with 8,000 men, to join the rest of the Imperial army under De Bournonville, based to the north near Frankfurt. When confronted by the victorious Turenne the Imperial army, which had advanced to below Heidelberg, retreated to Frankfurt, there to await the various contingents from the Empire, who were proving somewhat slow in coming.[93]

Meanwhile the contributions levied by the French on the local population in the Palatinate were not being paid and, when the French resorted to burning, the peasants, encouraged by their Elector, turned to a vicious guerrilla campaign against the invaders. Further burnings and devastations by the French resulted, and they laid waste the approaches to the French fortress of Philippsburg.[94]

On 23 August a council of war of the chiefs of the German forces was held at Frankfurt. The forces from Zell, Wolfenbüttel and Lüneburg, as well as those of the Bishop of Münster, who was now on the Imperial side, had presently arrived. The troops of the Elector of Brandenburg, who were mustering at Magdeburg, were still awaited, but as Turenne's army appeared to be much smaller than theirs, the Germans decided to march towards him and push him out of Alsace. At the end of August they crossed the Rhine at Mainz with about 30,000 men and 30 pieces of cannon; but they had erred in their estimate of Turenne's strength – they believed he had scarcely 12,000 or 13,000 men, when he had almost double that number and his artillery was equal to that of the Germans.[95] The Germans marched towards Strasburg, which they captured at the end of September.[96] In the meantime the Elector of Brandenburg was on his way with his army and, to pre-empt his joining with the German army under De Bournonville, Turenne attacked the Germans at Enzheim on 4 October; an inconclusive engagement, it did not prevent the Elector's arrival at Strasburg in the middle of October with 16,000 men. Here the Duke of Brunswick-Celle also arrived with 2,500 men so that the German army now amounted to 50,000; overall command lay with the Elector, but decisions had to be taken by majority vote.

In the Spanish Netherlands the campaigning season was now at an end and Turenne received reinforcements from Condé's army. But no major engagement resulted and at the end of November the various contingents of the German army went into winter quarters.[97]

Turenne, however, was not content – a winter campaign did not deter him. At the end of October he had taken up position at Dettwiller, between Saverne and Haguenot, to the north-east of Strasburg. At the beginning of December he learnt that the Germans had taken up their winter quarters at Schellestadt and Colmar, to the south-east of Strasburg. He crossed the Vosges mountains and descended upon the unsuspecting Germans, took them by surprise and found the Elector of Brandenburg with between 30,000 and 40,000 men between Colmar and Turkheim. Here the battle of Turkheim took place on 5 January 1675; the allied troops were forced to retreat to Schellestadt, abandoning their camp at Colmar; and between 10 and 12 January they recrossed the Rhine at Strasburg, which fell into French hands. The French now commanded the whole of the left bank of the Rhine from Basel to Mainz.[98] If Condé had proved his brilliance at Seneffe, Turenne had proved that he was his equal at Turkheim. No allied commander – even Montecuccoli fell short – could equal them.

---

1 Huygens, *Journaal, op cit.*, 16 October 1673, p.8.

2 D.J. Roorda, 'Prins Willem III en het Utrechtse Regeringsreglement' in *Van Standen tot Staten*, Utrecht, 1975, p.111.

3 Wagenaar, *Historie, op. cit.*, 14, pp.308–10.

4 *Ibid.*, pp.309–10.

5 M. van den Bijl and Quarles van Ufford, eds, *Briefwisseling van Godard Adriaan van Reede van Amerongen en Everard van Weede van Dijkveld*, Nederlandsch Historisch Genootschap, The Hague, 1991, pp.3, 5. Roorda, *Utrechtse Regeringsreglement, op. cit.*, p.106.

6 Huygens, *Journaal, op. cit.*, 22 October 1673, p.10.

7 Israel, *Dutch Republic, op. cit.*, pp.814, 444.

8 Roorda, *Utrechtse Regeringsreglement, op. cit.*, p.111.

9 *Vervolg van't Verwerd Europa, op. cit.*, pp.648–9.

10 *Ibid.*, pp.651–2. *'T Ontroerde Nederlandt, op. cit.*, II, pp.751, 754.

11 Roorda, *Utrechtse Regeringsreglement, op. cit.*, pp.108, 112. Sylvius, *op cit.*, p.217.

12 Hop & Vivien, *op. cit.*, pp.401–2.

13 Hop & Vivien, *op. cit.*, pp.421–2.

14 Wagenaar, *op. cit.*, 14, pp.314–16. *Correspondentie Willem III en Portland, op. cit.*, II, 1, p.336.

15 Wageneaar, *op. cit.*, 14, pp.316–17. Hop & Vivien, *op. cit.*, p.434.

16 The account which follows is based on Hop & Vivien, *op. cit.*, pp.423ff., and Wagenaar, *op. cit.*, 14, pp.318ff.

17 Wagenaar, *op. cit.*, 14, pp.325–7. *Vervolg van't Verwerd Europa, op. cit.*, Appendix pp.91–4.

18 Roorda, *Utrechtse Regeringsreglement, op cit.*, pp.116, 118, 119. Wagenaar, *op. cit.*, 14, p.327. M. Van der Bijl, *Utrechtse Weerstand, in Van Standen tot Staten*, Utrecht, 1975, pp.138–9.

19 Wagenaar, *op. cit.*, 14, pp.327–9. S. Groenveld, *Evidente Factiën in de Staet,* Hilversum, 1990, p.69.

20 Roorda, *Utrechtse Regeringsreglement, op. cit.*, pp.119–21.

21 *Vervolg van't Verwerd Europa, op. cit.*, p.837.

22 Roorda, *Utrechtse regeringsreglement, op. cit.*, pp.124–5. Van den Bijl, *Utrechts' Weerstand, op. cit.*, p.139.

23 *Correspondentie Willem III en Portland, op. cit.*, II, 1, p.519.

24 M.W. Hartog, 'Prinse Willem III en de Hertogshoed van Gelderland 1673–1675', in *Bijdragn en Mededelingen der Vereniging*, Gelre, LXVIII, pp. 127, 174–7.

25 Mignet, *op. cit.*, IV, pp.272–3, 277–80. Redlich, *op. cit.*, p.125. Rousset, *op. cit.*, II, p.3. D'Estrades, *op. cit.*, IX, Supplement, p.4.

26 Mignet, *op. cit.*, IV, pp.280–1. John T. O'Connor, *Negotiator out of season, The Career of Wilhelm Egon von Fürstenberg 1629 to 1704*, Athens, 1978, p.64.

27 G. von Antal and J.C.H. de Pater, *Weensche gezantschapsberichten*, The Hague, 1929, Pt I, p.104. Despach to Fagel, 25 January 1674.

28 Mignet, *op. cit.*, IV, pp.281–2. Mignet states that the Diet solemnly declared war on Louis in the name of the Holy Roman Empire. P.H. Wilson, *German Armies*, UCL Press, 1998, p.47, maintains that the Diet's decrees fell short of a formal *Reichskrieg*.

29 Quoted in Derek McKay, *The Great Elector, op. cit.*, p.216.

30 *Ibid.*, p.217.

31 Ernst Opgenoorth, *Friedrich Wilhelm: Der Grosse Kurfürst von Brandenburg*, Frankfurt, Zurich, I, 1971, pp.152, 154–5.

32 Israel, *The Anglo-Dutch Moment, op. cit.*, art. by Wout Troost, p.305.

33 Opgenoorth, *op. cit.*, I, p.152. McKay, *The Great Elector, op. cit.*, p.218.

34 Waddington, *op. cit.*, pp.345–6.

35 Israel, *The Anglo-Dutch Moment, op. cit.*, art. by Wout Troost, p.305.

36 Rousset, *op. cit.*, II, pp.18–20, 22–4.

37 *Ibid.*, pp.37, 12, 16. Knoop, *op. cit.*, p.12.

38 For this account see F.J.L. Krämer's articles in *Bijdragen voor Vaderlandsche Geschiedenis en Oudheidkunde*, 3.6, 1892 and 3.7, 1893.

39 *Correspondentie Willem III en Portland, op. cit.*, II, 1, pp.355ff.

40 De Jonge, *op. cit.*, III, 2, pp.4, 7, 9ff., 22, 34, 35.

41 Rousset, *op. cit.*, II, pp.114–16.

42 De Jonge, *op. cit.*, pp.28–9, 36, 38–9. *Correspondentie Willem III en Portland*, II, 1, *op. cit.*, pp.455–6.

43 Rousset, *op. cit.*, II, pp.121–3.

44 *Ibid.*, p.119.

45 *Correspondentie Willem III en Bentinck, op. cit.*, II, 1, pp.352–4.

46 Krämer in *Bydragen voor Vaderlandsche Geschiedeniss en Oudheidkunde*, III, 7, 1893, pp.59–60. *Correspondentie Willem III en Portland, op. cit.*, II, 1, pp.447–8 and p.447 n.3 in which Japikse elucidates the date of July which Krämer had wrongly attributed to August. See also p.530.

47 A. Lossky, *Louis XIV and the French Monarchy*, New Brunswick, 1994, pp.155–6.

48 *Relation Succincte de ce qui s'est passé de plus considérable sous le commandement de son Altesse Mgr. Le Prince d'Orange dans la Campagne de 1674*, Leyden, 1747. Although not cited as the author this was written by Du Moulin, pp.2, 6, 9. See further *Vervolg van't Verwerd Europa, op. cit.*, pp.914–15.

49 Knoop, *op. cit.*, pp.27–8.

50 Rousset, *op. cit.*, II, p.17.

51 *Correspondentie Willem III en Portland, op. cit.*, II, 1, pp.362, 363–4.

52 *Vervolg van't Verwerd Europa, op. cit.*, p.915.

53 *Correspondentie Willem III en Bentinck, II, 1, op. cit.*, pp.364–7.

54 Knoop, *op. cit.*, pp.39–40.

55 *Correspondentie Willem III en Portland, op. cit.*, II, 1, p.377.

56 Knoop, *op. cit.*, pp.39–40, 45–6.

57 Du Moulin, *Relation Succincte, op. cit.*, pp.27–8, 32–7.

58 *Ibid.*, pp.38–9.

59 *Ibid.*, pp.40–45, 58, 88.

60 *Correspondentie Willem III en Portland, op. cit.*, II, 1, pp.412–13. For the Austrian army's movement from the Roer and the position of the Prince's army see Knoop, *op. cit.*, pp.45–6.

61 *Correspondentie Willem III en Portland, op. cit.*, II, 1, pp.425–6, 430–1, 443–4. For the review of the troops at Louvain see *Vervolg van't Verwerd Europa, op. cit.*, p.920.

62 *Correspondentie Willem III en Portland, op. cit.*, II, 1, p.453.

63 Japikse, *Willem III, op. cit.*, II, p.25.

64 Knoop, *op. cit.*, p.63.

65 *Ibid.*, pp.58–60.

66 This account of the battle is primarily based on Prince William's despatches to his grandmother, Amalia von Solms (12 August), and to the States-General (14, 16, 18 August) – see *Correspondentie Willem III en Portland*, II, 1, pp. 457, 460–2, 463–7; and, for the French side, on Rousset, *op cit.*, II, pp.41ff. See also, with some caution, Knoop, *op. cit.*, pp.64ff.; and Japikse, *Willem III, op cit.*, II, pp.25ff.

67 Rousset, *op cit.*, II, pp.51–4.

68 Knoop, *op cit.*, p.81.

69 Krämer, *Ned.Spaansche Diplomatie, op cit.*, pp.165–7.

70 *Correspondentie Willem III en Portland, op cit.*, II, 1, pp.508–9.

71 *Ibid.*, pp.462–3, 467–8.

72 Mignet, *op. cit.*, IV, pp.364–5.

73 *Correspondentie Willem III en Portland, op. cit.*, II, 1, pp.477–8.

74 Knoop, *op. cit.*, p.99. *Correspondentie Willem III en Portland, op. cit.*, II, 1, p.476.

75 *Correspondentie Willem III en Portland, op. cit.*, II, 1, pp.481–2.

76 *Ibid., Correspondentie Willem III en Portland, op. cit.*, II, 1, pp.487–90. Burnet, *op. cit.*, II, OUP, 1900, p.68.

77 Knoop, *op. cit.*, p.100.

78 *Correspondentie Willem III en Portland, op. cit.*, II, 1, p.499.

79 Rousset, *op. cit.*, II, p.61.

80 Rousset, *op. cit.*, II, p.63.

81 See *Correspondentie Willem III en Portland, op cit.*, II, 1, pp.501ff.

82 *Ibid.*, pp.501, 515, 522.

83 Rauchbar, *op. cit.*, pp.370–73.

84 Knoop, *op. cit.*, pp.114–16. Rousset, *op. cit.*, II, p.65.

85 Knoop, *op. cit.*, pp.122, 129. Rousset, *op. cit.*, II, p.66.

86 *Correspondentie Willem III en Bentinck, op. cit.*, II, 1, p.512. Knoop, *op. cit.*, p.136.

87 Rousset, II, p.67.

88 Knoop, pp.137–9, 141, 143–4. The Dutch losses of 7/8,000 men, on a par with those of the battle of Seneffe, which Knoop cites, hardly seem credible, even if account is taken of the length of the siege. *Correspondentie Willem III en Portland, op. cit.*, II, 1, p.520.

89 *Ibid.*, II, 1, p.523. Rousset, *op. cit.*, II, p.67.

90 *Vervolg van't Verwerd Europa, op. cit.*, pp.116–17.

91 *Correspondentie Willem III en Portland, op. cit.*, II, 1, p.521. Ten Raa & Bas, *op. cit.*, VI, p.35.

92 Knoop, *op. cit.*, pp.107–8. Redlich, *op. cit.*, p.130.

93 Rousset, *op. cit.*, II, pp. 1–2, 7, 75–6.

94 *Ibid.*, pp.79–82.

95 *Ibid.*, pp.83–4.

96 Redlich, *op. cit.*, pp.19–20.

97 Rousset, *op. cit.*, II, pp.85–6. Redlich, *op. cit.*, p.132.

98 Redlich, *op. cit.*, pp.133, 135–6. Rousset, *op. cit.*, II, pp.101–6.

14 1674: SOVEREIGNTY: THE CHOICES

SOVEREIGNTY AND LOUIS XIV

Sovereignty could come to the Prince of Orange in several guises; he already possessed it in Orange itself, although it had become somewhat tenuous after the Principality had fallen into the hands of Louis XIV in 1673; there was the Dutch Republic; there was the Britain of Charles II; and now Louis dangled before him a further possibility, the Duchy of Limburg. The Count d'Estrades, the former ambassador to The Hague, had been appointed governor of Maastricht after its capture by the French and he retained his contacts in the Republic. One of these, the servitor of the Prince of Orange named Launoy, provided D'Estrades with information (for which he was well remunerated), sometimes with, and sometimes without, the knowledge of the Prince. Through him an unofficial channel of communications was established between the Count and the Prince, with Launoy providing additional intelligence of his own – including a great deal of military information such as, on 10 April, that the Dutch fleet with 10,000 men under the Count of Hoorn would descend on the French coast. He was thus not only a go-between but also a very informative spy.

In April 1674 he passed on the information to the Count that the Prince was determined to stick exactly to the treaties with the Dutch allies, the Emperor, Spain, and the Duke of Lorraine. This, *inter alia*, meant returning to the state of affairs prevailing at the Peace of the Pyrenees, that is to say, Louis would have to forgo all he had acquired from Spain under the treaty of Aix-la-Chapelle after the War of Devolution and all his conquests afterwards. Spain's cause was strongly supported by Waldeck and the Rhinegrave, who argued that there could be no security without maintaining the pact with the three allies.[1]

Louvois, nevertheless, brushed all this aside. He instructed D'Estrades, in May, to appeal, through the intermediary of Launoy, to the Prince's personal interests; once peace was made he would need Louis to maintain his authority in the Dutch Republic, which the Dutch States would seek to diminish the moment it was made. Louvois elaborated on this on 11 July. At the end of this year's campaign, so ran the arguments to be put to the Prince, the Dutch States would want to make peace for the sake of their commerce and to curb his authority; if such a peace were entered into before he had set out his measures with Louis it would be very difficult for the King to do anything for someone who had been so opposed to him; on the other hand, if the Prince had come to an accommodation with Louis prior to the peace, the King could make sure that the conditions would contain whatever measures he desired to maintain his authority or even to increase it.[2]

On receiving these overtures Prince William did not totally reject them. Characteristically, he kept his options open. It was now the end of July and a battle was in prospect – the battle of Seneffe indeed occurred on 11 August – and he told Launoy that his mind was fixed on these preoccupations and on acquiring repute in the field.[3]

Although the battle of Seneffe was a draw, Louvois was not the man to allow too much latitude to inconvenient facts and he represented the battle as a self-evident French victory. He wrote to D'Estrades on 15 August, suggesting that, in the light of this defeat, Prince William should present his terms for a peace on an unsigned piece of paper. If these were acceptable to the French 'the peace would be signed at Maastricht before anyone knew about it'.[4] The energetic unscrupulousness of Louis's Minister caused him on this occasion to overlook the predictable reactions of the Dutch States-General and of their allies, when this would be revealed to them, both of whom would need to ratify any treaty. In the meantime the mind of the Prince of Orange, who, in the interval, had become very suspicious of Launoy, was fixed on seeking another battle.

On 19 August Louvois again wrote to D'Estrades, once more depicting Prince William's personal position in the aftermath of Seneffe as parlous. Louis 'would insert amongst the conditions [of the peace] everything which would be most advantageous for the maintenance of the Prince's authority and for that of his posterity … instead of the Prince's position depending as it appeared at present on unstable circumstances, supported by factors which it was apparent could not last, it would find a solid support in the amity of his Majesty'. As far as terms were concerned, the French King was prepared, as they pertained to Germany, to return to the Treaty of Westphalia – which meant returning his conquests to the German States – and, as they pertained to Spain, to the Treaty of Aix-la-Chapelle, with the exception of Franche-Comté, which France would retain. It meant as well, of course, France's retention of all she had gained under the Treaty of Aix-la-Chapelle itself after the War of Devolution. And there was no mention of the restoration of the Duke of Lorraine to his duchy, which France had seized from him.[5]

This approach found no encouragement from Prince William.[6]

In the meantime, D'Estrades had also, since May, been holding parallel conversations in Maastricht with Johan Pesters, who had been the Pensionary of that town and hence was known to the Count. He was also a friend and relation of Fagel – for which reason, no doubt, the Prince had, at the end of April, nominated him as Griffier (secretary) of the Court of Utrecht, a position to which he was formally appointed by the States of that Province in the middle of October. Of these conversations Pesters kept Fagel informed.

Towards the beginning of August they took on a more solid form. D'Estrades emphasised his personal goodwill for the Dutch Republic and for the Prince of Orange and he indicated that he believed that he could dispose Louis XIV to enter into a reasonable peace – a confidence which was fully justified, as he was, in fact, acting with the full authority of the King. The terms he suggested for the allies were much the same as those conveyed via Launoy, but the French became more explicit on what they had in mind for the Prince of Orange personally; he would obtain Maastricht, with Overmaas and the dukedom of Limburg, and, as the Republic and the Prince were committed under their treaties to transfer Maastricht to Spain, this city would be obtained by the Prince in exchange for the debt owed to him by Spain. The Republic itself would obtain a treaty of friendship from Louis which would safeguard her commerce.

Although acting on behalf of Louis XIV, D'Estrades did not overlook his own interests. For his services he wanted to be appointed governor of Maastricht, as well as to a military command, and he also asked that a position be found for his son.[7]

Launoy was now dropped as the informal intermediary and more formal channels of communication were opened by means of Pesters. D'Estrades, meanwhile, had bribed not only Launoy but also Fagel's secretary or clerk, so that he – and his masters in France – knew what was passing between the Prince and the Pensionary. On 6 August Pesters left Maastricht to go to The Hague and both Fagel and the Prince were fully briefed on what had passed between him and the French Count. Fagel told him to inform D'Estrades that there was a disposition on the Dutch side to make peace, but William was less positive – he merely told Pesters to 'keep in hand the negotiations' and 'to pursue them as far as was practicable'.[8] There was thus at this stage a nice difference in emphasis as far as the Pensionary and the Prince were concerned; the former, who had the task of managing the Regents, particularly in Holland, was somewhat more pacific, the latter less so, although he did not ignore the Regents' commercial and financial concerns. It was a difference that was to grow more marked as time and events marched on, but it was never allowed to develop into an open breach between the two men.

Pesters's instructions for his negotiations with D'Estrades were based on a memorandum dated 1 September. This, it seems, was drawn up for Prince William's own guidance and its contents appear to have been conveyed to Pesters verbally. However, Launoy soon saw to it that a copy was in D'Estrades's hands, although it was incomplete. D'Estrades sent it on to France, where, still incomplete, it remains in the French archives.[9]

Prince William recognised, the memoir reads, that the French would try to drive a wedge between himself and the Republic's allies, but 'nothing in the world could cause me to be lacking in my word nor in the treaties which I have made'. The Dutch, the Emperor and the Holy Roman Empire had been gratuitously attacked and it was reasonable that they should receive compensation. He and the States-General were bound by treaty to restore Spain to what she had at the Peace of the Pyrenees. This stipulation could not be met unless satisfaction were accorded to Spain by the return of Franche-Comté and her acquisition of Ath and Charleroi either by direct cession or in exchange for St-Omer and Aire. This would address the disquiet felt by the Dutch States and by neighbouring princes arising from the great power of Louis XIV.

If an honourable agreement could not be reached at the present time the allied coalition should be maintained by whatever means possible to form a barrier against France.

As far as the places to be returned to the Dutch and to himself were concerned, the Prince anticipated, as indeed happened, that he would soon recapture Grave. But the only other Dutch town still in French hands, Maastricht, was, as he put it, an 'embarrassment', a delicate matter.

He turned to the suggestion floated by D'Estrades that he himself should acquire Maastricht by using the debt owed him by Spain, and on this he elaborated. He had no intention of allowing Spain to retain Maastricht. Once peace was established, and he was free from the Spanish commitment, he wanted to return to the model of a draft agreement which D'Estrades himself had made with his father as far back as 20 October 1650. This contemplated William II acquiring the Duchy of Limburg and possibly Maastricht as well. But, if he did not want Spain to have Maastricht, nor did he want France to have it either, with its command of the Maas and Rhine rivers.

The solution was for Louis to acknowledge that Maastricht should fall to himself as compensation for the losses he had suffered in the war. The debt the Spaniards owed him – 5 million, he said, in which currency is not clear – would meet the consideration for them to grant him the Duchy of Limburg, plus some further lands at Overmaas, at a price to be determined through arbitration. If this were refused he considered that he would be justified in using force to achieve his ends.

What he was after in acquiring the Duchy of Limburg was sovereignty. It could provide an alternative to Orange, should he lose the latter permanently.[10]

But the obstacles in arriving at an agreement with the French were too great. Louis was not prepared to concede Franche-Comté, unless an equivalent was offered, nor Ath and Charleroi; and on Lorraine the furthest the King was prepared to go was that this duchy might be submitted to arbitration on the conclusion of peace – on no account could the duchy be included in the peace treaty itself.[11]

The discussions, through Pesters and d'Estrades, continued and embraced the possibility of an armistice at sea and a Franco-Dutch trade agreement – the Prince was kept informed by the Dutch ambassadors in London, who included Coenraad van Beuningen, the Amsterdam Regent, of how much English neutrality in the war was benefiting English trade, at the expense of the Dutch.[12] Both the Prince of Orange and the Holland Grand Pensionary, Fagel, needed to take account of this; it was an added reason for leaving a channel of communication open for negotiations with France.

In October the French made an informal proposal that the Prince of Orange should marry Mademoiselle de Blois, the barely 11-year-old illegitimate daughter of Louis XIV and Louise de la Vallière. The Prince, according to Saint-Simon, is said to have replied that the Princes of Orange were accustomed to marry the legitimate daughters of great kings, not their bastards. However that may be, he rejected both this proposal and the later suggestion, made in November, that he should marry the Princess of Orléans. Both initiatives were made in the light of the heightened rumours circulating in England of a marriage between Prince William and his cousin, Mary, the daughter of the Duke of York. To see so important a client as James draw away from Louis's patronage system was anathema at the court of France, and the French counter-suggestions were laid as baits designed to frustrate this from happening.[13]

Here, for the time being, we shall leave this set of negotiations and turn to Britain and Charles II.

SOVEREIGNTY AND BRITAIN

His uncle's kingdoms, of course, presented a further possibility of acquiring sovereignty. Through his secretary, Pierre du Moulin, William was well informed about the state of affairs in his uncle's domains; and rumours reached him at the end of January 1674 that venereal disease was likely to render fruitless the second marriage of his other uncle, the Duke of York, to Mary of Modena.[14]

The signing of the Peace of Westminster in February 1674 presented the opportunity for him to open, or reopen, communications with English contacts. At the end of February he wrote to that congenial soldier, his old friend the Earl of Ossory, their friendship having not in any way been diminished by Ossory's service in the English fleet against the Dutch. The Earl had written that he was planning to visit the Dutch Republic as soon as the treaty was ratified, and the Prince replied, 'In the name of God, my dear Mylord, bring it to pass, because assuredly one of the things I desire most in the world is to see you, and that you should be able to bear witness that our army is not just made up of Holland rabble.' He himself wanted to visit England 'to assure the King of my very humble respects and to see all my friends, but that would have to be postponed until the end of the winter'.[15]

Charles II sent Sylvius to Holland to congratulate Prince William on his becoming hereditary Stadholder; and he also decided to send William Temple, the architect of the Triple Alliance with his well-known belief in an alliance with the Dutch, to The Hague as his ambassador. William wrote to Temple at the end of February expressing satisfaction at his appointment; and he also took the opportunity of Sylvius's congratulations to send Jonkheer van Reede on another mission to England to re-establish contact with his uncle – Van Reede had in fact been in England, probably in November 1673 when Parliament was sitting and making difficulties about voting money to continue the war, but of this mission no information has come down to us.

On the present occasion the Jonkheer's instructions (dated The Hague, 10 March 1674) were that the Prince wanted to be allowed to recruit troops for his army in Britain, and he wanted the King to recall those in the service of France; and Van Reede should raise the matter of the royal debts still owing to the House of Orange.

But behind this cover of routine diplomacy there was a more important matter; he was to inform himself, with the utmost secrecy, of the state of English public opinion regarding the Duke of York; anyone approaching him at Du Moulin's behest should be given audience and their advice employed to further the Prince's interests; and persons of consequence favourably disposed towards the Prince should receive encouragement and appropriate assurances.[16] The purpose, in short, was to establish a nucleus of a following for the Prince of Orange in his uncle's British kingdoms, and to ascertain to what extent the unpopularity of the Duke of York could be used to further this.

Some such following seems already to have existed. Van Reede's personal *aide-mémoire* notes his meeting several of the most prominent gentlemen of quality in the country. These favoured the marriage of the Prince to Mary, the elder of the Duke of York's two daughters. The memoir also says that the Duke of York himself was very much in favour of the match at this time, a view which was to prove vacillating.[17]

As we have seen both King Charles and his chief minister, Arlington, were convinced that the Prince of Orange had been conspiring with the English opposition; but they failed to find proof that men of substantial political consequence – as opposed to minor players – had formulated plans in conjunction with the Prince to oppose the court; and nor have the skilful researches of Professor Haley.[18] Nevertheless, as we shall shortly see, the Prince himself admitted that there were several such – and 'considerable', in his words – who made approaches to him with that end in view, although we may, at the same time, remark that it is a testament to his dexterity, and of the Grand Pensionary of Holland, that neither at the time nor to this day do we know who they were. In the absence of that knowledge it is difficult to assess either the political weight which can be attached to these contacts or the manner in which they operated.

There were certainly those in England who took the trouble to maintain good relations with William; these included, apart from Ossory, one of the Secretaries of State, Henry Coventry (the other, and more senior, Secretary was Arlington) and the Earl of Pembroke and, as his correspondence shows, William was just as happy to return their compliments.[19] With Ossory he went a degree further than the exchange of compliments; he was quite prepared, if he could, to use this bluff soldier to circumvent King Charles's objections to the Prince's recruiting British soldiers. Ossory, like Arlington, had married a daughter of Nassau Beverweert, an illegitimate branch of the Nassau family; he had served in the Irish army in the 1660s as well as in the English navy; and his father, the Duke of Ormond, head of the Butler clan in Ireland, had long held senior positions both in Ireland and in England dating from before the Civil War. But Ossory himself lacked the political acumen and weight to form the core of a Prince's party in Britain.

Van Reede, who arrived in London on 17 March, received a friendly reception from the King; but Charles, having been forced to break away from his French cousin with the Treaty of Westminster, did not wish to carry matters any further in favour of the Dutch. His aim now was to act as mediator between the opposing parties in the war on the Continent, although the enticement of Louis XIV remained as strong as ever.[20] He refused to allow the recruitment of troops for the Dutch army in his kingdoms and he refused to withdraw those serving with the French; and, as an indication, perhaps, of how seriously he took the threat of the Prince of Orange's involvement in English affairs, or perhaps because he did not wish to raise the suspicions of Louis – or both – he refused leave for Ossory to visit his nephew in Holland. Prince William wrote to the latter complaining of the 'rough' rebuff to his request to recruit troops in England, when he was doing so in every other neutral country; he was instructing Van Reede to try to do so by 'underhand' means and he asked Ossory to lend his assistance. The King's greater inclination for the interests of France than for those of the Dutch, the Prince said, was barely understandable.[21] Charles II was indeed in breach of the Treaty of Westminster, under a secret article of which he and the Dutch were bound not to aid their mutual enemies, directly or indirectly, including with troops.[22] The Prince himself wrote to King Charles at the end of May reminding him of this and reiterating the request to be allowed to raise troops in his kingdoms.[23]

We need to note that by December 1673 Ossory's father, the Duke of Ormond, and Shaftesbury were the leaders of the pro-Dutch party – Shaftesbury had spoken in favour of the Test Act in the spring of 1673 and the French ambassador in London, Colbert de Croissy, reported to Pomponne on 18 May that he was now *tout à fait Hollandois*, whilst on 22 June he told Louis XIV that Ormond was opposed to the French alliance.[24] Shaftesbury's position was opaque – in November he supported the King's plea for supplies to continue the Dutch war, which, however, did not prevent Charles from dismissing him from office, on the suspicion that he was lending tacit support to the English opposition. There was a strong personal animosity between the fervently anti-Catholic Shaftesbury and the King's brother, which was the occasion, it was believed at the time, for the dismissal. If it did not now, it soon did become Shaftesbury's vehement purpose to exclude James from the throne. Arlington, whose relations with both Shaftesbury and Ormond were friendly, was taken aback by this dismissal; he, too, became an enemy of the Duke of York; and he embarked on the promotion of the interests of the two possible rivals to James for the succession, the Prince of Orange and the Duke of Monmouth – in the case of the former, as it turned out, very maladroitly.[25]

There was now a figure rising to prominence in English politics, Thomas Osborne; soon to be created Earl of Danby, [26] he had become Lord Treasurer in June 1673, and he remained a figure of importance for the rest of William of Orange's life, and, indeed, afterwards, dying in 1712. Part of Van Reede's mission to England was to discuss the debt owed to the Prince of Orange by Charles II, which brought him into contact with Danby, as Lord Treasurer – Prince William wrote a letter of credence to him on behalf of Van Reede at the beginning of April. It was these negotiations that led to the Dutch war indemnity being assigned to Prince William in satisfaction of the debts owed by the Stuarts to the House of Orange – the negotiations continued until the beginning of 1675.[27] The satisfactory outcome of the negotiations provided a promising basis to establish amicable relations between Prince and Minister.

Danby's politics, too, were calculated to be of interest to Prince William. His political principles were spelled out in a memorandum that he prepared in October 1673; they were to promote Protestant interests at home and abroad; to adhere to the Triple Alliance and to endeavour to expand it through the inclusion of other Protestant powers; and, domestically, to pursue economy in financial matters.[28] In a further memorandum at the end of 1673 he concluded that no more money would be forthcoming either from the existing Parliament or any conceivable replacement 'till they were satisfied in their fears as to France'; he argued that the use of force against Parliament was unrealistic and the only practical course of action was to reach an accommodation with the existing Parliament, which meant the enforcement of the laws against both Catholics and nonconformists alike.

Domestically Charles II was prepared to follow Danby's advice on religious matters; and when Parliament was convened on 17 January 1674 Catholics were forbidden the court, and the laws were enforced against them.[29] At the same time Danby was successful in restoring the King's finances. He was the beneficiary of the expansion of English trade, the result, as we have already seen, not least of the handicap the Dutch suffered through their own continued involvement in the war – this, good harvests, and Danby's own measures enabled him to pay for the war and at the end of 1674 for the first time after the Restoration the revenues exceeded expenditure.[30]

The rise of Danby was accompanied by the waning of Arlington. In September 1674 the latter made the mistake of surrendering his post as Secretary of State to his client, Joseph Williamson, to take up the position of Lord Chamberlain; his aim was to reduce his commitments so that he could concentrate his energies; he succeeded in reducing his importance and his patronage to advance Danby.[31] William of Orange took the opportunity to congratulate Williamson on his elevation, thus opening a further line of contact with the English political class.[32]

But, whilst following Danby in religious and financial matters, Charles II was uneasy to do so in foreign policy; he felt himself in danger of being pushed by his Parliament to take active measures against his powerful patron and protector, Louis XIV, and, at the same time, he continued to be angered by the alleged intrigues of the Prince of Orange with the English opposition. Arlington thought that here he had the opportunity to make use of his family connections with the Nassau clan to restore his position; he proposed that he should be sent to Holland to persuade the Prince of Orange to make peace and to reveal the names of his contacts in Britain; if the Prince was agreeable to this the possibility could be floated of the marriage of William to Mary, the elder daughter of James, which would, if James had no surviving male children, bring him closer to the throne of England.[33]

And so Arlington departed on 27 November for The Hague accompanied by his wife, her brother Nassau-Odijk, her unmarried sister, Charlotte Nassau-Beverweert – who, according to Temple, 'had something in her humour and conversation very agreeable to the prince' – and the husband of another sister, Ossory. Sir Gabriel Sylvius too was of the party. At Danby's insistence his son, who had just succeeded him as Viscount Latimer consequent to his own elevation as Earl of Danby, also joined the party (with a warm complimentary letter from his father to the Prince), although he was frozen out of the negotiations that followed. According to Ruvigny, the French ambassador in London, the Duke of York, who entertained hopes of marrying Mary to the French Dauphin, had agreed only with reluctance to the marriage plans out of loyalty to his brother. The visit of this party was treated as a purely family affair and neither Arlington nor Ossory had any official diplomatic credentials.[34] But the Prince of Orange would have been extremely pleased to see Ossory at last, for whom he had in mind a position in the Dutch army.[35]

The mood of the Prince in advance of the party's arrival was described by William Temple with that diplomat's usual acuity in his despatches in November; at the personal psychological level the Prince found the life of the camp and campaigning congenial; 'he is pleased with the life he has led this summer, and loves the trade, and thinks himself better in health and humour, the less he is at rest'; the inactive life which peace would bring would not suit him; every small success in the field increased his authority among the people; and those who accompanied him on the campaign reported that no one believed more firmly than he did in predestination, which enabled him to regard with equanimity both the fatigues and the dangers of the campaign, and this also enhanced his soldiers' affection for him.[36] In short, the war was a stimulus to the Prince, and the stimulus was enhanced by his sense of divinely ordained destiny.

But whatever the exhilarations of waging war Prince William also had a hard-headed view of the difficult prospects of achieving peace, made more onerous by the commitments the Dutch had to their allies. Although he complained to Temple about the performance of the Spanish and the Imperialists he was nevertheless very clear that the States could not enter into a peace separate from the allies on any terms that the French could offer them; no general peace could be entered into which left the Spanish Netherlands defenceless against attack – guarantees would not do; Spain could not surrender Franche-Comté; the Spanish Netherlands would have to revert to the position under the Treaty of the Pyrenees, unless Aire or St-Omer were offered in settlement. All this was, of course, in conformity with what he had been imparting to D'Estrades, when, however, he also suggested that Aire and St-Omer could be exchanged for Ath and Charleroi, which would have strengthened the Spanish strategic position.

King Charles's offer to act as mediator had been accepted by Vienna and Madrid, as it had by Louis XIV, and Temple told the Prince that, as the author and guarantor of the treaty of Aix-la-Chapelle, Charles could not propose anything under his mediation that went beyond the terms of that treaty, 'or something equivalent'. In that case, the Prince said, ''twere better going on with the war, let it last as long, and cost as much, as it would'. He believed he had the support of all men of any sense in the Dutch Republic – although Temple, rather forthrightly, told him he doubted that.[37]

Moral obligations were intertwined with *realpolitik*; once abandoned by the Dutch it would be very difficult to reconstruct another grand coalition against Louis XIV and, quite apart from Spain, the Dutch had their own vital interests to preserve in securing the very vulnerable Spanish Netherlands against France. At the same time King Charles, the Prince said, 'could never shew him so much kindness, as to bring him out of this war with honour: if he would not, it must go on till some change happened in the condition of the parties, to make the peace more necessary on one side or the other…; he must perform what his own honour, as well as that of the States, was engaged in to their allies, let it cost what it would.' 'Honour' was an essential component of his *gloire* and the diminution of the one would bring with it the diminution of the other.

The terms he conveyed to Temple were, of course, unacceptable to France. But the Prince believed that it was in the interests of his uncle to safeguard the Spanish Netherlands and he also believed, or at least said, that Charles II was in a position to impose peace terms on France.[38] For Charles the overriding imperative was not to be divided from Louis XIV, however much an increasing body of influential opinion in England shared the Prince's views on the Spanish Netherlands.

Thus matters stood when the family mission led by Arlington arrived in The Hague. It started well enough, with the Prince resorting to Nassau-Odijk's house, where Arlington was staying, for nightly suppers. There was a preliminary meeting, confined to courtesies. But when subsequent meetings turned to matters of substance the mood changed. Despite Arlington assuring the King of the Prince's goodwill and affection for his uncle, Temple reports that Arlington found the Prince 'dry and sullen, or, at the best, uneasy', whilst the Prince complained of Arlington's 'arrogance and insolence' and that he treated him as 'a child … it was as if he had taken himself as the prince of Orange, and him for my lord Arlington'. In short, as the Prince of Orange – who had now also become one of the chief protagonists on the European scene – he was not prepared to be patronised by Charles II's Lord Chamberlain.

When the discussions between them turned to the possible peace terms to end the war they covered much the same ground as had those with Temple,[39] and advanced no further.

On his contacts with the English opposition in the late Anglo-Dutch war and after, Ossory's account relates that the Prince admitted that he had used 'his best endeavours to obtain, if not constrain, the king' to enter into the peace between the two countries, 'but not by anything tending to a rebellion'. He was, he told Ossory, certainly not involved in anything that could smack of rebellion after the peace had been entered into. Whilst he declined to reveal who his contacts were, he promised 'that if for the future anything came to his knowledge that might disturb the quiet of [his uncle's] kingdoms, he would give notice of it in time'. It came close to being, but was not entirely, disingenuous – Van Reede's activities in building up a following for the Prince stopped well short of instigating rebellion, there is no evidence that Du Moulin's did otherwise, and the 'quiet' of the kingdoms was – perhaps – a vague and very general term. At the beginning of 1676 the Prince did admit to Temple that 'during the late war, neither the States, nor he in particular, were without application from several persons, *and considerable* [my italics], in England, who would fain have engaged him to head the discontents that were raised by the conduct of the Court in that whole war, which he knew was begun and carried on quite contrary to the humour of the nation, and might perhaps have proved very dangerous to the Crown, if it [that is, the war] had not ended as it did.' Thus – the suggestion here is – the Prince had in fact been instrumental in saving the court from itself.

Because of the warm relationship that was known to exist between Ossory and Prince William he had been assigned the delicate task of sounding William out on his marrying Princess Mary. The Prince gently excused himself on the grounds that he was too involved with the war at the present time to be able to avail himself of the honour. Why did he react in this way and not pursue the marriage, as he was later to do? Ossory suggests that Charles's motives were to assist the Duke of York – a Protestant marriage, we may surmise, would help him out of the difficulties he himself had created through his Catholic faith. The *quid pro quo* for William was Mary's closeness to the throne; but the Duchess of York was pregnant at this time and, if she bore a son, Mary would be removed further down the line from that objective.[40] Moreover, at this time Fagel was setting moves afoot in the Province of Gelderland to offer William the sovereignty of that Province; that was a delicate enough matter in itself; and the calculation may have arisen in the Prince's mind that to raise the matter of a royal marriage at this time would have exacerbated historical suspicions of the House of Orange's monarchical ambitions – it would be better first to await the reaction of Dutch opinion to Fagel's schemes.

He, therefore, did not reject the suggestion outright; as usual, he kept his options open.

As for honest Ossory, he was soundly berated by James for his efforts, because, instead of imperceptibly sounding out William, as a polished diplomat would have done, he had, by using a comma instead of a full stop in a letter he showed the Prince, managed to appear as a crude supplicant, and had thus affronted royal prestige. It was as a soldier, not as a statesman, that William of Orange was looking to make use of his services.

After this there was very little for Arlington and his family entourage to do except to make the best of it, and to enjoy the entertainments provided for them by William himself, by Waldeck, and by Odijk. And that, delayed by bad weather for six weeks, they proceeded to do.[41]

Fagel took the opportunity to present Arlington with a draft offensive and defensive treaty between the States and England which was to take effect after the conclusion of the present war – a project, which, however, a startled and embarrassed Charles II, anxious, as always, about cousin Louis, hastened to repudiate when he received reproaches from the French ambassador in London.[42]

Upon the departure of Arlington's party in January 1675 Prince William returned to the barbed issue of his contacts with the English opposition, and wrote a personal letter to his uncle, very much following the line he had taken with Ossory – he would inform the King of all he could learn of his enemies' designs against him. In return he asked the King for true marks of his amity for both himself and for the States, 'whose interests at present are inseparable from mine' – an allusion to the King's using his influence as mediator in the peace negotiations to further the Dutch terms. He added his conviction that it lay within the power of the King to engineer a peace or to allow the war to continue.[43]

As a token of amity he agreed to dismiss Du Moulin from his service – the secretary's last draft letter for William is dated 27 November 1674. William sought a position for him as governor of Surinam, which appointment, however, was delayed by the States of Zeeland, and he was not able to take it up before he died in June 1676.[44]

To Ossory he wrote as well, in cheerful manner; he was to tell Lott – Charlotte van Nassau-Beverweert, for whom we have already noted his affection – that, notwithstanding all her heartlessness, he loved her with all his heart, and Ossory was to convey to her his reproaches for not yet writing to him nor even responding to his letter, in keeping with her promise when she left The Hague. He also hoped that she would soon declare herself on what she had promised she would think about on her departure, because Bentinck wanted to know where he stood, 'which seems to me very reasonable'.[45] We do not know for certain what this was, but, again, with Ossory, there was a light-hearted raillery which William tended to confine to his close intimates and which was at variance with the cold distance for which he was reputed.

But light-hearted raillery was not extended to Arlington; between him and the Prince a strong personal antipathy appears, for the time being, to have developed, the result, it seems, of Arlington's not according the Prince the respect and deference demanded by the stature he had acquired. On Arlington's part there was also the lingering suspicion that Du Moulin was continuing to be employed by the Prince, something William denied in a letter in March, although he said he was still seeing Du Moulin to tidy up his affairs.[46] But that did not prevent King Charles and Arlington continuing to think that William was still involved in his intrigues with the English opposition. In March, Temple recorded in his memoirs, Prince William came to him and told him 'in a great heat' that he had 'received the most impertinent letter from Arlington that ever was', accusing him of planning a trip to England to coincide with the next session of Parliament with the aim of 'raising heats in the Parliament, and commotions in the kingdoms'; a strong hint was dropped that it lay within the power of the King to inflict on the Prince the same fate as had befallen De Witt, an echo of the threat made to Van Reede in September 1672. The normally controlled Prince was in a great rage: the outcome, we may surmise, of both his word being doubted and of the threat to him physically, neither of which he would have regarded as being compatible with his honour, his dignity or his *gloire*.[47] However, by the beginning of June the family quarrel appears to have been patched up, as a friendly exchange of letters between the two of them demonstrates.[48]

At the beginning of 1675, therefore, neither the possibility of the marriage to Mary nor the possibility of acquiring sovereignty through the Duchy of Limburg had been cast aside; both were in abeyance. The mind of Prince William, however, was still occupied by the subject, and he had another object in view.

SOVEREIGNTY AND GELDERLAND

We have seen that when he had settled the Provincial constitution and administration of Utrecht – in a manner very much in his favour – the Prince did not have time, before he embarked on the military campaign of 1674, to do the same for the two other Provinces that had been wholly overrun by the French, Gelderland and Overijssel. For the time being he had appointed a military governor in Gelderland, the Count of Limburg-Stirum, whilst two members of his own Domestic Council, Wevelinckhoven and Wierts, had been sent to Overijssel; in both Provinces temporary appointments were made to the Provincial institutions through which to exercise rule.[49] The time had now come for a permanent settlement. And this settlement was being carefully orchestrated by his close associate, the Grand Pensionary of Holland, Gaspar Fagel.

The States of Gelderland were made up of three 'Quarters', Nijmegen, Arnhem and Zutphen; and when the temporary appointments were made to the offices in Nijmegen Fagel's half-brother, Nicholas Fagel, became the 'First Regent'. Their sister was also married to an important Nijmegen magistrate, who, in turn, had a son-in-law who was the secretary of the Nijmegen Quarter. At a meeting of the Nijmegen Quarter on 10 January 1675 Nicholas proposed that Gelderland's sovereignty should be offered to the Prince, subject to the Provincial privileges, immunities and liberties. This was hammered out into a formal offer made by the States of Gelderland, probably on 31 January – the authorities differ on the exact date when the hereditary title of Duke of Gelderland and Count of Zutphen was proffered to the Prince.[50]

William was staying close by, at Zuylenstein, when a delegation arrived with the offer, and, as the assembly of the Quarters required his consent to meet, which he had given, he was fully aware of what was happening. He did not, however, accept immediately but thanked the delegation and asked for a few days to consider. He then wrote to the three Provinces where he was Stadholder – Utrecht, Holland, and Zeeland – for their 'good and wise advice'. Utrecht, where his hold was the firmest, advised him to accept. But in the two other – and much more important – Provinces the position was much more ambivalent.[51]

On the night of 14/15 February Gaspar Fagel arrived at Arnhem with the views of the Holland towns. Although the majority were in favour, important towns such as Amsterdam, Delft, Leyden and Haarlem were against, the latter two despite their loyal Orangist sympathies. On the 15th the Prince arrived at Arnhem and, whilst awaiting the news from Zeeland, passed the time by giving a reception, attending a church service with music from an orchestra and choir, and engaging in his favourite relaxation of hunting.

In the absence of Nassau-Odijk, who usually represented him as First Noble in Zeeland, the Zeeland Pensionary, De Huybert, had received orders from the Prince not to use the vote which William had as First Noble.[52] It was plain, therefore, that he did not wish to exercise undue influence on the outcome; more, indeed, he seemed to be eager to test the true mood and opinion of Zeeland's political class.

When the Zeeland States met on the 15th the result was that one town had no view; two, including Flushing, which the Prince owned, were for acceptance; and three, including Veere, which he also owned, were against.[53]

In Holland the opinion was expressed that Prince William would have greater authority and favour amongst the people as Stadholder than as Sovereign, not least because he would incur the odium of having to raise taxes which would become his responsibility. In Zeeland that view was echoed – as Duke or Count the Prince would acquire no more authority than he already had. In both Provinces there were fears that granting sovereignty in Gelderland would give rise to pressure for Holland and Zeeland to follow suit, and there were some who feared that this would lead to domestic conflict.[54]

Although deferentially expressed it was clear from the underlying mood that there was no stomach amongst the Regents of these two Provinces for the Gelderland proposal. When, in 1672, the emissaries of Charles II had dangled sovereignty before him William had grasped the political reality that he was more powerful as Stadholder, with the support of the Regents, than he would be as Sovereign without it; and he must have realised this now, not least because these views were being expressed by influential Regents themselves. It was not an option to use his current prestige and his command of the army to push ahead with the project – it would have led to such dissent and such opposition from within the Regent class that it would have destroyed his power base within the Dutch Republic on which his war against Louis XIV rested. He had decided what to do when he was informed of opinion in Holland, before even he knew of the outcome in Zeeland. On 19 February he rejected the offer the States of Gelderland had made.[55]

It was a decision that was neither ideological nor visionary; it was purely pragmatic. The Prince was sufficiently a child of his times to value sovereignty, which, indeed, had many practical political attributes, and some form of which was essential to his own standing and that of his House. But he also had a shrewd grasp of political reality and, almost from the first moment he came to power in 1672 – indeed before, as it was inculcated in his education – he realised the enhancement to his power which a ruler could derive from working through, and not against, institutions representative of his country's political classes – and, conversely, of the diminution in his power if he did not do so. It was an insight of inestimable value when William invaded England in 1688. It seems commonplace now and it was an insight which was not his alone within the Dutch Republic then: but it was not the common wisdom of his times in Europe as a whole; that was to follow the model of the perceived Absolute Monarchy of Louis XIV, which seemed to harbour the ideal of the future, however illusory the absoluteness was in practice. That was the ideal of William's English uncles, and, although, by the skin of his teeth, Charles II survived, James II did not; and, in France, this road led, eventually, to the French Revolution.

William's insight on this score, however, was not revolutionary, but conservative and practical; he found at hand the representative institutions of the Dutch Republic and he used them; they were rooted in the Middle Ages, as was the English Parliament. It was Louis's concept of kingship and sovereignty – or, at least his successful application of it – which was new, and which so bedazzled contemporaries.

As soon as he sensed the direction of public opinion the Prince swiftly back-tracked. There had been echoes of his father's *coup d'état* and Temple reported the commotion that was being caused; funds were withdrawn from the Amsterdam Exchange Bank and there were sharp falls in the shares of the Dutch East India Company. William wrote immediately, on 20 February, to the States of Holland, defending himself against charges that he had promoted, and was pursuing, the war for his own self-advancement and that the acquisition of sovereignty in Gelderland was planned as a prelude to his doing the same in the other Provinces.[56]

The decision of the States of Zeeland was conveyed to the Prince in a letter dated 16 February; and this letter, the formal resolution passed at their meeting and their discussion were all printed and published. The effect this could have on public opinion roused the Prince to write a long reply, to which he must have devoted much thought, for it was not sent until 18 March; and it, too, was printed and published. It was, therefore, carefully crafted as propaganda, but it is interesting, none the less, or even because of this, as it reveals how the Prince of Orange saw, and justified, his special role.

The previous regime, his line was, had wanted to exclude him from the dignities which, very much in the interests of the country, had bedecked his ancestors; and, by depriving him of the prerogatives that properly belonged to him, they sought to reduce him to a position where he was unable to exert his authority for the country's good. Those who had boasted most about championing 'Freedom' were at the fore of those who wanted to submit to the enemy in 1672 on scandalous terms, as a result of which Religion, Freedom, Privileges – everything – would have been lost. Trusting to God's grace he had done his utmost to oppose this, although his properties, which lay beyond the country's borders, were more exposed than those of any other of its inhabitants. Everyone knew that the enemy had included amongst its peace terms the granting to him of the sovereignty of the whole country, and that he had rejected this.

Thus we can see here encapsulated Prince William's creed. He believed that, under God's grace, he was fighting for the Religion, the Freedom and the Privileges of the United Provinces. It was a task from which he was not to deviate for the rest of his life.

He told the Zeeland States that he had the 'utmost aversion' to obtaining sovereignty; if he had really wanted it he would not have sought the advice of any of the other Provinces, but could simply have taken it. Not the slightest indication had been given by either himself or by his entourage to induce anybody in Gelderland to make the offer. And he could assure the States of Zeeland that his aversion to sovereignty would never change.[57]

The whole *démarche* of the Gelderland offer of sovereignty remains wrapped in obscurity. If it was true, as the Prince asserted, that he did not initiate the proceedings it is nevertheless also true that he was aware of what was being initiated on his behalf. The leading role played by Fagel's relations points clearly to the Grand Pensionary and it seems inconceivable that Fagel would have made his moves without sounding out the Prince in advance. At the end of the previous year he had been very ill, which may have impaired his judgement, and it may be that he advised the Prince that support for his acquiring sovereignty was greater than proved to be the case. Temple says that as important a Regent as Van Beverninck told him he supported the proposal,[58] but the debates in the Holland and Zeeland States do not indicate anywhere near the enthusiastic support amongst the Regents generally that the Prince needed if he was to sustain the project. Amongst the populace as a whole as well there was profound suspicion, which continued to rumble to the point that the Holland States issued a decree in September forbidding, on pain of death, the spreading of the rumour, by word or in writing, that the Prince aimed at sovereignty, for fear that it would lead to disorder and resistance to taxation.[59] William had been away at the front, remote from opinion in the Dutch Republic, but before committing himself irrevocably – he was much more cautious in politics and in diplomacy than he was on the battlefield – he took the precaution of sounding out the views of the Regents, and he was able to withdraw in time.

However, rejecting sovereignty was one thing; taking the opportunity to institute radical changes in the constitutions of Gelderland and Overijssel to entrench his power and further his purposes was another. He accepted the hereditary offices of Stadholder of the two Provinces; and he proceeded to reorder their constitutions and their governing personnel on the same lines as he had done in Utrecht. In Friesland his cousin, Casimir, also became hereditary Stadholder.

The appearance of Provincial sovereignty in the three Provinces of Utrecht, Gelderland and Overijssel was maintained; but, in actuality, the representatives at the States of these 'sovereign' Provinces no longer, other than in form, appointed the Stadholder as their functionary; it was the hereditary Stadholder who, in reality, appointed them. On 20 April 1675 the States-General appointed him hereditary Captain- and Admiral-General of the Republic. And William did not abandon the possibilities of sovereignty; it was only within the United Provinces that he did so.

1 D'Estrades, *op. cit.*, IX, Supplement pp.6–8.

2 *Ibid.*, pp.910, 17.

3 *Ibid.*, p.20.

4 *Ibid.*, p.27.

5 *Ibid.*, p.32.

6 *Ibid.*, p.34ff.

7 Krämer, *De Geheime Onderhandeling van Mr. Johan Pesters in het jaar 1674*, de Navorscher 1892, pp.308–9, 311. Krämer's account is based on Pesters's personal report. For Pesters's relationship with Fagel see d'Estrades, *op. cit.*, IX, Supplement, p.41.

8 Krämer, *Geheime Onderhandeling, op. cit.*, pp.309, 311, 312, 313.

9 See Japikse, *Willem III, op. cit.*, I, p.332, n.1. The incomplete form is in d'Estrades, *Lettres, op. cit.*, IX, Supplement, pp.38ff. See also Mignet, *op. cit.*, IV, p.311, n.1. Japikse says the complete copy of the memorandum can be found in St-Léger Revue du Nord nos.37–8, February and March 1921, pp.33ff. Whilst these nos. are missing from the British Library Krämer, *Geheime Onderhandeling, op. cit.*, pp.313ff. is drawn from Pesters's own report and there is Japikse's précis on p.331ff. of his Willem III, *op. cit.*, I.

10 Lossky, 'Political ideas of Willem III', *Political Ideas and Institutions in the Dutch Republic*, Clark Library seminar, 27 March 1982, p.51.

11 Krämer, *Geheime Onderhandeling, op. cit.*, pp.313–14.

12 *Correspondentie Willem III en Portland, op. cit.*, II, 1, pp.494–5.

13 Krämer, *Geheime Onderhandeling, op. cit.*, pp.320–21. Rousset, *op. cit.*, II, pp.68–9.

14 Haley, *English Opposition, op. cit.*, pp.172–3.

15 *Correspondentie Willem III en Portland, op. cit.*, II, 1, pp.338–9.

16 Korvezee, *op. cit.*, pp.250–52. See also *Some select letters from his majesty King William III when he was Prince of Orange to King Charles II etc.*, S. & J. Sprint and J. Nicholson 1705, pp.13, 15.

17 Korvezee, *op. cit.*, p.256. See also Haley, *The English Opposition*, pp.192–3.

18 See for example Haley, *The English Opposition, op. cit.*, pp. 126–7, 201. Professor Hutton, citing Haley's biography of Shaftesbury, *op. cit.*, describes the reasons why King Charles suspected Shaftesbury of encouraging opposition to the Dutch war in the summer of 1673 as 'a mystery'. *Charles II*, p.308.

19 *Correspondentie Willem III en Portland, op. cit.*, II, 1, pp.339, 341.

20 Hutton, *op. cit.*, p.325.

21 *Correspondentie Willem III en Portland, op. cit.*, II, 1, pp.342–3.

22 Mignet, *op. cit.*, IV, p.269.

23 Select Letters, *op. cit.*, pp.17ff.

24 Barbour, *op. cit.*, pp.209, 213–14, 223.

25 Hutton, *op. cit.*, pp.308, 309, 313. Barbour, *op. cit.*, pp.214, 240, 241.

26 At this stage his title was Viscount Latimer. He became the Earl of Danby on 27 June 1674, by which title we shall refer to him.

27 Andrew Browning, *Thomas Osborne Earl of Danby and Duke of Leeds, 1632-1712*, Glasgow 1951, II, pp.38ff., II, 1, p.133.

28 *Ibid.*, I, p.63, II, p.117.

29 *Ibid.*, I, p.121, II, pp.63–4.

30 Hutton, *op. cit.*, p.322. Browning, *op. cit.*, I, p.129.

31 Browning, *op. cit.*, II, pp.129,131–2. Hutton, *op. cit.*, pp.321–2.

32 *Correspondentie Willem III en Portland, op. cit.*, II, 1, p.511.

33 Browning, *op. cit.*, I, p.141.

34 Browning, *op. cit.*, I, p.142–3. Mignet, *op. cit.*, IV, pp.323–5. Temple, *Works, op. cit.*, 1770, II, p. 289. *Correspondentie Willem III en Bentinck, op. cit.*, II, 1, p.525, II, 2, p.4, n.2.

35 *Correspondentie Willem III en Portland*, II, 1, p.524.

36 Temple, *Works, op. cit.*, 1754, IV, pp.66, 68.

37 *Ibid.*, pp.66–7. Temple records the Prince as saying that 'Spain cannot quit … anything in Flanders beyond the terms of the Pyrenees, unless it be Aire or St-Omer'. The Prince's memoir above which was prepared to brief Pesters in fact envisaged Aire and St-Omer being exchanged for Ath and Charleroi. See also Barbour, op. cit., p.247, n.21 for Arlington's despatches to Charles II, 24–27 November, which adds Oudenarde to Ath and Charleroi.

38 Temple, *Works, op. cit.*, 1754, I, pp. 205–6. Barbour, *op. cit.*, p.246.

39 Save that, according to Arlington, Maastricht would be ceded to France after the razing of the fortifications. See Barbour, *op. cit.*, p.247, n.21. This is at variance with the memoir above prepared to brief Pesters.

40 Thomas Carte, *The Life of James Duke of Ormond*, Oxford 1851, IV, pp.495ff. Barbour, *op. cit.*, p.248.

41 Temple, *Works*, 1754, I, p.214. Barbour, *op. cit.*, p.249 and n.25.

42 Barbour, *op. cit.*, pp.246–7. Mignet, *op. cit.*, IV, pp.326–7.

43 *Original letters from King William III, then Prince of Orange, to King Charles II, Lord Arlington, etc.*, Cornhill, 1704, p.85.

44 Haley, *The English Opposition, op. cit.*, pp.212, 215–17.

45 *Correspondentie Willem III en Bentinck, op. cit.*, II, 2, p.4.

46 *Select Letters, op. cit.*, p.95.

47 Temple, *Works*, 1754, *op. cit.*, I, pp.220–1.

48 Original letters, *op. cit.*, p.99.

49 M.W. Hartog, article in *Gelre* LXVIII, 1974–5, p.127.

50 Johanna Maris, article in *Gelre* LXXII, 1981, pp.164–5. Hartog, article cited pp.128–31. Hartog says Nicholas Fagel's proposal was made on 11 January and the States offer on the 30th. Maris says the offer must have been made on the 31st and agreed by the Quarters on the 29th, pp.165, 167 of her article. See also Wicquefort, *Histoire, op. cit.*, IV, p.752. Wagenaar, *op. cit.*, 14, p.345.

51 Maris, article, *op. cit.*, pp.162, 166. Hertog, article, *op. cit.*, pp.138, 140.

52 Hartog, article, *op. cit.*, p.140. Wicquefort, *Histoire, op. cit.*, IV, pp.757–8.

53 Hartog, article, *op. cit.*, pp.141–2.

54 Wagenaar, *op. cit.*, 14, pp.348ff.

55 Hartog, article, *op. cit.*, p.143. Maris, article, *op. cit.*, p.168. Wagenaar, *op. cit.*, 14, p.358.

56 *Correspondentie Willem III en Portland*, II, 2, pp.10–13.

57 Wagenaar, *op. cit.*, 14, pp.352ff. See also Sylvius, *Historien onses Tyds, behelzende Saken van Staat en Oorlog*, Amsterdam, 1685, pp.205ff.

58 Temple, *Works*, 1754, *op. cit.*, I, p.219.

59 Wagenaar, *op. cit.*, 14, p.366.

15 1675: THE EVENLY BALANCED FORTUNES OF WAR

BRANDENBURG AND SWEDEN

Turenne's success at the turn of 1674 in driving the German armies from Alsace to the eastern banks of the Rhine was followed by French diplomatic success in Northern Germany. After the expenditure of the usual 'douceurs' in the appropriate quarters the Swedes, driven by their need for money, and after much dithering, entered the war on the side of France. They raised an army of 14,000 men; but they were unable to feed it whilst it remained on their own soil; and thus, more in desperation than by design, its commander, Karl Gustav Wrangel, led it in January 1675, despite orders to the contrary, into the Great Elector's territories in Pomerania, where they lived off the country by levying contributions in both cash and feedstuffs.

But Frederick-William saw this as an opportunity as much as a threat – he thought it provided him with the chance to add Swedish Pomerania to his existing territories. He did not, however, hasten immediately from the Rhine to return to the defence of his own lands, but took his time to bring his army into shape from the safety of the winter quarters where they had been billeted outside his territories, and from where they in turn could obtain their sustenance at the expense of others. Gout delayed him further and, whilst he lay indisposed, he was visited by his nephew William of Orange at Cleves from 20 to 23 March, who reported to Waldeck that he found his uncle 'the best intentioned man in the world and wants to do all that one could wish for'. It was not until the middle of May that he arrived in The Hague to sign a treaty with the Dutch, the Emperor, Spain and the dukes of Celle and Wolfenbüttel. The Dutch undertook to send a fleet into the Baltic and the Emperor undertook to provide a small contingent in his support. In The Hague he was splendidly entertained by the Prince of Orange, by Amalia von Solms – who was shortly to die – and by his Dutch family; and he was enthusiastically acclaimed by the populace everywhere, particularly in Amsterdam.

By the spring the Swedish army had increased to 20,000 men and it was not until June that Frederick-William commenced his own march with 21,000. This he now did very rapidly, arriving at Magdeburg on the 22nd. On the 25th he gave battle and dispersed the Swedish army at Rathenau; this was followed by the battle of Fehrbellin six days later at which the Swedish army, in the course of the two-day battle, was routed. By the end of the year the Elector of Brandenburg was the master of most of Swedish Pomerania, although the great prize of Stettin, which he hoped could form a base for a fleet, did not fall into his hands until December 1677, with the rest of Pomerania at the end of 1678.[1] Denmark, too, had been active and captured Wismar and Bremen.[2]

A small Dutch naval squadron left at the beginning of June for Copenhagen. It stayed there until 23 August when it sailed off the coast of Pomerania, with the Danish fleet, to observe the Swedish navy and to hinder the transport of Swedish troops; in this they were successful and they were able to capture a considerable number of transports. With the approach of winter they returned to the Republic.[3]

On this northern front, therefore, the war went well for the Alliance. It was, however, at the expense of seeing troops withdrawn from the front on the Rhine and the Mosel.

ALLIED PREPARATIONS

Waldeck, with his prestige as a German prince, his military record and his knowledge of, and contacts in, the German courts, was sent to Vienna, where he arrived on 10 February, to discuss the forthcoming campaign with Montecuccoli, with the Austrian Chancellor Hocher and with the Spanish ambassador at Vienna. He reported back to Prince William on the 14th; the Austrian plan of campaign was that Montecuccoli would command a powerful army on the Rhine whilst the Brunswick dukes would act with the Duke of Lorraine on the Mosel. It was envisaged that the Prince of Orange and the Spaniards would act in the Low Countries, whilst Brandenburg and a number of Imperial troops plus Denmark would operate against Sweden.[4] However, it soon became apparent, at a subsequent meeting on 17 February, that the allies were going to be short of troops; 155,000 men were deemed necessary for their plans, and it looked as if the most they could find would be 114,000 – a shortfall of 41,000. No solution was immediately in sight and it was left to each of the allies to see what they could do to fill the gap.[5]

Prince William went himself to Cleves to discuss matters with Frederick-William and wrote to Waldeck on 22 March confirming his uncle's goodwill, as we have stated above. There was a worry about the dukes of Celle and Wolfenbüttel, however; the representative of these dukes, who attended the discussions, had said that they were contemplating sending their troops to Bremen to counter the Swedes, rather than to the Rhine, for which latter purpose they were receiving subsidies from the Dutch and the Spaniards; and William asked Waldeck, who had a good relationship with the Duke of Celle, to intervene with the dukes on his journey back from Vienna.[6] In the event a compromise was eventually agreed at The Hague in the middle of May, under which the Brunswick troops would operate in the region of Bonn, but could be switched to Sweden if necessary.[7]

The Dutch could provide a field army in excess of 30,000 men by the beginning of April; but, whilst the Prince was ready, his Spanish allies were not. Although nominally the Spanish army amounted to just under 50,000, the real strength of the formations fell considerably below what they should have been and, as they devoted all their infantry to garrisoning their towns, this left only their cavalry of a few thousand men available for the field army. The new governor of the Spanish Netherlands was Villa Hermosa, who had succeeded Monterrey in January.[8]

As usual, the French were able to begin their campaigning season early when D'Estrades captured Liège on 31 March; it lay on the Maas and had thus blocked French communications with Maastricht, which lay further up the river.[9]

But at this stage Prince William, after leaving Cleves and his meeting with Frederick-William, fell very seriously ill at The Hague with the smallpox, the disease that had proved fatal to his father and his mother. He was attended by Hans Willem Bentinck during the illness and he later told William Temple that whether Bentinck 'slept or not he could not tell, but, in sixteen days and nights, he never called once that he was not answered by [Bentinck] as if he had been awake'. No sooner was William recovering than Bentinck also fell ill with the disease, which he, too, survived.[10]

The Prince was thus unable to deal with affairs for three weeks and it was not until 23 April that he could make a first attempt to resume his duties. 'You can imagine', he wrote to Waldeck, 'what was neglected during this period but as this comes from heaven one must have patience.'[11] Fagel, who had much to lose from the fall of the star to which he had hitched his wagon, and who was already fearful of the forthcoming campaign, expressed his anxiety to Pesters: 'My God, my dear friend, in what state shall we all be if anything becomes his highness.'

William himself, on the other hand, was 'full of heart and aspiration, and dreams only of embarking on the campaign'. He was expecting to muster the infantry at Bergen op Zoom on 6 May, followed by the cavalry when forage allowed.[12] A dispute with the Spaniards as to whether the Prince should exercise command over their slender forces was settled, in practice, in his favour when Villa Hermosa agreed to follow all his instructions.[13]

THE CAMPAIGN

On the French side Louis was preparing to attend the campaign in person. He left St-Germain on 11 May and took command of his troops, amounting to more than 60,000 men, between Ham and Câteau-Cambrésis, to advance, on the 18th, to Quesnoy. Whilst the royal army followed the course of the Sambre, Marshal Créqui and the Marquis de Rochefort joined forces to besiege Dinant on the Maas, which capitulated on the 28th. News was received by the French that Montecuccoli was advancing on the Upper Rhine towards Strasburg whilst the Duke of Lorraine had positioned himself on the Lower Rhine between Bonn and Cologne. Facing these armies was Turenne.

On 6 June the French captured Huy, where the troops engaged in the siege operations were covered by Louis's field army, and on the 9th they moved further east to begin siege operations against Limburg, again protected by the army of the King, with Condé in charge of operations.[14]

The Prince of Orange meanwhile had arrived at Rozendaal on 20 May, where the Dutch army mustered for the campaign, leaving Prince Maurits of Nassau-Siegen behind in overall command of the forces remaining in the Dutch Republic.[15] On the 24th the army marched to Duffel; the Spanish contingent was small, despite the loan of several Dutch regiments to man the Spanish garrisons; and the Prince complained of the lack of packhorses because the responsible contractors, not having been paid, refused to meet their commitments, whilst the Province of Friesland also fell short in providing wagons in accordance with what had been promised. He was therefore handicapped, being unable to intervene in the sieges of Dinant and Huy through lack of both numbers and equipment.[16]

These were early signs that the financial strains of the war were beginning to make themselves felt in the Dutch Republic; a further indication was that the urgent request from Spain to send naval forces to assist her in the Mediterranean with the revolt in Messina was not met until the end of the summer, when De Ruyter was despatched; and even then no serious attempt was made, as happened the previous year, to exploit the discontents in Brittany, which were still festering. There was still no sign of serious opposition to the war amongst the Regents and the States of Holland had indeed agreed promptly to an extraordinary financial levy – in which Waldeck saw the hand of God, assuring Prince William that 'all would yet be well, however acrid the outlook'.[17] But when he examined the homeland defences of the Republic, Maurits of Nassau-Siegen reported the old failings, so prevalent when the war began: these had been sadly neglected through lack of funds.[18] Although Maurits was now addressing the situation the prevailing state of the defences was a consideration that influenced the Prince's strategy.

When the allied army arrived at Louvain on 7 June it mustered, including 5,000 Spanish horse, 35,000 men, a third, or even fewer, than the French.[19] Accordingly on 12 June, at the same time as news was received that Louis had begun to besiege Limburg, it was decided that the army should march east to Roermond, at the junction of the Maas and Roer rivers (not to be confused with the Ruhr, which flows into the Rhine) where it was anticipated that it would be reinforced by cavalry from the Brunswick dukes and from Lorraine. From this position it could both come to the aid of the remaining towns on the Maas, including Limburg, and defend the approaches to the Republic through Dutch Gelderland.[20] But it left Brussels and its surrounding towns dangerously exposed.

The Brunswick and Lorraine contingents joined the army on the 23rd, with the allied army having commenced its march the day before to hasten to the relief of Limburg; but it had not advanced far when, to Prince William's bitter disappointment, news was received that the town had surrendered. It was about 14 leagues from Roermond and the sound of the cannon had been heard there during the siege. There was nothing for it but to abandon the march and observe what the enemy would do next.[21]

The danger Brussels and the Spanish towns were in was an opportunity that the Prince of Condé did not miss. No sooner had Limburg been occupied on the 22nd than the French army, formally headed by Louis but in practice led by Monsieur le Prince, advanced via Tongeren, St-Trond and Tirlemont, in the direction of Louvain and Brussels, to the dismay of the inhabitants of the Spanish Netherlands.[22]

To head it off the allied army advanced as rapidly as possible by means of forced marches through heavy rain towards Aerschot, to the north-east of Brussels, where it arrived on 1 July and then reached Louvain on the 9th, both towns being close to Mechelen.[23] From there it marched, on the 21st, to Halle, to the south-west of Brussels, to shadow Condé who, from Ath, was threatening Brussels, Mons and Ghent. As a result of the forced marches many of the allied troops straggled behind, and at this stage the army was reduced to 25,000 Dutch and 4,000 Spaniards, although reinforcements were expected from both the garrisons and from the stragglers.[24]

On the 17th Louis XIV left the French army to return to Versailles;[25] with his inferior numbers the Prince of Orange had been compelled to keep a safe distance between the two armies and a battle between King and Stadholder was thus avoided.

Then, on 27 July, Turenne, reconnoitring a position opposite Montecuccoli's army near Sasbach, between Salsburg and Baden-Baden, was struck down and instantly killed by a cannonball.[26] Prince William wrote to Fagel, when he heard the news, that he regretted the death as that 'of a relation and of a great man'.[27] To meet the threat on his eastern frontier Louis despatched Condé, with a detachment of troops from the Spanish Netherlands, to take over command there. Créqui had already been sent at the end of June to defend Trier.[28]

Luxemburg took over from Condé in the Spanish Netherlands; depleted by the need to send contingencies to Brittany, to the Mosel, to Alsace and to Lorraine, he had about 40,000 troops. With the opposing armies in the Spanish Netherlands now being of about equal size, both were compelled to adopt a defensive stance.[29] In his march towards Halle the Prince of Orange had managed to capture Diest; and he made the best of this to manage public opinion in the Dutch Republic. He instructed Fagel to spread the news in the towns of Holland that the promptitude of his actions and Diest's capture had saved what would otherwise have been the inevitable loss of Louvain, Mechelen and Brussels. Pesters was given the same propaganda task in Utrecht, Gelderland and Overijssel, and the Prince of Nassau was to do the same in Friesland and Groningen.[30]

Seen in the light of the limited resources at Prince William's disposal compared with the French, his defensive strategy was, indeed, no mean achievement; and the towns Louis had managed to capture, which were situated in the south of the Spanish Netherlands, were not of great importance. Nevertheless one can detect an underlying anxiety in the Prince's demeanour – it was necessary to maintain morale in the Dutch Republic. As early as the beginning of June he had had to assure the States-General that he would not take undue risks in the forthcoming campaign.[31]

His aggressive instincts were, nevertheless, not wholly stilled. At the end of August he ventured south to capture Binche, between Mons and Charleroi, but was soon compelled to withdraw. He was unable to persuade the Spaniards of the advisability of besieging Liège, and in the middle of October he departed for the Republic, leaving Waldeck in command to wind up the year's campaign and see the troops into winter quarters.[32]

The physical demands made on the Prince were considerable and he had to adapt himself to whatever accommodation could be found on the march, whether a monastery or a nunnery, a manor-house or a peasant's abode, with weather ranging from continuous rain for a fortnight to the summer's heat, and with hunting his one form of diversion. By contrast the horsemanship of his secretary, Constantijn Huygens the younger, seems to have been but mediocre, and he frequently fell from his mount; as a gossip he was more adept. He established a cosy coterie where there was much to-ing and fro-ing amongst the Prince's retinue, and where – if the Prince was not present – the company were able to divert themselves with a stimulating interchange of stories and scandal, often with an earthy sexual undertow.

On the eastern front the allied armies achieved some success; on 11 August Créqui was defeated at the battle of Konz-Saarbruck, at the junction formed by the Mosel and Saar rivers, at the hands of Brunswick and Lorraine troops. He sought refuge in Trier, but there he was not secure for long; his troops, including officers, mutinied on 6 September and he was compelled to surrender. This was not something that could be tolerated by Louis XIV; when the defeated garrison arrived at Metz one in 20 of the cavalry and dragoons drew lots and were hanged on the spot.[33]

On the Upper Rhine, however, the Imperial army was contained by Condé, and Montecuccoli withdrew from Alsace, to which he had advanced after the death of Turenne, to take up position at Kandel in the Palatinate, to the south of Heidelberg.[34]

ABRAHAM WICQUEFORT, DU MOULIN AND THE ENGLISH OPPOSITION

When the Prince was on his way back to the United Provinces he received news of the legal proceedings against Abraham Wicquefort, the contemporary historian, whose works we have frequently cited, and who had been a close intimate of Johan De Witt; his activities ranged widely and he was also a diplomat representing various European courts, the writer of newsletters and the provider of intelligence. Prince William had become suspicious of the sort of intelligence he was furnishing when he obtained an inkling of his correspondence with German courts at his meeting with the Great Elector at Cleves at the end of March, or shortly afterwards. At his instigation Wicquefort was arrested, and further investigation revealed correspondence between himself and Sir Joseph Williamson, the English Secretary of State, in which Williamson was trying to establish who the Prince's contacts were with the English opposition. For whatever reason – whether he could, but was unwilling, or whether he was promising more than he could deliver – Wicquefort fell short in providing these names.

The dealings with the English opposition were obviously a sensitive subject and, on Fagel's advice, the Prince did not go to The Hague, but to his residence at Soesdijk, to distance himself from the court proceedings. He did go to The Hague at the end of October but, at the beginning of November, just before the court issued its judgement, as the Prince wrote to Waldeck 'on this accursed affair of Wicquefort', he again absented himself from the capital – as, on this occasion, Fagel did as well. It was customary for the court's sentences to be published, and at the end of September it had sent William for his comments a draft of its sentence in view of its 'delicate' nature, both as regarded the Prince himself in particular and the interest of the State in general; he declined to comment himself but he did suggest that they consult the Committee on Foreign Affairs (the *Secrète Besogne*), as a result of which certain names were deleted. What could be done was therefore done to draw a veil over the activities of the Prince and the Grand Pensionary in England.

Furthermore, when Du Moulin died in June 1676 the Prince took care to write from his camp in the Southern Netherlands to Fagel, noting that Du Moulin 'had several papers of great importance' and asking the Pensionary to make certain that they did not fall into the wrong hands, but to take them into his own safekeeping. Fagel arranged for Halewijn, one of the judges of the court of Holland, to seize his papers, and they are now amongst Fagel's own papers at the Rijksarchief in The Hague. But Professor Haley has observed that there are some notable omissions we know of from other sources and speculates that some may after all have fallen into the wrong hands – Du Moulin was robbed by his servants on his deathbed.[35] Alternatively Fagel and his associates may have engaged in some selective weeding, and perhaps this is the reason why our knowledge of the relationship between the Prince of Orange, the Grand Pensionary of Holland and the English opposition is not more extensive.

As for Wicquefort, he found a fate not wholly uncongenial. Although found guilty he managed to escape from his prison and found refuge in Celle, where, in 1680, he received permission to return to The Hague for six months, and, after his death, his children were accorded the restoration of his confiscated estate.[36]

DEATH OF AMALIA VON SOLMS

At a personal level there was sad news regarding Prince William's grandmother, Amalia von Solms. At the end of June Dr Rumpf told Constantijn Huygens in the camp that she was not well and had lost her appetite; at the end of July the news was no better, although her force of personality does not appear to have diminished and she refused a visit from her two daughters, the Princesses of Friesland and Zimmeren, who had offered to come to her in The Hague, on the grounds that they would only weep at her bedside and make her feel much worse. The formidable old lady died on 8 September aged 74.[37] Like her daughter-in-law, Mary, she had seen the political importance of maintaining great state to uphold the prestige of the House of Orange – golden utensils were used even at her ordinary meals – and William had to find 100,000 guilders to pay off her debts.[38]

SUMMARY OF 1675

As we survey the war years to date we can observe that the first two years saw the stature of the Prince of Orange enhanced by achievements that raised him, with Louis XIV, to one of the two foremost protagonists on the European scene; in 1672 Louis's invasion of the United Provinces, with overwhelming force, had been brought to a halt; and 1673 saw the expulsion of his armies from the Dutch Republic and the creation of the Grand Alliance, which had brought the war to the very frontiers of his kingdom and threatened it. In 1674 the opportunity this presented had been wasted through circumstances which were not the doing of the Prince of Orange. Now, at the end of 1675 – when the Prince was barely 25 years old – the campaign can best be described as a draw; the minor gains made by Louis in the Spanish Netherlands were offset by his losses on the German front and by the losses of his Swedish ally in the north. But the allied impetus had also been checked in its turn. And the balance of power was to tilt gradually towards the French King.

1 Mignet, *op. cit.*, IV, p.340. McKay, *Great Elector, op. cit.*, pp.220ff. For the Prince of Orange's stay at Cleves see Waddington, *op. cit.*, II, p.360, for his reception in the Dutch Republic see p.361, and for the capture of Stettin and the rest of Pomerania, pp.386, 396. For William's letter to Waldeck see *Wilhelm III von Oranien und Georg Friedrich von Waldeck*, The Hague 1873–80, II, pp.246–7.
2 Nimwegen, *op. cit.*, p.488.
3 De Jonge, *op. cit.*, III, ii, pp.45, 47.
4 Antal and Pater, *op. cit.*, I. p.157. *Correspondentie Willem III en Bentinck, op. cit.*, II, 2, p.10.
5 Antal and Pater, *op. cit.*, I, pp.158–60.
6 Müller, *Waldeck, op. cit.*, I, p.37, II, pp 246–7.
7 Japikse, *Willem III, op. cit.*, II, p.42.
8 Nimwegen, *op. cit.*, p.485.
9 Rousset, *op. cit.*, II, pp.142, 144.
10 Temple, *Works, op. cit.*, I, pp.223.
11 Müller, *Waldeck, op. cit.*, II, p.247.
12 D'Estrades, *op. cit.*, IX, Supplement, p.101.
13 H. Lonchay, *Correspondance de la Cour d'Espagne*, Brussels, V, pp.213, 218–20.
14 Rousset, *op. cit.*, II, pp.146–9.
15 Huygens, *Journaal, op. cit.*, p.28. *Correspondentie Willem III en Bentinck, op. cit.*, II, 2, p.33.
16 *Correspondentie Willem III en Bentinck, op. cit.*, II, 2, pp.32–4. Rousset, *op. cit.*, II, p.147. Lonchay, *op. cit.*, V, p.213.
17 Huygens, *Journaal, op. cit.*, p.29.
18 *Correspondentie Willem III en Bentinck, op. cit.*, II, 2, p.36.
19 Rousset, *op. cit.*, II, p.149. Nimwegen, *op. cit.*, pp.485–6.

20 *Correspondentie Willem III en Bentinck, op. cit.*, II, 2, pp.38–9, 41–2. Nimwegen, *op. cit.*, n.49, p.486. Huygens, *Journaal, op. cit.*, p.32.

21 *Correspondentie Willem III en Bentinck, op. cit.*, II, 2, p.43. Huygens, *Journaal, op. cit.*, p.34.

22 Rousset, *op. cit.*, II, pp.146–50.

23 Huygens, *Journaal, op. cit.*, pp.38–39.

24 *Correspondentie Willem III en Bentinck, op. cit.*, II, 2, pp.47–8. Nimwegen, *op. cit.*, pp.486–7. For the rain see Huygens, *Journaal, op. cit.*, pp.36ff.

25 Rousset, *op. cit.*, II, p.150.

26 *Ibid.*, p.160–1.

27 D'Estrades, *op. cit.*, IX, Supplement, p.155.

28 Nimwegen, *op. cit.*, p.487. Rousset, *op. cit.*, II, p.149.

29 Rousset, *op. cit.*, pp.190–1. Huygens, *Journaal, op. cit.*, II, p.49.

30 Rousset, *op. cit.*, II, p.152.

31 *Correspondentie Willem III en Bentinck, op. cit.*, II, 2, p.38.

32 Huygens, *Journaal, op. cit.*, pp.59, 73, 74. Müller, *Waldeck, op. cit.*, pp.248ff.

33 Rousset, *op. cit.*, II, pp.174–80.

34 *Ibid.*, II, p.187.

35 Haley, *English Opposition, op. cit.*, pp.217–18.

36 *Correspondentie Willem III en Bentinck, op. cit.*, II, 2, p.24 n.2, p.68, p.114. Haley, *English Opposition, op. cit.*, pp.198–9. Müller, *Waldeck, op. cit.*, II, pp.251, 261. Huygens, *Journaal, op. cit.*, pp.72–3.

37 Huygens, *Journaal, op. cit.*, pp.38, 47. *Correspondentie Willem III en Bentinck, op. cit.*, II, 2, pp.60–1.

38 Poelhekke, article in *Amalia van Solms, op. cit.*, p.126. Baxter, *op. cit.*, p.132.

16 1676: PEACE MOVES AND THE ENGLISH MARRIAGE

PEACE NEGOTIATIONS BEGIN AT NIJMEGEN

At the end of 1675 peace negotiations, with Charles II acting as mediator, were moving very slowly forward; but it had at least been agreed that the venue for the Peace Congress should be Nijmegen. William Temple succinctly summarised the diplomatic scene in a letter to his father on 12 December. Whilst France laid claim to all the conquests she had made, both in the War of Devolution and in the present one, Temple believed she would be prepared to cede a town or two in the Spanish Netherlands, provided she kept Franche-Comté, and she was prepared to leave both the Dutch and the States of the Holy Roman Empire in the position they were in before the war; Spain wanted to return to the Treaty of the Pyrenees; the Emperor, finding that he had the support of nearly all the German states and being subsidised by the Dutch and by Spain, was prepared to continue the war and would insist not only on the restitution of the Duchy of Lorraine – the other allies agreed with him on this – and Philippsburg, but also reparation for the damages suffered by the German princes on the Rhine; the Dutch wanted the restoration of Maastricht and a commercial treaty with France, but also wanted five or six towns restored to Spain to safeguard the Spanish Netherlands in exchange for Franche-Comté.

Temple's own view was that the complications resulting in the north from Sweden's intervention would not stand in the way of peace if all the other points could be agreed; but of that he was not very optimistic and he thought matters would need to be settled by another campaign.[1] In fact, the best part of three more years of war was to ensue before the Peace of Nijmegen was concluded, and we will need to trace the diplomacy of Prince William in those years through its interaction with the military events in the field and the internal politics of the Dutch Republic.

We will later be examining the mechanisms by which the Prince of Orange exercised power within the country; suffice it to say that at this time his control over military affairs was paramount and he and Gaspar Fagel also had a very strong grip on foreign policy, which, however, was gradually to weaken over time. But the extent to which he dominated affairs at this point is reflected in Temple's observation after William left The Hague to join the army for the 1676 campaigning season that 'this place is now as dead as I have seen any great town, or seat of public business', the Prince taking with him 'all the company that used to fill this place'.[2]

THE PRINCE BROACHES THE ENGLISH MARRIAGE

But before his departure for the camp there was one very important matter that he wished to raise with the English ambassador. Temple was summoned to Honselaarsdijk, the Prince of Orange's country house outside The Hague, at the beginning of April. In the garden there, in the course of a two-hour talk between the two of them with no one else present, the Prince raised the subject of his marrying; his preference had been to address this issue after the conclusion of peace, but that looked as if it could take some time, and he was coming under pressure from both his supporters and from the States-General to come to a decision. He was resolved to marry and he was inclined to a match in England, by which he meant Princess Mary; but before coming to a decision he wanted Temple's advice 'as a friend' on two points.

The first was political. He was receiving advice from his English contacts not to pursue the English marriage because it would be seen as identifying him too closely with a court which was so at odds with the mood of the country that, without a change of course, it was bound to run into difficulties. This was, in fact, a very prescient observation but Temple reassured him that 'the Crown of England stood upon surer foundations than ever it had done in former times'; and that he 'believed the people would be found better subjects than perhaps the King himself believed them'. The Prince stood a chance of bringing the court round to his views – Temple meant the need to contain Louis XIV – and if he did 'the most seditious men in England would be hard put to find an ill side' in this marriage.

The second point was personal and related to 'the person and disposition of the young Lady', which were very important to him. With a degree of self-knowledge – as rare in the 17th century as it is now – he admitted 'that he might, perhaps, not be very easy for a wife to live with … that if he should meet with one to give him trouble at home, 'twas what he should not be able to bear, who was like to have enough abroad in the course of his life.' This too was prescient – he would *not* be easy to live with, and it fortunately turned out that Mary's personal qualities could not have been more suited to the partnership they were to enter into. Temple's wife and his sister, who were friends of the Princess's governess, had always spoken highly of her; and, as it happened, Lady Temple was about to go to England on private business; in all secrecy she was deputed to carry letters from the Prince to Charles II and the Duke of York asking for permission to go to England immediately after the conclusion of the campaign to pursue the matter further; and during her stay in England she, in Temple's words, 'should endeavour to inform herself the most particularly she could of all that concerned the person, humour and dispositions of the young Princess'.[3]

Lady Temple was a relative of Danby, who was also an old friend of Temple. Through Temple, therefore, the means lay close at hand for the Prince to add considerably to the strength of his English contacts.

One factor, it has been suggested, that induced the Prince of Orange to pursue the marriage at this time when he had pushed it aside the previous year was that Mary was now 14 years old – of marriageable age, therefore – and that there was a possibility that she might marry the Dauphin of France if he did not make his move.[4] There might also have been the further factor that he had always professed the belief that it lay within England's power to bring France to a satisfactory peace, something which now looked as though it would be increasingly difficult to do by military means alone.

At this time, however, Charles II had strengthened his ties with Louis XIV. In August 1675 he had given an undertaking to Louis that he would dissolve Parliament if it tried to force him into a war with France or refused him supply, in which case Louis would pay him £100,000. The House of Commons did vote a small supply of £300,000, but it was in a sour mood that boded ill for the future – one bill in contemplation would have curbed the King's ability to raise taxes – and on 23 November Charles prorogued Parliament for 15 months. This was not a dissolution but Charles told Louis that he was under pressure from Danby to enter into a Dutch alliance and this persuaded Louis to pay the £100,000 in exchange for a new agreement in which Charles undertook not to enter into a treaty with the Dutch without French consent. It was entered into on 26 February 1676. Danby refused to be party to this; and Charles was reduced to writing out the agreement in his own hand, and signing it with only Lauderdale amongst his ministers participating in the proceedings when he acted as a witness. A tinge of farce coloured the melodrama when Charles could not find the signet ring, which he particularly wanted to use for sentimental, perhaps for superstitious, reasons – his father had had it on his finger when he mounted the scaffold for his execution – and he had to use a cipher instead. It is not surprising, therefore, that the Prince of Orange eventually told Temple in September that his uncle had refused his request to go to England before peace was entered into 'in terms something hardish' – the words the Prince used were in English.[5] The marriage proposal, therefore, remained, for the time being, in abeyance.

THE UNSUCCESSFUL CAMPAIGN

The omens for the 1676 campaign were not good. There was no hiding the weakness of Spain, and the despatch the Spanish ambassador in The Hague, De Lira, sent to Madrid on 10 December 1675 presented a bleak picture; affairs in the Spanish Netherlands were in total disorder; there was a complete lack of resources and it was impossible to pay the subsidies due to the allies; the Spanish army was not large enough and Spain had not paid the Dutch what they had promised for the Dutch fleet to be sent to the Mediterranean. The Dutch had informed him that without an extraordinary effort by the Spanish King to meet his engagements it would be impossible for them to incur new expenditure for the war.[6]

A Dutch envoy, Van Heemskerk, was despatched to Madrid in this same month, and arrived there in January 1676. He told the Spaniards that offensive action in the Spanish Netherlands would require a minimum of 20,000 men, apart from the garrison troops;

combined with 30,000 Dutch troops this could constitute a force capable of undertaking a siege with a covering field army. On the financial side the Dutch would be unable to meet the subsidies due to the Emperor and the German princes. The Spaniards said that they were awaiting the arrival from America of their treasure fleet, which had been delayed, but the Dutch envoy discounted the relief this would provide – any recruits the Spaniards were able to raise would be sent to Catalonia or to Sicily to deal with the French-supported insurrection. His assessment, however, was a little too gloomy. The threat of the Dutch entering into a separate peace elicited a promise from the Spaniards to provide 20,000 or 22,000 men.[7] Although it was not a promise that they were to meet in full, in the event they did provide 13,000 for the allied field army in Flanders.

On the Austrian side in December 1675 Prince William sent an outline plan of campaign to Vienna, which envisaged the formation of four allied armies: the main Imperial army to act on the Rhine; another corps, under the Duke of Lorraine, on the Mosel; a Spanish army (supported by Dutch, Münster and Imperial contingents) on the Scheldt; with the main Dutch army on the left and the Brunswick troops on the right-hand side of the Maas. In Vienna, however, lack of support from Montecuccoli ensured it came to nothing.[8] An overall coordinated plan was thus, once again, lacking.

In 1676 there was a material change in the high command both amongst the French and the Austrians; Turenne was dead and the Prince of Condé, beset by gout, retired from the scene, as did Montecuccoli, with the new Duke of Lorraine, Charles V – his uncle had died the previous September – taking over the command of the Imperial army. In France strategy was now to be much influenced by Vauban, and it marked a wholly different approach to war. In September and October the previous year he had written to Louvois elaborating on ideas he had long held, emphasising the need to rationalise and straighten the French northern frontier to create what he called a *pré carré*, that is to say a squared-off or straightened-out frontier. Account, he argued, should be taken of the relationships which the fortresses had to each other, of the rivers, of the lie of the land, of the ability to bring up support where it was needed. This most mathematical of military engineers made his meticulous calculations of the most economical use of fighting manpower through the reordering of the fortresses. Too many of the French ones – such as Charleroi and Oudenarde – were too far forward; at the same time Spain retained enclaves inside France such as Aire, St-Omer, Condé, Bouchain, Valenciennes and Cambrai. This higgledy-piggledy disorder should be cured on the basis of mathematical principles. In war, as elsewhere, the inception of the age of reason was beginning to make its mark.[9] And these principles were to underlie what Louis was in the end able to demand, and obtain, under the Treaty of Nijmegen which finally ended the present war in 1678.

It was decided to besiege the town of Condé, and energetic preparations were at once put in train. Louvois was determined to enter the campaign both before the enemy and stronger than the enemy. On 21 February the positioning of the armies and the commands were decided upon. Louis would command in person in Flanders, having beneath him his brother, Monsieur, the Duke of Orléans, and five marshals of France, including Créqui, Schomberg and Humières. The army, it has been calculated, amounted to nearly 62,000 men – although exactitude, as always, is lacking. Marshal Rochefort was to command on the Maas with about 19,000 men; and Luxemburg, now also a marshal, was to take command against Germany with 32,000.[10]

On 17 April the town of Condé was besieged by Créqui; the following day 8,000 pioneers, under the direction of Vauban, began working on the lines of circumvallation; and on the 21st Louis arrived, having left St-Germain on the 16th, to attend the opening of the trenches exactly on the day appointed. The assault on the night of the 25th/26th was followed by the surrender of the town. Where Vauban was concerned precision was all.

The royal army and the King then moved on as a field force to cover the siege of Bouchain, which the besieging army began on 2 May under the command of Monsieur, Créqui and Vauban; this consisted of about 13,500 foot and nearly 8,000 horse.[11] The army of the King, at this time, amounted to more than 45,000 men – including, perhaps, the infantry from the besieging army – without counting more than 4,000 horse which could be drawn from the army of Monsieur at six hours' notice.[12]

The Prince of Orange in the meantime had reached Rozendaal, the usual muster point for the Dutch army, on 11 April. On the 19th he arrived near Mechelen, to the north of Brussels, where he received news of the siege of Condé and determined to march to its relief. He had about 28,000 men and Villa Hermosa had managed to assemble about 13,000, a combined force in the region of 41,000. The allied army marched to Mons – on the way the Prince found time to draft his will and sent it to Fagel, who was one of the executors – but they heard en route that Condé had fallen. The difference in manpower between the French and allied armies was very considerable; but despite this it was decided to come to the aid of Bouchain, and to seek out the King of France and offer battle.[13]

On 10 May the allied army arrived close to Valenciennes and as they arrived so did the army of Louis XIV; both were drawn up in battle array within a cannon shot of each other. We do not know the exact numbers on each side at this point, but the French army was the larger.[14] The Prince's usual elation at the prospect of battle manifested itself. 'It is the most beautiful sight in the world to see two such mighty armies so close to each other on a level field' – thus the Prince of Orange to Fagel on 11 May. He did not believe it possible for the armies so closely marshalled to be able to leave the field without a battle.[15] A nervous Fagel may, perhaps, have felt less elation.

But no combat ensued. Louis's army looked to the King, on horseback and surrounded by his marshals and other high-ranking officers, for the signal to commence the action. He did not give it; instead he asked for advice. Louvois was the first to proffer it; the role of the

King's army was to cover the siege of Bouchain, not to attack but to defend, he said. Louis made no response; and, asked to give their views, three marshals added their voices to that of Louvois, with only one against. Defence it would be.[16]

On the allied side as well the aggressive enthusiasm of the Prince of Orange was curbed both by the Spaniards and by the Rhinegrave and Waldeck. At their urging there, too, a defensive posture was adopted, although this was at the cost of the frustrated Prince directing his ire at his Field Marshal, which clearly distressed Waldeck greatly; he wrote William a dignified letter saying that one day he would realise that the aspersions cast upon him were not merited, but whatever transpired the Prince would find him unaltered, true to his promises, and forever 'Your Highness's faithful servitor'.[17]

The *gloire* of the two heads of the armies was deeply involved. For the great King a retreat from battle would bring the appearance of pusillanimity; but a defeat in battle would bring an unbearable diminution in prestige. For the Prince of Orange the outcome was predestined, a glorious victory or, the alternative he would otherwise have wished for, a glorious death; but the military and political consequences of defeat for either side in this single encounter were immense – the possible capture or death of the King or the Stadholder, and at risk was the loss of the Spanish Netherlands or the invasion of France. It was understandable that their advisers urged caution.

The allies managed to prevent the capture of Valenciennes, but Bouchain surrendered on 11 May. For ten days the two hostile armies faced each other before the French withdrew on the 20th,[18] and a war of manoeuvre followed for several weeks.

On 4 July, following what had become his usual pattern during the annual campaigning seasons, Louis left for Versailles, leaving Schomberg in command of the army; it had been reduced by the despatch of 8,000 troops to Luxemburg in May and by further reinforcements of nearly 9,000 men, which were sent a few days before Louis's departure to Créqui, who had succeeded Rochefort on the Maas after the latter's death.[19]

These reinforcements were required to safeguard the Rhine frontier and Alsace against the new Duke of Lorraine, an outstanding general, of whom our story will have much to say, who commanded the Imperial army on the Rhine. In May the Imperialists, under the Prince of Baden, threatened Philippsburg, which lay on the Rhine to the north of Strasburg, and in due course a long siege of the town commenced on 22 June which, despite Luxemburg's efforts and a heroic resistance, finally led to its capitulation on 9 September.[20]

The diversion of the French forces to the east decided the Prince of Orange to embark on the siege of Maastricht, as he informed the *Secrète Besogne* and Gaspar Fagel on 3 July.[21] However, he had at his disposal only around 36,000 men – 16,500 Dutch troops and the rest contingents from Brandenburg, Palatine Neuburg, Brunswick, and 6,000 Spanish cavalry. After making provision for the besieging force he could allocate only 26,000 to a field army to both cover the siege and defend Spanish Flanders. Against the Prince's 36,000 the

French army in Flanders still amounted to between 40,000 and 45,000 men, and, once again, Waldeck had reservations about the undertaking.[22] We need to remember that throughout this year's campaign the Prince's forces had been inferior to the French; there was little he could do about this but face the situation with fortitude.

On 7 July he arrived before Maastricht and the siege began. However, the waters in the Maas were so low that there was difficulty in getting the artillery to the besieged fortress before the 16th, and it was not until the 19th that 30 pieces of cannon opened fire on the defences. Ominously the Prince received information from Villa Hermosa that the French army was marching into Flanders to make an attack there;[23] Marshal d'Humières was indeed bringing up the Flanders army to besiege Aire, with Marshal Schomberg in command of the covering field contingent. The French had decided that Maastricht – it had a garrison of 7,000 men and a determined commander – could hold out for the time being whilst the opportunity was seized to take on Aire. On 21 July the siege began; on the 31st the town capitulated.[24]

Three days later whilst he was in the trenches Prince William received a wound in his right arm, although it was slight. An alarmed States-General was once again compelled to write expressing their concern; if anything should befall His Highness, they pointed out, 'the whole State would be thrown into the utmost confusion and disorder',[25] which, indeed, was true. Militarily, politically and diplomatically everything radiated from the Prince and there was none who could obviously fill his place either in the House of Orange or amongst the Regents.

After the surrender of Aire the French calculated that it would take 21 days to come to the relief of Maastricht, and, despite their earlier confidence, they were now uncertain that the town could hold out for that time. Nevertheless they decided on coming to her aid without any further diversion, other than the capture by d'Humières of the small fortress of Linck. In fact the Prince of Orange wrote to Waldeck on 3 August that the siege was 'scarcely progressing as much as he would have hoped'. Leaving Aire on the 6th, Schomberg arrived at Tongres on the 26th and fired off all his 32 cannon as a signal to the Maastricht garrison of his arrival. The allies decided that they would have to raise the siege.[26]

It had not been well conducted, and the lapse of nearly two months brought the Prince no success, although it was true that the town was strongly fortified, well garrisoned and ably commanded by the Count de Calvo. William himself was no Vauban, and he did not at this stage have a highly skilled siege engineer to remedy this deficiency, as he was later to have in Coehoorn. On 15 August the Rhinegrave was wounded, and, although William at first thought it was not dangerous, he was now also deprived of the assistance of this commander on whom he had always relied heavily[27] – and the wound in fact was to prove mortal.

The field army of the allies, too, had been out-manoeuvred by the French, the result of their different objectives; Waldeck wanted to protect the army besieging Maastricht; Villa Hermosa wanted to prevent Spanish towns falling into French hands. They ended up dividing their forces, with Villa Hermosa positioning himself to defend the towns and with Waldeck taking up station at Brussels to await what the French would do. Thus dispersed, they were unable to check Schomberg's march. The Spanish cavalry did join Waldeck's troops when he marched to the aid of the Prince before Maastricht, but they could not prevent the relief of the town. Nor could the combined forces then impede Schomberg's ably conducted withdrawal. Leaving a garrison behind at Maastricht, he retired south along the Maas towards France and eventually reached Charleroi – the generous rewards he received for his services included the confiscated property situated in France of the dead Rhinegrave.[28]

Prince William was deeply disappointed and his disappointment appears to have affected his health; thin and feverish, he left the army on 11 September, before Schomberg had completed his withdrawal, and, travelling so fast with his escort that his secretary, poor Huygens, who was suffering from a bad bout of dysentery, could hardly keep up, he arrived at his country house at Honselaarsdijk on the 13th and at The Hague two days later to be received by the burghers of the town. The state of his nerves appears to have resulted in a further outburst against Waldeck; in a letter sent the day after the Prince's departure the Field Marshal felt the need to express the hope that 'I have not entirely lost the confidence Your Highness has of my good intentions' and he asked the Prince to grant him 'the liberty to speak as a man of probity without fear of a rough response which is not merited'.[29]

It did not, however, take Prince William long to recover his equanimity and his old resolve; he told Waldeck that the political mood on his return to The Hague was unfavourable, but that would not change his own position; he fostered no illusions, was his grim assessment, but everything in his power would be done to prepare for a good campaign the following year. And when he learnt there was a chance of engaging Schomberg in battle he hurried south only to find that Spanish opposition had allowed the French Marshal to slip away, and thus, without reaching the army and without loss of time, he returned to the Republic to face the task in hand.[30]

AMSTERDAM BEGINS TO TURN AGAINST THE WAR

It was indeed true that political opinion in the Dutch Republic was hardening against the war. The Amsterdam Regent, Gillis Valckenier, was increasingly opposed to the war and to the power which had devolved on the Prince of Orange as a result of the constitutional settlements in Utrecht, Gelderland and Overijssel. He therefore sought a reconciliation with his opponents in the Town Council, of whom Hendrick Hooft, the old supporter of De Witt, was the most important. At Valckenier's instigation an agreement for the future governance of the city, which was to settle the differences amongst the factions, was drafted in May 1676, and, although not formally adopted, it led to Hooft becoming a Burgomaster in 1677.[31] The duo of Hooft and Valckenier were to become the kernel of the Dutch peace party. D'Estrades had also for some time been in communication with another Regent, Van den Bosch, who became Amsterdam's Pensionary.[32] Of all the Holland towns Amsterdam was not only the most wealthy and powerful but also the most independent – her complicated constitution ensured that in practice the Prince exercised but weak and indirect influence over the election of the four burgomasters and that the burgomasters had a high degree of autonomy from the Town Council.[33]

Temple told Charles II on 2 September that he was unable to judge 'whether the Prince, and the persons at present in the government, will be able, after this disgrace of Mastricht [*sic*], to keep the spirits there in temper enough to carry on the war another year'.[34]

THE PRINCE DETERMINED TO CONTINUE THE WAR

Not long afterwards William summoned Temple from Nijmegen, where the English Ambassador had gone for the Peace Conference – Hieronymus van Beverninck was also there as part of the Dutch delegation and D'Estrades as part of the French. William and Temple met on the 16th at Soestdijk, the Prince's country house between Utrecht and Amersfoort, which was about a day's journey from Nijmegen and where Temple stayed for two days. Temple's letter to Charles II of 20 September gives an account of the conversations they held in which he presents himself as being in a rather avuncular and cosy, confidential relationship, drawing out the Prince's innermost thoughts; but we need to remember that William was perfectly well aware that all he said would be reported to the King; hence, stripping away Temple's gloss, we will find a clear, businesslike message from William to his uncle.

The message he conveyed was that he was determined to continue the fight despite the unfortunate result of the campaign and despite the pressures he was coming under. He 'knew very well' that it was the ill luck attendant on the position he held that 'whilst others committed the mistakes it was he that carried the shame'. Except for the few who 'knew the inside of the business', the rest of the world would blame him for the campaign's outcome. But despite the failings of the Spaniards he was determined to 'have his revenge another year'. He brushed aside Temple's question 'whether he thought the States were in humour, or the country in condition to go on with the war' with the assertion that, whilst he would not pretend otherwise than that 'they had a horrible mind to the peace', that had also been the position for the last two years. They were capable of continuing the war, especially if relieved from subsidising the allies – the subsidies did in fact cease – and, lacking a peace 'with some honour and safety', they would be drawn unobtrusively into persisting with the war – but, as he was to reveal later in the conversation, he was perfectly aware that in the absence of success this might not be beyond the next campaign.

He wanted peace himself and no personal interests of his own should delay it. But 'he could not tell how to come by it' (spoken in English). There was no hope of a peace emerging from the conference at Nijmegen for another four years, but if Charles wanted peace that winter the King would have to make it himself, by laying down the terms he expected and thought reasonable from the contending parties.[35] The initiative, in short, the Prince thought, lay with the King of England. It was indeed true that Charles in conjunction with the Dutch had, by means of the Triple Alliance in 1668, forced Louis XIV to the negotiation table at the treaty of Aix-la-Chapelle, which had terminated the War of Devolution. But that was a course which Charles, very sensibly from his point of view in the very different present circumstances, declined to take again now. He thought it was up to the French to state their terms or for the Congress at Nijmegen to negotiate the peace, otherwise, as Temple reported back to William on 31 October, 'his Majesty must content himself with having done what he could towards it'. The King also reiterated that he was not yet ready to see William in England – the time 'was not yet proper for it'.[36]

The resolution of the Prince to continue with the war stood side by side with his cold grasp of the realities. Although his belief was that the States could be drawn into fighting another campaign, that belief was qualified. As he also told Temple at their meeting at Soestdijk, the failure of his allies was causing him to despair of 'any good issue of the war' and 'without some great success [in the forthcoming campaign], he did not believe the States would be induced to continue it longer'.[37]

However, Regent support was, at this juncture, still forthcoming, with the Prince of Orange's determined doggedness bearing fruit. The influential Holland Regent from Alkmaar, the wine-loving Hieronymus van Beverninck, told Temple towards the end of October – 'after talking himself sober' – that if the Germans would advance into France the States would not make peace in 1677; they had taken their measures and found they could continue the war for another campaign with the same forces as in 1676 or, if occasion demanded, with even larger ones.[38]

1 Temple, *Works, op. cit.*, 1754, IV, pp.126ff.
2 *Ibid.*, IV, p.226.
3 *Ibid.*, I, pp.254–7, IV, pp.227–30.
4 Haley, article in *The Anglo-Dutch Rapprochement of 1677, English Historical Review*, 73 (1958), pp.616–17.
5 Mignet, *op. cit.*, IV, pp.367–84. Hutton, *op. cit.*, pp.329–33. Temple, *Works, op. cit.*, 1754, IV, p.283.
6 Lonchay, *op. cit.*, V, p.235.
7 Nimwegen, *op. cit.*, pp.488–9.
8 *Correspondentie Willem III en Bentinck, op. cit.*, II, 2, pp.72–3. Antal and Pater, *op. cit.*, I, p.179.
9 Rousset, *op. cit.*, II, pp.202–5. See also John A. Lynn, *Wars of Louis XIV*, London & New York 1999, p.75.
10 Rousset, *op. cit.*, II, pp.205–7. Knoop, *op. cit.*, II, p.183.
11 Rousset, *op. cit.*, II, pp.216–18. Rousset puts the besieging army at 19 battalions and 55 squadrons which, on the figures given by John Lynn of 712 men per battalion and 144 per squadron, produces 13,528 foot and 7,920 horse, a total of 21,444 men (see John Lynn, *op. cit.*, p.61).

12 Rousset, *op. cit.*, II, p.219. Louvois wrote to Luxemburg on 2 and 4 May that the King's army amounted to 15 squadrons and 40 battalions, which he said amounted to more than 45,000 men without over 4,000 cavalry from Monsieur. On Lynn's figures – see note 11 above – 15 squadrons = 2,160 men and 40 battalions = 28,480 men, a total of 30,640. Perhaps Louvois was also including the besieging army's infantry of 13,528 foot, which would bring the King's army up to 44,174 men.

13 *Correspondentie Willem III en Bentinck, op. cit.*, II, 2, pp.85, 91, 95, 96. Knoop, *op. cit.*, II, pp.185–6.

14 Rousset, *op. cit.*, II, p.222.

15 *Correspondentie Willem III en Bentinck, op. cit.*, II, 2, p.98.

16 Rousset, *op. cit.*, II, pp.221–2.

17 *Correspondentie Willem III en Bentinck, op. cit.*, II, 2, p.99. Müller, Waldeck, *op. cit.*, I, p.40. Huygens, *Journaal, op. cit.*, p.114.

18 *Correspondentie Willem III en Bentinck, op. cit.*, II, 2, pp.99, 104.

19 Rousset, *op. cit.*, II, pp.228–9, 232.

20 Rousset, *op. cit.*, I, pp.255–6, 265.

21 *Correspondentie Willem III en Bentinck, op. cit.*, II, 2, pp.116–17.

22 Nimwegen, *op. cit.*, p.494.

23 *Correspondentie Willem III en Bentinck, op. cit.*, II, 2, pp.119, 124. Rousset, *op. cit.*, II, pp.233, 257.

24 Rousset, *op. cit.*, II, pp.233, 257, 240. Nimwegen, *op. cit.*, p.495.

25 *Correspondentie Willem III en Bentinck, op. cit.*, II, 2, pp.125–6. Huygens, *Journaal, op. cit.*, pp.117–18.

26 Rousset, *op. cit.*, II, pp.240–1, 246. Müller, *Waldeck, op. cit.*, II, p.294. Huygens, *Journaal, op. cit.*, p.136.

27 Müller, *Waldeck, op. cit.*, II, p.309.

28 Japikse, *Willem III, op. cit.*, II, p.52. Nimwegen, *op. cit.*, pp.495–7. Rousset, *op. cit.*, II, pp.247–8.

29 Huygens, *Journaal, op. cit.*, pp.137, 142–3. Nimwegen, *op. cit.*, n.79, p.497. Müller, *Waldeck, op. cit.*, II, pp.313, 315.

30 Müller, *Waldeck, op. cit.*, II, pp.315, 316, 319.

31 Fruin, *op. cit.*, IV, pp.318ff.

32 Japikse, *Willem III, op. cit.*, II, pp.55–6.

33 See Fruin, *op. cit.*, IV, pp.310–12 and n.2, p.310.

34 Temple, *Works, op. cit.*, 1754, IV, p.279.

35 *Ibid.*, IV, pp.281–4.

36 *Ibid.*, IV, p.287.

37 *Ibid.*, I, p.281–2.

38 *Ibid.*, IV, pp.285–6.

17 1677: PEACE NEGOTIATIONS AND MARRIAGE

THE PEACE NEGOTIATIONS AND CHARLES II

William was determined not to give up on his endeavours to involve his uncle in the peace process. At the end of 1676 he invited Temple to come from Nijmegen to The Hague for a few days to continue their discussions. They met on 1 January 1677 and agreed that little was to be expected from the Nijmegen Congress. William again said that 'his Majesty was alone able to make the peace'. The Dutch States thought the peace 'absolutely necessary for them', but both Spain and the Emperor were even more opposed than they had been at the end of the last campaign. He himself also wanted the peace 'but did not know which way to go about it'. He appealed to Charles to let him know the conditions he sought or believed might deliver this outcome and he would then endeavour to 'concert it the best he could with his Majesty', adding the usual and characteristic caveat, 'so it might be done with safety to his own honour, and the interests of his country'.

Two days later Temple met with Fagel, who, like the Prince, complained bitterly of the conduct of the Dutch allies. He said that the Dutch could have any terms they wanted from France, whether it were the restoration of Maastricht, a commercial treaty, 'or any advantages to the house of Orange'. Personally he would agree to a peace separate from the allies with 'the greatest regret that could be, yet he did not see what else could be done, and did not know one man in Holland that was not of the same mind'. Everybody knew that France was not in a position to refuse whatever terms Charles II insisted upon, or risk his joining the war in conjunction with the rest of the allies.

The next morning, on 4 January, Temple went to see the Prince. When told of Fagel's observation that there was nothing else to be done but to make a separate peace and that he knew not a man in Holland who was not of his mind, the Prince interrupted him. 'Yes, I am sure I know one, and that is myself, and I will hinder it as long as I can; but, if anything should happen to me, I know it would be done in two days' time.' He agreed with Fagel that the outlook for the forthcoming campaign was not good, but who knew what might not happen. Charles II could make the peace before the campaign began but if he didn't 'for his part, he must go on, and take his fortune'. He had seen a poor old man that very morning in a boat struggling on a canal against the eddies created by the opening of a sluice gate; each time he came to his intended destination he was forced back again and this happened three or four times under the Prince's gaze, who concluded that he himself should do just as the poor old man did, without knowing the final outcome any more than he did.[1]

Charles II had good reason to resist the Dutch pressure to threaten military intervention to compel Louis XIV to enter into a general peace. As client to the French King his ties were much too close. The consideration that Louis could reveal the various treaties between them, particularly the Treaty of Dover and its religious provisions, may have carried some, but not too much, weight in Charles's mind, for, from Louis's point of view, it is difficult to see who could have been a more satisfactory holder of the English crown – which explains why Louis left this double-edged sword dangling but unused. But, nevertheless, it was from Louis that Charles received his subsidies; it was Louis who was his only European ally; and it was from Louis alone that there was even the remote chance, as the Dover Treaty had stipulated, of military assistance if Charles faced rebellion at home. There was the further consideration that Charles would need Parliamentary grants to engage in war, and past experience had taught him that this led to sorry outcomes – the funding had proved inadequate and the *quid pro quo* uncongenial.[2]

But Charles did yield to Dutch pressure to a degree. Fagel's threat of the Dutch entering into a separate peace with France played to English anxieties; there was the danger that a separate peace would bring with it the loss of the Spanish Netherlands and the dependency of the Dutch on Louis XIV, and thus a very radical change in the European constellation of power – 'there is nothing wee apprehend so much here as a seperate [*sic*] peace', Danby wrote to Temple on 8 January. Charles complained, through Temple, that the Dutch allies had been lobbying Members of Parliament 'and raising all men's spirits as high against the peace as they could; and that they had done it to such a degree, as made it very difficult for him to make any steps with France towards a general peace'. It would help if the Dutch ambassador, Van Beuningen, submitted a memorial on behalf of the Dutch government pressing him to pursue the peace and declaring that otherwise 'Flanders' – that is, the Spanish Netherlands – would be lost. This would address domestic suspicions that the purpose of his mediation was solely directed at furthering the interests of France. At the same time, through Van Beuningen, he offered the Dutch a defensive alliance on the conclusion of peace provided the Dutch did not enter into any engagements – with France – inconsistent with it.[3]

The Prince and Fagel reacted with alacrity – it was of course a constant of William's policy to prise Charles away from the grip of the King of France. They undertook to provide as soon as possible the memorandum Charles asked for on behalf of the Dutch States pressing him to pursue the peace negotiations and, pending this, an immediate letter, signed by William and Fagel, was sent to Van Beuningen, to conduct himself in such a way as to convey the same message less formally. This letter, it is interesting to note, was not communicated even to the *Secrète Besogne* – such was the degree to which Dutch foreign policy still, at this stage, lay in the hands of the Prince of Orange and the Grand Pensionary. At the same time, as Temple reported to Charles II on 15 January, William asked Temple to obtain Charles's views on the terms of the peace.

Temple pointed out that this would cause a delay and suggested instead that the Prince should give his own views, a course which, in any case, he believed would be more agreeable to Charles and would inspire greater confidence in the Prince's goodwill. After pausing for a moment, William replied that the terms should be on the footing of the treaty of Aix-la-Chapelle, except that France would obtain Aire and St-Omer in exchange for Ath and Charleroi. Maastricht and Philippsburg would be razed, the one by France, the other by the Emperor. As Temple pointed out, this would mean the restoration to Spain of Franche-Comté plus all the conquests made by France, as well as those she was likely to make, without receiving anything in return other than Aire and St-Omer. The Prince held out the possibility of swapping Franche-Comté for further towns held by France in the Spanish Netherlands – one would have to enquire what the French proposed. He accepted, however, that the French could not be brought to an agreement without the interposition of Charles II.

But, he then went on, in a dauntless display of defiance, if France would not consent to the terms he had proffered, or something close to them proposed by Charles, 'the war must go on, and God Almighty must decide it'. If France insisted on insupportable terms and if she thought the Dutch could be induced to make a separate peace 'let the Pensioner, or any else, tell [him] what they pleased, they should never do it whilst he was alive: and he would say one thing further … he had it in his power to hinder it…. If he died, he knew very well, it would be made the next day: but he did not trouble himself how the world was like to go when he was gone out of it.'

With that the Prince arose from his chair and, barring the civilities, the emotive interview was at an end.[4]

Whilst awaiting the reply from King Charles the Prince departed to divide his time between Soestdijk and the Orange hunting lodge at Dieren, the latter of which was six leagues from Nijmegen. Both of these had the advantage that he could converse less conspicuously with Temple there than he could at The Hague, where his discussions had given rise to suspicions amongst the Dutch allies that he was planning to negotiate a separate peace.[5]

Temple, meanwhile, still in The Hague, had a further interview with Fagel who, he found, continued precisely in the view that 'it must come to a separate peace'. He thought His Highness might be forced into it by the conduct of the allies, by the lack of success in the forthcoming campaign, and by 'the mutinies of the people, to which they were already but too much disposed at Amsterdam' because of the lack of progress being made at the Nijmegen Peace Congress.[6]

The reply from King Charles was not long in coming. He sent two letters directly to his nephew dated 18 and 19 January, with a further letter from the Secretary of State, Sir Joseph Williamson, also dated the 19th. Temple brought these to the Prince at Dieren, where he had been out hunting, and read them out on the 27th. The letters addressed two issues: the first was the proposal already made to Van Beuningen for a defensive alliance to secure the

Dutch against the French after peace was entered into and this was well received by the Prince. But the other issue was Charles's comments on the Prince's proposed peace terms on the basis of the Treaty of Aix-la-Chapelle. The King thought that it might be possible that Louis would agree to France's obtaining Cambrai, Aire and St-Omer in exchange for Ath, Charleroi, Oudenarde, Condé and Bouchain. Temple reported that the Prince's countenance changed when he mentioned Cambrai, but, having heard Temple through, he said dinner was ready and the matter could be discussed afterwards. Near the door, however, he said 'he must rather die than make such a peace'.

The meal being concluded, he told Temple that he had spoiled his dinner. He noted that the offer of the alliance came from the letter in Charles's own hand, whilst the comments on the peace terms came from Williamson only. It treated him as though Williamson 'thought him a child, or to be fed with whipped cream'; an approach, in the Prince's eyes, as calamitous in the Secretary of State, Williamson, as it had been in the Lord Chamberlain, Arlington. The Prince summed up the terms succinctly: Spain was being asked to cede Franche-Comté, Cambrai, Aire and St-Omer for the five towns mentioned. If the Dutch made peace on these terms they would lose their allies and become absolutely dependent on France, because if Spain were left in this state, the Spanish Netherlands could be defended neither by the Dutch nor by England, whenever the French should think fit to invade them. And, with the Spanish Netherlands lost, the Dutch could not possibly be defended by England against France and they would have to seek terms with Louis.

He made a further point: 'how lost he should be in honour, to his allies, and to all the world, by such a peace as this'. That was a consideration not just for the moment, but a far-seeing political consideration for the future. It was his conduct now towards his allies, despite all the pressures to abandon them, which constituted such an important part of his *gloire*. It would enable him in the future to rebuild the coalition – and on a grander scale – against Louis when the present one disintegrated.

He wrote a diplomatic letter to his uncle on 27 January gracefully thanking him for the offer of the alliance once peace was concluded, which he received 'with very great joy'. He referred Charles to Temple's report of their meeting for his views on the King's comments on the peace terms, save that he pleaded the King to allow him to 'exit from this war with some honour'.[7]

Charles responded through the medium of Sir Joseph Williamson at the beginning of February; but Temple fell ill and William had to travel to Groningen to mediate in a dispute between the town and the surrounding countryside, so that Temple and William were prevented from discussing the King's reply until the 25th at Soestdijk. When the Prince learnt that the letter came from Williamson his aversion to the Minister once again became apparent, but he nevertheless desired Temple to read out the particulars to him. The King was concerned that the Prince had misunderstood his suggestions to arrive at a peace; they were not 'propositions', which he had no authority to make. What he had suggested would create 'a kind of double frontier to Brussels'. The King asked William to think further on the matter 'and not let it fall so flat as he did by his last answer, without trying what it could be beaten out to … if his Highness had any other proposition to make to France, the King would very readily hand it over to them in the best manner he could.'

Williamson's style 'was', as Temple put it, 'always so disagreeable' to the Prince and he made no bones that it was so now. The unfortunate Williamson had now definitely joined Arlington amongst his English interlocutors whose manner he disdained. 'He said that the style of letting it fall so flat, was my Lord Arlington's; and the double frontier, as it were, for Brussels, was some of [Williamson's] whipp'd cream, and fit for children…. His answer was very plain, that he had thought enough of it, and had no more to say at this time.'[8]

As Temple wrote to Williamson the Prince was quite succinct on the difference between himself and Charles; the King wanted to treat from the baseline of what France possessed at the present time and the exchange of places should proceed from there; whereas the Prince wanted to treat from the baseline of the Treaty of Aix-la-Chapelle and the exchanges should follow from that.[9] The Prince was very sorry to disagree with the King but he was bound to his allies – his 'honour' was again invoked; he was not at all confident that he could have brought them round to what he had proposed, although he would have tried, and he would be glad to know of Charles's thoughts whenever they 'came nearer to his'.[10]

The campaigning season had now approached and, for the time being, the interchanges with England were left at that.[11]

THE 1677 CAMPAIGN: FURTHER SETBACKS

For the Dutch the 1677 campaign brought further losses and disappointments; and from the start William was perfectly aware that this was likely to be the case. Even as he held his discussions with Temple at Soestdijk he thought it likely that 'the guns were playing before Valenciennes'. He thought the town would be taken and possibly St-Omer as well; 'he expected a very ill beginning of the campaign, and to make an ill figure in it himself'. His hopes were based on the Germans: 'he was in, and must go through with it.'[12]

As early as 22 November in the previous year William had written to the Spanish diplomat, the Marquis of Grana, who had been sent to Vienna to undertake negotiations, to do what he could to ensure that Villa Hermosa was provided with the means to form an army in the Spanish Netherlands – he had in mind the transference of Austrian troops to assist him for this purpose. Without such an army the Spanish Netherlands, or the greater part, would 'assuredly' be lost, for he could not defend them by himself and they would have to plead for peace to the King of France, 'cap in hand'.[13] The suspension of Dutch subsidies to Austria caused the Emperor to refuse this request,[14] but belatedly and rather unexpectedly Spain, if not entirely rising to the occasion in time, nevertheless managed to do rather more than a pessimist might have anticipated.

Dutch strategy for the new campaign was based on a memorandum which Waldeck had drawn up in December 1676. This envisaged the need for above 70,000 men; between 10,000 and 12,000 of these would cover the Dutch Republic against a French attack from Maastricht; 35,000 would be used to lay siege to Charleroi and threaten an invasion of France; and Villa Hermosa with 26,000 men, consisting of 5,000 Spanish, 5,000 Dutch, 8,000 from Münster and 8,000 from Brunswick-Osnabrück, would defend the Spanish fortresses in Flanders.

At this stage the Dutch were helped by a felicitous *coup d'état* in Spain in January 1677, when Don Juan marched into Madrid and took over the government from the Queen Mother; more robustly disposed to the war – and prompted, perhaps, by a Dutch threat in December that if Spain did not provide an army neither would the Dutch – he undertook to provide 25,000 Spanish troops for the Spanish Netherlands; and in Brussels Villa Hermosa told Waldeck and Dijkveld that he was in negotiations with the Bishop of Münster and the Brunswick dukes – for whose subsidies Spain would be responsible.[15]

But long before these plans could reach a practical form the French, aided by their extensive system of magazines, were ready to commence operations even earlier than in 1676 – something that the Prince of Orange had anticipated. On 1 March Louvois appeared before Valenciennes – Prince William was a few days out in his calculations on when the guns would come into play – and that day Louis left St-Germain, himself to arrive before Valenciennes on the 4th. The weather was atrocious and caused the King to arrive without his baggage, and almost without accompaniment, with his accoutrements and his courtiers impeded on the roads; for the first night he was compelled to sleep fully clothed in his coach. He had around 63,000 men under his command and five marshals of France. There was no hope that Valenciennes could be rescued and on the 17th it was stormed and captured.[16] With the bulk of his army Louis then marched on Cambrai and his brother, the Duke of Orléans, marched on St-Omer. Cambrai lay on the river Scheldt where the French already possessed Bouchain, Valenciennes, Condé and Doornink. Louis arrived there on the 22nd and the trenches were opened with the aid of 8,000 peasants brought up from Picardy.[17]

On 11 March Prince William wrote from The Hague to the Duke of Lorraine, who was in command of the Imperial forces in Germany, to tell him that he had given the Dutch troops their marching orders to advance to the Spanish Low Countries to oppose, as best they could, the French, who had such a superiority of numbers over them – the Dutch could not impede them by themselves. 'The only means of saving the Low Countries is the diversion which Your Highness might be able to make into France.' On the 15th the Prince received confirmation from the Duke of Lorraine that he was indeed marching towards the Rhine in order to cross it and create the necessary diversion there.[18]

The Prince left The Hague on 20 March and arrived in the evening at Breda where he stayed for nearly a fortnight; he was being pressed by the Elector of Brandenburg for a meeting at Cleves, which however did not materialise; and he was also awaiting the completion of the mustering of the troops between Bruges and Ghent, under Waldeck's command, which was delayed by lack of shipping transport. He learnt there of the fall of Valenciennes and of the sieges of Cambrai and St-Omer; and the order was given for the Dutch army to advance on Ypres, at which point the decision could be taken whether there was a chance of relieving St-Omer. The Prince left Breda on 3 April and arrived near Ypres on the 5th.[19] The army was estimated to amount to 30,000 men, consisting, according to Waldeck, of only Dutch troops, although according to others there were also some Spanish.[20]

The decision was taken to continue the advance and on the 9th the army arrived at Marie Capel, a small village four hours from St-Omer, close to Mont-Cassel. On the way the Prince's secretary, Huygens, could at first hear the guns from the siege of St-Omer, and then, as they reached the mound of Cassel, he could see the smoke from the cannon. The following day the Dutch army marched towards St-Omer and camped on the Peene, a small stream, a short distance away from the French army, which that night was reinforced by a detachment sent by Louis. The two armies were perhaps of about the same size, about 30,000 men, although Müller says the French army was a third larger and, according to Japikse, by 5,000 men.[21]

The country was more or less flat, with hedges and ditches filled with water running through the terrain, and, here and there, small hills surmounted by windmills. The French army was drawn up in two lines, with a reserve. D'Humières commanded the right flank, Luxemburg the left, and in the centre was Monsieur, Louis's brother – although the usual precaution had been taken of providing him with a keeper, this time the Count du Plessis, a lieutenant general. On the Dutch side the Count of Hoorn was on the right wing, the Count of Nassau-Saarbrucken on the left and William and Waldeck in the centre.

The preliminary operations of the battle started as dawn broke on the 11th when Prince William sent a detachment of troops across the Peene to occupy the abbey of the same name, which lay on his right wing. Although initially successful in capturing the abbey the Dutch troops, too, were soon driven out by the French after a stubborn resistance, leaving the abbey on fire.[22]

At about 10 o'clock the main battle commenced, when the Prince managed to push back the French centre; but to do this he sent strong reinforcements from his left, which was protected by hedges and entrenchments, but left with few troops. These were now attacked by d'Humières who put them to flight. In the centre, too, the Dutch were pushed back, as was their right wing.[23]

Shielded by the cavalry, Prince William was able to organise an orderly retreat to Ypres, and he was not vigorously pursued by the enemy, who were distracted by looting the Dutch baggage train. Nevertheless, French estimates put the Dutch losses at 3,000 dead, 4/5,000 wounded and over 2,000 prisoners, with 1,200 dead and 2,000 wounded on the French side. Exaggerated though the French figures might be, the loss in men and *matériel* was considerable. Despite his usual display of personal bravery – his harness was twice struck by enemy bullets – the military reputation of Prince William was not enhanced by the engagement, as he feared would be the case when he had held his conversations with Temple. When he and Waldeck surveyed the scene on the morning of the action Huygens noted how surprised they were by the reinforcements that Louis had sent his brother; and a couple of days after the battle Waldeck let fall that the Dutch were deficient in generals.[24]

To the States William admitted that the French strength had been underestimated and he also attributed the outcome of the battle to the infamous behaviour of two regiments, Walenburg's and La Verne's, who, having been put to flight, threw into confusion three other regiments sent to their aid. The Walenburg regiment must have been distinguished by their grey attire, for the Prince told Huygens, 'Put away that grey hat. I don't want to see any more grey hats, I am put into a fright every time I hear the name of Walenburg.' He did indeed proceed, with characteristic severity, to discipline this regiment, nine men of whom, chosen by lot, were hanged.[25] But it was a punishment not unusual for the times.

The fate of Cambrai and St-Omer could not for long be in doubt; the former capitulated on 17 April and the latter on the 22nd.[26] The French did not, however, follow up these successes; and the reason was to be found in England.

Charles II had opened a new session of Parliament on 14 February, and, whilst initially all seemed to be going well, with a vote being passed for the continuation of additional excise taxes, the French advance into Flanders caused such alarm that an address was made to the King on 10 March by both Houses to enter into alliances to safeguard the Spanish possessions. Moreover, Danby put his weight behind this on the grounds that a French war would restore the trust of the nation. When Charles eventually agreed to act on 11 April if Parliament voted the necessary finance, the members displayed their lack of confidence in the King by saying they would do so once the alliances were in place. At this point Charles, on 16 April, adjourned Parliament. And thus, at this delicate juncture, with Charles precariously balanced between the war his Parliament demanded and the patronage of Louis upon which he laid so much store, Louis had a clear motive for not exacerbating the position of his royal client by engaging in further conquests in the Spanish Netherlands. Charles, for his part, accepted that Louis needed Valenciennes, Cambrai and St-Omer to bring him the security he needed on his frontier, but he appealed to him not to press on any further.[27]

With this Louis was happy to comply, and at the end of May he left for Versailles where he arrived on the 31st, leaving Luxemburg in command in Flanders with perhaps 50,000 men and with orders to remain on the defensive.[28] Créqui was in command on the Rhine and the Vosges, with perhaps 40,000 at the beginning of June, and he too had orders to avoid battle if he could. Schomberg was in command on the Maas with 9,000 men. As part of the defensive measures on France's eastern frontier a scorched-earth policy had been pursued the previous winter with a ruthlessness and efficiency that left the whole country between the Saar and the Rhine and the whole of the valley of the Saar up to the Mosel in a state of devastation.[29]

The pause in hostilities enabled William to replenish the losses he had incurred at Mont-Cassel. Furthermore, Villa Hermosa was successful, at the end of April, in concluding his treaties with the Bishop of Münster, who would provide 9,000 troops, and with the Hanoverian brothers, the Duke of Osnabrück (7,000 men) and the Duke of Celle (8,000), altogether 24,000, to which the Spaniards would contribute another 5/6,000 for a total of around 30,000. As William was expecting to provide a Dutch army of 30,000 the allies now at last had the two field armies that Waldeck had envisaged for the 1677 campaign. These were expected to be ready by the end of May or the beginning of June.

During the lull the Prince took the opportunity to keep an eye open for works of art which might be for sale and he bought some paintings by Rubens and Bruegel. There was also a constant coming and going from the Dutch and foreign elite visiting the Prince of Orange wherever he was situated – princes, envoys, Regents, members of the Orange clan and court, and military men from all over Europe.[30]

By the middle of July William had a Dutch army of nearly 27,000 men assembled near Dendermonde, to the north of Brussels, and with the Münster, Brunswick and Spanish troops the allied army amounted to nearly 63,000. The intention was for the Prince to lay siege to Charleroi, whilst Villa Hermosa would provide a covering field army. It was also the intention to cooperate with the Duke of Lorraine who, by taking up position on the Upper Maas, would both contain Marshal Créqui and at the same time perhaps also send a cavalry detachment to assist the siege of Charleroi.[31] The plan was clear-cut – the execution very difficult against commanders as competent as those at the disposal of Louis XIV.

On 6 August the Prince of Orange began the siege of Charleroi – garrisoned according to the Prince's estimate with 5,000 men – whilst Villa Hermosa provided cover against Luxemburg's army of about 50,000, positioned near Ath. Luxemburg did not hesitate; he left Ath, with Villa Hermosa following in his tracks, and on the night of 8 August he crossed the Sambre, which Villa Hermosa was too late to prevent, and advanced to Gerpinnes, where he established a very strong position to the south-east of Charleroi. At the same time Louvois, who had joined Luxemburg's army, ordered d'Humières, with 9/10,000 men collected from the French garrisons in Flanders, to position himself at Braine le Comte to the north-east of the town, thus cutting off the supply lines from Brussels; and the French were also able to frustrate the collection of forage essential for the subsistence of the allied army. The Spanish generals urged an attack on Luxemburg's position; uncharacteristically, the Prince of Orange disagreed – it was too strong and there was not the slightest hope of retreat in case of defeat. And thus, on 14 August, the siege was raised. Never afraid of aggression, the Prince recognised the occasions when it would be foolhardy. And on the

Maas Créqui also managed, on 2 August, to contain the advance of the Duke of Lorraine.[32] Neither side on that front was able to establish firm dominance, although Créqui was able to capture Freiburg in the middle of November.[33]

On 23 September the Prince left the army to make his way to the Dutch Republic. His attention was fixed on England, where the sentiments of much of the country were reflected by the large numbers of English volunteers who had joined the Dutch army for the siege, the Duke of Monmouth being almost the only one who arrived at the quarters of the Duke of Luxemburg.[34] After being adjourned in April Parliament had reconvened on 23 May. Once again Charles found it as adamant as before that alliances should be created to address the French menace in Flanders, and a Dutch alliance was specifically mentioned; but once again it refused to vote supply up front, and on 28 May it was again adjourned. William of Orange had not wanted to be seen by the King to be plotting with members of Parliament when they were sitting, and the adjournment provided him with the opportunity to send a personal messenger to the King, without arousing such suspicions.[35] The man chosen for the task was Hans Willem Bentinck, who had shown such personal devotion to the Prince when he lay ill with the smallpox, and who had gradually risen in his favour – 'I esteem him more than any other of my people', as the Prince put it in a letter of recommendation to Ossory on 8 June.[36]

BENTINCK'S MISSION TO ENGLAND

William and Bentinck had met with Fagel at Philippine, west of Antwerp, and then at The Hague in the middle of May, which points to Bentinck's mission being then discussed in a small, confidential circle – the Prince's relation Nassau-Ouwerkerk, who was of the party, nevertheless complained that Bentinck kept him uninformed. After William's return from The Hague Fagel and Hieronymus van Beverninck arrived on 26 May at his camp at Lokeren, between Antwerp and Ghent, their arrival coinciding with the receipt on the previous day of a despatch from Coenraad van Beuningen in London, which reported that, at long last, Charles II was disposed to make the first overtures to suggest peace terms, and that the ardour of the English people against France was increasing by the day. Fagel and Van Beverninck at least, therefore, were in close consultation with the Prince in preparing the Bentinck mission – and the trip to The Hague leaves open the possibility that other influential Regents may also have been sounded out.[37] Certainly relations between the Prince and Fagel at this time were particularly close despite their different emphases in foreign policy – the Prince was writing at this time asking the Grand Pensionary for his advice on how to reconstruct his Domestic Council, which dealt with his private affairs; and we have already seen that Fagel was one of the Prince's executors under his will.[38]

Bentinck arrived at the Palace of Whitehall late on 14 June, after dinner, and immediately paid a preliminary courtesy visit to King Charles and the Duke of York, from whom he received a warm welcome.[39] His instructions from the Prince[40] were to sound out the King on how he wished William to conduct himself, on the one hand, if the war continued or, on the other hand, if peace negotiations materialised. Whilst, the instructions ran, the Prince knew the King wanted peace, and despite the reasons that might induce William himself to prefer to continue the war, he was not averse to peace, and he was very happy to comply with the King's wishes; but he doubted whether the French, after such great successes, would be prepared to grant peace on acceptable terms. The Prince asked the King to indicate the terms on which, in his judgement, peace should be made, so that he could apply himself to persuading the allies to accord with the King's wishes. Bentinck had no powers to make any proposals himself – he was there to listen – but the Spanish Low Countries were in such a state that they could be preserved only through the assistance of His Majesty and not without the restitution of six or seven towns to Spain.[41] This implied the retention by France of four towns – an increase on the two which the Prince had suggested to Temple in January, and which, of course, reflected the disappointing outcome of the summer's fighting.[42] Bentinck was also instructed to sound out the King on what he wanted as a *quid pro quo* to join the allies in the war against Louis and he was to offer him Wynoxbergen and Dunkirk once these were captured from France. Finally, the Prince asked if he could make a visit to England – '*un petit tour en Angleterre*' – but there was no mention of his marrying Mary.

We are given a hint of the people in England with whom the Prince clearly thought it important to keep in touch, for Bentinck was also instructed to meet the Duke of Ormond (Ossory's father), Danby, the Duke of Monmouth, the Chancellor, Heneage Finch, and the Secretary of State, Henry Coventry.

The enhanced desire for peace amongst influential Dutch Regents was demonstrated by the Amsterdammer, Van Beuningen, the Dutch ambassador in London, when he indicated that Franche-Comté would not present a great difficulty. Prince William had been careful to make no mention of this in Bentinck's instructions; and Bentinck complained to him of Van Beuningen's exceeding his powers.

This apart, his mission was well received by King Charles and by the Duke of York, both of whom indicated that they would be pleased to see the Prince in England at the end of the campaigning season; and it was also left that the King would send an emissary to the Prince indicating his peace proposals.

One person with whom Bentinck, and through him Prince William, had formed a close bond was the Lord Treasurer, Danby, who was also Temple's patron; Danby wrote the Prince a warm letter on 11 June advising him to make his friendship with King Charles 'as inseperable [*sic*] as your interests are, if rightly considered'.[43]

One sign of the improvement in relations on the side of the King was that Ossory was at last given permission in August to visit the Prince and, indeed, he attended the siege of Charleroi.

Bentinck had not yet left London when Charles summoned the French ambassador, Courtin, to a secret meeting at the rooms of his head valet, Chiffinch, in the Palace of Whitehall, at which, apart from the ambassador and the King, only the Duke of York was present. In his despatch[44] to Louis of 21 June Courtin said that Charles had emphasised the animosity against France that existed in England, and that it would be impossible to resist Parliamentary pressure for him to join Louis's enemies if there was no peace before Parliament reconvened; he would face a general insurgency if no provision was made for the preservation of the Spanish Netherlands; and there was pressure of time on him to see the peace concluded, because he would need to reconvene Parliament to renew the excise duty on wine due to expire at Michaelmas 1678.

Against this background Charles went on to propose the terms which he believed would bring a peace agreement to pass. France should cede Maastricht to the Dutch and six towns to Spain – compared with Bentinck's seven;[45] she would retain five towns – one more than Bentinck[46] – and she would also obtain Franche-Comté, of which Bentinck had made no mention; the Emperor would cede Philippsburg to France; and France would withdraw from Sicily and return Lorraine to its duke, which, after the razing of the fortifications of Nancy and Louis's retention of the fortress of Marsal, could never in the future, Charles said, be in a position to undertake anything against France. And, in conformity with his usual practice, he did not let the opportunity pass to ask Louis for £200,000 – otherwise he would be compelled to have recourse to Parliament.

Louis's reply to these proposals, on 3 July,[47] was that he declined to cede two of the towns Charles II had suggested,[48] and that if he was to forgo three of the others he wanted equivalents for them;[49] this meant he was asking for as many as eleven towns compared with Bentinck's four and Charles's five. He was prepared to concede Maastricht and Sicily and he offered a compromise for Lorraine, with the exchange of Toul for Nancy, which he would retain fully fortified. As for the £200,000, negotiations for this could be put in hand linked to the adjournment of Parliament until at least 25 March 1678. Prince William's predictions that it would be difficult to obtain acceptable terms from Louis in Flanders were thus fulfilled; and the French reply played into the hands of English advocates – Danby at the head – of closer ties with the Dutch as the only means of forcing reasonable terms on the French King.[50]

After William's failure to take Charleroi Charles instructed Laurence Hyde, who was on his way to the Nijmegen conference, to make a detour to meet William at his camp. Hyde's instructions were to tell William that Charles declined to enter the war, whilst outlining new peace proposals from the King. Louis should return four towns[51] and retain seven[52] – three more than Bentinck had suggested, two more than Charles's original proposal and four fewer than Louis's counter-demands. On Franche-Comté he alluded to safeguarding the Prince of Orange's estates there, which were substantial.[53]

WILLIAM'S VISIT TO ENGLAND AND HIS MARRIAGE

Danby had taken the opportunity to write to Prince William on 27 August: 'Mr Hyde comes to Your Highnesse so fully instructed by His Majesty that I have nothing to adde upon that subject, saveing that when Your Highnesse should thinke itt convenient to discourse with the King yourselfe, I should hope to see things brought to a better accomodation by that means than any other.' On the same day he wrote to Bentinck that the King was 'extreame [*sic*] desirous to see the Prince'.[54]

Hyde arrived in the Prince's camp on 17 September for a one-day visit; and prompted, it seems, or perhaps reinforced in his own views, by the hint in Danby's letter that he should 'discourse with the King' himself, William rejected the proposals he brought, save that he appeared to Hyde to relent in the matter of Franche-Comté's going to France.[55] His mind was set on exercising his personal diplomacy by means of his visit to England, and he decided on his own immediate departure from the army, which occurred on 23 September.[56] As the brother of the Duke of York's first wife, Anne, Laurence Hyde was the uncle of the Duke's daughter, Mary, and it may be that William took the opportunity to touch on the marriage to Mary, which he had in mind.

The Duke wrote to him on 3 October, expressing his pleasure that William was coming to England; yachts would be on their way by the end of the week to pick him up; and the following day the court was going to Newmarket where James hoped to see the Prince very soon. As on his previous visit to England he would be accompanied by Ossory – the two friends had found diversion in the camp by gambling late into the night, keeping poor Huygens from his bed until two in the morning.[57]

On his arrival in the Republic William told Waldeck that he found matters on a strange footing, from which we may deduce that the lack of military success had stiffened the Dutch peace party.[58] He tried to assuage the suspicions of the allied ambassadors in The Hague by saying that the journey was being undertaken at the invitation of his English uncle to discuss the interests of the Dutch and the allies; he also told them that his expectations now were that Charles would not enter the war but that he hoped for the least disadvantageous peace terms that could be obtained. They were told by Fagel that the Prince had no powers to commit the States – some indication, perhaps, of the diminution taking place in the Prince of Orange's influence in foreign affairs – and Fagel also said that he did not think the marriage of the Prince would be discussed, so that on this issue Fagel himself was in the dark.[59] To the world the Prince wished to convey the impression that the purpose of the visit was purely diplomatic – which in a sense was almost true, the marriage, in his eyes, being part of the diplomacy, although that did not exclude the proviso that the bride would need to be compatible in personal terms. There may also have been another consideration – keeping his marriage plans from the world would pre-empt French attempts to frustrate them.

This did not prevent intense speculation occurring on both sides of the North Sea as to the purpose of the visit, causing the Secretary of State, Henry Coventry, to observe at Newmarket that 'the State and horse politics resemble one another, those appear most confident that know least'.[60]

The Prince asked the States of Holland and the States-General for their consent to his leaving for a stay in England of three or four weeks, which was granted on 13 and 14 October.

William left The Hague on 17 October and, escorted by Ossory, who as we have seen had been in the Prince's company since August, and by Sir Gabriel Sylvius, who had arrived with the English yachts, he landed at Harwich on the 19th.[61] His entourage included his relations Nassau-Odijk, the Counts of Nassau, of Solms and of Brederode, and a great number of the nobility.[62] Not tarrying on the way, he went straight to Newmarket where he arrived the same day; 32 coaches were required for the transport of the retinue.[63]

He was met by Arlington as he stepped from his coach and Arlington's country house, Euston, near Newmarket, enabled him to entertain the Prince there.[64] But the Prince refused to use Arlington as his chief intermediary for transacting the business in hand – much to the delight of Temple, whose attitude to Arlington was unmistakeably one of deep malice, and whose delight was rendered more exquisite by the knowledge that everybody else, including Arlington, had assumed that his Nassau connection would pre-empt him for the role. As, amidst a large throng, the Prince was descending a staircase on the way to the King he met Temple and Danby, and he whispered to them that it was they whom he wished to use as his confidants.[65] He was intent on building a firm partnership with these two; they were firmly tied together both by their political and personal friendship and by the family connection of Lady Temple; and Danby's views on the need for an Anglo-Dutch alliance to contain Louis XIV were close to his own.

The Prince was entertained at the races and in the hunting field;[66] and he paid close attention to the Duke of York, making a point of attending his *couchées* and *levées*.[67] On his side he was very kindly received by his uncles, but he refused to agree peace terms until his marriage was settled and he refused to agree to the marriage until he had had a chance to see Mary and form his assessment of her. Charles laughed 'at this piece of nicety' when told of it by Temple; but to humour the Prince he curtailed the sojourn at Newmarket and the court returned to London on 23 October, where the Prince was lodged in the Duke of York's chambers in Whitehall Palace, the Duke staying in St James's.[68] There was calculation in William's taking the position he did; if the peace terms were agreed before the marriage the marriage could have been used as a bargaining counter in the negotiations – and seen to have been so by the whole world. At the same time the marriage as bargaining counter was not something William's uncles would readily give up, and thus the issue was not immediately resolved, although talks of a general nature on peace terms did take place, without coming to any final conclusions.

The Prince met Mary at ceremonies to celebrate the Duke of York's birthday;[69] he was very pleased with what he saw – she was indeed a striking beauty – as well as with the results of the enquiries he had instituted; and on 26 October, after two days of talks on the peace terms, the Prince asked the Duke of York for her hand. Charles, whose consent, of course, would be required, tried at first not to commit himself and the Prince wrote to Fagel asking him to send a ship as the talks were not very promising and he would not be staying in England for long. The talks nevertheless continued, but when it was proposed to hold a plenary session on 31 October, or the following day William categorically refused until his marriage was agreed.

Temple found him after supper on the 30th in a very bad humour; 'he repented he had ever come into England, and resolved he would stay but two days longer, and then be gone, if the King continued in his mind of treating upon the peace before he was married; but that, before he went, the King must chuse how they should live thereafter, for he was sure it must either be like the greatest friends, or the greatest enemies.' When Temple conveyed this to the King early in the morning of the next day Charles said he 'never yet was deceived in judging of a man's honesty by his looks' and if he was 'not deceived in the Prince's face, he is the honestest man in the world, and I will trust him, and he shall have his wife'. When the Duke of York was told he was 'a little surprised', but agreed to obey the King; he may have been influenced by his wife's pregnancy, which – if it was a boy, as proved to be the case, although he died a month after his birth – held the promise that Mary would be removed as the next in the line of succession to the throne, and hence reduce the status of the Prince of Orange as a rival on the English scene. Bustling back to William, Temple was embraced by him and thus, if we follow Temple's own account – in which he undoubtedly emerges rather well – the matter was settled.[70]

But, in fact, the ready response of the King is explained by the fact that he had already settled the matter the evening before. He frequently conducted his interviews with the French ambassadors in the quarters of Louise de Kérouaille, his French mistress, and it was in these congenial surroundings – they were more sumptuous than those of the Queen – that he told the newly appointed ambassador from Louis, Barillon, who had succeeded Courtin, of his decision regarding the marriage. The marriage, he reasoned, would allay the rumours in England that his liaison with France was fundamentally aimed at changing the country's government and religion, rumours which had been caused by the conduct of his brother, the Duke of York. The marriage would confound those who were plotting to draw the Prince into their party against him, and would enable the Prince to base his ambitions on friendship with him and on his interests.[71]

The argument that domestic pressure led Charles to approve the marriage undoubtedly rings true – it was a reason for the marriage put forward by Danby for some time. But the second part of the argument that the Prince of Orange would from henceforth align his policy with that of his uncle was a misconception – William's intention, on the contrary, was that the King should align his policy with his. He was committed to the view that Louis was a present and future danger, and that he needed to be resisted in the interests of the United Provinces, of the United Kingdom and, hence, of the Stuart clan, whose power base was dependent on those two centres; and he was determined to do what he could to persuade his uncles that the only feasible course was to combine the two in opposition to the French King. The whole point of the marriage, indeed, from his point of view, was that it was part of that strategy.

Charles's judgement that the marriage would prove popular was borne out by the reaction of the crowds in London. The whole night of 1 November was marked 'in ringing the bells and bonfires, and the greatest expressions of joy'. It was a joy very much shared in particular by Temple, who savoured Arlington's discomfort at having no knowledge of what was afoot. But it was not shared by Louis XIV; it was said that he received the news 'as he would have done the loss of an army'. And it was not shared by Mary – when told of the marriage plans she fell into a prolonged spell of weeping.[72] But this was an augury not of an unhappy marriage, but of what, in due course, became as powerful a partnership as any in Prince William's life.

The wedding took place on the Prince's birthday, 14 November; and immediately afterwards business was resumed, with the principals fixing their minds, without any further ado, on the question of the peace terms, in which Danby and Temple were closely involved. To the Prince's argument that without strong defences for Flanders France would merely end the present war and start another, in which she would conquer Flanders in a single campaign, Charles responded that he thought that Louis 'grew past his youth, and lazy, and would turn to the pleasures of the court, and building, and leave his neighbours in quiet' – which perhaps was more akin to his own pipe-dreams than the thoughts of Louis XIV, and was hardly persuasive.

William was not to be moved; the French would only make peace now in order to break the alliance arrayed against them and would begin another war when circumstances were propitious; 'their ambition would never end, till they had all Flanders and Germany to the Rhine, and thereby Holland in an absolute dependence upon them: and … Christendom could not be left safe by the peace, without such a frontier as he proposed for Flanders, and the restitution of Lorraine as well as what the Emperor had lost in Alsace.'[73]

William made no great issue about the coalition's gains from Sweden being relinquished by his allies.[74] Charles and the Duke of York easily agreed on Lorraine and Alsace; but they saw a sticking point in France's returning Franche-Comté to Spain. Charles thought that on this William was being swayed by his own estates there (which, according to Temple, were 'greater and more Seigneurial than those of the Crown of Spain') and suggested that either he would guarantee them personally or get a good price for them to recompense the Prince. William, however, rejected this offer, saying his interests there should not stand in the way of the peace, and that he would rather sacrifice them for one more town for Spain on the

Flanders frontier[75]– it was, of course, a fine gesture, but no negotiations are at an end until the final treaty is signed and the Prince may well have expected that there would be plenty of time to safeguard his interests in due course.

It has been suggested that in standing his ground on Franche-Comté the Prince was taking up a negotiating position with his uncles to obtain better terms in Flanders. If this was the case he was to be successful; when he did finally yield on Franche-Comté Charles agreed to go back to the proposals Bentinck had brought with him in June, even though these were less favourable to Louis than the proposals Charles had subsequently made to him and which Louis had already rejected at the beginning of July.[76] Moreover, he gave William an undertaking that 'he would never part from the least point' of the proposals, and 'would enter into the war against France', if they were refused.[77]

The reason Charles was prepared to take this course was fear of Parliament. Although he had tried to appease Louis by coupling the announcement of Mary's marriage with the extension of the prorogation of Parliament to April 1678 the subsidy he was receiving from Louis was not very large and at some stage he would need Parliament to reconvene to renew the duty on wine;[78] and this promised to be an extremely stormy occasion unless he could demonstrate that he had been taking measures to curb Louis's advance into Flanders. It was, therefore, a considerable blow when Louis, on 30 November, instructed Barillon to reject the terms outright because, he said, they would leave his kingdom too exposed – a rejection confirmed by the special emissary Charles had sent to Louis XIV, the Count of Feversham, when he returned to London on 11 December.[79]

On the one hand Charles was now faced with the commitment he had made to the Prince of Orange that he would join the war if the proposals were rejected whilst, on the other hand, he was reluctant to cut himself loose from his long-standing commitment to the patronage of Louis XIV. He told Barillon he would rather lose a hand than turn against France but that 'his very servants would abandon him if he did not conform to the sentiments of the nation'; and the Duke of York, too, sadly told the ambassador that his brother could not act differently, otherwise 'all his subjects, without exception, other than he himself, would revolt against him'.[80] War on the one hand, Louis's patronage on the other: it was a vertiginous path that confronted the King of England.

For the time being he shifted towards Parliament and the Prince of Orange: he advanced the recall of Parliament from 14 April to 25 January 1678 and military preparations were put in hand.[81] Danby was instructed to write to the Prince, on 14 December. He and Mary had left London on 29 November, although, because of contrary winds, they did not arrive at Honselaarsdijk until 9 December. Charles's proposal as contained in Danby's letter was that he would join with the Dutch 'to oblige France to accept' the terms he and William had agreed upon when he was in England – that is, the Bentinck terms – if the Dutch would do the same regarding Spain.[82] This was a deliberate echo of the Triple Alliance of 1668, which Temple had negotiated, and which had forced Louis, by threatening English armed intervention, to desist from pursuing the War of Devolution. As a matter of fact Temple himself thought that, in the present circumstances, this form of armed mediation would not go far enough; only England's threatening war in full-scale alliance with all the coalition partners, not just the Dutch alone, would do the trick.[83]

But it was not the view of William, who had himself suggested the proposal contained in Danby's letter. That proposal was less categorical and more vague than the outright war which Parliament wanted against Louis. Hence Charles wanted it to be kept secret, and he wanted it kept, for the time being, from the States-General – at this stage, the King would accept the Prince's personal undertaking as sufficient commitment on the Dutch side. This, of course, was very readily forthcoming.[84]

On 25 December the Committee of Foreign affairs in London produced a draft of the Treaty, with the aim of having it ratified by the time Parliament met on 25 January, so that Charles could say that he had an alliance in place with the Dutch 'for the preservation of Flanders'. Once Prince William had found a favourable response from Spain to the terms, he confided them to some of the leading Regents. Negotiations were not complete by the 25 January deadline, so that Charles again prorogued Parliament to 7 February, and even then the treaty was not ratified until the beginning of March.[85] Although modelled on the Triple Alliance, that alliance had spelt out in detail the military measures which would be taken to force French compliance, if they were needed, and it had been accompanied by a defensive alliance; the present treaty was deficient in both these respects, although it was envisaged that the defensive alliance would follow.[86]

To the Prince of Orange it must have appeared that, at long last, he had succeeded in achieving at any rate a form of an English alliance, incomplete though it still was, something for which he had laboured ever since the French invasion of the Dutch Republic in 1672 – it looked as if Uncle Charles had been dragged away from cousin Louis. That was to prove not to be the case; but what he did have was the English marriage, which ultimately, when he and Mary became King and Queen of England, would give him the Anglo-Dutch alliance in the strongest form he could wish for.

1 Temple, *Works, op. cit.*, 1754, I, pp.290ff.

2 See also Haley, *The Anglo-Dutch Rapprochement, op. cit.*, pp.619–20.

3 Temple, *Works, op. cit.*, 1754, I, pp.298–9. IV, pp.319, 323. Haley, *The Anglo-Dutch Rapprochement, op. cit.*, pp.621–3. Browning, *op. cit.*, II, p.482.

4 Temple, *Works, op. cit.*, 1754, I, pp.299–301. *Ibid.*, IV, pp.310–14.

5 *Ibid.*, IV, p.318.

6 *Ibid.*, I, pp.301–2.

7 *Ibid.*, I, pp.305–7, IV, pp.327–30, 334–7. *Correspondentie Willem III en Bentinck, op. cit.*, II, 2, pp.144–5.

8 Temple, *Works, op. cit.*, I, pp.314–15.

9 *Ibid.*, IV, p.340.

10 *Ibid.*, IV, pp.340–1.

11 In Mignet, *op. cit.*, IV, pp.408–23, we can trace further negotiations between the Prince and D'Estrades through the medium of Pesters. According to these William, tempted by the acquisition of Maastricht and the sovereignty of Limburg, was prepared to concede Cambrai and make a separate peace if the Spanish refused. He was also prepared to enter into a peace separate from his German allies on the basis of restoring Franche-Comté to Spain in exchange for the restoration to Sweden of what she had lost in Germany, although he knew that this would never have been accepted by the German allies or Denmark (p.415 in particular). This is wholly at variance with William's negotiations with Charles II as consistently reported by Temple and it would have meant abandoning his allies, which he had every reason not to do – otherwise he could have come to an immediate agreement with Charles. Prof. Haley suggests that either William was not serious or Pesters 'exceeded his instructions' (Haley, *The Anglo-Dutch Rapprochement, op. cit.*, n.2, pp.623–4). Was Pesters perhaps reflecting the views of Fagel rather than the Prince? Or did D'Estrades's eagerness to promote his career make him avid to hear what he knew his masters wanted to hear when he reported back to Paris? In any case the Prince did not pursue the negotiations. For a different interpretation see Baxter, *op. cit.*, p.140.

12 Temple, *Works, op. cit.*, 1754, IV, p.341.

13 *Correspondentie Willem III en Bentinck, op. cit.*, II, 2, pp.136–7.

14 Troost, *Willem III, op. cit.*, p.132.

15 Nimwegen, *op. cit.*, pp.499–500.

16 Rousset, *op. cit.*, II, pp.283–8.

17 *Ibid.*, II, pp.290–1. Knoop, *op. cit.*, II, p.245.

18 *Correspondentie Willem III en Bentinck, op. cit.*, II, 2, pp.148–9.

19 Huygens, *Journaal, op. cit.*, p.144. Müller, *Waldeck, op. cit.*, p.336. *Correspondentie Willem III en Bentinck, op. cit.*, II, 2, pp 155–6.

20 Knoop, *op. cit.*, II, p.251. Müller, *Waldeck, op. cit.*, p.42.

21 Huygens, *Journaal, op. cit.*, p.150. Knoop, *op. cit.*, II, p.254. Müller, *Waldeck, op. cit.*, p.42. Japikse, *William III, op. cit.*, II, p.60.

22 Rousset, *op. cit.*, II, pp.296–7.

23 *Ibid., op. cit.*, pp.297–9. Japikse, *Willem III, op. cit.*, II, pp.60–1.

24 Knoop, *op. cit.*, II, pp. 256–7. Rousset, *op. cit.*, II, p.300. Huygens, *Journaal, op. cit.*, pp.151, 155.

25 Huygens, *Journaal, op. cit.*, pp.154–6, 159.

26 Rousset, *op. cit.*, II, pp.305, 307.

27 Hutton, *op. cit.*, pp.341–3. Rousset, *op. cit.*, II, pp.309–13. Mignet, *op. cit.*, IV, p.442.

28 Rousset, *op. cit.*, pp.313–14.

29 *Ibid.*, pp.313–15, 321. Knoop, *op. cit.*, II, pp.260, 266.

30 Huygens, *Journaal, op. cit.*, e.g. pp.178–9 and his daily coverage of the 1677 campaign as a whole. Huygens also records (p.161) a visit by the Prince to Sluys where Nassau-La Lecq, the brother of Nassau-Ouwekerk and Nassau-Odijk, was governor, and where *une debauche enragée* was supposed to have taken place with the participants tearing off each other's clothes. It is the only incident of this kind of which we have a record and Huygens was an inveterate gossip, but perhaps the Prince did take to the bottle on this occasion. To the modern mind this may provide a hint of homosexual overtones, but there is no further inkling of this in Huygens' diary –nor of drunkenness in the Prince.

31 Nimwegen, *op. cit.*, pp.502–3. *Correspondentie Willem III en Bentinck, op. cit.*, II, 2, pp.186–7.

32 *Correspondentie Willem III en Bentinck, op. cit.*, II, 2, pp.190–94, 199–205. Nimwegen, *op. cit.*, pp.503–4. Rousset, *op. cit.*, II, pp.327, 340.

33 Lynn, *op. cit.*, pp.151–2.

34 Rousset, *op. cit.*, II, pp.339–40.

35 Hutton, *op. cit.*, p.343. Haley, *The Anglo-Dutch Rapprochement, op. cit.*, pp.631–2.

36 *Correspondentie Willem III en Bentinck, op. cit.*, II, 2, p.176.

37 Huygens, *Journaal, op. cit.*, pp.164, 169.

38 *Correspondentie Willem III en Bentinck, op. cit.*, II, 2, pp.175–6.

39 *Ibid., op. cit.*, I, 1, p.7.

40 *Ibid.*, I, 1, pp.4–6.

41 Namely Valenciennes, Tournai, Courtrai, Oudenarde, Ath, Charleroi and Condé.

42 Cambrai, Aire, St-Omer and Bouchain.

43 Browning, *op. cit.*, II, pp. 389–91, 485–7. *Correspondentie Willem III en Bentinck, op. cit.*, I, 1, p.8.

44 Mignet, *op. cit.*, IV, pp.479ff. Haley, *The Anglo-Dutch Rapprochement, op. cit.*, p.635 says Danby was also present, but his reference to Browning, *op. cit.*, I, pp.237–44 does not bear this out.

45 Charleroi, Ath, Oudenarde, Courtrai, Tournai and Condé.

46 Valenciennes was added.

47 Mignet, *op. cit.*, IV, pp.485ff.

48 Tournai and Courtrai.

49 He was prepared to exchange Charleroi, Ath and Oudenarde for Ypres, Charlemont and Luxemburg.

50 Mignet, *op. cit.*, IV, pp.479–97. Haley, *The Anglo-Dutch Rapprochement, op. cit.*, pp.633–5.

51 Courtrai, Oudenarde, Ath and Charleroi.

52 Tournai, Condé, Cambrai, Aire, St-Omer, Bouchain and Valenciennes.

53 Haley, *The Anglo-Dutch Rapprochement, op. cit.*, pp.636–7. Temple, *Works, op. cit.*, 1754, I, p.332.

54 *Correspondentie Willem III en Bentinck, op. cit.*, II, 2, p.197.

55 Haley, *The Anglo-Dutch Rapprochement, op. cit.*, p.637. Temple, *Works, op. cit.*, 1770, II, p.412. Did Charles's allusion to safeguarding the Prince's estates in Franche-Comté have an influence on his decision? They would come completely under the control of Louis XIV if he acquired Franche-Comté and no guarantee would be worth much, but they could be swapped or sold for a safer equivalent elsewhere, as indeed Charles later suggested (see p.356).

56 Huygens, *Journaal, op. cit.*, pp. 222–3, 225. *Correspondentie Willem III en Bentinck, op. cit.*, II, 2, p.207.

57 Groen van Prinsterer, *op. cit.*, 2nd series, V, p.348, who uses Old Style for letters from England. *Correspondentie Willem III en Bentinck, op. cit.*, II, 2, p.208. Huygens, *Journaal, op. cit.*, p.211.

58 Müller, *Waldeck, op. cit.*, pp.342–3.

59 Haley, *The Anglo-Dutch Rapprochement, op. cit.*, p.639.

60 *Ibid.*, p.640.

61 *Correspondentie Willem III en Bentinck, op. cit.*, II, 2, p.208, nn.1, 2.

62 J. Basnage, *Annales des Provinces-Unies*, II, The Hague 1726, p.865.

63 H. and B. Van der Zee, *William and Mary*, Macmillan 1973, p.114.

64 Browning, *op. cit.*, pp.250–51, II, p.41.

65 Temple, *Works, op. cit.*, 1770, I, p.339.

66 Basnage, *op. cit.*, II, p.865.

67 Mignet, *op. cit.*, IV, p.507.

68 Temple, *Works, op. cit.*, 1754, I, p.340. Browning, *op. cit.*, I, p.251. Basnage, *op. cit.*, p.865.

69 Basnage, *op. cit.*, II, p.865.

70 Temple, *Works, op. cit.*, 1754, I, pp.340–41. Haley, *The Anglo-Dutch Rapprochement, op. cit.*, p.640–42. For the part which Bishop Burnet attributes to Danby in persuading the King and the Duke of York see Basnage, *op. cit.*, II, pp.866–7. Burnet, however, did not give this account to Basnage until 1714 and, as so often with the Bishop, the distance in time does not enhance confidence in his evidence.

71 Mignet, *op. cit.*, IV, pp.509–10.

72 Browning, *op. cit.*, I, p.252. Temple, *Works, op. cit.*, 1754, I, pp.341–2. Van der Zees, *op. cit.*, p.117.

73 Temple, *Works, op. cit.*, 1754, I, pp.342–3.

74 Haley, *The Anglo-Dutch Rapprochement, op. cit.*, p.643.

75 Temple, *Works, op. cit.*, 1754, I, pp.343–4.

76 Haley, *The Anglo-Dutch Rapprochement, op. cit.*, p.644.

77 Temple, *Works, op. cit.*, 1754, I, p.345.

78 Haley, *The Anglo-Dutch Rapprochement, op. cit.*, p.645.

79 Mignet, *op. cit.*, IV, pp.514–17. C.L. Grose, art. *The Anglo-Dutch Alliance of 1678*, English Historical Review, 39, Jan.–Oct. 1924.

80 Mignet, *op. cit.*, IV, p.520.

81 Browning, *op. cit.*, I, pp.255–6.

82 *Correspondentie Willem III en Bentinck, op. cit.*, II, 2, pp.214–15.

83 Prinsterer, *op. cit.*, 2nd series, V, pp.361–2. Temple, *Works, op. cit.*, 1754, I, pp.346–7.

84 Browning, *op. cit.*, II, pp.402–05.

85 Grose, article *op. cit.*, pp.354–6.

86 Japikse, *Willem III, op. cit.*, II, p.81.

18 1678: THE TREATY OF NIJMEGEN AND THE END OF THE WAR

CHARLES II'S TORTUOUS PROGRESS

Immediately after his departure from London, William received a series of warm letters from both his English uncles – those from James, who, with the prospect of war and therefore of command, was being lured from his French commitment, being particularly cordial.[1] Charles recalled the British troops in French service and allowed the Dutch to recruit amongst his subjects in their stead – although not overtly.[2] William was full of plans to give military effect to the Alliance. He wrote to Danby on 29 January 1678 – he had been communicating regularly with him since he left England – with his suggestions. England should provide a considerable fleet in the Channel and a strong squadron in the Mediterranean to impede French commerce as well as a land army as strong as possible either to cause a diversion by landing on the French coast or to be sent to Flanders, the latter being preferable.[3] English plans to use Ostend as a base for their troops in Flanders were delayed by Spanish suspicions that, once they were there, Ostend would be permanently lost to Spain, and it required the intervention of the Prince of Orange before the first English contingent landed there on 8 March.[4]

But it soon became apparent that the omens for close cooperation between the Dutch and the English were not good. The negotiations for the defensive alliance were soon met with objections from Amsterdam, which, at the end of January, Fagel told the Prince he was having difficulty in overcoming.[5] Although Amsterdam was being driven to peace by the weight of taxation and the effect of war on her trade she was also fearful of the increase in the authority of the Prince which, in her eyes, flowed from the English connection; the anti-Stadholder faction looked to France as a counterweight.[6] Then, whilst the Dutch nevertheless eventually ratified the treaty on 7 April, Charles II refused to do so in England.[7]

In response to English requests the Dutch Rear-Admiral, Cornelis Eversten, was sent to London in the middle of February with detailed instructions that developed the views William had initially outlined to Danby in his letter of 29 January. They envisaged wide-ranging Anglo-Dutch cooperation in the Mediterranean, in the North Sea, in the West Indies, and in support of Denmark; they displayed an imaginative grasp of the potentialities of sea power, but, alas, the Prince had to admit that the financial exhaustion of the Dutch Republic meant that she would have to look for formidable contributions from England.[8] Because of this no agreement was reached on cooperation in the English Channel, and, although agreement was reached for the Mediterranean on 4 April, the plans were overtaken by the French withdrawal from Sicily and the course of the peace negotiations.[9]

But in the meantime Louis was using his extensive resources and web of able diplomats to engage in intrigues with the political classes both in England and in the Dutch Republic. In England Danby had built up a considerable Parliamentary following, in which bribery played a substantial part. Nevertheless, he had his political opponents, a mixed assortment, with different motives, united only by their antipathy towards him. They included Arlington, Buckingham, Russelll and, most potent of all, Shaftesbury; and French bribery of Members of Parliament, and French propaganda, were now added to the mix. The French played on the English fear of a standing army and the threat that this could pose to English liberties. They were also able to dilute support for the Prince of Orange by presenting his marriage as having brought him closely within Charles's sphere of influence.[10]

Intent on wrecking Charles's relations with Parliament, the French connived with the opposition to devise a strategy to embarrass the King by paradoxically pushing him much further against France than he himself could possibly contemplate. When it met on 7 February, Parliament made an address to the King praying him to treat with France only on the basis of the Treaty of the Pyrenees, a suggestion so patently at variance with diplomatic – and military – realities that Charles could not possibly accept it; it would not in any case have been consistent with the Anglo-Dutch Alliance which had just been signed and which had moved on from the terms in the Pyrenees agreement, although Parliament was ignorant of this.[11] Meeting Barillon that evening, Charles whispered in his ear that he believed that he must have used bribes to achieve such an outrageous outcome.

However, Parliament in the middle of February did give its consent to raising 30,000 men and the fitting out of 90 ships,[12] and, at the end of the month, it did vote the King supplies for the first six months of a war,[13] which enabled Charles to commence raising troops. Barillon reported on 7 April that 15,000 men of the new levies were already on their way, apart from what the King already had in Ostend and Bruges – the other place in Flanders where British troops were congregated.[14] Colonel Howard of the guards with 1,200 or 1,300 men was at Ostend and the Duke of Monmouth, switching over from his service with the French King, was at Bruges with 1,700.[15]

In the interim, at the beginning of February, Charles had offered Louis modified peace terms – he could have Charlemont in place of Tournai, 'as a place', as Danby put it to Prince William when he wrote to him about the proposal, 'the Spaniard may best spare'. The messenger Charles used to convey the offer to Louis was the French envoy Ruvigny, the son of a previous ambassador in London, who knew the English scene well, who, as a Huguenot, was deemed by Louis to be an excellent vehicle for bribing English Members of Parliament, and who accordingly had been despatched to London to assist Barillon.

Sidney Godolphin was sent to Prince William to explain that the 'dilatory proceedings of Parliament' left the King no other choice, but Danby also wrote to him – so close had their relationship become – secretly advising him to reject the King's new proposals, and to burn his letter. At Danby's request the Prince sent him two letters; in the first, which was to be shown to the King, he indicated his antipathy to the proposal by saying, diplomatically, that he was *un peu surpris* by Godolphin's mission. His second letter was for the eyes of Danby only; it is interesting not only for the high degree of confidence that had developed between the two of them – it was one in a whole series of letters that they had been exchanging since the Prince's return from England – but also for the pressure he was under from the peace party in the States. He was apprehensive, if the substance of Godolphin's mission became known, that that pressure would increase; and he admitted that majority opinion on the Dutch side of the North Sea would accept the exchange of Charlemont for Tournai, and, even, less favourable terms, and it was going to be extremely difficult to get them to put up more money for the war. Nevertheless he thought it would be a mistake to soften the terms that he and Charles had agreed upon when he was in England. On the contrary if they had asked for more, as he had urged, they would by now have had the peace.

Ruvigny's mission – he left London on 11 February – included a proposal from Charles that, if the terms Ruvigny brought with him were accepted, he should propose an Anglo-French alliance in return for £600,000 from Louis.[16] Meanwhile Charles undertook not to send troops to Flanders until 10 March,[17] which would give time for Ruvigny's return with Louis's reply – but it would also buy time for the French and delay any English intervention in Louis's war plans. Charles's undertaking was conditional on Louis's not engaging in any sieges in the meantime, but this the French ignored, for what they had in mind was a striking demonstration of power to put an end to the war, and their plans were already well under way.

At the beginning of 1678 Louis had an army of 279,610 men, which meant that, after making provision for garrisons, he could bring over 163,000 into the field in the various theatres of war. It was the largest force he had ever had at his disposal. The most the Spanish and Dutch could hope to bring into the field in Flanders to oppose him was 46,000 men.

The efficiency of the French provisioning system was demonstrated to the world by the winter siege of St-Ghislain, which, commencing on 1 December 1667, was followed by its capitulation on the 10th. The helplessness of Waldeck to prevent it, together with the Dutch inferiority in logistics, was exhibited for all to see.

Then Louis, with a display of showmanship unusual even by his standards, left St-Germain on 7 February with his Queen and his court, as well as with the obligatory mistress – this time La Montespan. To keep his destination uncertain he made a long detour to Metz; there he held a grand review of his army, which served to heighten the drama, to intensify the suspense, and to display his prowess. As he headed towards the north-west, his destination still uncertain, the Queen, the ladies of the court and the courtiers were dispensed with at Stenay on the 27th, to go in their coaches – by easy stages – to Lille; and Louis – by contrast moving fast on horseback – finally arrived before Ghent on 4 March, where the siege, with an army of about 60,000 men, had commenced on the evening of the 1st. But war as theatre could take its toll. 'His Majesty is extremely fatigued,' it was reported just before his arrival at Ghent: 'he vowes that never in his life has he endured so much.'[18]

He was, however, well recompensed. On the 9th the town capitulated, followed two days later by the citadel, the French casualties being but few. This siege was soon followed, in more bloody fashion, by that of Ypres, which surrendered on the 25th.[19] The lead performer in these scenes, which, as usual, had been meticulously orchestrated by Louvois, returned to his ladies at Lille; and on 7 April, two months to the day after his departure, he was back at St-Germain.[20]

Responding to these events, William departed in great haste from the Republic on 1 March, taking hardly any baggage with him, to join the Dutch army at Mechelen.[21] From there he wrote bitterly to Danby on the 5th that events had at length reached the point that he had always feared, and of which he had so often given warning verbally and in writing. King Charles had lost the opportunity to impose the terms of peace. The conditions demanded would now be even less favourable than the concessions Charles had made, as conveyed to him by Godolphin, and every effort would now have to be made to gain by war what could have been gained by the peace. Affairs were starting to affect England closely, he told Danby, and he appealed personally to the Lord Treasurer to do all that lay in his power to lend him assistance.[22]

On 14 March Danby wrote to him that Charles II had been informed by Barillon, whilst the siege of Ghent was still in progress, that his peace proposals as agreed with Prince William when he was in England would be acceptable to Louis, provided Tournai, Valenciennes and Condé were added to the French share – what we will refer to as the 'Barillon terms'. Before proceeding further, Charles wanted to know the reaction to this from the States, and, using the Dutch as intermediaries, from the Spanish. Sidney Godolphin was again sent over to the Republic to ascertain the Dutch reply.

A little earlier, on 8 March, Laurence Hyde, the English envoy at the Nijmegen peace conference, who was then in The Hague, had a meeting with Fagel. Ghent had not yet fallen but was expected to do so and there was deep anxiety that this would be followed by Bruges and Brussels. So great was the consternation, said Fagel, that there were those in the Republic who were ready to submit to France on any terms. Fagel himself admitted that he had thought that no assistance could come from England to save Flanders in time. He clearly already knew of Barillon's terms, for he said if Charles II could procure a peace on the basis of the terms agreed between himself and the Prince with the addition of Valenciennes and Tournai, or one of them, he would be doing a great service to the States – and, he added, for the interests of the Prince, who was so weakened by the war that only peace could re-establish him.[23]

On 21 March Godolphin arrived at The Hague, and he and Hyde met Fagel the following morning, when they 'fully acquainted him' with Barillon's terms. Fagel informed them that a meeting of the States-General, on the 9th, had gone better than he expected in that they had forborne to declare their readiness to accept the French peace terms until they had heard more from England, and in the meantime they had agreed to the continuation of taxes. But this mood was dependent on what Charles II could achieve; Fagel was aware that the King's military preparations were likely to be so inadequate both in time and scale as to be of little help, and the German Emperor could do nothing considerable until May. For his part he was inclined to accept Barillon's terms, poor though they were, although he would not convey them to the States-General until he had the opinion of the Prince, which he seemed to think would be favourable. He also thought the governor of the Spanish Netherlands, Villa Hermosa, would be content; and he repeated that only an immediate peace could restore the Prince of Orange's position in the country.[24]

The pressure on the Prince was thus very great and he was prepared to yield, to a degree. On the 27th, the day after Godolphin had arrived at his quarters and met him, he wrote to Danby saying that Villa Hermosa had been sounded out and that he had agreed to ceding Valenciennes and Tournai. On their side the Dutch would agree to this as well, if France was prepared to proceed on this footing – which, however, he very much doubted. If they declined to do so then England should declare war on them 'without any loss of time'. But he did not disguise that he thought the peace terms 'pernicious' and that they could have ill consequences.[25] On the 31st he added in a further letter that he hoped means might be found of retaining either Tournai or Valenciennes for Spain.

THE DUTCH PEACE PARTY

At this time the Count d'Estrades was in touch with the Dutch opposition to the Prince. Hitherto Amsterdam had been divided between the followers of Gillis Valckenier and those of Hendrik Hooft, but now, fearful of the increasing power of the Prince of Orange, this twosome united against him. They were joined by a third, the Amsterdam Pensionary Jacob van den Bosch, who had been the secretary of Johan De Witt and who remained a fierce admirer of his regime; and it was he that D'Estrades used as his intermediary.[26] On 18 March Van den Bosch had written to the Count saying that he had been asked to attend a meeting of the 'most able of the magistrates' of Amsterdam, who asked him to use the Count's offices to reach an accommodation with Louis. D'Estrades responded two days later saying that he had no doubt the King would comply with that request, provided that the Province of Holland undertook to cease levying taxes for the war until the agreement to be entered into with him was ratified by the other Provinces, and that Louis should retain the conquests he had made since he had offered his peace terms (the Barillon terms) to Charles II. This meant that France would retain Ghent and Ypres, which was too much for even Amsterdam to swallow, and the peace party asked Louis to drop these two towns from his demands.[27] But nevertheless when the States of Holland met on the 25th to discuss the war budget for 1678, which had been prepared by the Prince and the Council of State, they very reluctantly decided that they could not raise the necessary finance for this and they resolved to send a delegation to the Prince of Orange to acquaint him of their decision, which of course raised the question of the need to reduce the size of the army and hence the need for peace.[28]

The delegation met the Prince at Antwerp on 1 April.[29] He told them that he knew from several letters from Fagel of the strong disposition that existed to make peace because of the lack of sufficient means to continue the war, and he had told Godolphin that although he judged the peace to be 'damaging, yes ruinous', if the peace could be concluded, with Tournai and Valenciennes ceded to Louis, the Dutch States would be content with the terms; but he asked the delegation for a delay of two weeks before deciding on reducing the army so that they could ascertain Charles II's response after Godolphin's return to England.[30] It was the best he could do in a situation that was still fluid and uncertain; Barillon's terms demanded three extra towns for France and the Prince had replied with only two, perhaps, indeed, only one, whilst the French also wanted to retain the conquests they had made since Barillon had submitted the terms – Danby told the Prince on 13 April that Barillon had informed him that after its capture France wanted to retain Ypres.[31]

Nor was the Dutch peace party all that confident in confronting the Prince; there were those who attended the Antwerp meeting who wanted to delete 'disgraceful' from the report of what the Prince had said about the peace. 'I see from their conduct', Fagel reported back to the Prince, 'that these good friends, who so hanker after and long for the peace, rather wish that it did not come into the open that Your Highness had opposed the terms.' Prince William thus still held a strong hand when it came to Dutch public opinion. But, nevertheless, Fagel doubted that the French would accept William's terms and, in that event, the peace party would undoubtedly make further concessions, 'although many honest folk would wash their hands of it'.[32]

The peace party were also making progress on another front. Reluctant though Charles II was to enter the war against France, he nevertheless made contingency plans if he was forced into it by Parliament. In that event he wanted to be sure of having the necessary allies. To that end he had, at the beginning of March, proposed a quadruple alliance between England, the Dutch, Spain and the Emperor. He found, however, that the Dutch ambassador in London, Van Beuningen, lacked the necessary diplomatic powers to enter into the negotiations; and the Dutch peace party were able to ensure that they were not forthcoming, so that when the representatives of the four powers were due for their first meeting on 5 April Van Beuningen was still without his credentials. There were further delays and these negotiations were overtaken by those for the peace at Nijmegen – for the peace party a successful conclusion.[33]

LOUIS XIV REJECTS CHARLES II'S PEACE PROPOSALS AND SUBMITS HIS OWN

In the meantime, in his characteristic zigzag fashion, Charles II was negotiating on two fronts. We have seen that Rouvigny left London for France on 11 February with Charles's request for a subsidy from Louis of £600,000. This had set off negotiations, with the French offering 6 million *livres* (about £500,000). When Godolphin returned from the Continent on 31 March with his soundings of the Dutch and Spanish reactions to the Barillon proposals, Charles decided, as the mediator in the peace negotiations, to put forward terms whose acceptance by Spain and Holland he would guarantee. Danby agreed to write to Montagu, the English ambassador in Paris, with these particulars, which he did on 4 April (25 March Old Style), and they included the condition that, if Louis accepted them, Charles should receive the 6 million *livres* for three years, that is to say, 18 million *livres* in total – this request was justified on the grounds that it would probably take three years before Parliament would be in any mood to grant him supplies after a French peace thus entered into. These proposals included the restoration to Spain of Condé, Ghent and Ypres, and Danby did not expect Louis to accept them, which indeed proved to be the case. It has also been suggested that he pitched high the sum payable to Charles, so as to give Louis another reason to reject the terms. However that may be, he had given Montagu a potent weapon with which to blackmail him, and this, at the appropriate time, was to be deployed against him – he, the accusation would be, was the instrument by which Charles had become the pensioner of France.[34]

Louis rejected Charles's terms and proposed his own, which he conveyed to his envoys at the peace congress at Nijmegen; an extract was publicly printed on 15 April. He was prepared to cede Ghent but would retain Condé, Valenciennes and Ypres. To summarise, his final position, therefore, was that he would retain seven towns – the original four offered by Prince William through Bentinck, except that he substituted Cambrai for Courtrai (thus Cambrai, Aire, St-Omer, Bouchain), Charles II's addition of Valenciennes, and Louis's own additions of Condé and Ypres. He would return eight towns to Spain but keep the much more important Franche-Comté; and his terms for the unfortunate Duke of Lorraine so infringed the Duke's territorial integrity that it would make him wholly dependent on the goodwill of France. The terms were not subject to negotiation and would have to be accepted by 10 May.[35] They were, indeed, incorporated into the Treaty of Nijmegen when it was signed.

DUTCH DISCUSSION OF LOUIS'S PROPOSALS

Of course, unless the Dutch made a separate peace, their allies would also have to agree; and when the allied envoys met in The Hague on 21 April they urged the Dutch to reject them. One of Louis's demands – that the Northern German territories Sweden had lost to Brandenburg, Denmark, the Bishop of Münster, and the Dukes of Brunswick in the war should be restored to her – in particular caused qualms amongst the Dutch. The States-General met on 27 April and Prince William arrived in The Hague on the 29th, where he held a series of meetings.

On the 30th, he addressed the States of Holland with his views. The Elector of Brandenburg, he said, had been promised that he would be recompensed by Sweden and now Louis demanded that he be abandoned; the Dutch were committed to restoring the Duke of Lorraine to his duchy in its entirety; and the French terms ran counter to the agreement only recently entered into with Villa Hermosa. 'Who', he asked, 'would ever treat with the Republic if it broke engagements so newly entered into?... I am of the opinion', he went on, 'that Peace should be made, provided it is made on conditions that do not carry with them inevitable ruin'; so bad were the French terms that the peace would provide no guarantee of security so that many more troops than were ever anticipated would be required to maintain it. 'I am aware of the bad state of the Republic; but I am at the same time persuaded that the evil is not without remedy…. As for myself', he ended, 'I will always obey the orders of the State; but I will never be in agreement with a Peace so ruinous and so infamous.'

Whilst the nobility supported the Prince, Amsterdam stated that her delegation had express orders to prefer a reasonable peace to the uncertain events of a war, and she carried the majority of the Holland towns with her. However, in the end only Amsterdam was prepared to make peace without the allies, and once more the Prince was able to obtain a delay, although he was swimming against an almost irresistible current. The decision was taken first to consult the allies, although the emissaries to be sent to them were, as Prince William noted, chosen from the two towns most eager for the peace.

Van Leeuwen, from Leyden, was sent to London to ask Charles II to drop the proposal for the quadruple alliance and to mediate in the negotiations on the footing of the French terms; and Boreel, from Amsterdam, was sent to reinforce Dijckveldt at Brussels to meet Villa Hermosa, to whom they submitted a memoir on 8 May saying that the States were disposed to accept the French terms if the allies agreed.

Prince William wrote to Waldeck on 12 May saying that everything in Holland proceeded with much confusion; it looked as though they would give up exerting themselves, and cast themselves into the hands of Providence, who, the Prince hoped, would have pity on them all. On the following day, indeed, the Dutch finally resolved to accept the French terms if the allies did so too.[36]

To give themselves time for the necessary consultations they had, on 3 May, asked Louis to extend his deadline from 10 May, which he agreed to do eventually, to the 27th.[37] On the 18th – when he spoke, rather quaintly, of committing his *principale gloire* into taking all possible steps towards peace – he made another concession and promised not to carry the war any further into the Spanish Netherlands; he was intending to stay in the vicinity of Ghent until the 27th, where he was prepared to receive a Dutch embassy.

On receipt of the message William hurried from his house at Honselaarsdijk to The Hague and vigorously opposed any such mission; the King was setting a trap to separate the States from their allies; and their honour, their good faith, their true interests, compelled them to remain true to their engagements. He had the support of the Holland nobles and he had the support of Dordrecht, of Haarlem, of Delft, and of Gouda, but it was to no avail. He was opposed by Amsterdam. This city proposed sending a deputation to be charged with obtaining an armistice of six weeks, whilst talks continued with the allies to dispose them towards peace.

Both the Spaniards and the other allies were prepared to negotiate the armistice, without, however, acceding to Louis's terms.[38] But on 27 May Danby wrote to the Prince, 'commanded by his Majesty', to let him know that Charles's affairs in England were in such a bad state, and his Parliament in such a bad humour, that he had not the slightest hope of being able to make an armed contribution in Flanders. The Prince should take his measures accordingly, and comply with the Dutch desire for peace. Charles asked that William should use his good offices to bring round the Duke of Villa Hermosa; and, as far as William's private interests were concerned, Charles had 'no doubt but they will bee fully preserved to Your Highnesse'.

This left the Prince no choice but to submit to sending the embassy, as requested by Louis.[39]

Blaspiel, the Elector of Brandenburg's representative in the Republic, remonstrated strongly with him. He replied that Amsterdam and other towns were blindly set on the peace; to him it appeared disadvantageous to both the Republic and to its allies; he was resolved to oppose it with all his might, and to push matters to extremes, but this resolve would meet with many difficulties and would be exposed to many dangers. Spain would not send any help, Germany would always send it too late, the King of England was himself indifferent, whilst he was embroiled with his Parliament, which alone was for the war, and Holland was tired out and exhausted. 'I am coming round', he said, 'at viewing the peace, totally shameful and ruinous though it be, as necessary, having regard to the little of the [Spanish] Low Countries which remains. Furthermore the people, anxiety ridden as they are, force us to it.'[40] The Prince of Orange, in short, appeared to be in two minds, caught between his belief that a peace on the terms being considered was 'shameful', and the practical difficulties of resisting it. His personal reputation, his standing in Europe, was at stake; and, like his uncle Charles, but in a different context, he too was going to have to pursue a zigzag course.

CHARLES II'S AGREEMENT WITH LOUIS

His uncle's zigzagging had brought him, for the time being, within the orbit of Louis XIV. For on 27 May, the same day that Danby had written to the Prince advising him to comply with the Dutch desire for peace, Charles had signed, personally, a new secret agreement with Louis; he undertook to remain neutral during the continuation of the war if the Dutch and the Spanish did not accept Louis's peace terms within two months. Under a separate article, which however was signed only by Barillon and not by Charles, Louis promised to pay him 6 million *livres* if he recalled all but 3,000 of his troops from Flanders and disbanded all but 6,000 – 3,000 of which were destined to quell disturbances in Scotland – and if he prorogued Parliament for at least four months.

Charles had been driven to his present position by the continual lack of cooperation from Parliament to which Prince William had alluded in his conversation with Blaspiel. It attacked the King's ministers, including Danby, for whose removal it petitioned the King, and it wanted him to wage war on Louis, but, at the same time, it refused to provide him with the funds to do so because of the fear of a standing army; and now the arrival of Van Leeuwen made it clear that the Dutch were set on peace. Charles's predicament was not helped by the refusal of Danby – and others, including Temple, who was in England and who pleaded illness – to sign the agreement with Louis, although Danby had conducted the negotiations; and once again Charles had to do so on his own.

There is one provision in the agreement which we may note. At Charles's request Louis undertook to allow the Prince of Orange the free enjoyment of all his property in the domains of the French King, the Principality of Orange included, upon the States-General's accepting the peace terms.[41] It appeared that Charles had obtained a safeguard for the House of Nassau's possessions, including those which, under Louis's peace terms, lay in territory that would become part of his dominions, those in Franche-Comté being particularly extensive, but it was a point that applied elsewhere as well. It was an inducement to the Prince to obtain his compliance, we may surmise, as much as a sop to Charles II's dynastic sense of solidarity; and whilst this agreement was intended to be secret – although rumours of its existence were soon current – Charles had taken care that a hint of the safeguards for his interests should be conveyed to the Prince in Danby's letter to him of 27 May.

DUTCH ACCEPTANCE OF LOUIS'S TERMS

The emissary whom the Dutch chose to send to Louis was Hieronymus van Beverninck, who had at first refused the task until persuaded by Prince William that he should do so. He arrived at Louis's camp at Wetteren, near Ghent, on 1 June, where he had a long audience with the King; he informed him that the Dutch were prepared to accept the peace terms and Louis offered an armistice to last six weeks, commencing on 1 July. Historians dispute whether Van Beverninck exceeded his instructions by promising that the Dutch would make peace even without the agreement of the allies. However that might be, his return to The Hague on 3 June was greeted as synonymous with the conclusion of peace, although the delegates to the States-General still needed to obtain the views of their principals. Villa Hermosa conveyed the consent of Spain, but the other allies – Brandenburg, Denmark, Lorraine and the Emperor – remained opposed.[42]

On 8 June Waldeck reported to the Prince the anxieties the Dutch Regents had about the relationship between himself and Amsterdam. He had received members of Holland's Delegated Council (*Gecommiteerde Raden*) at his camp at Mechelen, where one of them, Aerson, had assured him that the Amsterdam Burgomaster Falckenier was not irreconcilably against the Prince. Another, Bleswijck, told him that the lack of understanding was ruining the State and every sensible person was doing all he could to address the problem; but the Prince on his side could do his bit by extending his patronage to those who at the moment were being excluded and were without hope of advancement – he made a reference to employing the most able people, perhaps a hint at the unsatisfactory quality of William's existing clients – which was, indeed, a just observation. A third, Van Asperen, who was well disposed to the Prince, pleaded for moderation.

The Prince responded two days later in robust form – he knew that the members of the Delegated Council would still be with Waldeck and that his views (no doubt appropriately edited) could be transmitted to them. He had nothing against Amsterdam, he told Waldeck, provided she did not infringe his legitimate authority; but one would see who was the stronger if she did so encroach, which was certainly what Amsterdam wanted to do; that was why she wanted to make peace, without adequate safeguards, and which was why she was attaching herself to France to get French backing. Amsterdam, in short, in the Prince's eyes, and Valckenier in particular, was seeking to attack his power base, under cover of the peace, and they were allying themselves with France to attain that end.

But Waldeck's letter of 8 June had revealed that there were those amongst the Regents who wanted to avoid the looming confrontation; and the Prince left the way open for an accommodation, despite the firmness of his tone. He had no other intention, he said, but to live peaceably with the authority he had, without extending it further; and he would be very happy if Burgomaster Valckenier sought reconciliation with him. He was not going to give way to Bleswijck – all he was doing was furthering the concerns of his own party in Delft. But it was needful to bring the disputes to a satisfactory end. He had no other aim than the service of the State, whose interests he had always put above his own.

Subordinating his interests to those of the State, however, was one thing; totally abandoning them was another. He advised Waldeck that now was the time for Waldeck to look after his own private interests at the Nijmegen congress and to get the States-General to authorise the Dutch ambassadors to act on his behalf, as he himself had done.[43] Taking advantage of his cousin Nassau-Odijk's going to Nijmegen as one of the Dutch ambassadors at the peace congress, he wrote to Van Beverninck on 9 June to tell him that Odijk was briefed on his personal affairs – Odijk brought a memorandum with him – and he asked Van Beverninck to do what he could for his 'just claims'. Van Beverninck, who was not fully aware of the magnitude of the Orange possessions, replied on 14 June that he would do what lay within his power.

In the same letter he complied with William's request, conveyed via Odijk, to let him have his views on the diplomatic situation – a request that may have been a gesture on William's part to demonstrate, in response to what Waldeck had written on 8 June, that he was prepared to listen to the Regents and to keep the support of one as influential as Van Beverninck.[44] The latter thought the peace negotiations needed to be brought to a conclusion and that the Emperor, like the Spaniards, would come to the same decision and would consequently bring the Duke of Lorraine in their train; but they would blame the peace on the Dutch. Hence the Dutch should point to the wretched state of Spain and the insupportable burdens on themselves; they had done all they could, and more, to comply with their treaty obligations. As a sweetener the Dutch should offer to negotiate mutual guarantees of the peace treaties that were to emerge. As for Sweden, the Republic should do what was possible for her allies, in particular the Elector of Brandenburg.[45]

All this reflected underlying realities – the Dutch were financially exhausted (or, perhaps more accurately, the Regents would pay no more) and the state of Spain and the Spanish Netherlands was dire – but from the point of view of the Republic's allies it was not remotely palatable. It was something the Prince of Orange had anticipated three days earlier in a letter to Waldeck: 'do not imagine that any consideration for the allies will impede us; and France, seeing that we are so resolved, is leading us where she wills … I am doing everything an "honest homme" [sic] ought to do, but I foresee great complaints … and they will all have reason to complain.'

On 22 June the Dutch States, at a meeting attended by the Prince, instructed their envoys at Nijmegen to 'conclude and sign the peace treaty before the end of the month together with those of the allies who found themselves so disposed'. They wrote to Louis asking him to cease hostilities and to withdraw his troops to his own domains towards the end of the month.[46] They had thus at last agreed upon a separate peace, leaving their allies to take it or leave it.

The following day the Prince of Orange wrote to Louis saying that he would be very happy if he 'could contribute something to the re-establishment of the good correspondence of old between your majesty and this state'; and at the same time he took the opportunity of asking the King if he could instruct his envoys at Nijmegen to ensure that he could have a 'just satisfaction for all the losses and damages he had suffered during this war'. But Louis was in no mood to be too forthcoming. He was very satisfied, he replied on the 29th, to see the Prince taking the occasion of the forthcoming peace to reiterate 'the sentiments he was entitled to expect' from him; it provided a promising basis for believing that his future conduct would enable the King to accord him marks of his goodwill.[47] The right tone clearly, in Louis's estimation, was *de haut en bas*.

And, continuing in this vein, he was not going to be over-accommodating when it came to the article in the peace treaty relating to the Prince's personal interests. William pointed out to Van Beverninck that Spain had never met its commitments under the Treaty of

Münster to make restitution for his properties in Franche-Comté, and, since these were now being acquired by France, he asked for the safeguard that provision should be made in this article that France should take over Spain's obligations. The French were not prepared to go as far as this, but drew attention to the provision that was being made for the preservation of all His Highness's rights, privileges, prerogatives etc., in every sense, namely in Franche-Comté. Nor were they prepared to allow William the title of 'Seigneur Prince', with its stronger connotation of sovereignty, confining themselves to 'Monsieur le Prince d'Orange'. 'I know very well', was the Prince's caustic comment to Van Beverninck on 9 July, 'that we are not negotiating with the French, but are only having the law laid down, and so that article too will have to be bedded down in accordance with their approval.'[48]

THE PEACE TREATY POSTPONED

The Prince's comment was much to the point, because the French King was now engaged in pursuing a course of action which can only be described as 'doing a Louis'; he was acting very much in the same manner he adopted in 1672, when, with the Dutch apparently at his feet, he insisted on peace terms that were too monstrously extravagant. Until the peace treaty was almost on the point of being signed he had played a masterly diplomatic game, in London and in The Hague, by exploiting the oppositions in these countries and – by halting his military advance in Flanders – he had avoided frightening them. But then, just when the Dutch were about to sign on 27 or 28 June, it became apparent how he intended to stand by his commitment to Sweden that the places she had lost in the war be restored to her. To give effect to this commitment he had come to the conclusion that he had to be able to send troops through Cleves and Marck, the Grand Elector's territories, so that they could advance into Northern Germany to force Sweden's enemies, if necessary, to restore their conquests. And to keep his lines of communication open to achieve that end he decided he needed to retain the towns in the Spanish Low Countries that he had agreed to return to Spain, as well as Maastricht, which he was going to hand back to the Dutch, until Sweden's position was safeguarded, particularly by Brandenburg.

To the French envoys at Nijmegen it looked as though, playing on the all too evident Dutch desire for peace, they would be able to slip this provision into the terms that were about to be signed. Moreover, Louis also had, or so he believed, his agreement of 27 May with Charles II, under which Charles undertook to remain neutral if the Dutch and Spain did not accept his terms, so he should have been safe from English intervention. But then, the untoward boasting of the Swedish envoy made the new French proposals public. At Nijmegen consternation prevailed; at The Hague the States-General refused to sign; in London Charles II and Danby were bewildered.

It might take a long time before Sweden found her lost territories returned to her and, in the meantime, the French would retain the Spanish towns – and Maastricht – for an indefinite period. Furthermore, the presence of French troops in Cleves and Marck was only too reminiscent of the outflanking movement along the Rhine that the French invasion forces had executed in 1672, and even the anxieties of Amsterdam were stirred. The Prince of Orange and the war party were once more in the ascendant. And the joy of the allies of the Dutch was unbounded.[49]

But Louis refused to yield.

The Prince of Orange was quick to see that this meant the possible continuation of the war, as he wrote at the end of June to his close friend Ossory: 'at least if you [the English] remain firm and us as well'. He would keep Ossory, who had just returned to England, informed on how matters developed in case it was possible for him to join the Dutch army, as the Prince very much wanted him to do. On 4 July he wrote to Dijkveldt warning him of the possible extension of the war and asking him and Boreel, both of whom were in the Spanish Netherlands, to hold discussions with Villa Hermosa to take contingency measures, in that event, to come to the aid of Mons.[50]

Mons was not being besieged, but was being blockaded, by the Duke of Luxemburg as a means of maintaining pressure on the Dutch and on Spain. At Luxemburg's request Dijkveldt, Boreel and Villa Hermosa had joined him on 1 July – on the assumption that the peace treaty was on course to be signed – to discuss the evacuation of the Spanish towns and the blockade of Mons, in particular whether the allies should be allowed to import foodstuffs into the town. On the 3rd, when Luxemburg had received new orders following the breakdown of talks at Nijmegen, the allies found that he was prepared only to let through supplies which, in their view, were insufficient for the town to subsist on. The threat was, therefore, that famine would force its surrender if the negotiations at Nijmegen were to continue for any length of time. At this, Spain joined the Dutch in refusing to sign the peace treaty. Moreover, Van Beverninck wrote to the Prince on 4 July that D'Avaux, one of the French envoys at Nijmegen, had twice repeated that Louis would not return Mons if it fell into his hands before the signing of the treaty and before its ratification.[51]

On the 5th the Prince sent his adjutant-general, Colonel David Colyer, to Dijkveldt to consult with him, Villa Hermosa and the Count of Nassau, who was commanding the Dutch army in the absence of Waldeck, whose health had suffered as the result of the simultaneous loss of his son and son-in-law, and who was at his country house at Culemborg.[52] On the 6th Dijkveldt reported to William that provisions in Mons were sufficient for only 11 or 12 days, and, although a relief convoy was being prepared, it would not be able to increase the provisions by very much.[53] The pressure to bring relief to the town was therefore very marked and was to weigh heavily in the calculations of the Prince of Orange.

THE ANGLO-DUTCH TREATY AND THE SIGNING OF THE TREATY OF NIJMEGEN

Whilst William was making military preparations, Charles II had again changed direction. He decided that Louis's plan to retain the towns was unacceptable and he sent Temple to The Hague, on 12 July, to negotiate a military alliance with the Dutch and to resume negotiations for the quadruple alliance.[54] Why he did so remains a mystery – Professor Hutton suggests that he was trying to demonstrate 'his power to make trouble' to Louis and thus increase his bargaining position.[55] But in forming his alliance with the Dutch he breached his agreement with the French King of 27 May to remain neutral, and he also forfeited the chance of receiving Louis's subsidy, which was dependent on his withdrawing troops from Flanders, instead of, as he was now doing, sending troops to the English coast for transportation there.[56]

Temple's first move on arriving at The Hague was to meet the Prince of Orange. The Prince made it clear that Charles II's determination was key: only he could either dispose France to make peace or get the Dutch States to continue the war. The peace party had wanted to revert to the old alliance with France; and there would have been nothing he could do to prevent that, but for the refusal of the French to surrender the Spanish towns; this had changed the mood in the country. Nevertheless, if the French restored the towns before the war resumed the Dutch would accept the peace.[57]

A great debate ensued at The Hague and both the Orangist party and the French exerted the utmost pressure.[58] Even Amsterdam was not of one mind, with Hooft overriding Valckenier and supporting Van Leeuwen, who had travelled from England with Temple, and who was now part of the war party; Temple had also managed to persuade Van Thilt from Haarlem to join it.[59] Working with his usual dispatch, Temple managed to get the Anglo-Dutch treaty signed on 25 July; it gave France until 10 August to make peace, without the Swedish provisions, or face war with the Dutch and the English.

But in England Charles was yet again vacillating. Since 12 July Louis had indicated that he was open to suggestions for ways to safeguard Sweden's interests, as an alternative to retaining the Spanish towns.[60] A face-saving device came to hand in the form of the Swedish envoy, Olivekrans, who was in England and who was offered the bait of an English alliance and the marriage of the Duke of York's second daughter, Princess Anne, to the Swedish king. Olivekrans went to Nijmegen, where on 26 July he told the French plenipotentiaries that they should not delay signing the treaty on Sweden's account, provided the Dutch and Spain undertook to desist from aiding Sweden's enemies.

Barillon, the French ambassador in London, was in the meantime in touch with a shadowy figure in his pay, Du Cros, a former French monk, the envoy of the Duke of Holstein who was also employed by Sweden in an ancillary diplomatic capacity in London. It was, Temple was subsequently told, in the apartments of Louise de Kérouaille, Charles's French mistress, that Barillon hatched his scheme. Charles allowed himself to be persuaded that Du Cros was – probably fictitiously – empowered on behalf of Sweden to give the assurance that she was content not to insist on France's retention of the Spanish towns if England could guarantee Dutch and Spanish neutrality.

On 29 July the treaty with the Dutch that Temple had negotiated arrived in London for ratification and Charles saw in Du Cros a means of avoiding the confrontation with Louis which that treaty embodied. To Temple's considerable surprise the former monk appeared in The Hague on 5 August with instructions from the King to go to Nijmegen to inform Olivekrans of the English guarantee and to assist in the peace negotiations. Temple told Du Cros, for whom he made no effort to hide his intense dislike and contempt either in his subsequent memoirs or his contemporary correspondence, that Olivekrans had already preceded him in making these steps towards the peace, but nevertheless he complied with his instructions to wend his way to Nijmegen.[61]

On 4 August Louis instructed his envoys to accept an undertaking that the Dutch and Spain would not come to the aid of Sweden's enemies. Temple arrived at Nijmegen on 8 August, where D'Estrades, hoping for better terms, had not yet revealed these concessions. The next day the Dutch told the French that the English and Dutch armies would commence operations if the treaty were not signed the following day. D'Estrades yielded and in the afternoon of the 10th Van Beverninck wrote to Fagel that the articles of the peace treaty were being written in final form and would be signed that evening. In the event it was signed close to midnight, with, because of the haste, only the French and the Dutch signing, although it was stipulated that it would not be ratified until the agreement of Spain was also obtained.[62]

But the war was not over.

THE BATTLE OF ST-DENIS

Waldeck had returned to the army, arriving at Vilvoorde, near Mechelen, to the north-east of Brussels, on 19 July, and gave orders for reinforcements to be sent from the Dutch garrisons where they could be spared, whilst some troops were also forthcoming from the allies – Osnabrück, Brandenburg and Spain. On the 22nd he estimated the French strength at about 44,000 men compared with an allied strength of about 42,000, although a few regiments had yet to arrive. With these forces Waldeck thought an attempt could be made to supply Mons.[63]

Prince William was engaged in the diplomatic negotiations with Temple which led to the signing of the Anglo-Dutch treaty on 25 July. As soon as it was signed he left the next day with the utmost despatch, leaving Honselaarsdijk at 9am and arriving at Vilvoorde at 10pm. On 2 August the army began its march towards Mons.[64] On the 6th the Prince reported to the States-General from St-Quinten, to the south-west of Brussels, that Mons was coming under more and more pressure and that he intended to arrive in its neighbourhood on the following day; he was expecting to make a conjunction with the Brandenburg troops under General Spaen, who was two marches away, at which point his army would have the same strength as the enemy. The intention was to march as close as possible to the enemy and then take a further decision.[65]

On the 10th Huygens was told that letters had been received in the camp saying that the peace was as good as signed and Colonel Colyer told him it should have been signed on the 9th.[66] These, however, were but rumours and the Prince wrote on the 10th to the States-General that Spaen's troops had joined his army the day before and they were planning to march on the enemy on the 11th, and would then decide whether and how to attack.[67] With 15,000 German troops from Brandenburg, Münster and Brunswick, a contingent of Spanish cavalry and a few English troops, William had an army of some 45,000 men.[68]

On the 11th Van Beverninck wrote to the Prince from Nijmegen to report that he had received a resolution from the States-General dated the 8th instructing him and the Dutch envoys at Nijmegen to conclude the peace treaty and that this had been signed on the night of the 10th – but this letter was never received by Prince William. In the absence of any alternative, as Van Beverninck later attested, it had been entrusted to a Spanish courier who, however, never reached his destination.[69] On the 13th Huygens saw a printed copy of a letter of the 10th which Van Beverninck had written to Fagel saying that the treaty was being drawn up in final form so that it could be signed that evening – it had been printed on the orders of the States-General. Whilst Prince William was aware of this letter, the only firm evidence it brought was the likelihood that the peace would be signed, not that it actually had been.[70]

Thus, peace treaty or no peace treaty, a battle was about to be fought at St-Denis, near Mons.

On 9 August the Prince's army had made its conjunction with the troops of General Spaen and, in four consecutive marches, it had arrived, via Soignies, to take up position near Mons, where, on the 14th, the battle took place.[71]

Returning from making a reconnaissance at about 9am on the 14th, Luxemburg found the son of D'Estrades, who had arrived from Nijmegen and was waiting for him with the peace treaty in his hand. The Marshal held a council of war to discuss whether he should inform the enemy of this news; views were divided; but a letter was drafted, and the trumpeter who was to convey it through the lines mounted his horse and was about to depart when Luxemburg changed his mind and put the treaty in his pocket.

Honours in the battle were more or less even, with a slight advantage to the Dutch, but during the night Luxemburg decided to abandon the field to retire behind the River Haisne, to the south of which Mons lay, joining the besieging army in front of Mons, and leaving behind his dead, his wounded, his tents and his provisions.

Thus ended the battle of St-Denis. Dijkveldt wrote on the 15th, in his capacity as a Dutch field deputy, that he 'guessed' the allies had lost between 3,000 and 4,000 men dead and the same number of wounded. Rousset puts the allied losses at 3,000 to 4,000 and the French losses in dead and wounded at 2,500.

The Prince of Orange displayed his usual courage in leading his troops and exposing himself to the hazards of the battle in all quarters; '*à moi, à moi*' was his cry as he led his troops forward; and, in the evening, he was saved as an enemy captain, advancing upon him, was shot dead from his horse by the Prince's bodyguard, Nassau-Ouwekerk.

There was another relation at the Prince's side during the battle, his uncle Charles II's illegitimate son, the Duke of Monmouth, who arrived a quarter of an hour before the battle began and who may have fought as a volunteer. The English troops in the Spanish Netherlands did not perhaps fight in the battle, although there were English and Scottish regiments in Dutch service who did – recruitment of English and Scottish troops had resumed in the autumn of 1677 and they were placed under the command of Ossory. Dr Keay's biography of Monmouth, however, maintains that both Ossory and Monmouth fought at the head of troops in English service. Both of them certainly distinguished themselves, and that night, as William slept in his coach after the battle, Monmouth slept beside it wrapped up in his cloak. Monmouth later visited a survivor of the battle, Henry Sidney, a colonel who lay sick in Antwerp, and who was soon to develop a close relationship with the Prince of Orange.[72]

VINDICATION OF THE PRINCE

Ever since the battle, a long debate has ensued as to whether the Prince of Orange was justified in engaging in it. He had many indications that the peace was about to be signed at Nijmegen and yet he launched a bloody assault on Luxemburg's position with heavy loss of life – to what purpose?[73]

We need to remember that Mons was deemed to be an exceptionally important fortress, and that the French had indicated that they would keep it if they captured it not only before the peace treaty was signed but before it was ratified. Apart from the importance of the loss of the fortress in itself it could therefore be an important bargaining counter as negotiations continued after the signing and before the ratification of the treaty. The Prince had indications – very clear indications – that the peace was going to be signed, but he had no certainty. Louis had already swerved once when it appeared that all had been agreed when, at the last moment, he had insisted on retaining the Spanish towns until his Swedish allies had been safeguarded; there was no guarantee that something else would not now occur again. We need to remember, too, that the Prince was under pressure of time; his information was that the plight of Mons was very serious and that it could not hold out much longer.

Luxemburg did have definitive knowledge that the peace had been signed, but he did not let the Prince know. It would have been a reasonable assumption on the Prince's part that, if

Luxemburg knew, he would have been told, and that, if neither of them knew, an obstacle to signing had arisen. The evidence the Prince had was that the treaty should have been signed on the 10th and by the time the battle was fought on the 14th four days had elapsed without any news of any sort. That was more than ample time for a messenger to have reached either him or Luxemburg, as, in the case of Luxemburg, was in fact what happened.

The day after the battle, the 15th, as he was deliberating what to do next, William received a very short letter – it was no more than four lines long – which Fagel had sent on the 13th telling him that the peace treaty had been signed. We may, incidentally, note that that had taken only two days to reach him. As he complained to the States-General, they had been wondering in the army for several days why they had not received any news of the progress of the negotiations at Nijmegen; and Fagel's letter did not enlighten them much further. It contained no details of the terms of the treaty, and, in particular, of what had been agreed regarding the cessation of hostilities and the reprovisioning of Mons. He told his secretary that he could not think why the devil he was not being better informed and that he thought everybody in The Hague had gone mad. He didn't have the treaty, nothing: just four lines from the Pensionary. To Fagel he wrote that day that he did not know how the news of the battle would be received in the Republic, 'but I can tell Your Excellency before God that I did not know before this afternoon, through Your Excellency's letter of the 13th, that the peace had been entered into'. And, he ended, as he had no official notification from the State he would continue to do his best to relieve Mons.[74]

But by the morning of the 16th he had thought better of doing this by military means, and Dijkveldt was sent to Luxemburg to discuss the revictualling of Mons. Luxemburg told him that he had news that the peace treaty had been signed before the battle commenced and that he was therefore surprised that the allies had embarked on their attack. Dijkveldt said that they would not have done so if Luxemburg had told them about the peace and asked why he had not done so; to which the reply came that the French had 'a master too jealous of the glory of his arms to have approved turning away from a battle'.

The outcome of this conversation was that Luxemburg would write to Louis to ascertain his orders regarding Mons and in the meantime an armistice was agreed.[75] The following day Louvois authorised the lifting of the blockade and on the 19th the two armies commenced their march, the French to Ath, the allies to Brussels. So it was not until this point that the Prince of Orange was certain that Mons was safe.

The opportunity was taken for the exchange of civilities between the Prince and the Marshal, accompanied by their senior offices. 'The conversation', an eyewitness reported, 'revolved around generalities, on how without use each of them was about to become during the peace and on the need to dedicate themselves to hunting to occupy themselves.'[76]

The question has been asked why the Prince did not send an emissary to Luxemburg before the battle commenced to ascertain if he had news of the peace,[77] and to come to an agreement on an armistice at that time to ascertain Louis's intentions, as now occurred after the battle. We have no evidence that the Prince even considered the possibility. But he needed official information from his own side, not uncertain information from the enemy, and with the armies confronting each other and Mons in a perilous state he would not have wanted to allow any room for prevarication.

Another charge has been levied against him: that, for the perfectly noble reason that he believed the peace to be 'ruinous', he wanted to fight the battle to disrupt it. But the Prince of Orange was much too much the realist for that. He knew the Regents were set on peace come what may and that the battle would not deter them, as, in the event – the peace still needed to be ratified – it didn't.

THE TERMS OF THE TREATY OF NIJMEGEN AND THE END OF THE WAR

Abandoned by the Dutch, the Grand Alliance which had been so painfully constructed ceased to be viable and one by one the allies were forced into signing their own settlements with Louis XIV on disadvantageous terms. They were deeply disappointed, particularly the Elector of Brandenburg who, forced by the invasion of his territories by Louis's troops, and finding that the Dutch were not prepared to meet their treaty commitments to come to his aid, had to return his conquests to Sweden; and the Duke of Lorraine preferred to remain in exile rather than accept the terms demanded of him for the restitution of his duchy – Louis was to retain Nancy and the four strategic roads crossing Lorraine. The Imperialists retained Philippsburg, but Louis gained Freiburg and hence a substitute bridgehead across the Rhine.

Under their treaty the Dutch obtained Maastricht and an advantageous trade agreement with France; and, under a separate clause, the Prince of Orange was restored to his Principality of Orange and to his estates in Franche-Comté, Charolais and Flanders,[78] although there were many details which remained to be resolved.

In 1672 the continuation of the very existence of the Dutch Republic seemed unlikely. Under the leadership of the Prince of Orange she recovered from this, and at one stage it looked as if he could threaten Louis with the invasion of France itself. The failure of cooperation between the allies led to this opportunity being missed, and allowed Louis in his turn to make a recovery. Now, after a bitter seven years' war, the Republic was restored to the position she held before the struggle began, having held her own against the vast might of Louis XIV. The terms Louis obtained fell far short of those which lay at his feet in 1672 and which would have left the Spanish Netherlands his for the taking in their entirety. But it remained nevertheless that he had made very substantial gains at the expense of Spain, including Franche-Comté, and he had destroyed the Grand Coalition which had so painstakingly been constructed against him by the Prince of Orange. The Prince thought the present settlement in the present circumstances was a disgrace and dishonourable, and it would bring no security in the future; and in this he was to be proved right.

1 See Groen van Prinsterer, *Archives, op. cit.*, 2nd series, V, pp.351ff. For James's bellicosity see p.354.

2 *Correspondentie Willem III en Bentinck, op. cit.*, II, 2, p.226.

3 *Ibid.*, II, 2, p.228.

4 Browning, *op. cit.*, I, p.258. Grose, *op. cit.*, pp.362–3.

5 Groen van Prinsterer, *Archives, op. cit.*, 2nd series, V, pp.362–4.

6 G.H. Kurtz, *Willem III en Amsterdam 1683–85*, Utrecht 1928, pp.19–20.

7 Grose, *op. cit.*, pp.356, 357.

8 *Correspondentie Willem III en Bentinck, op. cit.*, II, 2, pp.231–4.

9 Grose, *op. cit.*, pp.365, 366.

10 Grose, *op. cit.*, pp.358–361. Browning, *op. cit.*, I, p.260. Mignet, *op. cit.*, IV, pp.532, 534.

11 Browning, *op. cit.*, I, pp.261, 262. Hutton, *op. cit.*, p.347.

12 *Correspondentie Willem III en Bentinck, op. cit.*, II, 2, p.235.

13 Browning, *op. cit.*, I, p.263.

14 Mignet, *op. cit.*, IV, p.543.

15 Basnage, *op. cit.*, II, p.880.

16 Mignet, *op. cit.*, IV, p.536. Browning, *op. cit.*, II, pp.418–24.

17 Grose, *op. cit.*, p.363.

18 Browning, *op. cit.*, I, p.265. Rousset, *op. cit.*, II, pp.477, 478, 485–9. Nimwegen, *The Dutch Army, op. cit.*, p.507 for the size of the Spanish and Dutch army. See Lynn, *op. cit.*, pp.153, 161, for the size of the French army besieging Ghent.

19 Rousset, *op. cit.*, II, pp.492, 493.

20 *Ibid.*, II, p.497.

21 Huygens, *Journaal, op. cit.*, p.226.

22 Browning, *op. cit.*, II, pp.424, 425.

23 *Ibid.*, II, pp.416, 576, 577.

24 *Ibid.*, II, pp.578–80.

25 *Ibid.*, II, p.428.

26 Fruin, *op. cit.*, IV, pp.402, 403. In January 1677 the Amsterdam Regents arrived at a 'friendly reconciling of all differences among them'. See Israel, *Dutch Republic, op. cit.*, pp.821, 822.

27 Mignet, *op. cit.*, IV, pp.548, 549.

28 *Secrete Resolutien 1653–1790*, The Hague 1791, IV, pp.43ff.

29 *Correspondentie Willem III en Bentinck, op. cit.*, II, 2, p.240, n.2.

30 *Secrete Resolutien, op. cit.*, IV, pp.45ff.

31 Browning, *op. cit.*, II, p.431.

32 *Correspondentie Willem III en Bentinck, op. cit.*, II,2, pp.241–2.

33 Grose, *op. cit.*, pp.366–9.

34 Browning, *op. cit.*, I, pp.272–3 & II, pp.345–9. Grose, *op. cit.*, pp.371–2.

35 Mignet, *op. cit.*, IV, pp.550ff.

36 Grose, *op. cit.*, pp.528–9. Huygens, *Journaal, op. cit.*, pp.250–2, 255–6. Mignet, *op. cit.*, IV, p.562. See also for the Swedish losses in North Germany, article by Pillorget in *Peace of Nijmegen 1676–1678/79*, ed. J.A.H. Bots, Amsterdam 1980, pp.227–8. For William's speech to the States of Holland on 30 April and the subsequent discussion amongst the Holland towns see Basnage, *op. cit.*, II, pp.915–17.

37 Grose, *op. cit.*, p.528.

38 Mignet, *op. cit.*, IV, pp.564–6.

39 *Correspondentie Willem III en Bentinck, op. cit.*, II, 2, pp.247–8. Mignet, *op. cit.*, IV, pp.566–7.

40 Mignet, *op. cit.*, IV, pp.567–8.

41 *Ibid.*, IV, pp. 569–70, 578–81. Grose, *op. cit.*, pp.534–5.

42 Mignet, *op. cit.*, IV, pp.583–7. Grose, *op. cit.*, pp.530–1.

43 Müller, *Waldeck, op. cit.*, II, pp.356–9.

44 Waldeck had written on 8 June from Mechelen and William's letter to Van Beverninck was dated the 9th from Honselaarsdijk so that there would barely have been time for Waldeck's letter to have been received by him. But Van Beverninck's letter is dated the 14th from Nijmegen, so that there would have been ample time for William to have sent instructions to Odijk after receipt of Waldeck's report.

45 *Correspondentie Willem III en Bentinck, op. cit.*, II, 2, pp.248–52.

46 Mignet, *op. cit.*, IV, p.585. Müller, *Waldeck, op. cit.*, II, p.362.

47 Mignet, *op. cit.*, IV, pp.587–8. In a despatch of 14 June to Pomponne, D'Estrades said that Nassau-Odijk, on behalf of the Prince, had invited him to go hunting at Dieren, so that the Prince could explain his conduct to Louis and offer him his services. D'Estrades said he refused on the grounds that it would arouse the suspicions of the friends of France amongst the Regents. But the depiction of an obsequious Prince is perhaps more consonant with D'Estrades's self-promotion than otherwise.

48 *Correspondentie Willem III en Bentinck, op. cit.*, II, 2, pp.253, 255–6, 259.

49 Mignet, *op. cit.*, IV, pp.589–93. In Mignet's version (pp.591–2) Beverninck appears as desiring to create no difficulty over the last-minute French proposal. But see Grose, op. cit., pp.536–7 & footnotes which cites a letter from Beverninck to Fagel in which he accused the peace party and Amsterdam merchants of raising French expectations that their demands would be accepted. See also this article for the States-General reaction and (n.5, p.537) for Charles's attempts to obtain clarification from the French. See also Fruin, *op. cit.*, IV, pp.410–11.

50 *Correspondentie Willem III en Bentinck, op. cit.*, II, 2, pp.254–5.

51 Fruin, *op. cit.*, IV, p.411. *Correspondentie Willem III en Bentinck, op. cit.*, II, 2, p.257.

52 *Correspondentie Willem III en Bentinck, op. cit.*, II, 2, p.257. Müller, *Waldeck, op. cit.*, II, p.363.

53 *Correspondentie Willem III en Bentinck, op. cit.*, II, 2, pp.257–8.

54 Grose, *op. cit.*, p.539 & n.3.

55 Hutton, *op. cit.*, pp.355–6.

56 Mignet, *op. cit.*, IV, p.601. Charles was now refusing to ratify the agreement of 27 May, which was sent for ratification by the French on 12 July, although he had signed it himself as king and thus the question whether it indeed needed English ratification is moot.

57 Temple, *Works, op. cit.*, 1754, IV, pp.367–9.

58 Grose, *op. cit.*, p.541.

59 Temple, *Works, op. cit.*, 1754, IV, p.371, I, pp.362–3.

60 Mignet, *op. cit.*, IV, p.595.

61 Grose, *op. cit.*, pp.545–6. Temple, *Works, op. cit.*, 1754, IV, p.401, I, pp.364–6. Temple was as puzzled as we may be as to why Charles II had thought it necessary to despatch Du Cros to duplicate what Olivekrans was already engaged in conveying at Nijmegen and with greater authority. Olivekrans told Temple that he was acting on the assurances Charles II had given him before he left England (Temple, *Works, op. cit.*, IV, p.409). The most likely explanation was that Charles's motive was to underline his potential usefulness to Louis by indulging Barillon in his intrigue.

62 Grose, *op. cit.*, p.548. Van Beverninck's letter to Fagel of the 10th is reproduced in Fruin and Knoop, *Willem III en de slag van Saint-Denis*, The Hague 1881, p.132.

63 Müller, *Waldeck, op. cit.*, II, pp.366–7, 368 & n.1, & p.369. Following Lynn, *op. cit.*, pp.60–1 I have taken 712 men per battalion and 144 per squadron for the French; and I have also done so – rather crudely – for the Dutch. (French: 42 battalions infantry, 85 squadrons cavalry plus a further 2,000 cavalry. Dutch: 36 battalions infantry, 114 squadrons cavalry.) About five Dutch regiments had not yet arrived by the 24th (p.371). Nimwegen, *op. cit.*, pp.532–3, shows the very large differences in regimental strengths which existed at the muster on 9 July 1677. The tactical unit was the battalion or the squadron of which the regiment could contain one or more in the French army and it seems likely that the Dutch practice followed the French.

64 Huygens, *Journaal, op. cit.*, pp.258, 264.

65 *Correspondentie Willem III en Bentinck, op. cit.*, II, 2, p.267.

66 Huygens, *Journaal, op. cit.*, p.268.

67 *Correspondentie Willem III en Bentinck*, II, 2, p.269.

68 Nimwegen, *op. cit.*, p.510.

69 Fruin, *op. cit.*, IV, p.384.

70 Huygens, *Journaal, op. cit.*, p.270.

71 *Correspondentie Willem III en Bentinck*, II, 2, *op. cit.*, pp.269, 271. Rousset, *op. cit.*, II, p.514.

72 Fruin and Knoop, *Slag van St. Denis, op. cit.*, pp.8ff. Knoop, *Willem III, op. cit.*, II, pp.301ff. Rousset, *op. cit.*, II, pp.512ff. Fruin, *Verspreide Geschriften, op. cit.*, IV, pp.424–5, n.2. *Correspondentie Willem III en Bentinck*, II, 2, pp.270–1. Huygens, *Journaal, op. cit.*, pp.270–3. Anna Keay, *op. cit.*, pp.186–7.

73 There is an extensive debate between Professor Fruin and General Knoop in *Slag van St. Denis, op. cit.*, and Fruin also covers the ground thoroughly in *Verspreide Geschriften, op. cit.*, IV, pp.377ff.

74 *Correspondentie Willem III en Bentinck, op. cit.*, II, 2, p.272. Fruin, *Verspreide Geschriften, op. cit.*, IV, p.427 contains

the Prince's answer to Fagel's letter. Fagel's letter is lost but see Huygens's *Journaal, op. cit.*, pp.274–5. Huygens also mentions that the Marquis de Grana told the Prince on the 15th that he had received notification of the peace.

75 *Correspondentie Willem III en Bentinck, op. cit.*, II, 2, pp.272–3. Rousset, op. cit., II, p.529–31. See also n.2 on pp.531–2 for the report of the French intendant, Robert, that William had no knowledge that the peace had been signed. Huygens, *Journaal, op. cit.*, p.274.

76 Rousset, *op. cit.*, II, p.532.

77 See Japikse, *Willem III, op. cit.*, II, p.104.

78 Mignet, *op. cit.*, IV, p.623–4.

19 1677–1681: MARRIAGE, THE ENGLISH SUCCESSION AND THE POPISH PLOT

The early days of William and Mary's married life unfolded as the military campaign and the tortuous negotiations of 1678 which led up to the treaty of Nijmegen, and which we have narrated in the previous chapter, took place. At the time of the marriage Princess Mary was 15 years old, tall, graceful and a beauty. But the relationship, which was to develop over time into a profound partnership at both the personal and the political level, did not start auspiciously. On 31 October 1677 her chaplain, Dr Lake, recorded in his diary: 'The Duke of York din'd at Whitehall; after dinner return'd to St James's; took Lady Mary into her closet, and told her of the marriage designed between her and the Prince of Orange; whereupon her highness wept all that afternoon and the following day.'[1] A couple of days later James and her uncle, King Charles, formally presented William to her, when the King told his nephew, 'It is not good for a man to be alone: I will give you a helpmeet',[2] the first of a series of jests which were to continue throughout the wedding solemnities, and which amused the King without relieving the despondency of the Princess.

The news of the wedding was received with enthusiasm by the London crowds. The Lord Mayor's show took place on 8 November and the processions, attended by the engaged couple and the royal family, were followed by a banquet which was noted for its sumptuousness.[3] The commonality in the Dutch Republic were also enthusiastic for the match; but many of the Regents less so – they remembered the marriage of William's father to his Stuart mother and the entanglements that entailed, whilst, with their minds set on peace, they saw an English alliance as an obstacle in the way of re-establishing their former alliance with the King of France. Nor were the old fears of the House of Orange's royalist ambitions stilled by this royal union.[4]

Nevertheless, on 6 November the Prince sent a member of his entourage, the Delft Regent, Stangerland, to the Republic to ask the consent of the Regents to the match. No consent was formally required, but he received an annual allowance of 40,000 guilders (£4,000) from the States of Holland, and he would also receive a gratuity of 800,000 guilders (£80,000) upon his marriage, both of which were dependent on their approval. This in the event was forthcoming from both the Holland States and the States-General and Stangerland returned to London with the news the day before the wedding.[5]

This took place on 14 November at 9pm in the Princess's bedchamber at St James's Palace. As if to underline the difference in age between bride and groom, it was Prince William's 27th birthday. Mary's governess, Frances Villiers, was ill with the smallpox; her sister, Princess

Anne, was about to succumb to the same disease – Frances died, though Anne survived – and the Duchess of York was in the last stages of pregnancy. The Bishop of London, Henry Compton, officiated whilst the King gave Mary away – and resumed his jests.

He urged Compton to make haste lest the Duchess of York should be delivered of a son and so the marriage would be disappointed. When the Prince followed the usual formula and promised to endow Mary with all his worldly goods the King told Mary 'to put all up in her pocket, for 'twas clear gains'. The bedding took place at 11pm and when the time arrived for the assembly to retire it prompted the King to draw the bed-curtains himself with a final sally of 'Now nephew to your works. Hey! St George for England', before he made his exit.[6]

The business side of the marriage was concluded the same day with the signing of the marriage contract, which very much followed the precedent set by that of William's mother when she married his father, William II. On William's side it was negotiated by Nassau-Odijk and Bentinck. Like William's mother, Mary was to receive a dowry of £40,000, and she was also to receive £2,000 a year as pocket-money; two residences, one in The Hague and one in the country, were to be provided for her; she would be allowed to practise the Anglican religion; and any children from the marriage would require the consent of the King of England to marry, and he would also appoint her entourage. The following day Bentinck arrived with a magnificent gift of jewels for the Princess; valued at £40,000, they were equivalent to the dowry Mary was to receive under the marriage contract.[7]

Three days after the wedding the Duchess of York, Mary of Modena, was delivered of a son, who was christened the next day with the King and the Prince of Orange standing as godfathers; he was to live for only a month. After the christening the departure of William and Mary was delayed by the birthday of the Queen on 25 November, where Mary appeared at the court ball richly attired in the jewels her husband had given her ten days before. He, however, may well have been preoccupied by the threatening scene on the Continent and Louis XIV's menacing manipulations, for he was paying her scant attention. With the wind in the wrong direction they still could not depart and 'the court began to whisper the Prince's sullenness, or clownishness'.[8] But views differed – on the 20th one courtier had remarked that 'the Prince is a very fond husband, but she a very coy bride, at least before folks'.[9]

They did finally leave London on the 29th, embarking with the King and the Duke of York on barges at Whitehall. When the Queen, Catherine of Braganza, tried to console the still tearful Mary by reminding her that she too had had to come to a strange country, and had not, until that moment, seen the King, Mary's cheerless reply was, 'But, madam, you came into England; but I am going out of England.' The royal party dined at Erith and the King and the Duke accompanied them until they were in sight of Gravesend, then returned to London.[10] But William and Mary had not proceeded far when contrary winds again disrupted their journey and they were not able to leave Margate until 8 December.

Nor were their afflictions over. Travelling in separate ships during a very rough crossing, they aimed to land at Rotterdam, but thick ice prevented this and they had to transfer to sloops to land near a small fishing village on the 9th, where the Prince himself carried his wife up the beach. Still their travails persisted; they had to walk over three miles before coaches summoned from The Hague brought them to Honselaarsdijk. There, at long last, they found the fires alight, the candles lit and a hot repast awaiting them.[11]

The journey had not been a happy introduction to married life, but a splendid reception was prepared for them in The Hague, where on 14 December they arrived in a gilded coach drawn by six horses. They paused at the entrance to the town, where the militia fired off their muskets, where there was a 31-gun salute, and where young girls in white sprinkled herbs and greeted them with song. As they moved further into the town through decorative arches the streets were lined with ebullient crowds and festooned with garlands. At night The Hague was lit by fireworks and lighted tubs of pitch so that the whole town appeared ablaze. And amidst it all the bearing and the beauty of the new Princess of Orange were remarked upon.[12]

But the mind of the Prince of Orange himself remained concentrated on business. 'Here we are arrived at the Hague', he wrote to his friend Ossory on that same day, 'with general acclamation from the whole world. I can little participate in this joy, having yesterday received the news of the taking of St-Ghislain.'[13] If Mary's personal appeal was already beginning to act as a counterfoil to her introspective husband, she was now to learn that his devotion to the task in hand was undeviating and it was not the least of her qualities that, in due course, she learnt to respect him for it.

But the negotiations which came to an end with the signing of the treaty of Nijmegen on 10 August 1678 had barely been completed when a vicious dispute about the succession to the English throne was about to be set in motion. It was to be stilled for a while, but when it arose again it culminated in the crowning of William and Mary as King and Queen of England at the beginning of 1689.

THE INCEPTION OF THE POPISH PLOT

Early on the morning of 23 August, Christopher Kirkby, an amateur dabbler in chemistry, who as such was known to his fellow dabbler Charles II, accosted the King in Whitehall as he was about to embark on his morning walk in St James's Park, and handed him a letter. Asked to explain, Kirkby told the King that there was a plot against his life. Returning from his walk, Charles further questioned Kirkby, who said that a Benedictine and a Jesuit lay brother were planning to shoot him and, should this not succeed, Catherine of Braganza's physician, Sir George Wakeman, would poison him.

That evening Kirkby met the King again and produced his friend Israel Tonge, as the source of his information, which in turn was based on the inventions of Titus Oates, whose background was as motley as that of Tonge and even less respectable; but whereas Tonge was a clergyman afflicted with psychological difficulties, Oates was an adventurer with a good memory and a plausible manner of delivery. At one stage he had converted to Catholicism and attended Catholic religious establishments at Valladolid in Spain and St-Omer in France, from the latter of which he had been expelled, and he had developed both a knowledge and a hatred of the Jesuits. At some stage, too, he must have abandoned his Catholicism. Although sceptical, Charles handed the matter over to Danby to investigate further.[14]

Danby at first thought the matter could be used to rally support for the King and to provide a reason for keeping the army in being. But he was hampered in his investigations by the informers' slowness in providing evidence,[15] and it was not until the afternoon of 8 October that Oates appeared before the Privy Council. The King had attended the morning session when Tonge appeared and did not impress, so that he clearly thought there was nothing to detain him from going to Newmarket. But in his absence Oates gave such a very assured performance that the Council decided to recall the King. The next day Charles caught Oates out when he was unable to give a true description of Don Juan, whom he said he had met in Spain and whom Charles had himself met during his exile, and he was also caught out on the geography of Paris. Nevertheless, the Council took several measures including warrants for the arrests of Catholic priests named by Oates and they also ordered the seizure of the papers of Edward Coleman, a Catholic who had been the secretary of the Duke of York and then of the Duchess, and who in the 1670s had corresponded with, amongst others of a suspicious nature, Père La Chaise, Louis XIV's confessor. These letters – later ones, it was assumed, had been destroyed – turned out to be treasonable. The letters also showed that the Duke of York had endeavoured to obtain the dissolution of Parliament in return for Louis XIV's gold, and that he aspired to the reconversion of the kingdom to the Church of Rome.[16] John Miller indeed attests that both the letters and Coleman's statements make clear that the letters were authorised by James and that when James told the House of Lords that he knew nothing of the correspondence he was lying.[17]

Then, on 27 October, whilst the tidings of a Catholic plot were rapidly spreading, the body of a prominent Justice of the Peace, Sir Edmund Berry Godfrey, before whom Titus Oates had twice sworn parts of his evidence, was found dead in a ditch on Primrose Hill; he had been strangled and run through by his own sword. The immediate inference was that he had been silenced by the Jesuits. Panic, pandemonium and hysteria now took hold and what has become known to history as the Popish Plot was launched on its destructive course.[18]

We may note, in passing, that William of Orange was keeping a close eye on these developments in his uncle's kingdom; on 11 October he had written to Henry Coventry asking to be kept informed about what was happening.[19]

The virulent passions excited by the plot had several components. There was the long tradition of anti-Catholicism and its association with absolute monarchy; there were the suspicions of Charles II's foreign policy and his relations with Louis XIV – which were not unfounded; there was James's open avowal of his Catholicism and the fear that he would endeavour to reintroduce his faith – to which Coleman's letters lent substance; there was the dread of Charles's army – it was still in existence; and there was terror at the prospect of a Popish insurrection accompanied by murder and every form of atrocity – of which Godfrey's murder appeared to be the harbinger.[20]

THE INITIATIVE PASSES TO PARLIAMENT

The initiative now passed from Danby and the Privy Council to Parliament, which met on 31 October. The House of Commons began its own investigations, and on 3 November ordered the arrest of five Catholic peers; and in the Lords, Shaftesbury, whose fierce opposition to James dated from the time when James refused to take the Anglican communion in April 1673, now emerged as a major figure in that House, which also began investigations. It soon became apparent that in Shaftesbury the plot had found the political leader who was now set on the destruction of the heir apparent to the throne.[21]

In the House of Lords, on 12 November, when James and the King were also there, Shaftesbury urged the removal of James from the Privy Council and from the King's presence. It was a move supported by Halifax and even by five bishops – the court could normally rely on the contingent of bishops in the Lords – including Bishop Compton, who had so recently married William and Mary. It was an opening gambit and Shaftesbury did not press it to a vote.[22] Nevertheless, on the 13th Charles did ask James to withdraw from the Council.

And on the 19th he made a further attempt to contain the agitation when he appeared before both Houses and told them: 'I am come to assure you, that whatsoever reasonable Bills you shall present … to make you safe in the reign of any successor (so as they tend not to impeach the rights of succession, nor the descent of the Crown in the true line, and so as they restrain not my power, nor the just rights of any Protestant succession) shall find from me a ready concurrence.'[23] This at once defined the dilemma facing those who were attacking James. Either they would have to find a way of limiting his powers if he became king, in which case it would be difficult to construct guarantees to ensure that the limitations could never be rescinded; or they would need to go to the further extreme of excluding him from the throne entirely, in which case they would need to choose a replacement. The most obvious candidates were Monmouth or Mary, the wife of the Prince of Orange, who was of course inescapably linked to her – but in this case the question of legitimacy would become even more pressing, especially in the case of Monmouth, who was born out of wedlock. Having taken the stance he now did at this very early stage, Charles was never to deviate from it during the whole crisis that now enveloped the nation, a remarkable instance of consistency in one who had, and has, a reputation for the opposite; and a testament to the political insight of which Charles was capable when he set his mind to it.

In the meantime a new Test Bill was passing through Parliament which would exclude Catholics from sitting in either House. In the House of Lords James asked that he be exempt from its provisions, indicating vague, but possibly dire, consequences if he was refused, which can be interpreted as a confused hint of civil war. The Lords supported him and Danby rallied enough support in the Commons to push through James's exemption from these provisions, but only by two votes.[24]

At the beginning of November, Oates, emboldened by his successes, accused the Queen of encompassing the assassination of the King, a story which, even in those feverish times, carried no credence,[25] although Shaftesbury had for long been an advocate of a royal divorce so that Charles could marry again and beget Protestant heirs. But the danger to the King was grave, for both Catherine's secretary, Richard Bellings, and one of the five Catholic peers imprisoned by the House of Commons in the Tower, Lord Arundell of Wardour, had been signatories of the secret Treaty of Dover.[26] In the case of Catherine's secretary it may have been a reason why Charles refused to follow the path to divorce.

William of Orange, in The Hague, continued to watch over events with anxiety: 'I await with great impatience', he wrote on 11 November to Henry Coventry, one of Charles II's two Secretaries of State, 'what will happen in Parliament.... There is still scarcely any appearance of a general peace, the French are retreating every day from their initial offers', and he feared the effect the internal disorders in England were having on England's ability to put restraining pressure on France.[27] The Peace of Nijmegen had not put an end to Louis's designs on the Continent – we will be examining these in detail in due course; but we need to be aware that the Exclusion Crisis in England and Louis's moves on the Continent were inseparably linked in the mind of the Prince, for whom England – now as always – was central to any strategy to contain the French King. The personal interest that he and Mary had in the fate of the Stuart dynasty was becoming more and more a critical component of this, whilst, as events unfolded, with James at their centre, they brought in their train acute moral dilemmas.

THE FALL OF DANBY AND EXILE OF JAMES

Danger was now encroaching on Charles II still more closely. The British ambassador in Paris, Ralph Montagu, had been dismissed from his post towards the end of July after the – inevitably somewhat complicated – consequences arising from his conducting of an affair with both Charles's former mistress, the Countess of Castlemaine, and her daughter.[28] Unfortunately Danby, despite his fundamentally anti-French stance, had been reluctantly persuaded by Charles to enter into negotiations with Louis for a French subsidy whilst at the same time asking Parliament for money to fight France – and his correspondence with Montagu relating to this was in Montagu's possession. Because of his anti-French policy the French wanted the removal of Danby – and the disbandment of Charles's army – and they united with members of the Parliamentary opposition who wanted the same thing, albeit for different reasons. In October Montagu reached agreement with Barillon, the French ambassador in London, to reveal the letters in exchange for French money.

Danby was aware of the intrigue and he and Charles decided on a pre-emptive strike. They had information on compromising meetings which Montagu had held with the Papal Nuncio in Paris, and they ordered the seizure of his papers – if Montagu had not succeeded in becoming a Member of Parliament they could also have ordered his arrest and thus removed him from the scene. The House of Commons, which was sitting, and where Montagu was present, was told; and Montagu then made his own counter-move. The box containing the fateful correspondence with the French had evaded the King's officers as it was not in Montagu's house when they made their search, and it was now produced in the House of Commons. Montagu selected the letter of 25 March 1678 (Old Style) in which Danby had outlined, on behalf of the King, Charles's proposals of peace to Louis, combined with the demand of a payment of 6 million *livres* a year for three years. The outraged House of Commons proceeded at once to the impeachment of the minister on Saturday 31 December; and the formal impeachment was delivered to the House of Lords on Monday 2 January 1679.[29] The evidence, it seemed clear, was that Danby had merely used the pretext of a war against France to raise a standing army, whilst, at the same time, the King of England would become a client of the King of France.

The letters Montagu had in his possession provided no evidence that Danby's correspondence with him had been authorised by the King – indeed, one of the charges brought against him in the impeachment was that he had acted against the King's wishes. But in the very short interval between the Commons voting for the impeachment and its delivery to the House of Lords, that is, on Sunday 1 January, Danby persuaded Charles to write at the bottom of his draft of the letter of 25 March 1678 the words 'I approve of this letter, C.R.'[30] Charles may well have decided to provide Danby with this defence in view of Danby's ability to reveal much more than this if Charles fell out with his minister; and he also did all he could to avoid Danby's impeachment with all the revelations that it could bring in its trail.

Although the articles of the impeachment were carried in the Commons by comfortable majorities – between 50 and 24 – the court retained its control of the House of Lords, which refused even to commit Danby to custody. To provide himself with breathing space, Charles decided to prorogue Parliament until 14 February 1679, and promised to disband the army.[31] Danby was satisfied with the way the impeachment was going, and he was opposed to the prorogation, which he felt made the case against him look worse; but it was his own position that concerned Charles and he determined to dissolve Parliament on 3 January 1679, one advantage of which was that it would for the moment halt the impeachment,[32] whilst there were also legal arguments for maintaining that the dissolution would terminate the impeachment entirely. There was no question of Charles's doing without a Parliament; he needed one to vote permanent money for disbanding the army and, until it was disbanded, no money could be expected from Louis XIV.[33]

Observing events from The Hague, Prince William did not forget his old ally, Danby. 'I am too much one of your friends', he wrote to him on 13 January, 'not to have learnt with extreme chagrin of the malevolent measures your enemies are attempting to inflict upon you in Parliament. I hope you will emerge from this to your profit, and I would be extremely delighted to be of assistance to you on this score, and on all other occasions where it is in my power to do so. Of all the accusations levied against you that of being in the interest of France is the least true', which indeed was the case; and in thus showing his support for Danby in his hour of need the Prince wrought well for the future. He hoped, nonetheless, as he told Ossory in the middle of February, that Danby would not seek refuge in The Hague, which would draw the Prince personally too far into English politics.[34]

The new Parliament, which met on 16 March, was a triumph for Shaftesbury. The 'little Earl' – he was diminutive in size – had his own, somewhat idiosyncratic, way of calculating his support in the new House of Commons under four headings: 153 members on the list were 'old' – that is from the old Parliament – and 'worthy'; 149 were 'new and honest'; 98 were 'old and vile'; 60 were 'new and bad'; and 36 new members were doubtful. This produced 302 opposition members against 158 supporters of the court, which, whilst not wholly accurate, was near enough the mark. Nearly half the house consisted of members who had not sat in the previous Parliament.[35] Prince William could not but be disturbed by the disorders in the kingdom of his uncle, to whom he still looked, as he had always done and always would do, as an essential component in curbing the power of Louis XIV. 'God grant', he wrote to Ossory, 'that [the disorders] should soon cease, otherwise France will in little time be master of the whole of Europe.'[36]

Even before Parliament met, Charles decided that he needed to bend to the wind; on 17 February he dismissed the unpopular Sir Joseph Williamson as one of the two Secretaries of State and replaced him with Robert Spencer, the Earl of Sunderland, whose aunt was married to Shaftesbury and whose sister was married to Halifax, and who, for good measure, was on good terms with the King's mistress, Louise de Kérouaille, Duchess of Portsmouth,[37] with her French connections – thus a nod to Louis XIV.

But he took an even more important step. He had failed to persuade James to return to the Church of England, through the intermediary of Sancroft, the Archbishop of Canterbury, and the Bishop of Winchester, whilst James had in his turn failed to persuade him to use the army to govern by force – its disbandment was already under way, the expedient having been resorted to, in the absence of permanent Parliamentary grants, of financing this by short-term measures including loans, which, of course, did not eliminate Charles's ultimate need for a Parliament. On 10 March, in return for signing a declaration denying that he had ever married Monmouth's mother, the King asked his brother to go into exile; and with this order James complied, setting sail for Holland on the 13th.

He arrived in The Hague on the 18th with the Duchess, and there, as he wished to travel incognito, he was welcomed in a low-key manner by the Prince of Orange before departing for Brussels on the 24th. 'I confess', William told Ossory, 'that his arrival has not caused me a little surprise. God knows what the consequences will be, as much for him as for the King.' At the end of April James and the Duchess paid another short visit to The Hague, so that contact with his daughter and his son-in-law was maintained.[38]

On 20 March Danby resigned; and in addition to the full pardon that Charles had already granted him on the 10th there was added a pension of £5,000 a year and a Marquisate. But these terms so scandalised even the House of Lords that it decided that, despite the dissolution of the old Parliament, Danby's impeachment remained in force; and the Commons demanded that he be taken into custody.[39]

Charles was driven to address both Houses on 1 April and he demonstrated the extent to which he was prepared to go to protect his servant. He told them Danby was innocent; he had commanded Danby to write the letters to Montagu; and he said that he had granted Danby a full pardon, adding defiantly that he would do so again, if necessary ten times over.[40]

It did no good. The Commons questioned the pardon and it looked as if the Lords would cease their resistance to Danby's confinement, upon which the King ordered him to go into hiding, followed the next day with the order to leave the kingdom;[41] then he would be out of the way of revealing any embarrassing secrets. With the first, but not the second, Danby at first complied, fearing that once out of the country he, like Clarendon before him, would never return.

Parliament then passed a bill ordering him to surrender himself, in the absence of which he would be attainted. Submitting to the threat and preferring to take his chances for the future over exile, Danby surrendered, with Charles's consent, to Black Rod on 25 April, and was committed to the Tower.[42] The first phase of the Popish Plot had deprived Charles II of his leading minister and had resulted in the exile of the heir to the throne.

SHAFTESBURY, EXCLUSION, THE TRIUMVIRATE

Sir William Temple had been recalled from his embassy in The Hague because Charles had wanted to appoint him as the second Secretary of State, but, in the current turbulent times, he had cautiously declined. Nevertheless he remained at the centre of affairs and he now suggested to the King a reformed Privy Council, in which he was to be supported by others such as Sunderland and the Duchess of Portsmouth, and which, Temple argued, would, through its composition, either appease Parliament or, if that failed, would lend the King greater authority if he prorogued or dissolved it. To this end he suggested that the Privy Council should be reduced to 30 members instead of 46, of which half should be office holders and the other half members of standing from both Houses of Parliament who represented every shade of opinion – the majority in the new Council, indeed, was to consist of persons who had recently opposed the court. One of these whom Temple persuaded the King to accept was Halifax, much against the King's initial reluctance, based on the leading role Halifax had played with the opposition in the House of Lords alongside Shaftesbury. To Temple's extreme chagrin the King then proposed to include Shaftesbury as well, on the grounds that he would be better in than out, and he became the Council's Lord President.[43]

Charles did not intend the new Privy Council to play too prominent a role: 'Odds fish!' he exclaimed – a favourite expression – 'they have put a set of men about me, but they shall know nothing.'[44]

Nor did Shaftesbury relent in his hostility to the Duke of York. On 9 May Charles and the Lord Chancellor spelled out to the two Houses of Parliament what he meant by his readiness to accept laws to safeguard Protestantism under his successor – with the same proviso as previously, 'so as the same extend not to alter the descent of the Crown in the right line, nor to defeat the succession'. The proposals were deliberately muddled, designed to enmesh Parliament so much in discussion of the details that it might end up not agreeing on anything at all. A Popish successor would be unable to make any ecclesiastical appointments, and he would need the consent of Parliament to change the membership of the Privy Council, the Lords Lieutenant or officers in the navy; but not officers in the army, Secretaries of State, the admiralty or the household. Shaftesbury had opposed these proposals when the Privy Council had discussed them, because he thought, according to Temple, 'that there could be no security against the Duke, if once in possession of the crown'; and in doing so he moved away from Halifax, who was a proponent of imposing limitations on the successor, whilst Shaftesbury was moving towards the total exclusion of James.[45]

James was in despair, writing to William on 14 May that the monarchy, 'as well as his Majesty's person', were in great danger, the threat in his eyes coming from the 'Commonwealth party', by which he meant Shaftesbury and Monmouth, and he told the Prince, 'I could wish you in England'.[46]

Shaftesbury's plans, and his intrigues, bore fruit; on 21 May the House of Commons voted for exclusion; and ten days later the Bill for exclusion passed its second reading by 207 votes to 128. Three leading magnates in the Privy Council, Sunderland, Halifax and Essex, who had 'more land than the King' and who became known as the Triumvirate, together with William Temple, were becoming perturbed at the extent of Shaftesbury's influence and his closeness to Monmouth, which they feared, according to Temple's account, would leave these two 'absolutely at the head of all affairs'. They decided to advise the King to prorogue Parliament. The trials of the five Catholic peers and of Danby led to disputes between the two Houses of Parliament over procedural matters and this gave Charles a pretext to prorogue them from 6 June to 24 August. The driving force was, of course, that the Exclusion Bill and the revelations that might come out of the trials were in themselves reasons enough for the King to take this course; he pursued it without discussing it first in Council as the Triumvirate and Temple wanted,[47] thus demonstrating how little weight he attached to this body.

Shaftesbury was outraged and exclaimed in the House of Lords that he would have the heads of the King's advisers, thus opening the breach between himself and Halifax.

DISCUSSIONS ON INVOLVING THE PRINCE OF ORANGE

A movement in favour of the Prince of Orange, with the Triumvirate at its head, was now developing. They were joined by Temple, with his long-standing pro-Dutch stance and close relationship with the Prince. On 10 June the good-looking and winsome Henry Sidney – something of a philanderer, who had had an earlier dalliance with Anne Hyde, the first wife of the Duke of York – was told by the King of his intention to send him as ambassador to the Dutch Republic. He was *persona grata* with the Prince – in February 1678, as we have seen, he had been the colonel of a regiment sent to Flanders, and their friendship dated from that time. He was Sunderland's uncle, although they were almost exact contemporaries, and much of their youth was spent together; he was also the uncle of Halifax's wife, and Sidney, Sunderland and Halifax had travelled jointly on the Continent in the company of Sidney Godolphin, another rising figure, and Henry Compton.

On the day of his appointment, according to Sidney's diary, 'Lord Sunderland, Halifax and I walked together, and talked much to the advantage of the Prince'. Six days later he and Sunderland agreed that it would be a good thing if the Prince should come to England in October – he thought the King would be for it – and take his place in the Privy Council and the House of Lords. By the beginning of July Halifax, too, thought the Prince should come to England and by the end of the month Essex expressed the same opinion. When Sunderland spoke to Sidney Godolphin he also was extremely supportive of the Prince's coming over. With the supple and subtle realism central to his character, and despite his apprehension of Shaftesbury's power, Sunderland told Sidney to advise the Prince that 'the Lord Shaftesbury is not of our party, but that he is a good tool to work with, and that there is nothing to be done in Parliament without him'.[48] Nor was the Duke of York averse to William's coming to England – in May he had expressed the view that this would be a source of strength for the monarchy.[49]

Thus Henry Sidney, at the very start of his embassy, was performing a dual role: on behalf of the King his mission was to negotiate a Dutch treaty to guarantee the peace of Nijmegen; on behalf of the Triumvirate he was to inveigle the Prince of Orange to play a role in English politics as a Protestant counterweight to the pretensions of the Duke of Monmouth and the artifices of the Earl of Shaftesbury.

Monmouth's cause was now helped by the outbreak of a Covenanters' rebellion in

Scotland; he was given command of the forces sent to suppress it, which he did with some ease, defeating the rebels at the battle of Bothwell Bridge on 2 July; and he returned in triumph to London, the popular hero. The Prince of Orange had offered to send over the six English and Scottish regiments in the Dutch service under Ossory, for which Charles II offered his thanks.[50]

CHARLES II'S PREDICAMENT

In the meantime the respite the King had bought with the proroguing of Parliament was coming to an end and the time was approaching for it to reconvene at the end of August. As Temple put it, 'The Duke of Monmouth was greater than ever: Lord Shaftesbury reckoned upon being so too, upon the next meeting of Parliament, and at the cost of those whom he took to be the authors of the last prorogation.' In the light of this the Triumvirate and Temple met and decided that the best course would be to dissolve Parliament and try the temper of a new one to be called in October. And with this the King agreed.[51]

There was some good news for the King. The various informers who had emerged in the course of the Popish Plot had succeeded in bringing to grisly execution, through hanging, drawing and quartering, Coleman and several Jesuit priests – in the latter case despite Charles's misgivings about their guilt – as well as others. But the trial now took place of the Queen's physician, Sir George Wakeham, and on 28 July he was acquitted. Titus Oates's plausibility was shaken and he and his fellow informers had lost an important part of their impetus;[52] but, as we shall shortly see, this was not to be the case with the political forces they had been instrumental in bringing into being, and which had acquired a life of their own.

With retrenchments on the one hand – including the disbandment of the troops, the laying off of ships, and savings in the household and in pensions – and with the expansion of trade on the other, the King's finances began to improve so that the Treasury commissioners were able to tell him that he had sufficient finance for the time being. But when he planned to raise a new company of guards, Essex, who had been closely involved in the retrenchments and who had detailed knowledge of the finances, expressed concern at the end of July about the adverse effect this would have on opinion and on the need 'of a supply to relieve your Majesty's pressing concerns', mentioning the reluctance of people to lend to the King.[53] During July and August Charles again turned to Louis XIV to see whether he could obtain subsidies from France, but, from Louis's point of view, there was no need to subsidise his cousin since his lack of military power and his position in England rendered him incapable of intervening on the Continent, either for or against him.[54]

And the same consideration operated in the minds of the Dutch with whom Charles, characteristically, was engaged in his simultaneous negotiations for a treaty to guarantee the Peace of Nijmegen[55] – his motives being the usual ones of raising his price against Louis whilst also demonstrating to English opinion that he was determinedly anti-French.[56]

When Sidney met the Prince of Orange on 10 August William assured him that the Dutch were 'better disposed towards England than you imagine'; the difference was that England only wanted a treaty to guarantee the Nijmegen Peace whilst 'we are willing to enter with you and Spain into the firmest and strongest league that can be proposed to us for the preservation of Europe, which it is evident to everybody is in great danger'. His objection to the guarantee was that it would bind the Dutch also to 'defend France if it were attacked by the Emperor or any body else'. He added that Amsterdam had swung round to an anti-French mood, although Van Beuningen soon enough informed Sidney that nobody would dare propose an English alliance for fear of France, and Van Beuningen himself 'could not advise it in the condition' England was now in.[57]

THE DUTCH AND FRANCE

The Dutch were also being offered an alliance by the French: they proposed an advantageous commercial treaty; and they also undertook to provide undertakings that the Spanish Netherlands would never fall into their hands – in the event of war with Spain they would refrain from operating there and they would not accept the territory either as an exchange or voluntary gift.[58] A faction in Amsterdam very much favoured such an alliance because of the commercial advantages, but overall Amsterdam's position was not yet fixed; her hard-headed view, as reported by Sidney to Halifax on 15 August, was that she would prefer a treaty with France rather than risking losing another devastating war, unless Dutch defence could be assured with the assistance of Spain and of England. Despite their initial objections to the guarantee treaty, the Prince and Van Beuningen tried to persuade Amsterdam of its merits; but their efforts were to prove unsuccessful when, in October, Amsterdam resolved that she was prepared to pursue this course only if the Dutch also entered into a defensive alliance with France. The Prince of Orange did all he could to resist any French treaty,[59] but to persuade Amsterdam – where, at the end of August, Sidney observed to Sunderland that Valckenier was all-powerful[60] – and her sympathisers to desist, the Prince needed to be able to demonstrate that she could rely on English strength; and thus he observed the course of the Popish Plot with continued anxiety. He told Ossory in the second half of August that English affairs were 'moving in a manner so strange that without a miracle I do not know how they can be redressed and what chagrins me the most is to see myself so impotent that I can contribute nothing on one side or the other.'[61]

RENEWED EFFORTS TO INVOLVE THE PRINCE IN ENGLISH AFFAIRS

Then, on 1 September, Charles II fell ill at Windsor with a high fever and there was every indication that his life was in peril. The Triumvirate were thrown into alarm that Shaftesbury and Monmouth would seize power with the backing of the army, which Monmouth commanded, small though it was. According to Temple they persuaded the

King to send for James, and on the 3rd Sunderland informed James of the illness; but it seems to have been James's close friend, Feversham, who persuaded him to return from exile. In somewhat melodramatic fashion, having made his journey in disguise in a black wig, he appeared in Charles's bedchamber at 7am on the 12th, where he fell on his knees, with both brothers in tears.[62] 'God grant', Prince William told Ossory, 'that his voyage falls out to his satisfaction', and he told Henry Sidney that, if he were the Duke, he would have acted in the same manner.[63]

With the King's health in so parlous a state the courtiers flocked to pay court to James, the heir apparent; a contemporary observer, Mountstephens – possibly Sunderland's secretary – noted from Windsor, 'It's believed for three days last passed [there] has been more kneeling within these walls than in the four months before.'[64] Charles's indisposition, however, was of short duration, the last sign of his 'ague' being around 6 September; and Mountstephens was soon informing Sidney that the King had changed his diet from 'water gruels and potions for mutton and partridges, on which he feeds frequently and heartily'.[65]

The Triumvirate also looked for salvation to the other side of the North Sea. Sidney met the Prince of Orange in The Hague on 15 or 16 September (his diary is not clear on which date) after dinner at the house of Nassau-Odijk and tried to persuade him too to come to England. The Prince, however, could see no advantage in it. He did agree that the Duke of York would never inherit the crown and that, if the succession was not settled in one way or the other, the outcome would be a republic. The next day after dinner at Honselaarsdijk Sidney resumed his attempt to persuade the reluctant Prince. 'I told him the Monarchy was absolutely lost, unless he recovered it,' Sidney records. William repeated his belief that James would never possess the crown and then apparently made a somewhat dramatic revelation: Sidney found he 'would be very willing to be put into a way of having it himself'. On the point of coming to England, he was sufficiently persuaded to ask Sidney to write to Sunderland to ask him for his view on what would be the best time for him to make the journey.[66]

On the point of his wanting the crown we need to pause. The Prince had a sound motive in confiding his thoughts to the English ambassador. Sidney was closely linked to three of the most important politicians in England, the Triumvirate, and was speaking on their behalf. Although he was now recovering, Charles's encounter with death emphasised in acute form all the dangerous scenarios which could emerge if he died; neither Monmouth, nor James, nor a republic, nor a civil war would provide the stable Britain with which William sought to contain Louis XIV. That left the possibility of William himself making an appropriate intervention, as the Triumvirate were pressing him to do, and, although ambivalent, he was clearly tempted by this course. But did he go as far as revealing to Sidney that he had ambitions for the throne itself? No less an authority than the eminent Dutch historian Dr Nicolaas Japikse maintained that it was 'fantasy' on Sidney's part.[67]

It is the contention of this book that a consistent thread running throughout William's career was that he did not exclude the acquisition of sovereignty if, in the case of the Dutch Republic and England, it had the backing of the relevant political nation, if it were in accordance with his *gloire*, and if it were politically feasible. But therein lay the rub – Dutch political circumstances at this time would not for a moment have permitted an attempt on the English throne, for which he would need an army at his back, and in the British Isles it would have meant risking civil war. 'Fantasy', thus, it certainly was on Sidney's part or, perhaps, a misinterpretation of the Prince's words or body-language.[68] But, if the crown was not feasible now, it might be in the future.

In England the King's brush with death had changed the political situation and the divisions there became even more acute. It had brought to mind the dire spectre of possible civil war, to avoid which many rallied around James, whilst, on the other hand, the fears of the Exclusionists were accentuated by James's closer approach to the throne.

Amidst these rising tensions we need to have regard to Charles II's loyalty to the Stuart clan and family, which some historians have tended to underestimate, attributing to him more cynical motives. Yet behaviour can be the subject of more than one motive and a deep vein of clan and family consciousness marks Charles's conduct throughout his reign, tempered, and frequently overridden, by political realities. There was his affection for his sister Minette, useful though she also was as a diplomatic intermediary; there was his admiration for his cousin Louis and his hankering to use him, the head of the much more powerful Bourbon clan, as a patron and protector for that of the Stuarts; and there was certainly a family feeling for William of Orange despite his exasperation at his nephew's taking his independent line against, in Charles's view, himself as the head of the clan. This clan feeling became particularly pronounced during the Popish Plot and it cannot be ignored as a factor in assessing Charles's conduct or in the conflicting loyalties of which it formed a part. A particular difficulty that he faced was that James's own very pronounced loyalty to clan and family was nevertheless overruled by his religion, which he steadfastly refused to recant.

There was a further conflict of loyalties within the clan, which was instanced by the contest between James, the King's brother, the legitimate heir to both the throne and the headship of the clan, and Monmouth, his illegitimate son, of whom the King was very fond. Faced with this dilemma Charles engaged in a balancing act, in which, however, he leant firmly towards his brother's side; he decided to exile both Monmouth – to the Low Countries – and James – but this time to Edinburgh to take over the government of Scotland; and he relieved Monmouth of his command of the army.[69] Monmouth was informed by the King on 20 September and left for Holland on 4 October, whilst James left for Brussels on the following day to bring back his wife. He was back in London on 22 October, having spent three days in The Hague, before departing for Edinburgh on 6 November.[70]

In view of these developments the Prince reverted to his view that the time was unpropitious to intervene in English affairs. On 28 September he told Sidney at Bentinck's estate at Sorgvliet that the situation at the English court had changed and it was now less necessary for him to go to England; before the Duke of Monmouth was sent into exile James wanted his presence in the country; but with his exile it would look as if the Prince 'intended to set up for himself'.

The next day he elaborated on this; with Parliament sitting he was sure it would attack the Duke of York, and if he were in England the Duke would lay the blame on him; alternatively, if the King found Parliament recalcitrant and dissolved it the whole country would lay the blame on him. But, keeping his options open and avoiding a direct rebuff to his 'friends', he was prepared to come, even in the depths of winter, if they saw 'a good occasion for it'. He was content for the moment to be recognised as third in line to the throne. In the meantime he advised the King at all costs to come to an accommodation with Parliament – an early recognition of the Prince's important insight that an English sovereign could be a formidable force on the Continent with Parliament's support, and a negligible one without it. It was not an insight that his uncles shared; on the contrary they took Louis's view – and he was regarded as the model of the age by many other contemporaries – that representative institutions were a cause of hindrance, not of strength.

On James, he elaborated his views; he was in favour of laws excluding all Catholic kings, without specifically mentioning James, from the succession and were he a member of the House of Lords he believed he would cast his vote that way.[71]

The contending members of the Stuart clan, James and Monmouth, did not meet when they were both in The Hague. Monmouth arrived first, on 6 October. He 'was mightily well received' the next day by William, being offered the Prince's town house, being invited to go hunting, and was dissuaded from going on to Hamburg, and he wrote to his father telling him of this good reception. He had shown William a letter from Charles in which the King had explained that his own expulsion was necessitated by that of the Duke of York. The following day he showed Sidney the letter 'which', Sidney observed, 'was very kind'. On his part William told Monmouth politely, but firmly, 'that if he thought of the Crown, he could not be his friend in that, but in everything else he would'. Later William explained the warm reception he had extended to him on the grounds that 'he used him no better than he thought he ought to do one that the King writ such kind letters to'. On hearing, on 9 October, that the Duke of York was coming to The Hague, Monmouth departed to Utrecht, near which, at Rhenen, Prince Rupert had a house.[72]

When the Duke of York arrived on 16 October with his Duchess he immediately took the Prince aside and conversed with him for about an hour, with which, according to Sidney, 'the Prince was not much satisfied'. The two Stuart brothers, James had made clear, thought they could live without Parliament. The next day an express arrived from the King granting James leave to go to Scotland and when he and his wife departed on the 19th, William and

Mary accompanied them as far as Maaslandsluys. From Prince William's point of view it was an unsatisfactory visit – the King 'bids adieu to all Parliaments'.[73]

The departure of his uncle and rival for Scotland, and its government, emphasised for Monmouth the difference in their treatment, with his own isolation and exile on the Continent. Soon he was denigrating the King and frequenting the company of exiled opponents of his father's regime. Nevertheless he continued to be entertained by the Prince, who took him hunting at Dieren, 25 miles from Rhenen, where Prince Rupert's house had been lent to him. This entertainment did not go unnoticed in London and when Sidney was later in England in December he and Temple 'talked of the Prince and the Duke of Monmouth being of a party', Temple saying 'how strong they would be'.[74] In November Monmouth decided to defy his father and his exile and returned to London, whereupon Charles deprived him of all his remaining offices and forbade him the court. In England, however, he remained. 'At least', the Prince wrote to Ossory, who we must remember was a very close friend indeed, 'people will now, I hope, be dissuaded that we have been intriguing together, since he left the country unknown to me, having told me he was going to Cologne'.[75] We may note that he laid no great store on Monmouth's veracity or reliability, and it would not have been wise, as Sidney and Temple seemed at this stage to have thought, to form an alliance with this charming but very lightweight figure. Nevertheless, he might have his uses and to these we shall come later in this narrative.

On 24 October Charles dismissed Shaftesbury from the Privy Council and the next day he prorogued the new Parliament, which was to have met on 9 November, until 5 February 1680 – and from December there was a series of further prorogations to November 1680. There was indeed an attempt at reconciliation between the King and the Earl, which, however, came to nothing. Upon its failure Shaftesbury told his friends that 'he would never more enter the lists at Whitehall till it was resolved there should be excluded from thence the Queen, Duke, Duchess of Portsmouth, and every other Papist that were but an inch long'.[76]

If it is ever maintained that the passions kindled by Luther and Calvin at the beginning of the Reformation in the first half of the 16th century were stilled by the advent of the Age of Reason in the second half of the 17th, Shaftesbury and his following bear witness to the contrary. And Charles would have to contend for another 18 months before he was able to tame the fierce 'little Earl'.

Viewing events in England, the Prince of Orange seems to have cast his hands up to heaven: 'One has to submit to God's will', he wrote to wrote to Waldeck on 29 October; 'perhaps it is just as well at present that we have not concluded the Guarantee Treaty.'[77]

BREAK-UP OF THE TRIUMVIRATE
He was right not to base his intervention in English politics too much on the Triumvirate, which, in November, disintegrated. Sidney was given permission by the King to return to

England for a short leave when he was able to witness this disintegration at first hand. Before his departure he met Prince William on 1 November, who told him of his concern at the prorogation of Parliament: 'We are all undone'. It was not to be expected, he indicated, that the Regents 'would take any measures till they saw us better settled. All we can hope is to hinder them from making an Alliance with France.' Furthermore, he added, he thought England herself intended 'to fall in with France'.[78]

Immediately on his arrival in England on the 8th Sidney was received by the King whom he found unhappy that William could not be persuaded to his view on the need to prorogue Parliament. Sunderland told Sidney that the conduct of Monmouth and Shaftesbury could 'not be endured'; if the King had died Monmouth would have seized the crown for himself or established a republic – it was this fear of course that had brought the Triumvirate into being. But Sunderland also told Sidney that Essex and Halifax were discontented at the prorogation. Temple, too, was discontented and talked of retiring. He was unpopular with the King and the Duke of York, both of whom saw him as the instigator of the Prince of Orange's views and both of whom thought Temple was preventing the Prince from falling in with Charles's policy; and James moreover suspected that the Prince 'intends to set up for himself'. On the 25th Sidney found Halifax disaffected by the activities of the French ambassador, by the influence of the Duchess of Portsmouth, and by the ascendancy of the Duke of York.[79]

We need to remember that Halifax and Essex were as much opponents of the Duke of York as they were of the Earl of Shaftesbury and of Monmouth, the point of difference up to now having been that the first two were in favour of limiting James's powers if he were to ascend the throne whilst the latter two wanted to exclude him entirely. Now their anxieties became more centred on the dangers of arbitrary government, Charles's reliance on France, and the threat from Catholicism. Sunderland, whilst fearing the combination of Shaftesbury and Monmouth, had nevertheless – and characteristically – kept his lines of communication open with both Shaftesbury and James.[80] Charles's prorogation of Parliament without consulting the Privy Council and his decision to exile James to Scotland, where he was both in command of that country and not too far distant, together with indications of their own declining influence at court, were developments which both Halifax and Essex were not prepared to accept. On 26 November Essex resigned as First Lord of the Treasury and drew closer to Shaftesbury, whilst Halifax suffered a deterioration in his health – perhaps even coming some way close to a nervous crisis. Temple, too, the architect, in his own eyes, of the reformed Privy Council, which he saw now was little regarded by the King, withdrew to cultivate his garden at Sheen. Halifax told him that 'though he could not plant melons as [Temple] did, being in the North, yet he would plant carrots [sic] and cucumbers, rather than trouble himself any more about public affairs; and accordingly he went down to Rufford', his estate in Northamptonshire.[81]

SUNDERLAND'S FOREIGN POLICY

Replacing the Triumvirate were, first, Laurence Hyde, Clarendon's second son, the brother of James's first wife and, as such, a client of James; he became the first commissioner in the Treasury, replacing Essex – with Essex's departure the Treasury ceased to be headed by one man and was put into commission; Sidney Godolphin, who joined the Treasury board as well, also rose to foremost influence, whilst Sunderland remained as one of the two Secretaries of State – with what was becoming recognised as his distinguishing wiliness he had swung back to the side of the Duke of York, whose star for the moment appeared to be in the ascendant. 'These three', says Temple, 'were esteemed to be alone in the secret and management of the King's affairs, and looked upon as the ministry.' They were known alternatively as 'the Chits', a reflection on their youth and inexperience, or as 'the Second Triumvirate'.[82]

In the new ministry the leading role in foreign affairs continued to be taken by Sunderland, a role which, as one of the two Secretaries of State, he had already performed under the first Triumvirate; he had, according to his biographer, certainly actively participated since August in the negotiations with France which he and Charles were conducting in parallel with the negotiations with the Dutch.[83] The Dutch had rejected Charles's proposals for a treaty guaranteeing the Treaty of Nijmegen and when Sidney returned to The Hague and met the Prince of Orange on 2 December his instructions left him with no counter-proposals to make.[84] The gap this left was filled by the French and on the 7th D'Avaux, the new French ambassador in The Hague, presented Louis's formal request for an alliance which, two days later, was presented to the States-General. D'Avaux had introduced himself on 1 October,[85] by which time he was already engaged in intrigues with the Amsterdam Regents and others to further the French alliance and oppose the treaty of guarante.[86] On the 13th Sunderland and Charles were much perturbed by Sidney's report that the Prince of Orange would be unable to prevent the Dutch negotiating this alliance.[87] Charles's whole negotiating position *vis-à-vis* Louis was dependent on the threat of his forming an alliance with the Dutch to check Louis's ambitions in Flanders, or, if the alliance could be extended to other European powers, his ambitions on the Continent as a whole; if the Dutch now entered into an agreement with France he would have no negotiating position left at all.

He had to act, and on 30 December 1679 (Old Style – hence 9 January 1680 New Style), Sunderland, on his instructions, wrote to Prince William telling him that 'there is nothing [the King] should more unwillingly see than an alliance between France and the States', and Sidney was being given instructions 'to use all means possible to prevent it'. Charles recognised, Sunderland wrote, that the prorogation of Parliament was being misunderstood on the Continent and that this was frightening people into submitting to France; but his reasons, Sunderland tried to explain, were in fact to allow time for the mood to change in England so that the next Parliamentary session would be more amenable. He would have over 40 ships ready in the summer, for which he did not need the aid of Parliament, and he undertook to summon it as soon as he could hope for a good session. When Parliament did meet he had no doubt it would provide him with the means 'to defend himself and his friends'; and if Louis did attack the Dutch it would be of such general European concern that all the other powers would turn against him.[88]

Although Temple wrote to William on 12 January 1680 that the prorogation of Parliament was inconsistent with endeavours to hinder a Franco-Dutch alliance, four days later, in a further letter, he seems to have been at least half persuaded by the King's logic: that if Louis engaged in war that would draw in the rest of Europe and that 'it would bee the best way to rally us all at home, which are both points your Highness will beleeve not ill grounded'. It certainly carried sufficient weight with the States of Holland to deter them from the French alliance; William had written to Waldeck on 11 January that the majority were inclined not to enter into any new engagements either with France or with England. And he added that he himself believed it was the best course to pursue at the present juncture.[89]

The King's finances continued to improve, and at the end of March James, who had been allowed to return from his Scottish exile at the beginning of the month,[90] told William, 'I hope things will mend every day, and that we shall make a better figur every where, now that his Ma. is able to subsist upon his owne revenu, without the help of a Parliament.'[91] Not all agreed, however, that he could; as we have seen, Essex did not, although Hyde, and another treasury commissioner, Sir Stephen Fox, did – provided there was no foreign war.[92] The difference in opinion created a doubt, a doubt which explains Charles's perception of his continued need for Parliament or, alternatively, to look to Louis for subsidies. Perhaps, too, he was persuaded of the need to be as conciliatory as possible and that the permanent dissolution of Parliament would be an act too provocative at this stage, which might incur the danger of civil war.

In the meantime Sunderland embarked on an ambitious plan for a grand system of anti-French alliances that would include Denmark and Brandenburg, Spain and Leopold of Austria, and the Dutch. To this both Charles II and the Duke of York lent their support, and Temple persuaded the King to add Sweden to the list with a view to recreating the Triple Alliance of old. We are missing Prince William's letters in which he expressed his views, but he was closely consulted by Temple, the King and Sunderland and from Temple's and Sunderland's correspondence we can clearly deduce his support,[93] although of course we are lacking his nuances. The aim of these negotiations was to present Parliament with a grand anti-French coalition as an earnest of the King's anti-French and anti-Popish intentions – the negotiations abroad were accompanied by fierce measures against the Catholics at home. But with the prevailing state of affairs in England Charles II was hardly an attractive ally for the continental powers and by the middle of 1680 Sunderland could achieve only an alliance with a weak and exhausted Spain, signed on 18 June.[94] The treaty contained an undertaking for Charles to send troops to the Spanish Low Countries if Spain were attacked; as he was in no position to do this and as the Spanish were unable to defend themselves it was a sham, and regarded as such.[95] In France Louis contemplated publishing the secret clauses of the Treaty of Dover, which would have done for Charles. However, he ultimately found that bribery was a more efficacious method of obtaining the King's defection to his side.[96] We may observe that the alternatives to having Charles II as his client in England were hardly attractive.

THE PRINCE IS PERSUADED TO COME TO ENGLAND

Sunderland needed a new plan to preserve his position, and to this end he arranged a meeting with Halifax on 25 June at Althorp, his country estate in Northamptonshire. Sidney was home on leave and on the 24th he and Sunderland left Windsor, scooping up Hyde and Godolphin on the way, to go to Althorp. The meeting went on for a week; all there agreed that Parliament should meet no later than November, with the Spanish and Dutch ambassadors getting to work on the members in the meantime; the King should ask for money only if it was needed for his foreign alliances; he would furnish safeguards against Catholicism, provided, however, that there was no change in the succession; and it was agreed that William of Orange should come to England – Sunderland's calculation, a little later expressed to Sidney, was that he would have more followers as the Protestant champion than would Monmouth, 'who intends to play that game'.[97]

At this point Shaftesbury delivered a deliberately public insult with an impudence that few others would have dared to match. He arrived in court at Westminster Hall on 6 July, and there, before the grand jury of Middlesex, he accused the King's brother, the Duke of York, of being a recusant and the King's mistress, Louise de Kérouaille, of being a prostitute. The King was able, through Lord Chief Justice Scroggs, to discharge the jury, whose sympathies against the court at Whitehall were well known, and by that means prevent the indictment of his brother and his mistress; but the damage was done.[98]

The brazenness of the insult severely impaired Charles's prestige – in 17th-century terms, his *gloire* – as much abroad as at home. In these circumstances not only Sunderland but Charles himself looked to the Prince of Orange to assist them with his reputation as the champion of Protestantism. Sidney was about to return to Holland, and on the night before his departure he was urged by Sunderland to use his 'uttermost endeavours with the Prince to come over' without whom 'nothing could be done'. Moreover if William did come Sunderland would answer for it that the Prince would have more credit with the King than anybody else.

Sidney arrived for dinner at Honselaarsdijk on 14 July, after which he had a long conversation with Prince William. But William presented an array of arguments against the idea of the English visit; he could not imagine what good it could do; he had 'no acquaintance nor no party' in England; he was concerned about his own reputation – his own *gloire*, therefore – in the Dutch Republic where he would 'be absolutely undone' if no agreement could be reached between the King and his Parliament; and if the mood was running against the Duke of York 'it would be impossible for him to stop it'. Nevertheless he did say that 'If the Duke was gone, he believed he could do something.' However, he was about to go to Germany to see the Brunswick dukes and the Elector of Brandenburg and he could not decide on anything until his return in September.

On 23 July Sunderland informed Sidney that 'the King is absolutely of the same mind we are about the journey hither' – so for the first time Charles had been made aware that the journey was being discussed, and he was in agreement with it. On the 31st letters were sent by Sunderland to Sidney explaining his stratagem for persuading the Prince of the rightness of pursuing this course; on 3 August Sidney showed the Prince what was intended for his eyes in this correspondence; and, after considering for a day, William gave his reply. It is not preserved but we know its nature from Sunderland's acknowledgement that 'The King is very satisfied with the Prince's answer.' William, in other words, was at long last persuaded that he should go to England.

The arguments that Sunderland had presented were, in essence, that two points needed to be addressed at the next session of Parliament. The first was to persuade it to support the alliances the King had made and that he was in earnest; the second was 'to settle Religion without meddling with the Succession'. On both these points the Prince could contribute 'extremely to the creating such an understanding between the King and his Parliament as may keep us from ruin'. What Sunderland was looking for was for the Prince to perform the role of 'Mediatour between the King and his People'. If he succeeded in this he would enhance his reputation; if he failed at least he would have shown that he had tried. No doubt, too, William had in mind the need to protect the rights of Mary and himself against the pretensions of Monmouth.

But before effect could be given to these plans William had departed for Germany and did not return until, as it turned out, 10 November, by which time events had intervened.[99]

THE PRINCE AND EXCLUSION

Sunderland's plans hinged on presenting to Parliament a strong alliance against Louis XIV; but, as autumn approached, and as it became apparent that this would not be forthcoming, he began to be persuaded that Parliament could only be satisfied by the exclusion of the Duke of York, and that he would need to bend with the prevailing wind. Henry Sidney, who of course was very much in his camp and who at this time was once more in London, wrote to Prince William on 17 October that the Duke 'hath of late so exasperated the people that they can scarce heare his name with patience; the King hath begone to perceive it these three months, and every day [is] more and more perswaded, that it is impossible to agree with his Parliament and stick to his brother'. The King in the event did stick with his brother but the important fact is that Sidney and Sunderland did not think he would.

When Parliament met on 31 October it was clear that it was indeed set on the course Sunderland had anticipated, and on 4 November William Russelll in the House of Commons proposed the motion for James's exclusion.[100] Meeting Henry Sidney and other friends in his chamber in Whitehall on the night of the 7th, Sunderland and they decided once more to turn to the Prince of Orange to rescue the situation; and three days later Sidney was asked to go back to Holland without delay to make the necessary representations.[101] Sunderland wrote to William saying that the state of affairs was 'such as requires greate help, and I know nobody can give any but you yourselfe, either to those at home or abroad'. Godolphin, part of the same group of friends, also wrote that they were 'of one mind, that nothing in the world can contribute soe much to a perfect entire settlement of the whole kingdome and establishment of the Kings authority as your Highnesses coming over … and … I am of opinion it is absolutely necessary to the supporting of your owne particular interests here' – that is, Mary's rights to the throne. The Dutch ambassador also reported suggestions of the Prince acting as a protector of the Protestant religion during James's reign, 'or some other expedient of this nature'.[102]

But when Sidney arrived at The Hague on 13 November, he found the Prince of Orange adamant, with a position that was at once complex, subtle and firmly realistic. He thought it very likely, he told Sidney, that if he did not go to England it would prejudice his position there, which in turn would redound on his position in the Dutch Republic; but he also thought 'excluding the Duke an injustice, and he would not advise the King to do it for all the world'. As we have seen, earlier in the year William thought that James was unlikely to attain the throne, and he had asserted before his departure for Germany that 'if the Duke was gone, he believed that he could do something'. He had also indicated that he believed that if he were a member of the House of Lords he would have voted for the exclusion of a Catholic successor, without specifically naming James.[103] This would have left James with the option of recanting his faith, and thus, the Prince may have thought, his exclusion would be a matter that lay in his own hands, and, in those circumstances, 'he could do something'.

He and James had been in frequent correspondence throughout the year, exchanging both family and political news – only James's letters survive – and by the autumn they became tinged with a poignant note. James had become increasingly conscious throughout September of the attack threatening him and he started to prepare for the worst, impeachment. By the middle of October he was convinced that the real target of his enemies was 'to destroy the monarky and all our family'. With the tension mounting and Parliament due to meet, Charles decided that if the exclusion of his brother was to stand any chance of being defeated the renewal of James's exile in Scotland was essential. 'Those whom I expected to be most my friends are no more so now', James wrote with dismay on 22 October, '…'tis Lord Sunderland and Mr Godolphin who presse it.' But, as always, he complied with the head of the clan: 'His Majesty must be obeyd,' he wrote on the 29th, 'I am afraide he will sone repent the measurs he now taks, for I see nothing but ruine to himself and monarky.' And the next day, the day before Parliament met, the King saw his brother off on his way to Kirkcaldy.[104]

William was in a great dilemma over the course he should take in the exclusion crisis, and he did constantly change his mind on, for example, coming over to England. In now deciding not to support the bald exclusion of James specifically, rather than Catholics generally, he seems to have been persuaded that the removal of his uncle in this manner would very considerably weaken the monarchy and the crown that his wife might inherit, and might even, as James suggested, result in the ultimate destruction of the monarchy and of the Stuart clan. It was one thing to have a general provision barring Catholics from the throne, with which any individual could comply; it was another to establish the precedent by which Parliament could specifically bar anyone it wished. It is worth noting that his decision not to support the exclusion of the Duke of York was at variance with the views of Gaspar Fagel, who, the Prince told Sidney on 14 November, 'would willingly have him quit the Duke, and hath writ his opinion to' Van Leeuwen, the Dutch ambassador in London.[105]

As the exclusion Bill moved through the House of Commons the issue was raised as to who would succeed to the crown if the Duke of York were excluded. The Bill as it stood did not specify, as the Exclusion Bill of 1679 had, that the succession should pass to James's *children* (my italics) as though he were dead. Spelling this out would benefit his daughter Mary; leaving the matter vague would benefit Monmouth. A compromise was found with the wording that the succession should 'descend to such *person* [my italics] … as should inherit the same in case the Duke were dead'. This left the succession to Mary now, but it also left open the possibility that a succeeding bill could nominate Monmouth later. In this form the Bill moved to the House of Lords.[106]

There, on 25 November, the debate continued late into the night amidst the glimmering light of the candles and of the fire, in front of which the tall form of the King stood. He had attended the debate throughout its duration, the greater part of seven hours, absenting himself only for short periods to eat his dinner and his supper. He put on an impressive histrionic performance, his body-language indicating his approval or disapproval of the speeches as they were delivered. And it was clear that he would not countenance the exclusion of his brother from the throne.

One other person contributed to the outcome: in a rhetorical feat, in which he delivered 15 or 16 speeches, Halifax – still adhering to the principle of limitations against exclusion – displayed a virtuosity that greatly impressed contemporaries, answering 'Shaftesbury and Essex as oft as they spoke'. Although the surviving records are too incomplete for us to form a clear judgement of their content – he appears to have set store by a practical scheme of limitations and by pointing to the danger of civil war, whilst casting adverse reflections on Monmouth – contemporaries appeared clear that he had got the better of Shaftesbury.

The outcome was not in doubt. By 63 votes to 30 the House of Lords rejected the Bill. One of those who voted for it was Sunderland.[107] He was motivated, according to his biographer, by the fear of impeachment; but he wrote to Prince William on 6 December, when limitations were being widely discussed, that he thought they would be considered either ineffectual or would endanger the monarchy, so that it is possible that he himself may well have been genuinely persuaded that exclusion was the only practical means of monarchical preservation. For the King it was 'the kiss of Judas'; but he did not, for the time being, dismiss him. Sunderland's position was well known as the proponent of the Prince of Orange's providing some sort of solution to the exclusion crisis in opposition to Shaftesbury's championing of the Duke of Monmouth; Kenyon has argued that both solutions were unwelcome to the King, but, of the two, he preferred William's, and it was not long before he indicated that he would accept the regency of William and Mary. So, despite the royal anger, Sunderland retained his place.[108]

One other significant event occurred – or, rather, did not occur; the traditional pope-burning procession in London, which was held two days after the Lords rejected the Exclusion Bill, passed without incident.[109] The violence of the London mob, which had played so notable a part in 1641 before the outbreak of the Civil War, was thus absent.

In the meantime the House of Lords prepared a bill severely limiting the powers of a Papist successor to the throne, including the suspension of the royal veto, and the appointment of all officials by Parliament or its nominees, measures that were in accordance with Halifax's principles, although his exact involvement remains unknown. These were naturally anathema to James, who thought limitations 'to be yett more prejudiciall to the monarky and our family than even that of exclusion'.[110] And from William's point of view he was right. He clearly expressed his concerns in a letter of 10 December, for on the 17th Sir Lionel Jenkins replied that the King wished him to be assured that his aim was to preserve the rights of the crown as far as possible and that the monarchy should remain hereditary and not elective.[111] William's overriding aim was to bring the power of England to bear on the Continent. Excluding Papists generally, if it was the only way to bring unity to the Kingdom, was one thing; but if the powers of the monarchy were once curtailed under a Papist it might not be too easy to restore them under a Protestant, and that was another thing altogether. To be left with a hollow monarchy was not what the Prince wanted.

THE PRINCE INTERCEDES: THE INSINUATION

On 2 December news reached The Hague that the House of Lords had rejected the Exclusion Bill, which put the Lords and the King in opposition to the House of Commons and which thus constituted a check on William's hopes of seeing the longed-for unity in his uncle's domains necessary to contain Louis XIV. On that day he wrote to Sir Lionel, the other Secretary of State besides Sunderland, thanking him for keeping him informed of events in England, 'but I am vexed to learn with what animosity they proceed against the Duke God bless him! And grant that the King and his Parliament may agree, without which I foresee infallibly an imminent danger for the King, the royal family, and the greatest part of Europe.'[112] The news caused great consternation in the Dutch Republic, which had been looking for English support against Louis, and both the shares of the Dutch East India Company and bonds fell in the markets.[113]

Gaspar Fagel – in favour of the exclusion of the Duke of York – and William – in favour of the exclusion of all Catholics without naming the Duke of York – now appeared to reach a compromise. When the States-General met to discuss the news Fagel persuaded it on the 4th to authorise the *Secrète Besogne* (the foreign affairs committee) to meet Sidney and 'to ask him to use his good offices … to ensure that Parliament was not prorogued or dissolved and that the differences which might exist between Parliament and the King were resolved in a friendly manner'. In this way Fagel ensured that the matter was removed from the cumbersome body of the States-General into the smaller forum of the *Secrète Besogne*, consisting of only eight members, of which he was one, thus enabling the situation to be carefully controlled by himself – and by the Prince.[114] But he and Prince William, working closely together, did not let matters rest there and they took a further step to convey the message which they wanted to pass to Charles II.

On the evening of the 4th the Prince advised Sidney to pretend to be unwell so that he would not be able to meet the whole of the *Secrète Besogne* but only Fagel and one other member, who turned out to be De Mauregnault, a close associate of the Prince; and he also advised Sidney to ask for a written memorandum of what these two conveyed to him.[115] This enabled Fagel to phrase the memorandum in terms exactly as he wished. The memorandum in fact – known from its heading as the 'Insinuation'[116] – was revealed neither to the other members of the *Secrète Besogne* nor to the States-General, despite emanating in the latter's name. It may not have been drafted by the Prince but there is no doubt that it carried his stamp[117] and that he used it as a means of persuading his uncle to come to terms with his Parliament; but at the same time it avoided his direct involvement, and enabled him, if need be, to distance himself from it.

Sidney met Fagel and De Mauregnault on the 5th and he received the Insinuation the next day.[118]

The Insinuation – it was written in French – began by indicating that the States-General were extremely uneasy that relations between the King and his Parliament were not conducive to the unity which they so ardently hoped for and which the exigencies of Christendom required. They neither wished, nor were able, to involve themselves in judging the cause of the difficulty, and even less the means that might serve to re-establish the unity so necessary and so desirable. They were entirely persuaded that the King would take no other measures than those which he thought the most useful for the direction of his affairs and the most appropriate for the good of his subjects.

But the danger in which they found themselves obliged them to speak. His Majesty was fully aware of the adversities which they were compelled to endure consequent to the peace (of Nijmegen) and the pressure they came under from France to enter into an alliance with them; His Majesty had not been agreeable to such an alliance and it would not have been in the interests of their two countries. He had assured them of his protection and that he would hazard all to deliver them from the ills which menaced them. Furthermore, he promised them that he would summon Parliament at such time as his affairs would permit, and to this assurance they deferred.

But the increasing disagreement between the King and his people plunged them into despair because the point of contention was of such importance, so great, so delicate and so domestic in its nature that they dared not involve themselves in discussing it. Since the peace the French had seized a greater number of villages than they were entitled to and the quarrel between His Majesty and his people was furnishing them with ample occasion to execute their designs. They could not but apprehend that they might be so unfortunate that a matter so uncertain as that of a future succession, where time might bring with it considerable alterations, could cause their entire ruin, and that the interest of Europe, of all the Protestant princes and principally of the Dutch State, could be sacrificed for something that was so uncertain. The King would be aware that laws passed by Parliament pertaining to the succession had previously in history not been put into operation. The King 'could perhaps extinguish this whole fire with a single stroke of the pen' – *un seul écrit* in the original French – which, however disagreeable and unpleasant, could afterwards be readjusted when all sorts of propositions could be listened to and found acceptable in a calmer atmosphere. Nothing would be so unfortunate as for His Majesty to sacrifice his Kingdom, his royal person and the unity of his people for something that perhaps would never come to pass.[119]

What exact terms the *écrit* should contain is not spelled out, but one reading could be that Fagel was hinting that, in order to re-establish unity with his Parliament, Charles II should bend to the exclusion of his brother now, in the belief that matters could be readjusted later – exclusion without exclusion.[120] It provided a compromise between William and Fagel and it could assuage William's conscience as regards the Duke of York. It might also – just – enable the rightful line of succession to be re-established in due course and thus prevent too great a weakening of the monarchy and the Stuart dynasty. There were obvious risks in all this, but William and Fagel may have thought them unavoidable, given the precarious state of affairs in Charles's kingdom. Charles himself, with a much closer knowledge of English affairs, did not see why he should take the risks, and he was to be proved right.

On the 5th or 6th Sidney sent copies of the Insinuation to Sir Lionel Jenkins and to Sunderland in French and an English version was published in England.[121]

On the 10th William wrote to Sir Lionel telling him that he had 'always wished a good intelligence between the King and his Parliament; and that I wished to have been able to contribute to it'. He also expressed his concern at the limitations being discussed on the powers of any Papist successor to the throne. 'I hope that his Majesty will not incline to suffer a thing to be done so prejudicial to all the royal family … it must not be imagined that, if they had once taken away from the Crown such considerable prerogatives as are talked of, they would ever return again.'

That same day Sir William Temple wrote to the Prince advising him that he could pursue one of three courses of action: he could come to England and support the exclusion of the Duke of York; he could continue to do nothing; or he could do what in fact the Insinuation came remarkably close to doing. If a new Parliament were summoned he should come to England and manifest his concern 'for some union' between the King and Parliament; he should declare that the 'interests of Christendom are lost without it' and that without English support the Dutch would turn towards France; that he could not propose the means of reconciling the King and Parliament, 'being a stranger to our affairs', and that neither he nor the States could meddle in the matter of the Duke of York, which was a domestic matter, but that both of them would exert their endeavours to 'procuring a happy union between the King and his Parliament, and of preserving the Protestant religion, both here and in the rest of Christendome, since in all other parts it must have its support from hence'. This third course of action seemed in Temple's view to be the only one left and, as we have seen from the Insinuation, it was so very much in line with the thoughts of the Prince himself that one wonders if it was totally coincidental – much of William's correspondence at this time, which we know from his correspondents' replies took place, and which appears to have been extensive, is missing and Temple's own letter was in response to something he wrote.[122]

On the 17th Sir Lionel wrote on behalf of the King in reply to William's letter of the 10th. Nobody was more chagrined than the King to see that the 'heats rays'd among his people' rendered both him and them 'not regarded (as otherwise they would be) abroad'. He had always been ready to pass any law and to do anything to satisfy his people 'in matters of religion and of their civil rights' and he had never refused any Bill 'tending to the security of our religion'. He assured the Prince, however, that he would take care that the rights of the crown would be preserved, 'as much as is possible, entire', and that the monarchy would not be changed from hereditary to elective, 'for so His Majesty conceives it may in processe of time come to passe, if the next in bloud and the right heir of the crown be once disabled and excluded by act of Parliament'.[123]

Van Leeuwen, the Dutch ambassador in London, who was also acting on behalf of the Prince, too had an interview with Charles, who gave him similar assurances. Nobody more than he himself, the King said, had a greater concern for the prerogatives of the crown, of which the rights of succession formed an essential part. If he had wanted to rescind these he would have given the succession to one of his sons, but he knew only too well that this was not at his disposal.

This interview was followed by one Van Leeuwen had with Halifax, who told him that he was a long-time *serviteur* of the Prince, whom he regarded as the only Prince on which the Protestant party could build, and for whom he therefore had a particular veneration. He knew perfectly well that the Duke of York could not reign in England and would never do so – he would be the first to oppose him. But the Prince needed to have a care of those who wanted to pass the act of exclusion now so that it would be established beyond dispute that Parliament had the power of exclusion which in two or three years' time could be exercised in favour of the Duke of Monmouth. His solution of limitations was directed solely at the Duke of York and should concern neither the Prince nor any other member of the royal family. To Van Leeuwen's suggestion that exclusion should apply only to Papists, Halifax responded that this came to the same as specific exclusion of the Duke; it would demonstrate that Parliament was able to dispose of the succession; and it could be turned against the Prince by excluding him on the pretext that he was a foreigner or some other similar reason.

Van Leeuwen then talked to Sunderland and Godolphin, who, Van Leeuwen said, 'sont dans le sentiment de Votre Altesse' and were much in favour of the act of exclusion – evidence thus that William was in favour of exclusion, however qualified in his own mind. But Godolphin indicated that he was beginning to be uneasy about the Duke of Monmouth, whose support was growing in the House of Commons. However, at this point in time the largest part of the House of Commons was reasonable, but it was very much to be hoped that they would be able to see the Prince and to get to know him, and that he came to England. He could be given the title of the Duke of Gloucester and in this capacity show himself to Parliament, that is, in the House of Lords.[124]

On the same day Sir Lionel Jenkins wrote to Sidney to say that the Insinuation had been ill-received in London by the Committee of Intelligence and by the King, as trespassing on domestic affairs. Jenkins was commanded to issue a reprimand to Sidney for allowing it to have been sent and to inform him that no reply would be forthcoming from the English government. Sunderland, too, wrote to him at the same time, saying that he was being accused of being its author.[125]

William clearly wrote to the Duke of York – his letter is lost – exculpating himself from the Insinuation, for James wrote to him in reply on 4 January 1681 assuring him, 'I easily beleve you had no hand in it' and accusing Sunderland and Sidney of being the instigators.[126]

At this time William was mistakenly informed by a letter from Van Leeuwen that Charles II was prepared to pass the Exclusion Bill. He at once indicated that, based on this information, he was, if the King was prepared to make a public declaration to this effect, ready to go to England the 'next day, if my Lord Sunderland thought it would do any good'. His own view was that he might be of service to the King in these circumstances – it seems he had in mind with himself acting as mediator; but Van Leeuwen's information proved to be mistaken, and Sunderland wrote in response to Sidney's letter that he believed the King would never pass the Bill.[127]

CHARLES II INTERCEDES: THE OXFORD PARLIAMENT AND THE END OF THE EXCLUSION CRISIS

On 20 January 1681 the King prorogued Parliament and on the 28th he dissolved it, with the new Parliament to meet at Oxford on 31 March. On 3 February Essex, Temple and Sunderland were dismissed from the Council.[128] A week later Conway took Sunderland's place as Secretary of State and took over Sir Lionel Jenkins's responsibilities for Dutch affairs, although Jenkins remained as the other Secretary of State.[129]

The elections produced no substantial change in the composition of the House of Commons, where the Whigs predominated.[130]

William saw the dissolution as further evidence of English disunity, with its fatal consequences for Europe. On hearing the news of the dissolution of Parliament on 2 February he told Sidney he feared a war and he hoped the first bullet would kill him, 'for he would rather lose his life than his reputation'. Furthermore, he believed the King had taken measures with France. On the 6th he wrote to Sir Lionel Jenkins indicating that he saw Christendom 'to be entirely ruined' and abandoned to Louis XIV: 'may God have pity on so many poor people'.[131] But when Laurence Hyde misinterpreted a letter he wrote on 10 March as favouring exclusion and showed it to the King – who uncompromisingly rejected it – he received a firm rebuke from the Prince, denying that he would ever interfere in a 'matter as important and delicate as that of Exclusion'. His advice was and remained that some expedient be found to unite the King and his Parliament and that the affairs of the King, of his Kingdom, and of all his allies were in a very bad state, but that he did not know what the remedy was.[132]

But Charles had in mind his own solution and Temple had got wind of it, as he revealed to Henry Sidney in a letter of 2 March; it was for the Duke of York 'to have the name of King after the King's death, but the kingdom to be governed by a Protector and Council, and the Prince of Orange to be the Protector'.[133] Thus Charles, too, had his form of exclusion without exclusion. Sir Lionel Jenkins had provided William with a hint of the King's intentions when he wrote on 28 January that he was commanded by the King 'that he hath a proposition to make this new Parliament, which he is sure your Hignesse cannott dislike of, and he hopes will be acceptable to all considerate honest men'.[134] The proposal may have originated with Halifax, who, according to his biographer, in any case approved it.[135]

By this time the court's opponents had acquired the name of Whigs – derived from extreme Presbyterians in the south-west of Scotland – and its supporters had acquired the name of Tories – from Catholic bandits in Ireland. Charles's opening speech to Parliament, delivered on 31 March, was carefully phrased for its propaganda value against the Whigs and it was published on the day he delivered it. His opening words were: 'The unwarrantable proceedings of the last House of Commons were the Occasion of My parting with the last Parliament; for I, who will never use arbitrary Government Myself am resolved not to suffer it in others.' This was, of course, an allusion to the break with the lawful succession that exclusion implied. But to indicate his reasonableness, and subject to his standard qualification about maintaining the rightful succession, he undertook to 'remove all reasonable fears that may arise from the possibility of a popish successor coming to the crown, if means can be found that in such a case the administration of the government may remain in Protestant hands', and he promised to 'hearken to any such expedient'.[136]

The way was thus prepared for Sir Thomas Littleton and others to expound the regency proposals in the House of Commons on 5 April – James was to be banished for life, with the government vesting in Mary, and, if James returned from exile, the provisions of the Exclusion Bill would apply. As Hyde wrote to Prince William, this was done with the full authority of the King, 'who commanded all his servants in the House of Commons, to promote them the most that was in their power'. But it was not well received by the House, most of whose members were committed to exclusion, and there were indeed sound objections to it, not least that James was likely to reject it and that its implementation would inevitably lead to a confrontation between the nominal King and William as the actual holder of power.[137] But by rejecting the proposal and by at once returning to exclusion the Whigs showed their intransigence and walked into the trap that Charles had laid for them.

William's suspicions of an agreement between Charles and Louis were well founded, although the negotiations, which had begun at the end of 1680, had not been finalised at the time the previous Parliament was dissolved, but by a secret agreement on 1 April, the day after the new Parliament met. It was a verbal agreement and had been negotiated by the King, Laurence Hyde and the French ambassador in London, Barillon. Charles undertook to extricate himself gradually from his Spanish alliance in return for 3 million crowns (about £375,000) in total, payable over three years. There was also a vague undertaking by Charles to resist Parliamentary pressure for anything inconsistent with the agreement. Hyde had asked for an assurance that Louis would make no attack on the Low Countries, or Strasburg, as Charles would then have to come to the aid of the Dutch, even without Parliament meeting, but he had to be content with a general assurance that Louis did not intend to break the peace or to involve Charles in measures prejudicial to his interests.[138]

On both sides, therefore, the agreement was extremely nebulous, and too much significance has been attached to it. Louis's subsidy of an average of £125,000 a year was a handsome addition to Charles's resources – it enabled him to spend £100,000 on Louise de Kérouaille over two and a half years[139] – but it should be seen in the context of his total average expenditure of about £1,175,000 and against ordinary revenue of about £1,100,000.[140] Charles, indeed, was already practically financially independent of both Parliament and of Louis XIV – and there is therefore no substance in the claim long maintained by historians that the agreement enabled Charles to live without Parliament and thus to dismiss it; and Louis, too, must have been aware that the subsidy was comparatively modest. Why then did the two monarchs enter into this verbal agreement? It should perhaps be seen as a token between patron and client, a gesture of reassurance from Louis that he was extending his protection – and a gesture from Charles that he was prepared to accept it.

This, however, amounted to little more than vague moral assurance; for, although James, through Barillon, on a number of occasions called upon Louis for his protection,[141] it must have been doubtful what practical assistance Louis would, or perhaps even could, have extended to his English cousins in the event of insurrection at a time when his own preoccupations were centred on his own frontiers.

To protect himself Charles relied on much more robust measures. He held the Parliament at Oxford, rather than at London, where he would be free from the mob and the rioting which had destabilised his father in 1641 and which had foreshadowed the onset of the Civil War – not that there was much evidence in any case that London this time was in rebellious mood.[142] But, with the precedent of the Civil War in mind, he also took extremely careful military measures.

With most of the army disbanded, the very small English standing army that remained in 1681 consisted of 5,240 troops; but that was sufficient. Of these, 1,250 were in garrisons, leaving 3,990, and of these Charles employed more than two thirds – 2,800 men – to protect himself, Oxford and London in the political coup that he was about to launch. On 1 April he had 660 troops in Oxford and there were a further 250 lifeguards stationed on the London to Oxford road. In and about the cities of London and Westminster he had put the Earl of Craven in command with 1,890 men, including 300 in the Tower of London.[143] Although Shaftesbury left London for Oxford with 200 well-armed attendants on horseback,[144] they were clearly no match for the preparations the King had made. With no need of Parliament for financial reasons the other reason for maintaining it, therefore – the fear of civil war – also no longer applied.

On 8 April, as the Commons were giving the Bill for exclusion its first reading, they were summoned to make their way up the staircase leading into the hall of Christ Church. There they beheld the King in his full regalia; and there they heard him dissolve Parliament for the last time in his reign.[145]

THE PRINCE VISITS ENGLAND

To Prince William's great grief his friend Ossory had died on 9 August 1680 – 'I have lost one of the best friends I had in the world', he wrote to the widow[146] – and there was a delay in appointing his successor to the command of the British troops in Dutch service. Charles II wanted first Lord Dumbarton – who was inappropriate because he was a Catholic – and later the Duke of Albemarle – who was inappropriate because he had too many other commitments;[147] and in the summer of 1681 William appointed Henry Sidney. On 3 June Sidney, who had fallen into disfavour for his involvement in the exclusion crisis, informed

William that he was to be recalled as envoy to The Hague.[148] His successor was to be Bevil Skelton, and Lord Conway also asked Prince William not to dispose of the command of the British troops.[149] On the 25th the Prince wrote to Charles telling him how much he regretted the recall of Sidney and asking him to reconsider the appointment of Skelton – who had been a rather too Francophile envoy in Vienna – as 'someone with whom I could not live with good understanding'; and as regarded the appointment of Sidney to Ossory's commands he would have been appointed earlier had it not been for the reluctance of the States-General to appoint another general in time of peace.[150]

Four days earlier he had decided in principle that he should go to England. His main anxiety was that Louis XIV was making threatening moves on Luxemburg as part of his policy of *Réunions* – to which we will come – and William had expressed his concern on this score to Laurence Hyde on the 17th.[151] In addition there were the irritants of Skelton and Sidney, which stood in the way of good relations with Charles. But before finally making up his mind he wanted Sidney to sound out Sir William Temple and Godolphin on the efficacy of the visit. Temple wrote to him that he did not believe that any conversations between the King and himself would be mutually satisfactory. But if William, nevertheless, did decide to come it would be useful to ascertain how personal relations ('personal dispositions') stood between him and Charles, and he could use the pretext that he wanted to clarify 'several ill offices that you believe have been done you towards his Majesty'. Godolphin was more positive and saw the visit not only as giving occasion to redress the disagreements over Skelton and Sidney, but as also providing an opportunity for William to exert a beneficial influence over English affairs.[152]

After his return to England Sidney reported on 8 July: 'It is very plain that you have had ill offices done you to the King; they make him believe that your Highness is the party that is most against him.' When he spoke to Halifax and Hyde both complained of William's letters 'being too high and too sharp'.[153] There was thus clearly a need to mend fences – all the more so in the light of Louis's menaces on the Continent.

By 9 July Charles had consented to the visit,[154] although the Duke of York was uneasy and he wrote to Barillon that 'he advised my friends to be alert'.[155] He later recorded his objections to the visit as being that it would encourage the Whig opposition, just 'when the King had them … under his feet', that it would upset the French, and that it was clearly the Prince's object to get the King to come to an agreement with his Parliament, which 'would quite blast [James's] expectations of ever seeing an end to his miseries'.[156] But to the Prince he wrote expressing his gladness on the grounds that it would enable William to be better informed of Charles's affairs.[157]

The Prince arrived at Windsor on 3 August, a Saturday, and on the following Sunday he had a meeting with the King for two hours, which continued the next day with Halifax, Hyde, Conway and Jenkins also attending. The Prince urged the need for English intervention on the Continent – we need to remember that Louis was threatening Luxemburg, which was of great importance for the security of the Dutch. Inevitably, however, this implied the need for a Parliament, which in turn implied agreement with the Whigs. When it was put to him that Parliament would reiterate its old demands he was at a loss for an immediate and satisfactory reply – he agreed exclusion was unacceptable; he agreed limitations were unacceptable. Upon being asked what then was his alternative policy, he was compelled to request permission to make soundings. For this he went to London on 7 August and stayed at Arlington's house, where he held separate conversations with each of the former Triumvirate, Sunderland, Essex and Halifax. As part of his counter-offensive against the Whigs, Charles had arrested Shaftesbury on 12 July, which left William Russell as the leading proponent in the Whig camp, and with him too the Prince held conversations.[158] But all these dialogues clearly proved abortive, for James wrote to him on 14 August in reply to a letter from William 'by which I see that those that came to speak with you at London cannot be brought to reason'.[159] These meetings with the Whigs must have tested Charles's patience and when, through the doings of William Russell, William accepted an invitation to dine with the opposition in the City of London, he overstepped the mark; a swift recall to Windsor on 11 August was his uncle's response. The prerequisite for a strong Anglo-Dutch alliance to intervene against Louis XIV was the unity of King and Parliament and hence reconciliation between the King and the Whig opposition. William had failed to achieve this, as Temple predicted he would.

But it looked as though some progress was nevertheless made. Halifax, Hyde, Seymour and the two Secretaries of State, Conway and Jenkins, were appointed as commissioners to confer with the Spanish and Dutch representatives in London. The outcome was that Charles undertook to issue a strong protest, jointly with the Dutch, against Louis's actions and he also undertook to summon his Parliament and declare war on France if Louis invaded the Spanish Netherlands. This fell short of the Anglo-Dutch alliance against Louis XIV which the Prince was aiming for, but with this commitment – itself illusory as it turned out – he had to rest content as he left for Holland on 15 August.[160]

---

1 *Diary of Edward Lake*, Camden Miscellany, I, Camden Society, 39, 1847.

2 Van der Zees, *op. cit.*, p.117.

3 *Ibid.*, p.119.

4 Fruin, *Verspreide Geschriften, op. cit.*, V, pp.58–9. Mignet, *op. cit.*, IV, p.545.

5 Van der Zees, *op. cit.*, p.120. Japikse, *Willem III, op. cit.*, II, p.70.

6 Lake, *op. cit.*

7 Japikse, *Willem III, op. cit.*, II, pp.70–1. Van der Zees, *op. cit.*, p.122. The claim made by the Van der Zees that the dowry was never paid seems to be contradicted by Danby's letter to the Prince of 30 September 1678, the Prince's letter to Henry Coventry of 11 October 1678 and Godolphin's letter to the Prince of 22 June 1680. Japikse thinks the money mentioned in the latter letter was in satisfaction of the Stuart debt, but the sum of £20,000 mentioned there and the £20,000 mentioned in Danby's letter do come to the £40,000 owing under the dowry. For these letters and Japikse's note see *Correspondentie Willem III en Bentinck, op. cit.*, II, 2, pp.282, 347 with n.4.

8 Lake, *op. cit.* The objectivity of Dr Lake may have been coloured by his failure to secure the appointment to the Princess's chaplaincy in the Dutch Republic. On 11 November he recorded that Mary was in tears not only because of the illness of her sister Anne, but also because of 'the prince's urging her to remove her lodgings to Whitehall, which the princesse would by no means be perswaded'.

9 Quoted in Hester Chapman, *Mary II Queen of England*, London 1953, p.77.

10 Lake, *op. cit.*

11 Van der Zees, *op. cit.*, pp.126–8.

12 Japikse, *Willem III, op. cit.*, II, pp.78–9. Van der Zees, *op. cit.*, pp.128–9. Chapman, *op. cit.*, II, pp.78.

13 *Correspondentie Willem III en Bentinck, op. cit.*, II, 2, p.214.

14 Kenyon, *The Popish Plot*, London 1972, pp.51–3 & for Tonge's and Oates's backgrounds pp.45ff.

15 Browning, *op. cit.*, I, p.291.

16 Kenyon, *op. cit.*, pp.66, 69, 70, 75. Hutton, *Charles II, op. cit.*, p.360–61. Jones, *Charles II, op. cit.*, p.130. John Miller, *Charles II*, London 1991, p.88.

17 Miller, *op. cit.*, pp.294–5. He also thinks the assumption that the later letters were destroyed was 'almost certainly wrong'.

18 Kenyon, *op. cit.*, pp.77–8. Jones, *Charles II, op. cit.*, p.130. Haley, *Shaftesbury, op. cit.*, p.458. The riddle of the murder of Godfrey has never been solved.

19 *Correspondentie Willem III en Bentinck, op. cit.*, II, 2, p.282.

20 See John Miller, *Popery and Politics in England, 1660–1688*, London 1973, p.159.

21 Haley, *Shaftesbury, op. cit.*, pp.469, 470, 330.

22 *Ibid.*, p.471.

23 Quoted in *ibid.*, p.480.

24 *Ibid.*, pp.480–82.

25 *Ibid.*, pp.483–5.

26 Jones, *Charles II, op. cit.*, p.132.

27 *Correspondentie Willem III en Bentinck*, II, 2, *op. cit.*, pp.285–6.

28 Browning, *op. cit.*, I, pp.286–7.

29 *Ibid.*, I, pp.300–07 and II pp.346–9. J.R. Jones, *The First Whigs*, London 1961, pp.28–9.

30 Browning, *op. cit.*, I, pp.307–9.

31 Haley, *Shaftesbury, op. cit.*, p.494.

32 Browning, *op. cit.*, II, p.310.

33 Jones, *The First Whigs, op. cit.*, p.34.

34 *Correspondentie Willem III en Bentinck*, II, 2, *op. cit.*, pp.289, 291.

35 Haley, *Shaftesbury, op. cit.*, p.500.

36 *Correspondentie Willem III en Bentinck*, II, 2, *op. cit.*, p.294.

37 Haley, *Shaftesbury, op. cit.*, p.501.

38 *Ibid.*, pp.501–2, Miller, *James II, op. cit.*, pp.91, 96. Browning, *op. cit.*, II, pp.90–1. For the disbandment of the army see Hutton, *Charles II, op. cit.*, p.366. *Correspondentie Willem III en Bentinck, op. cit.*, II, 2, pp.294–6.

39 Browning, *op. cit.*, I, pp.321–2, 317.

40 *Ibid.*, I, p.322.

41 *Ibid.*, I, p.323.

42 Jones, *Charles II, op. cit.*, p.142. Browning, *op. cit.*, II, p.329.

43 Temple, *Works, op. cit.*, 1754, I, pp.413–19. See also Hutton, *op. cit.*, p.371.

44 Haley, *Shaftesbury, op. cit.*, p.513.

45 *Ibid.*, p.517. Jones, *Charles II, op. cit.*, p.145. Temple, *Works, op. cit.*, 1754, I, p.422.

46 See Robb, *op. cit.*, II, p.134, and Baxter, *op. cit.*, p.165.

47 Haley, *Shaftesbury, op. cit.*, p.519–25. Temple, *Works, op. cit.*, 1754, I, p.423. Jones, *Charles II. op. cit.*, pp.146, 147–8. Henry Sidney, *Diary of The Times of Charles II*, ed. Blencowe, London 1843, I, p.29.

48 Sidney, *op. cit.*, I, pp.1, 4, 10, 13, 15, 19–20, 29. Article on Henry Sidney by David Hosford in *Oxford Dictionary of National Biography*, online edn, January 2013.

49 Troost, 'Willem III en de exclusion crisis 1679–1681' in *Bijdragen en Mededelingen betreffende de Geschiedemis der Nederlanden, deel 107* (1992) p.33.

50 Sidney, *op. cit.*, I, p.26.

51 Temple, *Works, op. cit.*, 1754, I, pp.429, 432.

52 Hutton, *op. cit.*, pp.377–8.

53 See the letter of Essex to the King of 31 July 1679. Sidney, *op. cit.*, I, pp.36–9.

54 Jones, *Charles II, op. cit.*, pp.150–51. Jones's account that Charles approached Louis 'in the hope of gaining subsidies that would give him at least temporary independence from his subjects' appears at variance with Hutton's view that Charles 'did not need a grant of money' (see his *Charles II, op. cit.*, p.379); in that case it is difficult at first sight to see why Charles was holding a general election rather than dispensing with Parliament entirely – unless he feared that thus dispensing with Parliament might involve him in civil war. C.D. Chandaman, *op. cit.*, pp.249–51, estimates that his revenue in the years ended in Michaelmas amounted to approximately £1.326m. in 1679, £1.353m. in 1680 and £1.282m. in 1681 against average expenditure which did not exceed £1.15m.; which, of course, supports Hutton's thesis. Nevertheless Charles's actions seem to indicate that *at this stage* he thought he needed financial support either by summoning Parliament or by approaching Louis. Chandaman estimates Charles's total indebtedness at his death at not less than £2.85m. (pp.268–9), and, as Essex's letter indicates, a reluctance to lend to the King to tide him over fluctuations in revenue may have been a factor, particularly if the revenues were also considered to be uncertain (see Miller, *Charles II, op. cit.*, p.330). The continued improvement in his finances was, in due course, reflected in his dismissal of the Oxford Parliament in 1681 – at which time, too, Charles may have thought the risk of civil war had receded.

55 *Correspondentie Willem III en Bentinck, op. cit.*, II, 2, p.296.

56 See Sidney, *op. cit.*, I, p.111.

57 *Ibid.*, I, pp.46–50.

58 See Groen van Prinsterer, *Archives, op. cit.*, V, *Despatch of the Dutch envoys in Paris to Prince William 1 September 1679*, pp.368–72.

59 Sidney, *op. cit.*, I, p.54. See also H.C. Foxcroft, *Life and Letters of Halifax*, London 1898, I, pp.183–4, in which Sidney's relevant letter is reproduced in slightly different form. Troost, 'Willem III en de exclusion crisis', *op. cit.*, p.30–2.

60 Sidney, *op. cit.*, I, p.66.

61 *Correspondentie Willem III en Bentinck*, II, 2, *op. cit.*, p.298.

62 The accounts of these events vary considerably. It is not clear from Temple, *Works, op. cit.*, 1754, I, p.438, whether all three of the triumvirate or only Halifax and Essex were involved in persuading the King to send for James. Foxcroft, *op. cit.*, I, p.187, says that all three were involved and that the summons was endorsed by the King. James, in his account, apologised to the King for coming without his leave (see Sidney, *op. cit.*, I, n.p.125). See otherwise Hutton, *op. cit.*, p.381. J.P. Kenyon, *Robert Spencer, Earl of Sunderland*, London 1958, p.30. Miller, *James II, op. cit.*, p.99. Haley, *Shaftesbury, op. cit.*, pp.545–7. Keay, *op. cit.*, p.219.

63 *Correspondentie Willem III en Bentinck*, II, 2, *op. cit.*, p.299. Sidney, *op. cit.*, I, pp.120–21.

64 Quoted in Kenyon, *Sunderland, op. cit.*, n.p.31.

65 Sidney, *op. cit.*, I, p.99. On his being Sunderland's secretary, see n.1, p.96.

66 *Ibid.*, I, p.130.

67 Japikse, *Willem III, op. cit.*, II, pp.145–6, n.3.

68 Stephen Baxter, *op. cit.* (pp.166–7 and n.15) cites the despatch of the French ambassador in The Hague, D'Avaux, to Louis XIV of 15 October 1679 conveying the information provided by Fitzpatrick, a French double agent who was being used by James as a messenger to William, to the effect that William had decided that Charles II would have to abdicate, and that, as James would not be tolerated as king, Parliament would summon him to the throne. Previously William had told Fitzpatrick that, despite his loyalty to Charles and James, he could not, if summoned by Parliament, refuse. But Fitzpatrick is a dubious source – not least because William's famous reticence and self-control make it unlikely that he would reveal himself to somebody like him, on matters of such importance, all the more so when they might be relayed back to James. Fitzpatrick's standing and character were completely different from those of Sidney. His 'ill reputation' is mentioned on 20 October in Sidney, *op. cit.*, I, p.163; he is described as a 'villain' by Essex on 15 November, p.179; and Sidney wrote to the Prince concerning the widely held view of his poor reputation (pp.183–4) at the end of November 1679 – all, admittedly, after D'Avaux's despatch of 15 October, but immediately after. Furthermore, as Baxter says, 'Fitzpatrick's task was to colour the messages he carried in such a way as to irritate [William and James] against each other'. More interestingly, Fitzpatrick's information was also that William was using a certain Freeman to maintain contact with the English Presbyterians and that Freeman had been used in Du Moulin's time, when Titus Oates had also come to the Prince's attention (Baxter, *op. cit.*, pp.166–7 together with nn.13, 14). D'Avaux also asserts that Freeman was used by the Prince at this time for another mission to England to persuade Parliamentarians to support the Dutch alliance as a means of detaching him from Louis XIV and making

him dependent on Parliament (*Négociations de M. Le Comte D'Avaux en Hollande*, I, Paris 1752, pp.14–15). Professor Haley has tried to track down who exactly 'Freeman' was, and what his specific activities were, without success; see his references to 'Freeman' p.227 of the Index to *The English Opposition, op. cit.*

69 Jones, *Charles II, op. cit.*, pp.152–4. Haley, *Shaftesbury, op. cit.*, pp.548–51.

70 Kenyon, *Sunderland, op. cit.*, p.32. Miller, *James II, op. cit.*, pp.100–01. *Correspondentie Willem III en Bentinck, op. cit.*, II, 2, p.299, n.4. Keay, *op. cit.*, p.221.

71 Sidney, *op. cit.*, I, pp.142–3. It needs to be borne in mind that at the time these conversations took place the Prince was anticipating that the new Parliament would meet on 9 November. In fact it was prorogued on 25 October until 5 February 1680 and then, by stages, to November 1680.

72 Sidney, *op. cit.*, pp.154–5 and n.p.193. Keay, *op. cit.*, p.228.

73 Sidney, *op. cit.*, I, pp.160–63.

74 Keay, *op. cit.*, pp.230–31. Sidney, *op. cit.*, I, p.190.

75 Miller, *James II, op. cit.*, p.100. *Correspondentie Willem III en Bentinck*, II, 2, *op. cit.*, p.303.

76 Haley, *Shaftesbury, op. cit.*, pp.549–51. Jones, *Charles II, op. cit.*, p.154. *Correspondentie Willem III en Bentinck, op. cit.*, II, 2, p.299, n.4 and p.303.

77 Müller, *Waldeck, op. cit.*, I, p.101.

78 Sidney, *op. cit.*, I, p.173.

79 *Ibid.*, I, pp.175–7, 187.

80 Kenyon, *Sunderland, op. cit.*, pp.29, 31.

81 Temple, *Works, op. cit.*, 1754, I, p.440. Kenyon, *Sunderland, op. cit.*, pp.31–4.

82 Temple, *Works, op. cit.*, 1754, I, pp.440–41. Hutton, *op. cit.*, p.384.

83 Kenyon, *Sunderland, op. cit.*, pp.36, 38.

84 Sidney, *op. cit.*, I, pp.187, 193.

85 *Correspondentie Willem III en Bentinck, op. cit.*, II, 2, p.284, n.2.

86 D'Avaux, *Négociations, op. cit.*, pp.20–21.

87 Kenyon, *Sunderland, op. cit.*, p.39.

88 Groen van Prinsterer, *Archives, op. cit.*, 2nd series, V, pp.463–4. The letter is misdated 30 December 1680 Old Style instead of 1679, as the context makes clear, as also does Godolphin's letter to the Prince of 1 January 1680 Old Style (pp.374–5). The King's finances were definitely improving, but the promise of over 40 ships without parliamentary grants seems either a bluff or a – bold – assumption that the fitting out would soon be followed by grants.

89 Groen van Prinsterer, *Archives, op. cit.*, 2nd series, V, pp.376–8. Müller, *Waldeck, op. cit.*, I, p.105.

90 Groen van Prinsterer, *Archives, op. cit.*, 2nd series, V, p.383.

91 *Ibid.*, 2nd series, V, p.387.

92 Miller, *Charles II, op. cit.*, pp.322, 330.

93 Kenyon, *Sunderland, op. cit.*, pp.41–2. Hutton, *op. cit.*, p.389. For Temple's and Sunderland's letters see Groen van Prinsterer, *Archives, op. cit.*, 2nd series, V, pp.375, 386.

94 Kenyon, *Sunderland, op. cit.*, pp.43, 46. Miller, *James II, op. cit.*, p.101. Hutton, *op. cit.*, p.389.

95 Miller, *Charles II, op. cit.*, p.326.

96 Petitfils, *op. cit.*, p.410.

97 Kenyon, *Sunderland, op. cit.*, pp.47–8. Kenyon, 'Charles II and William of Orange in 1680', *Bulletin Inst. Hist. Research*, 30 (1957), pp.95–6. See Sidney, *op. cit.*, II, p.77 (6 July) for Sunderland's observation of William as the Protestant champion.

98 Kenyon, *Sunderland, op. cit.*, p.49. Haley, *Shaftesbury, op. cit.*, pp.380–81.

99 Kenyon, *Bulletin Inst. of Hist. Research, op. cit.*

100 Kenyon, *Sunderland, op. cit.*, pp.54, 60, 61. Groen van Prinsterer, *Archives, op. cit.*, 2nd series, V, pp.422–5.

101 Sidney, *op. cit.*, II, pp.116–17, 119.

102 Groen van Prinsterer, *Archives, op. cit.*, 2nd series, V, pp.434–7.

103 Sidney, *op. cit.*, II, p.120.

104 Groen van Prinsterer, *Archives, op. cit.*, 2nd series, V, pp.417ff.

105 Sidney, *op. cit.*, II, p.121.

106 Haley, *Shaftesbury, op. cit.*, p.598.

107 *Ibid.*, pp.600–02. For Halifax's speech see also Foxcroft, *Halifax, op. cit.*, I, pp.246–7.

108 Kenyon, *Sunderland, op. cit.*, pp.64, 66, 68–9. Groen van Prinsterer, *Archives, op. cit.*, 2nd series, V, pp.442–3.

109 Miller, *Charles II, op. cit.*, pp.335–6.

110 Foxcroft, *Halifax, op. cit.*, I, pp.263–4. Groen van Prinsterer, *Archives, op. cit.*, 2nd series, V, pp.457–8. James to William 21 December.

111 Groen van Prinsterer, *Archives, op. cit.*, 2nd series, V, p.451.

112 Japikse, 'De "Insinuation" van de Staten-Generaal aan Den Engeleschen gezant van 5 December 1680', in *Bijdragen voor Vaderlandsche Geschiedenis en Oudheidkunde*, Sevende Reeks, Derde Deel, 1933, p.35. Sidney, *op. cit.*, II, pp.126–7.

113 Sidney, *op. cit.*, II, pp.132–3.

114 Fruin, *Verspreide Geschriften, op. cit.*, V, pp.76–7.

115 Sidney, *op. cit.*, II, p.131.

116 Its full heading was 'Insinuation Faite par des Députés des Etats-Généreux Dans une Conférence à Mons De Sydney, Envoyé Extr. D'Angleterre'.

117 Japikse, 'Insinuation', *op. cit.*, pp.27–8.

118 Sidney, *op. cit.*, II, p.131.

119 The text is in Japikse's 'Insinuation', *op. cit.*, pp.41–4.

120 Japikse in *Willem III, op. cit.*, II, pp.148–9, reasons that the vagueness of the *écrit* does not allow the conclusion to be drawn that the author of the Insinuation – who he thinks was Fagel with the agreement of William – was arguing for the exclusion of the Duke of York; and that this enabled William to deny that that was the intention of the Insinuation. Japikse does postulate that William had in mind the exclusion of all Catholics, without specifically naming James. As James refused to recant his religion one might counter that this was the same as specific exclusion. Nevertheless the option remained for James to do so, thus, we may agree, justifying William in his denial. His denial would be equally justifiable if the intention was to leave the possibility open of reversing James's exclusion in due course.

121 The French ambassador in The Hague, D'Avaux, said it was published at the behest of Sunderland. This version omitted the reference to the *écrit*. See Fruin, *Verspreide Geschriften, op. cit.*, V, n.p.79 and Japikse, 'Insinuation', *op. cit.*, pp.41–4. See also Sidney, *op. cit.*, II, p.131. Sidney says he received the Insinuation on 6 December (26 November Old Style) and sent it to Sunderland and Jenkins. Jenkins's acknowledgement of 17 December, however, refers to Sidney's letter of 5 December (p.145).

122 Groen van Prinsterer, *Archives, op. cit.*, 2nd series, V, pp.445ff.

123 *Ibid.*, 2nd series, V, pp.450–1.

124 Groen van Prinsterer, *Archives, op. cit.*, 2nd series, V, pp.451ff., Van Leeuwen to the Prince, 17 December 1680.

125 Sidney, *op. cit.*, II, pp.143–5.

126 Groen van Prinsterer, *Archives, op. cit.*, 2nd series, V, pp.461–2.

127 Sidney, *op. cit.*, II, pp.147–51 and I, pp.243–4, where Sunderland's letter is mistakenly dated 12 January 1680 rather than 1681.

128 Hutton, *op. cit.*, pp.397–8. Jones, *Charles II, op. cit.*, p.161.

129 Foxcroft, *Halifax, op. cit.*, pp.276, 278.

130 Haley, *Shaftesbury, op. cit.*, pp.626–7.

131 Sidney, *op. cit.*, II, pp.160–61, 164–5.

132 Groen van Prinsterer, *Archives, op. cit.*, 2nd series, V, p.484. The Prince's letter is missing; Hyde replied on 21 March, and the Prince on 11 April, see pp.493–4.

133 Sidney, *op. cit.*, II, p.177.

134 Groen van Prinsterer, *Archives, op. cit.*, 2nd series, V, p.472.

135 Foxcroft, *op. cit.*, I, pp.285–6.

136 *Ibid.*, I, p.287. Haley, *Shaftesbury, op. cit.*, p.633.

137 Foxcroft, *op. cit.*, I, pp.290–91. For Hyde's letter to the Prince dated 8 April see Groen van Prinsterer, *Archives, op. cit.*, 2nd series, V, pp.490–91. See also Conway's letter of the same date, pp.491–3.

138 Haley, *Shaftesbury. op. cit.*, p.636. Foxcroft, *op. cit.*, I, pp.285, 305 and n.4, p.305. Jones, *Charles II, op. cit.*, pp.166–7.

139 Miller, *Charles II, op. cit.*, p.352.

140 Chandaman, *op. cit.*, pp.253–4.

141 See, for example, Dalrymple, *op. cit.*, I, p.345.

142 Miller, *Charles II, op. cit.*, p.340.

143 John Child, 'The Army and the Oxford Parliament of 1681', *English Hist. Review 1979*, pp.580–87.

144 Haley, *Shaftesbury, op. cit.*, p.632.

145 Hutton, *op. cit.*, pp.400–01.

146 *Correspondentie Willem III en Bentinck, op. cit.*, II, 2, pp.317 n.3, p.353.

147 Groen van Prinsterer, *Archives, op. cit.*, 2nd series, V, pp.413, 425. Sidney, *op. cit.*, I, pp.xx, xxi.

148 Sidney, *op. cit.*, II, p.198.

149 *Ibid.*, II, p.200.

150 *Correspondentie Willem III en Bentinck, op. cit.*, II, 2, pp.391–2.

151 Groen van Prinsterer, *Archives, op. cit.*, 2nd series, V, p.507. Sidney, *op. cit.*, II, p.204.

152 Sidney, *op. cit.*, II, p.203. Dalrymple, *op. cit.*, 1.1.1, pp.67–72.

153 Sidney, *op. cit.*, II, pp.212–14.

154 Foxcroft, *op. cit.*, I, p.307.

155 Dalrymple, *op. cit.*, 1.1.1., pp.72–3.

156 Sidney, *op. cit.*, II, n.1, pp.220–21.

157 Groen van Prinsterer, *Archives, op. cit.*, 2nd series, V, p.511.

158 Foxcroft, *op. cit.*, I, p.307. Kenyon, *Sunderland, op. cit.*, pp.77–8. Sidney, *op. cit.*, I, n.1, pp.220ff. Haley, *Shaftesbury, op. cit.*, p.654.

159 Groen van Prinsterer, *Archives, op. cit.*, 2nd series, V, p.513. William's letter to James is lost.

160 Foxcroft, *op. cit.*, I, pp.308–9. For William's desire for an Anglo-Dutch alliance see Dalrymple, *op. cit.*, 1.1.1., p.74. Barillon's despatch of 1 October 1681. Hutton, *Charles II, op. cit.*, p.409.

QUEEN MARY.   WISSING.

Mary II when Princess of Orange, c. 1685, by Willem Wissing. Royal Collection

20 MARRIED LIFE, THE COURT AND THE MACHINERY OF POWER

Let us pause for a while and divert our attention from the political, the diplomatic and the military narrative and see how the onset of peace enabled William and Mary to settle down to married life, to observe how their court functioned and to examine how William exercised his power.

YOUTH AND UPBRINGING OF MARY

Mary, as we have seen, was born at St James's Palace on 10 May 1662. When she was nine her mother died and she and her sister Anne were brought up as Children of State. Charles II, anxious to offset the Catholicism of James, took great care that they should be strictly educated in the precepts of the Church of England. From these precepts neither of them was ever to deviate; and, in due course, it led to the abandonment of James by both his daughters. Henry Compton, the Bishop of London, whom we have seen officiating at Mary's wedding, had been appointed as the governor of the two princesses and thus his relationship with Mary was forged at an early age – it was to have important consequences for the future. The next six years the two girls spent at Richmond, the palace built by Henry VII, in the charge of Colonel Sir Edward Villiers – who was, however largely absent – and his wife Lady Frances Villiers. Lady Frances had six daughters who were brought up with the princesses. We shall hear more of two of them, Anne who married Hans Willem Bentinck and Elizabeth who – it was said – became the mistress of William III. They were taught French by a Frenchman, so that Mary became very proficient in the language, whilst another Frenchman also taught her to dance; and at this too she excelled[1] – it became one of the joys of her life. As we have seen, Lady Villiers died of the smallpox at the time of the marriage of William and Mary.

There were frequent trips to London, where the princesses mingled with the young ladies of the court. One was Sarah Jennings, clever, ambitious, self-willed, imperious, under whose influence Princess Anne fell. When Anne succeeded William and Mary to the throne of England this dependency became the basis for the career of Sarah's husband, John Churchill, the future Duke of Marlborough, whom Sarah was shortly to marry – and equally Churchill's career was to be destroyed when Anne changed from dependency to dull, sullen, stolid animosity.

Just as Anne developed a passionate relationship with Sarah Jennings so did Mary with Frances Apsley, who was nine years older. Her father, Sir Allen Apsley, lived at St James's Palace, and was Treasurer of the King's household and Treasurer-General to the Duke. With her Mary began a correspondence which started when she was about 11 and continued until she was 25; in it she calls herself Clorin – or sometimes Chlorine – whilst Frances is called Aurelia, names which may have been derived from plays, the one from Beaumont and Fletcher and the other from Dryden. In the letters Mary describes Frances as her 'husband' and herself as Frances's 'wife'[2] and the tone sounds today – as perhaps it did even in the second half of the 17th century – as somewhat cloying and saccharine. Thus – in Mary's own singular spelling and non-existent punctuation – 'to tell my dearest dear husband how much I love her wold be but to make you weiree of it for al the paper books and parchments in the world wo'd not hold half the love I have for you my dearest dearest dear Aurelia but when my Aurelia goes away she wil forget her pore wife here at St Jeames and find some mistres in her naiborhood'.[3] The – to modern ears – apparently lesbian overtones can be put aside; these are but sentimental outpourings in the style of the period. But it may be that to the more cerebral William the girlish sentimentality became somewhat tedious.[4]

Cerebral the letters certainly were not. Always gushing, they tended to a high point of court gossip, such as the affair the Duke of Monmouth was having, outside his marriage to the very rich Anna Scott of Buccleuch, with Eleonor Needham, whom he made pregnant[5] – she was a friend of Mary and of Frances Apsley.

WILLIAM AND MARY'S COURT

When Mary travelled to Holland her entourage included Elizabeth and Anne Villiers, a Villiers cousin, Lady Inchiquin, a lady-in-waiting, Jane Wroth, and Mary's nurse Mrs Langford. Henry Sidney wrote to Lord Rochester, 'It were worth your while to see the old ladies and the young beggarly bitches … suing for places about the Princess.' An attempt was made on behalf of John Churchill to buy him a place as well, but this was rejected by William who said that he forbade such dealings at his court. Sir Gabriel Sylvius became Mary's Chamberlain and Dr Lloyd and Dr Hooper were appointed her chaplains, both of them disapproving of the Calvinism prevalent in the Dutch Republic, which they regarded as too akin to non-conformism.[6]

William insisted on appropriate etiquette at his court. On his instructions only noble ladies and unmarried ladies who were relations of the Prince were entitled to be kissed by Mary on the cheek; to others she extended her hand for it to be kissed by them. When the husbands of those not so treated complained that their 'offices gave them equal rank with the nobility' the Prince replied that 'no office ennobles its possessor'. There was thus a clear determination on his part to maintain a certain distance between himself and the Regents. But Mary was able to act to a degree as a counterfoil; her 'freer gaiety of temper and fluency of conversation' was remarked upon in contrast with the Prince's manner.[7]

After the Peace of Nijmegen William took the opportunity to reorder his court. A list was drawn up of those entitled to eat at his table which included Bentinck, as the Prince's

Chamberlain, and Nassau-Ouwekerk, as his Master of Horse, and several spare places were laid for guests such as leading political figures, diplomats and army officers. Those entitled to eat at Mary's table included Lady Inchiquin, as head of the princess's household, and eight ladies-in-waiting, including Anne Villiers; another five English attendants, one Dutch, a chaplain and Sylvius. The court included 13 members of the nobility, 22 pages, 24 court officials, three lady's maids, 20 footmen, 32 attendants, 15 servants in the kitchen and 27 Swiss Guards. There was a secretariat, doctors, an architect, a keeper of paintings, a goldsmith and a large number of further servants at the various Orange houses.[8] An account relating to the beginning of 1688 says the Prince sat at a table laid for 12. The Princess ate on her own and at nine in the evening, after playing cards, she retired to sup privately with William.[9]

At the head of William's secretariat was Constantijn Huygens who, with his clerks, went wherever the Prince went, their luggage being carried in a separate cart. In 1679 Johan Pesters became the Prince's secretary for foreign affairs, especially to handle the correspondence from the ambassadors. He was also a member of the Prince's Council and a steward of his private affairs.[10]

The Prince's Council, the Domein Raad, supervised the extensive properties of the House of Orange – until 1686, it had been presided over by Constantijn Huygens's father, Constantine the elder. It met at The Hague and the Prince was kept well informed of its workings, with the not infrequent referral to him of final decisions. In 1680/81 his total expenditure came to just over 400,000 guilders (£40,000), of which his personal expenditure absorbed a little under one third, with Mary having an allowance of £4,000 a year – which she frequently exceeded.[11]

Seven miles from The Hague stood the imposing Orange country house, Honselaarsdijk, which the noted Dutch architect Jacob van Campen had had a hand in designing. It was extremely comfortable, and had marble bathrooms with running hot water. There, in the dining room, the Prince and his wife took their meals in public and there, in the audience chamber, the Prince gave his formal receptions. In the great gallery there hung portraits of the Nassau family, as well as a couple of Rembrandts.[12] The gardens were acclaimed and William used them when he wished to discuss sensitive matters of state in privacy.

There were two residences in The Hague, the Binnenhof, a large complex of buildings which was also used by the States-General, and the Noordeinde, which could be used to house guests. There was also the rustic Het Huis ten Bosch (The House in the Woods) just outside The Hague. It had been built by Amalia von Solms and on his marriage William had added two wings. It contained the Orange Hall with paintings by Honthorst and Jordaens and everywhere there were reminders of the Orange-Nassau and Stuart ancestry. It was the scene of William and Mary's first ball.[13]

Elsewhere there were a considerable number of other Orange residences; these included a castle at Breda, close to the Spanish Netherlands, another – in a dilapidated state – at

Buren, a country house at Geertruidenberg, and in Brussels there was a palace. In 1674 William bought Soestdijk in the Province of Utrecht from the Amsterdam Regent Cornelis de Graeff, the art connoisseur, who had organised the Dutch Gift to Charles II at the time of his Restoration in 1660. Much land was added to it – including the manor of Soestdijk, which was given to him by the Province of Utrecht – and it was to become a major country estate. In November 1684 William bought Het Loo in the Province of Gelderland and extended it into a palace, with an extensive park inspired by Le Nôtre.

Then there was Dieren, which was no more than a hunting lodge with a hall hung with antlers; but the hunting in the adjoining Veluwe forests was good and there the Prince of Orange was able to relax.[14] Henry Sidney described it as 'an ill house, but in a fine country'.[15]

There was much entertaining, of which hunting and shooting formed a major part and to which there are frequent references in Henry Sidney's diary – at Honselaarsdijk 'I was all day hunting with the Prince'; at Dieren 'The Prince went a hunting, and I went a shooting'; 'The Prince went a stag-hunting, and did not come home till late'.[16] Hunting was only allowed to the elite and invitations to his hunts were a useful source of patronage for the Prince.[17]

At the various residences there was card-playing; there were balls – Nassau-Ouwekerk entertained on a sumptuous scale at his hôtel in The Hague;[18] there was the theatre – William subsidised the French theatre to the tune of 5,000 guilders a year;[19] there was the fashionable Italian opera; and there was scandal – the Count of Nassau-Zuylenstein, the son of William's old governor, seduced Jane Wroth, impregnated her, and was forced to marry her. The culture of the court was profoundly French and its language was French – in 1697 one of Louis's emissaries reported that William's command of the language was excellent and that he spoke it without an accent.[20] Mary wrote her *Memoirs* in French. It was the language of the Dutch aristocracy, which they used amongst themselves – in communicating with the Regents William used Dutch.

All this served a political purpose. As William Temple wrote, the Prince of Orange stood for 'the dignity of this State, by publique Guards, and the attendance of all military Officers; By the splendour of his Court, and the magnificence of his Expense'.[21] Olaf Mörke has estimated that the Prince's court amounted to around 200 to 220 persons, about the same as a medium-sized German court of the period,[22] although the influence he wielded at this time on the European stage far exceeded that of all the German princes bar the Emperor, and, after he became King of England, it exceeded his as well. The court was part of the Prince's *gloire*, not the least important aspect of which was that he could be seen to use his prestige to perform the role of great patron, extending his 'protection', as was the common expression in the 17th century, to the ordinary people of the United Provinces[23] – a popular counterweight to the Regents. It was a role which in 1688 was to be extended to 'the English Nation' as well.

Profoundly French in its culture his court might be, but William was not alone in having married an English wife and having English connections. Bentinck was married to Anne Villiers, whose father, Sir Edward, was a nephew of the first Duke of Buckingham. Anne's brother, another Edward, was Mary's Master of Horse, and their sister was Betty Villiers, William's supposed mistress, but certainly a very close companion. One of Nassau-Ouwekerk's sisters had married Arlington and another had married Ossory, and was the mother of the second Duke of Ormond, the leader of the Butler clan in Ireland. Nassau-Zuylenstein's mother was a Killigrew and he himself had married Jane Wroth, albeit, as we have seen, under somewhat forced circumstances.[24]

To this life Mary seemed rapidly to adapt herself. In January 1678 Dr Lake received news from a correspondent in Holland 'that the Princess was grown somewhat fatt, and very beautiful withal'.[25] One of the best ways of getting to know her new country was to make use of the very comfortable barges drawn by horses at a leisurely pace along the abundant waterways, and this Mary did during the course of 1678. She occupied herself otherwise in playing cards, embroidery, drawing, gardening and reading. She also began collecting china, which she continued to do for the rest of her days.[26]

Romance was in the air, and in February Bentinck married Anne Villiers, thus tying yet more closely the bond that already existed between him and the Prince. William gave Anne a yearly allowance of 8,000 guilders and in 1682 this was increased by another 1,000 guilders for her duties as lady-in-waiting, backdated to November 1677. In 1683 she took over from Lady Inchiquin.[27]

MARY'S RELATIONSHIP WITH THE PRINCE

As her letters to Frances Apsley reveal, Mary had a strongly romantic nature, even if, at this stage, it was a very adolescent one; and it was not therefore surprising that she was soon in love with her reserved husband. It came as a shock to her that he soon had to depart for the wars, occasioned by the news that the French had invested Namur. Her uncle, Laurence Hyde, recorded, 'The princess parted very unexpectedly from her husband on 1 March 1678. He had been hunting all the morning, and as he came home to her palace at The Hague to dinner he received letters by the way that occasioned his sudden departure, of which the princess said she had not the slightest previous intimation.' She was able to go with her husband to Rotterdam, 'where', Hyde observed, 'there was a very tender parting on both sides'.[28]

A stunned Mary wrote to Frances Apsley on the 3rd, 'till this time I never knew sorrow for what can be more cruall in the world than parting with what on loves and nott ondly comon parting but parting so as may be never to meet again to be perpetually in fear for god knows when I may see him or wethere he is nott at this instant in a batell I recon him now never in safety ever in danger oh miserable life that I lead now.'[29] She was pregnant at the time, but more bad news followed. Her father wrote to William in April, 'I was very sorry to find by the letters of this day from Holland, that my daughter has miscarried; pray let her be carefuller of herself another time: I will write to her to the same purpose.'[30]

Soon she was pregnant again and she confessed to Frances in August that 'I have played the whore a little', adding, 'I woud nott have it known yett for all the world since it cannot be above 6 or 7 weeks att most'.[31] At the end of the year it was agreed that the States-General should act as sponsors to this Orange child; but, alas, Mary miscarried again. When is uncertain – the child was expected in March 1679 – and it has been suggested that it might have been a false pregnancy. For a while Mary's health deteriorated; and she was not to conceive again.[32]

By August she seemed recovered, for Henry Sidney wrote to her father that he found her so well 'that I cannot believe she wants any remedies', although all the same she intended to go to Aix-la-Chapelle to take the waters. She was back again by September when Sidney met her and the Prince at Breda.[33]

THE MACHINERY OF POWER

From this court William of Orange had come to wield huge authority not only in the United Provinces but on the European continent as a whole. Let us examine the means by which he did so.

In Dutch constitutional theory the most important military and financial matters required unanimity in the States-General; but in practice the Prince of Orange and Fagel not infrequently ignored this, unless the opposition stemmed from Amsterdam with her command of the purse-strings, and even then, as we shall see, it was not impossible for able politicians like the Prince and Fagel to out-manoeuvre the city. The States-General had secret committees (*Secrètes Besognes*) including those for military, nautical, financial and foreign affairs and for the two large Dutch trading companies, the West India Company and the East India Company, the latter of which was well advanced in building a semi-autonomous trading empire in the Far East. The committees were small, made up of seven or eight of the most important Regents, one from each of the Provinces, one or two from Holland, plus the Pensionary. The advice of the committees was usually followed by the States-General.[34]

There was also the Council of State, but it had an advisory role and its function was to carry out the resolutions of the States-General on military and financial matters. It presented a yearly war budget and it was responsible for the payment of the soldiers.[35]

The States of Holland consisted of 18 towns plus the nobles and these States, too, had their own secret committees, which were dominated by the most influential Holland Regents – Amsterdam was represented on all the most important of them. In Amsterdam the views of the burgomasters were usually the determining factor in the policy adopted and here the Prince of Orange had negligible influence over their nomination. The existing burgomasters and aldermen and the old burgomasters and old aldermen chose the four new burgomasters. The Town Council had no direct influence on the nominations so that in practice the burgomasters were extremely independent.[36]

But William of Orange was the Stadholder of five of the seven Provinces. He had a very tight grip on Utrecht, Gelderland and Overijssel, and could nominate his favourites there to the States-General and its committees. He also had great influence in Zeeland; and in Holland too his influence was considerable both through his power of nomination to the town councils – the councils would present him with a dual list from which he could choose his preferred candidates – and through his very considerable powers of patronage.[37] He set up a system of managers with one or two persons in each town whose task it was to try to control the list of nominations.[38] The Holland nobles, of whom the Prince himself was a member and over whom he presided, invariably supported him – the support being strengthened by both Frederick van Reede and Hans Willem Bentinck acquiring manors in Holland, which made them members of the nobility.[39]

The only robust opposition which could be offered the Prince came from Amsterdam and the two northern Provinces, Friesland and Groningen, where his cousin, Hendrik-Casimir, was the Stadholder. After the Peace of Nijmegen, whilst Amsterdam was unsuccessful in abolishing the secret committees, their members had to refer back to their provincial masters and they thus ceased to serve the purposes of William and Fagel, who resorted instead to more informal methods to obtain their ends.[40]

William was able to overcome the historic tendency for conflict to arise between his House and the Pensionary of Holland. Instead he forged a close partnership with Caspar Fagel, who made full use of his office's potential, who established a network of agents of his own and who never deviated in his support. A major contribution was Fagel's management of the States-General, of the Holland States and, until they lost their use, of their respective secret committees, along with his participation in foreign affairs – Dutch overseas representatives sent their more confidential missives not to the States-General, but to him.

In foreign affairs the Prince operated through a network which worked in parallel with, and frequently separately from, the Republic's official envoys. Their concerns extended to the personal interests of his House. Sebastien Chièze, for example, was engaged in William's financial claims in Madrid whilst also representing the Republic. He came from Orange, was a Catholic and spoke no Dutch. Van Citters in London made representations in London regarding the Orange Principality. An analysis of 20 associates that the Prince used for his diplomacy reveals a very cosmopolitan group: four were Catholics, and the nobility was strongly represented.[41]

In the armed forces, whose officers too were very cosmopolitan, drawn from all over Europe, with backgrounds from the nobility and gentry strongly represented, and who were often William's relations, the Prince's authority ruled supreme. The States-General Field Deputies, who were supposed to exercise political and financial control over the army, consisted of people who bent to the Prince's wishes.[42] The activities of the committees for the army and navy tended to be limited to whatever directions William thought it appropriate for them to receive, frequently through Fagel. The planning and the execution of the campaigns practically bypassed the States-General and the Council of State. On naval affairs William was absent during the summer on land campaigns and he therefore made plans, as much as he could, with well-disposed deputies of the States-General and members of the admiralty colleges, instructed the heads of the navy accordingly, and then left it to them to conduct the operations at sea.[43]

In Dutch constitutional theory the Prince was the servant of the Dutch States and never their sovereign; but in practice he exercised enormous influence over the choice of his nominal masters who selected him. But he was not only the holder of important offices in the Dutch Republic; he was also, as the Prince of Orange, an independent European sovereign prince. His own claims to the English throne were not negligible, and his wife's claims were stronger still. The reach of the Orange-Nassau clan's family connections and patronage extended across the continent of Europe and in England his web of connections, which he had always assiduously cultivated, could be forged into a formidable force. He was, furthermore, through his illustrious predecessors, the inheritor of redoubtable *gloire*, the political importance of which we have emphasised in 17th-century Europe, and this status he had further burnished and embellished since his rise to power in 1672.

These were the means that William of Orange sought to employ for the next stage in the struggle to limit the ascendancy of Louis XIV.

1 Chapman, *op. cit.*, pp.19, 27, 28. Van der Zees, *op. cit.*, p.58.

2 Chapman, *op. cit.*, pp 29, 31.

3 Benjamin Bathurst, *Letters of Two Queens*, London 1924, p.43.

4 As it does to the historian.

5 Chapman, *op. cit.*, pp.32–3.

6 *Ibid.*, pp.66–7.

7 *Ibid.*, p.79.

8 Japikse, *Willem III, op. cit.*, II, pp.116–18.

9 Fruin, *Aantekeningen, in Overblyfsels van Geheugenis*, Coenraad Droste, Leyden, 1879. p.454.

10 D.J. Roorda, *Rond prins en patriciaat : verspreide opstellen*, Weesp 1984, II, p.98.

11 Robb, *op. cit.*, II, pp.234–5.

12 Van der Zees, *op. cit.*, pp.130–31. Chapman, *op. cit.*, p.76.

13 Chapman, *op. cit.*, p.83.

14 Van der Zees, *op. cit.*, p.132.

15 Sidney, *op. cit.*, I, p.43.

16 *Ibid.*, II, pp.84, 94–5.

17 Mörke, article in *William III's Stadhouderly Court in the Dutch Republic in Redefining William III*, eds. Esther Mijers and David Onnekink, Aldershot 2007, p.235.

18 Fruin, *Aantekeningen, op. ci*t., p.476.

19 *Ibid.*, p 441.

20 Hatton, art. *Louis XIV and his Fellow Monarchs in Louis XIV and Europe*, London 1976, p.24.

21 Quoted in Mörke, *William III's Stadhouderly Court, op. cit.*, p.230.

22 *Ibid.*, p.230.

23 *Ibid.*, p.233.

24 Andrew Barclay, art. *William's Court as King in Redefining William III, op. cit.*, pp.244–5.

25 Sidney, *op. cit.*, I, n.p.62.

26 Chapman, *op. cit.*, p.83.

27 Japikse, *Willem III, op. cit.*, II, pp.126–7.

28 Bathurst, *op. cit.*, p.87.

29 *Ibid.*, p.89.

30 Dalrymple, *op. cit.*, I, p.209.

31 Bathust, *op. cit.*, pp.91–2

32 Robb, *op. cit.*, pp.131, 133. Chapman, *op. cit.*, II, p.93.

33 Sidney, *op. cit.*, I, pp.45, 131.

34 Dreiskämper, *Aan de Vooravond van de Overtocht naar Engeland.Utrechtse*, Historische Cahiers, Jaargang 17 (1996), IV, pp.10.

35 *Ibid.*, p.11.

36 *Ibid.*, pp.11–12. Fruin, *Verspreide Geschriften, op. cit.*, IV, pp.309–12. The Stadholder, i.e. the Prince, indeed nominated the aldermen in the first instance out of a double list of 14 presented to him yearly by the town council, from which he chose seven, but, once nominated, they could vote as they liked. The existing burgomasters and the existing aldermen and the old burgomasters and old aldermen, who chose the new burgomasters, were very much a self-perpetuating clique.

37 Dreiskämper, *op. cit.*, pp.13–14.

38 Groenveld, article in *William III as Stadholder:Prince or Minister? in Redefining William III, op. cit.*, p.23.

39 Roorda, *Rond Prince, op. cit.*, I, p.185.

40 Bruin, *Geheimhouding en Verraad*, The Hague 1991, p.270.

41 Roorda, *Rond Prince, op. cit.*, pp.172, 176–77, 187, 190. Groenveld, article in *Redefining Willem III, op. cit.*, p.24.

42 Roorda, *Rond Prince, op. cit.*, p.184.

43 Bruin, *op. cit.*, p.273.

21 THE PRINCE, DUTCH POWER CENTRES AND GERMANY

FRENCH INTRIGUES IN THE REPUBLIC

If William was convinced that the Treaty of Nijmegen would not put a stop to the ambitions of Louis XIV, Louis equally did not relent in his hostility towards him. When his ambassador, the Count d'Avaux, arrived in The Hague in the autumn of 1679 his instructions were to keep personal relations with the Prince to a minimum; to make plain the acute disfavour with which he was regarded by the King; and to intrigue with the opposition – D'Avaux called them 'the Republicans'. When the ambassador paid visits to the wife of Brederode, who was part of the Orange clan – her mother was the sister of Amalia von Solms-Braunfels – and to the wife of Sommelsdijk, who was also part of the Prince's circle, he was forbidden to do so again. His lobbying of the Holland towns in favour of the French treaty irked both Fagel and the Prince – Fagel regarded this interference as unprecedented and insufferable.[1]

HENDRIK-CASIMIR

There was another source of opposition to Prince William, whom we have already mentioned – his cousin Hendrik-Casimir, the Stadholder of Friesland and Groningen. When his father died in 1664 Hendrik-Casimir was seven years old and his mother, Albertine-Agnes, a daughter of Frederick-Henry, became his guardian until he came of age. He developed a strong antipathy towards his more able cousin William, all the more so as William encroached on what had been regarded as his sphere of influence; in 1672 the Prince became Stadholder of Westerwolde, which had previously been linked to Groningen; in religion the Prince supported the Voetian faction in Friesland, who were in opposition to Hendrik-Casimir and his mother, supporters of the Cocceian; and in 1677 a dispute arose over the taxation and financial administration of the Province of Groningen between the capital city of that name and the surrounding country – the Ommelands – in which the Prince took the side of the Ommelands, with Hendrik-Casimir supporting the city.[2] With the relationship exacerbated by constant quibbling, it was no surprise when the two Provinces of which Hendrik-Casimir was Stadholder – Friesland and Groningen – voted in favour of the French Alliance when it came before the States of Holland in January 1680.[3]

RELATIONS WITH AMSTERDAM

But, although the Prince and the peace party led by Amsterdam had disagreed fundamentally about the Peace of Nijmegen, it would be wrong to exaggerate both the strength of the opposition on other matters and the differences in the period immediately after the signing of the Treaty. At the end of December 1678 Temple had reported to Laurence Hyde that William was 'in perpetual conversation' with the Dutch Regents who 'were thought his enemies' upon matters before they came before the States-General or the towns, 'and during the assembly of the States of Holland, [he] dines every day with the deputies of one town or other, all of which, joined to the sense they have what a rascally peace they have made, and how true advices from the Prince they refused, has very sensibly increased his authority here'. The Prince explained his strategy to Temple: a good union between him and the States was so absolutely necessary for the preservation of both of them and, as he had failed to persuade them on the great matter of the Peace of Nijmegen, he preferred to give way on minor concerns to preserve that essential unity.[4] D'Avaux warned Louis in 1679 that although there were many 'Republicans' opposed to the Prince of Orange they were, with eight or ten exceptions, a feeble lot.[5] Even Valckenier 'and others of his party', Sidney wrote in August that year, 'say they find the Prince much in the right, and they in the wrong'.[6] As we have seen, on the question of whether a treaty should be entered into with France or a guarantee treaty with England, a compromise was in the event reached at the beginning of 1680 to enter into neither.

The Prince used Temple to sound out Amsterdam on the policy it wanted to pursue after the Peace of Nijmegen. Temple found Hooft, who died at the end of 1678, well inclined to maintain unity within the Republic and to support the Prince, as long as he represented the general interest. The only point of difference would be the reduction in troop numbers, although even there he agreed that they would first have to see what France did.[7] In fact the Prince was prepared to yield even in the military sphere. After the conclusion of the Nijmegen Peace Louis XIV reduced his army by half from 280,000 to 140,000 men, although the battalion structures were maintained and could be revived at short notice, and it remained a very large force in comparison with those of the other European states.[8] Financial constraints compelled the Dutch, too, to make substantial reductions, and plans were in hand as early as July 1678 – before the Peace had even been signed – with implementation becoming embodied in succeeding war budgets. At the end of 1679 William admitted to Waldeck that the finances were certainly in great disorder, and, although Amsterdam needed persuading not to press for greater reductions, neither side pushed it towards a rupture.[9] Amsterdam's consent was dependent on the building of new warships to safeguard the trade which was of such importance to her, and to this the States of Holland agreed at the end of May 1680.[10]

A further issue with Amsterdam was settled in diplomatic fashion. Naarden had shown how important this town had been in the defence of the country in 1672 and Prince William thought that its defences needed strengthening. In opposing these plans the Amsterdam Regent Coenraad van Heemskerk had expressed the view that his real objective was to use Naarden to overawe Amsterdam. He was a man of some importance and he was also a nephew of Coenraad van Beuningen. It was a delicate situation and the final outcome was settled by the Prince, who made use of another Amsterdam Regent rising to prominence, Nicolaas Witsen, as an intermediary. In effect William turned a blind eye to Heemskerk's remarks and left the issue of Naarden to be settled by the Holland States.[11]

In due course the emollient Witsen was, with his cousin Johannes Hudde,[12] to succeed Valckenier – who died on 5 November 1680, two years after Hooft – as one of the two leading Regents in Amsterdam. This provided the background against which the opposition of Amsterdam became in due course sufficiently muted to allow the Prince of Orange to invade England in 1688. Nevertheless, before these favourable circumstances developed further, fundamental disagreements on principles were again to arise between the Prince and the powerful town. They were centred on the relationship with Louis XIV and William's attempts to contain him, which ranged over the whole European scene.

BRANDENBURG AFTER THE TREATY OF NIJMEGEN

The Peace of Nijmegen destroyed the grand coalition that William had done so much to create to contain Louis. If he now sought unity in the Republic he also sought to repair relations with the former allies as far as he could; but, as he had always made clear, the manner in which the Dutch had abandoned them would do lasting damage and there were many obstacles to be overcome. But at the personal level he had worked shrewdly and well and with considerable foresight. His own well-known opposition to the Peace, which was hidden from none, left his own credibility and his own *gloire* untarnished.

Spain complained that Maastricht had not been ceded to her, as the 1673 Treaty stipulated – the Dutch States in return said they acquired the town in exchange for the substantial sums owed by Spain to the House of Orange and for naval expenditure incurred by themselves.[13] Spain, however, was in so weak a position and so dependent upon the Dutch that this was an issue that could be left outstanding.

More important and more difficult was the matter of the Elector of Brandenburg, who considered that he had been betrayed by his allies. In February 1679 the Emperor ended the war with France on the basis of the Treaty of Westphalia, which implied the return to Sweden of all the Elector's hard-won conquests in Pomerania. In March Louis XIV sent an army into Cleves to force his hand, and at the end of the month the States-General refused him any assistance.[14] At last Frederick-William, submitting to reality, signed the Treaty of St-Germain on 29 June 1679. The Pomeranian conquests were given back to Sweden, with the Elector obtaining some frontier adjustments in return.[15] He lost no time in planning his vengeance, and on 2 July he ordered Meinders, who had negotiated the Treaty of St-Germain, to remain in Paris, to negotiate the closest possible alliance with the King of France. 'It is not the king of France who forced me to the peace', he asserted to one of his courtiers, 'but the Emperor, the Empire, and my closest relations and allies, who however will repent of it one day, seeing what they have driven me to do, and their loss in this will be as great as mine.'[16]

He had no illusions about France. 'For France', he wrote to Schwerin on 11 August, 'we have, as is well known, no reason to have any special affection, let alone to further her aggrandisement, while the French yoke is well known to us', but the abandonment by the allies, particularly the Emperor, Spain and the Dutch, left France as the arbiter, so that there was no alternative but to seek his security in her friendship and alliance.[17] On 25 October France and the Elector signed a second, secret, treaty at St-Germain under which the French undertook to protect his territories, French troops were allowed to cross these and he promised to vote for the French candidate in any Imperial election. Important though this latter stipulation seems, it needs to be remembered that Leopold I was still comparatively young (he was 39 years old) and any election might not take place for some considerable time.[18]

At the same time the Elector did not entirely close the door on the Dutch; and nor did Prince William entirely close the door on him. In August 1679 he had written to the States-General complaining of his treatment and the Prince wrote in return a friendly letter a month later taking up his suggestion that representatives from both sides should meet to resolve the differences and even suggesting that he should meet the Elector personally.[19] The outcome of this was that Van Amerongen – he had, of course, a long acquaintance with the Elector, who had also stayed with him on his Dutch visit in 1675 – was sent to Berlin in the middle of December to begin a lengthy negotiation, which for the time being proved fruitless, and of which he fully informed the Prince. The two main issues were the outstanding subsidies owed by the Dutch to the Elector and the damages he suffered from the invasion by the French of Cleves and Marck, for which he wanted the Dutch to compensate him. Matters were not facilitated by the frequent attacks of gout to which he was increasingly susceptible.[20] Always fiery and irascible, he was now more so than ever; and the bond with him was loosened by the death in December 1679 of Prince Maurits of Nassau-Siegen in Cleves, where he had been the Elector's governor and whom he had served in so many other roles.[21] That other supporter of the Dutch connection, Polnitz, also died that year.[22]

The bond was loosened, but not broken. William did his best to maintain relations with the Elector and his court – he arranged for Meinders's son to be appointed Prebendary at the cathedral of Utrecht[23] – and in September 1680 he notified the Elector that he had received an invitation from the Duke of Celle to visit him and suggested that this could be combined with a visit to his uncle as well, the suggestion that he had made a year earlier. To this the Elector replied that nothing would be more agreeable for him than to see the Prince and hold talks with him personally – although he advised him to avoid Magdeburg or Halle, which William had suggested as venues, because of the plague and dysentery prevailing there.[24]

WILLIAM'S VISIT TO NORTHERN GERMANY

Thus the Prince embarked on his trip to Northern Germany. His purpose was diplomatic, to mend relations with his Elector uncle and to persuade him to join the anti-French alliance that Sunderland was trying to negotiate at this stage so that he could present Parliament with a grand anti-French coalition; and also – although we do not have direct evidence – to cement relations with the Brunswick dukes of Hanover with the same intent. In the event, there is no denying that the expedition also turned very much into a journey of pleasure. We know a great deal about the pleasure because of the diary kept by Constantijn Huygens, and much less about the diplomacy, particularly with the Hanoverian dukes; historians have played down the statecraft in favour of highlighting the diversions. It was not, however, in the nature of Prince William to have no serious intent. Certainly the composition of his retinue, which consisted almost entirely of members of the Orange-Nassau clan or its clients, suggests that prestige and the display of the extent of the clan's reach in Germany, bringing with it the hint of what it could do for the Dutch Regents if the Prince chose to put it at their disposal, were important motives. More important still, the lengthy time devoted to the visit – it lasted eight weeks – when there were many compelling matters afoot, not least in England, indicates the significance the Prince attached to it as an important diplomatic attempt to reconstruct the anti-French alliance.

CELLE

William began his journey on 16 September, having taken leave of the States-General on the 14th, and, travelling via his domains in Lingen, he arrived outside Celle on the 22nd.[25] There he was met by the Duke, George William – one of the three Hanoverian dukes – with a military escort, and conducted to the Duke's *château* at the end of the town. He bestowed fulsome greetings on the Duchess, who was covered in diamonds – she was very large for a woman, Huygens observed – and, according to Sir Gabriel Sylvius, who was of the party, she very much influenced her husband in the French interest. At the beginning of the year Sylvius had been sent by Charles II to the Hanoverian dukes to try to persuade them to participate in Sunderland's anti-French alliance.[26] The Prince's entourage also included Ginkel, the son of Amerongen; the Count of Solms; the Count of Nassau – a general in the Dutch cavalry – and William's cousin Nassau-Ouwekerk. Waldeck had also arrived; apart from his wide-ranging connections in Germany he had, as we know, particularly close relations with the Celle court, part of his earlier career having been devoted to its service. The Duke kept a good table and during supper music was played.

The next day the hunting began at 8 o'clock in the morning, and, with Waldeck there, Huygens assumed that business was discussed, although, if so, we have no record of it. The midday meal was lavish, with roast oysters, ortolans, cakes, hares, partridges and skylarks. Although Prince William had a cold and a headache this did not prevent him killing a considerable number of deer and attending a comedy – Huygens thought the actors not particularly good.

Sir Gabriel Sylvius, in the meantime, appeared very anxious to find out Mary's state of health and whether she was likely to have children. Whilst a long-standing client of the Orange family, from whose principality he hailed, he was acting in this instance, it was thought, on behalf of Charles II, who had in him an informer who could keep him abreast on this and, no doubt, other matters.

The Prince's party stayed three weeks in Celle; the hunting continued day after day – it was hard and dangerous riding, with many falls and scratched faces – and the entertainment was well maintained, although it did not cause William to neglect his political and diplomatic correspondence, as we can see from the archives. As in any court there were petty jealousies, with the younger Zuylenstein and Nassau-Ouwekerk resenting the favour the Prince showed Bentinck. And the Prince indulged his enjoyment of gambling at the table, which, like hunting, was one of his major forms of relaxation – gambling, indeed, and the calculation of odds, is no bad trait in a man of action, as Winston Churchill also discovered.

BRANDENBURG

Departing, William and his party travelled through muddy roads, small, dirty places and wild country to Brandenburg. Van Amerongen came to find him and when they met the Elector, who had also travelled to meet them despite his customary gout, they entered an open carriage, regardless of the pouring rain, to travel to Potsdam on 17 October. There they found the Electoral residence pleasantly situated on the Havel river surrounded by a large park planted with oak trees, and the Prince was ensconced in a well-ordered chamber. Whilst he conducted business with his uncle, Huygens took an excursion to Berlin and inspected the Elector's art collection, which included pictures by Van Dyck and Rubens – critical as ever, Huygens, whose father was a noted connoisseur, seemed doubtful of the attributions made for a large number of others. He also looked at the Elector's collection of prints, his library and his manuscripts. The improvement in the Elector's finances in the course of his reign enabled him to maintain a court in greater style; it was modelled on the Orange court, rather than Versailles, with the artists and craftsmen he used originating mainly from the Netherlands, which reflected Frederick-William's Dutch orientation despite his current diplomatic alignment with France. This continued despite the death of his first, Dutch, wife, William of Orange's aunt, Louise-Henrietta, in July 1667 and his subsequent marriage to Duchess Dorothea of Brunswick-Hanover nine months later.[27]

The stay with Frederick-William lasted a little under a week, until 23 October. Sir Robert Southwell, the English ambassador in Berlin, who had arrived there in May, had been trying to persuade him to join Sunderland's anti-French alliances.[28] Prince William tried to convince his uncle of the merits of this;[29] but Frederick-William thought relations between

Charles II and his Parliament would make England an uncertain ally.[30] Moreover, he had told Southwell of the threats that faced him: Sweden's enmity was 'immortal', there were the dukes of Brunswick and the Elector of Saxony who were eyeing some of his territories, and Jan Sobieski, the King of Poland, was a client of France – thus his need of an army, as he told Southwell.[31] French subsidies contributed to this and he was negotiating another treaty with France at the very time of William's visit. He was keeping the French envoy in Berlin, Rébenac, closely informed of his talks with his nephew; and we learn from this that William, as part of his negotiating tactics, offered to make Frederick-William's third son, Prince Louis, his heir.[32]

At the personal level William was well received and fêted, and if his main object was not achieved, nevertheless he did obtain some concessions from his uncle; the Elector undertook to submit to the arbitration of the States-General and England the dispute he had with Spain – his navy had captured a Spanish ship, the *Carlos II*, off Ostend because of the non-payment of the Spanish debt owing to him – and he promised to return the fortress of Schenkenschans to the Dutch.[33] But, for now, he was not to be deterred from seeking his security in France; on 1 January 1681 he signed another secret treaty with Louis which tied him more closely to the King, and which we will examine in greater detail below.

THE HANOVERIAN DUKES

The homeward journey of William and his party was in contrast to the comparative culture of Berlin and Potsdam and was marked both by a reminder of the savagery of the Thirty Years' War, whose marks still persisted, and by the backwardness that prevailed in the more remote areas of Germany – Huygens commented that generally they found all the places, great or small, dirty and muddy. At Magdeburg, over 30 years after the war had ended, only part of the town had been rebuilt, with the rest remaining in ruins following its sack, when it had been put to the torch and its inhabitants slaughtered, children included. At Wolfenbüttel, a bizarre, eccentric aura prevailed; the party was entertained by the Duke, part of the trio of Hanoverian dukes, with the local church choir singing rather loudly during dinner, accompanied by a small organ and violins; the previous Duke had been in the habit of setting his chancellor on a wooden horse, preparatory to inviting him to dinner; and the meat before their departure was more plentiful than well prepared.

On 26 October they arrived at Celle. There they found the entertainment was on the same lavish scale as on their outward visit, although again, perhaps, it was more distinguished by its robustness than by its refinement. An enormous repast – a pyramid of ortolans was put before the Prince of Orange – was followed by the slaughter of 60 foxes and four small boars, which were not hunted in the conventional sense but driven on to a contraption of ropes and planks held by two men which tossed them high into the air before they were despatched. In the evening there was a play, followed by a ball.

On the 29th they arrived at Hanover itself, where the Prince was received by its Duke, Ernst Augustus, with great ceremony and with a train of 26 coaches-and-six. William's quarters consisted of two antechambers and a bedchamber with high, painted ceilings; tapestries depicting the labours of Hercules adorned the walls, according to Huygens finely worked in gold but badly designed and excessive; and the bed and the chairs were covered in yellow damask fringed with silver. The food was well prepared but all the same not as good as at Celle. Nor was the hunting neglected, this time of boars.

Hanover was the most powerful state in North Germany next to Brandenburg, and Ernst Augustus now also ruled over the Bishopric of Osnabrück.[34] The Duke of Celle arrived and no doubt discussions were held with him and his brother Ernst Augustus; they and the Prince of Orange were all old comrades in arms, as were many in William's retinue, and it must be most probable that William tried to persuade them too to join Sunderland's anti-French coalition. But, if so, the two dukes, like the Elector of Brandenburg, were presumably not persuaded of the reliability of England as an ally – although we have no record of the conversations.

Waldeck did, however, tell Huygens in a long talk at the door of Huygens's chamber that he was being cut out of affairs by William and Fagel, who seemed to want to do everything themselves, and he was contemplating retiring to take care of his own interests. He very much doubted that, if William continued to indulge himself so much in his amusements and hunting, he would be able to re-dedicate himself to business, and this voyage of the Prince had produced no results.

There is, perhaps, a little in this. The Prince had been at the head of affairs throughout a gruelling war and he may have had a – justified – desire to indulge in some relaxation. But we have already argued that the reason for the voyage was far from frivolous; and, if no significant business developed, the relaxation was also part of the strengthening of personal relations with two of the most important dynasties in Germany, the House of Brandenburg and the House of Brunswick.

And, as for Waldeck, he too was human and, neither for the first nor for the last time, he was giving vent to pique which, perhaps inevitably, was bound to arise between men of strong personality and strong ambition. But soon enough his employment was resumed by the Prince personally – not by the Dutch States-General[35] – in incessant travels to the German courts, great and small, to oppose the plans of Louis in Germany and to bring them into a coalition against him with sufficient armed might. His correspondence with William revealed the closeness of their partnership, with the Prince confiding in him his innermost thoughts, and with Waldeck devoting his utmost energy to serving the head of the clan into which he had married. Indeed, both his unrivalled knowledge of the extreme complexity of the relations between the German princes and his own close association with so many of them, including the numerous scions of the House of Orange-Nassau, the Elector of

Brandenburg, the Brunswick dukes, and soon also with the Emperor himself, made him indispensable. It is reasonable to assume that the Prince and the Count discussed the intricate labyrinth of the German scene in detail whilst they were together in that country.

The Prince suffered from minor ailments on these travels – coming back from the hunt on one occasion he felt weak, turned pale and scarcely ate anything. But if he had been in serious ill-health he would not have been able to endure the demands of the hunting, with whole days spent in the saddle, or the travelling. He was much afflicted by piles – as the state of his underwear witnessed. But in 17th-century terms neither this nor the minor ailments were too great an indisposition; certainly he himself does not seem to have regarded them as such, for when he returned to The Hague – he arrived there on 11 November, having first gone to Soestdijk on the 7th – he wrote to Van Amerongen that he was in good health.[36] Many historians have claimed that William suffered from ill-health throughout his life, but there is no contemporary evidence at this stage of his career that he suffered abnormal disabilities by the standards of his time. The working holiday and the hunting seem to have done him good. Indeed, he seems to have enjoyed himself so much that he agreed to go for a second visit to Celle in April 1681, this time joined by Mary. But little business seems to have been conducted, let alone concluded – at least, that we know of. Waldeck was again there, but neither in his memoirs nor in his diary has he left any record of the occasion.[37]

Nevertheless, the hard hunting and the long feasting with these North German rulers led to a bonding at a personal level that was to be of crucial importance in the future.

1 D'Avaux, *Négociations, op. cit.*, I, pp.7–9, 20–1, 28–31. Müller, *Waldeck*, I, pp.101, 105. Wagenaar, *op. cit.*, 15, pp.48–50.
2 Israel, *Dutch Republic, op. cit.*, pp.820–1, 823.
3 Wagenaar, *op. cit.*, 15, pp.48–50.
4 S.W. Singer, ed., *The Correspondence of H.H. Earl of Clarendon, and of his brother, Laurence Hyde, Earl of Rochester*, London 1828, I, pp.37–8, 40.
5 D'Avaux, *Négociations, op. cit.*, I, p.19.
6 Sidney, *op. cit.*, I, pp.47–8.
7 Kurtz, *op. cit.*, p.22.
8 Rousset, *op. cit.*, III, p.5.
9 Japikse, *Willem III, op. cit.*, II, pp.134–5. Müller, *Waldeck, op. cit.*, I, pp.103ff.
10 Kurtz, *op. cit.*, p.27.
11 J.F. Gebhard, *Het Leven van Nicolaas Witsen*, Utrecht 1881, pp.154ff.
12 *Ibid.*, p.168.
13 The issue is dealt with at length in Wagenaar, *op. cit.*, 15, pp.5ff.
14 Troost, in *The Anglo-Dutch Moment, op. cit.*, pp.310–11.
15 Waddington, *op. cit.*, II, pp.428–9.
16 *Ibid.*, II, pp.437–8.

17 Martin Philippson, *Der Grosse Kurfürst Friedrich Wilhelm von Brandenburg*, Berlin 1903, III, pp.252–3 n.1.

18 Waddington, *op. cit.*, II, pp.441–2. Philippson, *op. cit.*, III, p.264. But Troost, in *The Anglo-Dutch Moment, op. cit.*, p.313, says there were 'Rumours that the health of Leopold I was declining'.

19 Wagenaar, *op. cit.*, 15, p.20–22. *Correspondentie Willem III en Bentinck, op. cit.*, II, 2, pp.298–9.

20 Much of Amerongen's correspondence is contained in *Correspondentie Willem III en Bentinck, op. cit.*, II, 2, pp.300ff. See also Philippson, *op. cit.*, III, p.271.

21 Wagenaar, *op. cit.*, 15, p.37.

22 Waddington, *op. cit.*, II, p.468.

23 *Correspondentie Willem III en Bentinck, op. cit.*, II, 2, pp.348, 357.

24 *Ibid.*, II, 2, pp.358–9.

25 For this voyage see Huygens, *Voyage de Cell* etc., 1680, *Werken van het Historish Genootschap Gevestid te Utrecht*, New Series, 46, from which many of the details of this account are drawn.

26 *Register op de Journalen van Constantijn Huygens den Zoon, Hist. Gen. Utrecht*, 3rd Series, 35, Amsterdam 1915, Entry for Sylvius.

27 McKay, *The Great Elector, op. cit.*, pp.233–4.

28 Philippson, *op. cit.*, III, p.276.

29 *Correspondentie Willem III en Bentinck, op. cit.*, II, 2, p.372.

30 Philippson, *op. cit.*, III, p.281.

31 McKay, *The Great Elector, op. cit.*, p.243.

32 Troost in *The Anglo-Dutch Moment, op. cit.*, p.316.

33 Waddington, *op. cit.*, II, p.454.

34 Müller, *Waldeck, op. cit.*, I, p.69.

35 *Ibid.*, I, p.70.

36 *Correspondentie Willem III en Bentinck, op. cit.*, II, 2, p.374.

37 Japikse, *Willem III, op. cit.*, II, pp.141–2. Müller, *Waldeck, op. cit.*, I, p.69.

22 1679–1682: NEITHER WAR NOR PEACE

Between 1679 and 1682 William of Orange was determined to continue to confront Louis XIV of France and the King's encroachments, as he saw it, on the integrity of Europe. In this he needed to have regard not only to the internal politics of Britain and the Dutch Republic but also to the relationships between the powers of Europe across the Continent. It was an intriguing and complex challenge and how he handled it, and its multifarious interactions, is the subject of this chapter.

LOUIS XIV'S *RÉUNIONS*

We have traced the Prince's focus on England and the exclusion crisis up to the end of his visit to his English uncles on 15 August 1681. These events in England were taking place at the same time as Louis XIV was inverting Clausewitz's famed dictum that war is the continuation of politics by other means; Louis, at this time, was using the peace to secure, to consolidate and to extend his frontiers in a manner which he had not been able to do by means of the Dutch War. The Treaty of Nijmegen had left many matters vague, and so too – Louvois's ingenuity was soon to discover – had the Treaty of Westphalia, which could be used to the advantage of France.

A conference had been summoned at Courtrai in December 1679 to clarify what the Peace Treaty had left undefined; and from the beginning it became clear that it was likely to continue interminably. In fact it lasted more than two years; and this suited Louvois, for the Courtrai conference dealt with matters in the Spanish Netherlands and his primary concern – for the moment – lay on the frontiers of the Mosel and the Rhine.[1]

In June 1679 he wrote to Louis that it was his intention to extend the King's domains through, as he put it, pursuing 'the true meaning' of the Treaty of Westphalia, and he used the same principle to reinterpret the Treaty of Nijmegen. For this purpose he made use of the Parlements – the sovereign courts – of Besançon, Brisach and Metz, soon to be called in common parlance the *chambres de réunions*. Their task was to investigate the historic documentation pertaining to the places and territories which the treaties had granted to France. It was not long before they discovered long-forgotten feudal and other rights that extended Louis's sovereignty far beyond what appeared to be the case and far beyond what had been accepted as the frontiers of France – the places subject to these rights were to be reunited to their true possessor, now the King of France, hence *réunions*. Those affected were not just minor gentry but included magnates such as the Elector Palatine, the Elector of Trier, the King of Spain – as the Duke of Luxemburg – and the King of Sweden – as heir to the Duchy of Zweibrücken. Some were dispossessed immediately, other were summoned to perform acts of homage, failing which dispossession followed.[2]

It was not Louvois alone who was engaged in the *réunions*. On 18 November 1679, Pomponne, Louis's more emollient Foreign Minister, was dismissed and replaced by Colbert de Croissy, the brother of his Finance Minister. A lawyer by background, he had been a Vice-President of the Parlement of Metz and an Intendant in Alsace where he had been engaged in the study of documents relating to the legal rights of the territories. He was rude and short-tempered, and the addition of his character traits to those of the ruthless Louvois was not calculated to ease the presentiments of those who had to deal with the King of France. With the exception of Strasburg, Alsace had, by August 1680, become part of France[3] – and Strasburg too was to follow just over a year later.

Apart from the diplomatic damage that these acquisitions caused, they, and what was to follow, played havoc with Vauban's plans for a *pré carré* – a regular and defensible frontier system based on rational principles – for the acquisitions were arrayed in higgledy-piggledy fashion.[4] If, as has been claimed, Louis's motives were essentially defensive, they were certainly muddled, and he managed to present himself as pre-eminently aggressive. In the eyes of many of his contemporaries, he was perceived as having obtained the summit of power and the insolence of pride was now doing its work. Certainly that was how the Prince of Orange saw it, and it is easy to see why.

His feelings were furthermore bound to be exasperated when, although it was not part of the *réunions*, Louis in 1680 ordered the occupation once again of his Principality of Orange – it had been occupied during the war as well. The town was now dismantled, sovereignty devolved to the King, and possession of the fief was put in suspense, pending the outcome of a court case to decide a claim brought by the Duchess of Nemours. When William sent Anthonie Heinsius to Paris to demand justice – he refused to submit the matter to Louis's beneficence – Louvois threatened Heinsius (who was in due course to succeed Gaspar Fagel as Pensionary of Holland) with the Bastille.[5]

BRANDENBURG AND SWEDEN

We have seen that on 11 January 1681 Louis had entered into another treaty with the Elector of Brandenburg. Under its terms the Elector guaranteed all the King's rights which he enjoyed *or ought to enjoy* (my italics) under the Treaty of Nijmegen, that is to say, he was giving Louis a blank cheque for his acquisitions under the *réunions*. Furthermore, both sides agreed to come to each other's aid if their territories, rights *or claims* (my italics again) were challenged, without enquiry into the merits of the case. The Elector received the promise of Louis's aid if he were attacked by Spain on the issue of the *Carlos II*; he received a higher subsidy, and he would receive French support for the claims of the sons of his first wife as heirs to the Prince of Orange.[6] This provided a *quid pro quo* for the Elector's commitment to vote for the French candidate in any Imperial election under his treaty with France of 25 October 1680.

But in Sweden things were moving the Dutch way. There the young King, Charles XI, reappraised the French alliance and concluded that unwavering adherence to it had contributed to Sweden's financial and military weakness. On 10 June 1680 Johan Gyllenstierna, the Swedish minister who had favoured the alliance, died and authority devolved on Bengt Oxenstierna, who became Chancellor. With his assistance the King addressed his finances to obviate the need for foreign subsidies and embarked on a series of reforms that aimed to weaken the aristocracy and establish royal supremacy. This meant peace in Europe, in so far as it was attainable, and Oxenstierna, who took over the conduct of foreign policy and who had been a Swedish representative at the conference of Nijmegen, deemed this inconsistent with Sweden's attaching herself to the warlike Louis XIV. Instead he wished to pursue a defensive foreign policy based on the maintenance of the Treaties of Westphalia and Nijmegen.

At the beginning of October 1680, with the agreement of the King, he informed the Council of the change of course. On April 1681 the Duke of Zweibrücken died and to the Swedish King's consternation he found that, when he laid claim to the Duchy as his inheritance, the Parlement of Metz judged it to be a fief of France; in August Louis XIV appropriated it as part of the *réunions*. Although in the following years he did not take actual possession the damage was done. Negotiations were already well under way with the Dutch – D'Avaux had got wind of them in March – and on 11 June Caspar Fagel presented the Swedish ambassador in The Hague with a definitive draft treaty, which, however, still needed to be approved by the States-General.[7]

LOUIS'S BLOCKADE OF LUXEMBURG

In July 1681, the French now also turned their attention not just to their eastern frontier on the Rhine and the Mosel but to their northern frontier with the Spanish Netherlands as well. The court of Metz lit upon the county of Chiny – the most important fief of the Duchy of Luxemburg, which belonged to the King of Spain – as having once belonged to the Bishopric of Metz.

It incidentally contained two manors of the Prince of Orange, of which he was to be dispossessed for refusing to pay allegiance for them to the King of France, and they were allocated to the Marshal d'Humières – a not indifferent matter for the Elector of Brandenburg either, for they had been promised to his son, Louis, under his agreement with France.

The Metz court's decision regarding Chiny was conveyed to the Prince de Chimay, the Spanish governor of Luxemburg, accompanied by the demand for the immediate withdrawal of Spanish troops from the county. Chimay, backed by the Prince of Parma, the governor of the Spanish Netherlands, refused, and this refusal was followed by four corps of French cavalry occupying Spanish territory, where they lived off the land. It was enough to persuade Chimay in August to withdraw some civilian and military personnel from Chiny, which was occupied by the French. But this proved an insufficient concession. The court of Metz ascertained that there was also a whole chain of subsidiary fiefs which covered the whole of the Duchy of Luxemburg, save for the town itself, and 14 or 15 isolated villages.[8]

It remained for Louis to establish a valid claim to Luxemburg itself and, as none existed, some ingenuity was required, which compelled him to adopt a roundabout route. On 4 August he demanded Aalst and a number of villages in Spanish Flanders on the grounds that he had captured them in the war and that they were accordingly his by right of conquest. Nevertheless, as they would have penetrated the 'barrier' which protected the Dutch under the Treaty of Nijmegen, Louis was prepared to exchange them for an equivalent elsewhere – Luxemburg was not specified, although it was assumed that this was what the French had in mind, even though this, too, presented a threat to the United Provinces. Spain pointed out that Louis had evacuated the places he claimed after the war and there was no mention of them in the Treaty of Nijmegen. But this availed her nothing – the French began a blockade of Luxemburg.[9]

The city possessed strategic importance for France, for Germany and for the Dutch Republic. The Prince of Orange was particularly aware of the threat it could present to the Republic – at the instigation of Fagel the States-General had warned Charles II as early as 21 March 'that although the town of Luxemburg seems to be situated far away, it is the only barrier that covers this State from that side'[10] – and it was an important reason for his journey to England in this very month of August, when he tried to enlist the support of the English King to confront the danger.

The assurances that the Prince received from Charles that he would summon Parliament and declare war on France if Louis invaded the Spanish Low Countries seem to have overcome the earlier suspicion he had expressed to Sidney in February that he thought Charles had taken his steps with France. This, as we know, was in fact the case and William had been duped by his uncle. According to D'Avaux he assured the States-General on his return of Charles's amity and that there was no collusion nor secret intelligence between the Kings of France and England. Charles, he said, had declared that, although the remedies at his disposal would take time because of the differences between him and his Parliament, nonetheless if all the representations that he made to Louis XIV were of no effect and if France continued with its *réunions*, he would declare war against Louis.

William asked the States-General to order their ambassador in France to make strong representations jointly with the English.[11] He also told the States of Holland that he had met several of the most esteemed members of both Houses of Parliament, whom he had advised to come to an accommodation with Charles and whom he had found appreciative of the very dangerous state of affairs on the Continent; they would be pleased to settle their differences with the King and the Duke of York; and he hoped that as soon as Parliament were recalled unity could be established in England.[12]

On the day the Prince made his address to the Holland States – on 21 August – they resolved that the treaty with Sweden should be concluded as soon as possible; and the other Provinces agreed – with the exception of Groningen, which was later joined by Friesland.[13]

FRENCH OCCUPATION OF STRASBURG

On the night of 27–28 September 1681 French dragoons occupied the redoubt on the Rhine closest to Strasburg; on the 30th Strasburg, which until now had remained an independent republic, surrendered to Louvois; and at 4 o'clock that afternoon the troops of Louis XIV took possession of the town. The King now controlled, with Philippsburg, the only two crossings over the Rhine.[14] On the same day his troops took possession of Casale, which the Duke of Mantua had ceded for 100,000 Spanish *pistoles*. Strasburg opened the way to Germany, Casale the way to Italy, and each respectively threatened the two branches of the House of Habsburg, Austria and – through its possessions in Italy – Spain.

Hearing the news the following day at his *coucher* Louis indulged himself in the pleasantry that, if Louvois spent the night there, Strasburg must now indeed be entirely secure. On 24 October he arrived with his usual magnificence, with his Queen, with the Princes and Princesses of the blood, and with all his household troops. He had been preceded four days earlier by his client, Wilhelm-Egon von Fürstenberg, the influential adviser to the Bishop of Cologne, who took his place as the Catholic Bishop of Strasburg.[15]

ASSOCIATION TREATY BETWEEN THE DUTCH AND SWEDEN

Under the pressure of these events the Dutch signed the treaty with Sweden on 10 October, with Groningen and Friesland abstaining. The treaty was to last 20 years and it envisaged that several other states should join the Dutch and Swedes. It stipulated that the signatories would maintain the peace on the basis of the Treaties of Westphalia and Nijmegen; should the peace be disturbed then the signatories would offer their good offices to reconcile the parties in conflict; and if this did not succeed they would resort to military means – although, and this was the weakness in the treaty, these were not spelled out. If one of the signatories were attacked as a result of their intervention the others would come to their aid. France could join this 'Association' and it was claimed that the treaty was not aimed at her.[16] That, however, was not the way France saw it and she exerted every endeavour to prevent its ratification.

D'Avaux entered into intrigues with Hendrik-Casimir to stiffen the opposition of Friesland and Groningen and he turned, too, to Amsterdam. But there he found that his arguments that the Association Treaty was essentially directed at France found no support. Van Beuningen, with his usual fiery animation, played an important role in persuading his home town to resist French blandishments – indeed, encountering some resistance at a meeting of the town council on 2 October, he threatened to resign, to sell all his property and to leave the country. In fact the town council had already, on 18 August, approved the Association, but all opposition was now removed and Van Beuningen persuaded first Witsen and then the other Regents to support the Association Treaty on 4 October. But the premise on which both Van Beuningen and Amsterdam acted was that England would also become a member, a false assumption, which was to have important consequences.

Whilst lacking the forceful character of Valckenier, Nicolaas Witsen and his relation, Johannes Hudde, were rising to prominence in Amsterdam. Hudde had indeed been a Burgomaster as far back as 1672, whilst Witsen was to become one in February 1682.[17] They were, however, overshadowed at this stage by Van Beuningen – an intensely religious Protestant – who was profoundly affected by an edict of Louis XIV on 17 June 1681, which induced children of seven years or more to become Roman Catholics against the wishes of their parents. The edict also worked on the mood of the other Regents in Amsterdam, who on 20 September passed a resolution granting citizenship to the increasing number of Huguenot refugees from France.[18]

The good relations at this stage between William and Amsterdam were reflected in an official visit which he and Mary paid to the city, where their lavish entertainment lasted three days.[19]

The Prince wrote to Waldeck on 23 October sending him a copy of the Association Treaty. Although, he said, it was only a simple guarantee of the Treaties of Westphalia – a reference to the lack of detailed military measures for its enforcement – it was a step towards creating a league, and, once one knew who was prepared to join it, one could easily embody stronger measures afterwards. The Emperor, he said, would join it, and so would England – he was to be proved wrong on this. Denmark and Brandenburg had been invited, he had written to Celle and Hanover, and he asked Waldeck if he knew of any other princes who might wish to be included.[20]

ATTEMPTS TO PERSUADE CHARLES TO INTERVENE ON THE CONTINENT

At William's urging Van Beuningen was despatched as extraordinary ambassador to London, where he arrived on 18 October 1681, to join the existing ordinary ambassador, Van Citters, and bring his force of personality to bear to persuade Charles II to join the Association.

There, after the dissolution of the Oxford Parliament, Charles had continued with his assault on the Whigs, but his measures remained incomplete and whilst that was the case he was not yet wholly master of his kingdom. It was true that a programme for replacing the Justices of the Peace left the Tories supreme by the end of the summer, but the local militias were still being restructured, plans for the replacement of sheriffs were still unfinished, and a commission for Church appointments was established only in July – it included Archbishop

Sancroft and Bishop Compton, who was then the Bishop of London. The work was still in the making; in particular new corporation charters were required to restructure the governments of the towns to reduce the influence of the Whigs and to influence elections to Parliament. The most important town was London, which remained under Whig control, and where the King's weakness was soon to be demonstrated. Here the sheriffs were elected, not appointed, and on 4 December a London Grand Jury, chosen by the sheriffs and dominated by Whigs, acquitted Shaftesbury.

The King's two most important ministers were Halifax and Hyde. Of these Halifax seemed on the surface the most significant, not least because of the speech he had made in the House of Lords which had led to the rejection of exclusion. But he was the proponent of limitations on James's powers if he became King, he wanted the recall of Parliament and he championed robust opposition to Louis XIV. In practice, back-stage, it was Hyde in foreign policy who wielded much the greater influence and it was he who was used by Charles in his clandestine negotiations with the French, of which Halifax was ignorant. As was his wont, therefore, Charles pursued two contradictory policies at the same time, but increasingly in favour of Louis.

On 21 October Halifax told the Prince on behalf of the King that although, 'in the condition he is in', it was in his interest to avoid war, 'as farre as it may be done by fayre and honourable means', nevertheless if Louis did anything further that appeared to be 'a plaine violation of the peace in relation to the Spanish Netherlands' he would be ready to join with the States to take 'proper' measures and he would recall Parliament.

On 26 October the Dutch ambassadors submitted a formal memorandum to the King asking him to join the Association. This put Charles in a difficult position; he had his commitments to Louis XIV, and he did not want to summon Parliament, but nor did he wish to be seen giving Louis a free hand on the Continent. He thus played for time and the Dutch memorandum was submitted to a commission, which engaged in drawn-out discussions with the ambassadors.

Finally, a draft reply was prepared, although Charles and Hyde first agreed it privately with the French ambassador, Barillon – Halifax and the other ministers remained in ignorance of this – after which it was submitted to the Dutch on 18 November. In this Charles sidestepped the issue by stating that once the Emperor, the King of Denmark and the most important princes of the Empire had entered the Association he would be ready to follow suit. To add force to this a declaration was added – the Dutch were in future to refer to it as the King's Declaration of 18 November – that Parliament would be summoned if any claim was made, or any considerable district or town was annexed, in the Spanish Netherlands. But Hyde had in fact assured Barillon privately that Charles had no intention either of entering the Association or of summoning Parliament, and Hyde claimed that 'what [the King] had said left him at liberty to act as he pleased'.[21]

The French now brought pressure on Charles to desist from opposing their seizure of Luxemburg. Although Charles retorted that it would force him to summon his Parliament, otherwise it would be said that 'he had betrayed the interests of England, and sold to [Louis] the most important place in the Low Countries', his resistance did not last long. On 1 December he undertook to raise no objections and for this he was to receive 1 million *livres* (£77,000).[22] Again, Hyde was the only one of Charles's ministers who had knowledge of this.[23] The Duke of York had written to William from his exile in Scotland on 6 November, in reply to a letter from his nephew, that he shared his alarm,[24] although by the early months of 1682 his views were to come into alignment with those of the King.

On 8 December a conference took place in London attended by the Dutch and Spanish ambassadors and by Halifax and the two English Secretaries of State, Sir Lionel Jenkins and the Earl of Conway – until he became Lord Privy Seal in October 1682 Halifax did not hold high office and acted solely in his capacity as a member of the Privy Council. At the conference the Spanish asked that Charles and the Dutch should each send 8,000 men to their aid, in accordance with their respective treaties with Spain. Halifax agreed the treaties should be observed and good faith should be kept, but when the meeting was reported to Charles he said he could not act until he was confident that Parliament would provide the finance, whereupon the Dutch ambassadors urged the immediate recalling of Parliament. A compromise was reached on the 10th under which it was agreed that a joint memorandum should again be presented to Louis at Versailles by the Dutch and English representatives requesting him to raise the blockade of Luxemburg – a memorandum which, of course, was rather at variance with Charles's recent undertakings to Louis.[25]

The King completely duped Halifax, who wrote to William that day that he hoped that the memorandum 'will incline your Hignesse not to despayre altogether so much of us, as you may have done for the time past…. I do truly believe that, if upon the representation intended to be made to the King of France, there shall not bee some reasonable satisfaction given in the matter of Luxemburg, his Ma. will call a Parliament, without which hee is in no condition of making good the least of his ingagements to his Allyes.'[26]

Hyde, although fully in cahoots with Charles's duplicity, nevertheless also wrote to the Prince saying that he did not expect a satisfactory reply from France and therefore reckoned on a Parliament being summoned in a short time.[27]

No immediate reply was received from Louis, a delay which was at first caused by the absence of a Dutch representative at Versailles. But a second delay arose when Louis refused to receive a joint memorandum and insisted on separate ones from each of the two countries. Halifax rightly concluded in a letter to William on 22 January 1682 that this trivial reason for postponement meant a refusal would be forthcoming and that, if that were the case, the only remaining remedy would seem to be the recall of Parliament.[28]

Charles in the meantime had hit upon a solution, as it seemed to him, to the dilemma with which he was faced. On 15 January Barillon reported to Louis that he had proposed that he should act as arbiter in the dispute between France and Spain under which he would induce Spain to cede Luxemburg to France as an equivalent for all Louis's other claims. The proposal was conditional on Louis's demolition of Luxemburg's fortifications and his agreement that England and the Dutch Republic should become guarantors of the treaty which was to embody the proposal.[29]

After separate memoranda were eventually presented to him by the English and the Dutch, Louis's response, by means of a *mémoir* from Barillon on 4 February 1682, was, as Halifax had anticipated, a rejection of the request that he lift the blockade of Luxemburg. Instead it embodied part of the proposal Charles had made to Barillon; he was prepared to forgo all his claims in the Spanish Netherlands in exchange for Luxemburg, whose defences he was prepared to demolish;[30] but there was no mention of Charles's arbitration. And in the meantime the blockade of Luxemburg continued.

Charles thus continued to be faced with his quandary – on the one hand there was his promise to William and the Dutch to summon Parliament, which he wished to avoid at all costs; on the other hand there was his commitment to Louis XIV not to oppose the seizure of Luxemburg. Faced with this choice he took a further step towards his French cousin and patron. On 6 February Van Beuningen and Van Citters reported that he was not prepared to call a Parliament.

DIVISIONS IN THE DUTCH REPUBLIC

Charles's refusal to call Parliament was to have a profound effect on Dutch politics, for it changed the views of Van Beuningen, which now began to diverge from those of the Prince of Orange. He was a much more potent force than any of the other Amsterdam Regents and he wrote to the Prince on the 10th saying that, as the King himself admitted that without Parliament he could do nothing to assist his allies, evidently, without England being in a position to act, France could do anything with sufficient certainty of success as to make her supremacy irresistible. He suggested that, as divisions within Germany stood in the way of reaching an overarching settlement of all the parties – Spain as well as Germany – who had outstanding disputes with France, Spain should be pressed to settle separately.[31] This ran completely counter to the Prince of Orange's policy of maintaining unity amongst Louis's opponents by negotiating the settlement of the German questions conjointly with the Spanish, thus blocking Louis's pursuit of a policy of divide and rule.

Like the English King, the Dutch, too, were soon to be faced with a quandary of their own. On 11 February 1682 the Spanish ambassador in The Hague, De Fuen-Major, delivered a memorandum reminding the States-General of their treaty obligations under which mutual assistance was promised if either side were attacked, and he now requested the aid of the 8,000 men stipulated by the treaty. We may note that William had managed to get the

William III as Prince of Orange, in garter robes, c. 1682, in the manner of Sir Peter Lely.
Chirk Castle, Wrexham

States of Holland to pass a resolution on 31 December 1681 to strengthen the Dutch army, although only for six months. To meet the Spanish request would naturally bring with it the risk of war with France and, although William thought that the request should nevertheless be complied with, he decided to sound out Nicolaas Witsen on the views of Amsterdam before the matter came before the Holland States and the States-General.

Witsen – we have his notes of the meeting with William, which also took place on the 11th – thought Dutch interests 'should come before all else and that nothing should, or could be, done, without England'. A definite reply to Spain should be delayed whilst further efforts took place at the English court and elsewhere, and during the delay an appropriate settlement, if that were possible, should be worked on. The Prince said it would not be possible to induce Spain to come to an agreement and she would rather surrender all – an allusion to Spain's swapping the Low Countries for an equivalent elsewhere, which would have brought Louis to the doorstep of the Dutch Republic.

Shortly afterwards the French ambassador, D'Avaux, submitted his own memorandum, in which he warned that the Spanish request could bring war in its wake.[32]

His lobbying was reflected in the bearing of Friesland, one of whose Regents, Van Sevenaar, approached Witsen on 16 February on behalf of the Province – she wanted to induce Spain to bow to the French proposals. Van Sevenaar had discussed these with D'Avaux and the resulting peace, he argued, would obviate the need for maintaining burdensome Dutch garrisons on the frontiers. In a reference to the methods used by the Prince of Orange and of Fagel in governing the country he complained that two or three people settled everything in the committees of the States-General; and that Gelderland, Overijssel and Utrecht gave way to the Prince on all points, whilst anyone in those Provinces who found themselves in disagreement absented themselves from meetings rather than give tacit approval by their attendance. Witsen, characteristically, responded with great politeness, but urged the need for unity and the need to stick to one line.[33]

DETERIORATING RELATIONS BETWEEN CHARLES AND THE PRINCE OF ORANGE

The extent of how far relations between the Prince and Charles II were deteriorating was now demonstrated. The new English ambassador, Thomas Chudleigh, had at last arrived in The Hague on 15 February 1682 to succeed Sidney – the gap following whose departure in June 1681 had been temporarily filled by Thomas Plott – and prior to the States-General meeting on the 17th he spoke with the Prince in approving terms regarding Barillon's *mémoir* of the 4th. This was met with the Prince telling him that 'he was surprised I should bring such a proposition now as it contained no more than' what had been offered by D'Avaux and Barillon three months previously and had been rejected as unreasonable. 'The States he was very sure would by no means like it.' He went on to say 'that everybody now did see but too

453

plainly that there was an intelligence' between France and England. There was a very sharp response, three days later, to this from Conway on Charles's behalf. 'I am commanded to tell you,' he wrote to Chudleigh, 'and you are to give this answer to the Prince of Orange that it is a method of proceeding which His Majesty did not expect from His Highness and that it is language which none but the worst sort of the King's enemies do give him here.'

There was thus a revival of Charles's fears of William's plotting with the English opposition. And we shall see that it was not going to go away, despite the Prince's attempt to exculpate himself by saying 'that what he had said was not spoken as his sense or belief, but as the sense of others'.[34]

WILLIAM'S MANAGEMENT OF THE STATES-GENERAL

William's control over the States-General at this time was demonstrated when it reflected his views and reacted to Barillon's *mémoir* on 17 February by urging Charles to call Parliament in conformity with his Declaration of 18 November 1681.[35]

On 20 February the Prince invited Witsen to an intimate and wide-ranging discussion, to which it is worth giving a little time.[36] It reveals his anxiety to maintain unity in the Republic in the face of the acute crisis that the blockade of Luxemburg had created, his determination to sustain a dialogue with Amsterdam, the finely balanced arguments on each side of the question on how to react – and the political guile of which he was capable when he set his mind to it.

The Prince, Witsen's notes read, said that the Dutch should keep the word they had given to Spain under their treaty obligations; if they did not do this nobody would ever treat with them again; and failure to do this at the Treaty of Nijmegen had resulted in them and Spain being defeated *en petit*. The Emperor and the German Empire would come to their side. This was by no means an unrealistic view at this stage; the Dutch ambassador in Vienna, Hamel Bruynincx, had reported on 15 February that the Emperor had 40,000 men with a further 22,000 recruits who would be ready in March; that spring Leopold sent 25,000 troops into the Rhineland,[37] and on 28 February he joined the Association Treaty. The Prince went on to argue that the King of England would be forced by his people and by his Parliament to second the Dutch, provided the Dutch were resolute. He was wrong in this assessment, but he was not alone – before March was out Barillon indeed told Louis that Charles would be forced to call Parliament by public opinion if the siege of Luxemburg persisted. The Prince continued that De Witt, who was no friend of his, had taught him, 'kings are permitted to vacillate somewhat, but republics not, if they wished to avoid total ruin'.

From Witsen's point of view there was no hurry – '*qui a tempo a vita*'; Dutch well-wishers in Europe needed to come out into the open, and perhaps agreement could be found with France; nothing could be done without England and she would first need to call Parliament and send troops, and Brandenburg should also participate.

Both Witsen and the Prince knew from Van Beuningen's and Van Citters's despatch of the 6th that Charles had refused to summon Parliament, but William argued that Charles's hand would be forced by his people if the Dutch took action to come to the assistance of Spain. Witsen said that should this not happen – they had seen in the past that Charles was capable of acting against his own interests and those of his people – the 8,000 men would be sent to the aid of Spain only to be destroyed. To William's response that this could be anticipated by keeping them garrisoned in the towns, Witsen pointed to the danger that they could be besieged before England was ready, even if she were prepared to act.

He admitted, however, that not everybody shared his views; His Highness had asked him to speak out, he was not giving any formal advice, but was only engaging in a frank discussion. That was his own position as well, said William, and he had not yet come to a firm view on the matter; for him the consideration that weighed most heavily was internal disagreement; he complained greatly about the behaviour of people in Friesland and Groningen and told of scandalous examples of their corruption and foreign intrigues. He added, between themselves, that as regarded Brandenburg, the French had corrupted everybody from the Elector down to the humble maid who washed the dishes – the Elector's own children complained of it.

When Witsen, however, did not budge from his view that Spain should reach an accommodation with France, William, with considerable wiliness, heightened the note of confidentiality between them on which he had already embarked. He spoke favourably of the Amsterdam Pensionary, Jacob Hop, whom he said he prized highly and whom, if he were a little older, he saw as a possible successor to Fagel, if the latter were to die; at the moment he thought the succession should pass to the Pensionary of Haarlem, Michiel ten Hove. Now, the Pensionary of Holland, like the Prince himself, was supposed to be a servant of the Holland States, yet here William was presuming to nominate, if not dictate, who should fill the most powerful position in the United Provinces next to himself – and he was simultaneously flattering Witsen by inviting him to share in the decision at his side.

Their conversation was interspersed with elegant French and Latin quotations, which further elevated the tone to one appropriate for two statesmen settling the affairs of their country between them. There was undoubtedly a genuine desire on the part of the Prince to use all his powers of persuasion to achieve unity, but, mixed with this, a firm impression remains that he was exploring – and exploiting – by means of flattery a certain weakness in the character of the Amsterdam Regent, which, from his point of view, was to have useful, indeed crucial, consequences in the future.

On 3 March, Thomas Chudleigh, in accordance with his instructions, submitted a memorandum on behalf of Charles II in which the King asked whether Barillon's *mémoir* could not form the basis for negotiation, especially if Louis permitted Luxemburg to be provisioned in the meantime so that it did not fall into his hands, and Charles thought this was so reasonable that it could not be refused. He could not agree with the States-General that his summoning Parliament was the only way to preserve the peace; he questioned whether war would enable England and the Republic to preserve Luxemburg for Spain or enable them to obtain more advantageous terms than those presented by Louis's proposals; and he questioned also whether any assistance that could be expected by means of Parliament could arrive in time.[38] It could not be clearer where Charles II's sympathies lay. Nevertheless, on the advice of Prince William, the States-General persisted in pressing him to call Parliament.[39]

On 5 March the States of Holland were due to meet again and in advance of this D'Avaux devoted half an hour to lobbying Amsterdam. The matter in dispute, he said, on which peace or war depended, hinged on Aalst and some countryside, and Louis had for long wanted to settle this amicably. When the Spaniards had specified what they wanted to retain at Nijmegen no mention was made of these places and, as Louis already occupied them, they fell to his lot. Luxemburg was being blockaded only to bring Spain to reason. Louis otherwise did not want it and would be content with a sufficient equivalent of whatever sort. The King of England was very much inclined to see the reasonableness of this, he claimed, as were five of the German Electors. The Dutch assistance of 8,000 troops could bring nothing to the party except war; Spain could barely add 2,000 men. If the Dutch sent 40,000 it would be a different matter, although it would inevitably lead to war. Any Spanish initiative would be met by Louis's armies occupying the Spanish Netherlands and retaining them − thus, the clear threat was, bringing him to the doorstep of the United Provinces. On the other hand, if agreement were reached he would make certain that all outstanding ambiguities contained in the existing treaties would be resolved and incorporated in a new treaty and guarantee. To this the Amsterdam delegates listened but did not respond.

Their predicament was not eased when they subsequently consulted the representatives of Spain, who assured them that if the Dutch refused the 8,000 troops she would take desperate measures − the threat on their side being that they would swap the Spanish Netherlands for an equivalent elsewhere which, too, would bring Louis to the Dutch doorstep.[40]

At a private meeting with the Amsterdam delegates the Prince complained of Charles II's conduct and his own firm religious convictions came to the fore. He firmly believed, he said, in Divine Predestination and could not believe 'that God had allowed this country to come so far only to allow it to be lost at this time'.[41]

For his part, Charles's old fears that Prince William was plotting with the English opposition had never gone away. At about this time Chudleigh was instructed to track down 'phaticall' members of the Whig party in Amsterdam and elsewhere; a private visit of Sidney to The Hague had also aroused the King's suspicions. 'His Majesty was very sensible', Conway wrote to Jenkins from Newmarket, 'that the Prince of Orange would not carry on affaires in Holland to such a height, nor goe so far to bring a war in Flanders, if he were not encouraged and directed to it by the disaffected party in England, among which he thinks Mr Sidney a great agent.'[42]

On 23 February William complained to Waldeck of the great timidity becoming evident amongst the Dutch, 'caused by the insufferable conduct of England, I vow it leads me to despair seeing that she is the sole cause of the dangers we are in'. On 5 March he wrote that 'The inexcusable conduct of England embarrasses us greatly, as you will see from the copy of [Chudleigh's Memorandum] which is enclosed.'[43]

On 6 March he had another confidential conversation with Witsen, who told him that D'Avaux's lobbying was merely designed to intimidate, and he then outlined the position of Amsterdam. The Dutch were of course committed to keeping their word to Spain, but matters had not yet come to the point where they were obliged to come to Spain's aid – to date there were hostilities without a declaration of war and the blockade of Luxemburg was but a means of exerting pressure and not of itself an act of war. The Dutch, together with the English, should negotiate with France, and during these negotiations Luxemburg should be assured of provisions and should not fall into French hands. The Republic, England and Germany should work together to arrive at a settlement between France and Spain. He thought that in the event of war Germany would be a weak and untrustworthy ally, because many German princes were on the side of France and the German Emperor himself needed all the military might at his disposal in Hungary – we will come to this.

He assured the Prince, however, that he should not draw the conclusion from all this that Amsterdam approved of France's conduct; one had to choose the lesser of two evils and Amsterdam's proposed answer to D'Avaux therefore was that the Dutch would try to persuade Spain to come to an accommodation, provided Luxemburg was meanwhile allowed to be provisioned and that negotiations were held with Germany conjointly.[44]

Amsterdam, therefore, had conceded the need for joint negotiations even though she was not prepared to accept that Spain had the right at this stage to request the Dutch troops under her treaty with the Republic, which was the Prince's position.

Witsen had put the essence of his arguments in a memorandum, which William had the opportunity to consider overnight. When the two of them met again between eight and nine in the morning of the 7th he admitted that the wording of the Spanish treaty allowed for the Burgomaster's interpretation, but one had to have regard not just to the words but to the intention. His belief was that French hostilities did indeed amount to war, that Spain therefore was justified in declaring war herself, and that she was morally justified in asking for the Dutch troops even in the absence of such a declaration. He added that France on several occasions had retreated from its extreme demands when faced with united opposition.

But 'I cannot speak in any other manner,' replied Witsen, 'I would be disavowed, and in any case it is my own view.' William, however, had support in the States-General, as both men knew,[45] and this would put pressure on Amsterdam.

It was against the background of these interchanges that, later on that day, the Prince delivered a great set-piece oration to the States of Holland, who now needed to come to a decision on the great question facing the Republic.

He began by defending himself against accusations that he wanted war. His personal affairs were more threatened than anyone else's if it went badly: he would not be able to remain in the Republic, and as commander he would be held personally responsible. He was well aware of the insufficiency of the Republic's military needs on land and sea and of the finances, and he would be mad to desire war, knowing all that. But that was no reason to be plunged into total ruin by panicking.

The position in Europe was this: nobody doubted that France's aim was to make herself master of the Continent, to establish a universal monarchy with a universal religion. There was no need for him to hold forth on her infractions of the Treaty of Nijmegen – whole books had been devoted to it. That was not to say that they should not negotiate, but it was a question of how. The danger was to enter into separate negotiations, as had happened at Nijmegen. He had warned them then of the consequences, which indeed the outcome proved.

He could not but view with sadness the state of affairs in England. It had hinged on the court there, as it still did, being able to check France. However, they chose not to do so, their conduct was abominable, and they needed to be constrained to follow their true interests. In the long run England could not allow matters to run their course and she would have to revert to her true concerns. That was certain to happen – if one did not shy away from pushing her to pursue the right course.

In Germany matters also left much to be desired, but they were not as bad as France gave out. There were many sympathisers there, with the Emperor foremost, and there were soldiers enough to be brought into support. Brandenburg alone stood in opposition and was responsible for the lack of German unity. She exercised a bad influence on Denmark, but Sweden was onside. Spain was the sick man who sought to be cured and who would be cured.

Was it likely if they delayed their decision that circumstances would improve? On the contrary, in both England and Germany, it would create a bad impression on those sympathetic to them if they held back – the only advantage that they would draw was that within a year or two they would have the good luck to be eaten last. It was ruinous for a republic not to keep her word.

Was there cause for intervention? Absolutely. One could interpret the treaty with Spain as requiring assistance only in the case of war. But blood had been spilled, the Dutch and English memoranda delivered to France had received no satisfactory answer, and the blockade of Luxemburg continued. Was that not war? At the end of the day greater regard was owed to the spirit than to the wording of the Spanish treaty. To Spain therefore the answer should be: we would send the 8,000 troops. We had always found that if we took the resolute course France would yield.

But to France we needed to demonstrate that we did not seek war and that, provided Luxemburg continued to be provisioned, we preferred to settle the differences amicably, which was to say that the Spanish differences should be settled jointly with the German. Otherwise we would fall into the mistake made at Nijmegen and be divided from our allies. England should be kept informed of our decision and we should continue to urge the summons of Parliament. Precisely to exercise influence there it was necessary to assist Spain without any hesitation.

That was the only hope for a successful negotiation. Otherwise they would have to submit to what France wanted, in which case Spain could be driven to desperate remedies and swap the Southern Netherlands for an equivalent elsewhere.[46]

A discussion followed this oration and the Holland delegates felt compelled to return for consultation to their towns, and it was not until 21 March that an agreed position was arrived at, which was also adopted by the States-General on the 23rd. It was a compromise between the views of William and Amsterdam. It was agreed in principle that the 8,000 men should be sent; however, as the treaty stipulated that, before war could begin, an attempt should be made to arrive at an amicable settlement, the Dutch agreed to assert themselves to persuade France to that end and Luxemburg should in the meantime be open to supplies. If Spain then showed herself willing to arrive at an accommodation but France did not, or if the French refused to lift the blockade, the 8,000 troops would be sent at once. Furthermore, the States-General stipulated that the negotiations should include the participation of the German Emperor.[47] Thus Amsterdam got her way that Spain should submit to negotiations, and the Prince that these should not be separate from those with Germany.

But then, suddenly, on 23 March, the date of the States-General meeting, Louis XIV lifted the blockade of Luxemburg and accepted the arbitration of Charles II.

Why did he do so?

LOUIS RAISES THE BLOCKADE OF LUXEMBURG

On the day the blockade was raised Louis wrote to Barillon that he was in no doubt that the Turks would invade Hungary in the course of the year and that he had 'decided to place the common good of Christendom before all those considerations which could have led him to force the submission of Luxemburg and its dependent territories, as an equivalent for his claims in Flanders'.[48]

In the opinion of William, as expressed to Waldeck on 2 April, this was nonsense; the vigorous action of the Dutch contributed more to Louis's decision than the 'Grand Turk'. He was determined to exploit this as much as possible, principally to demonstrate to 'our people that in speaking firmly and taking the high road one always achieves one's aims better'. It was also absolutely necessary to form a close bond with the German Empire.[49] On the 'Grand Turk' being a cover for Louis's real reasons William was indeed right, for

Louis did not hesitate to invade Flanders 15 months later when the Turks were advancing on Vienna.[50]

There was certainly pressure on Louis from England; Barillon reported that the blockade had alarmed English opinion and Charles II would not be able to postpone calling Parliament[51] – exactly William's prediction. But whether this was the whole truth of the matter is another question. We have seen that Charles's financial position was such that, without a war, he need not summon Parliament. Of this Louis must have had, at the least, a shrewd suspicion, and there was an inherent contradiction in Charles's offer of arbitration – if he was under pressure now to summon Parliament to intervene militarily to save Luxemburg what trouble would he not be in if he granted Louis the town under his arbitration? Pressure to summon Parliament was therefore a red herring advanced by Charles to obtain more cash from Louis.

However, there was a more cogent reason why Charles's offer would have had its attractions as an alternative way for Louis to achieve his objective, even if it took a little longer. Waldeck pointed it out to William on 21 April – as arbitrator the English King would be precluded from intervening in the dispute.[52] This would strengthen the case of the Dutch opposition to William of Orange – and also of the pro-French party in Germany in opposition to Leopold of Austria who, faced also with the Turkish menace, could come under irresistible pressure to settle in the west.

But John Wolf, Louis's eminent biographer, has surmised that there may also have been yet another, even more tempting motive behind the raising of the blockade, which lured Louis – to end the long dynastic struggle against the Habsburgs by an ingenious manoeuvre which would establish him or his son as Holy Roman Emperor. To examine this we need to turn to the court of Vienna and to the mounting menace from Turkey as it appeared at the time Louis lifted his blockade.

AUSTRIA, LOUIS XIV, THE TURKS AND THE *REICH*

In Vienna in the autumn of 1681 Leopold was faced with the persistent dilemma of having to choose whether he faced a greater danger in the west from France or in the east from Turkey. There his envoy in Constantinople was sending increasingly emphatic messages that, under the ambitious and aggressive Grand Vizier, Kara Mustapha, war preparations were under way and were directed at Austria. But the French occupation of Strasburg nevertheless decided Leopold to concentrate on the west[53] and on 28 February 1682, as we have seen, he joined the Association Treaty.

If for Leopold I the dilemma between choosing the east or the west was endemic, so was rebellion in Hungary. This was being led by Count Tököly, a Protestant renegade, who was being supported by the Turks – not only by the Turks but also, with money, by Louis XIV. And Louis was also encouraging the Turks to invade Leopold's territories. He had decided,

Wolf's argument runs, that Leopold stood no chance of creating an army large enough to resist that of Kara Mustapha and he tried to persuade John Sobieski, the Polish King, who hitherto had been, with his French wife, a client of France, to desist from coming to Leopold's aid. John Wolf has surmised that his motives during these years – 1682–3 – were to acquire the crown of the Holy Roman Empire for himself or his son. If the Turks captured the Habsburg lands in the east and invaded Germany, Louis would have the only army large enough to resist them and he would be able to pose as the defender of Christendom, the role historically performed by the Habsburgs; and his army, once in place in Germany, would enable him to secure the Imperial crown, which had also been historically theirs. The French historian Rousset makes the same point: Louis offered 30,000 men to assist Leopold against the Turks; privately he had in mind a further 30,000 and, if need be, yet another 30,000. Louis explained his reason for raising the blockade of Luxemburg to Marshal Créqui in April 1682: the Turkish assault would come the following year and he did 'not wish that those who should oppose the Turkish invasion could reproach me that my actions … had made it impossible for them to wage war successfully for the defence of Christianity'.[54]

It is indeed true that there were those in Vienna at the time who suspected that Louis's aims were precisely as outlined by John Wolf[55] and that by combining the Imperial with the French crown he would put an end to the Habsburgs and establish his monarchy 'over the whole of Christendom'; and we have seen that William of Orange was also convinced that 'universal monarchy' was Louis's design.

We have no direct evidence of Louis's motives and there may have been several considerations in his mind which indeed may have changed over time. But the Prince of Orange had to assess the facts as he faced them and react accordingly, and it is difficult for the historian to avoid the view that, if events had evolved to bring 'universal monarchy' within Louis's reach, now or later, he would not have seized it. In this he would not have been alone in the course of history.

FRANCE'S USE OF BRANDENBURG IN THE *REICH*

There is a further dimension to French diplomacy at the time of the lifting of the Luxemburg blockade. With Sweden's abandonment of her traditional role as a client of France Louis was building on his new alliance with Brandenburg to form a triple alliance between himself and Sweden's old enemies, Brandenburg and Denmark, and to use Brandenburg to lobby the German princes on his behalf.

Frederick-William was receptive, for he saw no alternative – two players with an important, perhaps an essential, role to perform in an anti-French coalition were hamstrung, Charles II because of his relations with Parliament and Leopold of Austria because of rebellion in Hungary. Thus the Elector signed the new treaty with France on 22 January 1682; further treaties were entered into between Brandenburg and Denmark on 10 February and between France and Denmark on 25 March, which thus completed the triple alliance almost simultaneously with the lifting of the blockade. Whilst the Brandenburg–Danish treaties did not specify that they were directed against their traditional enemy Sweden, with whom both of them had many scores to settle, the two allies did so regard it, and, although Louis was not prepared to support any moves against Charles XI, they nevertheless made their plans accordingly. Frederick-William received a larger subsidy and France undertook to limit her claims under the *réunions* to the territories she had acquired as at 1 August 1681, but including Strasburg, which she did not in fact acquire until September.

Shortly before the January treaty France had, on 2 January, submitted a written proposal at Frankfurt, where a conference was under way between the French, the Austrians and a deputation of the German *Reich* to settle the Franco-German disputes, in which Louis declared himself content with the position as at 1 August 1681 (plus Strasburg) if the Emperor and the Empire ratified the *réunions*. The Elector of Brandenburg had already been lobbying the German princes to this effect and continued his efforts. Whilst, assisted by promises of both French largesse and French intimidation, he received favourable responses from the Electors on the Rhine and Mainz, Trier, Cologne, and the Palatine, he did not do so from the Electors of Saxony and Bavaria, from the Duke of Hanover, or from the Landgrave of Hesse-Cassel.[56]

Raising the blockade of Luxemburg on 23 March 1682 did not end France's pursuit of the separate settlement of her disputes with Germany and Spain. Remember that Louis demanded from Germany the recognition of all his acquisitions as at 1 August 1681 plus Strasburg, and from Spain he demanded Luxemburg as an equivalent for all his claims in the Spanish Netherlands. In the case of Spain Louis knew that, if Charles arbitrated, he would come down on his side and, having settled with Spain on his terms, he would then be in a strong position to repeat the exercise with the Germans – or vice versa.

WALDECK'S *REICH* ALLIANCE

Just as determinedly Prince William continued opposing this system of divide and rule; and Waldeck was an important instrument in achieving his aims. On 6 March 1682, the Count, who was criss-crossing Germany and the German courts with all their complexities to bring more German princes into the Association Treaty, had written to the Prince saying all would be brought to naught if they could not stop a separate agreement between France and the Empire. William replied on the 24th that the most important thing was unity between the Dutch Republic and the Emperor and the *Reich* – to this end the more participants Waldeck could bring into the Association Treaty the better – and on 7 April he wrote that 'all our security and happiness depends on tying together' the German and Spanish negotiations. Rather curiously, in view of his opinion that Charles II had come to terms with France, he also said that he 'could not see how the Spaniards can refuse at present the arbitrage of England after France has offered it',[57] and it is not quite clear at what point in time he changed his mind on this.

Waldeck built on an earlier defensive alliance which he had succeeded in forming in September 1679 between some of the minor German princes – 'the Union' – in which members of the House of Nassau played a leading role, but which initially had at its disposal an armed force of only 2,000 professional soldiers, with the same number of militia. Although the Union almost at once formed an alliance with Hesse-Cassel, later further extended into a broader alliance of German states, with at its core the Franconian and Upper Rhine *Kreise* – for defensive purposes the *Reich* was divided into ten of these – Waldeck had found it very difficult to give either the Union or the alliance much substance.[58]

Nevertheless, the Union was an innovative organisation. Hitherto the *Reich* had had a list showing the contingent of troops, and their cash equivalent, which each ruler had to contribute for the defence of the *Reich* in case of war and which could be summoned by the Reichstag with the agreement of the Emperor. Instead of providing these separate contingents the members of the Union paid into a central treasury in Frankfurt to finance a single unified army with one set of arms, one set of uniforms and one set of drill under the command of Waldeck.

Waldeck envisaged extending this over the entire *Reich*. For practical reasons Leopold did not do this but modified the model; the central treasury and unified command remained but the details of who contributed what and how within the *Kreise* – which would have led to endless negotiations if done centrally – were left for them to determine; they would each have their own treasury, with the central treasury paying for the general staff, which the Emperor controlled, and the artillery train. The reformed system was introduced in stages between May 1681 and March 1682 and was to last until the *Reich* was abolished by Napoleon.[59] This system of defence for the *Reich* did not preclude either the Emperor or the more powerful princes having their own armies – between 1679 and 1682 Bavaria, Hesse-Cassel, Hanover and Saxony built up armies of between 7,000 and 15,000 men, which, unlike the *Reich* army, were standing forces.[60]

On 10 June 1682 Waldeck succeeded in transforming the Union into a new alliance with the Emperor at its head, known as the 'Laxenburg Recess' after the Emperor's summer residence where it was signed. It was a much more ambitious military alliance than the Union and it aimed at establishing a powerful army to defend the German *Reich*, with its signatories, in so far as they had not already done so, joining the Association. It envisaged the Emperor and the Elector of Bavaria committing 30,000 men on the Upper Rhine, the extended alliance committing 20,000 (including 3,000 Austrian cavalry) on the middle Rhine, and the Duke of Hanover being asked, together with some other German states, to commit 20,000 men on the Lower Rhine – thus 70,000 men deployed on the Rhine frontier with France.[61]

Waldeck was created a Prince of the Holy Roman Empire on 17 June – it brought with it a vote in the German Diet and it was therefore not inconsequential. In due course he was also to become a Field-Marshal in the service of the Austrian Emperor in command of some of these forces; this had been mooted for some time, but it required the approval of the Dutch States-General, which was long delayed by the opposition of Friesland and Groningen under the leadership of Prince William's truculent cousin, Hendrik-Casimir.[62]

Prince William welcomed these plans but he wrote to Waldeck on 20 July that what troubled him most at the moment were the movements of the Turks and those of the Hungarian malcontents; if these could be contained he had good hopes for their affairs, but otherwise he feared that the Empire would be forced into a treaty with Louis as shameful as it would be ruinous.

On 31 July he was anxious to clarify a misunderstanding that appeared to have arisen from a conversation he had with the Spanish and Austrian ambassadors in The Hague: that he was so concerned about a Turkish invasion that he would advocate putting the Franco-German disputes to the arbitration of Charles II. In fact, the furthest he was prepared to go, in those extreme circumstances, he explained to Waldeck, was to put them to the mediation of his uncle.[63]

TURKISH DECISION TO INVADE AUSTRIA

He was right to be preoccupied with the Turks, for on 6 August 1682 the Sultan met his Divan in his palace in Istanbul. There it was decided to contravene the peace treaty with Austria, which was not due to expire until 1684, and to plan for an invasion of Hungary in 1683 with all the forces that could be summoned from every corner of the Turkish Empire. In the meantime Tököly would be recognised as the King of Hungary under a Turkish Protectorate.[64]

Unaware of this, Leopold and his advisers met at Laxenburg on the 11th and decided to continue with their policy to resist Louis XIV in the west, whilst doing what they could to appease the Turks in the east. Leopold's viewpoint is reflected in a despatch from Bruynincx, the Dutch ambassador in Vienna, at the end of July; the understanding between the two branches of the Habsburg family, the Austrian and the Spanish, was closer than ever, he reported, and they saw the welfare of each in large part dependent on the other; Leopold, he said, undoubtedly thought Louis's long-term aim was to snatch the Imperial crown from his head; and the Emperor and his advisers were convinced that the Spanish and German disputes with France could only be settled jointly.

On 6 September, by when the Turkish intentions had become quite apparent, Bruynincx told Fagel that nevertheless Leopold, for now at least, was not in any way relaxing his measures against France – encouraged, Bruynincx thought, by the Spanish ambassador – and that the Duke of Lorraine was being despatched to take command of the troops on the

Rhine.[65] We have seen that in the spring of 1682 Leopold had sent 25,000 troops into the Rhineland. Between 1681 and February 1682 he increased the Austrian army by 30,000 men to 62,400.[66] When at the end of November William expressed doubts that Leopold could fight the Turks and France simultaneously, Waldeck provided a reassuring reply.[67]

On the diplomatic front the Emperor had succeeded during the course of 1682 in detaching Max Emanuel, the Elector of Bavaria, from the French alliance and promised him his daughter Marie Antoinette in marriage – their son was to become in 1698 a claimant to the throne of Carlos II of Spain.[68] In view of the Turkish menace he also managed to detach John Sobieski of Poland from France and the clientage of Louis XIV – in the spring of 1682 Sobieski undertook to stop France transmitting funds via Poland to the Hungarian rebels, whom he expelled from Poland, and at the end of March 1683 he formed an alliance with Austria under which he was to provide 40,000 men and the Emperor 60,000 against the Turks. To this the Pope, Innocent XI, also lent his support, seeing the alliance as a holy crusade, and provided funds both directly and by allowing Leopold and Max Emanuel to tax Church property.

Leopold remained steadfast in refusing to accept the *réunions*, which thus remained without international recognition, and he refused the offer from the Elector of Brandenburg of 16,000 troops against the Turks if he yielded to Louis's demands.[69] Furthermore, apart from himself, he persuaded the Franconian and Upper Rhine *Kreise*, Saxe-Weimar, Saxe-Gotha, the Duke of Neuburg and the Elector of Bavaria, to join the Association Treaty, as did Spain.[70] That treaty was strengthened on 18 March 1683 when the Emperor, Sweden and the Dutch Republic at long last spelled out the military support they would give each other under the Association – Spain was also a signatory, but in the event failed to ratify. Furthermore, Leopold entered into a treaty with Duke Ernst Augustus of Hanover on 14 January 1683 in which the Duke promised 10,000 men for the Lower Rhine–Mosel region, if required – motivated probably by his ambition to raise his Duchy to an Electorate by means of the Emperor's goodwill.[71]

THE AMBIGUITIES OF BRANDENBURG

In July 1682 the Elector of Brandenburg had sent a representative to Vienna with a brief tantamount to his *apologia* for the position he was taking. He pointed out the weakness of the Empire; the *réunions* were undoubtedly unjust but in the present state of division of the German states, for the most part disposed to peace, and with the difficulties of the Emperor, who was beset by rebels in Hungary and who was soon also to be beset by the Turks, there was only one road to salvation, which was to conclude a peace clarifying the ambiguities of the Treaties of Westphalia and of Nijmegen, which could then be maintained in the future by solid alliances.[72]

But we have seen that Frederick-William was no great lover of France and his sentiments were not ameliorated when Louis XIV yet again occupied the Principality of Orange on 17

August. Louis's pretext was a lawsuit which the Prince of Orange had with the House of Condé and a further explanation was given that the defensive walls of the town were being rebuilt. The Condé claim, of course, affected the House of Brandenburg's own possible inheritance of the Principality should William die without heirs – a claim agreed to by Louis under his Treaty with Brandenburg in January 1681. On the instigation of the Dutch States and of Amerongen – seconded by the Prince of Anhalt – the Elector remonstrated strongly at the French court. William wrote to thank him for this on 5 December and at the personal level relations between the Prince and the Elector were well maintained – helped no doubt by the interests of the extended clan and by Frederick-William's having sent his son, Louis, in July to study in Utrecht.

The Franco–Brandenburg relationship, always equivocal on both sides, became even more so. In June Frederick-William had met King Christian of Denmark and signed an offensive treaty against Sweden, although the timing of the attack was left open. For this, the Elector was aware, he needed further French subsidies and support.[73] The occupation of Orange cooled the Elector's view of Louis as well as that of his Minister, Fuchs, who had previously been regarded as pro-French. Towards the end of 1682 or the beginning of 1683 Fuchs drew up a memorandum advising him to pursue neither a stricter alliance with France nor to join the Association, but to follow a middle course with the main aim of preserving peace, whilst at the same time drawing French subsidies to strengthen his army. And this the Elector decided to do. As for Louis, he wanted to encourage Frederick-William's hostile stance towards Sweden as a means of distracting her from the Association, but at the same time he had instructed Rebenac at the end of 1681 to foster the Elector's hopes without lending them substance.[74] Andrew Lossky explains Louis's policy as residing in his belief that Sweden's true interests – her 'true maxims' as he called them – were to have France as her natural ally and that Charles XI's actions were but passing whims. There was also the fear that once Brandenburg and Denmark had settled with Sweden they would return to Leopold to seek Imperial sanction for their conquests from Charles XI in the *Reich*. What Louis wanted from his allies was not an attack on Sweden but to check the pro-Austrian Dukes of Hanover.[75]

LOUIS'S OCCUPATION OF ORANGE: THE PRINCE'S REACTION
The Prince of Orange's response to the occupation of his Principality was to appeal to the head of the Stuart clan. On 31 August 1682 he wrote to Laurence Hyde to intercede on his behalf with Charles II, whom, he said, he 'had implored for his protection and assistance … since I believe that if his Majesty does me the kindness of speaking a little firmly, and to demonstrate to France that the injuries against me concern him I would soon be delivered from them'.[76] His proverbial reticence gave way to profound anger and resentment. '*Eh bien, messieurs les Français m'accommodent bien*', he announced on 2 September to the company

asscmblcd at table at Hooghsoeren, one of his country residences. He proceeded to relate that a regiment of French dragoons had arrived at Orange, billeted themselves on the principal inhabitants and pillaged them on a daily basis, with orders to raze its defensive walls. With a countenance marked by exasperation he repeated four or five times that he needed patience until he was in a position to avenge himself, and that he hoped that he would not die until he had the means of doing so. It is the mark of his deep rancour that he repeated this in almost exactly the same words to Waldeck two days later. These were 'public injuries which the French inflict on me', he said to Waldeck – note the 'public'. They thus reflected on his *gloire* and we can observe that from this time the conflict between the Prince of Orange and the King of France became deeply and bitterly personal.[77]

The Treaty of Nijmegen had confirmed that he held Orange in full sovereignty and he regarded Louis's actions as a direct insult. He had the support of the States of Holland, including Amsterdam, who resolved on 5 October to send an embassy to Paris to object. The Dutch envoys in London were instructed to petition Charles to direct Preston, his ambassador in Paris, to cooperate with the Dutch emissary there to induce Louis to relent. Conway wrote to the Prince on 26 October telling him that Charles was resolved to support his interests and Mary's – 'which can never be separated from his own'; and on 3 November Chudleigh met William at Soestdijk and assured him that 'Preston would have orders to second and assist the Envoy of the States'.

It is unlikely that William was persuaded by these assurances, his view of the English court being reflected by his treatment of poor Lord Cornbury, Clarendon's eldest son, who was a visitor at his table on 11 October and to whom he refused to utter a word during the whole evening meal; the distraught 20-year-old was lodged in the local inn and was reduced to tears. Charles's promises of support by means of Preston were indeed of little value, for Preston was simultaneously instructed not to displease the French King. Charles's view was that what had been done could not be undone and he was also not certain that his nephew had right on his side.[78] Hence, in having to choose between the extended Stuart–Orange clan and his patron, the King of France, Charles came down on the side of the latter.

On 13 November Chudleigh reported that the Prince 'seems to look upon his town of Orange as lost in effect', because, although he did not think he would be dispossessed of it at this time, the French would see how their actions were received with a view to doing so in the future.[79] The failure of Charles to come to his aid on as important a matter as his sovereignty – with all the potential political consequences that it brought in its wake in Europe, in the United Provinces and in England – could only embitter the already acrimonious view he held of his English uncle. How acrimonious is reflected in a letter to Waldeck of 23 October, when he turned with venom on his uncle, 'All our ills derive from England, who will cause her own downfall and that of the whole of Europe, the court is presently worse than it has ever been, passing all imagination.'[80]

DEVELOPMENTS IN ENGLAND

There was indeed a detrimental development that had been slowly evolving at the English court during the whole of 1682 – the return to favour of Sunderland under the patronage of Louis XIV. Sunderland's grasp of foreign affairs was pre-eminent amongst English politicians, and Charles II had need of it. On his side Sunderland's financial situation was such that he needed the emoluments of office and he also sensed that the exclusionist and Whig tide was on the turn. On 14 March the Duke of York received notice that he was being recalled from his exile; he was soon with the King at Newmarket, having been enthusiastically received at Yarmouth and Norwich; and from there – against Halifax's advice – the King took him to London, a sign of Charles's own confidence in the turning of the tide. A month later James wrote to William that conditions in England are 'much mended within this twelve month and his Ma. is now master … and he need not feare nor endeavour to manage Lord Shaftesbury'. At the end of June Sunderland assured Barillon that, if he returned to office, no one would be more zealous than he in maintaining a strict union between the Kings of France and England and that there was no liaison between himself and the Prince of Orange – the exact opposite of his line when in office – and it must have taken all his polish to carry conviction in this brazen about-turn. However, Charles's French mistress, Louise de Kérouaille, whom Sunderland had always taken care to cultivate, was on a visit to France and she secured Louis's support.

There was an obstacle – James; for, it will be remembered, Sunderland had voted for his exclusion. However, there was also a solution – although it would require Sunderland to perform another suave about-turn. He repented his past faults to James, and he could also act as a counterweight to Halifax, which brought the necessary reconciliation with the Duke of York – it needs to be noted that, although brothers-in-law, Halifax and Sunderland had cultivated, since their time in office, a lively hatred of each other. Halifax indeed threatened to resign if Sunderland were returned to favour, but he was squared with the post of the Privy Seal and a marquisate – which in turn meant placating Laurence Hyde, who became the Earl of Rochester. On 6 August Sunderland kissed hands and returned to court. He rejoined the Privy Council at the end of September and the committee on foreign affairs at the beginning of November, but his informal influence was being felt before that; and thus it was that Charles II's pro-French foreign policy received a formidable boost.

There was one other nicety which Sunderland was not likely to overlook as a reassurance policy. On 11 August he wrote to Prince William to say that 'If any condition I can be in, may enable me to be serviceable to your Highnesse, there is no man alive that will more zealously embrace the occasion of it than I shall.'[81]

RELATIONS BETWEEN VAN BEUNINGEN AND THE PRINCE WORSEN

After an interval of six months, Spain at last responded to Louis's proposal that Charles II should arbitrate on her disputes with France. At the end of September 1682 she announced that she would accept the good offices of the English King, but on very different terms from those proposed by Louis. His proposal had been that Charles should arbitrate solely on the Franco-Spanish disputes. Spain now would merely accept his mediation, and then only jointly with the German disputes as well.[82]

On 29 September Van Beuningen took his disagreement with the Prince of Orange a stage further by writing a letter to the Burgomasters of Amsterdam; the Republic should do everything she could to avoid a break with France, because Charles II was not in a position to participate in a war. Because of the exhausted state of Dutch finances, war, he said, would be a disaster. The alliance between Brandenburg, Denmark and France threatened her trade in the Baltic; and with a Turkish war in prospect it was best to advise the Emperor and Spain to come to a swift settlement. He then added at the end of the letter that he had written on these lines to Van Heemskerk, now the Dutch envoy in Madrid, and that he had gone to work on the Spanish and Austrian ambassadors in London in the same spirit – to the extent of handing a memorandum to the former advocating Charles II's arbitration. At the beginning of October he expressed his thoughts in letters to Van Heemskerk in Madrid and to Hamel Bruynincx in Vienna, and on the 6th he confirmed what he had done in a letter to Fagel – all this without any authorisation from The Hague.

There his high-handed conduct in opposition to the Prince and the States-General naturally caused consternation – even Amsterdam had not until now spoken openly against William's policy. Nevertheless the States-General confined itself on 13 October to issuing a sharp reproof[83] rather than recalling him from his post; as William told Waldeck, three days later, although Van Beuningen's conduct was becoming insufferable he preferred to submit to that than face having him at home.[84] But his behaviour threatened dangers that William had for long warned against – on the 24th Waldeck reported that it was having repercussions in Germany by casting doubts on the reliability of the United Provinces as allies.[85]

William's perception of the damage Van Beuningen could do was reflected in a letter of 2 November to Waldeck: despite the States-General's disavowal, Van Beuningen's 'extraordinary conduct will infallibly produce the very war he believes he is preventing. As for myself, I fear the great mischief … occasioned by those who pose as working for peace. If greater faith were put in those who are reputed to be for war we would have had peace a long time ago and we could still have it. From England', he repeated, reverting to a now customary theme, 'you can only expect all the ill you can imagine. Thus you can see what trouble I will have to keep people here on the right path.'[86] One of his major concerns on the foreign front was no doubt reflected in a conversation Fagel had with Chudleigh on 13 November when the Pensionary said that, if the Dutch did not stand by Spain, Spain would swap their Low Countries for an equivalent elsewhere, 'and in such case', Chudleigh reported, 'he looks upon this State as lost to France too'.[87]

Van Beuningen continued in the same eccentric, high-handed manner, and his written correspondence, which had always reflected his verbal volubility, increasingly took on a manic tone, which perhaps tragically foreshadowed the madness to which he was ultimately to succumb. He assured Bruynincx that he had the confidence of the States-General, and the Spanish and Imperial ambassadors that the States were privately in agreement with him.[88]

William's forebodings on the domestic front were fully justified, for now Amsterdam, too, began to change course – and publicly. On 17 November her delegates at the Holland States were instructed to propose that Spain should be pressed to accept Charles's arbitration and that he should be requested to act simultaneously as mediator in the Franco-German disputes. All this, Amsterdam maintained, was in accordance with the Republic's established maxim of conducting her affairs *pari passu* with England. Her proposal was rejected by all the other members of the Holland States and by the States-General.[89]

But that was not to be the end of the matter.

1 Rousset, *op. cit.*, III, pp.16, 17.

2 *Ibid.*, III, pp.18, 19, 25, 26.

3 Lossky, *Louis XIV, op. cit.*, pp.169–70.

4 *Ibid.*, p.171.

5 Rousset, *op. cit.*, III, p.211.

6 Waddington, *op. cit.*, II, pp.471ff. and Philippson, *op. cit.*, III, pp.282ff.

7 See W.J.M. van Eysinga, 'Het Associatie Verdrag van 10 October 1681', pp.1, 11, in *Mededelingen Nederlandsche Akademie van Wetensschappen, Afdeeling Letterkunde, Nieuwe Reeks*, Deel 10, 1–9, Deel II, Amsterdam 1947. Waddington, *op. cit.*, p.482. Lossky, *Louis XIV, op. cit.*, pp.3, 164–5, 171.

8 Rousset, *op. cit.*, III, pp.40, 52–3, 212–14. For the Prince's manors in Chiny see Wagenaar, *op. cit.*, 15, p.58 and Troost, in *The Anglo-Dutch Moment, op. cit.*, p.317.

9 Rousset, *op. cit.*, III, pp.214, 215, 217.

10 Fruin, *Verspreide Geschriften, op. cit.*, V, p.89n.

11 D'Avaux, *Négociations, op. cit.*, I, pp.165–6.

12 *Secrete Resolutiën, op. cit.*, V, pp.89ff.

13 Eysinga, *op. cit.*, pp.3, 4. *Secrete Resolutiën, op. cit.*, V, pp.91ff.

14 Rousset, *op. cit.*, III, pp.40, 45, 47. Bérenger, p.5 in seminar *Les Relations Franco–Autrichiennes sous Louis XIV*, 9–11 March 1983.

15 Rousset, *op. cit.*, III, pp.139, 150, 151, 152, 153. Contrary to Louis's pleasantry Louvois did not in fact spend the night of the 30th in Strasburg, although he was wont to take great care of his personal security (see p.51).

16 Eysinga, *op. cit.*, pp.6–9.

17 See Van Beuningen's letters to Prince William of 11 and 17 September. Groen van Prinsterer, *Archives, op. cit.*, 2, V, pp.515–20. Gebhard, *op. cit.*, I, pp.168, 193, 204–5n. Fruin, *Verspreide Geschriften, op. cit.*, V, p.92. Kurtz, *op. cit.*, p.28.

18 Kurtz, *op. cit.*, pp.28–9.

19 F.A. Middlebush, ed., *Despatches of Thomas Plott and Thomas Chudleigh*, The Hague 1926, p.5 n.2.

20 Müller, *Waldeck*, I, p.115.

21 Foxcroft, *op. cit.*, I, pp.318 19, 321 3. Dalrymple, *op. cit.*, Pt 1, Bk 1, appendix pp.79–80. Kurtz, *op. cit.*, p.30. Hutton,

op. cit., pp.404–5.

22 Dalrymple, *op. cit.*, Pt 1, Bk 1, app. pp.81–85.

23 Foxcroft, *op. cit.*, I, p.327.

24 Groen van Prinsterer, *Archives, op. cit.*, 2, V, p.529. William's letter is lost.

25 Foxcroft, *op. cit.*, I, pp.327–32. Jones, *Charles II, op. cit.*, p.177.

26 Groen van Prinsterer, *Archives, op. cit.*, 2, V, p.534.

27 *Ibid.*, 2, V, p.536.

28 Foxcroft, *op. cit.*, I, pp.337–8.

29 *Ibid.*, I, p.336. Fruin, *Verspreide Geschriften, op. cit.*, V, p.95. Middlebush, *op. cit.*, XXVII.

30 Fruin, *Verspreide Geschriften, op. cit.*, V, p.97. A copy of Barillon's memoir of 4 February is contained in *Secrete Resolutiën, op. cit.*, V, p.115.

31 *Correspondentie Willem III en Bentinck, op. cit.*, II, 2, pp.433–4 and p.433 n.3.

32 Gebhard, *op. cit.*, I, pp.206–8, II, p.36. Kurtz, *op. cit.*, p.31.

33 Gebhard, *op. cit.*, II, p.389.

34 Middlebush, *op. cit.*, pp.41ff., 46, 552.

35 *Secrete Resolutiën, op. cit.*, V, p.116.

36 Gebhard, *op. cit.*, II, pp.40–3 and I, pp.211–17.

37 Von Antal and Pater, *op. cit.*, I, p.309. Bérenger, *op. cit.*, p.7.

38 Fruin, *Verspreide Geschriften, op. cit.*, V, pp.97–8. Middlebush, *op. cit.*, p.41.

39 *Secrete Resolutiën, op. cit.*, V, p.117.

40 Gebhard, *op. cit.*, II, pp.44–6, and I, pp.216–18. Witsen's note on p.46 regarding Cramprich, the Emperor's Resident in The Hague, 'Camprigt duytsland sal afwijken', is ambiguous but could mean that Cramprich had said that Germany would dissent.

41 Gebhard, *op. cit.*, I, pp.218–20.

42 Middlebush, *op. cit.*, pp.68–9, 70.

43 Müller, *Waldeck, op. cit.*, I, pp.132, 134.

44 Gebhard, *op. cit.*, I, pp.220–22.

45 *Ibid.*, I, pp.222–4.

46 Both Witsen and Heinsius, who at this stage was the Pensionary for Delft, made notes of the Prince's speech which are contained in respectively Gebhard, *op. cit.*, II, pp.46ff. and pp.55ff. and in *Van der Heim, Archief van den Raadpensionaris Antonie Heinsius*, The Hague, 1867–80, I, pp.49–52. Both Fruin (*Verspreide Geschriften, op. cit.*, V, pp.101–3) and Japikse (*Willem III, op. cit.*, II, pp.161–3) provide syntheses of these sources, which I have also consulted.

47 Gebhard, *op. cit.*, I, pp.228–9. Fruin, *Verspreide Geschriften, op. cit.*, V, pp.104–5. Japikse, *Willem III, op. cit.*, II, p.165.

48 V.L. Tapié, in *Louis XIV and Europe, op. cit.*, p.9.

49 Müller, *Waldeck, op. cit.*, I, p.143.

50 Tapié, *op. cit.*, p.9.

51 *Ibid.*, pp.8–9.

52 Müller, *Waldeck, op. cit.*, I, p.151.

53 Spielman, *op. cit.*, p.89.

54 John Wolf, *Louis XIV*, London 1968, pp.412–15. Part of the circumstantial evidence cited by Wolf are the treaties Louis entered into after 1679 with the Electors of Brandenburg, Bavaria, Saxony and Cologne requiring them to vote for Louis's candidate for the Imperial throne at the next election, p.414. Bérenger, *op. cit.*, p.12. Rousset, *op. cit.*, III, pp.229–30.

55 Von Antal and De Pater, *op. cit.*, I, pp.317–18, Bruynincx to Amerongen 30 April 1682 with copy in States-General archives.

56 Waddington, *op. cit.*, II, pp.483–7. Troost, in *The Anglo-Dutch Moment, op. cit.*, p.319. Lossky, *Louis XIV, William III and The Baltic Crisis of 1683*, California 1954, pp.5–6.

57 Müller, *Waldeck, op. cit.*, I, pp.135, 141, 145.

58 Its members included, apart from Waldeck and the Princes and Counts of the House of Nassau, the Counts of Hanau, Solms, Isenburg, Stollberg, Wittgenstein, Westerburg, Wied and Manderscheid. Prince Johan Maurits of Nassau-Siegen (just before his death), Prince William Maurits of Nassau-Siegen, and the Count of Nassau-Saarbrucken – all of whom were in Dutch service – were the members of the House of Nassau who played a leading role. Müller, *Waldeck, op. cit.*, I, pp.58–9, 60, 71.

59 Peter Wilson, *German Armies, War and German Politics, 1648–1806*, London 1998, pp.23, 63–65.

60 *Ibid.*, p.66.

61 Müller, *Waldeck, op. cit.*, I, p.84.

62 *Ibid.*, I, pp.87, 88, 181.

63 *Ibid.*, I, pp.182, 185.

64 John Stoye, *The Siege of Vienna*, London 1964, pp.15–16.

65 Antal and Pater, *op. cit.*, I, pp.323–6, 330–2.

66 Wilson, *op. cit.*, p.68.

67 Müller, *Waldeck*, I, pp.218–20.

68 Bérenger, *op. cit.*, p.7.

69 John P. Spielman, *Leopold of Austria*, London 1977, p.98. Bérenger, *op. cit.*, pp.7–8.

70 Eysinga, *op. cit.*, p.11.

71 Lossky, *The Baltic Crisis, op. cit.*, p.4 and p.47 n.9.

72 Waddington, *op. cit.*, II, pp.489–90.

73 McKay, *The Great Elector, op. cit.*, p.246.

74 *Ibid.*, pp.244–7. Waddington, *op. cit.*, p.500. Philippson, *op. cit.*, III, pp.313–14.

75 Lossky, *Louis XIV, op. cit.*, p.175 & *The Baltic Crisis, op. cit.*, pp.5–6, 14, 15, 21.

76 Singer, *op. cit.*, I, p.79.

77 For this see Huygens, *Journaal, op. cit.*, III, p.62. Müller, *Waldeck, op. cit.*, I, p.195. *Correspondentie Willem III en Bentinck, op. cit.*, II, 2, pp.505ff. Troost, in *The Anglo-Dutch Moment, op. cit.*, p.322.

78 Middlebush, *op. cit.*, pp.147–9 and pp.149–50 n.5. For the States of Holland resolution to send an embassy to Paris see Kurtz, *op. cit.*, p.35. For Cornbury see Huygens, *Journaal, op. cit.*, III, p.70.

79 Middlebush, *op. cit.*, I, pp.158–9.

80 Müller, *Waldeck, op. cit.*, I, pp.212–13.

81 Kenyon, *Sunderland, op. cit.*, pp.78–82, 85, 86, p.349 n.34. Miller, *James II, op. cit.*, p.109. Groen van Prinsterer, *Archives, op. cit.*, 2, V, pp.542–6, 559–60.

82 Franken, *op. cit.*, pp.200, 203–4.

83 *Ibid.*, pp.204–5.

84 Müller, *Waldeck, op. cit.*, I, p.209.

85 *Ibid.*, I, pp.213–14.

86 *Ibid.*, I, p.215.

87 Middlebush, *op. cit.*, pp.158–9.

88 Franken, *op. cit.*, pp.210–211.

89 *Ibid.*, pp.211–12.

23 1683–1684: CONFLICT WITH AMSTERDAM; THE 20 YEARS' TRUCE

VAN BEUNINGEN'S RETURN TO AMSTERDAM

On 1 February 1683 Van Beuningen was elected a Burgomaster of Amsterdam. This marked a phase in which the city was to become increasingly intransigent; indeed, his biographer has argued that he had gained influence with important groups in Amsterdam precisely because of his conflict with the Prince. He returned to the Republic from his English embassy on 17 March and wrote a paper entitled *Considerations*, in which he set out his views on the need to treat with France; he circulated it to leading personalities in the Republic. It infuriated the Prince of Orange, who maintained that, if all Van Beuningen said was true, there was nothing left but to submit to France. 'I am so indignant about the whole document', he wrote to Fagel on 1 April, 'that I cannot find sufficient words to express myself.... Although I am certain that Van Beuningen and I will from henceforth become irreconcilable I don't want to go into that; the one matter that saddens me is that the public good has suffered so much, and will suffer so much, solely on account of a turbulent spirit.' He anticipated that Amsterdam would summon a meeting of the Holland States and he asked Fagel to let him know when he wanted him in The Hague, 'because I shall not only come, but fly there … to prevent any harm' from Van Beuningen's doings.

In fact, at the meeting of the Holland States where the *Considerations* were discussed, the Prince used a more moderate tone and after the meeting Fagel went to Amsterdam to try to win back the city and her recalcitrant Regent – but, as we shall see, without success.[1]

MARRIAGE OF PRINCESS ANNE AND PRINCE GEORGE OF DENMARK

Charles II had showed fulsome approval of Van Beuningen in a letter to William of 12 March – 'I never saw anybody more ernest in all your concernes and interest than he is'. The tone of the letter was as friendly as he could make it; it was in reply to William's of 16 February – now lost – which Charles said he had received 'with great satisfaction' and he was very pleased that William agreed with him that peace was 'absolutely necessary for us both'. But, pleasantries aside, he persisted that 'I am of opinion that, if my advice had been followed, [the peace] had been farr advanced, and can yett see no other way of obtaining it but by the King of Spaines acceptance of the arbitration.' We have an early, very rough draft of William's reply which, with its alterations and contradictions, demonstrates how hard he struggled to stick to his principles whilst appeasing his royal uncle as diplomatically as he could.[2]

But before he could give the polished answer required, Charles had continued to move further into Louis's orbit. On 13 May the Duke of York wrote to William to inform him of the planned marriage of his younger daughter, Anne – the sister of Mary – to Prince George of Denmark. In due course it would become apparent that Prince George's placid, good-natured dullness was to render him both admirable as a husband for Anne and negligible as a political force. But the news at this time would not have been pleasing to Prince William; Denmark, as we have seen, was, together with Brandenburg, part of the French system of political alliances in Northern Europe. The plans of Brandenburg and Denmark, hypothetical as they remained without the necessary French support, nevertheless envisaged the destruction of the Swedish fleet and to this end the Danes had embarked on naval preparations.

News of this reached the Dutch in early 1683 and they began to take measures to restore their navy, which had been run down after the Treaty of Nijmegen – their concern was not only for their ally Sweden but also that Denmark and Brandenburg might combine to prey on their commerce as a means of indemnifying themselves for what, they argued, the Dutch owed them from the previous war.

Having refused to support his two northern clients in their wish to attack Sweden, Louis was under all the more pressure to assist them in other ways. He did this on two fronts: first, he sent a French squadron to stand by the Danes; and secondly, he advocated the match between George, the brother of Christian V, and Anne. This tightening of the Anglo-Danish bond would, he hoped, prove a deterrent to the Dutch in providing naval aid for Denmark, and, as far as domestic English politics were concerned, it would provide another Protestant close to the throne to counterbalance the Prince of Orange. Given George's character, he was to prove unsuccessful on the second count, and as a result of the poor state of the English navy and ambiguities at the English court he was also to prove unsuccessful on the first.[3] William's own plans in 1680 had envisaged Anne's marrying George of Hanover, which would have strengthened both his own ties with the Brunswick dukes and those of the Stuart clan.

In sending the French fleet to assist the Danes, Louis was undoubtedly taking a risk that the Danes would unleash the very war against Sweden that he wished to avoid. But without French backing the Elector of Brandenburg was persuaded that the Swedish enterprise would have to be put on hold and Louis, Andrew Lossky judges, calculated that Frederick-William would restrain his Danish ally.[4]

It was against this background that William now at last responded on 1 June to Charles's letter of 12 March. His struggle over the response was well worth the effort, for it succinctly encapsulated his position on Louis's encroachments. The grievous consequences of the peace of Nijmegen had demonstrated, he said, that, to come to a settlement with a predominant power, without those who had reason to apprehend it entering into appropriate alliances between themselves to counterbalance it, produced only an ostensible harmony and a false security. He was, however, in agreement with the King that peace was at present absolutely necessary and he was thus persuaded (so he said) that they shared the same aims; and, although he and the States had not advised Spain to accept the arbitration, they had not omitted always to represent to her the danger of a war. And he took the occasion to ask Charles to use his good offices, made possible by the Danish match, to prevent the conflict with Sweden.[5]

THE RYE HOUSE PLOT

On 2 July James informed William of the discovery of a plot against Charles and himself. The Whigs had been steadily on the defensive throughout 1682 and the King strengthened his grip on London; in July a rigged election produced two Tory sheriffs there, which gave control of the juries; in September another – also rigged – election produced a Tory mayor; and by the end of the year Shaftesbury had fled to Holland. With no Parliament and with few alternatives, a number of prominent Whigs including Shaftesbury, Monmouth, Essex, Russelll and Lord Grey of Warke contemplated an uprising in the autumn of 1682. At a lower level there were the inveterate plotter Robert Ferguson and the staunch republican John Hampden. Nothing came of all this immediately, but during June 1683 an informer called Keeling revealed a plot that had been planned to take place in March to assassinate Charles and James at Rye House on their return from Newmarket – it had been foiled because a fire in Newmarket had necessitated a return to London earlier than expected.

There were, in fact, two plots, one by old Cromwellians and Republicans of lower social status who aimed at killing the King and his brother, and a second which planned to overpower the guards and seize their persons. This second involved foremost Whig grandees, including those (other than Shaftesbury, who had died in Holland at the end of January) involved in the previous discussions regarding rebellion, among them thus also Monmouth. Russelll and Algernon Sidney – the brother of Henry, but of a completely different political persuasion, who also became involved – were executed. Essex cut his throat in the tower and Lord Grey managed to escape only through the negligence of his custodian.[6] In the meantime, when a distraught Charles heard of the involvement of his wayward but beloved son, he had arranged for his disappearance. Monmouth made his way to Toddington Manor, the family seat of his mistress, Lady Henrietta Wentworth, to whom he was devoted and she to him. He told the King of his arrival, but Charles ensured he was not arrested.[7]

The immediate effect of the Rye House plot was the disintegration of the Whig party, and the King's position in his realm, already strong, became stronger still.

At this time the Prince asked his uncle for permission to visit England and, when this was refused, he sent Bentinck instead.[8] Bentinck's task was to congratulate William's uncles on their escape from the Rye House plot, to present the Prince's compliments to the Prince of Denmark, and to sound out the King on European affairs.

Before his departure William entrusted him with a touching personal mission: on 19 July he sent him a lock of hair – presumably his own – which was to be inserted into a locket made by his court silversmith; it was to be sent to Dieren as a surprise for Mary, his instructions to Bentinck being 'say nothing to the Princess of what I have written, nor of the lockett'.[9]

THE SIEGE OF VIENNA; LOUIS'S OFFER OF A 30-YEAR TRUCE

At the same time as the Prince was preoccupied by these domestic occasions momentous events were taking place in eastern Europe. On 22 July William wrote to Bentinck that he had learnt of 'the unfortunate news from Vienna' – the Turks had laid siege to the city. The bulk of the Turkish army, leaving Adrianople on 31 March, had arrived at Belgrade on 3 May and, with reinforcements from all over the Turkish Empire, now amounted to around 100,000 men; they were further reinforced as they marched through Hungary under the command of Kara Mustapha, who had been appointed by the Sultan to that position on 13 May, when he was symbolically given custody of the Flag of the Prophet.

Leopold, in response, appointed Charles of Lorraine as commander of his forces and on 6 May reviewed his army of around 30,000 men at Pressburg. It was composed of some 10,000 men from the *Reich*'s *Kreise*, with the rest coming from Bavaria and Saxony. Brandenburg had made such exorbitant demands to participate that Leopold refused and, faced with the threat from Brandenburg at home, the Brunswick dukes in turn also did not take part. Too small a force to confront the Turks in a major battle, this army was pushed to the defensive. Kara Mustapha's original instructions from the Sultan were not to capture Vienna and to concentrate on securing Turkish Hungary; but on 25 June he decided to disregard his orders and to march on the city instead, and on 7 July news of his advance reached the Hofburg. Leopold decided to leave his capital that evening with his family and by 17 July they had reached Passau on the Danube. In the meantime, Count von Starhemburg arrived on the 8th in Vienna to take command of the city. On the 16th Vienna lay surrounded by the Turkish army.[10]

Louis XIV was not slow to take advantage of the fragility of the position of his Habsburg opponent. On 26 July the French ambassador at Regensburg offered a 30-year truce in lieu of a definitive peace treaty, on the basis of Louis's previous offer that he should retain all his acquisitions as at 1 August 1681 plus Strasburg. The offer remained open for acceptance until 31 August.[11]

William at first underestimated the import of these events both in eastern Europe and at Regensburg. The alarm here has passed, he told Bentinck on 27 July, since the matter concerning Vienna is not as bad as was first thought. The worst part 'was the extraordinary manner of the court's departure from Vienna and the fright induced in the army and the city by three thousand tartars'. He didn't think a Turkish siege was feasible unless the Emperor's army was first defeated or driven away; Brandenburg, he said, was sending assistance together with a mission by the Prince of Anhalt – this, as we have seen, proved abortive; and, on Louis's offer made at Regensburg, his view was that the 'well intentioned' in Germany would remain firm.

That was enough, for the time being, of serious matters, he said, and turned to give his friend a detailed relation of how things were at Dieren. Everything was going swimmingly, both in the garden and the plantation, but there was very little fruit and all the melons were spoiled because of the rains – and he then went on to give an exciting account of the hunting.[12]

Lighter matters still remained in the forefront of his mind at the end of the month, when hunting was again mentioned in another letter, in which he also took the opportunity to ask Bentinck to buy a good hunter for himself and a saddle horse for Mary.[13]

But by 2 August his correspondence had assumed a more measured tone. He was glad to hear from Bentinck that he hoped he had satisfied the King and the Duke of York regarding his own conduct and views, 'but I fear', he added realistically, 'that you flatter yourself a little'. However that should be, he would write to James. He asked Bentinck to tell the King that the accomplices in the Rye House plot would not only not be tolerated in the Dutch Republic but that they would try to seize them and send them to England, and they were cooperating with Chudleigh on this score. There were rumours that Monmouth and a companion were in the country but it was not known where they were now, or whether the rumours were true, but both Chudleigh and himself would do everything possible to discover their whereabouts.

He was sorry that the King was still persuaded of France's good intentions. He could not conceive how Charles could allow himself these impressions and that he seemed to judge it reasonable that the German Reich should sacrifice Strasburg for some such equivalent as Fribourg or some other place in Alsace – an idea Charles had floated past Van Citters on 2 July. He continued to think that the Germans would remain resolute in the face of Louis's Regensburg offer, and he also thought that the Emperor would refuse Louis's offer of military assistance against the Turks, which was being discussed in England, since Louis's army would be more feared in Germany than the Turks themselves.

There was a mild hint of reproof, for the Prince expressed surprise that Bentinck had not mentioned whether Charles had indicated the terms on which he expected Spain to settle with France, 'since it is that which touches us most closely and on which subject I discoursed with you several times before your departure'.

Bentinck should not forget his concerns about his Orange Principality, should the subject come up, 'because assuredly, if the King does not prevent it, I will be dispossessed, and it is only he who can save me from this blow, if only he will speak firmly to France'.

'After having written to you of serious affairs, I must turn to bagatelles,' William resumed.

Hunting inevitably again became the subject of the letter, but on this occasion also scandal. Somebody's daughter had become pregnant and Eppinger, the Lieutenant-Colonel of the Prince's regiment of dragoons, was said to be responsible. The Colonel declared by all the devils in hell that he had never slept with her. The father and the mother had become ill; the son demanded a duel. 'There are a thousand entertaining aspects to the affair too long to relate,' said the Prince, 'but it is extremely embarrassing and I can't see any way out.'[14]

As he had promised Bentinck, William had written to his father-in-law, James, on 2 August, with James sending a friendly reply four days later when he promised to do his part in maintaining a good understanding between William and Charles – 'but you must do your part to [*sic*]'. He then went on to relate that the marriage between Princess Anne and Prince George had been consummated the previous night.

William had written to King Charles on 6 July complimenting him on the progress his plans were making to change the charter of the City of London, and at about the time he wrote to James he also wrote to the King concerning the Rye House plot. Charles replied – on 9 August – thanking him for what he wrote concerning his 'deliverance', as Charles put it 'from the hands of those bloody villans'. But he was sorry to learn from Bentinck that William persisted in thinking that peace could not be obtained on France's terms. These, of course, would have meant Spain's ceding Luxemburg and William replied asking Charles to consider what the Spanish Low Countries would become without that fortress and what assurances or security the Dutch could have in a 'barrier' which would not be capable of the least resistance.[15] He regretted these differences, he told Laurence Hyde, now the Earl of Rochester: 'if all the happiness and security of this State did not depend on it, and (if I may venture to say so) even the true interests of his Majesty [and the Duke of York], I could yield to their opinions'; he would do this on all that concerned the internal affairs of the King; 'but I hope that in future they will have a little more faith in me on the subject of foreign affairs, since assuredly, from being nearer the scene of action, we are better informed'.[16]

A DIVERSION IN THE NORTH SEA

On the night of 11–12 August a Dutch squadron set sail for the North Sea. There had been a dispute between Prince William, who wanted to use it in aid of Sweden as a means of bolstering the anti-French coalition, and Amsterdam, who wanted to use it to protect the Republic's commerce. In June the issue was settled by rumours that an English fleet had set sail either to assist the Danes and the French or to attack the returning Dutch East India fleet. The fleet remained in the North Sea, but at a position so far south that it was not well placed either to meet the returning East India Men or to intercept any attack from French or Danish warships. On the other hand it was usefully close to the Baltic. As the Republic's Admiral-General Prince William was able give secret instructions to the Admiral of the Dutch fleet, Schepers, who reported that 'we are being held here in order to be rather near to the Baltic, and thus not to leave Sweden too far out of sight'. Andrew Lossky has suggested that the most likely explanation for these dispositions was that Prince William was engaging in a war of nerves – rumours were rife that the fleet was set on sailing to Gothenburg, and William did not deny them. But – apart from the war of nerves – he may also have been keeping his options open. He had previously secretly assured Charles XI of Sweden of Dutch naval support but if the fleet had sailed directly to Gothenburg it would have raised a storm of protest from Amsterdam. On the other hand, if war broke out in the Baltic he could have answered Amsterdam that there was a need to protect the substantial amount of Dutch shipping operating there. As it was, the rumours and the war of nerves were enough to do the trick, sufficiently to distract the Franco-Danish fleet, and hostilities were averted. On 14 September William ordered Schepers to return to Schoonevelt, off the coast of Zeeland, probably because it was running out of provisions, and on 12 October the French fleet also sailed for home.[17]

FRENCH TROOPS ENTER THE SPANISH NETHERLANDS

In Germany Louis's offer of a 30-year truce was beginning to find resonance at Regensburg; there a majority of the Electoral college – that is, the four Rhenish Electors plus Brandenburg – lent support to the French proposal, later to be followed, after long deliberation, by the Colleges of the Princes and of the Towns, albeit only in principle and without deciding on anything definitive.[18] In the meantime Louis was acting aggressively against Spain.

He had given Spain deadlines, repeatedly extended, to accept the arbitration of Charles II and, like the offer of the 30-year truce to the Germans, the last extension expired on 31 August. That evening Louis's emissary, Baron d'Asfelt, presented himself before the Marquis de Grana, who had replaced Parma, and declared that, as Spain had repeatedly declined the offer of arbitration from the King of England, 35,000 French troops would the following day enter her territories and live off the land; at the least sign of resistance Marshal d'Humières had orders to burn 50 villages up to the gates of Brussels; and the French would impose contributions of 3 million florins on the inhabitants of Spanish Flanders. A week before Louvois had issued orders in the name of the King that the occupied territories should be left in such a condition that they would be incapable of furnishing any supplies at all to Grana in the future.[19] Thus did Brutality and Refinement stroll arm in arm amidst the splendours of Versailles.

On 3 September the Spanish ambassador at The Hague handed over a memorandum which asked that the 8,000 men due under the Spanish–Dutch Treaty should be sent to Spain's assistance. The Prince informed the States-General that day that he had anticipated the French action and was planning to send troops to Brabant and Flanders as a precautionary measure. Amsterdam's view was that the Spanish request should be resisted as no state of war existed between France and Spain, an opinion in conflict with both the beliefs of Fagel and the Prince of Orange,[20] and indeed, although no formal war had been declared, with the underlying reality.

THE SIEGE OF VIENNA RAISED

Far away, in eastern Europe, Starhemberg had led a lionhearted defence of Vienna, which came perilously close to disaster; but now, two months after the siege began, forces from all over Germany and from Poland had come to the Emperor's aid. The wisdom of his withdrawal from his capital, which William of Orange had so strongly criticised, was now apparent; it enabled him to keep a government in being under his personal control to direct events, which would have been impossible if he had been locked up in the city. His and his allies' forces, including contingents from Bavaria and Saxony, were now assembled close by Vienna in overwhelming numbers – the Duke of Lorraine's army mustered some 40,000 men and that of Sobieski possibly a further 20,000; the Turks, who, according to Peter Wilson, had lost 40,000 men during the siege, had some 28,500 men plus an assortment of auxiliaries from Wallachia, from Moldavia and from the Tartars which were of uncertain value. On 12 September the allies descended on the Turkish camp from the surrounding hills and the army of the Grand Vizier was routed.[21]

In Versailles this was totally unexpected;[22] nor could Louis have anticipated the long-term consequences, which were to make of Habsburg Austria the great power essential to check his dominance of Europe. For the moment these effects would take time to develop, for Leopold would be first preoccupied in clearing the Turks from Hungary.

DISAGREEMENT ON REACTING TO LOUIS'S ACTIONS

Back in The Hague William and Fagel on 15 September pushed through the States-General a resolution to send the 8,000 Dutch troops to aid the Spaniards, despite the opposition of Friesland and Groningen and without Amsterdam's consent.[23] On 29 September the Council of State, led by Prince William, submitted a petition to increase the army by 16,000 men within four months. The Prince also looked around to raise troops from elsewhere and his thoughts turned to Sweden, where he knew Charles XI had surplus troops at his disposal. On 3 October – before William was aware that the French fleet had sailed for home – Schepers received orders to sail for Gothenburg. William's preference would have been for the Swedish troops to be sent to the Spanish Netherlands; but failing that they could have been sent to support the Brunswick dukes, who in turn could have sent assistance south to the Spanish Netherlands. But on his arrival at Gothenburg Schepers found Charles XI and his senior officers absent, with everything returned to a peace-time basis. It would have taken time to negotiate what Prince William wanted, and, at this late stage in the season, time was not on Schepers's side. He decided that he needed to return home; but he was already too late. Delayed by contrary winds, he did not put to sea until 4 November, and a storm destroyed seven of his ships of the line, with nearly 1,000 men – five of the ships from Amsterdam.

This disaster had not yet happened when the petition for 16,000 men was presented at the end of September. It had long been anticipated and caused no surprise, and Amsterdam decided not to confront the proposal head-on. Instead, on 5 October she resolved to ask what served the interests of the Republic best, peace on the basis that Luxemburg was ceded to France by Spain, or war between these two countries. In the latter case it was Amsterdam's contention that the Republic was not bound by her treaty with Spain – Spain had not exhausted all the means of arriving at an amicable settlement – and any assistance sent to the Spanish would go beyond her commitments. Before considering the petition therefore it behoved them to exert their best endeavours to explore the possibilities of peace.[24]

Van Beuningen informed Prince William of Amsterdam's decision. In a voice raised so high that a third person present overheard the altercation, the Prince responded that even if he were to share Amsterdam's opinion that Spain should cede Luxemburg, they would never be able to oblige her to do so.[25] On 21 October Amsterdam rejected the proposal of the new muster of 16,000 men on the grounds that it would lead to war and when the town's deputation informed William of this he laid the blame firmly at the door of Van Beuningen. He knew well enough what the intentions were of the 'heer van Beuningen', but he would frustrate them, 'or my name is not William'.[26]

SPAIN DECLARES WAR AGAINST FRANCE

By now a Franco-Spanish war had become unavoidable; on 12 October Grana gave the order that force should be met with force and Spanish parties emerged from their fortresses to pillage the villages of the French and to levy contributions on French territory. Louis forbade his subjects to pay these on pain of the galleys and ordered D'Humières to burn 50 houses or villages for every one in his country; six weeks later, this became 100 for one. On 26 October Spain declared war on the King of France, although the States-General were not officially informed by the Spanish ambassador until 14 December that war had been declared on the 11th.[27]

Nevertheless, Amsterdam continued to refuse the new muster of troops and she presented her case at the States of Holland on 4 November. There the Prince was standing behind the screen separating him from the main body of the hall, and, as Amsterdam was holding forth, he emerged from behind it. D'Avaux, he said, could not have spoken to the greater advantage of the King of France than Amsterdam had done. He had heard her saying that trade was the soul of the State. That was also his view, but the State should come first, for if the State were lost trade would follow. He was as deeply interested in the State – even more so than the entire magistrate of Amsterdam. As for Van Beuningen, he would not trouble himself with the chimeras and caprices of Burgomaster van Beuningen, who deserved to have his head cut down to roll at his feet.

So bitter had the dispute between the Prince and the Amsterdam Regent become that the Amsterdam deputies at The Hague advised Van Beuningen to refrain from coming to the town.[28]

On 5 November D'Avaux delivered a memorandum in which Louis offered one of five equivalents for his claims in the Spanish Low Countries, one of which was Luxemburg and its dependencies; another comprised Dixmude, Courtrai, Beaumont, Bouvines, Chimay, and the castellany of Ath. The three other alternatives lay in Spain, who was given until the end of the year to make her choice.[29] Simultaneously at the beginning of November the French laid siege to and captured Courtrai and Dixmude,[30] two towns which were specifically designated as 'barrier' towns under the Treaty of Nijmegen.[31]

As we have seen, Spain's reaction was to inform the States-General officially of her declaration of war. In the weak state she was in, it was a throw of desperation to force the Dutch to come to her aid.

Amsterdam remained resolute in her opposition to the new muster despite the pressure from other members of the States of Holland urging her to desist – all supported the new muster, except that Delft insisted on unanimity – and it was decided that a weighty delegation should be sent to her consisting of the Prince of Orange, three members of the nobility, including Bentinck, two each from nine towns, and the Grand Pensionary Fagel.[32] There was a touching attempt by Van Beuningen to explain his position to the Prince. On 12 November he wrote a moving letter deeply deploring the rift between them; he reiterated the reasons for the stance he was taking – not least that without the English navy the Republic would need to succumb to France – and expressing the hope that his innocence and uprightness in the service of the Prince and of the country would not remain forever concealed from His Highness.[33] But to these pleas the Prince of Orange was to remain implacable.

The auspices for the mission to Amsterdam were not good, as the news of the disaster to Schepers's fleet had arrived and William was charged with having exceeded his authority by sending the fleet without the assent of the States-General.[34]

The delegation arrived at Amsterdam on 15 November, where it remained whilst the cost of the stay was borne by the city. The courtesies were maintained; on the 16th the members of the delegation were conducted from their lodgings by coaches, accompanied by two of the Burgomasters and the town's own Pensionary, Jacob Hop, to arrive at the town hall, where the two remaining Burgomasters, one of them Van Beuningen, awaited them. Fagel set out the purpose of the mission and Hop asked if the delegates could remain for a few days to give Amsterdam a chance to formulate an appropriate reply. Meetings followed; the Prince of Orange was entertained to dinner on the 16th and reciprocated on the 18th (Van Beuningen absented himself from all the meals); but on the 19th it became apparent that Amsterdam, led by Jacob Hop, would not yield.

She argued that the new muster was not large enough to withstand the might of France and that a conference should be held with D'Avaux instead. Fagel said that Amsterdam was viewing the matter from the wrong perspective; it was not a question of either accepting the French conditions or engaging in a formal war, but merely of strengthening the army whilst negotiations were taking place; nor did he regard the French offer as constituting an ultimatum, as Amsterdam did. The talks stretched into the following day, with Amsterdam arguing that the lesser evil, accepting the French terms, should be preferred against the greater – the consequences of rejecting them.

On the 21st the Prince lost his patience; it was intolerable, he said, that a single member of the United Provinces should seek to govern the rest; it looked as though Amsterdam was too proud to review her position, once it had been challenged; and he departed with some of the delegation without taking his leave.

So concerned were the Amsterdam Burgomasters that a recurrence of the 1650 *coup d'état* executed by William's father would recur that Witsen was delegated to take defensive military measures.

And soon, in accordance with their view that talks should be held with D'Avaux, they were in correspondence with the French ambassador.

AMSTERDAM'S DEALINGS WITH D'AVAUX

In response to D'Avaux's invitation Hooft and Hop were delegated to go to his house to engage in discussions on 24 December 1683. These revolved around his memorandum of 5 November with the equivalents offered by Louis XIV. Louis was now prepared to extend the time for acceptance of these to 1 February 1684; and the options available if Spain did not reply by that date were also ventilated. No firm conclusions were reached and, in her defence, Amsterdam was later to argue that D'Avaux was told that, as she could not enter into any separate agreement with France, he would have to tell prominent figures in the Republic of his proposals. Of these contacts Fagel, and hence Prince William, were informed.[35]

But Amsterdam was involved in a dangerous exercise. D'Avaux's object, naturally, was to explore the divisions within the Republic to ascertain whether they could not be exploited to prevent her forcefully intervening on the side of Spain.

The ire of the Prince of Orange was aroused; he saw Amsterdam's actions as imperilling the safety of the country and thought that she was even flirting with something close to treason. On 31 December, at the States of Holland, he launched a powerful attack on both the city and on Van Beuningen. If Amsterdam continued on her course, he said, they would undoubtedly have war and the Republic would go under. He was accused of warmongering; he would not extol his efforts in avoiding war; but he was certain that Van Beuningen's methods would bring war about. Amsterdam sought to appease France and had a secret intelligence with her, which could not be tolerated. The issue now was whether, by means of Amsterdam, they should submit to France, which he would resist as long as he could. Freedom was being invoked by Amsterdam whilst at the same time everybody else was forced to desist from arming themselves.

He then issued a – probably unwise and heavy-handed – threat, and alluded to the fate that had befallen the De Witt brothers when they had been torn to pieces by the mob in 1672. April would not be upon them, he said, before the issue was decided in the streets and there was a repeat of 1672; it would then become evident whose heads were safe, and which Regents had kept to their oaths and done their duty and which had not. But he would not submit to France and he would safeguard the existing form of government with his blood.[36]

The nobility – almost certainly with Bentinck to the fore – provided unwavering support. Amsterdam wanted to lord it over everybody else, the nobles said; it was putting freedom and the welfare of the State at risk; those responsible should be named and the intelligence connections they had with France should be brought to light. In the meantime if Amsterdam could be persuaded to drop her objections to the muster of new troops, many difficulties could be prevented; otherwise it would have to be decided by majority vote.[37]

Amsterdam argued that the Republic was not at war with France and she was just as entitled to talk to the French envoy as to the Swedish. Such conversations were perfectly permissible provided that what concerned the Republic in general was revealed, which she had said she was prepared to do. Meanwhile she was sufficiently alarmed by the Prince's remarks for the Burgomasters to discuss measures to be taken by the civic guard and the militia.[38]

On the muster of new troops Amsterdam was not without her supporters. When the Prince and Fagel attempted to carry the measure through the States of Holland by majority votes they found resistance from six towns. They were able to reduce this to three – Amsterdam and Schiedam, with Delft voting for the muster but against the majority decision – and, on that basis, it passed on 31 January 1684. But Amsterdam regarded it as unlawful and refused to pay for her share of the troops.[39]

She underlined her determination on 1 February by re-electing Van Beuningen as Burgomaster,[40] after which the dispute with Prince William escalated further. Since 21 January a conference of the allies had convened at The Hague, which became known as The Hague Conference; it consisted of representatives from the Emperor, Bavaria, Spain, Sweden and the Dutch, whilst further representatives were expected from Saxony, the Brunswick dukes and the Franconian and Upper Rhine *Kreise*; but on the Dutch side only five Provinces were represented, with Friesland and Groningen refusing to join. On 7 February the States-General resolved, again without Friesland and Groningen, and against the opposition of Amsterdam, that it would accept only a general peace encompassing all the allies, which would be endorsed by a league of guarantee. The allies followed suit, but

Amsterdam thought it unjust that the five Provinces were standing in the way of reaching a separate settlement with Spain by insisting on a joint settlement with the *Reich*.[41]

Determined to push the confrontation up a notch, Prince William now again mismanaged the situation. A despatch by D'Avaux to Louis XIV of 9 January giving details of his discussions with Amsterdam was intercepted,[42] and ended up with the Prince – whether the interception was his doing or that of the Marquis de Grana is still a matter of dispute. The despatch was retained by the Prince for a while until he decided that the time was opportune to make use of it for a further onslaught on Amsterdam.

On 16 February he appeared at the States-General, saying that he had a matter of the utmost importance to impart; it concerned in particular Gerrit Hooft and Jacob Hop, and he asked that they should depart from the hall. Fagel then read out D'Avaux's intercepted despatch which, in fact, gave a very misleading account of his conversations with Amsterdam and, as some of it was not yet deciphered, a rather muddled one. But, as many of the Dutch delegates had an imperfect command of French, they gained the impression that there was a sinister accord between Hop, Hooft and the French ambassador, to which Fagel gave added impetus by giving the translation as adverse a gloss as possible. At first there was talk of arresting Hop and Hooft, who had returned to the meeting on the grounds that, as their names were not mentioned in the despatch, there were no grounds for excluding them. The meeting did resolve by five votes that Amsterdam's papers should be seized and sealed. But it was clear that there was also empathy for the city, for it was resolved that the papers were to be entrusted to the safekeeping of one of her own delegates.

THE FRENCH OFFER OF TRUCE TO SPAIN AND THE *REICH*

In the midst of this rumpus D'Avaux advised the States-General on 17 February of a French offer to Spain of a 20-year truce, with France retaining what she had acquired, an offer that had also been made to the German *Reich*. It may be that this offer had been prompted by the pressure arising from The Hague Conference of the allies. But, although the French now conceded that the disputes between the *Reich* and Spain should be settled jointly, the surrender of so many places was unacceptable to Prince William.

The rumpus about D'Avaux's despatch continued; attempts to keep matters secret were bound to fail in the Dutch Republic; a pamphlet war broke out and the country's divisions were clear for all the world to see. Amsterdam was able to defend herself vigorously and the Prince seems to have decided that the wisest course was to let this particular affair fizzle out.

William's position was becoming demonstrably weaker. On 28 February Amsterdam withdrew her delegates from the States of Holland[43] in protest over the D'Avaux despatch, which must have raised questions as to how the Union could continue to function without her participation and cooperation. In the States-General none of the Provinces except Gelderland and Utrecht supported the muster. Friesland, under William's cousin Hendrik-

Casimir, argued that there was no need for it and that a truce was a better option. Led by the towns of Middelburg and Goes, Zeeland was also opposed, although Goes gave way after the Prince wrote to them. In March he decided to go to Middelburg himself, but could make no headway and the Zeeland Pensionary, De Huybert, refused his request to push the resolution through by majority vote. Prince William was reduced to taking the chair himself, when, at the end of the month, the resolution was eventually passed by five votes to one, with Middelburg strongly protesting.[44]

In the meantime Amsterdam had resolved on 24 and 28 February to press for negotiations with France on the basis of the French offer of the 20-year truce. Other members of both the Holland States and the States-General argued that to put pressure on Spain to yield to the truce contravened the treaty of 1673. But they did not want to follow Spain in engaging in open warfare with France, and their hopes rested on The Hague Conference of the allies.[45] This decided at the end of February to ask England to propose to Louis a truce of seven or eight years, to be guaranteed by the allies. As far as the *Reich* was concerned they proposed various alternatives for Louis to choose and as far as Spain was concerned they offered Louis four more towns. The proposals remained academic, however, as they were rejected by Spain; and Charles II furthermore said they would be unacceptable to Louis and he declined to act as intermediary. Instead Chudleigh submitted a memorandum on 17 March to the States-General asking for their cooperation to persuade Spain to accept the terms of the 20-year truce.[46]

Three days earlier Prince William had persuaded the States of Holland to send extra troops to assist Spain, but once more against the adamant objection of Amsterdam, supported in this instance by Schiedam and Edam and with Den Briel and Purmurend demurring. He did manage to get it through the States-General, but, following what had become the usual pattern, only with the support of five Provinces, and without Friesland and Groningen.[47] Obviously he was finding matters increasingly heavy going.

And he was not being encouraged by the actions of the Elector of Brandenburg.

FREDERICK-WILLIAM OFFERS HIS MEDIATION IN THE HAGUE

Frederick-William entered a new alliance with France in January 1684, in which he undertook to attack the Brunswick dukes if they came to the assistance of Spain, and he also agreed to promote the acceptance of Louis's *réunions* in the *Reich*. He also supported Louis's offer of the 20-year truce, as the best available means of preserving peace in the *Reich*. At the same time he wanted to keep an eye on his interests in the Dutch States. As Waldeck remarked – and none knew the Elector better – these interests were substantial, because his children were the heirs presumptive of the Prince of Orange 'and it was only through these States that one of them could succeed to the Stadholdership of these Provinces'. He accordingly sent his minister, Paul Fuchs, to The Hague to confer with the Amsterdam Regents and to assess the situation.[48]

After an initial meeting in Amsterdam with Van Beuningen, who told him that the

Prince 'had more ambition, obstinacy, and self-confidence than was good', Fuchs had an audience with the Prince himself on 18 March, at which he explained that the Elector wanted to see if, through his good offices, he could not bring about a reconciliation of the misunderstandings existing in the Republic. Van Beuningen, he said, who felt acutely the disfavour he had fallen into with the Prince, well understood the need for a reconciliation provided that Amsterdam's rights and privileges were not affected and provided peace was maintained.

William replied that he did not want war, but the Spanish Netherlands were the foremost defence of the Dutch State, which she could not abandon. Once they were conquered, France could drive forward into the heart of the country. Above all France should not become master of Luxemburg, the only means by which the Spanish Netherlands could maintain communications with Germany. Louis had not the least right to what he had seized after the Treaty of Nijmegen. One would have to be blind not to see that it was the mastery of Europe that he coveted. It was true that the forces that could be arraigned against France fell far too short; and that from a worldly perspective the United Provinces and their allies could expect nothing but setbacks and defeats; but they would have to await, with patience and resolution, what God decreed. It was better to die with honour than to live in shame. As for himself, he was born and bred in adversity. Notwithstanding that, he was by God's Grace restored to the offices of his ancestors, despite his enemies. That same Grace would, he hoped, prevent his dying a hapless death, but if God in his wisdom decided otherwise, he would abide by his will.[49]

We have here, then, a further illustration of what motivated the Prince of Orange. Right was not on the side of Louis XIV, who wanted to dominate Europe – to establish a 'universal monarchy'; he was unshakeably convinced that he was God's instrument to prevent this happening; but, if God decided otherwise, his *gloire* demanded that he die in honour rather than live in shame. In the meantime he would fight on against all the odds, come what may.

The discord within his clan was something that the Prince felt acutely. 'One thing pains me in the extreme, that the Elector, who from my earliest youth has regarded me as his son, and whom I have esteemed as a father, now seems to be leaning towards the Amsterdammers, who regard it as part of their renown to contradict everything that I put forward.' As for Van Beuningen, he wanted nothing more to do with him – he had been insulted by him in the grossest manner,[50] which in the Prince's eyes, and in 17th-century terms, constituted a derogation of his *gloire* that was not tolerable.

Van Beuningen, for his part, told Fuchs at the beginning of April that the Prince and Fagel were hell-bent on war and that to achieve this they were prepared to cast aside the fundamental laws of the Provinces and the constitution of the Union. There was clear evidence, he went on, that there were plans to murder or kidnap him – he stayed inside his house and posted a guard at his door.

The Prince's stand was at the cost of his popularity. Fuchs said that one Province after another had come to thank him for his efforts on behalf of the peace party, not excluding Gelderland and Utrecht, and also Overijssel − the three Provinces over which the Prince exercised the tightest control − and the hatred of the populace for him and Fagel was increasing by the day.[51]

THE FRENCH BESIEGE LUXEMBURG AND SUBMIT NEW PROPOSALS

At the end of April the French laid siege to Luxemburg and Louis used this additional pressure to submit new proposals, contained in a memorandum from D'Avaux on the 29th in which Louis justified his claim to the city on the grounds that it lay outside the barrier stipulated by the Treaty of Nijmegen. If Spain surrendered Luxemburg by 20 May he would, of the places he had captured since 20 August 1683, return two, with their defences levelled, and retain three. Side by side with the concession there was a threat: if the Dutch came to the assistance of Spain he would give orders for the seizure of ships and goods belonging to Dutch subjects. Amsterdam's reaction was to resolve on the 30th that all Dutch troops above the 8,000 should be withdrawn from the Spanish Netherlands if Spain did not accept Louis's terms.[52]

William was making an assessment of the military options and initially took a pessimistic view; he wrote to Waldeck on 8 May, saying he doubted whether the Count could bring German troops to Luxemburg's aid in time and that the Dutch were too weak to do it on their own. 'It is a curse of heaven that our people are in such an ill mind or alternatively so ignorant as not to see that France is playing cat and mouse with us. However, if the good Lord wishes to see us lost we have well merited it and we must have patience.'[53]

One concession was elicited from Louis XIV. We have seen that on 17 February he demanded from Spain the retention of all his acquisitions, which would be accompanied by a 20-year truce, the same terms as he was offering to the German *Reich*. Although the demands contained in D'Avaux's memorandum of 29 April were more moderate than those of 17 February, there was no mention of the truce. On 9 May Louis conceded the point; the places stipulated in D'Avaux's memorandum of 29 April would be retained by him during the period of the truce, that is to say, they would not be yielded outright. Talks commenced between D'Avaux and representatives of the States-General, which dragged on with the Dutch deputies insisting that the truce be a general one, that it was to be on the same terms as for the German *Reich*, and that agreement be reached on the German places to be ceded.[54]

With these negotiations remaining unsettled, William's stance remained obdurate; he told the States-General on the 11th that they could abandon Luxemburg and do what they liked; but as far as he himself was concerned he would rather lose his life than let Luxemburg go and he would rather perish in front of the place than consent to its abandonment.[55] With the sensitive talks taking place with D'Avaux there was a nervousness amongst the Holland Regents as to what the Prince might do in the meantime. It caused the States of Holland −

probably at the instigation of Amsterdam – to ask him on 13 May not to allow the Dutch troops in the Spanish Netherlands to undertake any hostilities. To this William replied that this would be difficult and he could do so for only a limited period of time[56] – which was unlikely, of course, to have stilled the nerves jangling in the Holland States.

He continued to study the military options. On 22 May he wrote to Waldeck that he had spent the previous week in Vilvoorden – where the Dutch army was assembled – to consult with the Marquis de Grana, and there he had formulated plans. The 20 May deadline given by the French for Spain to surrender Luxemburg had passed without the States-General giving a final answer to France's proposals and this, William hoped, might give him time to rally wayward Dutch spirits to try to rescue the situation. It all depended on being able to save Luxemburg and he urged Waldeck to endeavour to do all he could to ensure that the troops of the Elector of Bavaria, the Landgrave of Hesse and the Allied *Kreise* could march promptly up to the Rhine. He could join him with eight or ten battalions of infantry and all the cavalry and the dragoons, and Grana could contribute about 3,000 men. The key was for Luxemburg to hold out long enough.[57]

With Imperial troops Waldeck estimated at the end of May that he could have 40,000 men at his disposal, although he had doubts whether there was a will to divert so many men from Germany.[58] Not the least of his difficulties was that there were doubts amongst the Germans that the Prince had the authority to carry the States-General with him.[59]

These doubts were borne out when, on 2 June, Amsterdam resolved that she would refuse to make payments stipulated under her allocation in the State of War (the Dutch War Budget) unless her specific consent was first given.[60]

CAPITULATION OF LUXEMBURG; LEOPOLD AND THE DUTCH ACCEPT THE TRUCE

All this notwithstanding, William travelled again to Vilvoorden to continue with his martial preparations. But by the time he arrived there the blow fell – Luxemburg had surrendered on 7 June. 'The loss is irreparable', he wrote to Waldeck on the 10th. But a second reverse was to follow – he heard on the 12th that the Emperor had agreed to accept Louis's offer of the 20-year truce. Leopold had decided that the opportunities presented by the Turkish defeat at Vienna and the effort now required to recapture Hungary overruled, for the time being, resistance to Louis XIV in the west. It is difficult to disagree with the wisdom of this course: if he had turned to the west now he would still have had the Turks in his rear; if he did so later, having won in the east, he could bring all his resources to bear against France. As it was, the truce did not give legal sanction to Louis's acquisitions; it was to be a joint truce, which was to apply to Spain as well; and, furthermore, as John Spielman has pointed out, it was an important concession to what Brandenburg had been asking for.[61]

But for William of Orange it was a great defeat. '*Au nom de Dieu considerez quel contretemps*', he exclaimed to Waldeck on 12 June. It drove one mad, he wrote, and it only required this to drive their people at The Hague into further extravagances. However, if that was God's will, they would have to submit to it; they would have the consolation of having done all they could for their respective countries.[62]

But it was one of his characteristics that he adapted to reality when he thought it inevitable. When caution was urged upon him by the States-General he replied on 20 June that his purpose was always to act in accordance with their intentions, and, as far as he could, he would avoid provocations leading to hostilities whilst he awaited the outcome of their deliberations – unless, he added, the French took aggressive measures.[63]

On 24 June the States-General accepted the truce by majority vote, with Gelderland and Zeeland protesting,[64] and on the 29th the treaty was signed, with the Dutch undertaking to refuse support to Spain if she refused the terms. Spain had authorised Leopold to negotiate a truce on her behalf and on 15 August Spanish and Imperial treaties were entered into at Regensburg. Under the Spanish treaty Louis, during the term of the 20-year truce, retained Luxemburg, Beaumont, Bouvines and Chimay, whilst returning Courtrai and Dixmude. Under the treaty with Leopold and the *Reich* Louis, likewise during the term of the truce, retained the *réunions* made before 1 August 1681 plus Strasburg and Kehl, returning the rest to their initial possessors.[65] The only consolation remaining to the Prince of Orange was that, unlike the Treaty of Nijmegen, the Dutch and their allies had acted conjointly.

1 Franken, *op. cit.*, pp.218–23. Groen van Prinsterer, *Archives, op. cit.*, 2, V, pp.572–3.

2 Groen van Prinsterer, *Archives, op. cit.*, 2, V, pp.566–71.

3 Lossky, *The Baltic Crisis, op. cit.*, pp.23, 24, 27, 28, p.57 n.121.

4 *Ibid.*, pp.30, 18–19.

5 *Correspondentie Willem III en Bentinck, op. cit.*, II, 2, pp.551–3.

6 Hutton, *Charles II, op. cit.*, pp.419–22. Miller, *op. cit.*, pp.366–7. Haley, *Shaftesbury, op. cit.*, p.699–700, 704. Groen van Prinsterer, *Archives, op. cit.*, 2, V, pp.577–8. Keay, *op. cit.*, pp.287–94.

7 Keay, *op. cit.*, pp.295–7, 300.

8 Baxter, *op. cit.*, p.188.

9 *Correspondentie Willem III en Bentinck, op. cit.*, I, 1, p.12.

10 Spielman, *op. cit.*, pp.99–100, 102. John Stoye, *op. cit.*, p.21. Bérenger, *A History of the Hapsburg Empire 1273-1700*, trans. C.A.Simpson, London 1994, p.328.Whaley, *op. cit.*, II, p.42.

11 Antal and Pater, *op. cit.*, I, p.365n. Müller, *Waldeck, op. cit.*, I, p.96. *Correspondentie Willem III en Bentinck, op. cit.*, I.

12 *Ibid.*, I, 1, pp.12–14.

13 *Correspondentie Willem III en Bentinck, op. cit.*, I, 1, p.14.

14 *Ibid.*, I, 1, pp.14–16. For Charles's suggestion that Fribourg should be accepted as an equivalent for Strasburg see *Correspondentie Willem III en Bentinck, op. cit.*, II, 2, pp.561–4.

15 Groen van Prinsterer, *Archives, op. cit.*, 2, V, pp.582–3.

16 Singer, *op. cit.*, I, pp.89, 90.

17 Lossky, *The Baltic Crisis, op. cit.*, pp.34–8.

18 Müller, *Waldeck, op. cit.*, I, p.96.

19 Rousset, *op. cit.*, III, pp.236–7.

20 Kurtz, *op. cit.*, pp.55–6. *Correspondentie Willem III en Bentinck, op. cit.*, II, 2, p.602.

21 Stoye, *op. cit.*, pp.257ff. Bérenger, *Hapsburg Empire, op. cit.*, p.330. See also Wilson, *German Armies, op. cit.*, pp.70–1 for the numbers involved, for which, as always, there is considerable variation.

22 Lossky, *Louis XIV, op. cit.*, p.173.

23 Dreiskämper, *op. cit.*, IV, p.16. Franken, *op. cit.*, p.224.

24 Kurtz, *op. cit.*, p.62. Wagenaar, *op. cit.*, 15, p.140. Lossky, *The Baltic Crisis, op. cit.*, pp.38–42.

25 Kurtz, *op. cit.*, p.63. It is Kurtz's opinion that the interview was probably the one related in D'Avaux, *Négociations, op. cit.*, I, pp.350–1.

26 Franken, *op. cit.*, p.225.

27 Rousset, *op. cit.*, III, p.238. Japikse, *Willem III, op. cit.*, II, p.180, says Spain declared war on 11 December, as does Kurtz, *op. cit.*, p.83 with the Spanish ambassador informing the States General on the 14th. See also Wagenaar, *op. cit.*, 15, p.148.

28 Kurtz, *op. cit.*, pp.67–8.

29 *Ibid.*, p.68.

30 Rousset, *op. cit.*, III, pp.240–1.

31 Israel, *The Dutch Republic, op. cit.*, p.832.

32 For this and what follows I have mainly relied on Kurtz, *op. cit.*, pp.71ff. and Japikse, *Willem III, op. cit.*, II, pp.178–81. Japikse says that everybody except Delft supported the muster (p.178). Israel, *The Dutch Republic, op. cit.*, p.831 says Leyden and Delft supported Amsterdam. Wagenaar, *op. cit.*, 15, p.141 says Delft was only insisting on unanimity and (p.145) he includes both Delft and Leyden amongst the nine towns making up the delegation.

33 *Correspondentie Willem III en Bentinck, op. cit.*, II, 2, pp.614–16.

34 Lossky, *The Baltic Crisis, op. cit.*, p.39.

35 Kurtz, *op. cit.*, pp.87, 88, 92.

36 Wagenaar, *op. cit.*, 15, p.159–60.

37 *Ibid.*, 15, pp.160–1.

38 Kurtz, *op. cit.*, pp.94–5.

39 Israel, *The Dutch Republic, op. cit.*, p.832. Wagenaar, *op. cit.*, 15, pp.177–9.

40 Franken, *op. cit.*, p.218.

41 Kurtz, *op. cit.*, pp.104, 117. Wagenaar, *op. cit.*, 15, p.219.

42 The following account is based on Kurtz, *op. cit.*, pp.98, 107–11. See also Wagenaar, *op. cit.*, 15, pp.179ff. Japikse, *Willem III, op. cit.*, II, p.184–5. Troost, in *The Anglo-Dutch Moment, op. cit.*, p.325.

43 Wagenaar, *op. cit.*, 15, p.191.

44 Kurtz, *op. cit.*, p.116. Israel, *Dutch Republic, op. cit.*, p.833. Wagenaar, *op. cit.*, 15, p.216.

45 Kurtz, *op. cit.*, pp.104, 117. Wagenaar, *op. cit.*, 15, p.222.

46 Kurtz, *op. cit.*, pp.117–18. The towns were Kortrijk, Dixmude, Beaumont and Chimay. Wagenaar, *op. cit.*, 15, p.222.

47 Kurtz, *op. cit.*, p.118.

48 McKay, *Great Elector, op. cit.*, pp.250–1. *Urkunden und Actenstücke, op. cit.*, XXI, p.69.

49 *Urkunden und Actenstücke, op. cit.*, XXI, pp.68ff. Wagenaar, *op. cit.*, 15, pp.201ff.

50 *Urkunden und Actenstücke, op. cit.*, XXI, p.71 and Wagenaar, *op. cit.*, 15, p.203.

51 *Urkunden und Actenstücke, op. cit.*, XXI, p.75–6.

52 Kurtz, *op. cit.*, p.127. D'Avaux, *Négociations, op. cit.*, II, pp.323ff.

53 Müller, *Waldeck, op. cit.*, I, p.265.

54 Kurtz, *op. cit.*, pp.128–9.

55 D'Avaux, *Négociations, op. cit.*, III, p.34.

56 Japikse, *Willem III, op. cit.*, II, p.189.

57 Müller, *Waldeck, op. cit.*, I, pp.268–9.

58 *Ibid.*, I, p.270.

59 *Ibid.*, I pp.274–5.

60 Kurtz, *op. cit.*, p.134.

61 Müller, *Waldeck, op. cit.*, I, pp.276–7, 278–9. Spielman, op. cit., p.116–17.

62 Müller, *Waldeck, op. cit.*, I, p.279.

63 Japikse, *Willem III, op. cit.*, II, p.190.

64 Kurtz, *op. cit.*, p.136.

65 Lossky, *Louis XIV, op. cit.*, p.174.

24 1683–1685: MONMOUTH; CHARLES'S DEATH AND JAMES'S SUCCESSION; BETTY VILLIERS

MONMOUTH

We need to turn now to the perplexing relationship between the Prince of Orange and the Duke of Monmouth. We have seen that following the revelations of the Rye House plot in the summer of 1683 Monmouth had taken refuge at Toddington Manor, the home of his mistress, Lady Henrietta Wentworth. Through the intermediary of Halifax there was a reconciliation between the Duke, his father and the Duke of York in November, when the King's joy was apparent for all to see. That joy, however, soon turned to exasperated anger when, having received his father's pardon, Monmouth refuted his confession. He was denied the court and by the beginning of 1684 he had fled to Brussels.[1] Of these happenings the Duke of York kept the Prince of Orange informed in a series of letters, including the King's instructions to his envoy in Brussels that Monmouth was to receive no military honours.[2]

His correspondence took a sharper tone after William went in the middle of May 1684 to Vilvoorden, a few miles north of Brussels, to review some of the Dutch troops; there he met Monmouth and his companion, Lord Brandon, who had been imprisoned in the Tower and who had escaped conviction for the Rye House plot because of lack of evidence.[3] At the end of the month James wrote to his nephew: 'I find by your letter that the Duke of Monmouth had been to see you.… I do think it odd enough for him to present himself to you, after his having been engaged in so horrid a conspiracy, for the alteration of the government, and ruin of the King and our family.' On 6 June he wrote to Mary: 'I must need tell you, it scandalises all loyal and monarchical people here, to know how well the Prince lives with, and how civil he is to the Duke of Monmouth, and Lord Brandon … in this affair methinks you might talk to the Prince (though you meddle in no others); the Duke of Monmouth, Lord Brandon, and the rest of that party, being declared my mortal enemies. And let the Prince flatter himself as he pleases, the Duke of Monmouth will do his part, to have a push with him for the crown.'[4] Mary's excuse that Monmouth had been pardoned by the King was dismissed on the grounds that 'all the world knows what an ill return he made the King for it, which obliged his Ma. to banish him his presence'.[5]

On 5 June Prince William again went to the Dutch army encampment at Vilvoorden, and stayed there until the end of the month, when the Twenty Years' Truce was signed.[6] According to D'Avaux he once more showed Monmouth exceptional marks of friendship; he ordered his troops to accord him the same honours as those for Waldeck; and when the

English regiments in Dutch service wished to comply with King Charles's orders not to show Monmouth any marks of respect he overruled them. After the signing of the truce he went on to Dieren for the hunting and took Monmouth and Brandon with him.[7]

On 4 July Van Citters, the Dutch envoy in London, conveyed Charles II's marked displeasure at William's treatment of his renegade son, and the English ambassador in The Hague, Chudleigh, received orders to raise the matter with him.[8] When he met Prince William the Prince said that he had accorded Monmouth the civilities due to his birth, being the King's son, whom the King had always loved and whose faults, yet again, he had pardoned; and he resorted to the mediation of Halifax to soothe his uncle's feelings.[9] He also asked Bentinck, whom as we have seen he had sent to London, to intervene with Charles, should the occasion arise, explaining his behaviour on much the same terms as he had used with Chudleigh. Monmouth, he wrote, was Charles's son 'whom he has pardoned for the faults which he may have committed, and though he has removed him from his presence, I know that in the bottom of his heart, he has always some friendship for him'.[10] But neither Halifax's nor Bentinck's mediation nor occasional letters of exculpation from William stopped the King's complaints. From the beginning of August 1684 until Charles's death on 16 February 1685 Van Citters, acting in this respect as the personal envoy of the Prince of Orange, sent despatch after despatch to the Prince containing Charles's complaints about the civil treatment William accorded the Duke.[11] Monmouth was undoubtedly continuously entertained by the Orange court during this period.[12] Why did the Prince do it?

Different explanations have been proffered. Foxcroft maintained that William's behaviour towards Monmouth had the secret sanction of Charles II who, towards the end of 1684, was planning to reduce the influence of the Duke of York and to promote that of Halifax and Monmouth, and that Prince William saw in this an opportunity at last of forging the English alliance. But this has been rebutted by Kenyon in some detail.[13] Burnet in his *History* says there was a scheme afoot to exile James afresh to Scotland and that Monmouth was summoned to England to be informed of this – although Burnet admits 'that how it was laid was so great a secret that I could never penetrate it'.[14] In her recently published biography of Monmouth Dr Keay says that William and Mary developed a genuine affection for the Duke and that they connived at Charles's scheme to banish the Duke of York and recall Monmouth, a scheme in which Halifax was closely involved.[15] Hugh Trevor-Roper's verdict was that 'The evidence is conflicting and irreconcilable.'[16]

Certainly there are a number of perplexing points. It must be doubtful that the illegitimate Monmouth would have brought the stability to England that William of Orange had so long aimed at – even if Charles were to declare him legitimate after all his previous denials. It does also seem inherently implausible that William would have wanted to see Monmouth in a powerful position in England, rivalling the claims of Mary and himself. And, even granted Charles II's predilection for playing a double game, supporting his brother James,

Duke of York, on the one hand and his son James, Duke of Monmouth, on the other, and then coming down on the side of Monmouth would have run counter to his whole conduct during the Popish Plot.

There is another possible explanation, a hint of which is to be found in the otherwise somewhat unreliable D'Avaux, who reported on 11 January 1685 that Prince William was continuing at all times to heap welcome on Monmouth and that, asthmatic though he was, and averse to all diversions, not least dancing, he nevertheless passed several nights in that pursuit in the company of Mary's ladies-in-waiting to entertain Monmouth. Bentinck, D'Avaux's account goes on, and other friends of William loudly put it about that the Prince made no move as regarded Monmouth but with the consent of the King of England, pointing out that Monmouth, who had just been to England, had seen the King in particular.[17]

Chudleigh, too, had reported much the same to Sunderland at the end of October when he said Monmouth had been expressly invited to Soestdijk, one of William's residences, and to Dieren for the hunting. All the Prince's 'creatures', according to Chudleigh, spread it around that the treatment of Monmouth was with Charles's 'private consent and approbation'; and that it was commonly believed that Monmouth stood very well with the King and was in his confidence, but that Charles did not want to show this openly for fear of upsetting the Duke of York. Prince William, said Chudleigh, knew this very well, and this was his way 'to make his court to the King'.[18]

All this would be consistent with William's court engaging in an exercise of disinformation. It would serve the useful purpose of alarming Louis XIV with the thought that Charles II was realigning himself with his nephew – anything that induced alarm in Louis was of course relish to the nephew. And it also reminded the Regents in the Republic of William's connection with the Stuart clan, that two-edged sword, one edge of which could be put at their disposal whatever disadvantages they apprehended from its other side.[19]

Apart from the Prince's resort to Halifax and Bentinck, he responded to Van Citters's fulsome despatches apparently on only three occasions. The first was on 2 October when he excused his failure to write with the rather weak reason that the King had been at Winchester and that he did not want to inconvenience him there with business. Writing to the King at the same time he said that seeing the Duke of Monmouth could not be construed as a crime; he could vow for the Duke that during the time he saw him he always spoke with the respect and veneration which he owed the King and he appeared as zealous for his service as any subject could be. But he did not address the King's complaint that his reception of his son was inappropriately fulsome, nor did he desist from continuing on that course. On 15 December he wrote again to the King in similarly bland terms without addressing the issue, merely saying that he did not believe he deserved the disgrace he had fallen into. And on 9 January 1685 he wrote to Van Citters saying that he was prepared to make submission to the King for anything Charles wished and to ask forgiveness for any offence he may have committed, but to admit guilt for something which he was persuaded did not proceed from ill intent nor was of ill consequence was not something that could be demanded from himself or any fair-minded man, and that he would never do. He feared the arrival of Monmouth at The Hague on 7 January would again be a pretext for suspicion, but he could assure Van Citters that he was not forewarned of Monmouth's arrival, far less that he had invited him. The Duke, he added, was preparing to leave for Hungary in the spring to attend the forthcoming military campaign against the Turks.[20]

The Prince was right that Monmouth's arrival would start the tongues wagging in London. On 26 January Van Citters reported that the north wind from St James's blew so hard and with such impetus that nothing could resist it and what was uttered against the Prince was so hostile that no one could counter it. Nor perhaps was this surprising for, as Charles complained, Prince William was slow in writing to the King himself and when he did so the letters were as bland as they could be. For the reasons we have given we can surmise – and it is no more than another surmise – that William had no intention of desisting from welcoming Monmouth for as long as he could get away with it and he presented this in public as signalling a secret understanding between him and his English uncle, despite Charles's exasperation.[21]

DEATH OF CHARLES II AND SUCCESSION OF JAMES II

Then the unexpected happened. On 12 February 1685 Charles was being shaved; he had a stroke; he fell to the ground. He was received into the Catholic Church on the evening of the 15th and the following morning he asked that the curtains be drawn so that he could see the sun rising over the Thames. And then he died.[22]

And the Duke of York became King James II.

James began his reign by striking a moderate domestic note when he lost no time in announcing to the Privy Council that 'I shall make it my endeavour to preserve this government both in church and state as it is by law established.' There was one major change in the ministerial team: James's brother-in-law, Rochester, became Lord Treasurer and Rochester's brother, Clarendon, succeeded Halifax as Lord Privy Seal, Halifax being demoted to Lord President of the Council. It was Rochester who was now the most important of the new King's ministers. But a dark horse remained, Sunderland, who, the moment Charles died, dexterously asked Barillon to seek 'marks of protection' from Louis XIV with regard to the new English King. This and his ability to influence Parliamentary elections assured his precarious survival as a Secretary of State.[23]

But James's attention was not only fixed on the domestic scene. On 18 February he had a private conversation with Barillon to tell him of his plans. For financial reasons he had to summon Parliament in May, but, he assured Barillon, he would hinder Parliament from meddling in foreign affairs and he 'would put an end to the session as soon as I see the members shew any ill will'. He was aware, he said, that without Louis's support and protection he could do nothing of what he designed for the Catholics and that his safety could be assured only if they were granted their liberty of conscience. The following morning Rochester expanded on this by indicating that James was looking to Louis for financial support if Parliament refused him the requisite revenues.[24]

Although Charles II had broken the triennial act of 1664 by not calling a Parliament – he had agreed with Louis in April 1681 that he would not do so – the life revenues granted to him could not be continued without Parliamentary approval. In the event the elections held during March and April returned 468 Tories and only 57 Whigs. This was partly the result of the campaign for new constituency charters which Charles had inaugurated – he had completed 51 new charters by the time of his death – and which James continued in the run-up to the elections, when he added a further 48, although modern research has concluded that the Tories would still have won the election by a good margin without this manipulation.[25]

At the beginning of his reign James had a fair-sized army at his disposal; when Tangier was abandoned its garrison returned to England, increasing Charles's army in England to nearly 9,000 men, with an additional 9,700 troops in Scotland and Ireland – over 6,000 in Ireland alone.[26]

And Charles left the royal finances in a very healthy state; his ordinary revenue plus the small French subsidy gave him £1.45 million a year and during James's reign his income averaged around £2.06 million from all sources between Michaelmas 1685 and Michaelmas 1688.[27]

James could not have expected a better inheritance. There had been one consistent thread running through all his brother's designs: ever since his restoration Charles had looked for financial support from outside the country to make himself independent of Parliament; he sought this first from the Dutch and then from Louis XIV, with a spell when he hoped the spoils of war on the Dutch could also provide a solution. All three failed, but by the end of the reign the increase in trade aided by better administration had brought his finances to the requisite level when he had no need of Parliament – albeit at the expense of being a weak player on the Continent. Once, by means of his Tory majority in Parliament, James had acquired his ordinary revenues for life he too would be independent of Parliament. In fact, events enabled him to do better than this and also enabled him to build up his military strength to a formidable level.

But until Parliament passed the necessary resolutions James's immediate finances were precarious, and he had had to resort to collecting the customs revenues before Parliament met and without its approval. It was also unknown what the outcome of the elections would be and, after Rochester's initial overtures, James's ministers set about obtaining money from Louis which would strengthen his hand in case Parliament should turn out to be recalcitrant.

Louis, indeed, had sent over 500,000 *livres* (about £42,000) after Charles's death and later increased it to 2 million *livres* (about £170,000) but refused its disbursement except in the case of rebellion. It was not until 19 May that Parliament met, when the size of the Tory triumph became fully apparent. James, therefore, in the meanwhile hedged his bets by being amenable to overtures from the Dutch.[28]

JAMES II'S RELATIONS WITH THE PRINCE AND THE DUTCH ESTATES

The result of Charles's death was that Mary became next in line to the throne after James – provided he produced no surviving children, which the record to date made unlikely – and from henceforth Mary was served on bended knee. William, too, was anxious to establish friendly relations with James and he sent Monmouth away from his court – Chudleigh gave orders for his arrest on 15 May – whilst at the same time sending his cousin Nassau-Ouwekerk to England.[29] This incidentally provided William with a suitable opportunity to write to congratulate Rochester on his promotion and thus keep his lines of communication open with James's most important minister.[30] Rochester, indeed, had made use of this at the end of April to drop a hint to the Prince that Monmouth had best be sent away.[31]

Ouwekerk conveyed a compliant message to the new King and James for his part stipulated three demands: there should be no further commerce with Monmouth – the Prince readily complied; the officers in the English and Scottish regiments in Dutch service with whom James was not satisfied should be dismissed – the Prince did not object; and thirdly, he should, in effect, follow James in his relations with Louis XIV – in response the Prince undertook not to act against his interests, which James appeared to swallow. The obnoxious – to William – Chudleigh was removed as ambassador at The Hague and the marginally less obnoxious Skelton took his place.[32] In June the Prince remonstrated against the appointment of Skelton and his preparedness to tolerate James's interventions in the British regiments had its limits – in the late summer he remonstrated against the recall of Henry Sidney from his command over the British troops in Dutch service, which was unsuccessful, and his replacement by Lord Carlingford on the grounds that he was a Catholic, which succeeded.[33]

Apart from Nassau-Ouwekerk, who was sent as the Prince of Orange's personal envoy, the States-General also sent James an embassy, consisting of Baron van Wassenaar-Duivenvoorde, Van Citters and Dijkveldt, which was received by James on 13 March, and whose task was to renew the Anglo-Dutch commercial treaties as well as the defensive treaty of 1678.[34] Of these negotiations the Prince was closely informed at every step.

MONMOUTH'S REBELLION

Although the embassy was well received the negotiations were held back, for James was soon faced with two insurrections, both of which were launched with a small number of ships from the Dutch Republic. One was led by the Earl of Argyll, who had fallen foul of the Duke of York when he was in Scotland over the introduction of the Scottish Test Act and who had fled to the Dutch Republic under sentence of death. At the beginning of March he met Monmouth, who, having first gone to the Spanish Netherlands after his father's death, had returned to Amsterdam. There he and Argyll agreed that Argyll would raise an insurrection in Scotland whilst Monmouth commanded one in England, with Whig dissidents raising insurrections in the north-west and London. In early May Argyll landed in western Scotland, where he presented no great threat, and by June he had been captured and executed.

On 11 June Monmouth landed at Lyme Regis, his ships carrying no more than 83 men with weapons for a further 1,500 – he was counting on his Whig supporters to raise another 15,000 or even 30,000. Argyll had managed to fit out three ships, followed a month later by Monmouth with another three, in both cases at the mouth of the Texel to the north of Amsterdam. There they lay outside the jurisdiction of the Amsterdam Admiralty. Skelton therefore had to resort to the States-General, and by the time he obtained the necessary orders to detain the ships Argyll's little fleet had sailed. When he learnt of the assembly of Monmouth's fleet he repeated his mistake; he again applied first to the Amsterdam Admiralty and was again referred to the States-General, and Monmouth's fleet too was allowed to get away.[35]

James had warned Prince William of Monmouth's plotting on 28 April[36] and William wrote to Rochester on the 30th assuring him, on his word of honour, that he did not know whether Monmouth was in Holland.[37] There were indeed rumours, he said, that he 'was wandering between Rotterdam and Amsterdam, and even that he had been in The Hague', but that he had been unable to track him down. On 25 May he was telling Rochester that 'I must confess to you that I never should have believed the Duke of Monmouth capable of such an action, after the assurances he made to me of the contrary when he took leave of me', and that, despite his most diligent enquiries, he was again unable to ascertain whether he was still in the country.[38]

On 1 June James had asked William to send the three Scottish regiments in Dutch service to Scotland to assist with the Argyll rebellion, to which the Prince gave a positive response on the 9th saying that he had received the States-General's consent that day.[39] On 27 June James asked as well for the three English regiments to be sent to England to address Monmouth's insurrection.[40] Again he received a positive response and the Prince sent Bentinck to England with instructions, in William's own hand, dated 4 July. In these the Prince offered to come over to England in person if that were considered useful and if there were need for generals or other officers he would send them too – he had no doubt that the States-General would approve, the next day or the day after, the sending of the three English regiments and he would see to it that they were sent at once.

But he also looked to a *quid pro quo* from James. Heed would need to be paid to the protocol of his own treatment with regard to the Prince of Denmark; Bentinck needed to talk to James's ministers about his properties seized by the French; and Bentinck was to sound out James and his ministers on the assistance he could expect from them once the rebellion was contained 'if my enemies in this country push me to extremities'. He was hoping therefore for a sort of family compact – he would secure James in his position if James secured him in his. The memoranda which Bentinck prepared for himself to guide his conversations with the English authorities repeat his and the Prince's concerns about the ties the Dutch opposition had with Louis XIV, the extreme measures to which they might resort, and the support William might expect from James if the opposition pushed matters too far.[41]

The States of Holland and the States-General indeed approved the sending of the English regiments on 6 July. The only opposition in Holland came from Delft and she soon too came into line.[42]

On 10 July James wrote to William thanking him for the offers he had made by means of Bentinck, but declining the suggestion that William himself should come to England on the ostensible grounds that he was required in Holland to 'keep all things well there'.[43] When William wrote to Bentinck on the 14th, he interpreted this as a rejection of all his offers, 'at least that is how I understand it', including presumably, that is to say, the family compact.[44] But this did not prevent Bentinck raising the issue again with Rochester later in July,[45] we must assume without any further success.

The campaign against Monmouth lasted only seven weeks but William was at first anxious about its progress and how long it might last, and he said he did not view it as so small a matter as it seemed to be regarded in England. His sympathies were not with Monmouth and he rejoiced at his final defeat at Sedgemoor on 16 July – Monmouth was betrayed after the defeat by Lord Grey of Warke, who had accompanied him on his ill-judged venture, and his execution on Tower Hill followed nine days later. The Prince hoped James would soon return the six English and Scottish regiments and he hoped also that none but he himself and his generals would now be allowed to determine who their officers should be – it would do him harm in the Dutch Republic if Catholic officers were appointed at James's behest.[46] This wish for the swift return of the regiments should perhaps be seen in parallel with William's worries about the Dutch opposition.

Although neither the English nor the Scottish regiments had seen action during the insurrections James expressed his appreciation of the prompt show of assistance demonstrated by the States and the Prince of Orange and at the end of August the Anglo-Dutch Treaty, renewing the old treaties, was signed.[47] In contrast to the assistance that he received from his nephew and the Dutch Republic, Louis on 26 July ordered the return of most of the funds which Barillon had been husbanding for James's support.[48] Earlier in the month Bentinck had even suggested that those in close attendance on James deduced from his manner that he thought Louis had assisted the rebels.[49]

James's position was now immeasurably strengthened. In May his speech at the opening of Parliament was well received; at the end of it James announced that the Earl of Argyll had landed in Scotland to launch his rebellion, which elicited cries of 'Long live the King'. On 5 June the Commons passed a Bill to grant him his ordinary revenue for life; it was followed by another which provided customs duties to pay off Charles II's debts and restore the fleet; and by a third, a month later, to provide revenues for five years to meet the costs of the Monmouth rebellion. Parliament in fact acted more generously than it intended, for it was not aware of the extent to which Charles II's revenues had increased and the Monmouth rebellion proved of shorter duration than it anticipated.[50] As a result James was able to retain the troops raised to confront the rebellion, so that by the end of 1685 his forces in England alone came to nearly 20,000 men.[51]

But the first signs of opposition were becoming apparent. James had commissioned nearly 100 Catholic officers for his expanded army[52] and Halifax challenged the legality of this under the Test Act. He refused to support either the repeal of this, or the repeal of the Habeas Corpus Act, which prevented imprisonment without due cause, and at the end of October he was dismissed from his offices. When James met Parliament on 19 November he made clear his intention to retain the Catholic officers. The House of Commons made it equally clear, in respectful terms, however, that this was contrary to the law and in the House of Lords speakers stressed, in the presence of James himself, the need to respect the anti-Popery laws, one of the speakers being Bishop Compton of London and another Lord Halifax. James's response was to prorogue Parliament after a session which had lasted ten days, and it was never to meet again during his reign. Bishop Compton was dismissed from the Privy Council and Sunderland took the place of Halifax as its Lord President.[53] The combination of this post with his position as one of the two Secretaries of State persuaded Barillon that his influence was worth a very substantial pension from Louis, which, after much haggling, came to 90,000 *livres* (about £7,000) and which nearly doubled his income.[54] The rise of Sunderland, now tied even more firmly to Louis XIV, was to challenge the position of Rochester.

BETTY VILLIERS

If the relationship between William and Monmouth is somewhat perplexing, that with Betty Villiers is too. Betty was one of the six Villiers daughters brought up by their mother Frances together with Mary and her sister Anne at Richmond Palace. She came over from England in the entourage of Mary as one of her ladies-in-waiting. Her mother was a daughter of the Earl of Suffolk and had married Sir Edward Villiers, but she died, as we have seen, of the smallpox at the time William and Mary married. Barbara Villiers, who

Elizabeth Villiers, Countess of Orkney, 1696, attributed to Sir Godfrey Kneller.
Private collection

became the Duchess of Castlemaine and mistress of Charles II, was a cousin. Betty's eldest brother, Edward, was Mary's Master of Horse and we have already mentioned that her sister Anne had married Bentinck. Betty was not beautiful and had a squint – Huygens sometimes describes her as 'the one with the squint'; but she was extremely intelligent – Dean Swift later described her in 1712 as 'the wisest woman I ever saw, and Lord Treasurer [Oxford] made great use of her advice'.[55]

There are various contemporary accounts of William's relationship with Betty, but they all lack authenticity. Here are the hard facts. On 22 October the Prince wrote to Rochester from Dieren saying that he was grieved to have to write concerning a matter which had arisen. He had heard many rumours that the Princess's chaplain, Dr Covell, was unreliable and he enclosed a copy of a letter that Covell had written to Skelton which had fallen into his hands. In view of the content he and Mary had no choice but to dismiss him from their household; and the Prince also complained about Skelton's engaging in such correspondence, asking that James should recall him. James agreed to this, although it was not convenient to do so immediately since there was a lot of unfinished business in which Skelton was engaged. Here is Covell's letter to Skelton: 'Your honour may be astonished at the news, but it is too true, the Princess's heart is ready to break…. We dare no more speak to her. The prince hath infallibly made her his complete slave…. None but pimps and bawds must expect any tolerable usage here.'[56] That day Bentinck wrote to Henry Sidney, also from Dieren, saying that Dr Covell had been for a long time a malicious spy in the Prince's household and since Mrs Langford (Mary's old nurse, who had also come with her from England) and a maid of honour, Anne Trelawny, were also involved they had been dismissed as well by Mary that morning.[57]

So much for the facts; now for the rumours and the speculations. A source most frequently cited is the *Mémoirs de Monsieur de B*.[58] According to this James II, piqued by William's refusal to endorse his repeal of the Test Act – never mind that this did not in fact occur until the end of 1686 – tried to break the marriage of his daughter Mary with Prince William by inciting Mary's jealousy. To this end he employed Skelton, and members of the Prince's household were induced to tell Mary that William had an attachment for one of her maids of honour, that is to say, Betty. When he stayed up late he told her that he was busy with his papers, and on one occasion, to test the truth of this, she waited for him at the bottom of the stairs communicating with the maids of honour's apartment. Finding her there at two o'clock in the morning the Prince reproached her and she responded only with tears and retired to her bed, from which the Prince absented himself for several days. Suspecting the members of his household, he arranged for the messenger carrying correspondence to James II to be intercepted, from which he learnt the whole purport of the plot. He asked the Princess to come into his study, and having closed the door, he assured her, by what was most sacred, that what he was engaged in was pure amusement and no misconduct had occurred ('*qu'il n'y a aucun crime*'). Mary, in tears, threw herself on his neck and the couple were reconciled, with those involved in the plot being dismissed. It is, at a stretch, possible that the Prince and Princess's conversation at the bottom of the stairs may have been overheard, but it is asking too much to believe that what was said behind a closed door in the study was also heard for the second time.[59]

A further version can be found in Coenraad Droste's *Overblyfsels van Geheugenis*.[60]

Fruin cites the sources of various rumours which were current of a plot in which James II and Skelton were supposed to be involved, which envisaged Mary escaping from William and marrying Louis XIV. But Mary was already legally married and so probably – although James would not have known this – was Louis XIV, to Madame de Maintenon.[61]

We thus have a collection of rumours, which vary in detail and which may well have fed off each other. We are no further in establishing the exact relationship with Betty Villiers, although most historians believe she was William's mistress. Perhaps, but there is no evidence of a physical relationship and it is quite possible that her attraction for William was her mind, her wit, and her wisdom. The quote from Bishop Burnet's *History* that the Prince 'had no vice, but of one sort, in which he was very cautious and secret'[62] has been much cited; it is usually mentioned as referring to a possible homosexual relationship with Bentinck or, later, with Joost Keppel; but it may equally apply to Betty Villiers. Even the Prince of Orange, that most reserved of men, needed somebody in whom he had *almost* full confidence – which was all that was granted him by the position he held. In the whole course of his life, there were no more than two or three people who filled this role – Bentinck and, as I surmise, Betty, and soon, to an ever greater degree until his confidence became total, Mary as well. Like Bentinck, Betty was to be well rewarded for her friendship when William became King of England.

There is one dimension of the relationship with Mary of which we need to be aware at this stage in her marriage. She, not William, was the next in succession to the Stuart throne. She was thus, in William's mind, though not in her own, a potential competitor for power in her uncle's kingdoms – although we shall see that this, in the following year, would change.

1 Hutton, *op. cit.*, p.422. Miller, *Charles II, op. cit.*, pp.375–6. A detailed account is in Keay, *op. cit.*, pp.303–17.
2 Dalrymple, *op. cit.*, I, pp.114ff. Groen van Prinsterer, *op. cit.*, 2, V, p.586.
3 Groen van Prinsterer, *op. cit.*, 2, V, p.586. Elizabeth Hamilton, *William's Mary: a biography of Mary II*, London 1972, p.137. Dalrymple, *op. cit.*, I, pp.118–19.
4 Dalrymple, *op. cit.*, I, pp.118–19.
5 Groen van Prinsterer, *op. cit.*, 2, V, p.587.
6 *Correspondentie Willem III en Bentinck, op. cit.*, II, 2, p.647 n.3.
7 D'Avaux, *Négociations, op. cit.*, IV, pp.15–16.
8 *Correspondentie Willem III en Bentinck, op. cit.*, II, 2, pp.642ff.
9 *Ibid.*, II, 2, pp.649, 650, 653.

10 Dalrymple, *op. cit.*, I, p.124.

11 *Correspondentie Willem III en Bentinck, op. cit.*, II, 2, pp.642–97 are devoted mainly to the subject.

12 Although we can discount much of what D'Avaux says – see for example *Négociations, op. cit.*, IV, pp.240ff. – driven as he was by his consistent and excessive zeal to denigrate the Prince of Orange on all fronts, probably to ingratiate himself with his master at Versailles.

13 Foxcroft, *op. cit.*, pp.420–34. See Kenyon's dismissal of Foxcroft's thesis, *Sunderland, op. cit.*, pp.104–6.

14 Burnet, *op. cit.*, London, 1818, II, p.224.

15 Keay, *op. cit.*, pp.324–8.

16 Trevor Roper, in *The Anglo-Dutch Moment, op. cit.*, p.488, n.8. Hutton, *Charles II, op. cit.*, pp.441–3.

17 D'Avaux, *Négociations, op. cit.*, IV, p.217. D'Avaux's account that Prince William went so far as to encourage a flirtation between Mary and Monmouth is so out of Mary's character – not to mention the Prince's – that we may discount it (p.225); similarly his account, which is often cited, of Mary's ice skating with Monmouth, skating on alternative legs with her skirts drawn up (p.241). He did not always resist the temptation to present William and Mary in an unfavourable light to his masters in France.

18 Middlebush, *op. cit.*, p.249.

19 D'Avaux, *Négociations, op. cit.*, IV, p.184 mentions that the Prince's supporters were encouraged by the rumours of a *rapprochement* between Charles and William which they spread to intimidate his opponents. D'Avaux provides different – conflicting – versions of such a *rapprochement*. See pp.133–4, 138–9 in which he brings both Van Beuningen into the scheming for such an outcome – English support was always central to Van Beuningen's foreign policy – and the Duke of York who, it seems, saw it – rather improbably, it has to be said – as a means of strengthening the King's position – or was it, even more improbably, his own? On pp.140–1 he develops the version taken up by Foxcroft that Halifax was the prime mover of the intrigue, his aim being to remove the Duke of York from the centre of affairs, as well as Rochester, and to substitute the Prince of Orange, with whom he would act in concert and become first minister. See also pp.183–92 in which Sylvius also plays a role in attempting a reconciliation between Charles and William.

20 *Correspondentie Willem III en Bentinck, op. cit.*, II, 2, pp.666–7, 676–7, 694. The Prince's letter to Van Citters of 9 January 1685 is completely at variance with D'Avaux's account, also of 9 January, which historians have often cited, that Monmouth arrived at The Hague at Van Citters's instigation, Van Citters having been so instructed by the Prince to satisfy the remonstrations of Halifax; that his arrival in The Hague was expected and that Bentinck brought him to the Prince after his arrival at eight in the evening; that William insisted that Mary, who had retired for the night, should dress again to receive him; and that he invited him to stay in Prince Maurits's palace – now the Mauritshuis – attended by all the servants he needed. D'Avaux may have been relying on gossip, or he may have been embellishing the story to show Prince William in a bad light, as he frequently does in the rest of his *Memoirs. Négociations, op. cit.*, IV, pp.211–12.

21 Kenyon suggests that there may well have been a *rapprochement* between Charles and William and that bringing Monmouth into the discourse is, in effect, a red herring which confuses the issue. Neither Charles nor James, this suggestion goes, wanted to see William, who was a member of the Stuart clan, go down before the Regents of Amsterdam in combination with Louis XIV and 'Though any final conclusion must await the production of further evidence there is nothing improbable in the theory that Charles and James were giving William underhand support in 1684', *Sunderland, op. cit.*, pp.104–6. This evidence is certainly not there in Van Citters's despatches which we have cited on p.493 and note 11 above – very much on the contrary, despite the occasional displays of benignity in Charles's demeanour.

22 Miller, *Charles II, op. cit.*, p.381. Hutton, *op. cit.*, p.445.

23 Miller, *James II, op. cit.*, pp.120–1. Kenyon, *Sunderland, op. cit.*, pp.111, 113.

24 Dalrymple, *op. cit.*, II, Appendix to Part I, pp.1–4.

25 Holmes, *The Making of a Great Power 1660–1722*, 1993, pp.165, 166, 168, 422.

26 *Ibid.*, p.170.

27 *Ibid.*, p.166.

28 Kenyon, *Sunderland, op. cit.*, pp.114–16.

29 *Correspondentie Willem III en Bentinck, op. cit.*, II, 2, pp.697–8. Middlebush, *op. cit.*, pp.252–3.

30 Singer, *op. cit.*, I, pp.115–16.

31 *Ibid.*, I, pp.122–3.

32 Miller, *James II*, p.138. Dalrymple, *op. cit.*, II, Appendix to Part I, pp 13–14.

33 Dalrymple, *op. cit.*, II, Appendix to Part I, pp.18, 29, 30, 31, 32.

34 *Verbaal van de Buitengewoone Ambassade van Jacob van Wassenaar – Diuvenvoorde – Arnout van Citters en Everard van Weede van Dijkveld, Hist. Gen. Utrecht*, N.S.2, 1863, pp.11, 46.

35 Robb, *op. cit.*, II, p.209. Miller, *James II, op. cit.*, p.139. *Oxford Dictionary of National Biography*, article by Tim Harris on Monmouth. Keay, *op. cit.*, pp.337, 441, 442.

36 Dalrymple, *op. cit.*, II, Appendix to Part I, pp.19–20.

37 Singer, *op. cit.,* I, pp.124–5.

38 *Ibid.*, I, pp.126–7.

39 *Ibid.*, I, p.128.

40 Dalrymple, *op. cit.*, II, Appendix to Part I, pp.22–3.

41 *Correspondentie Willem III en Bentinck, op. cit.*, I, 1, pp.20–1, 25–8.

42 *Ibid.*, I,1, p.21.

43 Dalrymple, *op. cit.*, II, Appendix to Part I, p,23.

44 *Correspondentie Willem III en Bentinck, op. cit.*, I, 1, p.24.

45 *Ibid.*, I, 1, see Bentinck's 'Points to be discussed with Rochester' dated 18 July, p.27.

46 *Ibid.*, I, 1, pp.22, 28. Keay, *op. cit.*, pp.364–6.

47 Verbaal, *op. cit.*, pp.121, 122, 138.

48 Kenyon, *Sunderland, op. cit.*, p.118.

49 *Correspondentie Willem III en Bentinck, op. cit.*, I, 1, p.23.

50 Miller, *James II, op. cit.*, pp.136–7.

51 Holmes, *op. cit.*, p.171.

52 Miller, *James II, op. cit.*, p.143.

53 Foxcroft, *op. cit.*, I, pp.448–51, 454, 458–9.

54 Kenyon, *Sunderland, op. cit.*, pp.126–7.

55 See Fruin, *Aantekeningen, op. cit.*, p.435–6.

56 Quoted in Fruin, *Aantekeningen, op. cit.*, pp.462ff. and in Sidney, *op. cit.*, II, p.254 n.1.

57 Sidney, *op. cit.*, II, pp.253–5. William's letter to Rochester and Covell's letter to Shelton are also contained in Singer, *op. cit.*, I, pp.163–6, together with Rochester's reply in which he conveys James's preparedness to recall Shelton.

58 *Mémoirs de Monsieur de B., Hist. Gen. Utrecht*, 19, 1898, pp.62ff.

59 *Ibid.*, pp.83ff.

60 Fruin, *Aantekeningen, op. cit.*, pp.435ff.

61 *Ibid.*, pp.460ff. For Louis's marriage to La Maintenon see John Wolf, *op. cit.*, p.332.

62 Burnet, *op. cit.*, 1818, II, p.313.

25 AUGUST 1684 TO LATE 1686: DUTCH UNITY; THE COALITION; JAMES'S CATHOLICISING POLICIES

Although it was not apparent at the time, the signing by the Dutch of the Twenty Years' Truce on 29 June 1684 and by the Emperor and Spain on 15 August was to mark the apex of Louis XIV's ascendancy in Europe. To challenge that position the Prince of Orange needed to forge greater unity in the Dutch Republic to rebuild the Grand Coalition against the French King, and to keep a close scrutiny on events evolving in Britain.

Shortly after the Twenty Years' Truce was signed William wrote to Waldeck on 28 August 1684 that Amsterdam was making him discreet offers of accommodation, an affair so delicate that he could not put it in writing.[1] He was referring to conversations that had taken place a little earlier, the initial intermediary for which was the obscure Dr Maréchal, of whom otherwise nothing much is known. Maréchal was acquainted with Van Beuningen, who had previously used him to intercede on his behalf with Prince William. It seems that Van Beuningen took the initiative in sending Maréchal to Dieren where the Prince of Orange had retired to lick his wounds after the signing of the truce.

On his return Maréchal asked Van Beuningen, at William's behest, what Amsterdam's future intentions were. Van Beuningen responded that the restoration of an understanding with the Prince was very necessary, as was the maintenance of the Prince's lawful authority in accordance with the country's constitution, and that if agreement could be reached on that basis one could let bygones be bygones. The Prince indicated that with this he was content.[2] To his fellow Burgomasters Van Beuningen argued that they should make use of the Prince's authority to serve their interests – far from curtailing it they should maintain it.[3] What he had in mind, in part, was the ability of the Prince of Orange to use his influence to further Amsterdam's commercial and financial interests, and to this we shall come.

But there was another reason. The Amsterdam Burgomasters chose Witsen, who would have been more acceptable to the Prince than Van Beuningen, to hold talks with him and Fagel; and Witsen wrote to them from The Hague that 'everyone here calls out that the Republic is lost, if disunity continues'. Nine months later Van Beuningen, who had never been a champion of France, was to express the same view very clearly to the Elector of Brandenburg's envoy, Fuchs, who was in Amsterdam in May 1685: 'the Amsterdammers', he said then, 'were so far from wanting to curtail the Prince's authority that they regarded the destruction of the State as inevitable if they now fell out with His Highness. The power that he possessed, exceeding that of his predecessors, was conferred upon him in time of war and turmoil; but one could not reduce it now, without putting the welfare of the State into the scales.'[4] In short, the threat from Louis XIV was by no means over and the traditional role of the House of Orange in times of danger would need to be maintained.

Witsen and Fagel met on 25 August 1684 and the mood was encouraging, although Fagel pointed to differences over the military budget that needed to be resolved. When he consulted the Prince, William indicated his readiness to enter into an amicable understanding with Amsterdam – but 'the friendship should not be plastered over, but be reflected in deeds and to come from the heart'. His one demand was that the size of the army was to remain unchanged from that fixed by the Budget for 1685, although Fagel indicated that even here this might not be his last word.

Waldeck did present a difficulty, however; although now serving the Emperor, he still drew his stipend from the States, very much against the will of Amsterdam, who saw him as a warmonger. The Prince could not yield on this front without abandoning a key client, but on the army numbers he indicated that although his advice would be to retain the recent recruits for two months rather than a further month he was prepared to concede the point. Against that he asked that the regiment of dragoons be kept until the end of the year, which Amsterdam, in her turn, conceded.[5]

In the meantime, the Princess of Anhalt, the mother-in-law of William's cousin Hendrik-Casimir, the Stadholder of Friesland and Groningen, was taking steps to heal another notable division in the Dutch Republic, the long-standing dispute between the two cousins. As a daughter of Frederick-Henry she was an aunt of both Prince William and Hendrik-Casimir, who had married her daughter, Amalia von Anhalt, in November 1683. She paid a visit to Amsterdam accompanied by Hendrik-Casimir and the Amsterdam Burgomasters took the opportunity to use her as an intermediary with Prince William to assure him of their amity. From him she received an encouraging response and he said he looked forward to seeing both the Amsterdam representatives and his cousin at the forthcoming meeting of the States of Holland.[6]

In pursuance of this Prince William met an Amsterdam delegation at the end of November in which he did not deny that he had had many occasions to complain about Amsterdam but 'that he preferred the public to his private interests', and he wished that unity in the future would be based 'on such fundaments that it would be of long duration'. As regarded Hendrik-Casimir, he viewed this as of domestic concern and not for discussion with third parties, but he indicated that this would be settled to mutual satisfaction.[7]

And so it was. Waldeck agreed terms, which were embodied in a contract on 21 March 1685, with Van der Waeyen, Hendrik-Casimir's adviser, who had great influence with him. Hendrik-Casimir would have powers of appointment in the Friesian and Groningen regiments and, on his side, he undertook to support William in both his foreign and his domestic policy.[8]

In the meantime, however, two other issues arose which ensured that the harmony between the Prince and Amsterdam was not unalloyed.

The first was that the Prince managed to remove opponents from the town councils in Utrecht, in Leyden, in Delft and in Dordrecht which, particularly in the case of Dordrecht, unsettled Amsterdam; she was concerned about the rights of the towns and, where they were Holland towns, the sovereignty of the States of Holland; but she nevertheless accepted the outcome.[9] William made use of the old statesman Van Beverninck to reorder the town councils and the two of them pursued a policy of balancing the competing factions. The outcome was at once a step further in the consolidation of Prince William's power and in the forging of closer unity in the Dutch Republic.[10]

The second issue arose over the war budget. In May 1685 Amsterdam wanted to reduce the size of the army to 30,000 men to save 2 million guilders and use the savings for the navy, which could defend her commerce. William agreed as regarded the navy, but not on the reduction of the land forces. Unanimity was required in the States of Holland to pass the Budget and, with the support of Leyden and Delft, Amsterdam prevented its adoption.

Fagel, however, used his ingenuity to find a way round. The States of Holland was composed of two Quarters, the Northern and the much richer Southern, which consisted of 11 of the 18 Holland towns. Each of the Quarters had a Standing Committee which was responsible for collecting taxes, and here unanimity did not apply. Fagel accordingly arranged, on 12 June 1685, for the Southern Quarter to approve, by five votes to four, the payments to the army on its old footing. He thus managed to give effect in practice to the 1685 war budget without the approval of Amsterdam, the States of Holland or the States-General.[11]

Amsterdam realised that confrontation with Prince William and Fagel had brought her no further forward. She would need to come to some sort of accommodation. She needed the support of the Prince for the abolition of taxes on the export of grain, in which she was heavily involved; and she also needed that support for increases in the tariffs on imports and exports and to augment the licences issued to permit trade with enemy powers; these latter were referred to as the 'Convooyen en Licenten', and they were used to finance the convoys that protected Dutch shipping. They were insufficient, however, to pay fully for the navy and they had to be supplemented by subsidies from the States-General, which caused resentment from the land Provinces.[12]

As regards the navy the States-General had in 1682 approved the building of 36 warships, but now in 1685 lack of funds had produced no more than 18 incompletely built ships, and there were plans afoot to bring the strength of the navy up to the 96 ships regarded as the minimum required to protect Dutch commerce around the globe.[13]

It was against this background that William sent a member of his court, Gravemoer, to Amsterdam to make soundings on the war budget for 1686 before it came to the States-

General. On 15 October 1685 Gravemoer met Jacob Hop and informed him that the Prince was prepared to make savings, if they were not too onerous, in the army's budget. On 16 November there was a meeting at The Hague between the Prince, Witsen and Hop at which William agreed to the setting up of a committee to examine what savings could be made, and the two Amsterdam representatives declared that Amsterdam would, on that basis, support the 1686 war budget. On 21 December the States of Holland unanimously approved the budget and the appointment of the committee to look at the savings; and on the 24th the States-General also gave its consent. On 9 January 1686 Fagel saw to it that the States-General unanimously approved the increase of the tariff on imported grain by half, so that the export of grain, in which Amsterdam was so involved, could remain untaxed.[14]

Thus at the end of 1685 and the beginning of 1686 some sort of compromise was reached. Amsterdam had obtained what she wanted on the export of grain, but not the increase in the 'Convooyen en Licenten' nor the additions to the navy, and William had seen the war budget through for 1686, but not for subsequent years, and he had to concede that the committee look at savings.[15]

The Prince of Orange and the City of Amsterdam continued to be separated by considerable differences, but they had come to realise that they needed each other and they were on the way to build a precarious, but practical, *modus vivendi*, on a day-to-day basis, between them.

MOVES TOWARDS THE RECREATION OF THE ANTI-FRENCH COALITION

Earlier in 1685 the first steps had also been taken to restore the Grand Coalition against Louis XIV. In December 1684 General Spaen, an old comrade-in-arms of the Prince of Orange, had come to The Hague on behalf of the Elector of Brandenburg and engaged in conversations with the Prince and Fagel. This prompted William in January 1685 to send a Huguenot pastor-refugee, François Gaultier, on a secret mission to Berlin to discuss the idea of a Protestant coalition. Gaultier could not have come at a more propitious time: Charles II had been succeeded by his Catholic brother James in England; Louis XIV was increasing his persecution of the Huguenots in France; and Leopold, as his army drove back the Turks, was persecuting the Protestants in Hungary. In all this Frederick-William saw the triumphant march of Catholicism against the Reformed Religion and he toyed with the idea of an invasion of England by the Prince of Orange with 10,000 men. He now abandoned his plans for attacking Protestant Sweden – for this, when it came to the point, he had received no support from Louis, and now was not the time, with Protestantism under threat, for the Protestant powers to take each other to pieces.

His objectives now became twofold: to strengthen, by whatever means lay at hand, Protestantism in Europe and to confront the over-mighty Louis XIV. These two objectives were connected but to achieve them he did need to compromise in seeking the support of Catholic Austria. He was also forced into a second compromise; on 26 May 1685 the Protestant Elector Palatine died and was succeeded by the Catholic Philipp-William of Pfalz-Neuburg, whose succession to a large part of the inheritance was challenged by Louis XIV on behalf of his sister-in-law, the Duchess of Orléans; this turned Frederick-William into one of the new Elector's most ardent champions.

In July talks about assisting Leopold I against the Turks and forming an alliance were being actively pursued, and Frederick-William also sent an envoy to Sweden, who was well received, with a view to forming a Grand Protestant Coalition.

He had not ignored the Dutch. On 8 May he signed his instructions for Fuchs to return to the Republic. The grave circumstances prevailing in Europe, the instructions read, made necessary an understanding with the Prince of Orange and the Dutch States; the old intimacy between the Houses of Brandenburg and Nassau should be re-established and the Stadholder's support should be sought regarding the States; as far as the latter were concerned he wanted to gain them by means of the confessional tie and the necessity to come to the aid of their persecuted co-religionists; and, of course, the old outstanding Brandenburg claims for compensation arising from the previous war should be addressed. In a supplementary *mémoir*, Frederick-William also addressed the means of safeguarding the rights of his sons by his first marriage to William's aunt, given the possibility of William's dying without children.[16]

William, of course, welcomed the *rapprochement*, but he was aware of Amsterdam's sensitivity about measures hostile to France and he therefore resorted to Amerongen, the ambassador in Berlin, who was well regarded by the Elector and who had a good relationship with Van Beuningen, to act as an intermediary with Amsterdam. The financial terms raised no difficulties between the Prince and the town, but the fourth clause of the proposed treaty, which stipulated that the signatories would maintain the peace against 'potential disturbers', did. D'Avaux objected that this was, like the Association Treaty of 1681, directed against France, and he lobbied Amsterdam on this account. The town responded that she did not intend to give the least umbrage to Louis XIV and ratification of the treaty was delayed until 5 October 1685. Troost has maintained that it was Louis's Revocation of the Edict of Nantes, which forbade the exercise of Protestantism in France, that persuaded Amsterdam to ratify the Brandenburg Treaty. But Petra Dreiskämper has pointed out that the Revocation in fact occurred on 22 October, thus after the ratification, and we may conclude, therefore, that it was Van Beuningen's desire to reach agreement with the Prince on the war budget that was the trigger for Amsterdam's agreeing to ratify the treaty with the Elector.[17]

Frederick-William responded to the Revocation with his own Edict of Potsdam. Having deplored the persecutions in France against the Protestants, he promised them exile in his estates; and he was proof against all Louis's protestations.[18]

And on 4 January 1686 he signed an Agreement with Austria that promised a minimum of 7,000 troops for the war in Hungary, in exchange for subsidies, and he also agreed a payment from Austria for his claims against Spain, arising, like his claims against the Dutch, from the previous war.[19]

Bit by bit the new coalition against Louis XIV was beginning to take shape.

JAMES II'S CATHOLICISING POLICIES

When James prorogued Parliament at the end of November 1685 he took the first steps towards dissolving the alliance between the Crown and the Anglican Church which, after the exclusion crisis, had been at the heart of Charles II's Tory counter-attack against the Whigs. Whilst Rochester, a member of James's clan and his brother-in-law, whose power base rested with the Anglican nobility and gentry and with the Church, remained his foremost minister for the time being, Sunderland championed the promotion of Catholicism as a means of challenging his position and advancing his own.[20]

Sunderland made use of three factors. First, he formed a close alliance with three Catholics to whom James was likely to turn for advice: his Queen, Mary Beatrice, yet more Catholic than James himself; Father Petre, who had brought up his illegitimate children; and James Talbot, the Earl of Tyrconnell, a forceful and ambitious Irish Catholic politician who was to become a major proponent in advancing the Catholics in Ireland, although, from Sunderland's point of view, he was an equivocal ally. Secondly, he established a power base in an unofficial Catholic council which, under his predominance, extended its scope until the business it transacted became more important than that transacted in either the Privy or Cabinet Councils. And lastly, through Barillon, he continued to cultivate Louis XIV.[21]

Throughout 1686 James – and Sunderland – pursued their policies to promote Catholicism, thus further alienating the Anglican party and Rochester, who nevertheless clung tenaciously to power. From the outset of James's reign the clergy had engaged in anti-Catholic sermons and he had endeavoured to persuade the Archbishop of Canterbury, William Sancroft, and other bishops to curtail them, without any marked success. In May John Sharp, the Rector of St Giles in the Fields, which lay in the diocese of Bishop Compton, preached a strongly anti-Catholic sermon, and James instructed Compton to suspend him, a task that Compton refused. The bishops having failed him in controlling the clergy, James decided to resort to other means. In July he established the Ecclesiastical Commission under the pliant judge George Jeffreys, who had gained notoriety for his harsh treatment of the Monmouth rebels and who had been made Lord Chancellor. The Commission, which many regarded as the successor of the Court of High Commission (declared illegal by Parliament in 1641 and 1661) and which was therefore seen as illegal itself, was to be used to curtail the anti-Catholic sermons and to allow admissions to the universities of non-Anglicans both as students and as dons. Catholic penetration of Oxford began in July with the appointment of John Massey as Dean of Christ Church and in September the Commission suspended Bishop Compton.[22]

Throughout the year James was turning away increasingly from the Anglicans, who were

James II, c. 1683–90, by Sir Godfrey Kneller. Government Art Collection

proving such a disappointment, for support and moved instead towards the Dissenters, one of whom was the Quaker William Penn. In March legal steps against the Quakers were suspended and by August other Dissenters were also able to meet freely. James, however, wanted to go further and repeal the penal laws and the Test Acts entirely. For this he would need Parliamentary approval and he knew that he would not get it from the existing Parliament. To obtain the Parliament he wanted he would need to gain control of the constituencies by dismissing Tories from the local offices through which it could be exercised and replacing them with Dissenters and Catholics. But this the Test and Corporation Acts were specifically designed to prevent, and to achieve his ends James would need to resort to dispensing and suspending powers of the law under his royal prerogative, which would prove to be controversial.[23]

In Ireland Tyrconnell was purging the army and the government of Protestants and substituting Catholics instead, and he also succeeded in having Rochester's brother Clarendon removed from the Lord Lieutenancy of Ireland and, in December, taking his place.[24] At the end of September James in England began a purge of his court, of the government and of the army of all those who would not support religious toleration, and on 22 October a committee of the Privy Council was charged with removing all opposition Members of Parliament, together with their relatives and friends, as Justices of the Peace – nearly two thirds of those who replaced them were Catholics.[25] And at the beginning of January 1687 Rochester, having refused the opportunity that James gave him of converting to Catholicism, was dismissed, his dismissal following that of his brother, Clarendon, by five days.[26] Not only therefore was James destroying the alliance with the Anglicans, he had begun to break up the Stuart clan as well. Sunderland was in the ascendant.

At this time James began interviewing in his closet members of both Houses of Parliament about their views on the toleration of Catholics – it became known as 'closeting'. One of these was Danby, who at long last had been released from the Tower by Charles II in February 1684, although his formal impeachment was not dropped until May 1685,[27] and he had been without court employment since. When James pressed him to pledge his vote for the repeal of the Test Acts he replied that 'my answer is that I look upon these Laws as the security of our religion and therefore I cannot concur'.[28] Another, in March 1687, was the Member of Parliament for Dover, Admiral Arthur Herbert, who was noted for his lax lifestyle; when likewise pressed by James to pledge to vote for the repeal of the Test Acts, he replied that his honour and his conscience prevented it; and when James, unwisely given his own mistresses, said, 'Nobody doubts your honour, but a man who lives as you do ought not to talk about his conscience', his response was, 'I have my faults, sir: but I could name people who talk much more about conscience than I am in the habit of doing, and yet lead lives as loose as mine.' He was dismissed from all his offices, on which he was sorely dependent.[29] Like Danby, he now became a staunch member of the opposition.

JAMES'S RELATIONS WITH PRINCE WILLIAM

In September 1685 members of Prince William's Council, which dealt with his personal affairs, had lodged a formal complaint with the States-General about violence committed in the Principality of Orange by French troops, and at their request the States had undertaken to make representations through both their ambassador in Paris and through the ambassadorial team negotiating the defensive treaty with James II in London. This the Dutch ambassadors did in London at the end of September immediately prior to their return to the United Provinces.[30] The Prince himself wrote to James II on 11 October and James replied on the 20th that he would instruct his new ambassador in Paris, Sir William Trumball, to take the matter up as soon as he arrived in France.[31]

Sunderland kept the Prince informed of Trumball's efforts on his behalf.[32] At the end of 1685 and the beginning of 1686 Trumball gave Sunderland a full report of the representations he was making, in conjunction with the Dutch ambassador, at the French court. Louis's Foreign Minister, Croissy, told him that Louis had left the Prince undisturbed 'so long as his conduct might deserve it' but now that he had opposed Louis so openly he had changed his mind. Louis hoped that James 'would not interpose in a thing wherein he had no interest, but leave [him] free to do as he thought fit in his own dominions', adding further 'that the right of sovereignty did not belong to the Prince of Orange, but to the House of Longueville', despite the specific terms to the contrary in the Treaty of Nijmegen. In January James wrote to William saying he was sorry that Trumball had received no better an answer and that 'I shall still continue doing my part in pressing it' but Sunderland also indicated to Prince William that 'he does not expect much from it'.[33]

This exasperated William. The Principality of Orange, as we have frequently emphasised, was of huge importance to him, which was, of course, the reason why Louis exerted great efforts to wrench it from his grasp. The Prince wrote to Rochester on 12 February 1686 in terms that did not hide his resentment. He could not accept the view Rochester had expressed that there was nothing more to be done. If that was all that James could do it would have been better if he had never become involved, 'for what will the world say, if it sees that his Majesty suffers one who has the honour to be his son-in-law and his nephew to be ill used … and does not resent it'. He could not accept that more vigour could not be shown and he ended ominously, perhaps even menacingly, 'I confess that this matter affects me very deeply, and if I do not see myself protected now, I have nothing to expect in the future.'[34] Thus not only the Stuart clan but the wider Stuart-Orange-Nassau clan was showing signs of fragility.

Nevertheless, until the second half of 1686 reasonable relations were still maintained between uncle and nephew. Whilst in March James complained to William that rebels from Monmouth's insurrection had been able to obtain refuge in the United Provinces, William was able to reassure him in May that both the States of Holland and the States-General would abide by their defensive treaty with him to banish them from their territories; and James expressed his gratitude for the part William played in obtaining this result.[35] At the same time William sent Hugh Mackay, who, at James's instigation, had been appointed Colonel of the Scottish regiments in Dutch service, to assure him of his goodwill, which was well received by the King.[36]

But in August the underlying discord came to the surface. James nominated the Earl of Carlingford to command the six British regiments in Dutch service, which, as he was a Catholic, William refused.[37] At the same time, James was planning to send as a replacement for Skelton as ambassador in The Hague a Catholic Irish adventurer, whose original name was White and who, according to Burnet, acquired the title of the Marquis d'Albeville from the Spaniards in part payment for his services as a spy – he was to take up his post in January 1687.[38] On 2 August Van Citters reported from London that D'Albeville had confided to him that James was planning a rupture with the Dutch.[39] D'Albeville was incompetent, and the main criterion for his appointment was that there was a dearth of suitable Catholics to fill James's assignments, whilst Van Citters's French was deficient and he may have misunderstood what D'Albeville told him; but he had also begun reporting that James was fitting out a great fleet and that it behoved the Dutch to be on their guard. On 13 August Van Citters sent over a document entitled 'the Remonstrance' to The Hague which ostensibly contained the arguments that the pro-French party and the Catholics in England were putting to James. An attack on the Dutch, so the Remonstrance argued, should take place now whilst Leopold was still preoccupied with the Turks; and James should change the English succession in favour of a Catholic, with Louis XIV being better than Mary, and with the English being better off as vassals of Louis than as slaves of the Dutch.

The Remonstrance was dismissed as a forgery by James – as indeed it might well have been – but it alarmed the Dutch, who had it printed. James's efforts at strengthening his fleet had, as it happened, not been very great but the fright the document instilled in the Dutch seems to have encouraged him to make more formidable preparations as a deterrence from intervention in his kingdoms. James, in fact, had no interest in any war; it would have meant recalling Parliament to finance it; and it would certainly have frustrated his plans to catholicise his kingdoms. But his naval preparations and the rumours of war were all to the good as far as William of Orange was concerned in his efforts to persuade the Dutch Regents to re-arm.[40] How much credence he himself gave to the rumours we do not know, although he might have thought that James's behaviour would inevitably push him into the arms of Louis XIV.

BISHOP BURNET'S OBSERVATIONS ON WILLIAM AND MARY

There is evidence for this view in Bishop Burnet's *History of His Own Time*. Burnet had arrived in the United Provinces in May 1686,[41] having sought voluntary exile on the

Continent, where he had been for some time after falling into disgrace with both Charles II and James II for his political opposition. According to his own account, he was invited to wait on the Prince and Princess of Orange and thereafter, again according to his account, he was taken into their confidence. The Prince feared, says Burnet, that James II's behaviour was such that the distrust by his people that he was engendering would force him 'into a French management, and engage him into such desperate designs as would force violent remedies'.

Some of the Bishop's observations on both William and Mary are worth noting. For Mary his admiration was total. 'The Princess possessed all that conversed with her with admiration. Her person was majestic and created respect. She had great knowledge, with a true understanding, and a noble expression. There was a sweetness in her deportment that charmed, and an exactness in piety and virtue that made her a pattern to all that saw her…. She had read much, both in history and divinity.'[42]

As regards William, he records one of the Prince's insights, which retains its resonance. 'I was afraid', writes the Bishop, 'lest his struggle with the Louvestein party … might have given him a jealousy of liberty and of a free government. He assured me it was quite the contrary; nothing but such a constitution could resist a powerful aggressor long, or have the credit that was necessary to raise such sums as a great war might require.' It was his explanation of how two and a half million Dutchmen, with their apparently anarchic, but representative, institutions, were able to confront the 20 million Frenchmen under Louis's apparent absolutism – and to find the finance too.[43]

Two other observations of the Prince are worth noting. He disapproved of the renewal of the town charters with which first Charles and then James used to pack Parliament 'and expressed his sense of a legal and limited authority fully', in other words a limited monarchy. In religion he was in favour of toleration, if only for the practical reason of 'quieting our contentions at home', and, although he wished some of the ceremonies of the Church of England might be laid aside, he had no intention of imposing his own Calvinistic notions of predestination on the country.[44]

CREATION OF CLOSE ATTACHMENT BETWEEN WILLIAM AND MARY

There was one development, of great significance, that Burnet's presence in The Hague brought about – at least if we believe his account, and there is no reason not to. Burnet raised with Mary the position the Prince would hold if she came to the Crown: 'I told her, a titular kingship was no acceptable thing to a man, especially if it was to depend on another's life; and such a nominal dignity might endanger the real one that the Prince had in Holland.' Mary had no hesitation in deciding on her reply and asked Burnet to bring the Prince to her so that he could hear what it was. As the Prince was out hunting this meeting occurred the following day. 'She did not think', under the laws of God, 'that the husband was ever to be obedient to the wife; she promised him he should always bear rule.' But there was a *quid pro quo*: 'she asked only that he would obey the command "of husbands love your wives", as she should do that, "wives, be obedient to your husbands in all things".' If, therefore, there was a relationship between Betty Villiers and the Prince it should not be at the expense of William's love for her.

The significance at the political level was equally as marked as it was at the personal; any doubt that Mary might be a contender for power was now removed.[45]

Thus at both levels the partnership between William and Mary was consolidated, a consolidation within their side of the Stuart clan which contrasted with the divisions that James had started to instigate within the British constituent of the clan on the other side of the North Sea. With any danger of disunity between William and Mary removed they would prove an increasingly attractive alternative focus of power in preference to the head of the clan.

THE PRINCE'S OPPOSITION TO JAMES'S POLICY

It now also became apparent that the underlying tensions between the two sides of the clan on either side of the North Sea, already noticeable under Charles II, but reasonably contained at the commencement of James's reign, were again coming to the surface in more forceful form. In November James sent over the Quaker William Penn to Holland to persuade William to support his policy of religious toleration for both Dissenters and Catholics. It was an unwise choice; for Penn, according to Burnet, 'was a talking, vain man…. He had such an opinion of his own faculty of persuading, that he thought none could stand before it; though he was singular in that opinion; for he had a tedious luscious way, that was not apt to overcome a man's reason, though it might tire his patience.' He was certainly not very successful with the Prince, who was readily prepared to see toleration of worship granted to both Dissenters and Papists – he thought 'conscience was only subject to God' – provided it was proposed and passed by Parliament, and he was prepared to lend his assistance to that end. But, as for the repeal of the Test Acts, he regarded that as a betrayal of the Protestant religion; the Acts provided security, indeed the only form of security, when the King was a Catholic. The bait which Penn dangled before him that James would 'enter into an entire confidence with him' had no effect.[46] He was immovably opposed to the central tenet of James's policy.

At this time there was another visitor from England, swashbuckling, outgoing and a staunch Whig, Charles, Lord Mordaunt, who, according to Burnet, tried to persuade William to launch an expedition to England. However, 'he represented the matter as so easy, that this appeared too romantic to the Prince to build upon'. Instead William promised to keep an eye on English affairs whilst putting those in Holland in such a position as to enable him to act when it became necessary. In the meantime, if James tried to change the established religion or infringed Mary's rights of succession he would see what he could do.[47]

As Van Citters reported on 18 October, Mordaunt's generous reception and entertainment by the Prince did not go unnoticed in England; there rumours were circulating that

Mordaunt was acting under instructions from other English malcontents to concert plans with the Prince of Orange. There, he also reported, rumours were circulating as well that there were plans afoot to put James's illegitimate son, the Catholic Duke of Berwick, on the throne, in preference to a Protestant successor, should James die; Tyrconnell's measures and the catholicisation of the nation, the rumours averred, might make this possible.[48] No doubt William will have discounted the plausibility of these stories, but his complaisance would change once a more credible Catholic contender emerged.

BRANDENBURG MOVES TOWARDS THE ANTI-FRENCH CAMP

We have seen that the Great Elector had signed a treaty with Leopold of Austria in January 1686. That was not to be the end of the matter – Frederick-William was determined to move further into the anti-French camp. In this same month he proposed a 20-year defensive pact to the Emperor. There was a stumbling-block – he wanted to swap his claims to Silesia for Schwiebus and this Leopold was not prepared to concede. However, the Elector's heir, Prince Frederick, looking to Austria for support for his succession when the time came, entered into a secret arrangement, which was kept from his father, under which Frederick promised to return Schwiebus upon his succession in exchange for a monetary payment. On 1 April the Twenty Years' Treaty was signed by Brandenburg and Austria. It was a defensive treaty under which, if their states or their rights came under attack, they would come to each other's assistance. They would similarly come to the aid of the Empire and of the new Elector Palatine, to part of whose territories, as we have seen, Louis was laying claim on behalf of his brother, the Duke of Orléans, who had married the previous Elector's daughter. The Great Elector also undertook to support the House of Austria's claims to the Spanish succession and the Imperial crown.[49]

The month before, on 20 February, Brandenburg and Sweden had also signed a defensive treaty of ten years to defend the terms of the Peace of Westphalia, the Regensburg Truce and the integrity of the Empire.[50]

Somewhat carried away, the Elector even envisaged an invasion of France by 57,000 Brandenburg and Dutch troops, which would take advantage of the discontents in France – Catholics, Huguenots, the Paris Parlement, and the Princes of the Blood all – to bring Louis XIV to heel.[51]

Nothing, of course, came of these chimerical reveries of the irascible old gentleman. But he did maintain contact with William of Orange. He went to Cleves, where William arrived on 4 August, and on the 7th uncle and nephew conferred for three hours. A week later there was a grand revue of Dutch troops on the Dutch side of the border near Nijmegen, in which the Elector participated in his carriage with the Electrice at his side.[52] William was unable to bring Mary with him because of the precedence that James II insisted she should have over the Elector's wife at the ceremonies. Rather than cause any embarrassment

Mary decided to stay away.[53] The occasion no doubt served to reinforce the old intimacy between the Elector and the Prince, the purpose of the meeting being in the Elector's words 'to discuss things with you in a better and more trusting manner'.[54] But no record of their discussions survives. Subsequent to these events William took care to provide the Elector's eldest son by his second marriage, Philippe, with lavish entertainment at his court during his extended stay in the United Provinces, with all the Dutch nobility in attendance.[55] D'Avaux reported rumours that William had promised Philippe's mother and the Elector that he would arrange for Philippe to succeed to his offices in the Republic and that the visit was intended as a means of his gaining sufficient popularity to that end, the feasibility of which D'Avaux rightly dismisses.[56]

THE LEAGUE OF AUGSBURG AND AUSTRIAN SUCCESSES AGAINST THE TURKS

A little earlier, on 9 July, a defensive League, the League of Augsburg, was signed between prominent members of the German Reich. Foremost were the Emperor, the King of Spain in his capacity as the Duke of Burgundy, the King of Sweden, on behalf of his territories in the Reich, and the Elector of Bavaria. It included the *Kreise* of Bavaria, Franconia and Swabia and it was designed to fulfil Waldeck's hopes when he formed the Laxenburg League, which had now reached the end of its term – Waldeck, indeed, played an influential role in creating the new League and so, possibly, did the Prince of Orange. Evidence is lacking, although the Prince did send Eckhart, a member of his Private Domains Council, to Regensburg as his personal representative. The League's object was to maintain the Truce of Ratisbon (Regensburg) and the Peace of the Empire – a response to Louis's claims on the Palatinate. It envisaged raising an army of 60,000 men with Waldeck as Field Marshal. However, whilst Austria was still preoccupied with the Turks it remained militarily insignificant for the time being, even after the later adhesion of the Elector of Palatine and the Upper Rhine *Kreis*, and for this reason and also because he was not yet ready for a complete break with France, the Elector of Brandenburg did not join it.[57] Nor did the Dutch Republic – Fagel and Prince William told the Emperor's ambassador, Cramprich, that it needed the accession of Brandenburg and Brunswick-Lüneburg.[58] But the League was to acquire substance in the future.

Austria's preoccupation with the Turks indeed was beginning to change. Leopold's forces, aided by Brandenburg troops and contingents from the Empire – 34,000 men – pushed the Turks back in Hungary and in September they captured Buda. Whilst no peace agreement was reached with the Turks on satisfactory terms and whilst Leopold's Privy Conference decided, on 19 April 1687, to continue the war,[59] for Louis XIV the signs of the re-establishment of unity within the German Reich and of the accretion of Leopold's power, which it was already clear would follow from the Turkish defeat, were ominous indications for the future.

1 Müller, *Waldeck, op. cit.*, I, pp.293–4.

2 G.H. Kurz, *Willem III en Amsterdam, 1683–1685*, Utrecht 1928, p.141. Witsen, *op. cit.*, I, p.272. Witsen says the initiative came from the Prince and so does Fruin, *Verspreide Geschriften, op. cit.*, V, p.126. But we have William's letter to Waldeck above saying Amsterdam was making him offers.

3 Witsen, *op. cit.*, II, p.163.

4 *Ibid.*, II, p.87. Japikse, *Willem III, op. cit.*, II, pp.203–4.

5 Witsen, *op. cit.*, I, pp.273–8.

6 *Ibid.*, I, p.282. Fruin, *Verspreide Geschriften, op. cit.*, V, p.129.

7 Witsen, *op. cit.*, I, pp.282–3.

8 Israel, *Dutch Republic, op. cit.*, pp.836–7. Fruin, *Verspreide Geschriften, op. cit.*, V, pp.129–30.

9 Japikse, *Willem III, op. cit.*, II, p.202.

10 Israel, *Dutch Republic, op. cit.*, pp.837–9.

11 Dreiskämper, *op. cit.*, p.11–12, 20–1.

12 *Ibid.*, pp.34, 31, 32.

13 *Ibid.*, p.33.

14 *Ibid.*, pp.26–7.

15 *Ibid.*, pp.28–9.

16 For all this see Waddington, *op. cit.*, II, pp.534ff.

17 Troost, art. in *The Anglo-Dutch Moment, op. cit.*, pp.328–9. Waddington, *op. cit.*, II, pp.546–7. Dreiskämper, *op. cit.*, p.25. The Revocation was in fact signed by Louis on 15 October, sent to the Intendants on the 17th, and registered by all the Parlements on the 22nd, see Rousset, *op. cit.*, III pp.477–8.

18 Waddington, *op. cit.*, II, p.350.

19 *Ibid.*, II, p.551.

20 Miller, *James II, op. cit.*, p.148.

21 Kenyon, *Sunderland, op. cit.*, pp.122, 123, 128 (and n.+). Miller, *James II, op. cit.*, pp.149–50.

22 Miller, *James II, op. cit.*, pp.154–6. Holmes, *op. cit.*, p.13.

23 Miller, *James II, op. cit.*, p.156.

24 *Ibid.*, pp.157, 163.

25 Kenyon, *Sunderland, op. cit.*, p.139. Miller, *James II, op. cit.*, p.164.

26 Miller, *James II, op. cit.*, p.163. Kenyon, *Sunderland, op. cit.*, p.144.

27 Browning, *op. cit.*, II, pp.355, 371.

28 Quoted in W.A. Speck, *James II*, London 2002, p.53.

29 Macaulay, *History of England*, Everyman Edition, reprinted 1927, I, pp.666–7.

30 *Verbaal, op. cit.*, pp.135–42.

31 *Correspondentie Willem III en Bentinck, op. cit.*, II, 2, p.720.

32 *Ibid.*, II, 2, pp.722–7.

33 Dalrymple, *op. cit.*, II, pp.46–8, 53–4.

34 Singer, *op. cit.*, I, pp.168–9.

35 Dalrymple, *op. cit.*, II, Appendix to Part I, pp.55–6.

36 *Correspondentie Willem III en Bentinck, op. cit.*, II, 2, pp.731–2.

37 *Ibid.*, II, 2, p.736.

38 *Ibid.*, II, p.737 n.2, 744 and n.4. Burnet, *op. cit.*, 1818, II, p.334.

39 *Correspondentie Willem III en Bentinck, op. cit.*, II, 2, p.737.

40 Miller, *James II, op. cit.*, pp.162–3. See also Troost, *William III, op. cit.*, pp.181–2 whose interpretation of Van Citters's correspondence is somewhat different from Miller's.

41 Miller, *James II, op. cit.*, p.158.

42 Burnet, *op. cit.*, 1818, II, p.313–14.

43 *Ibid.*, II, pp.314–15.

44 *Ibid.*, II, p.315.

45 *Ibid.*, II, pp.316–17.

46 *Ibid.*, II, pp.317–18.

47 *Ibid.*, II, pp.395–6.

48 *Correspondentie Willem III en Bentinck, op. cit.*, II, 2, p.742.

49 Mckay, *Great Elector, op. cit.*, pp.255–6. Waddington, *op. cit.*, pp.552–7. Spielman, *op. cit.*, p.124.

50 Waddington, *op. cit.*, II, p.538.

51 Philippson, *op. cit.*, III, pp.422–3.

52 Waddington, *op. cit.*, II, pp.566–7.

53 *Correspondentie Willem III en Bentinck, op. cit.*, II, 2, p.738–9.

54 Troost, in *Anglo-Dutch Moment, op. cit.*, p.330.

55 Fruin, *Aantekeningen, op. cit.*, pp.446ff.

56 D'Avaux, *Négociations, op. cit.*, V, pp.269–72, 312.

57 Waddington, *op. cit.*, II, pp.564–5. For Waldeck's and William's roles see Müller, *Waldeck, op. cit.*, II, pp.11–13.

58 Onno Klopp, *Der Fall des Hauses Stuart*, Vienna 1876, III, pp.242–3.

59 Spielman, *op. cit.*, I, pp.126–7.

26 1687: THE PRINCE INTENSIFIES CONTACT WITH THE ENGLISH OPPOSITION; OPEN BREACH BETWEEN WILLIAM & MARY AND JAMES

DIJKVELDT'S MISSION TO ENGLAND

The reports that fleets were being fitted out in England and France and that these could be directed at the Republic decided the States of Holland and the States-General in January 1687, at the behest of Prince William, to send Dijkveldt on an embassy to England to ascertain the truth of the rumours, whilst assuring James II of Dutch goodwill.[1] Fagel, incidentally, used the reports to push through the war budget for 1687.[2] Dijkveldt's instructions are lost, although Burnet claimed that he drafted them and that Dijkveldt followed them closely. According to Burnet's *History* the envoy was to engage in dialogue with a wide range of people whilst at the same time remonstrating diplomatically but firmly with James on the course he was pursuing, at home and abroad, and to see whether it was possible to forge a closer understanding between himself and the Prince. An appeal to the Tories should be made by assuring them that the Prince would support the Church of England, and to the Whigs by holding out the promise of toleration for Dissenters if Mary came to the throne.[3] Clearly, part of his task would need to be conducted clandestinely and Dijkveldt was eminently well chosen; he had been part of the Dutch mission to London in 1685 which had successfully negotiated the Anglo-Dutch defensive treaty and which had been well received by James II; but the length of its stay no doubt also contributed to Dijkveldt's being able to cultivate a wide range of contacts amongst the English elite.

On 17 January 1687 James II's new ambassador, D'Albeville, arrived in The Hague.[4] He conveyed James's request that the disgraced Burnet be forbidden the Orange court, and this was complied with, but nevertheless communications with him continued to be maintained by means of Dijkveldt and another of William's confidants, Hallewyn, who kept him informed of the news from England – Burnet suspected that the Anglicans kept in touch with him by means of Bishop Compton.[5]

Dijkveldt arrived in England on 23 February but a – perhaps conveniently – sore foot and protocol delays in receiving D'Albeville in The Hague, which also meant delays in receiving Dijkveldt in London, meant that he did not have his first interview with James until 3 March[6] – delays which may have been useful in sounding out his English contacts. At this interview James assured Dijkveldt that he 'never had the intention to break with the States nor to declare war upon them. These were the rumours of evil-minded persons'.[7]

A rather curious incident then took place. On 17 March the Countess of Sunderland, Sunderland's own wife, took it upon herself to write to the Prince of Orange personally. She warned William that seductive offers would be made to Dijkveldt promising an Anglo-Dutch alliance, and that William would be granted the right of nomination to civil and military appointments, this to include Ireland, if he instructed Dijkveldt and his co-ambassador, Van Citters, to issue a declaration in his name supporting the repeal of the Test Acts.[8] Although William hardly needed telling, she pointed out the trap behind this – once the declaration was issued it would be binding on the Prince whilst the *quid pro quo* could be evaded. Burnet indeed indicates that Sunderland put this offer to Dijkveldt, spelling out that the Anglo-Dutch alliance would be directed against France.[9] Dalrymple suggests that the letter was dictated to his wife by the deeply devious Sunderland, who wished to reinsure himself with the Prince of Orange by issuing a warning against the moves he himself was carrying out, although Kenyon rejects this – the Countess, he says, was motivated by her conscience and religious convictions.[10] Princess Anne had no doubts what she thought of the character of the Sunderlands, wife and husband, and expressed them to her sister Mary: 'Sure there never was a couple so well matched as she and her good husband, for as she is throughout in all her actions the greatest jade that ever was, so is he the subtillest workinest [*sic*] villain that is on the face of the earth.'[11]

William issued his instruction about the manner in which he wished Dijkveldt's negotiations to be conducted by means of letters to Fagel, who, in his capacity as the Pensionary, transmitted them onwards to the envoy. James's religious policy, said William, should be treated with great sensitivity; it should not be raised until shortly before the end of the mission and after consultation with 'the well intentioned', that is with the English opposition whom Dijkveldt was cultivating, and not until it was clear how James would handle Louis XIV's treatment of the Principality of Orange. At the end of March Dijkveldt reported 'the steadfast resolution of the King to annul the test and penal laws in one way or the other' and said that he wanted William to concur with this. Before giving a negative reply, William thought Dijkveldt should try to see whether it would be possible to satisfy James with an assurance from him and Mary that Catholics would not be prosecuted for the assumption of offices against the law. He didn't think it would work but it was worth a try. Dijkveldt should also try to obtain a satisfactory answer on the question of Orange. He didn't think that would work either, as he anticipated that James would want to bargain his support on Orange for William's support for his religious policy, 'in which he would be very deluded, for I will rather suffer anything than do anything against my honour and conscience'.[12] By 13 April, indeed, he took the view that there was no point in awaiting James's reply on Orange, because any promises would be subsequently nullified by his stance on the religious question.[13]

JAMES II'S DECLARATION OF INDULGENCE

On 28 March James II had announced his intention of allowing a universal liberty of conscience – he had already dispensed individual Dissenters, such as William Penn and his family, from the penal laws – and this was followed on 14 April by his Declaration of Indulgence, which suspended the Test and Corporation Acts and the penal laws. There were about 40 of these, which *inter alia* prevented Nonconformists from attending the universities, under which they were fined if they did not attend the Anglican Church and under which it was treason to try to convert anyone to Catholicism. The Declaration was issued in consultation with Dissenters and William Penn may have been instrumental in its drafting.[14]

William was unsure how to convey his – of course negative – reaction to the Declaration to the King; on 27 April he told Fagel he wanted to consult him and he was to tell Dijkveldt that instructions would be conveyed to him by the postal courier on 1 May; alas, these we do not have.[15] He did however tell D'Albeville – hence, it was to be expected, for onward transmission to James – in the middle of May that Catholicism could not become dominant in England without James breaching both the laws and his promises, and without, he feared, 'causing disorders which would imperil the monarchy'; he was prepared to grant Catholics the same degree of liberty that they enjoyed in the Dutch Republic, but he would never consent to their dominance.[16] Burnet says that Mary spoke to D'Albeville with such firmness that 'she was more intractable on these matters than the Prince himself'. As for James, he told Dijkveldt during his stay in England that he was the head of the family and that the Prince ought to comply with that, but instead he had always set himself against him.[17] At their final interview on 10 June Dijkveldt was asked to convey to the Prince and Princess King James's request that they approve the repeal of the Test Acts and the penal laws, or, as a minimum, their suspension under his Declaration of Indulgence.[18]

On his return to Holland Dijkveldt carried a letter for William from James dated 7 June in which he says that he had spoken to Dijkveldt of 'your private concerns [that is to say of Orange], of which he will give you an account, as also of the public affairs here [the religious issue] … and told him (what I think) I have reason to expect from you, for the good of the monarchy, as well as our family, which he has promised to tell you, so that I need not write it'.[19] We can assume from this that James either regarded whatever Dijkveldt had told him at their final interview as not quite final or that he was determined, stubbornly, to ignore it.

But a reply was soon forthcoming from the Prince himself which could leave no further doubts on the matter. On 17 June he thanked James for his promise of support regarding Orange. On the point of religion he said that there was no one more averse to persecution than he was, 'but at the same time … I can never resolve to do anything contrary to the interest of the religion which I profess; and that therefore I cannot concur in what your

Majesty asks of me'. James's response was that, as what Dijkveldt had conveyed to the Prince on his behalf had not changed the Prince's mind, there was no point in him trying to do it by letter; but he did complain that Dijkveldt had not got the right measure of affairs in England because he gave too much credit 'to some that do not wish me and the monarchy well'.[20]

DIJKVELDT AND THE ENGLISH OPPOSITION

Dijkveldt had indeed consulted widely, Whigs and Tories, Catholics and Dissenters. For this he made use of the house of the Earl of Shrewsbury. His contacts included Halifax, Nottingham, Admiral Herbert and Mordaunt as well as 'the Immortal Seven', who in the following year, 1688, famously issued the invitation to William to invade England, that is to say the Earl of Shrewsbury, the Earl of Devonshire, Danby, Compton, Edward Russelll (another admiral), Henry Sidney and Lord Lumley.[21]

One development may perhaps have been that the conspiracy in the English army against James II in 1688, which was to have such deleterious effects for the King, now began to take tentative shape.[22] Certainly John Churchill, later created the Duke of Marlborough, who played a deciding role in the conspiracy, took advantage of Dijkveldt's return to Holland to bring with him a letter for the Prince. He and his wife, Sarah, were close confidants of Princess Anne, who, as we have seen, was married to Prince George of Denmark, and for a long time into Mary's reign, when she succeeded William and Mary, the Churchills' influence over her was the foundation of the second leg of John Churchill's career. Until now that had been based on the patronage of James II, and the Churchills were preparing the ground for a possible change of sides – they asserted because of the claims of their religion.

'The Princess of Denmark', Churchill wrote on 27 May, 'having ordered me to discourse with Mons. Dykvelt, and to let him know her resolutions, so that he might let your Highness, and the Princess, her sister, know, that she was resolved, by the assistance of God, to suffer all extremities, even to death itself, rather than be brought to change her religion, I thought it my duty to your Highness and the Princess Royal [Mary], by this opportunity of Mons. Dyckvelt, to give you assurances under my own hand, that my places and the King's favour I set at naught, in comparison of the being true to my religion. In all things but this the King may command me, and I call God to witness, that even with joy I should expose my life for his service, so sensible am I of his favours.' He excuses his impertinence in writing, 'I being of so little use to your Highness', 'but that I think it may be a great ease to your Highness and the Princess to be satisfied that the Princess of Denmark is safe in the trusting of me; I being resolved, although I cannot live the life of a saint, if there be ever occasion for it, to shew the resolution of a martyr.'[23]

It was a remarkable gesture and, given Churchill's dependence on, and obligations to, James, a very risky one, especially when it was committed in writing – he could after all have conveyed the message through Dijkveldt verbally, although that would, of course, have lacked the same impact. After the breach with James's brothers-in-law, Clarendon and Rochester, a further breach in the Stuart clan was now opening up, this time even closer to home, with his daughter Anne showing her repugnance for his religious policy. Signs of this breach had indeed become manifest a little earlier during Dijkveldt's visit when Anne wrote a long letter to Mary on 23 March in which she reported that James had cancelled her request to pay a visit to Holland; that she was anticipating that he would put pressure on her to change her religion; that she was resolved to 'undergo anything rather than' do that; and in which she warned that neither William nor Mary should visit England for 'if you or the Prince should come, I should be frightened out of my wits for fear any harm should happen to either of you'.[24]

The letter from Churchill was not the only one in Dijkveldt's voluminous postbag; there were indeed letters from Clarendon and Rochester as well, as there were from Nottingham, Danby, Halifax, the Earl of Devonshire and the Earl of Shrewsbury. Sunderland also did not omit a formally obsequious, though short, missive.[25]

On 26 June Bishop Compton also wrote: 'It is not only for your near relation to the crown, that you are so much prayed for here, but for your usefulness to it. For if the King should have any trouble come upon him, which God forbid, we do not know any sure friend he has to rely on abroad, besides yourself.' Compton, in short, was looking to William to save James from himself.

There was also a sad letter from the Earl of Bedford, the head of the powerful Russelll family, whose son William had been executed for his participation in the Rye House plot and who was a cousin of Edward Russelll. The Earl expressed gratitude for the messages of 'compassion' which he had received from Dijkveldt on the Prince's behalf and the Prince's 'gracious disposition to comfort an unfortunate family, which I should be less concerned for than I am, if I could doubt any branch of it would ever fail in any point of duty to your Highness' person'. It was a strong hint.

In August James's Queen, Mary of Modena, wrote to William with the news of the death of her mother, the Duchess of Modena. William took the occasion to send his cousin, Nassau-Zuylenstein, to England to offer his condolences[26] and the opportunity this visit presented was also taken to continue to develop the contacts which Dijkveldt had fostered during his.

JAMES'S PLANS TO PACK PARLIAMENT

James, meanwhile, having decided that he could expect no cooperation from the existing Parliament, decided to dissolve it in July and he started preparations to pack a new one, a process which he thought would take six months. In August he began by reversing Charles II's removal of Whigs from positions in the London livery companies – who constituted the Parliamentary electorate – and by removing the less supportive Lord Lieutenants in the counties.[27] Three questions were put to Members of Parliament, Deputy Lieutenants,

Magistrates, important gentry and office holders: were they prepared to live peacefully with their neighbours of whatever religion; if they were elected to Parliament would they support the repeal of the Test Acts and penal laws; and would they vote for Parliamentary candidates who were so committed? The answers, when they came in, were muddled and, not unexpectedly, ambiguous; but it was clear that support for James's religious policy was weak. Those who gave unsatisfactory answers were removed from office and their places taken by Dissenters and Catholics. Many of those thus removed had been put in place by Charles II to facilitate the Tory reaction after the Popish Plot[28] and helped to provide James with his sympathetic Parliament in 1685. His policies had now pushed the Tory Anglican sympathies of these men beyond what they could tolerate, which did not prevent James from advancing further on his course. In November he commenced revising the lists of sheriffs who supervised the Parliamentary elections, again inserting both Catholics and Dissenters; and work commenced on purging the corporations so that their constituencies could be packed as well.[29] With his ability to appoint peers the aim therefore was to assure James of both Houses of Parliament.

But how effective these measures might have been in procuring the compliant Parliament dependent on himself that James aimed for we do not know, for the elections were never held. William of Orange was naturally anxious to ascertain the likelihood of their success and one of Zuylenstein's tasks was to seek out the views of leading figures in England on this. Certainly the opinion of Nottingham and Halifax, expressed to William, was that they were unlikely to work;[30] and at this time Halifax published, anonymously, his famous pamphlet, *Letter to a Dissenter*, in which he pointed out that the Dissenters' aspirations were likely to be secured on much more solid ground with the accession of Mary and that the Protestants, if unity were preserved between Anglicans and Dissenters, were sure to prevail in the long run because of their weight of numbers.[31] William would have been further informed of affairs in England when both Henry Sidney and Shrewsbury visited him at Het Loo in September.[32]

PUBLIC BREACH BETWEEN WILLIAM & MARY AND JAMES II

In the meantime William was prompted to engage in the propaganda battle and to issue what was, in effect, a religious manifesto to the people of Britain.

For some time a Scottish advocate, James Steward, had been in correspondence with Fagel. He was a Dissenter, an old opponent of James when he was Duke of York, who had participated in Argyll's rebellion, and who had taken refuge, after its failure, in the Dutch Republic, where he fostered an acquaintance with Fagel. William Penn persuaded him to return to England, promising him he would be forgiven and would be well received at the English court, and, after his welcome there, he was used as an intermediary to persuade William and Mary of the merits of the Declaration of Indulgence seen from a Dissenting point of view. By July he was engaged in this task, using Fagel as an intermediary, to whom he wrote a number of letters. Fagel's initial reluctance to engage with him was overcome when he was persuaded by Steward that he was acting with the backing of James II. Fagel realised that this presented an ideal opportunity for William and Mary to declare in unmistakeable terms – and publicly – what their views were on the religious question agitating the British people. With the full agreement of Prince William he drafted a reply in Latin, which was translated into English by Gilbert Burnet, and sent to James Steward, thereafter to be printed and published.[33]

Dated 4 November, the letter is in Fagel's name[34] but written on behalf of William and Mary; it was thus a joint manifesto and indicates how much Mary had come to the fore. The letter makes it clear that it is a direct response to James II, 'since you [James Steward: he spelt it 'Stewart'] say that your Letters were writ by the King's knowledge and allowance'.

The view of William and Mary, says the letter, is that no Christian should be persecuted for his conscience and they therefore agreed that Papists – in England, it should be noted, Scotland, and Ireland – should be allowed to pursue their religion with the same liberty as was allowed them in the United Provinces, that is to say with full liberty of conscience. They would also agree to the repeal of the penal laws, provided that they should continue to apply to exclude Catholics from Parliament and all ecclesiastical, civil and military offices so that the Protestant religion was secured. They could not, however, agree to the repeal of the Test Acts, which were there to secure Protestantism.

Dissenters, too, should be allowed the full exercise of their religion, and, under William and Mary's proposals, as Lord Polwarth, then a Scottish exile living in Utrecht, noted, the Test Acts would only apply to Catholics and not to them, thus enabling them to stand for office, including Parliament.[35]

The reason why the Test Acts should apply to Catholics was spelt out: 'their Highnesses are convinced in their consciences', the letter reads, 'that both the Protestant Religion and the Safety of the Nation, would be exposed to most certain Dangers, if either the Test, or those other Penal Laws should be Repealed; Therefore they cannot consent to this, nor concur with his Majesty's will; for they believe, they should have much to Answer for to God, if the consideration of any present advantages should carry them to consent and concur in things which they believe would be not only dangerous but mischievous to the Protestant Religion.'

It was a very clever manifesto; it appealed at once to Catholics and to Dissenters, both of whom would be granted freedom of worship, and to Anglicans, who would see their religion secured. It therefore appealed to all three religious sectors of the population in contrast to James's appeal to Catholics and Dissenters at the expense of Anglicans – which was, in any case, an inherently weak coalition because many Dissenters were as suspicious of Catholicism as were Anglicans. It appealed also to all three nations in the British Isles. And the granting of liberty of conscience to Catholics appealed as well to those Catholic allies on the Continent whom William was seeking to array against Louis XIV.

The opposition of William and Mary to James II's religious policy was now officially public and, as the letter was printed in English, in Dutch and in Latin, it was designed to reach the widest possible audience across Europe. It may be, as we shall see in the next chapter, that the manifesto emerged at the same time as William was moving close to a decision that he needed to invade England.

The letter did not prevent James from trying to convert Mary to his Catholic views. The opportunity to make the attempt seems to have arisen from Mary's having told D'Albeville that she would like to know what principal motives lay behind her father's conversion.[36] James wrote her a number of letters and sent her literature over a period of time, which continued until March of the following year, when both parties seemed to conclude that they had exhausted the subject.[37] Mary kept her sister Princess Anne, Bishop Compton, and through her Chaplain, Dr Stanley, William Sancroft, the Archbishop of Canterbury, informed; and she also told Prince William, who was so impressed, 'not thinking I was capable of such a thing', as Mary wrote in her *Memoirs*, that it 'did not a little flatter my vanity'.[38] Although he was admittedly always an admirer, Burnet was impressed, in his account of the interchange, with her learning and understanding of the Anglican religion,[39] as was Dr Stanley.[40]

In the autumn James's plans to break the Anglican monopoly over the universities of Oxford and Cambridge culminated in the expulsion of the President and 25 fellows of Magdalen College, Oxford, and the steady substitution of Catholics.[41]

On 12 November he drew up a list of the sheriffs who presided over the county elections, in which he inserted both Catholic and Dissenter names; and, at the same time a commission was established to purge the corporations so that these too could be manipulated.[42]

And then rumours began to circulate during the month that James's Queen, Mary Beatrice of Modena, was pregnant, and on 24 November they were confirmed.[43] Mary had frequently miscarried and she might do so again; but, nevertheless, until now the next in succession to the throne were the two Protestant princesses, Mary and Anne, who provided the hope that James's catholicising measures would not survive his demise. Now, if the child were a boy, the prospect arose that the next occupant to the throne would be yet another Catholic who would be able to consolidate James's work. He would be a much more legitimate contender for the throne than Monmouth had ever been, let alone Berwick. And the removal of Mary as next in line to the throne was naturally of the greatest importance for Prince William of Orange. It lent further weight to the considerations pointing to an invasion of England.

---

1 Fruin, *Verspreide Geschriften, op. cit.*, V, p.151. His source: D'Avaux, *Négociations, op. cit.*, VI, p.29.

2 Dreiskämper, *Vooravond, op. cit.*, p.43.

3 Burnet, *op. cit.*, 1818, II, pp.334–5.

4 Muilenburg, *The Embassy of Everard van Weede, Lord of Dykvelt, to England in 1687*, University Studies of the University of Nebraska, XX, July-Oct 1920, Nos 3 & 4, p.12.

5 Burnet, *op. cit.*, 1818, II, p.334.

6 Muilenburg, *op. cit.*, p.26.

7 *Ibid.*, pp.27–8.

8 Dalrymple, *op. cit.*, II, Book V app., pp.58–61.

9 Burnet, *op. cit.*, 1818, II, p.337.

10 Dalrymple, *op. cit.*, II, Book V app., p.58. Kenyon, 'The Earl of Sunderland and the Revolution of 1688', *Cambridge Hist. Journal*, xi, 1955, pp.293–6.

11 Sidney, *op. cit.*, II, pp.265–6.

12 See William's letters to Fagel, 15, 27 & 30 March 1687. *Correspondentie Willem III en Bentinck, op. cit.*, II, 2, pp.746–8.

13 Letter to Fagel 13 April. *Correspondentie Willem III en Bentinck, op. cit.*, II, 2, pp.749–50.

14 Miller, *James II, op. cit.*, pp.339–40. Barry Coward, *The Stuart Age England 1603–1714*, 2003, pp.339–40. Speck, *op. cit*, p.52. Holmes, *op. cit.*, p.170.

15 *Correspondentie Willem III en Bentinck, op. cit.*, II, 2, pp.750–1.

16 Miller, *James II, op. cit.*, pp.175–6.

17 Burnet, *op. cit.*, 1818, II, p.337.

18 Kenyon, *Sunderland, op. cit.*, p.157.

19 Dalrymple, *op. cit.*, Book V app., p.54. Kenyon (see note 18 above) gives the date of Dijkveldt's final interview with James as 30 May. Dalrymple dates James's letter as 28 May. I have converted both dates to New Style, but under both versions James's letter precedes the final interview, which suggests that Dijkveldt did not convey a categorical refusal by William to support the Declaration of Indulgence.

20 Dalrymple, *op. cit.*, Book V app., pp.54–6.

21 Muilenburg, *op. cit.*, pp.41ff. Burnet, *op. cit.*, 1818, II, p.339.

22 John Childs, *The Army of James II and the Glorious Revolution*, Manchester 1980, p.141.

23 Dalrymple, *op. cit.*, Book V app., pp.62–3. The punctuation is Churchill's own (unless Dalrymple has miscopied it)

24 Winston Churchill, *Marlborough, His Life and Times*, London 1933, I, pp.237–9.

25 Dalrymple, *op. cit.*, Book V app., pp.63–72.

26 *Ibid.*, pp.74–5.

27 Kenyon, *Sunderland, op. cit.*, pp.159, 161.

28 *Ibid.*, pp.171–2. Miller, *James II, op. cit.*, pp.178–9.

29 Speck, *op. cit.*, pp.58–60.

30 See their letters to William, *Dalrymple, op. cit.*, II, Book V app., pp.77–80, 82–85.

31 Foxcroft, *op. cit.*, 1, pp.487 (and n.6), 488. For the views of modern historians see Speck, *op. cit.*, p.68 n.30.

32 Sidney, *op. cit.*, II, p.265. *Correspondentie Willem III en Bentinck, op. cit.*, II, 2, p.761.

33 Fruin, *Verspreide Geschriften, op. cit.*, V, pp.161–2. Burnet, *op. cit.*, 1818, II, pp.360–1. *Correspondentie Willem III en Bentinck, op. cit.*, I, 1, pp.33–4.

34 'A Letter Writ by Mijn Heer Fagel, Pennsionary of Holland To Mr. Iames Stewart, Advocate, giving an Account of the Prince and Princess of Orange's Thoughts concerning the Repeal of the Test, and the Penal Laws.' Text in British Library under this heading.

35 See Polwarth's letter to Bentinck, *Correspondentie Willem III en Bentinck, op. cit.*, I, 2, p.602.

36 See James's letter to Mary dated 4 November (14th OS). *Lettres et Mémoires de Marie, Reine d'Angleterre*, Mechtild Bentinck, 1880, pp.4ff.

37 *Ibid.*, p.65.

38 *Ibid.*, p.60.

39 Burnet, *op. cit.*, 1818, II, pp.354, 348ff.

40 Singer, *op. cit.*, II, pp.486–8.

41 Holmes, *op. cit.*, p.173.

42 Speck, *op. cit.*, pp.58–9.

43 Kenyon, *Sunderland, op. cit.*, p.167.

27 1688: THE INVASION OF ENGLAND

THE PRINCE UNDER PRESSURE OF TIME

At the news of Mary Beatrice's pregnancy William despatched Henry Sidney from Holland to ascertain the exact facts and to assist Bentinck in a more clandestine design – the development of a secret intelligence network in England and Scotland, which Bentinck had begun in December 1687. Sidney participated by playing a coordinating role and forwarding correspondence – much of it went to Dr Hutton, the doctor in the Orange household, or to others close to Bentinck or William. Amongst the correspondents are to be found, apart from Sidney, the Earl of Devonshire, the Earl of Carlyle and the Scot James Johnston, Burnet's cousin, who, after 1688, became William's Secretary of State for Scotland, but the informants came from a variety of backgrounds. Every care was taken to maintain secrecy, with the use of invisible ink, encryption, false names, false addresses and anonymous correspondents. It was by this means that William and Bentinck were kept very fully informed of affairs in Britain, and they formed a very useful supplement to the extensive despatches from Van Citters, which, however, were not safe from interception, with Van Citters himself always under close scrutiny.[1]

From this network William learnt in January 1688 that the majority of James's ministers were doubtful of his success in packing Parliament and that the factional divisions amongst the Catholics ensured that 'nothing will be concluded at present' at the King's court.[2] But conflicting advice had come from Sidney the previous December when he wrote to Bentinck, 'Tis certainly believed by all our wise men, except Milord Halifax, that we shall have a parliament, and they say, more certain[ly], that it will be a packed one, chose only by those that return it.' He went on to say 'that the Prince should take his measures what he will do in that case, for we must never expect to see a free parliament under the present state of affairs'.[3]

Prince William was therefore coming under acute pressure from two sides: there was the pregnancy of Mary Beatrice, which, if it produced a surviving son, would remove Mary as next in line to the throne, and there were James's plans for packing Parliament.

JAMES II'S PERCEIVED THREAT TO THE DUTCH REGENTS

By the beginning of 1688 Fagel's letter to James Steward, which so clearly set out William's and Mary's opposition to James's religious policy, was in public circulation. It set off an angry reaction from the King. On 27 January he directed D'Albeville to ask the States-General to return the English and Scottish regiments in their service and on the same date he wrote to William asking him to do his part to expedite their embarkation.[4] D'Albeville had suggested their return in April of the previous year on the grounds that they provided a means for William to recruit men who were disloyal to James[5] – William indeed had resisted James's demands for Catholic officers and instead had recruited the discontented from England and Scotland, Huguenots fleeing from Louis's France, and the Protestant officers whom Tyrconnell had dismissed from the Irish army.[6] James was reluctant to take on more men – he was able to finance the 20,000 men he already had, but an additional 3,000 was more than he was prepared to contemplate.

The solution that presented itself was to ask Louis XIV to take the regiments into French service, to form, in the French Catholic environment, a loyal – to James – Anglo-French brigade which he could call upon in case of need, but which would, in the meantime, be financed by the French King. Louis, however, had had unfortunate experiences in the past when much the same system prevailed under Charles II, who had inconveniently recalled these troops in 1674 and 1678. Instead Louis was ready to pay for the upkeep of the troops in England and he assured James of his assistance if he needed it to preserve his position in his kingdoms. James did not expect that all the troops would be prepared to serve under him in England, but he looked to the Catholics and those disaffected towards the Prince of Orange to do so, and Louis accordingly was asked to pay for 2,000 and not the full 3,000 in Dutch service.[7]

The States-General feared that James's request could be a prelude to his taking hostile action against them,[8] and, after a month's delay, they replied on 19 February – 'with the most wise advice of the Prince of Orange' – that the present conjuncture of affairs did not allow them 'to part with such an important part of their army, enlisted at so great expense'.[9] James's claim rested at first on the troops being his subjects and therefore subject to his commands, and then – when he found it – on an agreement entered into between William and Ossory in 1678, under which the regiments could be recalled as required.[10] On the first point the States-General eventually replied at the end of April that the laws of nature allowed men to serve where they pleased, and, as regarded the Ossory agreement, this had never been ratified by them. They therefore did not feel themselves bound by it and, in any case, it envisaged the recall of the troops only in an emergency – as was the case during Monmouth's rebellion – and it made no mention of a permanent recall.[11]

In the event it appears that around 104 officers out of between 213 and 234, mostly Catholics, obeyed James's summons to return to England, and there they were re-employed in three new regiments formed on the understanding that Louis would pay for them. But very few of the rank and file followed their officers, the numbers fell well short of the 2,000 that Louis had assumed, and even these were largely filled by a mere switch of 1,000 from the Irish army and not from the depletion of the forces at William's disposal. Louis accordingly reneged after two months' payments.

For William of Orange it was pure gain; the departing officers were soon replaced by

Protestants loyal to himself and, in the event, he would have at his disposal 3,000 loyal and mainly British troops for his invasion of England later in the year, from which he could draw propaganda benefits.[12]

There was a further benefit accruing to the Prince; it looked as though James, in alienating himself from the Dutch, was moving closer in the direction of an alliance with Louis XIV, a threat made more acute by his large navy – Van Citters reported that he had a fleet of 38 men-of-war – and a not inconsiderable army. James was in fact far too preoccupied with affairs in his own kingdoms to wish to engage in continental entanglements, and Van Citters and Johnson told Bentinck that he could not wage war. Nevertheless Fagel was able to persuade the secret committee for naval affairs to double the size of the Dutch fleet by building 21 ships in addition to the existing 21[13] – the States-General had indeed authorised the building of 36 warships the previous August,[14] but the perceived threat from James no doubt stiffened their resolve to complete the building programme. D'Avaux had reported to Louis on 1 January that William had put in hand the fitting out of men-of-war – he cited 20 – to be ready in the spring; and he had no doubt that William was aiming these preparations at encouraging the opposition in England by demonstrating a fleet off the English coast which could support them and offset any naval assistance Louis might send.[15] In the event, when William mustered the invasion fleet which was to land his army in England later in the year there were 52 warships available as escorts.[16]

THE REGENTS AND LOUIS'S COMMERCIAL MEASURES

Tensions had certainly been rising for some time between the Republic and France, which lent force to suspicions that this could lead to an Anglo-French assault, as in 1672.

Long-standing religious factors did not make for a propitious background. The persecution of the Huguenots in France, which began in 1679 and which culminated in the revocation by Louis of the Edict of Nantes in October 1685, led to the emigration of 200,000 Protestants,[17] many of whom sought refuge in the United Provinces. There the melancholy tales of their sufferings elicited both the sympathy and the alarm of their co-religionists. The revocation of the Edict was followed by French intervention in Savoy, where there were not many Protestants, but whose mountain valleys provided refuge for those fleeing from France. Its Duke was forced, with the aid of French troops, to pursue a policy of persecution of his own.[18]

But, whilst Louis's actions alienated opinion throughout Protestant Europe, including Brandenburg and Britain, amongst the mercantile Dutch it was his economic rather than his religious policies[19] that did most harm. To persuade the Dutch Regents to enter into the Treaty of Nijmegen Louis had undertaken to return to the low tariffs existing in 1664. After the treaty, Dutch imports flowed into France whilst Dutch ships dominated the trade of carrying French wines, spirits and salt for export. The Huguenot refugees brought not only capital with them but also commercial skills which benefited the Dutch at the expense of the French. In August 1687 Louis forbade the import of Dutch herrings unless salted with French salt. The following month he reintroduced Colbert's high tariffs of 1667, which, in particular, doubled the rate for fine cloths, and this had a special impact on Leyden.[20]

Amsterdam's initial reaction, however, was conciliatory. When in October D'Avaux attended a lavish dinner in the city, Hudde took him aside to assure him that he would devote the last drop of his blood to maintain good relations with Louis and a toast was drunk by the four Burgomasters to the union between the King and the Republic and to confusion to those who wished to overturn it. But the ambassador nevertheless issued a warning to his master that, if the Prince of Orange supported the complaints of the merchants for the next six months, the results would be lasting and very advantageous to him – certainly funds would be found to equip 50 ships at sea.[21] In November D'Avaux warned the King that 60,000 Dutchmen depended for their subsistence on the herring industry and that retaliatory measures were being considered, principally tariffs on French wines.[22]

His master, however, persisted in taking adverse measures and ignored Dutch protests. In March 1688 Leyden complained in the States of Holland about the effective ban on the sale of their fine cloths to France and by May Fagel was able to argue that, diplomatic efforts having failed, stronger measures needed to be considered.[23] But still Amsterdam remained unconvinced.

THE PRINCE CONTEMPLATES THE ENGLISH INVASION

We have no direct evidence of when William decided to invade England. We do, however, have an authoritative account from the respected 18th-century Dutch historian Jan Wagenaar, which is based on notes kept by Witsen. These notes have now been lost, but they were available to Wagenaar. At the beginning of 1688, or, according to Wagenaar, earlier, Fagel cast a fly over Witsen and two or three other members of the Delegated Council of the States of Holland. He told them that he was minded that His Highness should go to England, to restore order to the confused situation there, especially if he was asked to do so by prominent figures in the country. Fagel added that in these circumstances the Dutch State should support the Prince, without elaborating further. The delegate from Delft, a member of the Tromp family, whispered into Witsen's ear, 'The Prince seems to want to play the role of little Monmouth.' Witsen, says Wagenaar, faced a dilemma; on the one hand he promised to remain silent, on the other hand Dutch ships bound for France would be sailing towards their ruin, if the Prince's crossing to England proceeded.[24] A vacillating man, Witsen, as we shall see, was to vacillate until the last moment.

We should note Fagel's point about the Prince being asked to intervene in England by prominent figures there. In 1672 he had contemplated accepting sovereignty in the United Provinces, but only if it were offered to him by the political nation. We are not suggesting that he had yet decided to seek the Crown in England; but he was clear from the start that, if he were to intervene in England, it was to be with the consent of the English political nation, or, at least, at the request of as influential and representative a body as circumstances allowed. When, in the event, sovereignty did come his way, much of the ground had been prepared – albeit in serendipitous fashion – for the argument to be advanced that it was at the hands of the English political nation that it was bestowed.

The Prince was careful to use Fagel to sound out Witsen and did not do so directly himself. He was a man to keep his options open whenever he could; an invasion of England would be an extremely complex operation which would need to be prepared on a number of fronts, and from which it might be necessary to retreat until retreat itself was no longer possible.

How he set about the task – in James's British Isles, across the continent of Europe, and in the Dutch Republic, whilst always heeding the moves of Louis XIV – we must now examine.

THE PRINCE'S ENGLISH VISITORS

On 29 April, William wrote to Bentinck from Het Loo that Arthur Herbert and 'the two Russellls', that is, Admiral Edward Russelll, who was the cousin of Lord William Russelll (executed during the Popish Plot), together with – probably – the Admiral's father, had been there, adding, 'I will not tell you what they told me, since that is better done verbally.'[25] According to Burnet, Admiral Russelll 'was desired by many of great power and interest in England to speak very freely to the Prince, and to know positively of him what might be expected from him…. The Prince answered, that if he was invited by some men of the best interest, and the most valued in the nation, who should both in their own name, and in the name of others who trusted them, invite him to come and rescue the nation and the religion, he could be ready by the end of September to come over.'[26]

A little later in his *History* Burnet elaborated that in the discourse between the two men the Prince 'said he must satisfy both his honour [read *gloire*] and conscience, before he could enter into so great a design, which, if it miscarried, must bring ruin both on England and Holland: he protested, that no private ambition nor resentment of his own could ever prevail so far with him, as to make him break with so near a relation [James II], or engage in a war, of which the consequences must be of the last importance, both to the interests of Europe and of the protestant religion; therefore he expected formal and direct invitations. Russelll laid before him the danger of trusting such a secret to great numbers. The Prince said, if a considerable number of men, that might be supposed to understand the sense of the nation best, should do it, he would acquiesce in it.'[27]

Russelll returned to England and began organising the invitation the Prince asked for. The Prince wanted Henry Sidney to be the chief coordinator. 'But', as Burnet put it, 'because he was lazy, and the business required an active man, who could run about', he recommended his cousin, Johnston, for the task.[28]

JAMES'S SECOND DECLARATION OF INDULGENCE AND THE SEVEN BISHOPS

Shortly after these visits to Het Loo James issued his second Declaration of Indulgence on 6 May, announcing at the same time that he would summon Parliament in November or earlier; and on 14 May he ordered the clergy to read out the Declaration in the churches on two successive Sundays, on 30 May and 6 June in London and 13 and 20 June in the country.[29] Most of the London clergy refused to comply and on 27 May six bishops presented a petition to James – it had been penned, and signed, by Archbishop Sancroft at a long meeting at Lambeth Palace which preceded the presentation, although he himself was not present when it was submitted because, as a result of his refusal to cooperate with James's catholicising measures,[30] he had been banned from court. Nor, because he had been suspended from his office, was Bishop Compton, who had also participated at the Lambeth Palace meeting.[31] The most senior of the six bishops who waited upon James was William Lloyd, who had been Mary's chaplain in The Hague.[32] The six declined to comply with the King's Declaration 'among many other considerations, from this especially, because the Declaration is founded upon such dispensing powers, as hath often been declared illegal in Parliament; and … your petitioners cannot in prudence, honour, or conscience so far make themselves party to it.'[33]

Printed copies of the petition appeared almost at once – by 30 May at the latest. On that day the refusal of the London clergy to read out the Declaration was almost total; and soon another eight bishops sent in their support; out of the 25 dioceses in England and Wales without vacancies only four were committed to James.[34] On 18 June the seven bishops who had signed the petition appeared before the Privy Council and were committed to the Tower, where they were conveyed along the river by one of the royal barges. Popular opinion was enthusiastically in their favour. 'Both banks of the Thames were lined with multitudes, who, when too distant to be heard, manifested their feelings by falling down on their knees,' Van Citters reported.

According to Carswell the Prince of Orange in Holland was being kept informed by the bishops themselves.[35] The significance of what was happening was immediately clear to him. He wrote to Bentinck on 4 June, 'I enclose for your information letters from … England; this affair of the Bishops could rapidly bring matters to a turning point', and on the 7th he sent his friend further letters from England, expecting more at any moment; he was agog to know the outcome, '*ce qui pouroit aller loin*'.[36] On the 10th Dr Stanley wrote to Sancroft on his and Mary's behalf expressing their appreciation of the bishops' actions, which they had 'vindicated' to D'Albeville.[37]

Then, on 20 June, Mary Beatrice gave birth to a son.

BIRTH OF THE PRINCE OF WALES

Rumours about the genuineness of the pregnancy had begun to circulate not long after its announcement. At the end of January Clarendon recorded in his diary that 'it is strange to see how the Queen's great belly is everywhere ridiculed, as if scarce any body believed it to be true'.[38] Princess Anne wrote to Mary on 24 March, 'I cannot help thinking Mansell's wife's great belly [Mansell was her code name for James II] is a little suspicious. It is true indeed, she is very big, but she looks better than ever she did, which is not usual; for people when they are so far gone, for the most part, look very ill.... Her being so positive it will be a son, and the principles of that religion being such, that they will stick at nothing, be it never so wicked, if it will promote their interest, give some cause to fear there may be foul play intended. I will do all I can to find out, if it be so; and if I should make any discovery, you shall be sure to have an account of it.' Six days later she wrote that the likelihood was that Mary Beatrice would produce a son, 'there being so much reason to believe it is a false belly. For, methinks if it were not, there having been so many stories and jests made about it, she should, to convince the world, make either me, or some of my friends feel her belly; but quite contrary, whenever one talks of her being with child, she looks as if she were afraid one should touch her. And whenever I have happened to be in the room, as she has been undressing, she has always gone in the next room, to put on her smock.' Nobody would be convinced the child was hers unless it was a daughter. Anne herself certainly wouldn't unless she actually witnessed the birth.[39]

As it happened she did not, for the child was born a month before it was due and Anne was at Bath, where she had gone after miscarrying and did not return to London until 25 June.[40] And neither her suspicions[41] nor those of many others were stilled – Johnston wrote, 'the generality of the people conclude all is a trick'.[42]

Princess Mary also had her doubts from an early stage. Mary Beatrice had written to her personally about the pregnancy during its preliminary phases when she was still not certain about her condition. James also wrote, but in a manner so assured, 'at a time when no woman could be certain', as Mary says in her *Memoirs*, 'which was enough to raise some suspicion'. She was not concerned for herself, she wrote, but she could not remain indifferent to the consequences for the Protestant Church which a Papist successor implied. Beside the Church there was the love for her husband, although – whilst she regretted she did not have three crowns to bestow on him – she was not blind to his faults. But she knew his virtues too and she shared his views.[43]

Partly because of the political importance of her position in the Stuart clan and partly because of the strength of her now mature personality, Mary was coming increasingly to the fore in the partnership with William and her views, and her motivations, are increasingly a factor of which we need to take account.

When Anne did arrive in London she wrote to Mary on 28 June relating the suspicious circumstances surrounding the delivery of the child. 'After all this, 'tis possible it may be her child; but where one believes it, a thousand do not. For my part, except they do give it very plain demonstrations, which is almost impossible now, I shall ever be of the number of unbelievers.'[44]

Modern historians have no doubt that James Francis Edward Stuart was James II's legitimate heir. But given the issues at stake – on both sides – the immediate doubts were justified at the time and they were, of course, of huge political significance.

But, oddly, this significance was not immediately exploited by the Prince of Orange. Bentinck's wife being ill, William sent Nassau-Zuylenstein on another mission to England to offer his congratulations to James and his wife.[45] He arrived in England on 3 July.[46] There he made contact with the signatories of the formal letter which William had asked for inviting him to come to England, and which Henry Sidney and Johnston were now organising.[47]

THE IMMORTAL SEVEN AND THE INVITATION TO INVADE ENGLAND

A preliminary hearing of the Seven Bishops by the Judges on 20 June was attended by such a throng and such a tumult that Van Citters anticipated an insurrection.[48] On 9 July the trial proper began in Westminster Hall before a large crowd, including the Marquis of Halifax, Danby, and 29 other peers, whose sympathy for the bishops was vocally demonstrated. When Sunderland, who had just converted to Catholicism, arrived as a witness he was greeted with cries of 'popish dog'.[49] The bishops were represented by a strong, and the government by a weak, legal team.[50] On the 10th, the jury gave its verdict – not guilty, 'upon which', Clarendon recorded in his diary, 'there was a most wonderful shout, that one would have thought the Hall had cracked'.[51] Another contemporary said, 'the Marquis of Halifax waving his Hat over his head cry'd Huzzah' and the 'Acclamations of Joy' spread throughout London. Bonfires were lit and even the soldiers camped at Hounslow Heath shouted their approval.[52]

That night the formal invitation to William of Orange to come over to England was signed. The signatories, who signed in cipher, were the Earl of Shrewsbury, the Earl of Devonshire, the Earl of Danby, Baron Lumley, Bishop Compton, Admiral Russelll and Henry Sidney, the 'Immortal Seven' as Dalrymple called them.[53]

Burnet says that Admiral Russelll, on his return to England after his conversations with William in Holland at the end of April, had first approached Shrewsbury, and then Lumley.[54] Sidney had tried Halifax, but received no encouragement, Halifax thinking the planned invasion was impractical and rash.[55] Sidney's approach to Danby, however, was successful and Danby brought in Compton. They advised approaching Nottingham, with his 'great credit with the church party' who was at first receptive, but then withdrew on grounds of conscience. Finally the Earl of Devonshire was approached, who accepted with enthusiasm.[56]

Nottingham's change of mind presented a security risk and a discussion was held as to whether he should be shot, 'in such a manner, that it should appear to have been done by highwaymen'. The plan was dropped on his assurance that he would not betray the secret.[57]

Amongst senior officers in the army, according to Burnet, Sidney also persuaded

Churchill, Kirke and Trelawney to join in the conspiracy – Trelawney bringing in his brother, the Bishop of Bristol, and Churchill Princess Anne and Prince George of Denmark.[58]

The signatories to the invitation were a disparate assortment – Devonshire had even supported the impeachment of Danby on several occasions. High political office had been held only by Danby, and that some time ago. Compton stood reasonably high in the Church as the – suspended – Bishop of London. Edward Russelll had resigned as an Admiral as long ago as the Rye House plot, when his cousin, William Russelll, was, as we have noted, executed – 'murder', Edward called it, of a 'man I passionately loved'.[59] Apart from Halifax and Nottingham, two other heavyweights, the Hyde brothers, Clarendon and Rochester, the leaders of the High Anglican party and the uncles of the Princesses Mary and Anne, were missing from the signatories – although Clarendon was in touch with Zuylenstein on several occasions after his arrival.[60]

The letter noted with satisfaction that they had learnt from Admiral Russelll and Zuylenstein that the Prince was willing to come to their assistance. Since the situation was deteriorating every day they urged prompt action. 'Nineteen parts of twenty' of the people of the country were so 'dissatisfied with the present conduct of the government, in relation to their religion, liberties and properties (all of which have been greatly invaded)' that they wanted change. They would rise against the government if they were protected against being overpowered before the rising could get under way. The 'greatest part of the nobility and gentry' were just as dissatisfied, and some of the most considerable would join the Prince at his first landing, bringing their supporters with them. If the Prince brought a sufficient force with him to protect the dissidents there was no question but that they would quickly increase in number to double the army at James's disposal, even if his army remained loyal. But they had good grounds for believing that in these circumstances his army would be very much divided – many officers were discontented, and there was strong anti-Papist sentiment amongst the common soldiers. In the navy it was almost certain that not one in ten of the seamen would be prepared to serve. However, measures being taken to alter the personnel of both the officers and the men meant this favourable situation would not last, and there were also the consequences to be apprehended from a packed Parliament, including measures against the King's opponents. On top of this, if a packed Parliament did not produce the results James desired, more violent measures could be expected.

These considerations led them to believe that the present situation made now the right time to act, 'although', they added, 'we must own to your Highness there are some judgments differing from ours in this particular'. This seems to be a reference to Halifax and Nottingham, both of whom wrote to William at the beginning of August. Halifax said he thought that James's designs for Catholicism – 'the great design', as he called them – were not making any progress and a packed Parliament, on which James's party was relying, was 'subject to so many accidents and uncertainties, that according to human probability we are secure'. Nottingham said that the birth of the Prince of Wales, further designs against the Seven Bishops, the reorganisation of the army and the calling of the Parliament were matters for reflection, 'but I cannot apprehend from them such ill consequences to our religion, or the just interests of your Highness, that a little time will not effectually remedy, nor can I imagine that the Papists are able to make any further considerable progress.'[61]

The conspirators were acutely alive – as well they might be – to the obvious hazard attending the whole expedition, with the preparations and the need to inform the States-General providing warning for James and his supporters both to strengthen their defences and to take into custody those they suspected of planning to join the Prince.

There was one point of criticism in the letter, and it related to the political significance of the suppositious birth of the Prince of Wales, which William had overlooked – or perhaps he was biding his time. The compliments which he and Mary had presented on the birth of the child – 'which not one in a thousand here believes to be the Queen's' – were detrimental to their cause, since it would need to be one of the chief reasons they would have to advance for the invasion.[62]

Disguised as a common seaman, Admiral Herbert carried the letter to Holland in a small, agile packet boat, which was also used to convey couriers and secret correspondence to Prince William on a regular basis. It may well have been by this means that Bentinck was told that, as the letter from the Immortal Seven intimated, James would, by the winter, have a strong army and a compliant Parliament. With him Herbert also brought a covering letter from Sidney, in which Sidney offered to come over himself, asked for Zuylenstein to remain in England until William gave his response – hidden in the country to avoid raising suspicion – and advised recruiting for the invasion the services of Marshal Schomberg, one of Louis XIV's marshals, who as a Huguenot, had removed himself from France to the service of Brandenburg.

On his arrival on Friday 16 July Herbert went at once to Prince William at Honselaarsdijk, and the whole day following was devoted to conferences to which Bentinck and Dijkveldt were summoned. Further meetings followed, including with Fagel and with one of the Burgomasters of Amsterdam. Van Citters was called back from London for consultations.

One immediate consequence was that the advice contained in the letter of the Immortal Seven relating to the birth of the Prince of Wales – it was reiterated by one of Bentinck's secret correspondents – was heeded. The party which D'Albeville had organised to celebrate the child's birth was boycotted and prayers for him were no longer delivered in the chapel of the Princess of Orange.[63] She wrote to Anne with a long list of questions regarding the circumstances of the birth, and Anne's answers were hardly designed to still the doubts.[64]

LEOPOLD I'S TRIUMPH OVER THE TURKS

Let us, for now, leave England in this feverish state and contemplate the scene on the Continent. We have seen that in 1684 the Twenty Years' Truce of Regensburg (Ratisbon) was entered into under which Louis retained most of the gains acquired under the *réunions* – but the acquisitions were precarious and had no legal recognition. In Leopold of Austria's eyes the truce was just that, it was not permanent and it was entered into whilst he dealt with the Turks in the east, after which he could once again confront the hereditary Bourbon enemy in the west. Following the raising of the siege of Vienna and the capture of Budapest Leopold's armies crushed the Turks at Mohacs in 1687, after which they advanced into Serbia. In Turkey there was upheaval and the Sultan was dethroned. The conquest of practically the whole of Hungary was reflected in the crowning of Leopold's son, Joseph, as the hereditary King of the country in December 1687.[65] Leopold, that easily underestimated Habsburg Emperor, was well on the way to rehabilitate his House as a pre-eminent European power, a position which the Thirty Years' War, the decline of Spain and the rise of France had done so much to undermine. It was a rehabilitation that was to last until the First World War.

THE ARCHBISHOPRIC OF COLOGNE AND THE THREAT TO LOUIS

Leopold's increasing *gloire* had a magnetic effect on the German princes. It was manifest in the formation of the League of Augsburg two years before, it was manifest in the contributions made by the Princes, the Reichstag and the Imperial *Kreise* to the Hungarian campaigns, and it was manifest in the desertion from the French camp of such important German princes as the Elector of Brandenburg and the Elector of Bavaria. It was manifest, too, in Louis XIV whose gaze became fatally fixed on his eastern frontier, from where the threat of the resurgent power of the Habsburg enemy was most acute. He had to look to his own *gloire* and to the clients which he still retained.

One of these was the Archbishop Elector of Cologne, Maximilian Henry of Wittelsbach, who was also the Bishop of Liège and Münster. Cologne and Liège, in particular, were of the first strategic importance; Liège, with its territories cutting deep into the Spanish Netherlands, had been the launch pad for Louis's invasion of the Dutch Republic in 1672; and Cologne's position on the Rhine made it key to the defence of France itself. Münster also, with its borders marching with the eastern borders of the Dutch Republic, was not strategically negligible, although it was now not so easily within the reach of France as it had been in 1672. As an Elector, moreover, the Archbishop carried a vote in the Electoral College which chose the Emperor. Maximilian Henry's chief adviser, who kept him in the French camp, was another client of Louis, Wilhelm-Egon of Fürstenberg, whom Louis had so theatrically installed as Bishop of Strasburg and whose release from Austrian captivity was so adamantly insisted upon by the King in the Treaty of Nijmegen.

Maximilian Henry was now rapidly ailing and as a first step in securing Fürstenberg's succession Louis arranged for him to be elected as co-adjutor of Cologne in January 1688, where he received 19 votes out of 24 in the cathedral chapter. Unfortunately for Louis the election needed the authorisation of the Pope and with the Pope, Innocent XI, he had fallen out.

One dispute between them concerned the authority the Pope was able to exercise in France in matters spiritual, which Louis, supported by the Gallicans in the French Church, maintained should be limited by French custom and French constitutional practice. Related to this issue was the question of the *régale*, whether the Pope or the King was entitled to the revenues of vacant benefices. A second dispute arose over the juridical rights exercised by the French ambassador in Rome, which granted immunity from the Roman police authorities within the ambassadorial quarters, the extent of which was liberally interpreted by the French. This was exploited by lawless elements and the Pope was determined to put an end to it. He was successful in persuading every country, except France, to relinquish their similar rights. A new French ambassador, Lavardin, was appointed in November 1687, following the death of his predecessor, and he proceeded to Rome with an armed escort to resist the Pope's demands. Innocent excommunicated him, followed, in January 1688, by the secret excommunication of Louis himself. Croissy, Louis's foreign minister, threatened the Papal Nuncio at Versailles with the seizure of the Papal enclave at Avignon. It was therefore no surprise, in these circumstances, that Papal confirmation for Fürstenberg's election as co-adjutor of Cologne was not forthcoming.[66]

Then, on 3 June, Maximilian Henry died. Fürstenberg was also interested in being elected to Liège and Münster, and to a third bishopric, Hildesheim, where Maximilian Henry had been bishop; but of these Cologne and Liège were regarded by his French patron as of primary importance and Louis ordered 4,000 cavalry to station themselves within reach of Cologne.[67] Here the other contender was Clement, another member of the Wittelsbach family, who had been bishops of Cologne since 1580. He was the brother of the Elector of Bavaria, now allied to the Austrian Emperor, whose daughter he had married. Clement was only 17 years old and because of this and because he already held two other bishoprics – despite not being in clerical orders – he needed Papal dispensation. The Pope granted him this, which meant he could be elected by a simple majority, whilst Innocent XI refused a similar concession to Fürstenberg as he already held the bishopric of Strasburg, and he would therefore require a two thirds majority; even then he would still need final Papal approval, although refusal without a very strong reason would be difficult in these circumstances.[68]

Faced with this predicament, Louis decided on 6 July to send the Marquis de Chamlay to Rome, in great secrecy and under an assumed name, to seek a private audience with the Pope to request his support for Fürstenberg.[69] On 19 July, whilst Chamlay was at Venice awaiting the outcome of the election, the result was declared; Fürstenberg with 13 votes had received fewer than the required two thirds majority and Clement had eight fewer than the simple majority which he needed. The Pope would therefore have to decide, and on 10 August he refused Chamlay the required audience. On 18 August the French learnt that Fürstenberg had also failed to win Liège.[70]

Louis decided on force. Chamlay was recalled from Rome and the French troops at Maintenon were given their marching orders: one section under Marshal d'Humières was to march on Flanders to form a corps of observation, and the rest were ordered to the German frontier.[71]

GERMAN ALLIANCES AND PREPARATIONS FOR THE AUSTRIAN ALLIANCE

For some time William of Orange, too, had been making his plans in Germany. In the second half of 1687 he had sent the President of his Domain Council, Simon van Petticum, to the court of Brunswick-Lüneburg. This was an entirely private mission on behalf of the Prince himself – Van Petticum was instructed by the Prince to say nothing of the purpose of his journey to Jacob Hop, the Pensionary of Amsterdam, who was on an official mission from the States-General to Berlin to address the differences the States had with Denmark.[72] On his return journey in January 1688 Van Petticum received assurances from the Duke of Celle's first minister that the Duke was firmly '*dans le bon party*' and that the Dukes of Wolfenbüttel were tied to him. As regarded his meetings with the Hanoverians, he did not think that the Duke of Hanover had any treaty with France; nor, with the Emperor's armies victorious, was he minded to do so. His show of non-commitment had no other aim but to extract money from the Emperor, Spain, or the States, or from all three.[73]

No concrete agreements materialised at this time, but the ground was prepared for future negotiations. Van Petticum had also extended his journey to Berlin with a view to the Prince of Orange's mediating a reconciliation between the Elector of Brandenburg and his Crown Prince, Frederick. Frederick had removed himself from his father's court following the death of his younger brother, Ludwig, whom he thought his stepmother had poisoned. The mediation was successful in establishing at least some sort of peace, and this gesture to heal the family quarrel, from so close a relation as the Prince of Orange, was much appreciated by the Crown Prince;[74] this no doubt helped to secure his commitment to the Prince's cause when he succeeded his father later in the year.

There was a further development. Van Petticum was specifically instructed to take the opportunity to cultivate a close relationship with Marshal Schomberg, who was then in the service of the Elector. William's eye was therefore on him even before Henry Sidney recommended his recruitment for the invasion of England.

The Elector was affronted in January by Louis XIV's attempts to get Fürstenberg elected as Bishop of Cologne – it was, he protested, as though Leopold of Austria were installing his appointee as Bishop of Rheims or Paris – and in March he offered to station 9,000 troops in Cleves to cover the eastern approaches to the Dutch Republic.

Then, on 9 May, he died. As he lay dying his instructions to his heir, Frederick III (later

Frederick I in Prussia), were 'defend and increase the glory I bequeath you'.[75] He had, therefore, the same concept of *gloire* as Louis XIV and the Prince of Orange.

The Great Elector's death occurred shortly after William had indicated to Admiral Russelll that, if he received the appropriate invitation, he could be ready to sail for England by the end of September. He reacted swiftly to the news from Brandenburg and on 17 May he wrote to Frederick that he was sending Bentinck as his personal emissary to offer his condolences and his good wishes for the new Elector's succession.[76] Bentinck was soon in Berlin. At the same time Amerongen was at Aix-la-Chapelle, where the Elector of Saxony was taking the waters, to induce him to enter into a defensive alliance. In this Amerongen was not successful and nor, for the time being, was Jacob Hop, who took over the negotiations in September; but Amerongen had also informed Bentinck on 28 May that he thought Frederick of Brandenburg favoured such an alliance.[77]

At the beginning of June William wrote to Bentinck telling him that he was ready to meet Frederick personally if that was necessary to conclude the negotiations, and asking him to prepare the way for this. At that time Bentinck was planning to return to the Republic with the initial intention of travelling via the Brunswick dukes and the Landgrave of Hesse-Cassel. William told him that after his departure Hop could deal with the negotiations relating to the renewal of the old alliances of 1678 and 1685 – which were in fact renewed on 30 June – but that the secret negotiations, 'especially as regards the affairs of England', would be handled by himself through Thomas Danckelmann, the brother of Eberhard, Frederick's chief minister, and Von Diest, the Brandenburg envoy in The Hague. We do not know at what point Bentinck had been specific regarding the designs for England; but we do know that plans were far advanced for the hire by the Dutch of auxiliary Brandenburg troops, for William told Bentinck on 4 June that the money for this was ready – Eberhard Danckelmann sent the receipt on the 23rd – and it is not easy to see how this could be kept separate from the English issue.[78]

In the event Bentinck had to forgo his visits to the Brunswick dukes and Hesse-Cassel. The Prince had personally informed him of the tragic death of the Bentincks' little son, Willem, named after the Prince, and of the grave illness of his wife. When she took a turn for the worse he told him, on 12 June, to return home at once.[79] Furthermore, Thomas Danckelmann was engaged in negotiations in Vienna from which he could not be spared,[80] and the new Elector of Brandenburg was preoccupied both with receiving the homage of his new subjects[81] and the lavish ceremonies attendant on the funeral of his father – it did not take place until 22 September and cost 150,000 *écus*, enough, grumbled Schomberg, to have raised four regiments.[82] The negotiations with Brandenburg, therefore, slowed for the time being.

Talks in Vienna were more promising. These were conducted on William's behalf by Freiherr von Görz, the Chamberlain of the Landgrave of Hesse-Cassel; he was chosen because he was a good friend of Waldeck, with whom he had worked closely, and he would be less conspicuous than any alternative in the secret negotiations about to commence. He travelled to Vienna in the middle of May and only the Emperor, his Chancellor, Stratman, and the Spanish ambassador, Borgamainero, were privy to the talks. Leopold's main preoccupations were addressed: the threat to his House from the ancestral Bourbon enemy, the Habsburgs' traditional championship of Catholicism, their inheritance in Spain and their position in Germany. Applying himself to these concerns, Görz emphasised the threat to the Dutch Republic – and hence to Germany and the whole of Europe – which would arise from an alliance between James II and Louis XIV; assurances were given that William would not tolerate any persecution of Catholics in England; and one of the aims of the alliance at which William was aiming was to safeguard the Emperor's claims to the Spanish inheritance and the election of a member of his House as King of Rome. The talks went well and on 4 September Leopold indicated, as the Dutch had already done on 20 July, that he wanted to adhere to the existing treaties and to enter into a new defensive alliance. Even if the latter was not signed until well into 1689, the import was clear – the Emperor and William were well on the way to reconstructing the Grand Alliance against Louis XIV which he had managed to destroy by means of the Treaty of Nijmegen.[83]

Bentinck had returned to The Hague on 19 June[84] and this enabled him to participate in the urgent consultations between Prince William and his advisers triggered by Admiral Herbert's arrival on 16 July with the invitation to invade England. If William was to do this by the end of September, as he had previously promised Herbert, time was of the essence. He could not afford any further delay in obtaining the German alliances and Bentinck was once again despatched to complete the work on this which he had begun.

Prior to his departure Bentinck wrote, on 20 July, to Eberhard von Danckelmann that 'affaires in England are beginning to become extremely pressing and they are now in such a crisis that His Highness dare not delay in making preparations so that he is not taken by surprise by the unforeseen'. To that end Bentinck was being sent to Hesse-Cassel and to Hanover to negotiate treaties with those princes for the loan of their troops, and he asked what Frederick III's intentions for Brandenburg were. On the same day he wrote to Johan Ham, the States-General Resident in Berlin, telling him too that affairs in England were expected to reach a crisis, 'in which case we cannot sit still or the Republic and Religion will be lost. The Elector of Brandenburg has demonstrated all his zeal and earnestness on that score and told me on a number of occasions that he would do his uttermost [*tout pour le tout*] to assist the Prince, and the time had now come for him to do his part.' The Dutch State 'would intervene in the English matter with all its might' and for this it would need Brandenburg to provide help and back-up. So important and secret was the matter that Ham should confine his correspondence on this to the Prince and himself – that is to say, it was to be kept outside the purview of the States-General.[85]

On 22 July he travelled to the Landgrave of Hesse-Cassel, with whom he concluded a treaty to provide troops for the Dutch army; on 5 August treaties were also entered into with Celle and Wolfenbüttel, although not, for the time being, with the third Hanoverian Duke, Ernst Augustus. On the 6th he concluded a treaty, through Fuchs, with Brandenburg and a treaty was also signed – this time with Waldeck as intermediary[86] – with the Duke of Württemberg on 4 August.

The line of argument Bentinck used with Fuchs is worthy of note because it was very similar to that which Fagel later employed with the States of Holland when he sought their support for the English invasion. James II and Louis XIV, Bentinck maintained, were putting together plans under which James would first establish Catholicism in England to confirm his ascendancy there, after which he and Louis would make themselves masters of the Netherlands and, subsequently, Germany – a sort of replay, in short, of 1672. Pressed by the English opposition to James, which Bentinck depicted as formidable, the Prince had decided to intervene and 40 warships and five frigates were being fitted out for this purpose. The Prince had not yet brought the matter before the States-General, but the most influential people had been consulted, and, said Bentinck, bending the facts not a little, he was being urged on unremittingly by Hudde, Witsen and Geelfink. There was no difficulty as far as finance was concerned and the small number in the know had authorised the Prince to recruit as many men as he could.

Bentinck was in fact pushing at an open door, as Fuchs had received instructions from his master to be accommodating. Frederick III would provide men for the Dutch States' army whilst recruiting replacements for his army in Cleves in exchange for Dutch subsidies. He did expect recognition in William's will – which, however, at this stage, Bentinck was able to leave in the air.[87]

All the treaties provided for the provision of troops to the Dutch Republic and were entered into in the Republic's name in exchange for subsidies, but the States-General, at this stage, was neither aware of the treaties, nor therefore, as yet, of the subsidies. They were not informed by the Prince until 20 September, his justification being the need for secrecy. It is a sign of the authority he was perceived to wield in the United Provinces – which Bentinck no doubt exaggerated as he had with Fuchs – that the German princes were in principle prepared to enter into their alliances on this basis, although the agreements would need to be ratified in due course by the States-General. All of them were Protestants and they thus complemented the Catholic alliance which was being simultaneously negotiated with the Austrian Emperor. They provided a force of just over 13,000 men for the Dutch army, to which were added another 6,000 troops from Sweden by an agreement reached on 12 September.[88]

Japikse's contention that William at this time spoke to nobody outside the Republic about his plans to invade England, nor allowed anybody else to discuss them – but without excluding discussions of English affairs in general terms – is clearly not tenable in the light of Bentinck's conversation with Fuchs.[89] On the other hand, I do not share Lucile Pinkham's view that the old Elector of Brandenburg knew as early as the winter of 1687/8, as I do not believe that Prince William had decided on any definite plans by that time.[90] Görz, as she asserts, was also in the secret (but at the beginning of June, not early July as she says).[91] It must seem probable that the other German princes who agreed to lend troops to the Dutch were similarly informed.

WILLIAM OF ORANGE, WITSEN AND AMSTERDAM

We must now look at how William was managing the internal politics of the Dutch Republic. We have noted that at the beginning of 1688, or earlier, Fagel had hinted to Witsen at the possibility of Prince William's crossing to England, to which Witsen had given a vacillating response. The time had now come to sound him out again on his views and those of his fellow Amsterdam Burgomasters. Towards the middle of June William sent Dijkveldt to Amsterdam, where he held a meeting with Witsen and Hudde at Hudde's house – a third Burgomaster, Geelfink, was out of town. Dijkveldt pointed to the danger that James II represented, depicting him as 'a confirmed enemy of this State and of the Reformed Religion'. The Burgomasters answered that the precautions being taken – a reference to the military and diplomatic measures under way – would soon head off the danger and that circumstances might change. They strongly advised against a pre-emptive intervention in England now – at the least they should wait until the spring of 1689. To act now would make it look as though the Dutch were starting a religious war and this would alienate the Catholic powers in Europe. The country could not be denuded of its army, as well as its commander-in-chief – the Prince of Orange – without leaving it exposed to a French attack, which could lead, as in 1672, to popular disturbances. Two days later Dijkveldt wrote to Witsen asking him to attend a meeting with Prince William himself, whose response, Dijkveldt said, was '*aut nunc, aut nunquam*', now or never.

Before the meeting Witsen had a conversation with Dijkveldt and Bentinck who assured him of the support of the English elite for the Prince. The following day the interview with the Prince took place. William told Witsen that he had not yet come to a firm decision on intervening in England, but he said the difficulties had been exaggerated; the money could be found from the 4 million guilders voted earlier in the year for improvements to the fortresses; across the North Sea the job could be done within a week or two; any delay would enable James to strengthen his position; and the venture would be undertaken by himself, not the Dutch State, which would need only to lend him its support. What this meant in effect was that William, as the Sovereign Prince of Orange and with his and Mary's claims to the English throne, would act as principal with the Dutch State acting as auxiliary – a very 17th-century concept; in 1672 Spain gave auxiliary aid to the Dutch against Louis's invasion without herself declaring war against France.

The discussion lasted a long time and was resumed the following day. Finally, the Prince asked Witsen for his support for the undertaking – that is, to act as an auxiliary – provided he were not a principal to it. Witsen said that he would need to consult the two other Burgomasters, Hudde and Geelfink – the Prince had vetoed his consulting the fourth Burgomaster, Appelman, on the grounds that he was too much in the French camp. The reply came that the three Burgomasters could not advise for or against the enterprise; however, they did take up William's suggestion of the previous day and said they were prepared to act as auxiliaries, if that were consistent with their oaths of office and their duty. But they did not think such a proposal would get through the Amsterdam Town Council. It was as tortuous a response as could be imagined, and far from heroic, but it served the Prince's purpose. The auxiliary support of Amsterdam and the Dutch State would be enough – although he would still need to push their formal consent through the necessary representative bodies at the right time.

Fagel, in the presence of Prince William, exerted his best endeavours to elicit a firmer response from Witsen, emphasising, as was his wont, the religious aspect. 'The English matter', he said, 'was a religious matter, and God himself would extend his protection.' Witsen, however, was not to be moved, however many references to the Scriptures were invoked. The Prince finally brought the business to a conclusion by reiterating that he had not yet finally made up his mind; in the meantime he would make all the necessary preparations for the expedition, using the money voted for the fortresses, and he would not inform the States until shortly before his departure.[92] It is a moot point whether the three Burgomasters in whom the Prince confided in fact conveyed his plans to the Amsterdam Town Council – in the opinion of Petra Dreiskämper they did not, but kept the secret to themselves.[93] In support of this contention is the fact that there were objections in the Town Council that they had been kept in the dark when the Council was finally informed of the intention to invade on 26 September, although that does not exclude a select number being in the know.

There are two points we need to note: the first is that, in order to obtain Amsterdam's support, the invasion of England was to be undertaken by the Prince of Orange in his personal capacity as a sovereign prince and a leading member of the Stuart family with claims to the English throne – Mary's claims were even stronger. The proposal was that the Dutch Republic would act as an auxiliary and not as a principal – although, at this stage, that assistance still remained in the balance and without it the whole enterprise would not have been feasible. The Prince acting as principal brought the additional advantage that it could be presented, in England, as not being an invasion by the Dutch – not indeed even as an invasion at all – but as one part of the Stuart clan coming to the rescue to resolve the difficulties caused by the other part. The second point we need to note is that by the middle or towards the end of June, William was still keeping his options open. Nevertheless, preparations for the invasion were now under way and bore their own momentum.

THE ENGLISH INVASION: PREPARATIONS

The preparations for the invasion of England were of necessity extremely extensive and could not be hidden, whilst, at the same time, it was necessary to disguise their purpose from James II and Louis XIV. Fortunately the death on 3 June of the Archbishop of Cologne and the escalating crisis this led to, with Louis's despatch of his cavalry to the Electorate, provided the cover William and Fagel needed to build up the Dutch forces. The 4 million guilders originally destined for the fortifications were soon available – the States of Holland passed the necessary resolution on 16 July. At the same time, according to D'Avaux, the States-General appointed a small delegation to liaise with the Prince on how best to address the Republic's defences; it consisted of his confidants and he entrusted them with his plans, so that the troops could easily be switched to the English invasion force in due course. Although D'Avaux says this was a States-General delegation it seems unlikely that it excluded Holland representatives entirely. The need to counter the French threat was also used to obtain authorisation from the States-General to ready the Dutch fleet.[94]

Speed was of the essence, as the invasion would need to be launched before the winter set in. Admiral Herbert had arrived in The Hague on 16 July and on 29 October the vast invasion fleet was to set sail. At the centre of the planning during that brief period were the Prince and the trio of his closest advisers, Bentinck, Dijkveldt and Fagel, although the latter was now very ill.

Around the middle of August Bentinck was sent by William on a secret visit to Amsterdam to make another attempt to obtain a firmer commitment from the three Burgomasters for the English expedition, and also, importantly, to make plans for the fitting out of the fleet by means of Hiob de Wildt, the Secretary of the Amsterdam Admiralty, who had succeeded his father, and whose vast experience had been accumulated over nearly 30 years. De Wildt was thus in the know, as his collaborators must have been.

Bentinck told Witsen and Geelfink – Hudde was absent because of illness – of his recruitment of the 13,000 troops from the German princes, with the intention of gaining their support for the formal sanction for this from the Holland States. But on this point the two Burgomasters allowed themselves no more than a polite but negative reply. Bentinck then tried to argue that the birth of the new Prince of Wales in England had implications not only for the Prince of Orange, but for the whole Dutch State; to which the Burgomasters answered that that was not what the Prince and Fagel were saying. At dinner afterwards the Burgomasters pointedly refused to drink to the success of the expedition.[95] They were, then, still maintaining their stance of neither supporting nor opposing the plans of Prince William.

The Prince told Bentinck, on 25 August, that if Amsterdam would not take the necessary steps to sanction the German recruits in the States of Holland, Leyden could take the initiative – they were the ones who were pressing the hardest for trade reprisals against the

French, the taking of which could serve as the pretext for the recruitment. It was, however, necessary to keep open the lines of communication with Amsterdam, 'with whom we are up to now in concert in all matters', which we can interpret as meaning that, in the absence of her open opposition, he could rely on her tacit support – provided she did not waver.[96] That she, or, more precisely, the three Burgomasters in the know, did not waver, indeed, was crucial; De Wildt played a key role regarding the naval preparations, which he could not have done against Amsterdam's active opposition, and that would have frustrated all the other preparations as well. Geelfink indeed was, until the autumn of 1688, an influential member of the Amsterdam Admiralty and could thus have proved a major obstacle.[97] As we have indicated above, De Wildt's collaborators must have been in the secret and there must have been a substantial number of others who turned a blind eye at the least; there was additionally the States-General delegation mentioned by D'Avaux.

In the same letter the Prince expressed his anxieties about the German recruits, whose speedy march towards the Dutch Republic was essential amidst all the German internecine rivalries. The Duke of Hanover's consent would be needed to allow the Brandenburg troops to pass through his territories – if he refused they could always pass through the country of Münster, where, in July, the new Archbishop, Frederick Christian von Plettenberg, had been chosen instead of Fürstenberg. Brandenburg herself would need to grant permission for the opening of lines of communication for the Celle troops to pass back and forth through her territories – in writing, for Celle perhaps might not trust Brandenburg's word. The prospects of obtaining troops from Saxony were not looking good, but Bentinck should write to persuade Frederick III of Brandenburg to put pressure on the Saxon Duke – this, as we have seen, despite William's doubts, was to lead to a satisfactory outcome, as were the negotiations with Hanover initiated through the same channel. On equipping the fleet he was concerned about the tardiness exhibited by Zeeland, where his cousin Nassau-Odijk held sway on his behalf. Despite this he did not trust him – Fagel would need to talk to him, but not let him fully into the secret regarding the English plans.[98]

Enclosed with the letter was a memorandum from Admiral Herbert with William's annotations dealing with intelligence in England. Sidney was soon expected in the Republic and there was a need for someone else to take his place in coordinating the English opposition and intelligence network. Herbert suggested Dijkveldt, but the Prince said he could not be spared, and, pending Sidney's advice on his arrival, he could think of no one better than 'the good' Dr Hutton, the doctor in his household who had been active in corresponding with the English agents. Herbert was to send people with knowledge of the west and north coasts of England to do a reconnaissance there; he was to be responsible for recruiting English naval officers to join the Dutch service; and Van Citters was to take charge of intelligence regarding the disposition of the English army and fleet, in which task he was to be supplied with information from the existing intelligence network.[99]

On the evening of 27 August Sidney arrived in great secrecy, having travelled with Shrewsbury in a hired boat. A long conversation with William followed which lasted until midnight. William instructed Bentinck to meet Sidney two days later at Teilingen, the safest place for security reasons, and to bring Herbert with him. The most pressing decision, which Bentinck was to agree with Sidney and Herbert, was Sidney's replacement in England.[100]

One of the letters Sidney brought with him was from John Churchill. It was dated 4 August (14th New Style): 'Mr Sidney will let you know how I intend to behave myself … I think it is what I owe to God and my country. My honour I take leave to put into your Royal Highness's hands, in which I think it safe. If you think there is any thing else that I ought to do, you have but to command me, and I shall pay an entire obedience to it, being resolved to die in that religion that it has pleased God to give you both the will and power to protect.'[101] Churchill's commitment – in writing – was thus total, and he was to play a key role in undermining both James's morale and his overall position when he defected to the Prince of Orange after the invasion. We have already noted two other officers associated with Churchill, Charles Trelawney, the brother of the Bishop of Bristol – one of the dissenting bishops who had refused to comply with James's Declaration of Indulgence – and Percy Kirke, important components of the military conspiracy. Both had served with Churchill during the Dutch war and in Tangier. His brother, George Churchill, an officer in the navy, was instrumental in furthering the conspiracy there.[102]

The tremendous strain the Prince was under was revealed in his letter to Bentinck of 29 August[103] – to no other person, except Mary perhaps, would a man so noted for his reserve have been so open concerning his psychological state of mind. A number of factors had been building up. The Duke of Württemberg had divulged that he was raising troops for the Prince, 'a great blunder', as William put it, 'setting speculation alight'. More importantly, the Dutch envoy in Paris had reported a French military concentration, which, in William's view, it would be a mistake to interpret as being aimed at Cologne – he believed it was directed at the Dutch and it therefore had implications for the expedition being planned. He referred to a letter from Danby – presumably brought over by Sidney; it is now lost – suggesting postponing the expedition until the spring of 1689, it seems in response to these French military moves. This in itself raised a question-mark, the Prince said, but to add to the conundrum rumours were beginning to spread and they were behind in their preparations. With all these 'dreadful uncertainties', he had 'more need than ever of Divine direction', not being clear in his mind on the road to follow. He had therefore still not definitely decided on launching the invasion – the options were still open.

Sidney had brought with him a draft Declaration, or Manifesto, to be issued at the time the invasion was launched, and the Prince asked Bentinck 'to confer long and hard' with Fagel and Dijkveldt on its contents, which, in his view, needed much alteration. You will observe, he told Bentinck, that 'it throws me entirely on the mercy of a Parliament …

although I know well enough, it cannot be otherwise', but 'to put one's fate in their hands is not a small hazard'. It would need to be shown to George Melville, a Scotsman who had come to the Republic and who was to become Secretary of State for Scotland in 1689.

He went on to deal with naval matters in the letter and points raised by De Wildt – emphasising the need to balance the call to victual the ships in good time against the fear of publicising what they were doing. In a postscript he added that two matters had been overlooked, the need to bring a printing press and the need to strike coins or bring them with them; Fagel and De Wildt needed to be consulted.[104]

If there had been any doubts in his mind on the timing of the expedition, they did not last long and Fagel dissuaded him from postponing it. On 31 August he was in complete agreement with the Pensionary that *la grande affaire* should be undertaken now. At this point therefore the die was cast and he ceased to keep his options open. Pressure, said the Prince, should be put on De Wildt regarding the manning of the fleet – it was that which he most feared would retard them. On the question of the coinage an effigy of Mary and himself could appear on it, but when it came to the technicalities of foreign exchange he expressed himself totally ignorant and others would have to decide.[105]

On 4 September he once again wrote to Bentinck unburdening himself of the huge responsibilities he was facing. He asked him to tell Fagel to prepare the ground for the towns to sanction the recruitment of German troops. Amsterdam still remained an uncertain quantity and he suggested that Dijkveldt should go there or meet Hudde in the country to coordinate matters, 'because I am always in apprehension of this great city'. The French troop movements remained a great worry: 'if they muster a substantial army corps in the Bishopric of Cologne and another on the Maas I do not know where we shall be' – the Governor of the Spanish Netherlands, the Marquis de Gastañaga, had written to him the previous day expressing his acute anxiety concerning these territories. He was worried that the German princes would be distracted by Cologne and would not supply the troops they had promised; he was worried that the Dutch would not allow him to embark on the English expedition with so much to fear on the Continent; and, as for the Spanish Netherlands, they could be totally lost, Marshal d'Humières being only a single march away from Brussels and Antwerp if he chose to undertake it. He thought that French support for Fürstenberg was a feint, their real intention being to frustrate the English design. 'I vow all this causes me terrible tribulation and anxiety, fearing that our design will be aborted, whilst over here we will be drawn into a great war.' The one good bit of news was that it looked as though the Swedes would provide 6,000 men.[106]

THE GERMAN ALLIANCES: THE FINISHING TOUCHES

The following day he departed for Minden for the long-planned meeting with Frederick III of Brandenburg, where he arrived on 7 September. The meeting on the whole was cordial and Frederick undertook to use his endeavours to push the negotiations with the Duke of Hanover and the Elector of Saxony in a favourable direction. There was one disappointment from Frederick's point of view; the Prince remained silent on the question regarding his appointment as William's heir should anything untoward befall him on the English expedition. The silence is explained not least because of the difficulties it would have caused with William's cousin, the Stadholder of Friesland, Hendrik-Casimir, a split with whom, at this point, when he was exerting his utmost to build up unity in the Republic, would have been most damaging. On the 9th William went to Celle where he went hunting with the Duke, his old comrade-in-arms, and he also had a meeting with the Landgrave of Hesse-Cassel.[107] These meetings prepared the way for the formation of the Concert of Magdeburg, a union against France, which put the finishing touches to William's system of Protestant alliances of German princes.

At the end of the month Frederick sent his envoy, Schmettau, and the Prince of Anhalt to the Elector of Saxony to put the case that, whilst it was too late to save Philippsburg, Frankfurt needed to be preserved, otherwise the French would fall on Coblenz, Cologne and the Netherlands and the independence of the German Empire would be destroyed. The most influential figure at that time at the Saxon court, Marshal Fleming, assured them that the Saxon infantry was ready to march in eight days. The Saxons aimed to conduct the war on the Middle Rhine, while Austria would have responsibility for the Upper and Brandenburg for the Lower Rhine.[108]

At about the same time Frederick sent Fuchs to Celle where he met the Duke of Hanover, whose daughter Frederick had married as his second wife. Frederick, at a previous interview, had persuaded Ernst Augustus that, if France took offensive action against the Empire, he would come to its aid and, Frederick instructed Fuchs, that 'the case contemplated had now come to pass'. Ernst Augustus agreed.[109] On 22 October Brandenburg, Saxony, Hanover and Hesse-Cassel signed the Concert of Magdeburg, with the signatories undertaking to bring 22,000 men into the field to march on Frankfurt.[110]

JAMES AND LOUIS XIV

In the meantime William had, by 13 September, returned to Het Loo 'sain et sauf et extremement obligeant envers moy', as Mary recorded.[111]

Events had not stood still during his absence. To understand the background to these we need to take a short step back to England. During May James, concerned by the Dutch naval preparations, had commenced fitting out 20 new ships of his own. At the beginning of June Louis, who wanted James's support for the election of Fürstenberg, offered 15 or 16 French ships to join the English fleet. For James, however, to be seen to be associated with France would add to his unpopularity in England, and he informed Barillon that he wanted to postpone any decision until Dutch intentions became clearer. Nevertheless he allowed the offer to be leaked, so that the impression of an Anglo-French understanding gained currency – a political gift to William of Orange, of which he made full use.

On 24 August D'Albeville returned to London on leave from The Hague and brought with him information strongly indicating that William intended to invade England, confirmed by the information that D'Avaux was sending from The Hague to Barillon in London. But although English naval preparations were intensified Sunderland told the Papal Nuncio, D'Adda, on the 31st that he thought Louis was exaggerating the dangers in order to put pressure on James to lend his support for Fürstenberg, whilst James himself did not think the States-General would back William in the pursuit of his personal ends. When Louis sent another envoy, Bonrepos, to meet James at Windsor on 4 September to reiterate his warnings and to renew the offer of naval assistance, James, a few days later, told him there was no need for it that year. One factor influencing his decision, apart from the unpopularity of a French alliance generally, was that it would have been unpopular in the English fleet as well – there were still memories of the battle of Solebay in 1672, at which James had been in command, when the French had declined to take part in the action.[112] Sunderland, speaking on his own account, then suggested to Bonrepos that France and England should launch a joint attack on the Dutch, as they had done in 1672, in which case the defeat of the Dutch trading competitor would offset the unpopularity of the French alliance. But Louis's gaze was on his eastern frontiers and the 1672 precedent had no attractions for him – it had not, indeed, been very auspicious.[113] His fleet, which was based at Toulon in the Mediterranean, remained there.

Then James and Louis managed to muddle the individual lines of diplomacy each was pursuing, the muddle becoming all the greater through James's lack of control over his ambassador in Paris, the same Skelton whom he had previously employed in The Hague. D'Albeville on 8 September delivered a memorandum to the States-General asking them what they intended by their naval preparations at such an unfavourable time of year. The next day D'Avaux also delivered two memoranda. The first, despite James's non-acceptance of Louis's offer of naval assistance – at least for that year – declared that, if the Dutch naval preparations were aimed at England, then Louis wished to make it clear that his ties with James bound him to support the King and to regard the first sign of hostility from the States against England as an open breach of the peace with himself. The second memorandum declared that Louis would come to the defence of Fürstenberg, and of Cologne, against any of Fürstenberg's enemies.[114]

This was the state of affairs when William returned from Minden. D'Avaux's first memorandum had, in fact, been delivered at the instigation of Skelton without James's authorisation. James, when he found out, recalled him to England and shut him up in the Tower of London,[115] but the damage had been done and it confirmed the suspicions, long lingering in Dutch minds, that there was a secret understanding between James and Louis, as there had been in 1672 between Louis and Charles II, to attack the Republic. James's subsequent denials of this to Van Citters[116] did nothing to erase the suspicions and William of Orange naturally made the most of the gift handed to him. There is no evidence that he did not believe it himself; and, if he but knew it, Sunderland, when he spoke to Bonrepos on his own account, was suggesting exactly the same course of action to the French at this very time. Nor did James's disavowal bring him any compensating benefits; following his rejection of Louis's naval offer, Louis would have been strengthened in his view that his decision, which in any case he had already taken, to concentrate on the Rhine was the correct one. James could be left to his own devices.

AMSTERDAM OUTFLANKED: HER RELUCTANT CONSENT

Despite the outcry against an Anglo-French alliance against the Republic there were still signs of resistance from within Amsterdam. Whilst he was still at Minden William had written to the Amsterdam Council telling them that he had put the finishing touches to the German alliances and that now was the time for them to support retaliatory measures against French goods at the forthcoming meeting of the States of Holland. When the Amsterdam Council met on the 14th, however, to the consternation of the Prince it was divided and the retaliatory trade measures against France were not approved.[117] 'I am very concerned about the timidity of some of them and the maliciousness of others', he told Bentinck that day, and the manner in which the Burgomasters spoke to Dijkveldt worried him.[118]

But the lobbying of the other towns he had instructed Fagel to undertake earlier in the month was bearing fruit and the Amsterdam opposition would be outflanked, step by step – a reversal of the position that led to the Treaty of Nijmegen, when Amsterdam had rallied the key towns against the Prince and Fagel. On 18 September, at a secret session of the States of Holland, the Prince reported on the agreements he had entered into for the loan of troops from the German princes, which he emphasised could be at the disposal of the State at very short notice if the agreements were ratified. He had needed to act in secrecy, he said, because of the notorious lack of confidentiality that prevailed in the Republic. The steps taken by James II and Louis XIV so threatened Religion, Freedom, Trade – the entire welfare of the country – that it needed to look to its defences and the sooner the troops were taken into the service of the State the better.[119] The meeting adjourned to ascertain the views of the towns and on the 20th the States-General in secret session was also informed of the troop agreements.[120]

On the 21st Amsterdam did resolve that it was necessary to take on the troops in view of the threats emanating from Louis, but only for defensive purposes – they should not be used for any offensive action against 'other potentates' – and she still wanted to make a last attempt, by means of D'Avaux, to get the French measures against Dutch imports rescinded. On 22 September the States of Holland approved the agreements.[121] Gelderland

and Overijssel agreed on the 25th; Zeeland was to agree on the 30th and on 4 October Hendrik-Casimir was to secure the approval of Friesland. In all these cases much had been made of the supposed understanding between James II and Louis.[122] Furthermore, on the 25th the States-General resolved to increase each company of foot in the Dutch army by 16 men and of horse by 22, a total increase of about 10,000 men.[123]

But until now only three of Amsterdam's Burgomasters, and possibly a few other Regents, but not the Town Council as a whole, were aware of Prince William's plans for the invasion of England. Now her decision on that could no longer be avoided.

On 26 September the Amsterdam Council met to address this momentous question. We have the notes kept by Hudde of the meeting and we know, therefore, the acute tussle in his mind and, no doubt, in the minds of his colleagues. The Amsterdam representatives on the *Secrète Besogne* in The Hague reported that Prince William had resolved to intervene in England and had outlined his reasons for doing so – he had done so on 24 September. His arguments were subsequently amplified by Fagel to the States of Holland and we will examine them when we come to their meeting. The pertinent point now, however, is to see what it was that decided Hudde and his colleagues to support the Prince.

There were weighty considerations against the Prince's proposals – the huge risks of the undertaking, the adverse financial and economic consequences to be anticipated from the war, and the vacuum in the leadership of the country left by the Prince's absence in England, all of which Hudde noted. He weighed against all these points the Prince's reasons for the invasion; but what finally decided him to come down on William's side was the unanimous support for him from the *Secrète Besogne* in The Hague, the intensity of that support, and the support for him from the commonality and the preachers, which was manifest. He thought that the Prince's project would proceed in any case; that, if Amsterdam did not support it, she would receive no thanks in the case of success but would receive the blame in the case of failure, and that in both cases she would not only incur the disfavour of the Prince but also of all the other members of the States of Holland, of the commonality, and of the Church.[124] These considerations also decided the rest of the Town Council, for they resolved 'to support His Highness, as matters had been so advanced by the other members of the States of Holland that they could now not be stopped'. Some on the Council complained that the three Burgomasters in the secret had not kept them informed, but others acknowledged that the premature revelation of the invasion plans would have been a great security risk.[125] D'Avaux indeed learnt of the plans on the 27th, the following day.[126]

It was not enthusiastic support and it came only because the Prince and Fagel had outmanoeuvred the great city by arraigning the rest of the country, the people and the preachers against her. At the beginning of September D'Avaux had analysed the state of public opinion in the Province of Holland for Louis XIV; apart from the alarm arising from Louis's support for Fürstenberg in Cologne and the need to defend themselves, the majority were bellicose, some because they were supporters of the Prince of Orange, some because of religion, and some because of the concern for commerce. The small number of a pacific disposition could not, or dared not, oppose the Prince.[127] But, all this notwithstanding, Amsterdam would still not vote for reprisals against France and, as we have seen, her decision to support the Prince had not been based on France's actions against the Republic's commerce.

Then Louis outdid himself. At the end of September he ordered the seizure of all Dutch shipping in French ports, which were then full of Dutch ships assembled to transport the French wine harvest. The despatch of the Dutch ambassador in France reporting this is dated 27 September and the States of Holland did not learn of it until the 30th, thus after the Amsterdam meeting held on the 26th. On 3 October, at last, the reprisals from Amsterdam were forthcoming and her Town Council voted for the seizure of French ships in Dutch ports, followed, on the 15th, by a ban on French imports.[128]

THE STATES OF HOLLAND AND THE STATES-GENERAL CONSENT TO THE INVASION

Amsterdam having approved the invasion of England, it was now the turn of the States of Holland to follow suit. The Prince at this time was personally engaged in initiating the embarkation of the troops; this he did on 26 September, the day Amsterdam gave her approval but before Holland or the States-General did so. The arguments accordingly were put on his behalf by Fagel to the Holland States on 29 September.

Louis XIV and James II, Fagel contended, were in cahoots aiming to smother the Reformed Religion. The closeness of their relationship was demonstrated by D'Avaux's *mémoir* of 9 September in which Louis had declared that his ties with James bound him to support the English King. No one could doubt that the two kings were bent on destroying the Dutch State and that they were only awaiting the right moment to do so. They had tried to persuade Leopold of Austria to abandon the Dutch for an English alliance by appealing to his Catholicism – heresy would be extirpated both in England and the Republic. In England one of two things would happen: either James would triumph in the domestic disputes or the 'Nation' of England would. If James triumphed the Dutch would have him as well as Louis about their necks. If the 'Nation' prevailed it would form a republic, for which the precedents, as far as the Dutch were concerned, were in any case not good – the reference was to the first Dutch war – and if they did not come to the aid of the English 'Nation', as the English had good reason to expect, they would be seen as having abandoned it in its hour of need. If the intervention in England led to complications Louis would have to divert a large part of his resources to England to prop up James and he would be less able to threaten the Dutch and others on the Continent. There was a characteristic Fagel touch – there was a moral obligation to come to the aid of those who professed the Reformed Religion.

The Prince had no wish to hide his own interest in intervening. Everyone knew what expectations he and his wife had in the succession to the English throne and how greatly concerned they, as Princes of the Blood, were that the dispute between the King and 'Nation' should not exclude them from the throne. If the King prevailed the Reformed Religion would be suppressed and those of that religion would be excluded from the succession. The whole English 'Nation' had a pronounced aversion to the court and there was a good chance of success arising from intervention. His Highness was resolved, with the blessing of God, to come to the aid of the English 'Nation', to preserve the Reformed Religion and the 'Nation's' liberties and rights, and to do so in the name of himself and Her Royal Highness.

He did not want to usurp the throne, but to ensure only that, by calling a free Parliament, in accordance with the laws of England, the Reformed Religion could be secured, harmony restored, and the infringements of the 'Nation's' freedoms and rights redressed, so that the King and the 'Nation' could live in a state of mutual understanding and be of profit to her friends and allies, particularly the Dutch State.

He could not undertake this task, in which the Dutch State itself had so great an interest, without seeking the help of its fleet and manpower, acting in no other manner but in an auxiliary capacity.[129]

And so the States of Holland resolved: they would act as auxiliaries in making the Dutch fleet and manpower available and the intervention would take place in the Prince's name. In coming to this decision they took account of the, in their minds, undoubted intention of both James and Louis to subvert both the Dutch State and the Reformed Religion, which it would be grossly irresponsible not to pre-empt.

On 2 October they resolved to pay the German troops, whom the Prince had recruited, out of the fortifications fund of 4 million guilders, with each of the Provinces replacing the sums in accordance with their quotas, so that the money for the fortifications was not diminished; and on the 9th they further resolved that the 4 million should also be used to finance the Prince's expedition to England, on the same terms. Finally, on the 14th they approved taking over the 6,000 troops from Sweden.[130]

Meanwhile, on 8 October, the States-General also approved the expedition to England.

LOUIS XIV'S DEPLOYMENTS

These developments in the Republic were taking place in parallel with Louis XIV's deployments, which took place during September and which could not fail to have their effect on the mood of the Dutch.

Louis's mind, as we have said, was firmly fixed on his eastern frontier. Louvois had written to Marshal d'Humières on 21 September that it appeared from all the news emanating from Holland that the Prince of Orange was on the point of embarking for England, where, it was said, measures had been taken to force James II to leave his kingdom within three weeks.[131]

But there was little that Louis could do to assist his English cousin. His fleet remained at Toulon in the Mediterranean to assist in a possible invasion of the Papal States, and he perceived the main threat to his kingdom to lie on the Rhine, so that a thrust through the Spanish Netherlands to attack either Maastricht or the Dutch Republic, or both, would have been a distraction from the main task in hand.

To that he was already firmly committed. On 10 September, 6,000 French troops had entered the Electorate of Cologne, although they were too late to prevent Schomberg from occupying the city of Cologne itself with 3,000 men on the 21st. On the 15th French troops entered the Papal enclave at Avignon. On the 24th Louis issued a manifesto in Rome and in Regensburg citing the obstinate refusal of the Empire to transform the Truce of Regensburg into a permanent peace, the rejection of the legitimate claims of the Duchess of Orléans in the Palatinate, and the formation of a menacing league on his frontiers. He was constrained, he argued, to occupy Philippsburg, the last remaining gateway into France from the east, but he merely wanted to use it as a pledge. His intentions were pacific: if his opponents were prepared to translate the Truce of Regensburg into a permanent peace he was prepared to cede Philippsburg, and even Freiburg, which he had held for a long time, after dismantling their defences; the claims of the Duchess of Orléans could be met by suitable compensation; and he was prepared to accept Clement as co-adjutor of Cologne if Fürstenberg were recognised as the Archbishop Elector. These terms were to remain open for acceptance for three months.

At the same time, apart from his moves on Avignon and Cologne, his troops occupied the bishopric of Liège, there to take up defensive positions, whilst an army under the nominal command of the Dauphin began the siege of Philippsburg. Stoutly defended for four weeks by the brother of the Stahremberg who had successfully defended Vienna, it was compelled to capitulate on 29 October.

Louis's aim was a swift coup which would establish him in a position of strength on the Rhine. It would help to keep the Turks in the war, which would handicap Leopold in switching his troops to the west, and it would force through legal recognition of the *réunions*. This, he had calculated, would secure his eastern frontiers without a long military effort being required. Instead he had initiated the Nine Years' War.[132]

THE INVASION OF ENGLAND: THE DETAILED PREPARATIONS
He had also cleared the way for William of Orange to finalise his plans for the invasion of England. When completed the invasion force consisted of 53 warships, about 10 fireships, and about 400 other transport vessels. There are various estimates of the number of troops who actually landed, but 21,000 seems a reasonable estimate, of whom 5,000 were volunteers – the bulk of them English and Scots, but also 600 Huguenot officers and the rest a widely gathered cosmopolitan mixture, not excluding many from France. The English and Scots

volunteers had amongst them a large number of aristocrats, gentry and gentlemen, but also a ragbag of professional conspirators, amongst them survivors of Monmouth's rebellion. Three ships were required to transport the 'English Lords', who included Shrewsbury. The English and Scottish regiments in Dutch service contributed 3,710 men and in the Dutch regiments many were German. The House of Orange itself provided five battalions of foot – one provided by Nassau-Zuylenstein – and three regiments of cavalry guards. The extended clan also produced a Brandenburg battalion commanded by Prince Albert Frederick of Brandenburg. If we add the crews on the warships – among them English sailors and pilots – and those manning the transports, the total invasion force seems to have amounted to around 40,000 men and around 5,000 horses. The preparations were done at formidable speed, beginning in June and completed in October. Amsterdam provided more than half the ships and naval manpower, with Rotterdam being the other major contributor. At the end of July the States-General voted for the near-doubling of the navy's manpower with the recruitment of an extra 9,000 sailors in less than a month. The hiring of the transports began at the end of August and this too was completed in less than a month.[133]

Bentinck, in charge of the logistics, covered every detail: oats for the horses, 2,000 saddles, biscuits for 16,000 men for two weeks, 10,000 cheeses at 6 lbs each in weight, 50 hogsheads of brandy, 1,600 hogsheads of beer, pipes for the men, tobacco for the men, 10,000 pairs of shoes – the list goes on.[134]

Somehow the money to finance the invasion, which Van der Kuijl puts at 7.3 million guilders by the end of January 1689,[135] was found. Burnet says that in the light of the tensions in Cologne Fagel had in July persuaded the States-General to raise, by means of a loan, the 4 million guilders to repair the Dutch defences on the Rhine and the Ijssel to which we have already referred.[136] As we have also seen they resolved in October to use this money for the German troops and the English expedition. In the interim the Prince may also have used his own resources and credit; he had arrived at a settlement with Spain for the amounts owing to him from that country and we find him writing to Bentinck at the beginning of September that he approves De Wildt's suggestions for the remittance of his money from Spain – De Wildt needed only to write to William's agent there.[137] D'Avaux's information in May was that the settlement had been signed and that under the terms of payment, as far as he could ascertain, 300,000 guilders were to be paid cash down with thereafter a yearly payment of 150,000 guilders until the debt was cleared.[138] Furthermore the Prince was lent 2 million guilders by the Portuguese Jew Francisco Lopez de Suasso.[139] On the naval side, the finances of the five Admiralty Colleges were considerably enhanced in the course of 1686 by the farming out of customs duties which, as D'Avaux had reported to Louis in January, meant the navy could be expanded without recourse to the States-General under the pretext of the need to provide convoys for Dutch shipping.[140] Shrewsbury, who was by no means well off, made a contribution amounting to perhaps £3,000.[141]

In the meantime communication was re-established with the English opposition. The gap left by the departure of Sidney was at last filled by the despatch of Jacob van Leeuwen, Bentinck's secretary, who arrived in London on 11 September and met Edward Russelll, Lumley and Danby. From this William learnt that Bonrepos had told James that the Dutch armaments were aimed at him and that, nevertheless, James had rejected the offer of French assistance. For security reasons Van Leeuwen himself was advised by the conspirators not to linger in England and that information would be sent to Bentinck by secure means. On his return he brought with him information on the English fleet, which he put at 27 fighting ships (excluding fireships), with 17 in the course of being re-equipped or being fitted out, a total of 44 ships excluding the fireships. The English were working day and night but it would need more than ten days to complete the preparations. His figures were nearly accurate in total, although not in detail, the actual overall size of the English fleet on 1 October being 21 with 22 being fitted out, a total of 43, excluding fireships. However, as we shall see, the English fleet which in the event took station to confront the Dutch was to be considerably smaller than this. Van Leeuwen also brought with him the important and accurate information that James's army was positioned around London within a day's march of the capital. He also reported that the Earl of Bath commanded at Plymouth and that the Duke of Berwick, James's illegitimate son – by Marlborough's sister Arabella – commanded at Portsmouth.[142]

On 20 September William summoned Lieutenant-Admiral Evertsen and Vice-Admiral Almonde to attend him in the greatest secrecy at Bentinck's house, Zorgfliet, where they were not to arrive until after dark, at 7pm, to receive his orders.[143] We have no record of the meeting, but it seems implausible, as both De Jonge and Japikse maintain, that it was not until this moment that these two commanders were made aware of the Prince's plans for the invasion of England.[144] But it is extremely likely that they were then informed of the command structure of the invading fleet, to which we will come in an instant.

On 26 September William inspected the troops assembled at Mookerheide and gave them their marching orders, without, for security reasons, telling them of their final destination – they were informed of this only at the last moment. For the same reasons they headed for different embarkation points.[145]

On 6 October – two days before the States-General gave their approval for the expedition – Herbert was formally appointed commander of the invasion fleet, with Evertsen as his deputy, although both of them were to exercise joint command until such time as they encountered the English fleet. At that point the Dutch flag would be lowered and the flag of William and Mary raised. Herbert was instructed by the Prince to do everything possible to avoid conflict with the English fleet and to persuade its personnel to change sides. A short letter to be distributed to the English officers and seamen was prepared to induce them to do this: 'You are made use of only as Instruments to bring this Nation under

Popery and Slavery by means of the Irish and other Foreigners, that are assembling for your Destruction.'[146]

In a memorandum which he submitted at this time Herbert expressed the view that the fleet was more than sufficient to counter any force James II could deploy to sea that year. He emphasised the need for it to have as English a flavour as possible, and as many English seamen and officers should be recruited as was feasible. There were only two possible landing places, the north and the west of England, but he thought the north so dangerous that he hardly believed it practicable; however, the Thames might be considered as a third possibility. At the end of the day, he asserted, it was the wind which would be the deciding factor, taking account of how James II deployed his army.[147]

Bentinck drew up a list of places which could be considered suitable for landing, beginning in the north and ending in the west.[148] He may also have been the author of an anonymous memorandum dated October 1688 to an English agent which stated that, in view of James's army being positioned around London – as Van Leeuwen had reported – any landing in the north could be no closer to London than Yorkshire and any landing in the west no closer than Devonshire. The memorandum also stated that it was intended that there should be one landing in the north and one in the west.[149]

On 10 October everything was almost ready for the vast invasion fleet to set sail and William now judged it opportune to issue his Declaration,[150] on which so much labour had been expended, justifying his invasion of England. We shall refer to this as his First Declaration, for, in due course, two others were to follow. It is of such constitutional importance in English history – it greatly influenced first the Declaration of Rights and subsequently the Bill of Rights – that we ask for the reader's indulgence in summarising it below.

The peace and happiness of any state, it declared, could not be preserved if the laws, liberties and customs as by law established were openly transgressed and annulled. Where it was endeavoured to introduce a religion contrary to law those 'most immediately Concerned' were indispensably bound to maintain the established laws, liberties and customs and, above all, the established religion, and to ensure that the inhabitants of the state were not deprived of their religion or civil rights. The King's 'Evil Counsellors' were subjecting his realms quite openly to arbitrary government, and there then follows a lengthy enumeration of complaints against specific transgressions by these counsellors: the exercise of the King's dispensing powers; the annulment of the Test Acts; the establishment of the illegal Ecclesiastical Commission; the 'turning out' of the President and Fellows of Magdalen College, Oxford, from their 'freehold' contrary to the provisions of Magna Carta 'that no man shall lose life or goods, but by the Law of the Land';[151] the abrogation of the Municipal Charters; the subvention of the judges; and the subvention of the army by appointing Papists to military offices. By these means the 'Evil Counsellors' planned to achieve 'their wicked designs, by the assistance of the Army, and thereby enslave the Nation.'

'The dismal effects' were evidenced in Ireland, 'where the whole government is put in the hands of Papists'.

Then there was the birth of James's and Mary of Modena's son amidst 'so many just and Visible grounds of suspicion, that not only wee ourselves, but all the good Subjects of those Kingdomes, doe Vehemently suspect, that the pretended Prince of Wales was not born by the Queen'.

Since William and Mary were so interested in the matter, with their rights to the succession, and since the English Nation had testified their affection and esteem for them, they could not excuse themselves from espousing the interests of the inhabitants and from doing all they could to maintain the Protestant religion, and the laws and liberties of their kingdom, and to secure for the inhabitants the continued enjoyment of their just rights. They had been asked to do this by many Lords, both spiritual and temporal, and by many gentlemen and other subjects of all ranks.

He was bringing over a force sufficient to secure him from the 'Evil Counsellors'. His expedition had no other design but to have a free and lawful Parliament as soon as possible. The two Houses of Parliament would need to procure an agreement between the Church of England and the Protestant Dissenters and to secure all those who lived peacefully under the government as good subjects from all persecution on account of their religion, Papists not excluded. An enquiry would be held into the birth of the 'Pretended Prince of Wales, and of all things, relating to it and the Right of Succession'.

His sole object was 'the Preservation of the Protestant Religion, the Covering of all men from Persecution of their Consciences, and the securing to the whole Nation the free enjoyment of all their Lawes, Rights and Liberties, under a Just and Legall Government'.

As soon as the state of the Nation allowed he would send back all the foreign troops he had brought with him.

Finally, a Parliament would also be called in Scotland and he would study how to bring Ireland 'to such a state, that the Settlement there may be Religiously observed; and that the Protestant and British interest may be preserved'.

There are two points we may note. The Declaration addressed itself to very specific issues; there was no appeal to abstract rights.[152] And, just as practical, the promise of religious toleration, including for Papists, was not only designed to create unity within England, but was also directed at the Catholic powers of Europe from whom William sought support, a call for unity within the new Grand Coalition which he was forming against Louis XIV.

On 11 October William notified Herbert that all the troops would have been embarked by the 15th so that they should be able to choose to set sail the following day. But that was not to be, the stormy weather and a contrary wind preventing it. This necessitated a change of plan, as William informed Herbert on the 15th; originally it was intended that the warships would precede the transports to clear the way; now both the warships and the transports would sail together.[153] He made his will on the 15th and on the 16th added a codicil making generous provision for Bentinck and his children.[154] On the 28th he expressed his chagrin to Fagel at the contrary winds and took the opportunity to thank him for 'all his friendship and services, which I cannot begin to acknowledge to the degree I should'.[155]

He took care to explain what he was doing to the two branches of the Habsburgs. On the 29th he wrote to the Marquis de Gastañaga, the Governor of the Spanish Netherlands, with whom he had established a good line of communication, assuring him that it was not his intention, whatever his enemies asserted, to dethrone the King of England nor to extirpate Catholicism in his kingdoms. 'But I find myself obliged in honour and in conscience to go there to maintain the law and religion of his subjects, and to maintain liberty of conscience according to the laws.' He would have welcomed the participation of Gastañaga in the enterprise but he had to have regard to the sensibilities of the English.[156]

He wrote in similar terms to the Austrian branch of the Habsburgs. The misunderstandings between James II and his subjects, he wrote to Leopold, have reached such a pitch as to threaten a formal rupture, which obliged him to intervene at the repeated behests of 'many Peers and other considerable persons of the kingdom, as well ecclesiastical as secular'. He needed to take 'some troops' with him as protection. 'I assure your Imperial Majesty by this letter … I have not the least intention to do any hurt to his Britannic Majesty, or to those who have a right to pretend to the successions of his kingdom, and still less to make an attempt upon the crown, or to desire to appropriate it to myself.' He would endeavour by means of a lawfully assembled Parliament to secure the Protestant religion and the liberties and rights of the clergy, nobility and people; and by this means he hoped that a good union could be established between the King and his subjects so that they could contribute to 'the common good'. 'I will employ all my credit to provide that the Roman Catholics of that country may enjoy liberty of conscience … and provided they exercise their religion without noise, and with modesty, that they shall not be subject to any punishment.'[157]

Mary had been summoned by the Prince to The Hague, where she had arrived on 6 October. There she found William in good health, 'apart from his cough which inconvenienced him but not so much that he could not prepare everything for his expedition', the first time that we have evidence of the Prince's coughing as a feature of his health. Preparing for his departure, William told Mary on the 25th to consult Waldeck, Fagel and Dijkveldt during his absence. Should anything befall him she should marry again – it went without saying not to a Papist. It was a tender farewell and the Prince was in tears. In due course Mary was able to recover sufficiently from her confusion to assure him that she had never loved anyone other than him and she would never love another. Besides, having been married for so many years without it pleasing God to bless her with a child, she believed that was sufficient reason not to comply with his request. The following day they had dinner together at Honselaarsdijk and the Prince left, leaving Mary with the unhappy thought that, perhaps, she might never see him again.[158]

That day he also took formal farewell of the States-General; he told them that he was not undertaking so heavy a task for his own personal glory, but that 'his sole object was to honour God, and to preserve the Welfare of our Fatherland, and the Christian Religion'.[159] On the 27th, whilst a general fast was ordained which was observed with such zeal that it cut across faiths – the Jews observed it and the Spanish ambassador caused Masses to be said for the happy success of the enterprise – the last dispositions were made for the sailing of the fleet.[160] The Prince gave his orders to Herbert; the fleet was to escort the invasion force to the disembarkation points on the coast of England; it would be headed by the Prince's frigates, followed by Evertsen's squadron to starboard and Almonde's to port with Herbert's taking the rear – with the transports, it may be inferred, in the middle; in case of attack the warships would interpose themselves between the enemy and the transports; after disembarkation a detachment of frigates would escort the transports back to the Maas and Texel; and, if the wind allowed, the fleet would sail to Scotland to create a diversion there, or, if the winds made that impracticable, it would instead make a diversion in the west.[161] We may note from this that the option was kept open as to where the landing should take place – it could hardly be otherwise, as all would depend on the winds – and that the original idea contained in the anonymous memorandum to the English agent in October of there being two landings was changed to a diversion after the main landing had occurred – although this too, in the event, was dropped.

THE LANDING AT BRIXHAM: SOVEREIGNTY ACHIEVED

On the 29th the warships and the bulk of the transports put to sea from Goedereede, followed on the 30th by the rest of the transports from the Briel, with the Prince on board a brand-new frigate of 30 guns, also named the *Briel*. There he was accompanied by his naval advisers Lieutenant-Admiral Schepers and Vice-Admiral van Stirum. With a south-westerly wind the assembled fleet set sail for the north coast of England. The varied assortment of vessels stretched as far as the eye could see as they passed the beach at Scheveningen, where thousands had assembled to watch them sail by. All seemed set for a favourable voyage. But during the night a heavy storm blew up from the south-west, dispersing the whole fleet. When morning broke the Prince could do no other than take the necessary measures for the ships and vessels to return to port where best they could.[162]

Apart from the horses – about 300 of which perished from suffocation, as the hatches were battened down in face of the storm[163] – the damage was not great and the dispersed fleet was soon reassembling, although Herbert is unlikely to have had his mood improved by Burnet's writing him at length that it was all due to his dissolute life;[164] the one-eyed admiral had notoriously kept a harem when earlier in his career he had been posted to Tangier, which, we might speculate, probably rather enhanced than otherwise his well-known popularity in the English navy. The Prince did come under pressure to revert to the original plan that Herbert should take the Dutch fleet over to England to fight its English counterpart, or blockade it, in order to afford safe passage to the transports. William rejected this on the grounds of the loss of time at this late stage in the season. It was indeed already very late and with each day that passed the pressure on him mounted. Whilst awaiting a more favourable wind he was able to spare a couple of hours to say another farewell to Mary. Then, after an anxious wait of 11 days after the first attempt to depart, on 11 November the wind changed to the east, the *Briel* fired a gun as a signal for the fleet to weigh anchor, and it set sail again from Hellevoetsluis, amidst the thunder of the guns, the blowing of trumpets and the loud huzzahs of the soldiers, the sailors and the large crowds which again had assembled. It was watched by Mary from the top of a tower, from which, however, she could observe only the masts.[165]

The previous day Huygens had heard that Fagel's health was bad and was worsening every day.[166]

At a council of war held on the *Leyden*, anchored off Hellevoetsluis immediately before the fleet set sail, attended by Herbert, Bentinck, Evertsen and Russelll but not by the Prince, although no doubt the others were acting with his authority, it was decided that the landings for the invasion should be at Southampton, Poole, or Exmouth, or, if the wind changed to the south-west, the fleet would sail north.[167] All of this was very general and the next day, Friday the 12th, William wrote at one o'clock to Bentinck, who had gone to The Hague to say farewell to his sick wife; he deeply regretted Bentinck's absence at this crucial moment and feared he would not be able to join him because of the high winds and seas, but, if his friend could get a message to him, he wanted his advice on where exactly to land and at what stage the warships should take up a separate station from the transports.[168]

In fact, the easterly wind had enabled the fleet to sail to the north-east where four of the Immortal Seven had their power bases in Yorkshire (Danby), Derbyshire (Devonshire) and Durham (Nottingham and Lumley), and where they had assembled.[169] But on 12 November, the day William wrote to Bentinck, the fleet turned south-west. Historians have speculated on the reasons. Israel and Parker think it was because the strong wind made it inadvisable to land on the north-east English coast; so does Powley, who, alternatively, suggests that Herbert and the Prince had been informed of the exact position of the English fleet at the Gunfleet – an Ostend fisherman had reported that it lay 'between Harwich and the London river' (although Huygens discounted this as a mistake) – and realised that the wind would prevent it from coming out to hinder his own force – as we have seen, Herbert was always opposed to a landing in the north in any case; Dalrymple says that the whole manoeuvre was a stratagem of the Prince of Orange to induce James II to send troops to the north; and C. Jones says that William had already decided to sail down the Channel but because there were dangers in doing this at night the fleet had first sailed north to await daybreak.[170] The deciding evidence that it was the strong wind which prevented the landing in the north is provided by Israel and Parker who cite a letter from William, written after the landing at Torbay, in which he says, 'If we had landed in the north of England we would have found various things easier; but the strong easterly wind that we encountered did not allow this.'[171]

Huygens recorded on 29 October that letters from Van Citters reported great lack of enthusiasm in the English fleet; and on 5 November his diary mentions that Burnet told him that a skipper, who had sailed through the fleet, which then lay at the Buoy of the Nore at the mouth of the Thames, found the men from two of the English ships declaring that they would never fight the Dutch, and they had drunk the Prince of Orange's health. There were certainly members of the military conspiracy in the English navy, but coordination from separate ships was difficult and they were ineffective. The commander, Lord Dartmouth, was aware of 'caballing', and reported it to James at the end of October and the beginning of November. Nevertheless, he also told the King that 'I apprehend nothing but a readiness in all the Commanders to do their duty by your Majesty'. It was not a view he was to change and, at a much later date, he assured Burnet that whatever stories he had heard he was confident that both the officers and men in the English navy would have fought very heartily.[172]

As it happened the Dutch fleet sailed right past its English counterpart, which at that point had taken up station at the Gunfleet, south-west of the coast at Harwich; there both the wind and the tide prevented it from coming out to confront the Prince of Orange's invading force. At dawn on Saturday the 13th Dartmouth could see 13 of its warships on the horizon, the wind so strong that they sailed with almost bare masts. Captain Tennant, observing them from his frigate the *Tiger*, wrote to Pepys telling him he thought them 'too many for our fleet'.

William's armada sailed on to the Straits of Dover, where, on that Saturday, it stretched from the French to the English coasts, witnessed by throngs of spectators on either side. 'It was a very clear and pleasant day', John Whittle, the army chaplain, recorded in his diary. As they passed Calais and Dover the guns fired their salutes, for which purpose some men-of-war sailed very close to Dover and others to Calais. On the decks the Dutch regiments stood in parade order amidst the sound of the trumpets and the rolling of the drums, which played on for three hours. Leading the procession was the Prince of Orange in his frigate the *Briel*, with one man-of-war preceding it and two others accompanying it on either side. His flag, with the English colours, contained the device 'The Protestant Religion and liberties of England', with beneath '*Je Maintiendrai*'.[173] Always a master of propaganda, there were moments, too, when the Prince knew how to rival Louis XIV in arranging a spectacular display of pageantry to serve his ends.

Before sailing through the Straits a council of war had decided to change formation so that the transports now led, with the warships taking up the rear to protect them from the English fleet.[174] On 14 November at four in the morning Lord Dartmouth was indeed able to set sail in pursuit. It is estimated that he had with him 28 men-of-war and 12 fireships.[175] But he was thus much outnumbered by the Dutch fleet, which had set sail with 53 warships, even if we make allowance for losses on the way.

That fleet, reaching the Isle of Wight on the 13th after it had sailed through the Channel, passed the island during the night.[176] On the 14th the Prince told Herbert that, on the advice of the pilots, he was resolved to land most of his forces at Dartmouth and the rest at Torbay; Herbert's fleet was to cover the landings against the English fleet. Herbert seems to have advocated Exmouth but on the advice of Mr Gilbert, one of the pilots, that the wind was too strong for this, Dartmouth and Torbay it remained.[177] 14 November would have been an auspicious day to land, from the Prince's point of view, being both his 38th birthday and the anniversary of his marriage. But his English entourage hoped for the following day, the 15th, being 5 November under the Old-Style English calendar, and thus Gunpowder Day. On the night of the 14th the fleet followed the Prince's brightly lit ship, with three lanterns on its stern. The lights of the fleet's own lanterns covered the sea, and appeared like so many stars, dancing to and fro. As it happened the strong easterly wind caused the fleet to overshoot the mark on the 14th – it might have been the error of the pilot – and the fleet sailed right past Torbay.

It looked as if the disembarkation would now have to take place at Plymouth, which would have necessitated advancing inland through the desolation of Dartmoor, with winter approaching; furthermore it was commanded by the Earl of Bath, who, although he had indicated to Russelll he would join the Prince, might be somewhat dilatory in doing so until he could judge the lie of the land – which indeed subsequently proved to be the case. A distraught Admiral Russelll bid Burnet to go to his prayers, for all was lost.

And then, all of a sudden, the wind turned south 'and a soft and happy gale of wind', says Burnet, 'carried in the whole fleet, in four hours' time, into Torbay', on Gunpowder Day.

The wind, the Protestant Wind, which, in its caprice, had at first made life so difficult for the Prince of Orange before he could set sail from Hellevoetsluis for the second time, had thereafter blown in exactly the right direction during the four days of the voyage. When Burnet landed and met him after his landing at Brixham, near Torbay, William asked him if he did not now believe in predestination, or as Burnet put it:

> Heaven's favourite, for whom the skies do fight,
> And all the winds conspire to guide thee right.[178]

Five months later, on 21 April 1689, after the collapse of the regime of James II and his flight to France, William and Mary were crowned King and Queen of England. Sovereignty had been achieved.

1 Kenyon, *Sunderland, op. cit.*, p.167. *Correspondentie Willem III en Bentinck, op. cit.*, I, 2, pp.597–9 and p.599 n.2. David Onnekink, *The Anglo-Dutch favourite: the career of Hans Willem Bentinck, 1st Earl of Portland (1649–1709)*, 2007, p.42.

2 Onnekink, *Bentinck, op. cit.*, p.44.

3 Quoted in Kenyon, *Sunderland, op. cit.*, p.174.

4 *Ibid.*, pp.178–9. Miller, *James II, op. cit.*, p.184. Dalrymple, *op. cit.*, II, Book V app., pp.139–40.

5 Miller, *James II*, p.183.

6 Childs, *op. cit.*, p.130.

7 *Ibid.*, pp.131–2.

8 Miller, *James II, op. cit.*, p.184.

9 Quoted in John Carswell, *The descent on England: a study of the English Revolution of 1688 and its European background*, London 1969, pp.120–1.

10 See James's letters to Prince William of 26 February (16th O.S.) and 12 March (2nd O.S.) in. Dalrymple, *op. cit.*, II, Book V app., pp.140–1.

11 Childs, *op. cit.*, p.132.

12 *Ibid.*, pp.132–5. Dalrymple, *op. cit.* Book V app., pp.134–9.

13 Onnekink, *Bentinck, op. cit.*, pp.44–5.

14 De Jonge, *Zeeweesen, op. cit.*, IV, 1, p.51.

15 D'Avaux, *Négociations, op. cit.*, VI, pp.116–17.

16 Carswell, *op. cit.*, p.172.

17 Bluche, *op. cit.*, pp.405–6.

18 Wolf, *op. cit.*, pp.421–2.

19 See for this, Israel, in 'The Dutch Role in the Glorious Revolution' in *The Anglo-Dutch Moment, op. cit.*, pp.111–12.

20 *Ibid.*, pp.114–15. Carswell, *op. cit.*, pp.118–19.

21 D'Avaux, *Négociations, op. cit.*, VI, pp.100–2.

22 *Ibid.*, pp.108–9.

23 Israel, *Dutch Republic, op. cit.*, pp.844–5.

24 Wagenaar, *op. cit.*, 15, pp.425–7. Gebhard, *op. cit.*, I, pp.317–19.

25 *Correspondentie Willem III en Bentinck, op. cit.*, I, 1, pp.35–6.

26 Burnet, *op. cit.*, 1818, II, p.377. Both Foxcroft and Baxter suggest that William was compelled to intervene in England because he feared that a rebellion against James, which he himself did not control, could have created a Republic. Both base their views on Burnet's contemporary memoirs concluded on 26 December 1687. See Foxcroft, *op. cit.*, I, pp.492–3, Baxter, *op. cit.*, pp.230–1, Foxcroft, 'Supplement to Burnet's History of My Own Time', Oxford 1902, pp.261–3. But these are Burnet's own reflections, not a report of what William told him; at best they may reflect William's ruminations rather than his considered view. Baxter also says that 'Russelll told [William in May] that the English would wait no longer, that if William did not support them they would rise anyway.' But it is not, as he says, in Burnet's account of the May – in fact April – meeting; see p.377 cited above and pp.396–7 cited in note 27 below. Given the slowness with which the English rallied to William after his landing a rising without his considerable military support seems unlikely.

27 Burnet, *op. cit.*, 1818, II, pp.396–7.

28 *Ibid.*, II, p.397.

29 Miller, *James II, op. cit.*, p.182. Kenyon, *Sunderland, op. cit.*, p.194.

30 *Inter alia* he had refused to sit on the Ecclesiastical Commission, which he considered illegal. See Robert Beddard on Sancroft in *Oxford Dictionary of National Biography*, OUP 2004–16.

31 Miller, *James II, op. cit.*, p.185. Carswell, *op. cit.*, p.138.

32 Carswell, *op. cit.*, p.138.

33 Quoted in Carswell, *op. cit.*, p.139.

34 *Ibid.*, pp.139–40. Kenyon, *Sunderland, op. cit.*, p.194.

35 Carswell, *op. cit.*, p.143.

36 *Correspondentie Willem III en Bentinck, op. cit.*, I, 1, pp.40–2.

37 Singer, *op. cit.*, II, pp.488–9.

38 *Ibid.*, II, p.156.

39 Dalrymple, *op. cit.*, II, Book V app., pp.171–2.

40 Singer, *op. cit.*, pp.169, 177–8.

41 See her letter to Mary 28 June in Dalrymple, *op. cit.*, II, Book V app., p.175.

42 Quoted in Macaulay, *Hist. England*, London 1906, I, p.783 n.*.

43 *Lettres et Mémoires de Marie, op. cit.*, pp.61–3.

44 Letter to Mary 28 June, in Dalrymple, *op. cit.*, II, Book V app., p.175.

45 Onnekink, *Bentinck, op. cit.*, p.45.

46 Singer, *op. cit.*, II, p.178.

47 Dalrymple, *op. cit.*, II, Book V app., p.107.

48 Macaulay, *op. cit.*, 1906, I, p.785.

49 Kenyon, *Sunderland, op. cit.*, pp.198–9.

50 Macaulay, *op. cit.*, 1906, I, pp.789–90.

51 Singer, *op. cit.*, II, p.179.

52 Miller, *James II, op. cit.*, p.187. Foxcroft, *op. cit.*, I, pp.507–8. Browning, *op. cit.*, I, p.385.

53 Dalrymple, *op. cit.*, II, Book V app., p.107.

54 Burnet, *op. cit.*, 1818, II, p.397.

55 *Ibid.*, p.397. Against Burnet's version Foxcroft, *Halifax, op. cit.*, I, p.509 says Halifax was 'of course, entirely ignorant of the affair'. But his close relationship with Sidney and the tenor of his long correspondence with William make it unlikely that he was not approached. It also seems implausible that the anonymous letter in Dalrymple, *op. cit.*, II, Book V app., p.105, which states that 'Halifax hath been backward in this matter', 'may', as Foxcroft suggests, 'refer either to the Prince's projects or the trial of the bishops' (n.2). For Halifax's letter to William in August (25 July O.S.) see Dalrymple, pp.116–17.

56 Burnet, *op. cit.*, 1818, II, pp.397–8.

57 Speck, 'The Orangist conspiracy against James II', *Hist. Journal* 30, 2 June 1987, p.456.

58 Burnet, *op. cit.*, 1818, II, p.398. John Childs, *The Army of James II and the Glorious Revolution*, Manchester 1980, Supplement to Burnet's *History, op. cit.*, p.291.

59 Quoted by D.D. Aldridge in *Oxford Dictionary of National Biography*, OUP 2004–16.

60 Singer, *op. cit.*, pp.179, 182.

61 Dalrymple, *op. cit.*, II, Book V app., pp.116–18. Letters dated 25 and 27 July (O.S.), written within two days of each other and so similar we may wonder whether they were cooordinated.

62 *Ibid.*, pp.107–10.

63 *Ibid.*, pp.111–12. D'Avaux, *Négociations, op. cit.*, VI, pp.168–74. Onnekink, *Bentinck, op. cit.*, pp.45–6. That Bentinck's secret correspondents corroborated the letter of the Immortal Seven is hardly surprising, given Johnston's and Sidney's roles.

64 Dalrymple, *op. cit.*, II, Book V app., pp.177–83.

65 Symcox, 'Louis XIV and the Outbreak of the Nine Years War' in Ragnhild Hatton, ed., *op. cit.*, p.183. Spielman, *op. cit.*, I, p.128.

66 Symcox, *op. cit.*, pp.188–90. Bluche, *op. cit.*, pp.303–4. Rousset, *op. cit.*, IV, pp.59–60, 62–64.

67 Rousset, *op. cit.*, IV, p.65. Symcox, *op. cit.*, p.193.

68 Symcox, *op. cit.*, pp.193–4. Rousset, *op. cit.*, IV, pp.71–2.

69 Rousset, *op. cit.*, IV, pp.72–3. Symcox, *op. cit.*, p.194.

70 Symcox, *op. cit.*, pp.194, 197. Rousset, *op. cit.*, IV, p.85.

71 Rousset, *op. cit.*, IV, pp.87–9.

72 *Correspondentie Willem III en Bentinck, op. cit.*, II, 2, p.756.

73 *Ibid.*, II, 3, pp.1–3.

74 *Ibid.*, II, 2, pp.762–5, II, 3, p.1. McKay, *Great Elector, op. cit.*, pp.239–40.

75 McKay, *Great Elector, op. cit.*, pp.257, 258, 261.

76 *Correspondentie Willem III en Bentinck, op. cit.*, II, 3, p.14.

77 Troost, *Bentinck, op. cit.*, p.48. *Correspondentie Willem III en Bentinck, op. cit.*, I, 1, p.40, note 6.

78 *Correspondentie Willem III en Bentinck, op. cit.*, I, 1 pp.39–40 and p.40 n.4, I, 2, p.126. Lucile Pinkham, *William III and the Respectable Revolution*, Cambridge, Harvard University Press 1954, p.115.

79 *Correspondentie Willem III en Bentinck, op. cit.*, I, 1, p.43.

80 Pinkham, *op. cit.*, p.118.

81 *Correspondentie Willem III en Bentinck, op. cit.*, I, 2, p.127.

82 *Ibid.*, I, 2, p.158.

83 Redlich, *op. cit.*, p.328. Müller, *Waldeck, op. cit.*, pp.26ff. (which Redlich largely follows).

84 Onnekink, *Bentinck, op. cit.*, p.48.

85 *Correspondentie Willem III en Bentinck, op. cit.*, I, 1, pp.131–3.

86 *Ibid.*, I, 1, p.50.

87 Fuchs's report on his meeting with Bentinck dated Hamburg 27 July. Leopold von Ranke, *A History of England principally in the Seventeenth Century*, Oxford 1875, IV, App. II, pp.90–9, and Instructions to Fuchs pp.89–90.

88 Pinkham, *op. cit.*, pp.118–19, 121. Ten Raa & Bas, *op. cit.*, VI, pp.119–20, 270–3. According to this Brandenburg supplied 5,900 men, Celle and Wolfenbüttel 3,951, Hesse-Cassel 2,400 and Württemberg 1,000 horse. These figures are confirmed by Israel, 'Dutch role', in *Anglo-Dutch Moment, op. cit.*, p.107 n.5.

89 Japikse, *Willem III, op. cit.*, II, pp.244–5.

90 Pinkham, *op. cit.*, pp.119–20.

91 *Ibid.*, p.122. *Correspondentie Willem III en Bentinck, op. cit.*, I, 2, p.143.

92 Wagenaar, *op. cit.*, 15, pp.427–31.

93 Dreiskämper, *op. cit.*, p.61.

94 Wagenaar, *op. cit.*, 15, pp.431–4. *Correspondentie Willem III en Bentinck, op. cit.*, I, 1, p.44, note 3.

95 Wagenaar, *op. cit.*, 15, pp.435–6. De Jonge, *Zeeweesen, op. cit.*, III, 2, p.431.

96 *Correspondentie Willem III en Bentinck, op. cit.*, I, 1, pp.44–5.

97 De Jonge, *Zeeweesen, op. cit.*, III, 2, p.431.

98 *Correspondentie Willem III en Bentinck, op. cit.*, I, 1, p.45.

99 *Ibid.*, I, 1, pp.46–7.

100 *Correspondentie Willem III en Bentinck, op. cit.*, I, 1, p.47. Dorothy Somerville, *The King of Hearts: Charles Talbot, Duke of Shrewsbury*, London 1962, p.45.

101 Dalrymple, *op. cit.*, II, Book V app., p.121.

102 Childs, *op. cit.*, p.148.

103 *Correspondentie Willem III en Bentinck, op. cit.*, I, 1, pp.48–50.

104 *Ibid.*, I, 1, pp.48–50.

105 *Ibid.*, I, 1, p.53. The Prince's meaning is not absolutely clear; he uses the word 'divises' which could either mean the motto on the coinage or foreign exchange. But he also expresses his ignorance, which is more likely to be true of foreign exchange than mottoes.

106 *Ibid.*, I, 1, pp.54ff.

107 *Ibid.*, I, 2, pp.133ff.

108 Ranke, *op. cit.*, IV, p.415–16.

109 *Ibid.*, IV, p.416.

110 Redlich, *op. cit.*, p.32.

111 *Lettres et Mémoires de Marie, op. cit.*, p.78.

112 Kenyon, *Sunderland, op. cit.*, pp.203ff.

113 *Ibid.*, p.210.

114 Wagenaar, *op. cit.*, 15, pp.438–9.

115 Kenyon, *Sunderland, op. cit.*, p.213.

116 Wagenaar, *op. cit.*, 15, p.440.

117 Israel, 'Dutch Role', in *Anglo-Dutch Moment, op. cit.*, p.117.

118 *Correspondentie Willem III en Bentinck, op. cit.*, I, 1, p.57.

119 *Secrete Resolutien, op. cit.*, V, pp.224ff.

120 Dreiskämper, *op. cit.*, p.64.

121 *Secrete Resolutien, op. cit.*, V, p.228.

122 Israel, 'Dutch Role', in *Anglo-Dutch Moment, op. cit.*, p.118.

123 Fruin, *Verspreide Geschriften, op. cit.*, V, p.180.

124 Gebhard, *op. cit.*, I, pp.331, II, pp.169–74. For the date of 24 September when William informed the *Besogne* of the States of Holland of his intention to invade England, see Groenveld, 'The Dutch Side of the Revolution', p.240 in Beddard, ed., *The Revolutions of 1688*, Oxford 1991.

125 Wagenaar, *op. cit.*, 15, p.441.

126 Groenveld, *The Dutch Side of the Revolution, op. cit.*, p.240.

127 D'Avaux, *Négociations, op. cit.*, VI, pp.207–8.

128 Dreiskämper, *op. cit.*, p.62.

129 *Secrete Resolutien, op. cit.*, V, pp.229ff.

130 *Ibid.*, V, pp.229ff.

131 Rousset, *op. cit.*, IV, p.103.

132 Jean-Christian Petitfils, *Louis XIV*, Editions Perrin, 2008, p.493.Wolf, *op. cit.*, pp.443–4. Müller, *Waldeck, op. cit.*, p.37. Redlich, *op. cit.*, p.328.

133 Israel and Parker, 'Of Providence and Protestant Winds', in *Anglo-Dutch Moment*, pp.335, 337, 351–4. Carswell, *op. cit.*, pp.169–70. Beddard, *A Kingdom without a King*, Oxford 1988, p.21.

134 *Correspondentie Willem III en Bentinck, op. cit.*, I, 2, p.604.

135 Arjen Van der Kuijl, *De Glorieuze Overtocht naar Engeland in 1688*, Amsterdam 1988, p.48.

136 Burnet, *op. cit.*, 1818, II, p.414.

137 *Correspondentie Willem III en Bentinck, op. cit.*, I, 1, p.56.

138 D'Avaux, *Négociations*, VI, pp.151–2. D'Avaux says 'livres', but he was in the habit of using 'livres' co-terminously for guilders. See, for example, p.175.

139 Groenveld, *The Dutch Side of the Revolution, op. cit.*, p.241.

140 De Jonge, *Zeeweesen, op. cit.*, IV, 1, p.26. D'Avaux, *Négociations, op. cit.*, VI, pp.117–18.

141 Somerville, *op. cit.*, pp.45–6.

142 *Correspondentie Willem III en Bentinck, op. cit.*, I, 2, pp.607–10. For the size of the English fleet see Edward Powley, *The English Navy in the Revolution of 1688*, Cambridge 1928, p.29.

143 *Correspondentie Willem III en Bentinck, op. cit.*, II, 3, p.40.

144 De Jonge, *Zeeweesen, op. cit.*, III, 2, pp.444–6. Japikse, *Willem III*, II, pp.252–3. Implausible because the two admirals, or at least Evertsen, could hardly not have been involved in the detailed naval preparations.

145 *Correspondentie Willem III en Bentinck, op. cit.*, I, 1, pp.57–9. Van der Kuijl, *op. cit.*, p.43.

146 *Correspondentie Willem III en Bentinck, op. cit.*, II, 3, pp.41, 42, I, 2, pp.613ff. The Prince of Orange's Letter to the English Fleet. Translated from the Dutch. Miscellaneous Tracts 1603–1795, British Library (See also *Correspondentie Willem III en Bentinck, op. cit.*, I, 1 pp.59–60). So important did William deem the avoidance of battle with the English fleet that he had instructed Bentinck on 26 September so to tell Herbert and to repeat it until it had sunk in! *Correspondentie Willem III en Bentinck, op. cit.*, I, 1, p.58.

147 *Correspondentie Willem III en Bentinck, op. cit.*, I, 2, pp.610–13.

148 *Ibid.*, I, 2, pp.617–18.

149 *Ibid.*, I, 2, pp.618–19.

150 *Miscellaneous Tracts 1603–1795*, British Library.

151 In 17th-century terms the Fellows' loss of their positions was seen as an infringement of their property rights.

152 The 'Rights' and 'Liberties' the Declaration referred to were specific and were established by law or custom – 'Privileges' was an alternative term often used in the 17th century for both these words.

153 *Correspondentie Willem III en Bentinck, op. cit.*, II, 3, pp.44, 45.

154 *Ibid.*, II, 3, p.47.

155 *Ibid.*, II, 3, p.48.

156 *Ibid.*, II, 3, pp.49–50.

157 Dalrymple, *op. cit.*, Book V app., pp.152–3. Translation as there given. The letter bears no date but is clearly written at about the time of William's departure.

158 *Lettres et Mémoires de Marie, op. cit.*, pp.80–2.

159 Van der Kuijl, *op. cit.*, p.52.

160 *Lettres et Mémoires de Marie, op. cit.*, p.82.

161 De Jonge, *Zeeweesen, op. cit.*, III, 2, pp.495–6.

162 *Ibid.*, III, 2, pp.459–60. Carswell, *op. cit.*, pp.176–7.

163 Israel and Parker, 'Of Providence and Protestant Winds', in *Anglo-Dutch Moment, op. cit.*, p.354 n.61.

164 Carswell, *op. cit.*, p.178.

165 *Lettres et Mémoiers de Marie, op. cit.*, pp.82–6. Burnet, *op. cit.*, 1818, II, p.423. De Jonge, *Zeeweesen, op. cit.*, III, 2, pp.463–4. John Whittle, *Exact Diary of the late Expedition of His Illustrious Highness The Prince of Orange into England*, London 1689, p.28.

166 Huygens, *Journaal*, 21 October 1688–2 September 1696, *Hist. Gen. Utrecht*, New Series 23, 1876, 10 November.

167 *Correspondentie Willem III en Bentinck, op. cit.*, I, 2, pp.623–4.

168 *Ibid.*, II, 3, p.53.

169 Troost, *William III, op. cit.*, p.200 and n.42. See also Israel and Parker, 'Of Providence and Protestant Winds', *op. cit.*, pp.359–60 and p.360 n.84.

170 Israel and Parker, 'Of Providence and Protestant Winds', *op. cit.*, p.360. Powley, *op. cit.*, pp.79–80. Dalrymple, *op. cit.*, II, p.292. C. Jones, 'The Protestant Wind of 1688', *European Studies Review*, 3, July 1973, p.215. Huygens, *Journaal 1688, op. cit.*, 11 November.

171 Israel and Parker, 'Of Providence and Protestant Winds', *op. cit.*, pp.340–1.

172 Huygens, *Journaal 1688, op. cit.*, 29 October & 5 November. Burnet, *op. cit.*, 1818, II, pp.426–7. Powley, *op. cit.*, pp.67–9.

173 Powley, *op. cit.*, pp.80–1. Carswell, *op. cit.*, pp.181–2. Whittle, *Diary, op. cit.*, pp.30–1.

174 De Jonge, *Zeeweesen. op. cit.*, III, 2, p.465.

175 Powley, *op. cit.*, p.82.

176 *Ibid.*, pp.81–2.

177 *Correspondentie Willem III en Bentinck, op. cit.*, II, 3, p.53. Powley, *op. cit.*, p.82.

178 Burnet, *op. cit.*, 1818, II, pp.424–7.Whittle, *Diary, op. cit.*, pp.32–3.

William III as New King of England, c. 1690, by Sir Godfrey Kneller.
National Galleries of Scotland, Edinburgh

Epilogue

When William of Orange invaded England in 1688, he still had more than 13 years to live and great – arguably, even, his greatest – achievements still lay before him. The literature on his contributions to the parliamentary development of the English constitution, the 'Glorious Revolution', is vast. As we have indicated, the earliest instructions for his education enjoined him to work with the representative institutions of the Dutch Republic and this advice, despite many serious disagreements, he ultimately came round to heeding. As Tony Claydon has so perceptively indicated, it was a good grounding for his handling of the representative institutions of England.

The wars with Louis XIV continued; despite the attempts of the two antagonists to find an agreement, they floundered on the vexed question of the Spanish succession. When William died in 1702 the Duke of Marlborough succeeded in large measure to the military, diplomatic and political leadership in Britain and the Dutch Republic which William had undertaken. As indicated in the text there was a quasi-*condottiere* element in this role which Eugene of Savoy also performed on behalf of Leopold I of Austria. He and Marlborough succeeded in containing the hegemony of Louis XIV in Europe and at one stage Louis's Paris itself was seriously threatened.

William and Mary formed a formidable partnership at the political level until her early death, in 1694, with the Queen taking the reins of government during William's frequent absences abroad or in Ireland. At the personal level too their cultural contribution, with the palaces at Hampton Court and Het Loo, with their gardens, and Mary's collection of Chinese porcelain, can still be seen today.

I have not addressed the topic of homosexuality. Rumours of William's homosexuality did not begin to circulate in England until 1689 and a detailed examination therefore falls outside the scope of this book, which deals with his life before that date. However, it is significant that it was at this very time that the enmity towards William from supporters of James II after his departure began to emerge, and they had every incentive to spread the rumours of homosexuality. If these rumours had had substance, surely it is surprising that they were not spread much earlier. The very occasional suspicion once or twice faintly hinted at by Constantijn Huygens, Jr., does not signify – Huygens was an inveterate gossip and was suspicious of everybody.[1] The fact was that William was devoted to Mary – at whose death he collapsed and had a nervous breakdown – and he was devoted to Betty Villiers, whom he richly rewarded. This has to be set against his alleged relationships with Bentinck – who was famously uxorious – and Keppel – who was notorious for his promiscuity with women. The probabilities must be against the rumours.

The wars that Louis began in 1667 terminated at last with the treaties of Utrecht and their associated treaties, the final one of which was signed in 1714. Louis died in 1715. The French Revolution commenced in 1789, and swept away the *ancien régime* of which Louis was the foremost protagonist. The great king's grave at St-Denis, in the suburbs of Paris, together with the graves of many of his predecessors, were desecrated and his bones were scattered.

The bones of William III remain at peace in the Henry VII chapel in Westminster Abbey close to those of the two Marys, his mother and his wife.

1 Troost, *Willem III, op. cit.*, p.25.

BIBLIOGRAPHY

Of Works Cited in the Text

The author is particularly grateful for the details of:

The translation of Charles II's letter to Prince William in Ch. 1, note 58, taken from P.C.A. Geyl, *Orange and Stuart*.

William's education cited in Ch. 2, note 127, from Martinus Nyhoff, *Mémoires de Constantin Huygens*, The Hague, 1873.

Pomponne's character sketch of the Prince cited in Ch. 7, note 7, from H.H. Rowen (ed.), *Relation de mon Ambassade en Holland*.

Aitzema, L. van, *Saken van staet en oorlog*, The Hague 1669

Aldridge, D., 'Edward Russelll', *Oxford Dictionary of National Biography*, Oxford 2004

Antal, G. von, & Pater, J.C.H. de, *Weensche gezantschapsberichten*, The Hague 1929

Arlington, Lord, *Arlington's Letters to Sir William Temple*, ed. Thos. Babington, London

Barbour, V., *Henry Bennet Earl of Arlington, secretary of state to Charles II*, Oxford 1914

Barclay, A., *William's Court as King in Redefining William III*, Aldershot 2007

Basnage, J., *Annales des Provinces-Unies*, The Hague 1726

Bathurst, B., *Letters of Two Queens*, London 1924

Baxter, S., *William III*, London 1966

Beddard, R., *A Kingdom without a King*, Oxford 1988

– (ed.), *The Revolutions of 1688*, Oxford 1991

– 'Sancroft', *Oxford Dictionary of National Biography*, Oxford 2004

Bédoyère, Guy de (ed.), *The Diary of John Evelyn*, Woodbridge, 1995, repr. 2002

Bentinck, M., *Lettres et Mémoires de Marie, Reine D'Angleterre*, The Hague 1880

Bérenger, J., art. in *Louis XIV and Europe*, London 1976

– 'La Politique des Réunions et les Consequences', Seminar on *Les Relations Franco-Autrichiennes Sous Louis XIV* under the direction of Jean Bérenger, 9–11 March 1983

– trans. C.A. Simpson, *A History of the Habsburg Empire 1273–1700*, London 1994

Bijl, M. van der, 'Utrechtse Weerstand', *Van Standen tot Staten*, Utrecht 1975

– 'Johann Moritz von Nassau-Siegen (1604–1697), eine vermittlende Persönlichkeit in Oranien-Nassau', *Die Niederlande und das Reich*, ed. H. Lademacher, Münster/Hamburg, 1995

– & Ufford, Quarles van, eds, 'Briefwisseling van Godard Adriaan van Reede van Amerongen en Everard van Weede van Dijkveld', *Nederlandsch Historisch Genootschap*, The Hague 1991

Blok, P.J., *Geschiedenis van het Nederlandsche Volk*, Groningen 1892–1908, 1899

Bluche, F., *Louis XIV*, Blackwell 1990

Bontemantel, H., ed. Kernkamp, *De Regeering van Amsterdam*, The Hague 1897

Boxer, C.R., *The Anglo-Dutch Wars*, London 1974

Brieven aan De Witt: Brieven aan Johan de Witt, vol. 2, 1660–1672, *Historisch Genootschap te Utrecht*, Series 3, No. 44

Brieven van De Witt: *Brieven van Johan De Witt, Historisch Genootschap te Utrecht*, 3, 25, II, 1909

Browning, A., *Thomas Osborne Earl of Danby and Duke of Leeds*, 1632–1712, Glasgow 1951

Bruin, G. de, *Geheimhouding en Verraad*, The Hague 1991

Burnet, G., *Bishop Burnet's History of his Own Time: from the Restoration of King Charles II to the Conclusion of the Treaty of Peace at Utrecht in the Reign of Queen Anne*, 4 vols, London 1818

– Burnet's *History of my Own Time*, 2 vols, Oxford 1897–1900

Calendar of State Papers, Domestic 1670, ed. M.A. Everett Green, 1895

Carswell, J., *The Descent on England: a study of the English Revolution of 1688 and its European background*, London 1969

Carte, T., *The Life of James Duke of Ormond: Containing an Account of the Most Remarkable Affairs of his Time, and Particularly of Ireland under his Government*, Oxford 1851

Chandaman, C.D., *The English Public Revenue 1660–1688*, Oxford 1975

Chapman, H., *Mary II Queen of England*, London 1953

Childs, J ., *The Army of James II and the Glorious Revolution*, Manchester 1980

Churchill, W., *Marlborough, His Life and Times*, London 1933

Claydon, T., *William III*, Pearson 2002

Colenbrander, H.T., *Bescheiden uit vreemde archieven omtrent de groote Nederlandsche zeeoorlogen 1652–1676*, The Hague 1919

Costerus, B., *Historisch Verhaal*, Leyden 1756

Courtenay, T.H., *Memoirs of the Life, Works and Correspondence of Sir William Temple*, London 1836

Coward, B., *The Stuart Age England 1603–1714*, London 1980

Dalrymple, J., *Sir John Dalrymple Memoirs of Great Britain and Ireland*, London 1790

D'Avaux, Jean Antoine de Mesmes, *Négociations de M Le Comte D'Avaux en Hollande*, 1679–1684, ed. E. Mallet, Paris 1752, 1753

Davenport Adams, W.H. , *The White King*, London 1889

De Jonge, J.R., 'Briefwisseling tuschen Hieronymus van Beverninck en de Raadpensionaris Johan de Witt in het jaar 1672', *Verhandelingen en Onuitgegeven Stucken betreffende de Geschiedenis der Nederlanden*, Delft 1825

– *Geschiedenis van het Nederlandsche Zeewesen*, The Hague 1833–48

De Witt, Johan, *Uit de jeugd jaren van stadhouder Willem III*, The Hague 1925

– Letters: see Brieven

D'Estrades, Comte, *Lettres, Mémoires et Négociations de Monsieur Le Comte d'Estrades,* London 1743

Deursen, A. Th. van, art. in *Nassau en Oranje*, Alphen 1979

Dicconson, W. (ed.), *Mémoires de Jacques II*, vol. II, Paris 1824

Dijk, H.A. van, *Bydrage tot the Geschiedenis der Nederlandsche Diplomatie*, Utrecht 1851

Dreiskämper, P., 'Aan de Vooravond van de Overtocht naar Engeland', *Utrechtse Historische Cahiers*, Jaargang 17, 1996

Du Moulin, *Relation Succincte de ce qui s'est passé de plus considérable sous … le Commandment de son Altesse Mgr. Le Prins d'Orange de la Campagne de 1674*, Leyden 1745

Ekberg, C., *The Failure of Louis XIV's Dutch War*, University of North Carolina Press 1979

Elizabeth of Bohemia, *Letters of Elizabeth, Queen of Bohemia*, Bodley Head, London 1953

Everett Green, M.A., *Princesses of England*, London 1855

Eysinga, W.J.M. van, 'Het Associatie Verdrag van 10 October 1681', *Mededelingen Nederlandsche*

Akademie van Wetensschappen. Afdeeling Letterkunde. Nieuwe Reeks Deel 10.1-9, Deel II, Amsterdam 1947

Feiling, K., *British Foreign Policy 1660–1672*, London 1930

Fouw, A. de, *Onbekende Raasdpensionarissen*, The Hague 1946

Foxcroft, H.C., *Life and letters of Halifax*, London 1898

– Supplement to *Burnet's History of My Own Time*, Oxford 1902

Franken, M.A.M., *Coenraad van Beuningen's Politieke and Diplomatieke activiteiten in de jaren 1667–8*, Institut voor Geschiedenis der Rijksuniversiteit te Utrecht, 1996

Frijhof, W., & Spies, M., *Dutch Culture in a European Perspective*, Royal van Gorcum, 2004

Fruin, R.J., *Aantekeningen in Overblyfsels van Geheugenis*, Leyden 1879

– *Verspreide Geschriften*, The Hague 1901

Fruin & Knoop, *Willem III en de slag van Saint-Denis*, The Hague 1881

Gardiner, S.R., *History of the Commonwealth and Protectorate, 1649–1660*, London 1894–1901

Gebhard, J.F., *Het Leven van Nicolaas Witsen*, Utrecht 1881

Geyl, P.C.A., Orange and Stuart 1641–72, London 1969

Godley, Eveline, *The Great Condé*, London 1915

Gonnet, C.J., *Briefwisseling tusschen de Gebroeders (Willem, Martinus, Adriaen) van der Goes, 1659-1673*, 1899, 1909

Grew, M., *William Bentinck and William III, Prince of Orange: the Life of Bentinck, Earl of Portland from the Welbeck Correspondence*, London 1924

Groen van Prinsterer, G., *Archives ou Correspondance inédite de la Maison d'Orange-Nassau*, Leyden 1847

Groenveld, S., *Evidente Factiën in de Staet*, Hilversum 1990

– 'The House of Orange and the House of Stuart, 1639–1650: A Revision', *Historic Journal* 34, 1991

– 'William III as Stadholder: Prince or Minister?' *Redefining William III*, Aldershot 2007

Grose, C.L., 'The Anglo-Dutch Alliance of 1678', *English Historical Review*, 39, 1 July 1924

Grouvelle, Ph.A. (ed.), *Oeuvres de Louis XIV: Mémoires Historiques et Instructions de Louis XIV pour le Dauphin*, Année 1661, Paris 1806

Haijer, J.E., 'De moord op de Gebroeders De Witt', *Spiegel Historiael*, July/August 1967, 2de jaargang nr.7/8

Haley, K.H.D., *William of Orange and the English Opposition 1672–4*, Oxford 1953

– 'Anglo-Dutch Rapprochement', *English Historical Review* 73, 1958

– *The First Earl of Shaftesbury*, Oxford 1968

– *An English Diplomat in the Low Countries*, Oxford 1986

Harris, T., 'Monmouth', *Oxford Dictionary of National Biography*, Oxford 2004

Hartog, M.W., *Prinse Willem III en de Hertogshoed van Gelderland 1673–1675*, Gelre LXV art. in Gelre LXVIII, 1974–75

Hatton, R.M. (ed.), *Louis XIV and Europe*, London 1976

– *Louis XIV and his Fellow Monarchs*, London 1976

Heim, H.J. van der, *Archief van den Raadpensionaris Antonie Heinsius*, The Hague 1867–80

History of Parliament: The Commons 1660–1690, section on Henry Benett

– section on Downing

– section on Thomas Clifford

– vol. III: section on Robert Peston

Holmes, G., *The Making of a Great Power 1660–1722*, London 1993

Hop, C., & Vivien, N., *Notulen gehouden ter Staten-vergadering van Holland (1671–1675) door Cornelis Hop ... en Nicolaas Vivien ... uitg. door dr. N. Japikse, Historisch genootschap Utrecht*, ser. 3, no. 19

Hosford , D., 'Henry Sidney', *Oxford Dictionary of National Biography* online edn, Jan. 2013

Hutton, R., *Charles the Second: King of England, Scotland, and Ireland*, Oxford 1989

Huygens, C., Jr., 'Journaal', *Historisch genootschap Utrecht*, 1881

– 'Voyage de Cell etc., 1680', *Werken van het Historish Genootschap Gevestid te Utrecht*, New Series, 46

Huygens, C., Sr., *Mémoires de Constantin Huygens*, The Hague 1873

Israel, J.I. (ed.), *The Anglo-Dutch Moment*, Cambridge 1991

– *The Dutch Republic: Its Rise, Greatness, and Fall 1477–1806*, Oxford 1995

Israel & Parker, 'Of Providence and Protestant Winds', *The Anglo-Dutch Moment*, Cambridge 1991

Jansen, H.P.H., art. in *Nassau en Oranje*, ed. C.A. Tamse, Alphen 1979

Japikse, N., *De Verwikkelingen tuschen de Republiek en Engeland van 1660–1665*, Leyden 1900

– *Johan De Witt*, Amsterdam 1915

– (ed.), *Correspondentie van William III en van Hans Willem Bentinck*, The Hague 1927–37

– *Prins Willem III, De Stadthouder-Koning*, Amsterdam, 2 vols, 1930, 1933

– art. '"Insinuation" van de Staten-Generaal aan Den Engeleschen gezant van 5 December 1680', *Bijdragen voor Vaderlandsche Geschiedenis en Oudheidkunde*, Sevende Reeks, Derde Deel, 1933

– *De Geschiedenis Van Het Huis Van Oranje-Nassau*, The Hague 1937–38

Jones, C., 'The Protestant Wind of 1688', *European Studies Review* 3, July 1973

Jones, J.R., *The First Whigs*, London 1961

– *Charles II, Royal Politician*, London 1987

– *The Anglo-Dutch Wars of the 17th Century*, London 1996

Keay, Anna, *The Last Royal Rebel: the Life and Death of James, Duke of Monmouth*, London 2016

Keblusek, M., 'Mary II', *Oxford Dictionary of Biography*, Oxford 2004

Kenyon, J.P., 'The Earl of Sunderland and the Revolution of 1688', *Cambridge Hist. Journal*, xi, 1955

– 'Charles II and William of Orange in 1680', *Bulletin Inst. Hist. Research*, 30, 1957

– *The Earl of Sunderland*, London 1958

– *The Popish Plot*, London 1972

Kernkamp, J.H., *De Reis van Prins Willem III Naar Engeland in het jaar 1670*, The Hague 1948

Klopp, Onno, *Der Fall des Hauses Stuart*, Vienna 1876

Knoop, W.J., *Krijgs- en geschiedkundige beschouwingen over Willem den Derde*, Schiedam 1895

Korvezee, Elisabeth, 'De Zending van Frederik van Reede Naar Engeland in de jaren 1672–1674', *Bijdragen voor Vaderlandsche Gechiedenis en Oudheidkunde*, 6th ser., Part 7, The Hague 1928

Krämer, F.J. L., *De Nederlandsche-Spaansche diplomatie voor de vrede van Nijmegen*, Utrecht 1892

– *Geheime Onderhandeling van Mr. Johan Pesters in het jaar 1674*, de Navorscher 1892

Kroon, A.W., *Jan De Witt contra Oranje 1650–1672*, Amsterdam 1868

Kuijl, A. van der, *De Glorieuze Overtocht naar Engeland in 1688*, Amsterdam 1988

Kurtz, G.H., *Willem III en Amsterdam 1683–85*, Utrecht 1928

Ladurie, E. Le Roy, *The Ancien Régime*, Blackwell 1998

Lake, E., *Diary of Edward Lake, Camden Miscellany*, I, Camden Society 1847

Legrelle, A., *La diplomatie française et la succession d'Espagne*, Paris 1888

Letter to James Steward: 'A Letter Writ by Mijn Heer Fagel, Pennsionary of Holland To Mr. Iames Stewart, Advocate, giving an Account of the Prince and Princess of Orange's Thoughts concerning the Repeal of the Test, and the Penal Laws'. Text in British Library under this heading.

Levi, A., *Cardinal Richelieu and the Making of France*, London 2000

Lister, T.H., *Life and Administration of Edward, First Earl of Clarendon*, London 1837

Lonchay, H., *Correspondance de la Cour d'Espagne*, Brussels 1923–37

Lossky, A., *Louis XIV, William III and The Baltic Crisis of 1683*, California 1954

– 'Political ideas of Willem III', *Political Ideas and Institutions in the Dutch Republic*, Clark Library seminar, 27 March 1982

– *Louis XIV and the French Monarchy*, New Brunswick 1994

Lynn, J.A., *Wars of Louis XIV*, London and New York 1999

Macaulay, T.B., *History of England*, Everyman Edition, repr. 1927

MacCulloch, D., *Reformation: Europe's House Divided 1490–1700*, London 2003

Maris, J., art. in *Gelre* LXXII, 1981

McKay, D., *The Great Elector*, Harlow 2001

– 'Small-power diplomacy in the age of Louis XIV: the foreign policy of the Great Elector during the 1660s and 1670s', *Royal and Republican Sovereignty in Early Modern Europe*, eds Oresko, Gibbs & Scott, Cambridge 1997

Mettam, R., *Power and Faction in Louis XIV's France*, Oxford 1988

Middlebush, F.A., ed., *Despatches of Thomas Plott and Thomas Chudleigh*, The Hague 1926

Mignet, M., *Négociations Relatives à la Succession d'Espagne sous Louis XIV*, 4 vols, Paris 1835–42

Mijers, E., & Onnekink, D., eds, *Redefining William III,* Ashgate, Aldershot 2007

Miller, J., *Popery and Politics in England 1660–1688*, London 1973

– *Charles II*, London 1991

– *James II*, Newhaven & London 2000

Miscellaneous Tracts 1603–1795, British Library

Monsieur de B., *Mémoires de Monsieur de B., Historisch Genootschap te Utrecht*, 19, 1898

Montpensier, Mlle, *Mémoires de Mademoiselle de Montpensier*, Paris 1891

Mörke, O., 'Das Haus Oranien-Nassau als Brückenglied in Oranien-Nassau', *Die Niederlande und das Reich*, ed. H. Lademacher, Münster/Hamburg, 1995

– 'William III's Stadhouderly Court in the Dutch Republic', *Redefining William III*, Aldershot 2007

Muilenburg, J., *The Embassy of Everard van Weed, Lord of Dykvelt, to England in 1687*, University Studies of the University of Nebraska 1920

Müller, P.L., 'Nederlandsche Eerste Betrekkingen met Oostenrijk 1658–1678', *Verhandelingen der Koninklijke Akademia van Wetenschap*, Amsterdam 1869

– *Wilhelm III von Oranien und Georg Friedrich von Waldeck*, The Hague 1873–80

Nimwegen, O. van, trans. Andrew May, *The Dutch Army and the Military Revolutions*, Woodbridge 2010

O'Connor, J.T., *Negotiator out of Season, The Career of Wilhelm Egon von Fürstenberg 1629 to 1704*, Athens 1978

Ollard, R., *Man of War: Sir Robert Holmes and the Restoration Navy*, London 1969

Onnekink, D., *The Anglo-Dutch Favourite: the Career of Hans Willem Bentinck, 1st Earl of Portland (1649–1709)*, Ashgate, Aldershot 2007

Onroerde Nederland: *'t Onroerde Nederland*, Amsterdam 1676

Opgenoorth, F.W., *Der Grosse Kurfürst von Brandenburg*, Frankfurt/Zurich 1971

Original Letters from King William III, then Prince of Orange, to King Charles II, Lord Arlington, etc., Cornhill 1704

Pagès, G., *Le Grand Électeur et Louis XIV 1660–1688*, Paris 1905

Panhuysen,L., *Rampjaar 1672*, Amsterdam/Antwerp 2009

Pepys, S., *Diary of Samuel Pepys*, London 1875

Petitfils, J.-C., *Louis XIV*, Paris 2008

Philippson, M., *Der Grosse Kurfürst Friedrich Wilhelm von Brandenburg*, Berlin 1903

Pillorget, R., ed. J. Bots, 'La France et les Etats Allemands au Congrès de Nimègue', *The Peace of Nijmegen 1676–1678/9*, Amsterdam 1980

Pinkham, L., *William III and the Respectable Revolution*, Cambridge, Mass., Harvard University Press 1954

Plowden, A., *The Stuart Princesses*, Sutton 1997

Poelhekke, J.J., Frederik Hendrik, *Prins van Oranje: een biografisch drieluik Zutphen*, Zutphen 1978

– art. in *Nassau en Oranje*, Alphen 1979

– 'Amalia van Solms', *Vrouwen in Het Landsbestuur*, ed. C.A. Tamse, The Hague 1982

Pontbriant, A. de, *Histoire de la Principauté d'Orange*, Avignon 1891

Powley, E., *The English Navy in the Revolution of 1688*, Cambridge 1928

Pribram, A.F., *Franz Paul Freiherr von Lisola, 1613–1674*, Leipzig 1894

Ranke, L. von, *A History of England principally in the Seventeenth Century*, Oxford 1875

Rauchbar, J.G. von, *Leben und Thaten des Fürsten Georg Friederich von Waldeck, 1620–1692*, 1867–70

Redlich, O., *Weltmacht des Barock Osterreich in der Zeit Kaiser Leopolds I*, Vienna 1961

Register Journalen, Huygens, Jr.: 'Register op de Journalen van Constantijn Huygens den Zoon', *Historisch Genootschap te Utrecht*, ser. 3, 35, Amsterdam 1915

Reresby, J., *Memoirs*, Royal Historical Society, 1991

Resolutiën: *Resolutiën van consideratie der Ed. Groot. Mog. Heeren Staten van Holland ende West-Friestland genomen zedert den aenvang der bediening van den Heer Johan de Witt*, Amsterdam & The Hague 1719

Robb, N., *William of Orange*, London 1962

Roorda, D.J., 'Prins Willem III en het Utrechtse Regeringsreglement', *Standen tot Staten*, Utrecht 1975

– *Partij en Factie*, Groningen 1978

– *Rond prins en patriciaat: verspreide opstellen*, Weesp 1984

Rousset, C., *Histoire de Louvois et de son administration politique et militaire*, Paris 1861–63

Rowen, H.H., ed. *Pomponne Relation de mon Ambassade en Hollande*, Utrecht 1955

– *The Ambassador Prepares for War*, The Hague 1957

– *John De Witt, Grand Pensionary of Holland, 1625, 1672*, Princeton 1978

– *The Princes of Orange: the Stadholders in the Dutch Republic*, Cambridge 1988

Samson, P.A., *Histoire de Guillaume III*, The Hague 1703

Scheurleer, H., *Brieven geschreven tuschen de Heer Johan de Witt ende gevolmaghtigden van den Staadt*, The Hague 1724

Seaward, P., 'The House of Commons Committee of Trade and the Anglo-Dutch War, 1664', *Historical Journal*, vol. XXX, 1987

– *The Cavalier Parliament and the Reconstruction of the Old Regime*, Cambridge 1989

Secret Resolution: *Secrete Resolutien 1653–1790*, The Hague 1791

Ségur, P. de, *La jeunesse du Maréchal de Luxembourg*, Paris 1900

– *Le Maréchal de Luxembourg et le prince d'Orange 1668–1678*, Paris 1900

Select Letters: *Some Select Letters from His Majesty King William III when he was Prince of Orange to King Charles II etc.*, S. & J. Sprint and J. Nicholson 1705

Sidney, H., ed. Blencowe, *Diary of The Times of Charles II*, London 1843

Singer, S.W. (ed.), *The Correspondence of H. H., Earl of Clarendon, and of his brother, Laurence Hyde, Earl of Rochester; with the Diary of Lord Clarendon from 1687 to 1690 ... and the Diary of Lord Rochester during his embassy to Poland in 1676*, London 1828

Somerville, D., *The King of Hearts: Charles Talbot, Duke of Shrewsbury*, London 1962

Sonnino, P., *Louis XIV and the origins of the Dutch War*, Cambridge 1988

Speck, W.A., 'The Orangist conspiracy against James II', *Hist. Journal* 30, 2 June 1987

– *James II*, London 2002

Spielman, J., *Leopold I of Austria*, London 1997

Stoye, J., *The Siege of Vienna*, London 1964

Strickland, A., *Lives of the Last Four Princesses of the House of Stuart*, London 1872

Swart, K.W., art. in *Nassau en Oranje*, Alphen 1979

Sylvius, L., *Historien onses Tyds, behelzende Saken van Staat en Oorlog*, Amsterdam 1685

– *Willem de Derde*, Amsterdam 1694

Symcox, G., 'Louis XIV and the Outbreak of the Nine Years War', *Louis XIV and Europe*, ed. Ragnhild Hatton, London 1976

Sypesteyn, J.W., *Nederland and Brandenburg in 1672 en 1673*, The Hague 1863

Sypesteyn, J.W., & Bordes, J.P. de, *De Verdedeging van Nederland*, The Hague 1850

Tapié, V.L., 'Louis XIV: Methods and Foreign Policy', *Louis XIV and Europe*, ed. Ragnhild Hatton, The Hague 1976

Temple, W., *Letters written by Sir W. Temple, Bart., and other ministers of state, both at home and abroad: containing an account of the most important transactions that pass'd in Christendom from 1665–1672*, publ. Jonathan Swift 1700

– *The Works of Sir William Temple*, Edinburgh 1754, London 1770

Ten Raa & de Bas, *Het Staatsche Leger 1568–1795*, Breda 1911

Tex, J.I. den, *Oldenbarnevelt*, Cambridge 1973

Treasure, G.R.R. , *Mazarin, The Crisis of Absolutism in France*, London & New York 1997

Trevelyan, G.M., *William III and the Defence of Holland 1672–4*, London 1930

Troost, W., *William III, the Stadholder-King: A Political Biography*, Ashgate 2005

– 'William III, Brandenburg, and the Construction of the Anti-French Coalition', *The Anglo-Dutch Moment*, Cambridge 1991

– 'Willem III en de exclusion crisis 1679–1681', *Bijdragen en Mededelingen betreffende de Geschiedemis der Nederlanden*, Deel 107, 1992

Urkunden und Actenstücke Friedrich Wilhelm von Brandenburg, ed. Heinrich Peter, Berlin 1864

Veeze, B.J., *De raad van den Prinsen van Oranje tijdens de minderjarigheid van Willem III, 1650–1668*, Assen 1932

Venetian State Papers, 1640–42, XXV, XXVI

'Verbaal van de Buitengewoone Ambassade van Jacob van Wassenaar-Diuvenvoorde, Arnout van Citters en Everard van Weede van Dijkveld', *Historisch Genootschap te Utrecht*, New Series 2, 1863

Vervolg van't verwerd Europa, Amsterdam 1688

Waddington, A., *Le Grand Electeur Frédéric Guillaume de Brandenbourg. Sa politique extérieure, 1640–1688*, Paris 1908

Wagenaar, J., *Vaderlandsche Historie,* Amsterdam 1794

Wedgwood, C.V., *William the Silent: William of Nassau, Prince of Orange, 1553–1584*, London 1944

– *The Trial of Charles I*, London & New York 1964

Whaley, J., *Germany and the Holy Roman Empire*, Oxford 2012

Wicquefort, A. de, *Histoire des Provinse-Uni*, Amsterdam 1861

– 'Mémoires sur la guerre faite aux provinces-unies en l'année 1672', *Bijdragen en mededeelingen van het historisch genootschap gevestigd te Utrecht*, XI, 1888

Wijnne, J.A., *Geschiedenis Van Het Vaderland*, Groningen 1872

Wilson, C., *Profit and Power,* Longman's Green 1957

Wilson, P.H., *German Armies*, London, UCL 1998

Wolf, J., *Louis XIV,* London 1968

Wood, A., 'Athenaexonienses', *Fasti*, London 1820

Worp, J.A. (ed.), *Briefwisseling van Constantijn Huygens*, The Hague 1916

Zee, van de, H.& B., *William and Mary*, London 1973

Zuylen van Nyevelt, S. van, *Court Life in the Dutch Republic, 1638–1689*, London 1906

Index